An Introduction to ECONOMIC Thinking

An Introduction to ECONOMIC Thinking

Richard H. Leftwich

Professor of Economics
Oklahoma State University

Holt, Rinehart and Winston, Inc.

New York   Chicago   San Francisco   Atlanta
Dallas   Montreal   Toronto   London   Sydney

To Judy, Greg, and Brad

Preface

What to teach beginning students in economics and how to teach it are perennial and unsolved problems. It would be foolish of me to pretend that I have the answers and that they are contained in this book. I have put together my approach to the problems and, for economics students that I have taught, it seems to have worked reasonably well.

I think we must recognize that we cannot cover the whole broad scope of the discipline of economics in depth in the principles course. But it appears that this is what we have been trying to do in recent years and, correspondingly, principles of economics books are becoming basic economics encyclopedias. To attempt to teach in depth all that is typically included is to invite frustration and disappointment on the part of both students and instructors. For most beginning students I suspect that extended discussions of methodology and of sophisticated analytical models are simply irrelevant. In my judgment a thorough grasp of a limited number of elementary principles, together with the economist's way of thinking about things, will do much more toward building economic literacy.

This, then, is not a complex book and there are indeed omissions of a number of topics that are currently fashionable in principles textbooks. Yet I believe it is complete enough to provide the fundamental background for a reasonably correct analysis of both our current and our recurring economic problems. I believe, too, that if the principles contained herein are mastered those desiring to do so will have little difficulty in moving into more advanced, complex, and sophisticated realms of analysis.

Many have made contributions to the writing of this book and, stubborn man that I am, I have not been willing to accept all of their good suggestions. I have, however, rejected all of their bad ones and must, therefore, take full responsibility for the complete list of the book's shortcomings. I want to thank especially Professor Joseph J. Klos of Oklahoma State University for his incisive criticisms and suggestions for the entire work. Others who have been of very significant help include Professor Rudolph W. Trenton of Oklahoma State University and Mr. Loren Scott and Mr. James Green, graduate students in economics at Oklahoma State University. Mrs. Sandra Grimes has been very patient and very efficient in typing the various drafts of the manuscript.

—R.H.L.

November 1968
Stillwater, Oklahoma

Contents

Suggestions for a One-Semester Course

The condensation of introductory economics to a one-semester or a one-quarter three-hour course is a herculean task for an instructor. For those who want to—or for some reason or other must—attempt it a suggested outline follows. The number of pages included is considerably more than half of the entire text. However, the materials omitted are the more difficult analytical parts of microeconomics and macroeconomics where the going is slow in the two-semester or the two-quarter course. The materials included will provide a solid, rigorous one-semester course.

Suggested Outline

Part 1   An Overview of Economic Activity and Analysis

Part 2   Microeconomics: Markets for Goods and Services

Part 3   Microeconomics: Markets for Resources

PART 1 An Overview of Economic Activity and Analysis

There are many facets to the study of economics. In order to achieve a depth of understanding, we shall examine each one in turn as we proceed through this book. But we shall find that the analysis of any one area is not independent of the others, and that our grasp of each is enhanced by some knowledge of the others. Chapters 1–3 provide an overview of economic activity and analysis. Hopefully, they will give us a place to hang our hats—a place to which we can return time and again to make the apparently different aspects of economics fall into proper place within an over-all framework of knowledge.

What Economics Is About

CHAPTER 1

You discovered long ago that what you have to spend is not sufficient to obtain as much as you would like to have of the many goods and services available. Your diet is probably varied but it is unlikely that you can afford champagne and gourmet food day in and day out. Your wardrobe is somewhat less than perfect for the kind of life you want to lead, and the room in which you live is not exactly a palace.

In short, you are confronted with the fundamental principle upon which economic activity rests—the wants of mankind are unlimited while the means available for satisfying those wants are not. Individuals and societies must determine how they are going to use the relatively scarce means available to them. They must determine which of their many desires they will apply their means to attain and the extent to which the chosen desires will be fulfilled. Steel used in making automobiles is not available for construction purposes and land used for growing wheat cannot at the same time produce corn. In this introductory chapter we shall consider the nature of economic activity, and we shall take a brief look at some of the economic problems that confront us from day to day. We shall then differentiate between the analysis of economic activity and the policies aimed at solving economic problems.

ECONOMIC ACTIVITY

We devote much of our time to different kinds of economic activity. We earn our incomes by engaging in the production of the goods and services that society wants and in turn we use what we have earned to satisfy our own wants as fully as we can. In a society in which there are millions of people, almost as many different goods and services desired, and a great many different means of contributing to the processes of production, patterns of economic activity develop as an integral part of the social fabric. These patterns become exceedingly complex, frequently obscuring cause and effect relationships. Think of our task, then, as one of sorting out these relationships in order to understand how our economic system works, to determine its shortcomings, and to devise means of improving the operation of the system. The first step is to examine systematically the elements involved in economic activity. These are (1) human wants, (2) resources, and (3) techniques of production.

Human Wants

We have mentioned already that there are no limits to the range of goods and services that people want. We hear from time to time that we in the United States are surfeited with material things, but this is not so in any sort of absolute sense. Why do people want higher wages and salaries? Why do we have so many slums? Why do we wage a war on poverty? Not many people are so affluent that additional quantities of goods and services would add nothing to their satisfactions.

Human wants arise from several sources. Those of a biological nature are always in the foreground. We require certain minimum amounts of food and protection from the elements—shelter and clothing—in order to stay alive and to function. But a full stomach does not end our desires for food, nor does an eight-room house fully satisfy our wants for housing. Once our basic needs are met we want more variety and more elegance in the goods and services used to meet these needs. Consider the desire for variety in entertainment. Among university coeds, too, although there will be some degree of conformity in types of clothing worn, within those types every effort will be made to avoid duplications in patterns and color schemes. Social pressure, too, generates wants. For example, the purchase of a color television set by a neighbor makes us feel that we should have one too. Additionally, as we engage in the activities necessary to satisfy a given desire, new wants are born. Who wants to move into a new house without buying at least a few new pieces of furniture? Does the pursuit of a bachelor's degree create wants that would otherwise never have come into being for an individual?

These unlimited human wants are the mainsprings of economic activity. All economic activity is carried on for the purpose of fulfilling people's desires. It is directed toward satisfying as fully as possible the wants of individuals, of groups, and of the entire society.

Resources

The extent to which wants in any society can be fulfilled is determined largely by the availability of the ingredients that can be put into processes of production. What do you have that can contribute toward the production of goods and services desired by the society in which you live? You certainly are able to do physical labor and, given the opportunity, you may be able to put a little mental effort into the economic machine. You may also own a piece of land or other property that you can rent out to others. Or perhaps you own a few shares of stock, making you part owner of the assets of some corporation, and you let the corporation use your part of these assets to produce its products.

Resource Classifications

We call the ingredients that go into the production of goods and services *resources,* and for convenience we classify them into two broad categories: (1) *labor* and (2) *capital.* Each category contains a great many subcategories which may differ widely: corporation executives and garbage collectors, for example, both fall within the labor classification. While the classification is useful for many purposes, undue importance should not be attached to it. It is primarily a device to help us keep our thinking orderly when we consider resources.

Labor consists of all the muscular and mental effort that mankind can put into the productive processes. It includes what common laborers are able to do, but it is also made up of the capabilities of actors, musicians, artists, university professors, lawyers, accountants, railroad engineers, and so on. Labor, then, represents all productive efforts rendered directly by human beings.

Nonhuman resources are called *capital.* We include as capital all kinds of tools such as pencils, notebooks, hammers, pliers, and nails; machinery; and buildings. We shall place so-called natural resources in the capital category also, although some economists prefer to set these up in a third category called *land.* Natural resources consist of farm land, space for residential and industrial sites, mineral deposits, water, fish and wildlife, forests, and other such items. Inventories of goods comprise still another type of capital resource. For example, grocery inventories are a part of the capital resources of a supermarket and stocks of iron ore make up a portion of the capital resources of a steel mill.

A substantial part of the capital resources of the economy consists of *intermediate goods*—goods produced to be further used in production processes rather than directly by consumers. Steel, for example, is not consumed directly but is fabricated into any number of products that are then used by consumers. Thus resources may be used to produce other resources that are in turn employed to produce resources that are then used in the production of consumer goods and services. Pyramiding of this kind is common in the productive process.

Scarcity of Resources

We know from everyday experience that the quantities of resources available for producing goods and services are inadequate for fulfilling our unlimited wants. If resources were not scarce relative to wants they would not command a price; that is, they would be free like the air we breathe. That consumers and, in turn, producers are willing to pay to put resources into the productive process is evidence that they are scarce and are not to be had simply for the taking.

It is easy to see that there is an upper limit to the size of the labor force. The total population of an economy, if nothing else, would be the ultimate limiting factor. But there are a number of factors that restrict the labor force to something like one fourth of the total population. These include the age distribution of the population, its state of health, attitudes toward employment of women and children, whether or not aristocrats and would-be aristocrats are willing to get their hands dirty, and other factors of a similar nature.

The quantity of capital that an economy has available to place in production is also limited, but by a somewhat different set of factors. An economy may experience a paucity of natural resources—for example, many of the areas of North Africa and the Middle East. But scarcity of machines, buildings, tools, and other intermediate goods is even more significant. We might ask ourselves how an economy accumulates a stock of capital goods to put into productive processes. Generally, in order to do this, an economy must use existing resources that could have been used for the production of consumer goods to produce intermediate or capital goods instead. The production of intermediate goods thus involves a sacrifice of some quantities of consumer goods, unless unemployment of resources exists in the economy and these unemployed resources can be put to work. As consumers, we may not be willing to tighten our belts sufficiently to release the quantities of resources needed to bring about large relative increases in the economy's stock of capital. The poorer a country, the more difficult capital accumulation becomes.

Techniques of Production

The amounts of goods and services that can be produced with given quantities of labor and capital depend, of course, on how well those resources are used. Two students with the same degree of intelligence, the same books, and in the same surroundings may perform at different levels on an examination. The difference may well be in the techniques of study used by each. Similarly, with given quantities of resources one shoemaker may turn out a larger quantity of shoes than another because he employs superior techniques. In the same way, the general level of technological know-how varies among countries. The economies of Asia, Africa, South America, and the Middle East are behind those of western Europe and the United States in this respect.

By production techniques we mean the methods, knowledge, and means available for converting resources into want-satisfying goods. Engineering is generally thought of as the discipline most directly concerned with this process, which includes the development of new energy sources, improvements in construction methods, more efficient plant design and layout, development of new products, and anything else that increases the want satisfaction attainable from available resources. But we are also concerned with techniques of production in economics. Since resources are scarce relative to wants, we concern ourselves with whether or not the "best" techniques are used. The best techniques are those that enable given quantities of resources to yield the highest outputs of goods and services, or, to put it the other way around, those that permit given quantities of goods and services to be produced with the least expenditure of resources. We shall come back to these points again and again in a variety of contexts.

GOALS OF ECONOMIC ACTIVITY

The primary economic goal of most societies is to achieve a standard of living as high as its resources and its techniques of production will allow. Having made this statement, we must qualify it immediately. No society is likely to focus single mindedly on maximizing average living standards. There are other values to be achieved in "the good life," and the fulfillment of some of these objectives may require backing away from the achievement of the highest possible living standards. Preservation of a free as opposed to a totalitarian society, for example, may require that some resources be diverted from the production of want-satisfying consumer goods and services toward the production of armaments. Too, the United States has supported income-redistribution measures—the farm program, progressive taxation, minimum wage legislation—which many people believe have held the total output of the economy below what it would be in their absence, in order to secure a greater measure of economic justice. But most modern societies most of the time are interested in continually raising the levels of want satisfaction they can achieve.

Through newspapers, television programs, conversations, and other contacts with the rest of society we are reminded that the economic system operates imperfectly. Problems arise, the solutions to which make up a set of subgoals toward which economic activity is directed. What are some of a country's major economic problems? *Unemployment* is surely an important one. Another is *economic instability.* A third is *low levels of growth and development,* particularly in the poorer countries of the world. A fourth is presumed *injustices in income distribution*—in the way the economic system treats certain individuals and groups in the society as compared with others. A fifth problem centers around what *type of economic system* will best promote the goals toward which society wants to work. Let us examine the subgoals in greater detail in order to grasp more securely the dimensions of the problems that systematic economic analysis must attack.

Full Employment

The economy of the United States has experienced some difficulty in keeping its labor force and its productive capacity fully employed. During the depression of the 1930s, 25 percent of the labor force was unemployed. From 1958 to 1966 the unemployment rate was more than 5 percent. As individuals and as a society we are concerned, since unemployment implies hardship for fellow-human beings and perhaps for ourselves. It also means that the economy is turning out smaller quantities of goods and services than it is capable of producing and that our standard of living is lower than it need be.

What are the causes of unemployment? What can be done to decrease it? Economists are not entirely in accord on either point, but they do agree that identification of the causes is a prerequisite to taking intelligent action to mitigate the problem. Unless we can diagnose the disease we are not likely to get far in curing it.

Economic Stability

Economic instability, characterized by periods of recession and periods of inflation, is cause for much uneasiness in a society. A *recession* refers to a reduction in economic activity in which unemployment will increase, and it presents the possibility of becoming a serious depression such as that of the 1930s. *Inflation,* on the other hand, is characterized by rising prices and is ordinarily, but not necessarily, associated with high levels of economic activity. Both recessionary and inflationary periods have occurred in the United States since 1940, but none has been as severe as those of the 1800s or, of course, the Great Depression of the 1930s.

Economists believe they have learned much in recent years about economic instability and how to control it. In fact, many feel that our present state of economic knowledge is such that there will never be another depression of the magnitude of the Great Depression. Other economists, however, are more cautious and maintain that although we may know how to prevent future depressions, the political climate may impede or even prevent the application of this knowledge. Nevertheless, we continue to have periods of inflation and of recession. At the very least, we must be able to prevent them from getting out of hand; hopefully we can make them less and less damaging. We must learn all we can about the causes and consequences of recession and inflation in order to decrease their adverse effects on living standards.

Economic Growth and Development

We expect modern economic systems to provide rising standards of living over time. We want growth and development to take place particularly in the poorer countries of Latin America, Africa, and Asia, but most of us anticipate that living standards in Europe and the United States will rise as well. What are the forces that produce economic growth? What annual growth rate can reasonably be expected in the United States and in other countries? Why are growth rates so low in the underdeveloped nations? What, if anything, can be done to accelerate growth rates in the latter? Is economic aid from the advanced to the less advanced countries in order, and if so, how and in what quantities should it be provided?

There is much to be learned about the processes of economic growth and the obstacles that lie in its path. Growth processes as such should be amenable to economic analysis, but many of the factors that hinder economic development are outside the province of economics proper, lying rather in the fields of political science, sociology, psychology, and cultural anthropology.

Economic Justice and Economic Security

As individuals and as a society we are concerned with the twin problems of economic justice and economic security even though we are seldom clear as to what we mean by these terms. In a very broad sense, *justice,* or lack of it, is inferred from the treatment received by one person in economic affairs as compared with that received by others. *Security* refers to a guarantee of some minimum level of consumption. Some measure of security is ordinarily thought to be necessary for the individual in the interests of economic justice.

A great many questions arise with respect to what is just and what is not. Should people share equally in the economy's output or should they share in proportion to their contribution to the productive processes? If they are to share equally, what incentive does an individual have to make his maximum contribution? If they are to share in proportion to their contribution, security for many goes out the window. Many people do not own sufficient quantities of resources to earn a large enough share of the economy's output to keep them alive. Consider those who are permanently disabled and who own no capital. Problems of economic security and of economic justice cannot be solved with economic theory alone, although theory is an important ingredient in arriving at satisfactory solutions.

Ideas of what constitutes security and what constitutes justice depend upon the value judgments of individuals and groups in society, that is, upon their particular view of how things should be. We have not been able to reach a consensus in these areas and, consequently, in the United States we have a broad range of governmental and private arrangements designed to achieve some measure of security and justice. Among these are social security laws, the system of graduated income taxes, minimum wage laws, and laws providing for free public education. In the private sector we have insurance of many types. One of our main tasks from the point of view of economics is to subject such arrangements to thorough examination in order to determine whether or not they accomplish their objective. In addition, we need to assess their impact on the over-all level of economic activity.

Economic Systems

What type of economic system is most conducive to "the good life" as envisaged by people all over the world? Obviously people and societies hold widely differing opinions on this subject—indeed the Cold War has largely turned on this issue. Which will lead to the highest living standards, the socialistic system of the Soviet Union and Red China, the free enterprise system as represented by the United States, or some combination of the two? Which will come closest to fulfilling society's complex of economic and noneconomic goals?

Although we shall not define the terms "socialism" and "free enterprise" with precision at this point, let us consider the characteristics of each of these economic systems. In the *socialistic system* the economy is state directed, that is, the means of production are owned and controlled by the state. In the *free enterprise system* the means of production are owned privately. Economic activity is carried on through the volition of and under the direction of private individuals and groups. Neither the socialistic system of the Soviet Union nor the free enterprise system of the United States is pure in form. For example, recent evidence indicates that the U.S.S.R. is making increasing use of private ownership of some resources, while in the United States we find that some industries are socialized—the postal services and many municipal utility companies are cases in point. Final choices of the type of economic system that will predominate have not been made in either sphere of influence and likely will never be made. But societies are continually making choices that move them in one direction or the other, and these choices should be made as intelligently as possible.

ECONOMIC ANALYSIS AND ECONOMIC POLICY

Legislative bodies as well as groups of private individuals are constantly engaging in activities designed to remedy defects in the operation of the economic system. Some of these measures accomplish their objectives, but some produce results and by-products that are unexpected and unwanted. For example, for many years Congress has been concerned with the problem of low average incomes in the agricultural sector of the economy, and thus a farm program built around price supports for key storable farm products has been built up in order to increase farm incomes relative to other incomes in the economy. The general public as well as a number of Congressmen have expressed surprise that surpluses of a number of farm products have accumulated, and in addition, many are also surprised to learn that the wealthier farmers on the large farms receive the bulk of price support payments while smaller, poorer operators receive very little. The problem illustrated here is that those who attempt to remedy the economy's defects do not always understand how the economic system operates and thus the ramifications of their actions. For this reason we must distinguish clearly between economic analysis and economic policy. We need to understand both and to ground the latter on the former.

Economic Analysis

Economic analysis is the process of making sense out of economic relationships. Economists examine and record economic behavior and economic events in order to establish causal relations among the data and activities they have observed. Some of their conclusions are reached through reasoning deductively from more general to more specific events. As an illustration, the Cold War requires military preparedness, which in turn requires the use of steel. Thus, economists reason, an increase in military activities will increase demand for steel. Other causal relationships are established inductively, with analysts inferring from a series of events that certain relationships must exist. Suppose that over a number of years it is observed that increases in prices and increases in the total money available for spending in the economy always occur simultaneously. Economists might then reason that these conditions are causally related, or perhaps that they have common causes.

Tentative statements of causal relationships are called *hypotheses.* Such statements need to be tested again and again in order to determine whether or not they are valid. They can be weighed for logical consistency and they can be tested empirically in the world of facts. As a consequence of testing they may be verified, modified, or rejected.

Hypotheses that have withstood repeated testing and that seem to be able to explain or to predict economic activity with a fair degree of accuracy become known as *principles.* It must be emphasized, however, that principles are not necessarily absolute truths but rather should be thought of as subject to correction and refinement.

The general body of economic analysis is made up of principles designed to explain causal relationships among what are believed to be the more important economic variables. All possible variables surrounding all possible economic events obviously cannot be taken into account because of the limitations of the human mind. Principles are essentially simplifications of complex relationships and are intended to indicate what will happen most of the time in most cases, but almost any principle is subject to exceptions.

Economic analysis serves three main purposes. First, by explaining relationships among various economic variables it is a valuable aid in understanding the operation of an economy. Second, it aids in predicting the consequences of changes in economic variables. Finally, economic analysis serves as the fundamental framework for economic policy-making—indeed, if wise policy-making is to occur, it must be based on correct economic analysis.

Economic Policy

Economic policy refers to conscious intervention in the economic processes by government or by private groups in order to affect the results of economic activity. Associations of employers may agree not to "pirate" each other's labor, that is, not to try to hire each other's employees, in order to prevent wages from rising; labor organizations may use coercion to raise the wage levels of their members; Congress enacts laws that influence the behavior of businesses, employees, and consumers.

Such legislation includes antitrust laws, social security laws, farm legislation, tax laws, and many others.

Whereas economic policies of private groups in the economy are generally pursued with the intent of furthering the interest of those groups, we have every right to expect that government policies will be in the interests of the general public. To put it another way, we anticipate that government policies will increase economic efficiency. Although greater efficiency may result from a number of such measures, a healthy skepticism is in order, too. Individual Congressmen often have different ideas of how the economy should operate—and so do their advisers and the witnesses at their hearings. In addition, their economic analysis is not infallible. This is not to say that governmental policy-making usually goes off on the wrong track but rather that the more sound the economic analysis underlying governmental policy-making, the more effective that policy-making is likely to be. Yet there will always be conflict in this area.

SUMMARY

This chapter introduces the study of economics. Economic activity stems from the unlimited range of man's wants and the comparative scarcity of means available for fulfilling them. Wants arise from any sources, including biological necessity, desires for variety, social pressures, and want-satisfying activity itself. The means available for fulfilling wants comprise the resources of the economy and its technology. Resources are the ingredients that go into the processes of production and can be classified into a labor category and a capital category. Labor includes all human efforts that contribute to production while capital consists of resources that are nonhuman in character. By technology we mean the know-how and the means available to a society for converting resources into want-satisfying goods and services. The level of want satisfaction, or the average standard of living, that a society can attain depends upon the quantities and qualities of its available resources as well as the level of its technology.

The ultimate economic goal of a society is ordinarily the achievement of a standard of living as high as its resources and production techniques will permit. A number of subgoals related to problems that arise in the operation of the economic system can be identified. These include full employment of resources, economic stability, economic growth and development, economic justice and security, and determination of the type of economic system that best serves the purposes of the society.

The relation between economic analysis and economic policy must be clearly understood. Economic analysis is concerned with the establishment of causal relations among economic events. Its purposes are to help us understand how the economy operates, to enable us to predict what the consequences of changes in economic variables will be, and to serve as the basis for economic policy-making. Economic policy refers to the conscious attempts of private groups and governmental units to make the economy operate differently than it would in the absence of those attempts. Wise economic policy must rest on sound economic anaylsis.

EXERCISES AND QUESTIONS FOR DISCUSSION

1. During the course of a day make a list of the things you would like or would like more of but cannot afford. Why is your income (or your family's income) inadequate to make these purchases?
2. Per capita income, or average income per person, in India is less than $100 per year. What explanations can you offer for this relatively low standard of living?
3. Look through a current issue of your favorite news periodical, noting the articles pertaining to economic issues. Classify these articles under the five problem areas discussed in the chapter.
4. What do you think were the main causes of the relatively high rate of unemployment (over 5 percent of the labor force) between 1959 and 1964?
5. Which of the following are examples of socialism and why: (a) a municipally owned power plant; (b) the U.S. postal service; (c) American Telephone and Telegraph Company; (d) the federal government's farm program; (e) Medicare.
6. Evaluate this statement: "That may be all right in theory but not in fact."

SELECTED READINGS

Boulding, Kenneth E., *Economic Analysis,* 4th ed., Vol. 1. New York: Harper & Row, Publishers, Inc., 1966, Chap. 1.
Heilbroner, Robert L., *The Making of Economic Society.* Englewood Cliffs, N. J.: Prentice-Hall, Inc., 1962, Chap. 1

How an Economic System Works

CHAPTER 2

Consider your morning coffee break. It had its origins some time ago with investment in a piece of land in Brazil, Columbia, or some other tropical country. Labor and machinery cleared the land and brought it under cultivation. Coffee trees were planted and cultivated, bearing fruit after some five years. The berries were picked and pulped, leaving only the seeds or beans. These were hulled, peeled, sorted, sacked, shipped to the United States, cleaned, blended, roasted, and ground. The student union purchased the ground product and made it into the brew you drink. In addition to the resources used in the direct production process sketched above, still others were needed for the containers, railway cars, trucks, and ships in which the coffee product was transported through its different stages of manufacture. Still other resources were needed to construct the machinery and the buildings that were used at every point in the production of the coffee you drink.

A modern economic system is enormously complex. Thousands of economic operations are required to produce almost any product, and all of these processes must be efficiently coordinated. We attempt in this chapter to strip away the complexities and get down to the bare essentials of economic activity so that we may begin to understand how an economic system works. We shall consider first the functions that every economic system must perform and we then shall take a brief, preliminary look at how different types of systems perform them. Third, we shall construct a simple model of a free enterprise system.

THE FUNCTIONS OF AN ECONOMIC SYSTEM

Most economists list three basic functions that every economic system must perform. First, the system must determine what goods and services are to be produced as well as their order of importance. Second, it must organize productive effort so that the goods and services selected are produced in the proper quantities. Finally, it must determine how the finished output is to be shared among the members of the society. All societies are confronted with these same central functions, but the methods used to achieve them can differ widely.

Determining What Is to Be Produced

The fundamental economic problem of unlimited wants and scarce means of satisfying them makes it necessary for an economic system to have some method of determining not only what goods and services are to be produced but also their order of importance. We find two basic methods of performing this function in use in the world today. In the first instance the function is performed by the private action of the individuals making up the society and in the second by the state, that is, by the government or its agencies.

In a society that depends upon private action, consumers themselves determine the comparative values of goods and services through the price system. Individuals spend their available purchasing power however they wish, and each dollar spent is a vote on what is to be produced. The more urgently consumers want specific items, the higher will be the prices of these items relative to those of other items. Less urgently desired items command relatively lower prices. The more abundant the quantity available of any one product, the lower its price will be. Changes in consumers' preferences bring about changes in the prices of goods. For example, if the desires of housewives for television sets rise relative to their desires for dishwashers, they will channel their spending away from the latter toward the former and prices of television sets will rise while those of dishwashers will fall. The array of prices established for goods and services reflects the relative per unit values of the quantities currently available to consumers as a group.

In economies in which the state determines what is to be produced much detailed planning is necessary. In making estimates of future production needs, difficult questions arise concerning whether larger quantities of some products are in order. For example, a decision to step up automobile production is also a decision to increase the quantities of sheet metal, rubber tires, copper wire, batteries, and other items used in their manufacture. Since the resources of the economy are limited, additional quantities of these items can be had only if the quantities of other products are reduced. But by how much must they be reduced? Even with high-speed computers the task confronting the planners is a difficult one.

Government planning of what is to be produced may be based on (1) consumer desires, (2) governmental decisions as to what is best for the public, or (3) government aims and objectives apart from what the public wants. When governments attempt to plan in accordance with consumer desires, they may make use of a price system to register those desires, although it is not essential that they do so. Where government planning is based on governmental decisions as to what is best for the public, arbitrary decisions are made as to what is to be produced, and production quotas are established for each item in a vast array of goods and services. There is likely to be a move toward narrowing the types, models, and styles available in order to simplify planning—for example, a consumer may not be able to obtain the red necktie he desires. When government objectives are given priority, conflicts between these objectives and the desires of consumers are sure to occur. The government may find military strength essential to maintain itself in power when the public would prefer that more consumer goods be produced instead. Or the government, looking toward the future, may want to divert resources away from consumer goods and services at the present time in order to accumulate capital and increase future productive capacity while consumers want more goods and services now.

Actually, we see combinations of the two methods of determining what is to be produced in use throughout the world. In the United States consumer choice is the predominant method, but it is tempered by governmental decisions in a number of areas. For example, there are legal prohibitions against the sale of certain drugs; governmental units make decisions with regard to road building; and a number of other examples could be cited. In the Soviet Union government planning is the predominant method of allocating resources, yet even here consumer choice plays at least a limited role.

Organizing Production

Every economic system must have some means of mobilizing productive effort in order to turn out in appropriate quantities the goods and services desired. The organization of production has two main aspects. One is the process of moving resources away from the production of goods where they contribute less to consumer desires and into the production of goods where they contribute more. The other is the attainment of the greatest possible efficiency by individual production units or business enterprises in the economy. Again we can think in terms of two alternatives. Private individuals can be left to organize production on their own or the state can undertake the task.

Can we avoid chaos if individuals are left to their own devices—to work wherever they desire and to place the capital they own in employments of their own choosing? Even if chaos can be avoided, the task of getting the right resources to the right place at the right time seems highly remote. But we have omitted the price system from our thinking. The price system and the profit motive, maligned as they are, perform the task of organizing production in an unobtrusive, automatic way. It is evident that businesses can make higher profits by producing goods that consumers want most rather than those that consumers want least. Further, the most profitable businesses pay the highest prices for labor and capital resources while the least profitable businesses are those that resource owners prefer to avoid. We, as resource owners, move our labor and capital away from the lower-paying areas toward the higher-paying ones. As production of what consumers want most is expanded and of what they want least is contracted, prices and profits fall in the former and increase in the latter, diminishing the incentive of resource owners to make further transfers.

The profit motive also provides the prime incentive to private businesses to operate efficiently. The greater the value of output that can be obtained from a given value of resources, the more efficient the production process. Or, what amounts to the same thing, the smaller the value of resource inputs necessary to produce a given value of product output, the more efficient the process. It follows that the more efficient an enterprise is in its operations, the more profit it will make; hence the quest for profit spurs a drive for efficiency.

Organization of production by the state will be neither automatic nor unobtrusive. The magnitude of the planning task is almost overwhelming simply by virtue of the millions of decisions that must be made. Suppose that the state planning agencies have determined what goods and services are to be produced and have established production quotas for each that are within the capabilities of the economy, given its resources and its level of technology. How can one get workers who prefer the seaside to work in the mines? How can one decide on the degree of mechanization to use in road building as compared with that to use in agriculture? How far should one go in producing intermediate goods, and what kinds of intermediate goods should be produced? What if someone makes a mistake with respect to the amount of natural rubber that can be imported and an insufficient number of tires are available for the automobiles that are being produced? Of course, these problems also arise under a price system, but the price system corrects them before they become critical.

What are the incentives for efficiency in the operation of individual production units in the state-planned economy? Bonus incentives and promotion possibilities for managers and workers can be and are used to some extent. It is also common for the state to establish production quotas and for penalties to be assessed if these quotas are not met. But individual units may not be free to obtain resources in the kinds and quantities that will contribute most to efficient operation. They are usually obliged to accept whatever they can get, that is, whatever is allocated to them.

In the organization of production most economies will use some combination of the two alternatives discussed above, although it is apparent that some rely more heavily on one than on the other. The economy of the United States is largely price directed, but at a number of points governmental decisions are superimposed on, or substituted for, the price mechanism. The Soviet Union illustrates the opposite emphasis.

Distributing the Product

Every economic system must provide a method of determining how its citizens are to share in the economy's output. This function too can either be performed by private enterprise or by the state.

Here too the private approach utilizes the price system as the controlling device. How does it work? You know that the part of the economy's total yearly output that you can claim depends on the yearly income that you earn. Your income, in turn, depends upon how much labor and how much capital you put into the production process and the prices (wage rates, interest, dividends, rents, and so on) you receive for them. Most of us believe that we are not paid enough for our resources, but by and large we receive for them about what they contribute to the value of the economy's output. If one employer is not willing to pay that much for them it will be profitable for another to do so. But a fuller explanation of this point must wait.

The distribution of the economy's output thus depends on the distribution of income. In turn, the distribution of income depends on the distribution of resource ownership and the prices individuals receive for placing their resources in production. People well endowed with capital and labor resources and who place these where they contribute much to the value of the economy's output will have large incomes relative to others and will receive large shares. The Rockefellers and the Fords are cases in point. People with few resources that they utilize poorly receive low incomes and small shares.

In the state-planned approach income distribution can be whatever the state wills it to be. As a first approximation it might think in terms of rationing equal quantities of each product to each member of the society, but this would not be a satisfactory arrangement. People differ in their preferences and in their consumption patterns for a variety of reasons—different ages and residence in different parts of the country are two important ones. Indeed, if all were to share equally in the economy's output, how could workers be induced to move from employments where they want to be into employments where they are needed?

Economies such as the United States that rely primarily on the private approach make considerable use of state-planned distribution measures. Similarly, state-planned economies such as the Soviet Union make some use of the private approach. In the United States the government redistributes income in a number of ways—through progressive taxation, free public education, the farm program, and others. In the Soviet Union equal sharing in distribution is not followed in practice. Distribution is partly fixed as the state determines what is to be produced—what parts of total output are to be military hardware, heavy industrial goods, consumer goods, and so on. Wages and prices are rather rigidly controlled, but there are differentials between skilled and unskilled workers. Sometimes certain managerial positions or certain professions carry bonuses in order to attract more persons into them. These differences in income make it possible for some people to obtain greater shares of what is produced than others.

TYPES OF ECONOMIC SYSTEMS

The private approach to the three functions of an economic system is provided by a *free enterprise* type of economic system while the state-planned approach is typical of *socialistic* economies. Although a detailed discussion of these alternative types of systems is out of order at this point, we should have some grasp of the fundamental characteristics of each. The economic system that evolves in any particular society is not the consequence of decision-making on economic grounds alone. In fact, political and philosophical issues are likely to predominate—witness the Russian Revolution in 1918; and in some cases, such as Nazi Germany and Facist Italy of the pre-World War II days, personal aggrandizement on the part of an individual may be the molding force. But our concern here is with the economic aspects of the different systems.

The Free Enterprise System

The right of private persons and private organizations to own things is the foundation of a free enterprise economic system. We call this the *institution of private property*. Generally, legal guarantees are given to private individuals, partnerships, corporations, and other associations to own capital resources and consumer goods of almost all kinds. Individuals also own their own labor power, although this would not be so if slavery were permitted.

The fundamental methods by which such an economy operates are voluntary exchange and cooperation by private individuals and organizations. Why do people work 40 hours a week, week in and week out? They do so primarily because the time and effort they give up are worth less to them than the money they receive for working. The same proposition holds for the willingness of people to exchange capital resources for income. Producers who pay for the services of labor and capital must also feel that those services are worth more to them than what they pay out to resource owners. Unless both parties gain, the exchanges would never occur. Why do you give up purchasing power you have in exchange for goods and services? Again because the items you purchase must be worth more to you than the purchasing power you give up, otherwise you would not make the trade. The seller too must believe that the money he receives will be of greater benefit to him than the goods and services he gives up. Exchange occurs whenever and wherever two or more parties believe that they can benefit from the transaction.

Individuals or groups cooperate with each other whenever they believe they can gain more from working together than from working individually. You help your neighbor move his refrigerator; in turn he helps you haul a dead tree out of your yard. People in a society join their labor and their capital in more extensive productive efforts—in the manufacture of automobiles, houses, airplanes, and almost everything else that is needed.

In the exercise of voluntary exchange and cooperation there are three areas in which people are free to act either as individuals or in groups. First, as consumers people are free to purchase whatever goods and services they want within the limits of their income. Second, as resource owners they are free to sell or hire out their resources for income wherever they can find takers. Third, they are free to establish business enterprises for the production and sale of any desired product or service, and they can terminate those enterprises whenever they see fit to do so.

Largely because of its emphasis on individual freedom and voluntary exchange, many people conclude that the free enterprise system operates in a highly disorganized way. This, however, is not the case. As noted in the preceding section, prices and profits provide the guiding mechanism: the things that consumers value most highly are also those that it is most profitable to produce, and those valued least are produced at losses. The termination of enterprises and the contraction of productive capacity occurs in the latter while new enterprises and expansion of productive capacity occurs in the former. The profitable enterprises attract resources away from those incurring losses by paying more to resource owners. The mechanism is automatic, and although it is not perfect in its operation, neither is it chaotic.

The free enterprise system places a high premium on individual freedom of choice and action. Individuals are thought to be the best judges of the economic objectives of the society. Economic activity, guided and directed by prices, is motivated by the pursuit of self-interest. Each consumer attempts to spend his income in such a way as to maximize his individual well-being, and each business firm attempts to maximize its profits. Individuals as resource owners seek to maximize their incomes. Pursuit of individual self-interest in these ways is thought to lead to the greatest common economic welfare of the society as a whole.

The Socialistic System

Government ownership or control of the economy's resources underlies the socialistic type of economic system. The government owns such capital resources as land, buildings, and machinery, but since ownership of labor power is hard to separate from the individual who furnishes it, control of labor resources rather than outright government ownership is the usual case.

In the socialistic system government planning is used to organize economic activity. The government plans what is to be produced and it operates enterprises in different lines of production accordingly. Business enterprises can be established, labor resources can be directed, and capital resources can be allocated in whatever way government officials believe they will make their maximum contribution to the economic objectives specified by the state. Distribution of the product, too, will be in accordance with government's over-all economic plan.

The socialistic system is based on the philosophy that individual self-interest should be subordinated to the interests of the society as a whole. The government is thought to be the best judge of what constitutes the best interests of the society and, therefore, of its economic objecives. As a consequence, important restrictions may be placed on individual freedom. Consumers may find that their choices of some products, along with the quantities available for purchase, are curtailed when state objectives and consumer objectives are in conflict. The government may give planes higher priority than cooking utensils and may divert aluminum from the production of the latter into the construction of the former. Individuals may not be free to go into the occupations of their choice. Potential nuclear physicists may be diverted toward medicine or some other profession depending upon the number of physicists the government decides should be trained. Workers may not be able to move to the geographic area they desire because the state needs people with their qualifications elsewhere. On the face of it, there appears to be more compulsion by the state and less voluntary action on the part of individuals in the socialistic economy than in the free enterprise system.

Mixed Systems

In practice we find neither the free enterprise nor the socialistic economic system in its pure form. The United States leans heavily toward the free enterprise type of economy, but government regulation, control, and even ownership of production facilities are common. On the other hand, the Soviet Union, while predominantly socialistic, uses the market mechanism to accomplish some of its economic tasks.

In the United States governmental units influence in some way almost one fifth of the economy's output. Since some government action has the effect of redistributing income, patterns of consumer demand are affected. In addition, regulatory and control activities affect what many industries are able to produce and the prices they can charge. Regulation of the airlines by the Civil Aeronautics Board, of the railroads by the Interstate Commerce Commission, and of communications by the Federal Communications Commission are examples. Further, the government, having reduced consumer demand through taxes, spends those tax receipts to build roads, buildings, and dams and to provide services such as police protection and national defense, items that individuals might not purchase if they were free to spend the tax dollars directly.

In the Soviet Union almost all production facilities are state owned and operated. Workers are paid wages, however, and differentials have been established between professional and manual workers as well as between the skilled and the unskilled in order to provide incentives for developing labor potential. These measures, however, are supplementary to others taken in order to insure that supplies of different kinds of labor are developed as the state desires. Goods are sold in state-owned stores at set prices, but the prices are controlled by the state and so do not perform the function of reflecting how consumers value different goods and services relatively. It has recently been proposed in the Soviet Union, notably by an economist by the name of Liberman, that production units should be given some form of profit motive in order to stimulate efficiency.[1]

[1] See *Time*, Vol. 85 (February 12, 1965), pp. 23–29.

A MODEL OF A FREE ENTERPRISE SYSTEM

In this section we shall develop a highly simplified model of a free enterprise system. Its purpose is to identify the main operating units of such an economic system and to explain how they interact. Hopefully it serves as an introduction to economic analysis. However, the model presented here is not intended to provide a complete explanation of how the economy works. Indeed, it does not take into account an important factor in the operation of a free enterprise system—the government—but rather embraces the private sector of the economy only.

Classification of Economic Units

There are two groups of economic units that interact or engage in economic activity. These are households on the one hand and business enterprises on the other. Both are familiar concepts. *Households* consist either of family units or of unattached individuals who do not live with families. *Business enterprises* include individual proprietorships, partnerships, and corporations.

Since everyone in the economy belongs to some household unit, households play two roles in economic activity: (1) they are the consumers of the economy's output—its food, automobiles, houses, barbers' services, and books; and (2) they are the owners of the economy's resources—its labor and its capital. Much of the economy's capital is owned by corporations, but these are in turn owned by households, so that the entire available supply of capital is owned either directly or indirectly by households.

Business enterprises are the units that carry on the production of goods and services at all levels and stages. They include the family farm, the supermarket, and companies turning out sophisticated computers or electronic devices. The production processes carried on by business enterprises consist of the processing or conversion of resources either into final usable form or into states closer to that form. The economic activity of this group of units includes buying or hiring resources, processing or combining them, and selling the resulting goods and services.

Not all of the economy's population is embraced in the business enterprise group of economic units. Many resource owners prefer not to operate firms but instead to sell or hire out what they own to those who do. Sometimes a household unit is also a business enterprise. A neighborhood grocery store and a family farm are cases in point. But these firms present no analytical difficulties. We simply view their activities as

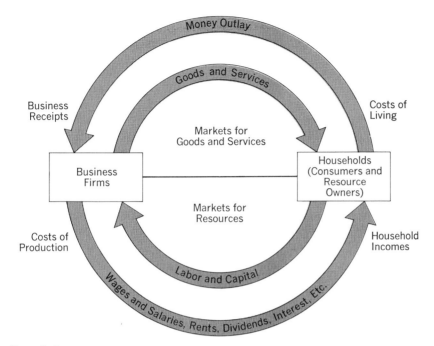

Figure 2-1
The circular flow.

households in the same light as we look at other household units and we analyze their behavior as business firms in the same way as we analyze other business firms.

Interaction of Economic Units

The well-known circular flow diagram of Figure 2–1 brings the two groups of economic units together and provides a convenient means for exploring the interaction that takes place between them. Consumer groups are represented by the box on the right and business firms by the one on the left. Resources or resource services flow from households to business firms and are converted into consumer goods and services.[2] Goods and services then flow to households in their roles as consumers. As consumers pay for the goods and services purchased, a money flow

---

[2]In the interests of simplicity we shall ignore the possibility that some resources may be used to produce net additions to the economy's stock of capital. In technical language we are working with a *stationary economy* in which productive capacity neither increases nor decreases.

is established in the opposite direction—toward business firms. The money flow continues around the circle from business firms to households as the former pay for the resources they use in the production of goods and services. Thus a physical flow of resources, goods, and services moves around the circle in one direction while a money flow moves around it the other way.

The money flow takes on different but closely related aspects at different points in the circle. As it is paid out by consumers for goods and services it is *costs of living*. As it reaches business firms the same flow becomes *business receipts*. Business receipts are paid to resource owners for the use of labor and capital in production. After materials, labor, and other operating costs are met, whatever is left of business receipts goes to the owners of enterprises in payment for the use of their physical plant and equipment. The money flow as it is paid out by business firms represents *costs of production*. When households receive it the same flow becomes *household incomes,* or what consumers have available to spend.

The Two Sets of Markets

Households and business enterprises interact in markets or places of exchange. These can be separated into two categories: (1) markets for goods and services, represented by the upper half of Figure 2–1, and (2) markets for resources, represented by the lower half.

In the consumer goods market the physical flow of goods and services is linked to the opposite flow of money by prices. Prices of goods depend on the amounts that consumers are willing to spend for the goods and the quantities available for purchase. Suppose that 1000 identical automobiles are sold and that a total of $3 million is spent for the entire lot. The average price per automobile obviously must be $3000. If more were spent—say, $4 million—the average price would be $4000. If only $2 million were spent, the average price would be $2000.

If we extend the analysis to cover all goods and services sold and all purchasing power spent for them, several simple but important propositions emerge. The total value of goods and services flowing from business firms to households must equal the money flow going in the opposite direction. If the money flow rises, that is, if households increase their rates of spending, but the physical volume of goods and services sold does not, then prices must rise. A decrease in household spending with no change in the physical volume of sales means that prices must fall. On the other hand, if the money flow is constant while the physical volume of goods and services declines, prices must rise, whereas if the volume of goods and services increases, prices must fall.

The same relations hold in resource markets. The flow of resources and their services to business firms is linked to the reverse flow of money by resource prices, although we seldom talk in terms of the "price" of resources. Generally we refer to the price of labor as *wages. Dividends* are prices paid to corporation stockholders for the complex of resources that they permit the corporation to use. *Interest* is the price paid for borrowing funds used by businesses to invest in capital equipment. In many instances when a firm uses resources that it does not purchase, for example, land and buildings, the prices for their use are called *rents.* But whatever name we give to the prices of different resources, a change in the spending of business firms on given quantities of resources will cause price changes to occur in the same direction as the change in spending. Given the total spending of business firms on resources, decreases in the quantities of resources made available will increase their prices while increases in the quantities will decrease their prices.

An Application of the Model

There are many uses to which the foregoing model can be put. Let us apply it to the problem of economic instability. As a starting point, suppose that the money flow around the circle is constant—that consumer outlays or costs of living are equal to consumer incomes and that business outlays or costs of production are equal to business receipts. Suppose also that initially the flow of goods and services from firms to households and the flow of resources and resource services from households to firms are constant. These conditions mean that average price levels are constant also.

What happens if the public develops a depression psychosis? Fear of depression induces people to save money for anticipated hard times ahead. In addition, if people believe that prices are going to fall in the near future, they will spend as little as possible at present prices, postponing purchases to the anticipated future period of lower prices. The reduction in household spending is a reduction in the money flow from households to business firms. Firms find their sales volumes lagging and inventories of goods building up. They reduce prices in order to limit the reductions in volume and the inventory build ups. Thus far, then, we find that a fear of depression reduces total household spending, which in turn reduces the volume of goods sold and the prices received for these goods.

When we turn to business firms we discover that since sales volume and business receipts have fallen, businesses desire to contract production. Since the promise of profits has faded and the funds available for obtaining resources have declined, firms want smaller quantities of resources.

Households now find that some of the resources they own are unemployed, so they reduce asking prices in order to limit the magnitude of unemployment. Some unemployment, coupled with lower resource prices, means that consumer incomes are decreased. Consumer spending is likely to be further reduced, and the decline in economic activity may become progressively worse.

The downward movement may eventually be halted and reversed, however. Suppose that the public, and particularly business enterprises, begin to feel more optimistic about the future of the economy. Businesses may then decide to expand production of goods and services. Since expansion requires higher levels of resource use, there may be some slight increase in resource prices as firms attempt to attract larger quantities of resources. However, if unemployment is serious. employment opportunities alone may be sufficient to put larger quantities back in production. In any case, the increased expenditures of firms generate higher consumer incomes, thus providing incentives for households as consumers to increase their spending on goods and services. Prices tend to rise, as does the volume of goods purchased. Greater spending by consumers means larger receipts for businesses, which in turn spark expansion of production and increased business expenditures on resources. Progressive expansion of economic activity occurs in much the same way as progressive contraction.

A special situation may develop in which increases in spending are reflected solely in price increases with no expansion in resource employment or in the output of goods and services. Suppose, for example, that economic activity has expanded to the point at which all available resources are employed. Further increases in consumer spending on goods and services can serve only to raise prices, since it is not possible to increase the quantities of goods available. Similarly, since further increases in business spending cannot increase the quantities of resources available, the prices of resources are driven higher. This is roughly the situation that existed in the inflationary period of 1966–1968.

Micro- and Macroeconomics

The circular flow model is useful in distinguishing between the two main branches of economic theory: (1) *microeconomics*, or price and allocation theory, and (2) *macroeconomics*, or national income analysis. Both are used extensively in the areas of study into which economics has traditionally been divided—money and banking, public finance, international trade, economic development, industrial organization, manpower economics—the precise division depending upon who is doing the dividing.

Microeconomics, as the name implies, is concerned with parts of the economy rather than with the economy as a whole. It is the economics of individual units, households and business firms, as they carry on their activities in the two sets of markets. The pricing and output of the goods and services that make up the flow from firms to households are also the concern of microeconomics, as are the pricing and employment of each of the many resources that constitute the flow from households to firms.

Macroeconomics, on the other hand, examines the economic system as a whole rather than in terms of individual economic units or specific products, resources, and prices. As such, it is the aggregate flows in Figure 2-1 that are important rather than the items that make up each flow. Macroeconomics is particularly concerned with problems of economic stability—with the causes and control of depression and inflation—and is relevant to the aggregate level of employment. It is concerned also with problems of economic growth and development.

SUMMARY

All economies must perform three basic functions: (1) determine what goods and services are to be produced and their priority; (2) organize production; and (3) distribute the goods and services through some sort of sharing arrangement. In the world today two methods are used to perform these functions. One is the private approach while the other is the state-planned approach.

The private approach utilizes the price system and the profit motive to guide economic activity. The system works automatically, though not perfectly, as individual economic units engage in economic activity, trying to make the most of what they have. The U.S. economy best illustrates the use of the private approach.

The state-planned approach is based on governmental decision-making. The system does not work automatically but requires detailed planning and coordination by a great many individuals and groups throughout the economy. A price system may be used to some extent to assist in the planning and organizing process. The Soviet Union provides an example of the state-planned approach.

The private approach is that of a free enterprise type of economic system. Such a system rests on the institution of private property and accomplishes its ends through voluntary exchange and cooperation. It places a high value on individual freedom and employs self-interest as its primary motivating force.

The state-planned approach is that of a socialistic economy. In this system the government owns the capital resources of the economy, controls labor, and owns and operates its business enterprises. Rather than individual self-interest, the interests of society as a whole as the government conceives them are paramount.

In a simple circular flow model of a free enterprise economy, leaving the government out of account, economic units can be classified into two groups, households and business firms. A flow of resources and their services moves from households as resource owners to business firms. At this point resources are made into goods and services that then flow from firms to households as consumers. A flow of money moves in the opposite direction. The two flows are linked together by prices as households and business firms interact in markets for goods and services and in markets for resources. The model can be used to present a highly simplified analysis of economic instability and is also helpful in distinguishing between micro- and macroeconomics, the two main facets of economic theory.

EXERCISES AND QUESTIONS FOR DISCUSSION

1. What are some industries in the United States in which the state determines prices and organizes production?
2. Explain how the U.S. government redistributes income through progressive taxation, free public education, the farm program, and Medicare.
3. Classify each of the following situations as a micro- or a macroeconomic problem, explaining your answer in each case.
   a. The Ford dealer in your city sets a price on a Galaxie 500.
   b. Food Canning, Inc., decides to lay off 1200 men during the winter slowdown in business.
   c. Uncle Harry debates whether or not to install a modern meat counter in his corner grocery store.
   d. The Federal Reserve Board decides to tighten credit.
4. In his State of the Union address in January 1968, President Johnson asked for a surtax of 10 percent on personal incomes to help combat inflation. How would this measure affect the circular flow?
5. Who runs a free enterprise type of economic system?

SELECTED READINGS

Boulding, Kenneth E., *Economic Analysis,* Vol. 1, *Microeconomics.* New York: Harper & Row, Publishers, Inc., 1966, Chap. 2

Heilbroner, Robert L., *The Worldly Philosophers,* rev. ed. New York: Simon and Schuster, 1961, Chap. 2.

Lange, Oskar, and Fred M. Taylor, *On the Economic Theory of Socialism,* B. E. Lippincott, (ed.) Minneapolis: University of Minnesota Press, 1938

Smith, Adam, *An Inquiry into the Nature and Causes of the Wealth of Nations.* New York: Random House, Inc., Modern Library edition. Book 1, Chap. 2.

Business Firms

CHAPTER 3

Since business firms play a major role in the economic activity of a free enterprise economy, we must at this point examine the nature and functions of these institutions. What part do business firms play in over-all patterns of economic activity? What is their organizational structure? What is the current business firm population in the United States? These are the questions considered in this chapter.

ECONOMIC ACTIVITY OF BUSINESS FIRMS

In the preceding chapter we introduced business firms as the production units of the economy. But what does this mean? What constitutes production? The primary objective of economic activity is to satisfy man's wants as fully as possible from the limited means available—from the resources of the economy and from its usable technology. Production refers to any activity that moves or transforms resources from their current places or forms to places or forms that are either closer to the satisfying of wants or that make them more useful in accomplishing this objective. Schematically, production is often thought of in terms of using technology to transform resources into finished goods. With some refinements this conceptualization is essentially correct. When we think of an individual business firm we are usually considering only one link in a long chain of production processes, each of which brings raw and semi-finished materials closer to their ultimate users. But production for the economy as a whole is not complete until what is being produced is actually in the hands of its ultimate user. We call the outputs of processes farther removed from the ultimate consumer *lower-order goods and services* and those that are closer *higher-order goods and services.*

The extractive activities in the economy provide examples of firms producing lower-order outputs. Firms engaged in mining crude oil, iron and copper ore, lead, and zinc are typical, as are those engaged in agricultural pursuits. Most such outputs require further processing before they are ready to be consumed.

At the other extreme, retail stores produce higher-order outputs. Some people have difficulty thinking of a retail store as engaging in production at all, but fundamentally its activity is the same as that of a manufacturing firm. The resources it uses are items not yet accessible to the final user, and these include inventories in the hands of wholesalers and manufacturers, labor, and buildings and equipment. These resources are utilized to put products where they are accessible to consumers; that is, to complete the production process.

Between these extremes are firms operating at many different levels of production. Basic steel firms use iron ore and other resources to make steel ingots, which may be sold to processing firms and steel fabricators to be converted into forms useful in making many different products. Milling companies turn wheat into flour, cereal, feed for livestock, and other items that are further processed before being sold to consumers. The outputs of a great many firms are the resource inputs of a number of other firms as lower-order goods go through the many production processes necessary to make them useful to consumers.

Profit expectations provide the primary incentive for establishing and expanding business firms. Firms are born and flourish in areas where revenues from the sale of goods and services exceed the costs of all resources used in producing them. Where losses occur, that is, where revenues are less than the costs of all resources used, firms contract and die. The profit incentive may be tempered by or supplemented by other incentives—the safety of diversification into several product fields, the desire to obtain a large sales volume, the prestige of ownership of a business, and others—but firms will not remain in areas where losses persist over long periods of time.

FORMS OF BUSINESS FIRMS

With respect to legal organization, there are three major types of profit-seeking firms in the United States: (1) the sole proprietorship, (2) the partnership, and (3) the corporation. There are, of course, non-profit-seeking organizations that use resources to provide goods and services. These include religious, charitable, philanthropic, scientific, and educational institutions. This chapter focuses on the former, but it should be kept in mind that the latter exist also, frequently in the same three legal forms.

The Sole Proprietorship

Sole proprietorships are individually owned business firms. Many corner grocery stores, filling stations, barber shops, doctors' offices, and farms are in this category. One individual owns most of the capital resources of such a business—its building, equipment, and inventories of goods in process—although lease or rental arrangements may be made for some. The proprietor also usually operates the business. As one of three alternative forms of organization, the sole proprietorship has its pros and cons.

The Pros

The most common reason for a businessman to choose the sole proprietorship form of organization is the *ease with which it can be established.* What does it take to establish a farm? Usually all that is required is a decision to do so plus the means of financing the minimum amount of capital resources necessary to get started. For a grocery store no more is required. In most states barbers, dry cleaners, plumbers, doctors, morticians, and tavern owners must have in addition a license in order to set themselves up in business, although this requirement holds as well if the business is a partnership or corporation.

Proprietors have greater *freedom and flexibility* in making a wide variety of decisions than the managers of other forms of business organizations simply because there is no one other than themselves to whom they are accountable for their actions. On 63rd Street in Chicago a sign reading, "Gone Fishing, Be Back Saturday" appeared regularly on the locked door of a candy store. Could the manager of a corporation or most partnerships get by with actions of this sort? The proprietor is free to switch from one line of business to another. He can withdraw money from the business for his personal use or he can invest more money in the business as he desires.

The Cons

The most important restraints placed on a sole proprietor are (1) his limited access to funds for investing in the business and carrying on its operations and (2) his inability to separate his business assets from his personal assets for liability purposes. A sole proprietor about to get a good thing going may find that he has *difficulties in securing funds* that will convert his dreams into reality. To set up a business in the first place he must have money available to purchase the minimum amounts of capital resources—land, buildings, and equipment—necessary to operate. If he wants to expand the business, still more money is needed, both to increase his productive capacity and to pay the additional costs of operating at higher levels of output. He has access to two types of financing: (1) equity financing and (2) debt financing.

Equity financing refers to the financing of a business through the acquisition of ownership interests in it. The owner uses whatever savings he may have to purchase his plant and equipment and to operate it. Over time, if the business does well, some of the profits, or the excess of receipts over the costs of all resources used in the production process, can be used to finance expansion. The limitation on the equity financing available to the proprietor is set by the extent of his personal assets or his personal fortune.

Debt financing refers to funds that the owner of the business borrows. A single proprietor may go to a bank, to a savings and loan association, or to some other type of lending institution, but the amount that he can borrow will depend upon the lending institution's evaluation of him and his business prospects. Most proprietors are not able to obtain much in the way of long-term loans simply because their long-term prospects are uncertain. Thus borrowing by proprietorships is largely in the form of short-term loans to carry on current operations, for example, to finance inventories.

Debt financing of a slightly different sort may be used also in carrying on current business operations. The proprietor of a grocery store may purchase canned goods on credit from a wholesaler, agreeing to make payment in 30, 60, or 90 days, depending upon the terms of the agreement. Short-term credit of this kind can be quite important for sole proprietors, but it may be largely offset by credit that the proprietor in turn extends to his customers.

Unlimited liability of the proprietor for debts of the business constitutes the second disadvantage of the sole proprietorship. The proprietor cannot separate claims by creditors upon his business from their claims on his personal belongings. If the proprietor does not pay his business debts, his creditors can legally attach not only his business property but also such personal property as his house and his automobile up to the extent of their claims. This creditors' weapon is double-barreled. If the proprietor's wife runs up personal debts for mink coats, jewelry, and the like, her creditors can attach the business property. Most states provide some relief for the debtor, however, by specifying a minimum value of property that is not subject to attachment.

The Partnership

As defined by the Uniform Partnership Act which most states have enacted, a partnership is a voluntary association of two or more persons who as co-owners operate a business for profit. Co-ownership means that the assets of the business are owned by the partners as a group rather than by the individual partners; one partner cannot pick out which specific assets are his and which belong to the other(s). Similarly, business liabilities are group liabilities. Operation of the business for profit means that this is the objective of the group, even though losses may in fact be incurred. Though somewhat more complex, the characteristics of the partnership are similar to those of the sole proprietorship.

The Pros

The partnership is also born easily, since its existence does not require approval by any governmental unit. Only an agreement among the partners is necessary. This may be written or oral; in fact, it may even be inferred from the activities of persons carrying on some business activity jointly. A written agreement drawn up by a lawyer is ordinarily used, since it provides some measure of protection to each partner from the others. Among other things, it spells out what each partner is to put into the business in the form of money, managerial effort, or capital goods, and it usually specifies the ratio in which profits or losses are to be shared as well as the distribution of business assets in the event of dissolution. If the agreement has been properly drawn up and one or more partners fail to live up to their specified obligations, the others can sue.

A further advantage of the partnership is that *it lends itself more to specialization of talents* than does the sole proprietorship. Partnerships are often formed to take advantage of complementary skills. A medical partnership may be formed by an obstetrician and a pediatrician; a legal partnership may include a skilled trial lawyer and one whose specialty is contracts and negotiable instruments; an accounting partnership may be formed by an accountant who directs the office work and a nonaccountant with good public contacts. A partnership, taking advantage of complementary fields of specialization, may prosper where any one of the partners working alone would fare badly.

The Cons

One of the most serious drawbacks to the partnership is *unlimited liability* of each partner for the debts of the firm. If a partner absconds to Brazil with all of the firm's liquid assets, the remaining partner(s) are personally liable for the business debts. As in the case of the sole proprietorship, the personal property of any one co-owner can be attached by creditors to satisfy their claims against the business. Partners caught in a situation of this kind can take legal action against the villain—if they can get him back to the court with the appropriate jurisdiction—but this in no way diminishes their individual responsibilities to creditors.

Closely related to the unlimited liability principle is the *agency rule* of partnerships. In the general type of partnership arrangement, any one of the partners may act in the name of the firm, committing the firm to those actions. The firm is bound even though the partner acts without the consent of the others and even though the action is outside the area assigned to him by the partnership agreement. Limited partnership arrangements are possible, however, in which certain individuals of the firm are designated as limited partners, with circumscribed areas within which they can commit the firm legally.

Partnerships encounter much the same kinds of *financing limitations* as sole proprietorships, although the partnership has an advantage in equity financing in that there are more co-owners to provide it. Debt financing, too, may be easier, since creditors know that they will have recourse to more than one individual should the firm default on its payments. Nevertheless, limits are set by the personal assets of the partners and by the amounts that financial institutions are willing to lend the business. An understandable reluctance on the part of the business to grow by taking in more partners arises from the unlimited liability principle and from the agency rule.

The Corporation

Most large business enterprises are organized as corporations. A corporation can be thought of as an entity separate and apart from the individuals who own it. From a legal point of view in many ways it functions like a person. It can contract debts or extend credit in its own name; it can hold title to property; it can be taxed; and it can sue and be sued. But what makes this organizational form so attractive for large enterprises?

The Pros

One advantage of the corporation is that *ownership of the business can be transferred* among individuals independently of the life and operation of the business. When ownership of a sole proprietorship or any part of a partnership changes hands, the old business ceases to exist and a new one is established. Frequently the death of an owner will result in the dissolution of the firm. On the other hand, if one buys a share of Republic Steel Corporation stock he becomes a part owner of the firm. The purchase of the share does not affect business operations and neither does its sale. Every stock market transaction is a transfer of ownership, and to a large extent the impact on business operations of the firms involved is either negligible or slight, since the stock purchased or sold is a small porportion of the total amount outstanding for any one firm. Stockholders do, however, elect boards of directors, and these in turn appoint the corporate officers. Obviously the transfer of a large enough block of stock of a corporation can change the composition of management and the course of business operations, but the continuity of the firm's business—its legal obligations to others and their obligations to it—is unaffected.

Another attractive feature of the corporate form of business is the *limited liability* of owners for business debts. If the corporation's gross income is not sufficient to meet its expenses and its debt obligations, the most that a stockholder can lose is what he has invested in his stock. Business creditors have no claim on the personal assets of any owner. They can force the firm into bankruptcy and divide the proceeds from the sale of its assets, but this is as far as they can go. The corporate structure is an effective device for insulating any one owner from the actions of other owners or of management.

Corporations also possess a greater *capacity for obtaining financial backing* than do proprietorships and partnerships. Equity financing is accomplished partly through the sale of stock. Debt financing can come from loans to the corporation, credit extended to it, or the sale of the corporation's bonds. The case with which shares of stock can be transferred and the limited liability of stockholders makes incorporation an attractive way of bringing together equity funds to start a business or to expand it. The firm can have a very large number of stockholders—American Telephone and Telegraph has over two and a half million—and the holdings of each can be almost as large or as small as the individual desires. It is not at all difficult for a successful company to issue and sell additional shares of stock to obtain money for expansion.

Corporations frequently use retained earnings to finance expansion, and this too is a form of equity financing. After a firm has paid all of its expenses—costs of resources hired or purchased from others—whatever it has left from its total receipts belongs to its owners. A corporation may pay all of these net earnings to stockholders as dividends, or it may elect to pay out a part of them only, holding the rest as retained earnings. If it follows the latter course, retained earnings may be used to finance expansion of the firm. Since these earnings really belong to the stockholders, their use for this purpose can legitimately be thought of as equity financing.

The corporation can also use debt financing to a greater extent than either the proprietorship or the partnership. It has special capacities for obtaining loans from financial institutions and issuing and selling bonds. The greater stability of the corporation, arising out of its ownership structures and its equity-financing capabilities, makes it a better risk on the average and enables it to borrow more easily from banks or other institutions.

Bond sales provide an important source of borrowing for corporations. A *bond* is a promise to pay to its purchaser at the end of a stated period of time a certain sum of money, with interest to be paid on the sum at regular intervals. The purchaser of the bond is in effect making a long-term loan to the corporation. When the bond reaches its maturity date and is paid off, the debt of the corporation is, of course, cancelled.

The Cons

The corporation is a little *more difficult to set up* than the proprietorship or the partnership, but this frequently cited disadvantage should not be overemphasized. Governmental approval, usually state but in some cases federal,[1] is required, but it is ordinarily automatic if the proper organizational steps have been completed. Prospective stockholders apply for a charter to the government of the state in which their principal office is to be located. Among other things, the application contains the name of the corporation, its purposes, the location of its principal office, the amount of stock it is authorized to issue, and the subscribers to its initial issue of stock. Upon approval by the appropriate state agency, the application becomes the corporation charter. Stock is issued and the first meeting of the stockholders is held. By-laws for the operation of the corporation are adopted and a board of directors is elected. The directors appoint the corporation officers and the corporation is ready to engage in the economic activities for which it was established. Since the provisions of the charter and of the by-laws can be amended easily, no great handicap is placed on the corporate form of business by legal organizational requirements; the process of organization is just more cumbersome than that for the other forms of businesses.

A more significant disadvantage of the corporation is the *treatment accorded it by tax laws,* both federal and state. Corporations pay corporate income taxes on their net earnings. When net earnings are distributed as dividends to stockholders, the latter pay personal income taxes on all dividends received except for a small exemption. The owners of the corporation thus find two tax bites taken out of the income of their business. Proprietorships and partnerships pay no business income tax on their net

---

[1]National banks, for example, are chartered by the federal government.

earnings; rather, net earnings are taxed only as personal income of the owners.[2]

Another alleged disadvantage of the corporation is that *corporate management and corporate ownership are distinct from one another.* The managers may be owners or stockholders, too, but they typically hold a small minority of total shares outstanding. Thus, if they so desire, the managers can pursue courses of action contrary to that desired by stockholders. To whom is the possibility of separation of ownership and control a disadvantage? It probably plays little part in the initial decision of whether to organize a business as a corporation or as a proprietorship or partnership. In a large enterprise managers may take actions such as paying themselves large bonuses that benefit them at the expense of the stockholders, but by and large both groups are interested in making the firm a profitable enterprise. Much controversy surrounds the issue of ownership versus control, but not much in the way of definitive conclusions have been reached.

THE BUSINESS POPULATION

How many business firms are there in the United States? How do the three organizational forms rank in importance? Does the dominant form of organization differ for different kinds of productive activity; that is, is it likely that one will be more adaptable to one kind of production while another is paramount in a different line?

Business Population by Organizational Form

From the discussion of the preceding section, under what form of business organization would you expect to find the greatest number of firms in the United States? Ease of organization and financial limitations on growth and expansion would point to the sole proprietorship as the most likely candidate. Available information, presented in Table 3–1, indicates that this is indeed the case and has been throughout the time period covered by the table. Somewhat less than one tenth of all business firms are partnerships and somewhat more than one tenth are corporations. The other four fifths are sole proprietorships.

The absolute number of firms may be a little surprising. There are over

---

[2] Much can be said on both sides about the "fairness" or "justice" of so-called double taxation of corporate net income. Most arguments for it maintain that the privileges or advantages of doing business as a corporation justify it. Arguments against it are to the effect that all forms of business enterprise should be accorded the same tax treatment.

TABLE 3-1

Business Firms in the United States by
Form of Organization, Selected Years

YEAR	SOLE PROPRIETORSHIPS (THOUSANDS)	PARTNERSHIPS (THOUSANDS)	CORPORATIONS (THOUSANDS)	TOTAL (THOUSANDS)
1947	6,624	889	552	8,065
1953	7,715	959	698	9,372
1957	8,738	971	940	10,649
1959	9,142	949	1,074	11,165
1960	9,090	941	1,141	11,172
1961	9,242	939	1,190	11,371
1962	9,183	932	1,268	11,383
1963	9,136	924	1,323	11,383
1964	9,193	922	1,374	11,489
1965	9,078	914	1,428	11,420

SOURCES: *Statistics of Income, 1964,* U.S. Treasury Department, Internal Revenue Service, pp. 122, 124, 128; *Statistics of Income, 1965 Preliminary,* U.S. Treasury Department, Internal Revenue Service, Corporation Income Tax Returns, p. 2 and U.S. Business Tax Returns, pp. 1, 2.

11 million in existence. Since the total population of the United States is in the neighborhood of 200 million, there is a business firm for almost every 20 persons. The total number has been expanding steadily over the years and all three forms have shared in the growth, although the corporate form shows the highest rate of increase of the three.

Organizational Forms and Size of Firms

We would expect sole proprietorships to be small businesses and Table 3–2 confirms this expectation. Over six out of nine sole proprietorships had gross or total incomes of less than $10,000 in 1962; over two out of nine had gross incomes of $10,000–$50,000; the number with higher income levels was relatively small; and those in the under $50,000 per year classes accounted for 42.39 percent of sole proprietorship income.

Although many corporations are small, we would expect most large businesses to be corporations. If we look at the number of firms with gross receipts of $1 million or more per year, the overwhelming proportion—about 90 percent—are corporations. Further, these corporations received over 96 percent of the total gross income earned by all firms in this gross receipts category.

Most partnerships are found in the under $500,000 per year total receipts classes. Medium-sized firms in the $50,000–$500,000 bracket, comprising somewhat less than one third of all partnerships, received a little over 50 percent of all partnership income; however, in this income range, corporations were much more numerous and received two and one-half

TABLE 3-2
Business Receipts and Number of Firms by Form of Organization and Adjusted Gross Income Classes, 1962*

SIZE OF BUSINESS RECEIPTS	SOLE PROPRIETORSHIP			PARTNERSHIP			CORPORATION		
	NUMBER OF FIRMS	BUSINESS RECEIPTS (THOUSANDS OF DOLLARS)	PERCENT OF TOTAL BUSINESS RECEIPTS	NUMBER OF FIRMS	BUSINESS RECEIPTS (THOUSANDS OF DOLLARS)	PERCENT OF TOTAL BUSINESS RECEIPTS	NUMBER OF FIRMS	BUSINESS RECEIPTS (THOUSANDS OF DOLLARS)	PERCENT OF TOTAL BUSINESS RECEIPTS
Under $10,000	5,738,683	18,959,511	10.63	301,849	1,113,065	1.54	183,567	470,835	.05
$10,000–$50,000	2,530,491	56,669,021	31.76	317,002	8,001,102	11.06	296,234	6,403,321	.72
$50,000–$500,000	761,752	84,823,411	47.54	268,120	36,432,583	50.39	528,960	90,347,661	10.09
$500,000–$1,000,000	15,442	10,512,308	5.89	12,357	8,449,407	11.69	94,857	64,069,934	7.16
$1 million and over	4,671	7,456,232	4.18	7,232	18,307,627	25.32	104,986	733,828,634	81.98
Receipts not reported	131,547			25,621			59,438		
Total	9,182,586	178,420,483	100.00	932,181	72,303,784	100.00	1,268,042	895,120,385	100.00

* Data in this form are not available for later years.
SOURCE: Statistics of Income, 1962, U.S. Treasury Department, Internal Revenue Service, pp. 34, 120, 233.

TABLE 3-3
Distribution of Business Firms and Business Receipts by Form of Organization and Type of Economic Activity, 1965

STANDARD INDUSTRIAL CLASSIFICATION	SOLE PROPRIETORSHIP			PARTNERSHIP			CORPORATION		
	NUMBER OF FIRMS (THOUSANDS)	BUSINESS RECEIPTS (MILLIONS OF DOLLARS)	PERCENT OF TOTAL BUSINESS RECEIPTS	NUMBER OF FIRMS (THOUSANDS)	BUSINESS RECEIPTS (MILLIONS OF DOLLARS)	PERCENT OF TOTAL BUSINESS RECEIPTS	NUMBER OF FIRMS (THOUSANDS)	BUSINESS RECEIPTS (MILLIONS OF DOLLARS)	PERCENT OF TOTAL BUSINESS RECEIPTS
Agriculture, forestry, and fishing	3,225	32,160	16.13	128	5,024	6.83	28	7,256	.64
Mining	36	943	.47	15	866	1.18	13	12,172	1.08
Construction	705	19,308	9.68	58	7,003	9.52	113	56,085	4.97
Manufacturing	186	7,267	3.64	37	5,596	7.60	187	505,235	44.75
Transportation, communication, and utilities	297	5,527	2.77	18	1,315	1.79	60	86,782	7.69
Wholesale and retail	1,854	97,190	48.74	235	34,373	46.71	442	363,096	32.16
Finance, insurance, and real estate	539	7,022	3.52	249	6,845	9.30	390	61,590	5.45
Services	2,208	29,789	14.94	169	12,442	16.91	188	36,775	3.25
Total[1]	9,078	199,385	99.89	914	73,588	99.84	1,428	1,129,075	100.00

[1] Estimates are rounded and may not add to totals. Not shown separately, but included in the appropriate totals, are data for the industry classifications "Wholesale and retail trade not allocable" and "Nature of business not allocable."

SOURCE: *Statistics of Income, 1965, Preliminary,* U.S. Treasury Department, Internal Revenue Service, U.S. Business Tax Returns, pp. 1, 2, and Corporation Income Tax Returns, pp. 14–19.

times as much gross income. It is interesting to note that almost one fourth of all partnership income was earned by the less than 1 percent of all partnerships receiving gross income of $1 million per year or over. The bulk of these are in the area of retail and wholesale trade.

Organizational Forms by Type of Economic Activity

Are different types of productive activity likely to foster one organizational form over others? Examine Table 3-3, in which the standard industrial classification of types of economic activity is used. In agriculture the sole proprietorship is clearly predominant in terms of both number of firms and in amount of total income earned by these firms. The same situation prevails in the services area.

Why is this the case? In agriculture the explanation seems to be that a farm business is rather easy to establish. Neither a large amount of money nor a high degree of skill is required to operate in the field, although both may be necessary if the endeavor is to be profitable. In services we find a wide variety of activities—medical, legal, personal, repair, recreation, lodging, and others. In many of these areas large-scale organization does not yield clear-cut advantages. The nature of the business often makes it a one-man show, and at the same time financial requirements for establishing and operating the business may not be great enough to warrant incorporation.

In all of the other activities sole proprietorships outnumber each of the other two forms of organization while corporations have the largest amounts of income received. The pre-eminence of the corporate form is especially evident in mnaufacturing; in transportation, communications, and utilities; and in wholesale and retail trade. In these areas large firms are generally much more efficient than small ones, and the corporation provides the vehicle for financing them.

The data we have do not indicate that the partnership form is preferred in any of the areas. Incorporation is a little more complex than drawing up a partnership agreement and offers much greater financial advantages. Partnerships are often a transitory step in the evolution of growing firms from the sole proprietorship to the corporate form.

SUMMARY

Business firms are the economic units that engage in production; that is, in activity that moves or transforms resources to a place or form nearer to that in which they are ultimately used. The outputs of production processes farther removed from the satisfying of consumer wants are called lower-order goods while those closer to the satisfying of consumer wants are higher-order goods. Business firms produce outputs at all levels, from extraction of raw materials to the placing of goods in the hands of their ultimate consumers. Profits provide the incentive for the creation and operation of business firms.

From a legal point of view there are three forms of business organization: (1) the sole proprietorship, (2) the partnership, and (3) the corporation. Sole proprietorships are business firms owned by one person or one family. Partnerships are firms owned by two or more individuals but which are not incorporated. Corporations are businesses set up as legal entities that can operate as a sort of legal person.

The sole proprietorship form has both advantages and disadvantages. Among the advantages are the ease with which it can be established and the freedom and flexibility it offers with respect to decision-making by its owner-manager. Its disadvantages are that funds for financing expansion and operation of the business are limited in amount and that the proprietor has unlimited liability for business debts.

We distinguish between equity financing of a business and debt financing. The former means that funds are provided the business by owners or in exchange for ownership interests. Debt financing means that the business obtains funds by borrowing or by going into debt.

Partnerships, like sole proprietorships, are easily formed. They have broader possibilities for specialization of managerial talents and for equity financing than have sole proprietorships. The disadvantages of a partnership are unlimited liability of each partner for partnership debts, the agency rule, under which any one partner can take actions binding the partnership, and limited sources of financing.

The advantages of a corporation are easy transferability of ownership interests, limited liability of owners for business debts, and much broader sources of financing than are available to the other two organizational forms. On the other side of the ledger, corporations are somewhat more complex to establish; their incomes are subjected to more onerous tax treatment than that of proprietorships and partnerships, and there is usually a separation of ownership from control of the corporation.

We find that in the United States there are more than 11 million business firms in existence. Four fifths of these are sole proprietorships, less than one tenth are partnerships, and more than one tenth are corporations. Most sole proprietorships have a gross income of less than $50,000 per year. Over 90 percent of firms with gross incomes of over $1 million per year are corporations. Partnerships are more numerous in the under $500,000 gross income classes than in the over $500,000 classes.

With respect to types of economic activity, the sole proprietorship is predominant in agriculture and in the services in both number of firms and amount of total income received. It also outnumbers the other organizational forms in every other major category of the standard industrial classification; however, corporations predominate in income received in each of the other categories. The partnership is predominant in none, neither in number of firms nor in income received.

EXERCISES AND QUESTIONS FOR DISCUSSION

1. Evaluate the statement: "Separation of ownership and control is common in U.S. corporations because in only a very few instances does any one stockholder control 51 percent of the voting stock."
2. Mr. Jones goes into the business of making lamp shades. What kind of business organization is implied by each of the following situations:
   a. He invests $30,000 of his own money and hires Mr. Smith along with 10 other men to work for him.
   b. He invests $30,000 of his own money, borrows $20,000 from Mr. Smith, agreeing to pay it back over a five-year period at 6 percent interest, and hires Mr. Smith along with 10 other men to work for him.
   c. He, his wife, Mr. Smith, and Smith's wife apply for a state charter for their business. They sell 1000 shares at $50 per share. Mr. Jones manages the business while Mr. Smith and 10 other men work for him.
   d. He invests $30,000 of his money and $30,000 of Mr. Smith's, with the agreement that they will share equally in the profits of the business. Jones manages the business, and Smith along with 10 other men work for him.
3. Indicate whether a business firm is using debt financing or equity financing in each of the following cases:
   a. It sells a $10,000 long-term bond.
   b. It sells 1000 shares of stock at $10 a share.
   c. It obtains a loan of $10,000 from the First National Bank.
   d. It obtains a loan of $10,000 from a friend of the manager.
   e. It uses $10,000 out of last year's earnings.
   Explain your answer for each case.
4. Five individuals get together to form a flying club and to purchase an airplane jointly. Should they form a partnership or a corporation? Explain your answer in detail.

SELECTED READINGS

Berle, A. A., and G. C. Means, *The Modern Corporation and Private Property.* New York: Commerce Clearing House, 1932.
Churchill, Betty C., "Business Population by Legal Form of Organization," *Survey of Current Business,* Vol. 35 (April 1955), pp. 14–20.
Weston, J. Fred and E. F. Brigham, *Managerial Finance.* 2d ed. New York: Holt, Rinehart and Winston, Inc., 1966, Chaps. 1–3.

Markets, Demand, Supply, and Prices

CHAPTER 4

Prices play a stellar role in economic analysis, although this is not always apparent to us as buyers or sellers of goods and services. When we buy textbooks or clothing or entertainment, what is most apparent to us is that we would prefer lower prices. As sellers of used books, labor services, and well-worn automobiles we seldom receive prices as high as we would like them to be. What causes prices to be what they are?

This chapter focuses on the principles that apply not only to the pricing of consumer goods and services but also to the determination of wage rates, land rents, and the returns on capital goods. The market situation that forms the framework of price determination as it is discussed in this chapter is a simplified one called *pure competition* and its main characteristics will be explained at appropriate points. In a purely competitive market setting the price of any product, service, or resource is determined by the interacting forces of demand and supply. We shall analyze demand and supply in turn and then demonstrate how they interact to determine price. The chapter concludes with an examination of the elasticity of demand.

MARKETS

Is a market a physical place where buyers and sellers make contact with each other and engage in exchange? It may be, but this is a marked oversimplification. Buyers and sellers need not confront each other physically as they do at an auction or in a grocery store. Many kinds of transactions can be carried out by telephone or by mail. The important point is that a market exists wherever buyers and sellers of a product or service are in touch with one another and can engage in exchange.

The areas embraced by different markets vary widely depending partly upon the nature of what is being exchanged. The markets for some items are local. People seldom travel beyond the neighborhood, to say nothing of the city itself, to get a haircut. Other markets are regional. For milk and fresh dairy products, the possibility of spoilage precludes shipment across the continent. Some markets are national in scope. Light airplanes from all over the nation are listed in trade publications, and a prospective purchaser or seller will go almost anywhere in the country for an advantageous exchange. Still other markets, like that for such well-known securities as American Telephone and Telegraph stock, operate on an international basis.

The extent of a market will depend, too, on whether we are thinking of it in terms of a short or a long period of time. Over a short period— say six months—accountants in the Wichita area may not be willing to consider employment in other cities because their homes, their families, and their friends are in Wichita. For this time period the market for accountants would be local. But if business activity in the city should become permanently slack, for example, if Boeing and other aircraft manufacturers moved elsewhere, better long-term earning possibilities in Kansas City or Denver might very well entice accountants away from Wichita. The extent of the market is correspondingly broader, but a time period of several years may be required to make it so.

DEMAND

The behavior of buyers in the market for a specific good or service is summed up in the term *demand*. We often speak of demand for a product as being some quantity of it that people need, but we shall find that the quantity demanded or needed is not invariate. Rather, it is determined by several factors that will be explored in some detail in this section.

Demand Schedules and Demand Curves

The determinants of demand are best explained in terms of a *demand schedule* or a *demand curve*. Suppose we ask ourselves how much margarine per year will be purchased in a given market. An immediate and important observation comes to mind—the quantity that will be taken depends upon its price. From everyday experience with many goods and services we know that at higher prices less will be taken than at lower prices. This *law of demand* is usually illustrated with a demand schedule or a demand curve showing the quantities that will be purchased at all alternative prices, other things being equal. Such a demand schedule is presented in Table 4–1.

The demand schedule must be read correctly. Note that in the table the quantity column shows the *rates* at which buyers are willing to purchase the product; that is, it shows the quantities per month they are willing to purchase. Unless we specify the time period during which the quantities will be taken, the figures in this column have no real meaning. For example, at a price of 70 cents the schedule states that buyers are willing to take 4000 pounds. If the time period were not specified, we could infer 4000 pounds per month or per year or per day, and the information would be meaningless. However, the quantity column states that the product will be purchased by buyers at a rate of 4000 pounds per month and this is information that makes sense.

TABLE 4–1
Hypothetical Demand Schedule for Margarine

Price of Margarine (cents per lb.)	Quantity of Margarine (lbs. per month)
100	1,000
90	2,000
80	3,000
70	4,000
60	5,000
50	6,000
40	7,000
30	8,000
20	9,000
10	10,000

The quantity column shows rates of purchase at *alternative* possible prices. Thus if the price were 70 cents per pound, purchasers would be willing to take only 4000 pounds per month; but if the price were 60 cents per pound, they would be willing to take 5000 pounds per month. Each price–quantity combination must be thought of as a separate and distinct alternative showing the total amount that buyers will take per time period at the indicated price.

A *demand curve* conveys the same information as a demand schedule, but it shows the information graphically instead of arithmetically. The demand schedule of Table 4–1 is plotted as a demand curve in Figure 4–1. Price per pound is measured along the vertical axis and pounds per month that would be purchased are measured along the horizontal axis.

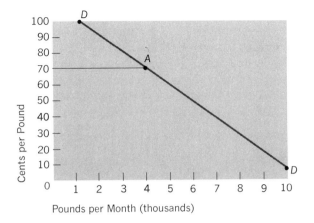

Figure 4–1
A demand curve for margarine.

Any point on the demand curve shows the quantity that would be taken at a particular price, or, alternatively, the price that consumers would be willing to pay for a particular quantity. For example, point *A* shows that at a price of 70 cents per pound, purchasers would be willing to take as much as 4000 pounds per month. It also indicates that for a total of 4000 pounds per month purchasers would be willing to pay as much as 70 cents per pound.

The Law of Demand

The law of demand, which states that more of a product will be purchased at lower prices than at higher prices, is not startlingly new to any of us, but the proposition is an important one in economic analysis. One of its most important implications is that for any given product, price can go high enough to induce purchasers voluntarily to limit their total purchases to the quantity available. This rationing function of price will be discussed in more detail later. Why do purchasers buy less at higher prices than at lower prices? In a way this seems a little like asking why water runs downhill, but our understanding of demand will be more complete if we look at the forces that are operative.

As higher prices of a product are considered by prospective purchasers, a *substitution effect* is at work. The higher the price of steak relative to that of pork chops, the less satisfaction a given expenditure on steak will yield relative to the same expenditure on pork chops—or the more satisfaction the expenditure will yield relatively when spent on pork chops instead of on steak. Thus as the price of steak rises, pork chops are substituted for steak and the total quantity of steak purchased decreases.

Additionally, there is usually an *income effect* at work. An increase in product prices when the dollars that purchasers have to spend is fixed reduces the quantities that can be purchased. A rise in the price of steak reduces the purchasing power of consumers, causing them to buy less steak as well as less of many other goods and services. The income effect ordinarily reinforces the substitution effect, making quantities purchased of any good or service vary inversely with the price.

Changes in Demand

The concept of a demand curve must be sharpened in order to avoid confusion over terminology. Suppose that DD in Figure 4–2 is the demand curve for fluid milk in the San Francisco area. Price is initially P_1 and the corresponding quantity purchased by consumers is X_1 gallons. Now suppose that price falls to P_2 and quantity taken increases to X_2. Has demand for fluid milk changed? Alternatively, suppose that a new calcium diet catches on in the area, increasing the intensity of consumer preferences for milk, so that at price P_1 consumers now want X_2 rather than X_1 gallons. Has demand for fluid milk changed?

If we refer to both of the foregoing circumstances as a change in demand, we invite analytical chaos. They are quite different situations. At the outset, then, we shall assign specific terminology to each situation and adhere to it throughout the book. We shall call the first case a *movement along a given demand curve,* or *a change in quantity demanded* because of a price change, and the second case a *change in demand.*

We should think of the term demand as referring to an entire demand curve. It expresses the functional relationship between the price of a product and the quantity of the product that buyers in the market

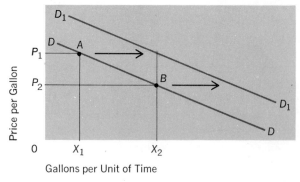

Figure 4–2
A change in demand.

are willing to take, other things being equal or constant. Thus a movement from *A* to *B* in Figure 4–2 is not a change in demand according to our terminology.

A change in demand means a change in the position or slope of a demand curve. In Figure 4–2 if the demand curve moves from DD to D_1D_1, an *increase in demand* has occurred. This increase may result from such factors as an increase in consumer incomes, anticipation of an imminent increase in the price of the product, an increase in the price of powdered milk, or a decrease in the price of cereals. Conversely, a movement of the demand curve from D_1D_1 to DD represents a *decrease in demand.* The causes of a decrease will be the opposite of those that bring about an increase in demand. It is worth noting that when we define demand for a product, stipulating that "other things" remain constant, we are in no sense leaving the possibility of changes in the "other things" out of consideration. We are setting up an analytical apparatus that permits us to take explicit account of such changes.

"Other Things Being Equal"

We have just noted that the price of a product is not the only factor that affects the quantity of it that consumers in the market are willing to purchase. Several other forces are operative, the most important ones being consumer preferences, consumer incomes, consumer expectations, and the prices of related goods. A change in any one of these will change the quantity of the product that consumers are willing to purchase even if there is no change in the product price. Consequently, to establish how differences in the price alone of a product affect the quantities that consumers will take, we must rule out changes in these "other things." Only if the other things are held constant can we establish a demand curve showing a unique set of quantities that consumers are willing to take at alternative prices.

Consumer preferences refer to the intensities of consumers' desires for products. The preferences of consumers for some items change rather slowly over time. Housing and staple food items are examples. For other items preferences may change rather rapidly, for example, styles of women's clothes. Changes in preferences change the demand curves for products. A given demand curve for one product can be established only on the assumption that preferences are constant at the time the curve is established.

Consumer incomes are thought of in demand analysis as the entire amount of money available for the group of consumers in the market to spend per time period. They consist of earnings plus whatever credit sources are available. Obviously, in order to estabish a unique set of quantities demanded at alternative prices of a product, the total dollar purchasing power of the group of consumers must not change. If incomes change either up or down, the demand curve itself will move to the right or to the left.

Consumer expectations also affect the quantities of a product that consumers will take at alternative prices. Suppose that consumers develop an expectation that the price of the product in question will rise sharply in the near future. They are likely to increase their rate of purchase at the present price over what it would have been had the change in expectations not occurred; that is, the demand curve shifts to the right. The state of consumer expectations must be assumed constant for a given demand curve to be established for a product.

The effect of changes in the *prices of related goods* on the quantities taken of a given good at alternative prices depends upon the nature of the relationship. Related goods may be complements or substitutes. *Complementary goods* are those that must be consumed together, such as tennis rackets and tennis balls. *Substitute products* are those such as beef and pork that can be consumed in lieu of one another.

Suppose that we are trying to establish a demand curve for tennis balls. We have determined that at a price of 50 cents per ball the market will take 1000 balls per month. But now the price of rackets suddenly doubles. Tennis players cut down on their rates of purchases of rackets and on their tennis activity. The quantity of balls that consumers will take at 50 cents each drops to some figure such as 700 per month. Thus a rise in the price of one of two complementary goods will decrease demand for the other, so in defining the demand curve for one the price of the other must be held at a constant level.

Substitute products affect each other the other way around. A rise in the price of pork will cause people to increase their consumption of beef if beef prices remain unchanged. Consequently, the price of pork must be assumed to remain constant when we establish the demand curve for beef.

SUPPLY

We use the concept of *supply* to analyze the sellers' side of a market, and many of the points developed in demand analysis can be carried over to the supply side. We first examine supply schedules and supply curves and then identify the "other things being equal." Finally, we differentiate between movements along a supply curve and changes in supply.

Supply Schedules and Supply Curves

What determines the quantities of margarine that sellers will place on sale in a given market? Obviously price will be an important determinant, but additional factors are also operative. In order to handle all of them analytically we define supply of a product as *the quantities that all sellers are willing to place on the market at alternative prices, other things being equal.* A hypothetical supply schedule for margarine is given in Table 4–2 and is plotted as a supply curve in Figure 4–3.

TABLE 4–2
Hypothetical Supply Schedule for Margarine

PRICE OF MARGARINE (CENTS PER LB.)	QUANTITY OF MARGARINE (LBS. PER MONTH)
10	2,000
20	3,000
30	4,000
40	5,000
50	6,000
60	7,000
70	8,000
80	9,000
90	10,000
100	11,000

Whereas demand curves generally slope downward to the right, supply curves ordinarily are upward sloping. The reasons for this are not hard to find. First, at higher prices it becomes more attractive to sellers to place goods on the market rather than to hold them in inventory. Second, at

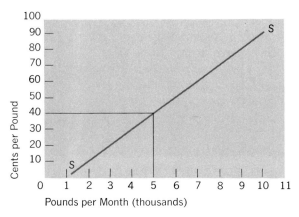

Figure 4–3
A supply curve for margarine.

higher prices the most profitable sales levels for existing producers are ordinarily greater than they are at lower prices. Third, higher profit possibilities attract new sellers into the field, expanding still more the total quantities made available for sale at higher prices.

Changes in Supply

The same considerations apply to supply as apply to demand in differentiating between a movement along a supply curve and a change in supply. We shall use the term supply to mean an entire supply curve. Accordingly, a movement from C to D in Figure 4–4 is not a change in supply but a change in *quantity supplied* as a result of a change in the product price. The supply curve has not moved.

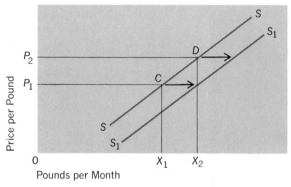

Figure 4–4
A change in supply.

A *change in supply* is represented by a change in the position or shape of the supply curve, such as that from SS to S_1S_1 in Figure 4–4. An *increase in supply* is a movement or shift of the supply curve to the right, while a *decrease in supply* is represented by a shift to the left. These shifts are caused by changes in the "other things."

"Other Things Being Equal"

As with demand, in order to establish a unique functional relationship between the price of a product and the quantity of it that sellers will place on the market, there are "other things" that must be held constant. These are, of course, the factors other than price that influence the quantities that sellers want to sell. The most important are (1) resource prices, (2) the range of production techniques available to producers of the product, and (3) producer expectations. Changes in any or all of these factors will affect the quantities per time period that sellers will place on the market at any given price.

Consider first the effects of different *resource price levels* on supply. Suppose that at current resource prices the sellers of Figure 4–3 are willing to place 5000 pounds of margarine per month on the market at a price of 40 cents per pound. Now suppose that prices of the resources used in making and marketing the product fall by 10 percent. Sellers can now place the 5000 pounds on the market at a lower price, or at the same price they can place a larger quantity on the market. Either alternative should be interpreted as a move off the supply curve *SS*. Thus in defining a given state of supply or a given supply curve resource prices must be held constant.

Similarly, if *production techniques* become more efficient, production of any particular quantity of a product per month becomes less expensive for producers. This amounts to saying that at any given price such as 40 cents per pound, sellers can place more than 5000 pounds per month on the market. It is clear then that in establishing a specific supply curve the state of production techniques must be held constant.

Changes in *producer expectations* operate in much the same way as do changes in consumer expectations. Suppose again in Figure 4–3 that initially at some such price as 40 cents per pound producers, expecting no price changes, would place 5000 pounds of margarine on the market. Now suppose that a decrease in the price of butter is believed to be just around the corner. Larger quantities of margarine will be thrown on the market at 40 cents and a movement to the right of supply curve *SS* occurs. In order to stake out a given supply curve, then, producer expectations must remain constant.

DETERMINATION OF MARKET PRICE AND QUANTITY EXCHANGED

Buyers and sellers interact in markets to determine product prices. Demand curves bring together the forces motivating buyers, while supply curves accomplish the same thing with respect to sellers. In this initial discussion of price determination the market is assumed to be one of pure competition, a market form less complex than others to be discussed later. We shall explain first the concept of pure competition. Next, we shall see how the price and the quantity exchanged of a product are determined under given conditions of demand and supply. Finally, we consider the impacts of changes in demand and supply on market price and quantity exchanged.

Pure Competition

There are three essential conditions that must be met in a market if it is to be one of pure competition: (1) there must be many buyers and many sellers of whatever is being bought and sold in the market; (2) there must be no collusion among buyers or sellers; and (3) there must be no price fixing.

The condition that there be many buyers and many sellers in the market means that there must be enough of each so that any one buyer or any one seller is insignificant relative to the market as a whole. What does insignificance mean in this context? On the buying side it means simply that no single buyer takes enough of the product to influence product price. How important are your purchases of bread at the neighborhood supermarket? Are they important enough for the store to sell to you at a penny less than the posted price rather than to lose you as a bread customer? Similarly, insignificance on the selling side means that an individual seller cannot by himself influence price. Suppose you are a cotton farmer. You can sell only at the going market price—or below. If you try to charge more per bale than the market price, no one will buy from you, since cotton is available from others at the market price.

The absence of collusion is largely a self-evident concept. It means that buyers do not "gang up" on sellers to force them to sell at lower prices and that sellers do not "gang up" on buyers to force them to buy at higher prices.

The absence of price fixing is closely related to the foregoing points. Prices in purely competitive markets are free to move up and down. They are not set by guidelines, minimum wage or price laws, price ceiling laws, or by such private organizations as sellers' associations or labor unions. They are responsive to changes in demand and supply.

Equilibrium Price and Quantity

Suppose we bring the buyers and sellers of margarine together to see how the price and quantity exchanged are determined in a given market. The demand schedule of Table 4–1 appears as columns (1) and (2) of Table 4–3, while the supply schedule of Table 4–2 is shown as columns (2) and (3) of Table 4–3. The meaning of column (4) will become clear shortly.

What will happen if the price of margarine is initially toward the upper end of the range of alternative possible prices—say at 70 cents per pound? The demand schedule shows the reactions of the buyers as a group. They are willing to take only 4000 pounds per month. However, according to the supply schedule, sellers will place 8000 pounds per month on the market at that price, and a surplus of 4000 pounds per mouth, shown in column (4), will come into existence.

Surpluses in the hands of individual sellers set in motion forces that drive the price down. One seller believes that if he lowers his price to slightly less than 70 cents, buyers will favor him and he can unload his surplus. But each of the other sellers thinks the same. In the absence of collusion, they undercut each other. The price drops to 60 cents per pound but surpluses still occur. The undercutting process continues and the price drops to 50 cents per pound. At that price buyers want to buy and sellers want to sell 6000 pounds per month. Because surpluses are no longer being brought into existence, the incentive to undercut no longer exists. Sellers can sell all they want to bring to market at that price.

What happens if the market opens at 30 cents per pound? Buyers want 8000 pounds but sellers are willing to place only 4000 pounds per month on the market. Altogether consumers are 4000 pounds short of what they would like to buy each month at that price. Any individual consumer, unable to get as much as he wants at the going price, will reason that if he offers sellers slightly more than 30 cents per pound they will prefer to sell to him and his personal shortage will be alleviated. Other buyers reason the same way and the price is bid up to 40 cents per pound. The higher price then causes consumers to reappraise their positions and to cut the total amount they are willing to take to 7000 pounds. Sellers, finding the 40 cent price more profitable than the 30 cent price, expand the total monthly amount that they place on the market to 5000 pounds. However, since consumers are still 2000 pounds short of what they would like to have each month, an incentive exists for them to bid the price even higher.

TABLE 4–3

Hypothetical Demand, Supply, and Market Price of Margarine

(1)	(2)	(3)	(4)
			SURPLUS (+) OR SHORTAGE (−)
QUANTITY DEMANDED (LBS. PER MONTH)	PRICE (CENTS PER LB.)	QUANTITY SUPPLIED (LBS. PER MONTH)	(LBS. PER MONTH)
1,000	100	11,000	(+) 10,000
2,000	90	10,000	(+) 8,000
3,000	80	9,000	(+) 6,000
4,000	70	8,000	(+) 4,000
5,000	60	7,000	(+) 2,000
6,000	50	6,000	Neither
7,000	40	5,000	(−) 2,000
8,000	30	4,000	(−) 4,000
9,000	20	3,000	(−) 6,000
10,000	10	2,000	(−) 8,000

At 50 cents per pound, buyers cut the amount they are willing to take per month to 6000 pounds, and sellers expand the quantity they are willing to place on the market to the same amount. The incentive to bid the price higher has been eliminated.

This price and this quantity exchanged—50 cents and 6000 pounds per month—are called, respectively, *the equilibrium price and quantity*. At any other price forces are set in motion that tend to drive the price back to the equilibrium level. This is the level toward which the price will gravitate and settle as long as demand and supply remain as shown by Table 4–3.

This analysis can be presented easily and quickly by means of a demand curve and a supply curve drawn in the same diagram. In Figure 4–5 note that at price level P_1, consumers take quantity X_1 per month, while sellers place quantity X'_1 on the market. Thus sellers find themselves accumulating surpluses at a rate of X'_1 minus X_1 per month. This situation

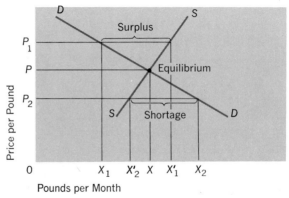

Figure 4–5
Equilibrium price and quantity.

induces individual sellers to undercut each other, thus forcing the price down. As the price falls, sellers bring smaller and smaller quantities per month to market while at the same time buyers purchase larger and larger quantities. Finally, when price has fallen to P and quantity exchanged is at X, there is no incentive for buyers or sellers to make further changes in the price and the quantity exchanged.

If the price were initially at P_2 rather than at P_1, buyers would want to buy quantity X_2. Sellers bring to market X'_2, and a shortage of X_2 minus X'_2 per month occurs. This provides an incentive for individual consumers to bid up the price. As the price rises, sellers are induced to place larger quantities per month on the market, whereas buyers are induced to ration themselves to smaller and smaller quantities. When the price level reaches P and the quantity exchanged is at X, the incentives for change no longer exist.

Changes in Demand

In the dynamic world in which we live we do not expect demand for any specific good or service to remain permanently fixed. Consumer preferences change; incomes increase; price changes in some goods cause demand changes for related goods; expectations change; and so on.

Suppose we look at the impact of a change in consumer preferences away from chicken and toward beef. In Figure 4–6(a) the initial demand for and supply of beef are D_bD_b and S_bS_b, so that P_b and B are the equilibrium price and quantity exchanged. The initial demand for and supply of chicken are D_cD_c and S_cS_c in Figure 4–6(b), making P_c and C the equilibrium price and quantity exchanged.

The shift in preferences increases the demand for beef to $D_{b_1}D_{b_1}$, creating a shortage of BB' at the original price P_b. Consumers bid against each other for the available supply, driving the price up. As the price rises, consumers restrict or ration their purchases more and more while sellers place larger and larger quantities per month on the market. When the price reaches the P_{b_1} level, the quantity that buyers want to buy will be the same as the quantity that sellers want to sell. Thus P_{b_1} and B_1 are the new equilibrium price and quantity exchanged. We can draw from this analysis the general principle that *an increase in demand ordinarily will increase both the price and the quantity exchanged of a product or service.*

In Figure 4–6(b) the demand for chicken decreases from D_cD_c to $D_{c_1}D_{c_1}$, resulting in a surplus of $C'C$ pounds per month at the initial price P_c. Sellers undercut each other to get rid of their individual surpluses. As the price falls, consumers increase the quantities they are willing to buy. Sellers curtail their sales levels as the production and sale of chicken becomes less profitable. At the price level P_{c_1} and the quantity exchanged C_1 equilibrium under the new demand conditions is established. The

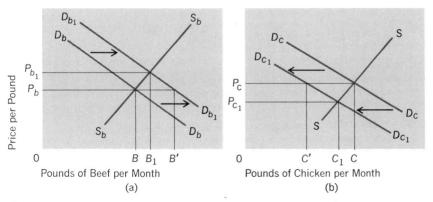

Figure 4–6
(a) Effects of an increase in demand.   (b) Effects of a decrease in demand.

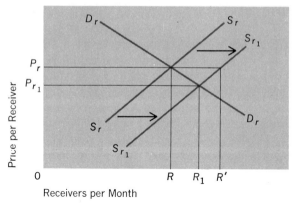

Figure 4–7
Effects of an increase in supply.

general principle illustrated here is that *a decrease in demand ordinarily will decrease both the price and the quantity exchanged of a product or service.*

Changes in Supply

Changes in the conditions of supply of specific goods and services take place constantly in the economy. New resources are being discovered and existing ones are being improved. New products are developed and resources are diverted from other products toward the production of the new ones. New techniques of production are developed. Resource prices change as conditions of demand for and supply of them change.

We shall look first at an increase in supply. In Figure 4–7, D_rD_r and S_rS_r are the initial demand and supply curves for color television receivers and P_r and R are the equilibrium price and quantity. Now suppose that as manufacturers become more familiar with production processes, cost-saving technology is developed. The supply curve will shift to the right, to some position such as $S_{r_1}S_{r_1}$. At the initial price P_r surpluses of RR' per month will accumulate. The surpluses trigger undercutting by sellers and the price falls, increasing the quantities that consumers are willing to buy and decreasing the quantities that sellers will produce and place on the market. At price P_{r_1} and quantity R_1, equilibrium is reached. The appropriate principle to draw from the example is that *an increase in supply ordinarily will decrease the price and increase the quantity exchanged of a product or service.*

Turning now to the impact of a decrease in supply, let us suppose that in Figure 4–8 we initially have the demand curve and the supply curve for apple pickers' services at D_aD_a and S_aS_a. The initial equilibrium price or wage rate is P_a and the quantity of labor exchanged is A man hours per week. A significant part of the apple picker supply is assumed to come from outside the country, with the foreign workers being given special work permits during the apple harvest season. Now suppose that legislation is enacted prohibiting the use of foreign apple pickers. This is equivalent to raising the prices that must be paid to domestic apple pickers in order to induce the same quantities of labor as before to seek this kind of employment. Or, from another angle, it decreases the quantities of apple picker labor available at each of the alternative possible wage rates. From either view supply decreases to some position $S_{a_1}S_{a_1}$, and at the price P_a there will be a shortage. Employers, faced with labor shortages, will bid against each other for the available supply. As wage rates rise more man hours of (domestic) apple picker labor are made available and apple growers want to hire smaller quantities. Wage rates will rise to the new equilibrium level of P_{a_1} and quantity exchanged will be A_1. The principle here is that *a decrease in supply ordinarily will raise the price of a product or service and decrease the quantity exchanged.*

Changes in Both Demand and Supply

From the analysis of changes in demand and supply we can easily add four corollaries to the principles already deduced. (1) If both demand and supply increase, the quantity exchanged will increase but the price may increase, decrease, or remain the same. (2) Conversely, if both demand and supply decrease, the quantity exchanged will decrease and again the price may increase, decrease, or remain the same. (3) An increase in demand accompanied by a decrease in supply will increase the

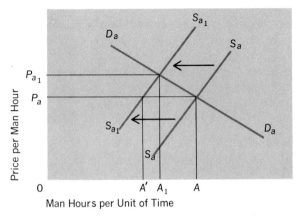

Figure 4–8
Effects of a decrease in supply.

price but the quantity exchanged may increase, decrease, or remain the same. (4) A decrease in demand accompanied by an increase in supply will decrease the price, and again the effects on quantity exchanged depend upon the circumstances of the specific case. It may be useful for the student to draw graphs for these four cases and to experiment with them. The important point to keep in mind is that for any given pair of demand and supply curves there is an equilibrium price and quantity exchanged. A change in demand or supply or both generally leads to a new equilibrium price and quantity combination.

ELASTICITY

We know that given the demand curve a change in the price of a product usually brings about a change in the quantity demanded even though there is no change in demand. Also we know that given the supply curve a price change usually brings about a change in quantity supplied even though there is no change in supply. But in both cases the door is left open for wide variations in the quantity response to a change in price. To sellers and buyers, as well as to economic analysts, the matter of responsiveness and quantity demanded or quantity supplied to price changes is a significant one. The measure of responsiveness is called *elasticity*. The concept of demand elasticity is more useful in economic analysis than that of supply elasticity, so we shall discuss the former in greater detail.

Elasticity of Demand

An analysis of elasticity of demand falls logically into three parts. First, how is the *responsiveness* of the quantity demanded to changes in the price of a product measured? Second, how do the *effects* of price changes on total spending on a commodity differ for different degrees of responsiveness? Third, what are the *forces that affect the responsiveness* of quantity taken to changes in the price of a product?

Measurement of Elasticity

The degree of responsiveness of quantity demanded to price changes, or the *measure of elasticity of demand,* is found by dividing the percentage change in quantity by the percentage change in price for small price changes. The number resulting from this computation is called the

TABLE 4-4
Elasticity of Demand for Hamburgers

(1) PRICE (CENTS PER HAMBURGER)	(2) QUANTITY (HAMBURGERS PER DAY)	(3) ELASTICITY
100	100	(−) 9
90	200	(−) 4
80	300	(−) 2⅓
70	400	(−) 1½
60	500	(−) 1
50	600	(−) ⅔
40	700	(−) 3/7
30	800	(−) ¼
20	900	(−) ⅑
10	1000	

elasticity coefficient, or, more simply, *elasticity of demand.* It can be easily determined given the demand schedule or demand curve for the product being considered. Suppose that the market demand schedule for hamburgers in a small town is that of columns (1) and (2) in Table 4-4. If the price were to fall from 80 cents to 70 cents, the quantity demanded would rise from 300 to 400 per day. The percentage change in quantity is a negative 33⅓ percent, found by dividing the 100-hamburger change by the original quantity of 300. Similarly, the percentage change in price is a positive 12½ percent. Dividing the negative 33⅓ percent by the positive 12½ percent, we find the elasticity coefficient to be a negative 2.67.

All of this is more conveniently done with algebra. Let the Greek letter delta (Δ) mean "the change in." The change in quantity is thus referred to as ΔX. The original quantity is X. The percentage change in quantity is thus $\Delta X / X$. Similarily, if ΔP is the change in price and P is the original price, the percentage change in price is $\Delta P / P$. If we let the Greek epsilon (ε) represent the elasticity coefficient, then

$$\varepsilon = -\frac{\Delta X / X}{\Delta P / P}$$

Why the minus sign? Since the quantity demanded varies inversely with the price, either ΔX or ΔP must be negative in sign. They cannot both be positive or both be negative at the same time. Plugging the values of the preceding paragraph into the formula, we find

$$\varepsilon = -\frac{100/300}{10/80} = -\frac{100}{300} \cdot \frac{80}{10} = -2\frac{2}{3}$$

for the decrease in price from 80 to 70 cents.

Suppose the movement of price is from 70 to 80 cents rather than from 80 to 70 cents. The original price is 70 cents and the original quantity is 400 hamburgers. Thus

$$\varepsilon = -\frac{100/400}{10/70} = -\frac{100}{400}\cdot\frac{70}{10} = -1\tfrac{3}{4}$$

We obtain two different elasticity figures depending upon which way we move between the two price–quantity combinations.

Actually, the discrepancy appears because of the relatively large size of the price change. If the percentage price change had been extremely small, say less than 1 percent, it would have been negligible. Elasticity computations for price changes of 5 percent or larger are subject to considerable error. The smaller the relative price change for which elasticity is computed, the smaller the error will be.

Problems arise, however, in which elasticity must be computed for relative price changes large enough to result in discrepancies like that of the example. In these cases we can find and use an average elasticity coefficient that falls between the two computed above. Economists use two or three different methods of computing such an average, but an easy and convenient one is to use the lower of the two quantities to compute the percentage change in quantity and the lower of the two prices to compute the percentage change in price. In terms of algebra, the elasticity formula becomes

$$\varepsilon = -\frac{\Delta X/X_0}{\Delta P/P_1}$$

in which X_0 is the lower of the two quantities and P_1 is the lower of the two prices.

Using this formula to compute the elasticity of demand for hamburgers, we obtain an elasticity coefficient lying between the negative $2\tfrac{2}{3}$ and the negative $1\tfrac{3}{4}$. The percentage change in quantity is $33\tfrac{1}{3}$, the quotient of 100 hamburgers divided by 300 hamburgers. The percentage change in price is a negative $14\tfrac{2}{7}$. Thus the elasticity coefficient is a negative $2\tfrac{1}{3}$, and is more representative of elasticity for the price range of 80 to 70 cents than either of the two previously computed. The elasticities in column (3) of Table 4–4 are all computed in this way.

Turning now to Figure 4–9, we can visualize the formula for elasticity measurement in terms of the demand curve. Starting at an initial price of P_0 and a quantity demanded of X_0, let the price fall to P_1. Quantity demanded increases by ΔX to X_1. Using the lower of the two quantities as the divisor, we find that the percentage change in quantity is $\Delta X/X_0$. Using the lower of the two prices as the divisor, we find that the percentage change in price is a negative $\Delta P/P_1$. Thus between prices P_0 and P_1,

$$\varepsilon = -\frac{\Delta X/X_0}{\Delta P/P_1}$$

For most demand curves elasticity is high toward the upper end, low toward the lower end, and decreases as price decreases. This situation can be most easily illustrated with a linear or straight line demand curve like that of Figure 4–9. Suppose that for the price change from P_0 to P_1, ΔP and ΔX are the same as they are for a price change from P_2 to P_3. When price changes from P_0 to P_1 the percentage change in quantity is great because X_0 is relatively small. The percentage change in price is small because P_1 is relatively large. Consequently, elasticity is relatively high. But for a price change from P_2 to P_3, the percentage change in quantity is much smaller because X_2 is much larger than was X_0. The percentage change in price is much larger because P_3 is much smaller than was P_1. In this second case the percentage change in quantity is smaller, the percentage change in price is larger, and the elasticity coefficient is smaller than in the first case. Obviously, for price changes moving down the demand curve to the right, elasticity will be decreasing.[1] These observations are verified by the elasticity computations in Table 4–4.

Elasticity coefficients can be classified usefully into three groups. When they are numerically greater than one ($\varepsilon > 1$), ignoring the sign, we say that demand is *elastic*. When coefficients are numerically equal to 1 ($\varepsilon = 1$), we say that demand has *unitary elasticity*. And when coefficients are numerically less than 1 ($\varepsilon < 1$), we say that demand is *inelastic*. For example, the demand schedule of Table 4–4 and the demand curve of Figure 4–9 are elastic in the upper regions and inelastic in the lower re-

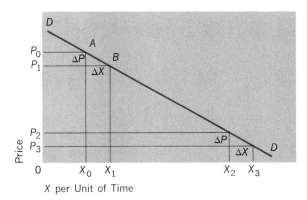

Figure 4–9
Demand elasticity computations.

[1] This will be so for demand curves with less curvature than that of a rectangular hyperbola. If the demand curve has the shape of a rectangular hyperbola, for every change in price the percentage change in quantity taken will equal the percentage change in price and the elasticity coefficient will be -1.

gions. Between the prices of 60 and 50 cents on the demand schedule, elasticity of demand is unitary. For a linear demand curve such as that of Figure 4–9, unitary elasticity is found at the midpoint; however, this is not necessarily the case for demand curves that are nonlinear.

Effects of Price Changes on Business Receipts

When economists, legislators, sellers, and others consider the market demand for a product they are interested in what will happen to total business receipts (equal to total consumer expenditures) for the product when the price is changed. The demand for wheat is a case in point. A most important question for farm policy decisions is what will happen to the total receipts of wheat farmers as a group if a farm program curtailing the supply of wheat is put into effect. Given the demand for the product, the effects of supply changes and the consequent price changes on total receipts of sellers depend upon the elasticity of demand.

Consider the demand schedule for wheat together with the total re- ceipts column in Table 4–5. Note that price decreases for which elasticity is greater than 1 increase total receipts of wheat sellers. Note also that price decreases for which elasticity is less than 1 cause total receipts to decrease. For price increases in both cases the effects on total receipts are just the opposite. When elasticity for a price change is unitary, total re- ceipts will not be affected by a price change.[2]

TABLE 4–5
Demand, Elasticity, and Total Receipts for Wheat

ELASTICITY OF DEMAND	PRICE OF WHEAT ($s PER BU.)	QUANTITY (BU. PER WEEK)	TOTAL RECEIPTS ($s)
	1.00	1,000	1,000.00
$\varepsilon > 1$	.90	2,000	1,800.00
	.80	3,000	2,400.00
	.70	4,000	2,800.00
$\varepsilon = 1$	.60	5,000	3,000.00
	.50	6,000	3,000.00
	.40	7,000	2,800.00
$\varepsilon < 1$	.30	8,000	2,400.00
	.20	9,000	1,800.00
	.10	10,000	1,000.00

[2] Why is this so? Consider the elasticity formula—the percentage change in quantity di- vided by the percentage change in price. This means that if demand is elastic, a 1 percent increase (decrease) in price generates a greater than 1 percent decrease (increase) in quantity demanded. The quantity change is thus in the *opposite direction from* and has a greater impact on total receipts than the price change. Can you apply this same line of reasoning to the case in which $\varepsilon < 1$? $\varepsilon = 1$?

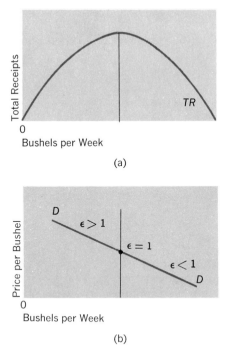

Figure 4–10
Price changes, demand elasticity, and total receipts.

Suppose that we look at the same problem with reference to Figure 4–10. The quantity scales of Figure 4–10(a) and (b) are assumed to be identical. The vertical scale of the bottom diagram measures product price while that of the upper diagram measures total receipts of sellers. The curves TR and DD are, respectively, the total receipts curve for sellers of wheat and the demand curve for wheat. For decreases in price in the region of the demand curve where elasticity is greater than 1 total receipts rise. For decreases in price where elasticity is less than 1 total receipts fall.

If we ask ourselves now what the effects on total receipts of wheat farmers will be of a governmental farm program that decreases the supply of wheat, or if a farm organization withholds supply from the market, we know that the answer turns on the elasticity of demand. In Figure 4–11 suppose that S_1S_1 is the uncontrolled wheat supply curve and that the government succeeds in reducing it to $S'_1S'_1$. Total receipts of wheat farmers will *rise* because the elasticity of demand for the price increase is less than 1. On the other hand, suppose that S_2S_2 is the uncontrolled supply curve and that the government is able to reduce it to $S'_2S'_2$. In this case the receipts of wheat farmers will decrease, since elasticity of demand

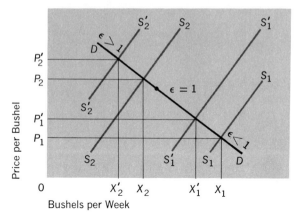

Figure 4–11
Effects of supply decreases under different elasticity conditions.

for the price increase is greater than 1. A farm program designed to increase the total receipts of wheat farmers by reducing the supply of wheat will work only if the elasticity of demand for wheat is less than 1.

Determinants of Elasticity

What are the main factors determining whether elasticity of demand for a product is large or small? One of the most important is the *availability of substitutes* for the product to consumers. If several good substitutes for brand X of cigarettes are available, a slight rise in the price of brand X will cause a large switch by consumers to the substitute brands. If the substitute brands are not available, a slight rise in price may cause smokers to smoke somewhat less, but the decrease in quantity taken obviously would be much smaller.

The *importance of a product in consumer budgets* has some influence on elasticity of demand. This factor is most applicable to products occupying positions of insignificance. Pepper provides an example. If the price of pepper were to double, what would happen to the quantity taken off the market? The decrease would not be large because, at double the present price, expenditures for the amount now purchased would still not be large enough for consumers to give it great consideration.

Elasticity of Supply

Not much beyond definition of elasticity of supply is necessary for our purposes. Like the demand elasticity coefficient, that for supply is found

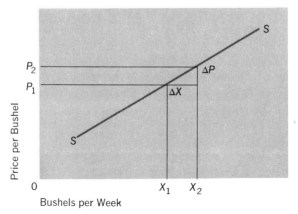

Figure 4-12
Supply elasticity computations.

by dividing the percentage change in quantity by the percentage change in price for a small change in price along a given supply curve. In Figure 4-12 supply elasticity for an increase in price from P_1 to P_2 is usually written in the following form:

$$\eta = \frac{\Delta X / X_1}{\Delta P / P_1}$$

The more responsive quantity supplied is to changes in the price of the product, the larger the elasticity coefficient will be. We may note also that the supply elasticity coefficient will be positive in sign for an upward-sloping supply curve, since ΔP and ΔX represent changes in the same direction. They are either both positive or both negative, and thus in either case η must be positive.

SUMMARY

This chapter explains the bedrock fundamentals of economic analysis, which include the concept of a market, the nature of demand and supply, the determination of the price of a product or service in purely competitive markets, and the concept of elasticity.

A market for a product or a service exists when buyers and sellers make contact with each other and engage in exchange. The market area varies from local to global, depending upon the nature of what is being exchanged and/or upon the time period under consideration.

Demand for an item refers to the quantities of it that consumers are willing to buy per unit of time at alternative possible prices, other things being equal. Demand information can be summarized in the form of a demand schedule or a demand curve. In identifying a specific demand curve for a product, such "other things" as consumer preferences, consumer incomes, consumer expectations, and the prices of related goods must not change. A change in any one of these will cause the demand curve to shift to the right or to the left.

Supply refers to the quantities of a good or service that sellers will place on the market at alternative prices, other things being equal. It is represented by a supply schedule or a supply curve. Changes in resource prices, in the level of technology, and in producer expectations will cause increases or decreases in supply.

The interaction of buyers and sellers in the market determines the equilibrium price and quantity exchanged of a product in purely competitive conditions. If price is below an equilibrium level, shortages will occur and buyers will bid up the price. If price is above equilibrium, surpluses will cause sellers to undercut each other. Changes in demand or supply or both will cause changes in the equilibrium price and quantity exchanged.

Elasticity of demand refers to the responsiveness of quantity demanded to changes in the price of a product. It is measured by dividing the percentage change in quantity demanded by the percentage change in price for any small price change. Demand may be elastic, of unitary elasticity, or inelastic, and the magnitude of elasticity will determine what happens to total receipts of sellers for price increases or for price decreases. Factors important in determining the elasticity of demand for a product are (1) the availability of substitutes and (2) the importance of a product in consumers' budgets.

Elasticity of supply is a less useful concept than elasticity of demand. It refers to the responsiveness of quantity placed on the market to changes in the price of a product and is measured in the same way as is elasticity of demand.

EXERCISES AND QUESTIONS FOR DISCUSSION

1. Of the following conditions, which would increase a student's demand for hamburgers?
   a. An increase in the price of hot dogs.
   b. An increase in his monthly allowance.
   c. A fall in the price of hamburgers.
   d. A note from the family lawyer that he has inherited $10,000.
   e. A bad piece of pork at a university cafeteria.
   f. A vow to stop smoking.
2. Would you expect the elasticity of demand for the following items to be large or small?
   a. Insulin for diabetics.

    b. Carrots.

    c. Matches.

    d. Automobiles.

    e. Sparkly toothpaste.

    f. Toothpaste.

3. Evalute the following statements:

    a. If demand for a good decreases and supply remains constant, price will rise and quantity taken will decrease.

    b. If supply decreases and demand remains constant, price will rise and quantity taken will decrease.

    c. If supply decreases and demand decreases, price will fall and quantity demanded will fall.

    d. If demand increases and supply decreases, price will fall but one cannot be sure of the direction of change of quantity.

SELECTED READINGS

Boulding, Kenneth E., *Economic Analysis,* 4th ed., Vol. I. New York: Harper & Row, Publishers, Inc., 1966, Chaps. 7 and 8.

Radford, R. A., "The Economic Organization of a P.O.W. Camp," *Economica,* Vol. XII (November 1945), pp. 189–201

Smith, Adam, *The Wealth of Nations,* Edwin Cannan, ed. New York: Random House Modern Library edition, 1937, Chaps. VI and VII.

PART 2   Microeconomics: Markets for Goods and Services

In this part of the book we begin a detailed examination of the several faces of economic theory. We shall cover the markets for goods and services—the upper half of the circular flow model pictured in Figure 2–1. Since our subject matter will be individual consumers, individual firms, and specific industries or product groups, it properly belongs to the area of microeconomics. But it is only a part of the complete area; the remainder—markets for resources—is developed in Part III.

The objective in Part II is to shed light on the mechanisms in a free enterprise economy that determine what is to be produced and that organize production. We shall be concerned with the economic analysis of how it works and, toward the end of Part II, with economic policy measures enacted by the government, presumably to make it work better. The chapters on consumer demand focus on the forces underlying the demand concept introduced in Chapter 4, while those on the principles of production and the costs of production are intended to do the same thing for the supply concept.[1]

[1] This will not be completely evident until we get into Chapter 9. In Chapters 9, 10, and 11, the determinants of prices and, consequently, of outputs of goods and services are examined much more thoroughly and under a much wider variety of circumstances than in Chapter 4. Chapters 12, 13, and 14 evaluate the effectiveness of the mechanisms as well as current major policy measures.

Consumer Behavior and Demand, I

CHAPTER 5

What is it that determines how an individual allocates his available purchasing power among a number of different goods and services? And why is it that he will take more of a given product at a lower price than he will at a higher price? You have probably not given much thought to these questions, and raising them is almost like asking why an apple falls down instead of up. But pursuit of the latter question paid off handsomely in terms of fame if not fortune for Sir Isaac Newton. Similarly, for a beginning economist there are important principles to be derived from an examination of such questions.

In the late 1800s economists developed what has come to be known as the utility theory of demand, and the analysis in this chapter follows the lines that they staked out. The indifference curve analysis of the next chapter provides an alternative (or perhaps a supplementary) explanation that is generally preferred today. Yet various aspects of utility theory are used broadly in both economic analysis and economic policy-making, so that it seems worthwhile to see what the theory has to offer.

THE CONCEPT OF UTILITY

Suppose we call the satisfaction a consumer obtains from consuming a good or service its *utility* to him. An increase or a decrease in his weekly rate of consumption of any one product, say his food intake, will increase or decrease his utility. If we pursue this causal relationship, we can distinguish between the *total amount of utility* or satisfaction received from whatever quantity he consumes per week and any *changes in utility* that may occur when he changes his rate of consumption from one level to another. We shall examine each of these more closely.

Total Utility

What can we say about the way in which the consumer's total utility from the consumption of a product or a service varies as his consumption level of the product is changed? Suppose we conduct a hypothetical experiment on a consumer who has been placed under our control. The product to be tested is beef, measured in pounds. The environment in which we keep the consumer is maintained as constant as possible: we hold his consumption of other products at constant levels; we have a psychiatrist whose sole function is to prevent changes from occurring in his mental attitudes; we have a social director who sees to it that his social contacts from week to week will not influence his beef consumption; and his level of physical activity over time is not changed.

Now, over a series of weeks we change the consumer's weekly level of beef consumption and we record the resulting levels of total utility from the product.[1] Table 5-1 shows a set of results conforming to what we would expect ordinarily. As the number of pounds of beef consumed per week increases, total utility yielded the consumer by it will increase too— up to a point. At some quantity—11 pounds per week in the example— the consumer is receiving as much utility as he is capable of receiving from this product. He is saturated with it, and we call that quantity his *saturation point.* The information contained in Table 5-1 is plotted graphically in Figure 5-1(a).

Marginal Utility

The change in the total utility a consumer receives from a product when his consumption level of it is increased or decreased by a small amount is called *marginal utility.* This is the first of the many marginal concepts that we shall use throughout the book. All of them are the same

---

[1] We are confronted immediately with a rather messy problem that has created considerable discussion among economists over time and that has never been satisfactorily dispensed with. Is utility measurable in the *cardinal* sense; that is, in such a way that we can say definitely that four units of utility represent twice as much as two? Or can we speak of utility magnitudes in an *ordinal* sense only; that is, in such a way that numbers assigned to them indicate which are greater and which are smaller without conveying any information about how much? For pedigogical purposes, we shall act as though it were cardinal, leaving the controversy for more advanced study, and assume that the consumer can inform us for each quantity of beef the number of units of utility it yields him.

TABLE 5-1

Total and Marginal Utility Schedules for Beef

	(1) QUANTITY OF BEEF (LBS. PER WEEK)	(2) TOTAL UTILITY	(3) MARGINAL UTILITY
	1	10	10
	2	19	9
	3	27	8
	4	34	7
	5	40	6
	6	45	5
	7	49	4
	8	52	3
	9	54	2
	10	55	1
Saturation Point	11	55	0
	12	54	$(-)1$

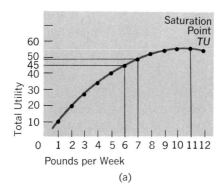

(a)

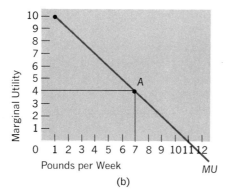

(b)

Figure 5-1

The utility from beef consumption.

mathematically and a thorough understanding of the one at hand will remove a good many bumps from the road ahead. Mathematically we can think of marginal utility as the *rate of change* of total utility as the consumer changes his consumption level by small increments.

The marginal utility of beef to our beef-eating consumer can be computed readily from the total utility schedule of Table 5–1. Consider the six-pound level of consumption. From column (2) of the table we note that a change from the six-pound level to the seven-pound level increases total utility from 45 to 49 units of utility. Or, if we start at the seven-pound level and move back to the six-pound level, total utility decreases from 49 to 45 units. In either case the change in total utility is four units for the one-pound change. This is the marginal utility of the seventh pound and is so recorded in column (3) of the table. Marginal utilities of beef to the consumer at other consumption levels are found in the same manner and round out the column.

What we can do with the table we can do also with its graphic counterpart. Consider the six-pound-per-week consumption level in Figure 5–1(a). The *TU* curve shows the consumer's total utility as 45 units. If the consumption level were raised to seven pounds, it shows that the consumer's total utility will rise to 49 units. The upward movement with reference to the total utility axis—four units of utility—is the marginal utility of a seventh pound of beef to the consumer.

Now consider Figure 5–1(b). The horizontal or quantity axis is identical to that of Figure 5–1(a), but along the vertical axis we measure *changes* in total utility per one-unit change in the consumption level; that is, we show *marginal utility*. To locate the marginal utility curve we first find the numerical magnitude of marginal utility at each consumption level and then we plot the coordinates. For example, by plotting marginal utility at the seven-pound-per-week consumption level we get point *A*. (Determine for yourself that the other points tracing out *MU* are computed and plotted correctly.)

Diminishing Marginal Utility

In the foregoing example the marginal utility of beef to the consumer decreases as his weekly level of consumption increases. Is it reasonable to expect that this will be the case for most goods and services to most consumers? It will be impossible to provide an unequivocal answer here; we can only appeal to our everyday experience. What about shoes? If you have only one pair of shoes per year to consume, will you get a large increase in satisfaction from an additional pair? How would your answer differ if you had five pairs per year available to you initially? In all probability a sixth pair would add less to your total utility than a second pair, and if you think through the list of items you purchase regularly, diminishing marginal utility will prevail for most. It seems to be common enough for us to speak of the existence of the *principle of diminishing marginal utility.* In Figure 5–1(a) the principle is evidenced in the concave-downward shape of the *TU* curve. In Figure 5–1(b) the downward slope to the right of the *MU* curve is the graphic representation of it.

Some goods or services may be perverse, however. Suppose you are an avid golfer. One game per year is too little to keep in practice and two are not much better. But as you increase the yearly number of games you play, each one-game increase may add more to the total utility you receive from golf than the preceding one did; that is, marginal utility may be increasing. Still, even for golf games, there must be a saturation point. If this is so as the consumption level approaches it, marginal utility must be decreasing even though for lower levels of consumption it is increasing. (Study Figure 5–1(a) and see if you can redraw it to reflect this situation. At the saturation point what is the magnitude of marginal utility?)

Consumer Preferences

If we had the patience and if the consumer on whom we are experimenting would hold still long enough, presumably we could obtain total utility curves and the corresponding marginal utility curves for all of the things he is interested in consuming. All together these would provide us with a set of graphs rather staggering in number picturing the consumer's pattern of preferences. Suppose we simplify the matter conceptually by looking at only two of his marginal utility curves, those illustrated in Figure 5–2 for product *X* and product *Y*.

What do these two diagrams tell us? The consumer is easily saturated with product *X*. Its marginal utility (but not its total utility) falls to zero at a low level of consumption. Suppose that *X* is strychnine used for

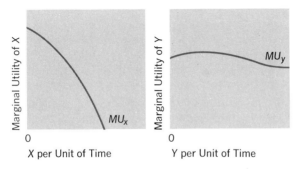

Figure 5–2
A consumer's marginal utility curves.

medicinal purposes and the consumer is a heart patient. Small consumption levels may yield very high marginal utilities, but the additions to satisfaction fall off very rapidly as the dosage is increased. Product *Y,* on the other hand, is an item with which the consumer is not easily saturated. As the consumption level is increased, the additions to total utility decrease very slowly. The consumer is obviously a woman and product *Y* is clothing.

PRINCIPLES OF INCOME ALLOCATION

In your role as a consumer what do you consider to be your major problem? Undoubtedly it is one of inadequate income to purchase as much as you would like of different goods and services. Or, to put the problem in a slightly different way, given your income you want to spend it on items available to you so as to secure as much satisfaction as possible from your purchases. This is the premise underlying the theory of consumer behavior; that is, the objective of the typical consumer is to allocate his income among different goods and services in such a way that he maximizes his satisfaction from the consumption of all of them. The given data of the problem are the individual consumer's income, his preference pattern, and the prices of whatever is available to be purchased.

Again we shall impose on an unnamed consumer, using him as a subject for experimentation and observation. His preferences (his utility schedules or curves) are given and remain constant, that is, they do not shift, while the experiment is in progress. These are presented in schedule form in Table 5–2. His income or purchasing power per week is nine dollars and does not change. To simplify matters we shall let the consumer live in a two-commodity world in which only food and clothing are available. The price of food is two dollars per bushel and the price of clothing is one dollar per yard. Both food and clothing can be purchased in half units if this seems to be desirable.

What allocation of the consumer's income between food and clothing will maximize his satisfaction, or his aggregate utility, from the two? Suppose the consumer were to spend everything on clothing, thereby obtaining nine yards per week. His aggregate utility is 63 utility units, found by adding marginal utilities for the quantities to and including nine yards of clothing.[2] Marginal utility of a yard of clothing is three at this level of consumption. The consumer is likely to be warm but hungry and to con-

---

[2] If you do not understand why the total utility of any specific quantity is found by adding marginal utilities for all units to and including that quantity, look again at Table 5–1 and Figure 5–1 and reread the textual explanation of both the total and marginal utility concepts.

template the food supply. If he were to give up a dollar's worth of clothing, his utility would fall by three units—the marginal utility of the ninth yard. If that dollar were spent on food, he would obtain $7\frac{1}{2}$ units of utility —the marginal utility of the first half bushel of food. Consequently, he would experience a net gain of $4\frac{1}{2}$ units by transferring a dollar from clothing to food.

Further gains can be obtained from further transfers. By giving up the eighth yard of clothing the consumer sacrifices four units of utility, but as the dollar withdrawn from this use is spent on the remaining one half of the first bushel of food, he picks up $7\frac{1}{2}$ units of utility for a net gain of $3\frac{1}{2}$. Similarily, the transfer of another dollar from the seventh yard of clothing to the first half of the second bushel of food yields a net gain of two utility units. Then, if the sixth yard of clothing is given up in return for the rest of the second bushel of food, still another net gain of one utility unit occurs.

No further gains in aggregate utility or satisfaction are possible. The exchange of the fifth yard of clothing for one half of the third bushel of food would cause a one-half unit net loss in aggregate utility. Similarly, if one half of the second bushel of food were given up for the sixth yard of clothing, a net utility loss of one unit would occur. The satisfaction-maximizing allocation of the consumer's income between food and clothing is four dollars for two bushels of food and five dollars for five yards of clothing. At this point the marginal utility of a dollar's worth of food and the marginal utility of a dollar's worth of clothing are each seven units of utility.

We have uncovered the principle underlying maximization of satisfaction by an individual consumer—he must allocate his income among the

TABLE 5-2
Marginal Utility Schedules for Food and Clothing

Food		Clothing	
QUANTITY (BU. PER WEEK)	MARGINAL UTILITY (MU_f)	QUANTITY (YDS. PER WEEK)	MARGINAL UTILITY (MU_c)
1	15	1	11
2	14	2	10
3	13	3	9
4	12	4	8
5	11	5	7
6	9	6	6
7	7	7	5
8	5	8	4
9	3	9	3
10	0	10	0

different goods and services available to him in such a way that the marginal utility per dollar's worth on one is equal to the marginal utility per dollar's worth of every other one. We can state these conditions in the form of simple equations for our two-commodity world. First,

$$\frac{MU_f}{P_f} = \frac{MU_c}{P_c}$$

in which MU_f is the marginal utility per bushel of food at his current consumption level; P_f is the price per bushel; MU_c is the marginal utility per yard of clothing at his current consumption level; and P_c is the price per yard. Note that in the example the marginal utility per dollar's worth of each is seven units of utility. Second, the income limitation of the consumer is expressed as

$$f \cdot P_f + c \cdot P_c = I$$

in which f and c are the consumption levels, respectively, of food in bushels and clothing in yards and I is the consumer's available purchasing power. These statements are not restricted to the two-commodity world but can be extended to as many goods and services as a consumer may desire. All we need to do is add terms to the equations.

The principle of diminishing marginal utility was probably obscured by the mechanics of the foregoing analysis. Nevertheless, it was there; look at Table 5–2. If the principle were not operative, the conditions we have listed as determining maximum satisfaction for the consumer might not hold. Look again at the consumer's *equilibrium position*—his satisfaction-maximizing position—in Table 5–2. Suppose now that the marginal utility of food and clothing were increasing as shown in Table 5–3 instead of decreasing. The consumer could make net additions to his aggregate utility either by transferring dollars from food to clothing or by transferring dollars from clothing to food; and, depending upon which way he begins to transfer, he will end up spending his entire income on one product.

Consumers are not always successful in making the precise satisfaction-maximizing adjustments reached in the example. Sometimes they are not sure whether the marginal utility of a dollar in a proposed use would be greater or less than that in a present use. Experience in consuming a product may not live up to what the consumer anticipated when he decided to buy it. Tradition and habit may inhibit transfers of dollars. Sometimes consumers are ill informed as to what is available or misinformed as to the satisfaction that some goods can be expected to yield. Still, it seems reasonable to believe that most consumers most of the time are trying to place their dollars where they will contribute the most to satisfaction. (If you had an extra five dollars to spend this week what would you do with it?)

TABLE 5-3
Marginal Utility Schedules for Food and Clothing[a]

	Food		Clothing	
QUANTITY (BU. PER WEEK)	MARGINAL UTILITY (MU_f)		QUANTITY (YDS. PER WEEK)	MARGINAL UTILITY (MU_c)
1	12	1		3
2	14	2		4
3	15	3		5
4	16	4		6
5	17	5		7
6	18	6		8
7	19	7		9
8	20	8		10
9	21	9		11
10	22	10		12

[a] This table is presented solely to demonstrate the effects on the consumer's allocation of income if the principle of diminishing marginal utility were not operative. Since we assume in this chapter that the principle is operative, this table should be disregarded for all purposes except the one for which it is presented.

PRINCIPLES OF DEMAND

The inverse relationship between the price of a product and the quantity of it that consumers will take per unit of time was introduced in Chapter 4. Now, with the aid of the analysis developed in the preceding section, a more detailed explanation is possible. Market demand for a product is composed of the demands of individual consumers, so again we confine our attention to the consumer on whom we have been experimenting.

We are concerned with discovering what determines the demand curve of an individual consumer for any specific product and why it is expected to slope downward to the right. As we experiment with the consumer there are several conditioning factors that we want to hold constant in order to get at the unique way in which the quantity taken will vary as the price of the product changes. These are (1) the consumer's preferences—his utility schedules, (2) the consumer's income, and (3) the prices of related products. Suppose now that we limit the consumer to a two-commodity world;[3] his preferences to those of Table 5–2; his income to nine dollars per week; and the price of clothing to one dollar

[3] This limitation is not really necessary but it does greatly simplify the problem—perhaps too much.

TABLE 5-4
Demand Schedule for Food

P_f ($S PER BU.)	f (BU.)
2	2
1	6

per yard. All that remains is to confront the consumer with different prices of food and record the quantity he takes at each price when he is allocating his income between the two products in such a way that he is maximizing satisfaction or aggregate utility.

Repeating an earlier experiment, suppose we confront the consumer initially with a food price of two dollars per bushel. He maximizes satisfaction by taking two bushels of food and five yards of clothing, the marginal utility per dollar's worth of each being seven units of utility. We have established one point on his demand curve for food: at a price of two dollars each he will take two bushels. This is listed as the first row of the demand schedule shown by Table 5-4 and is plotted as point A in Figure 5-3.

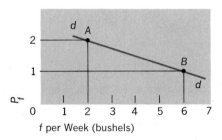

Figure 5-3
Consumer demand curve for food.

Now suppose we change the price of food to one dollar per bushel. At two bushels of food and five yards of clothing the consumer is no longer maximizing aggregate utility. In the first place, he is not spending all of his purchasing power and, second, the marginal utility of a dollar's worth of food exceeds that of a dollar's worth of clothing. The former is now 14 utility units while the latter is still 7.

The consumer can add to his aggregate utility by spending the two extra dollars available to him on the third and fourth bushels of food. He would prefer these to the sixth and seventh yards of clothing because of their higher marginal utility per dollar's worth to him. But he is not yet maximizing satisfaction. At four bushels of food and five yards of clothing the marginal utility per dollar's worth of food is 12 units of utility while that of a dollar's worth of clothing is only 7.

Still more can be added to aggregate utility by the transfer of expenditure from clothing to food. If the fifth yard of clothing per week is given up and the dollar thus made available is spent for a fifth bushel of food per week, there is a net gain of four utility units. Further, if the fourth yard of clothing is foregone and the sixth bushel of food per week is taken in its place, a gain of one utility unit occurs. The marginal utility per dollar's worth of each is now 9.

The consumer is now maximizing satisfaction and a second point on his demand curve for food has been established. A one dollar transfer of expenditure in either direction would decrease his aggregate utility. At one dollar per bushel the consumer will take six bushels of food, giving us the second row of Table 5-4 and point *B* in Figure 5-3. We have demonstrated the principle that the consumer will take more of a product at a lower price than he will at a higher one. With more extensive marginal utility schedules in which quantities are more finely graduated, a number of points on a consumer's demand schedule could be determined in a similar manner and plotted as a demand curve.

A review of the derivation of the two points on the consumer's demand curve for food will reveal that two forces were at work causing quantity taken to rise as the price declined. On the one hand the price decline from two dollars per bushel to one dollar per bushel increased the consumer's purchasing power—his dollars spent on food go farther than they would previously. We call this an *income effect,* an increase in his *real income* or purchasing power even though his *money income* is fixed. (Have you ever thought of the fact that decreases in the prices of things that you buy constitute an increase in your real income?)

On the other hand, the decrease in the price of food relative to the price of clothing increases the marginal utility of a dollar's worth of food relative to that of a dollar's worth of clothing. Since the former now becomes greater than the latter, the consumer is induced to substitute dollars' worth of food for dollars' worth of clothing in his expenditure pattern. This is called the *substitution effect.* (What would be your reaction to a decrease in the price of steak relative to the prices of other meat, poultry, and fish dishes at your favorite cafeteria?) In the example given the entire increase in the quantity of food the consumer takes comes from a combination of the income effect and the substitution effect.

INDIVIDUAL CONSUMER DEMAND AND MARKET DEMAND

Market demand for any good or service originates in the wants of individual consumers. Conceptually, the market demand curve that we met in Chapter 4 is built up from individual consumer demand curves for the product under consideration. The forces underlying individual consumer demand curves have just been examined.

Relation between Market and Individual Consumer Demand

The market demand curves for particular products are built up from individual consumer or household demand curves for those products. Market demand originates in the wants of individual consumers. Each consumer of product X has his own demand curve for it. By putting together the demands of all consumers we arrive at market demand for the product.

A market demand schedule is illustrated in Table 5–5. For purposes of simplification suppose that Mr. A and Mr. B are the only consumers of product X. As the table indicates, we simply add together the quantities per unit of time that both would be willing to take at each alternative price level in order to obtain the market demand schedule. Note that at any price above eight dollars Mr. B is the entire market. A table of this kind can be readily extended to as many consumers as there are in the market for a particular product.

TABLE 5–5
Individual Consumer and Market Demand Schedules for X

Mr. A		Mr. B		Market	
P_x X PER UNIT OF TIME		P_x X PER UNIT OF TIME		P_x X PER UNIT OF TIME	
$10	0	$10	1	$10	1
9	0	9	2	9	2
8	2	8	3	8	5
7	4	7	4	7	8
6	6	6	5	6	11
5	8	5	6	5	14
4	10	4	7	4	17
3	13	3	8	3	21
2	17	2	9	2	26
1	22	1	10	1	32

In Figure 5–4 the construction of a market demand curve from those of individual consumers is shown graphically. At price P_2 neither Mr. A nor Mr. B would take any of the product. At price P_1 Mr. A would take none of the product but Mr. B would take quantity x'_1. Thus at price P_1 quantity X_1 for the market as a whole is the same as quantity x'_1 in Mr. B's diagram. Between price P_2 and price P_1 the market demand curve is identical to that of Mr. B, since he is the only one in the market through that price range. At price P_0 Mr. A would take quantity x_0 and Mr. B would take quantity x'_0. Together they would take quantity X_0, the sum

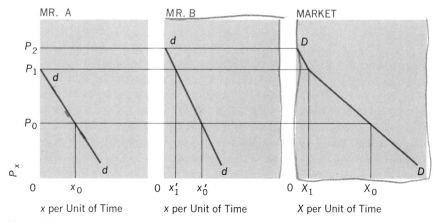

Figure 5–4
The market demand curve.

of quantity x_0 and quantity x'_0. All other points on the market demand curve are determined in the same way—by adding horizontally the amounts that both would take at each possible price level. Thus the market demand curve is found by summing horizontally the individual consumer demand curves for the product. Again the process can be extended to as many consumers as there may be in the market for the product.

SUMMARY

The utility theory of individual consumer behavior and demand is examined in this chapter. The preferences of a consumer are described by his total and marginal utility curves for goods and services. The total utility yielded to him by any specific commodity increases as his consumption of it per unit of time is increased up to the saturation point. Marginal utility of the product, defined as the change in total utility per unit change in the consumption level, decreases as the consumption level approaches the saturation point. This principle of diminishing marginal utility is basic to the analysis of individual consumer behavior and demand.

A consumer tends to allocate the purchasing power available to him among different goods and services in such a way that he maximizes his aggregate utility or satisfaction from all of them. This is accomplished when (1) the marginal utility per dollar's worth of one is equal to that of every other one and (2) when his entire purchasing power is utilized.

When the consumer is maximizing satisfaction he is said to be in equilibrium.

The consumer's demand curve for a product shows the quantities he will take at alternative prices, given his preferences, his income, and the prices of other goods. Under the given circumstances we specify a price for the product, let the consumer reach an equilibrium position, and read off the quantity of the product that is taken at that price. Then we change the price, let the consumer re-establish equilibrium, and read off the quantity that he will take at the new price level. A series of such price-quantity observations constitutes his demand curve for the product. Ordinarily it is downward sloping to the right. The change in quantity taken when price changes stems from a combination of an income effect and a substitution effect.

The market demand curve for a product is constructed from individual demand curves for it. At each price level the quantity point on the market demand curve is the summation of the quantity points on individual consumer demand curves.

EXERCISES AND QUESTIONS FOR DISCUSSION

1. A small boy is given $2.25 to spend an hour at Plenti-Fun Amusement Park one evening. It is an unusual amusement park in that only two activities are offered, the roller coaster rides, which are 50 cents each, and trips through the fun house at 25 cents a trip. Given the following utility schedules, how many roller coaster rides and how many trips through the fun house will the boy take? How will the combination of rides change if the charge for a roller coaster ride drops to 20 cents? Can you find two points on the boy's demand curve for roller coaster rides from this information? What conditions would you include in "other things equal" when you construct the demand curve?

Marginal Utility Schedules for
Roller Coaster Rides and Trips through the Fun House

Roller Coaster Rides		Trips through Fun House	
RIDES	MU_R	TRIPS	MU_T
1	40	1	18
2	32	2	15
3	24	3	12
4	16	4	9
5	9	5	7
6	4	6	5
7	2	7	2
8	0	8	1

2. Adam Smith in *Wealth of Nations* wrote about a diamond-water paradox. He said: "Nothing is more useful than water; but it will purchase scarce anything; scarce anything can be had in exchange for it. A diamond, on the contrary, has scarce any value in use; but a very great quantity of other goods may frequently be exchanged for it." Upon reading this statement a later economist, Alexander

Gray, wrote of Smith: "The wiley bird had never heard of marginal utility."
Gray gave the clue to the solution to this paradox. Can you solve it?
3. Black, Thompson, and Hood are landscaping their yards and are in the market
for palm trees. These three men are the only persons in the economy who want
to buy palm trees and the following are their demand schedules:

Black		Thompson		Hood	
P_t	Q_t	P_t	Q_t	P_t	Q_t
$40	1	$40	0	$40	0
35	2	35	0	35	0
30	3	30	1	30	1
25	4	25	3	25	2
20	5	20	5	20	3
15	6	15	7	15	4
10	7	10	9	10	5
5	8	5	11	5	6

Construct the market demand curve for palm trees.
4. Phil Parker's wife was constantly nagging him to ask his boss for a raise. One
morning he screwed up his courage, asked for it, and received in return a pat on
the back and a plea to be patient. On the way home that evening as he read the
Wall Street Journal he discovered that the general price level in the past month
had dropped by 3 percent. On arriving home he burst through the front door with
the announcement that he had received a raise. Was he telling the truth?

SELECTED READINGS

Fellner, William, *Modern Economic Analysis*. New York: McGraw-Hill Book Com-
pany, Inc., 1960, Chap. 14.
Marshall, Alfred, "Value," *Readings in Economic Doctrines*, Vol. 1, H. L. Balsley, ed.
Patterson, N. J.: Littlefield, Adams, and Company, 1961, pp. 119–121.
Watson, Donald S., *Price Theory and Its Uses*. 2d ed. Boston: Houghton Mifflin
Company, 1968, Chap. 4.

Consumer Behavior and Demand, II

CHAPTER 6

In the 1930s a pair of British economists, sparked by the controversy over whether utility is measurable in a cardinal sense, came forward with an approach to the theory of individual consumer demand that avoids the concept of utility altogether.[1] Their *indifference curve approach* is widely used as an alternative to the utility approach of Chapter 5. We shall develop it here to attack again the questions of the last chapter—what determines the consumer's allocation of income among different products, and why do demand curves slope downward to the right. In so doing we shall start from scratch, completely ignoring the preceding chapter, except for the section relating individual consumer demand to market demand for a product.

CONCEPTS OF INDIFFERENCE CURVE ANALYSIS

Two fundamental concepts are employed in indifference curve analysis. One of these, the *consumer's indifference map,* has to do with the consumer's preferences, or what he would like to do. The other is his *line of attainable combinations* or his *budget line,* which provides information on the restrictions he encounters in pursuing the satisfaction of his wants.

[1] J. R. Hicks and R. G. D. Allen, "A Reconsideration of the Theory of Value," *Economica* (February, May 1934), pp. 52–76 and 196–219, respectively.

The Indifference Map

A consumer confronted with different combinations of mixed goods and services should be able to give us some information regarding the relative importance to him of each combination. He should be able to list the combinations he prefers, and he should also be able to indicate at any given point in his preference ranking those combinations of goods for which he has equal preference or those that he expects would yield him equivalent satisfaction.

As an example, suppose we select a consumer for observation and limit him to a two-commodity world in which only food and clothing are available. In Figure 6–1 bushels of food are measured along the horizontal axis and yards of clothing are represented by the vertical axis. Any point in the quadrant formed by the two axes represents a combination of food and clothing.

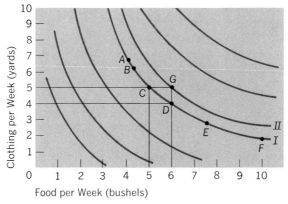

Figure 6–1
A consumer's indifference map.

Some combinations in the quadrant will be preferred by the consumer over others. Combination *C* contains five yards of clothing and five bushels of food per week. Combination *G* contains five yards of clothing and *six* bushels of food. Clearly the consumer would prefer *G* to *C*, since both contain the same amount of clothing but *G* contains a greater amount of food.[2] Other combinations preferred to *G* and still others less preferred than *C* can be located on the graph.

There must be other combinations of food and clothing that the con-

---

[2] There is a possibility that at five bushels of food the consumer is *saturated* with it—that is, that additional units per week would add nothing to his enjoyment of food—but we shall assume for the present that the saturation point is not reached for either product.

sumer believes would yield the same satisfaction as combination *C*. Suppose he informs us that this is so for the bundle of goods represented by *D*. In comparing *D* with *C* we find that it contains one less yard of clothing and one more bushel of food per week. Apparently the consumer believes that the loss in satisfaction occasioned by the decrease in clothing consumption would be just offset by the gain in satisfaction coming from the increase in food consumption. Suppose that still other combinations equivalent to *C* are represented by *A*, *B*, *E*, and *F*. If enough such equivalent combinations were plotted, they would trace out the *indifference curve* labeled *I* in Figure 6–1. An indifference curve through point *C* is the locus of points representing all the combinations of food and clothing that the consumer considers to be the equivalent of *C*—he would be indifferent if required to make a choice among those points.

All combinations believed by the consumer to be equivalent to combination *G* are represented by points making up indifference curve *II*. Since combination *G* is preferred to combination *C*, then all combinations represented by indifference curve *II* must be preferable to all of those represented by *I*.

A graph such as Figure 6–1 contains a large number of indifference curves. The entire set is called the consumer's *indifference map* and it presents a graphic picture of his preference structure. Every preference rank is represented by an indifference curve; any curve farther from the origin than another represents a set of equivalent combinations preferred to the set of equivalent combinations of the lower curve. In drawing an indifference map we usually draw in only those indifference curves needed for the analysis at hand.

Characteristics of Indifference Curves

The indifference curves forming a consumer's indifference map have three important characteristics: (1) they slope downward to the right; (2) no two indifference curves will intersect; and (3) they are convex to the origin of the indifference curve diagram. How do we know that these characteristics prevail?

Downward Slope

If the consumer is not saturated with either of the products shown on his indifference map, it follows that an indifference curve will slope downward to the right. Suppose a student consuming both football games and dances has one football game per season taken away from him. The new combination of the two, containing the same number of dances but one less football game, would be less preferred than the old. However, since the student is not saturated with dances, additional dances could be added until a third combination just equivalent to the original one is discovered; that is, it is possible to add enough dances to his recreation schedule to just compensate for the loss of a football game. This is what the downward slope of an indifference curve means.

Look again at combination *C* in Figure 6–1. If a yard of clothing is taken away from the consumer, a bushel of food must be added to avoid moving the consumer to a less-preferred combination. This brings the consumer to combination *D*, which is equivalent to combination *C* and must necessarily lie below and to the right of *C*.

Nonintersection

Two indifference curves on the same indifference map of a consumer cannot intersect. The combinations of goods shown by one indifference curve—the one farthest from the origin—are preferable to those of the other, otherwise both could not exist. Now consider the combinations shown by the less preferable curve, say indifference curve *I* in Figure 6–1. Any preferred combination must contain at least as much of one product and more of the other than some one of the combinations on the less preferable curve. This condition in itself rules out the possibility of intersection. We cannot infer from this that two indifference curves are everywhere the same distance apart. They may approach each other without intersecting.

Convexity to the Origin

The more a person consumes of any one product relative to another the less important a unit of it will be to him relative to a unit of the other. In Figure 6–2 compare the consumer's desires at combination *A*, at which point he is consuming large amounts of clothing relative to food, with what they would be at combination *C* on the same indifference curve, at which point he is consuming small amounts of clothing relative to food. At combination *A* the consumer would surely be willing to give up more clothing—say three yards—to get an additional bushel of food than he would at point *C*.[3] At point *C* we suppose that he is willing to give up only one fourth of a yard of clothing for an additional bushel of food per week. If this is indeed the case, then as we consider combinations lying on the same indifference curve from *A* to *C*, the consumer would be willing to give up less and less clothing to obtain additional bushels of food as his weekly consumption of clothing is decreased while that of food is in-

---

[3] We have not proved anything here; we are simply relying on casual observations to support the point.

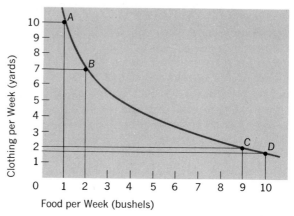

Figure 6–2
Diminishing marginal rate of substitution.

creased. This state of affairs is represented graphically by an indifference curve that is convex to the origin. A thorough study of the indifference curve in Figure 6–2 will make this point clear. What would the indifference curve look like if the consumer were willing to give up more and more clothing in exchange for each additional unit of food per week?

At any point on an indifference curve we call the amount of one product that the consumer is just willing to give up to obtain an additional unit of the other his *marginal rate of substitution* of the latter for the former. From point A to point B in Figure 6–2 the marginal rate of substitution of food for clothing, or MRS_{fc}, is 3. From C to D it is $\frac{1}{4}$. Between A and D it is decreasing as clothing is given up and as food is added to the weekly consumption pattern. This phenomenon is referred to as *the principle of the diminishing marginal rate of substitution of one product for another.*

The Line of Attainable Combinations

What are the major restrictions that you encounter as a consumer? The answer comes easily enough—your income is too small. From a slightly different point of view, given your income, the prices of goods and services are too high for you to purchase as much as you would like.

This problem can be expressed in a form compatible with the consumer's indifference map. Limiting the consumer to a two-commodity world, food and clothing, suppose he has 50 dollars per week to spend; the price of food is 1 dollar per bushel and the price of clothing is 2 dollars per yard. If he spends all of his income or purchasing power on clothing, he can purchase 25 yards per week. This possibility appears as point *A* in Figure 6–3(a). If the consumer were to decide that eating, too, is desirable, he could obtain 10 bushels of food by giving up 5 yards of clothing. Giving up the clothing would release 10 dollars of his purchasing power which could be spent for the 10 bushels of food. The consumer would then be at point *B*, purchasing 20 yards of clothing and 10 bushels of food each week. He can increase his consumption of food to 20 bushels by giving up another 5 yards of clothing. Substitution of food for clothing can be continued in this way until the consumer is taking no clothing and 50 bushels of food—spending his entire income on food. All possible combinations of clothing and food available to him lie on or under the straight line *AE*, which is called appropriately his *line of attainable combinations,* or his *budget line.*

The rate at which the consumer is able to substitute food for clothing is determined by the ratio of the price of food to the price of clothing. With the price of clothing at two dollars per yard and that of food at one dollar per bushel, the ratio is one half, meaning that one-half yard of clothing must be given up to obtain an additional bushel of food, or that two bushels of food must be given up to obtain an additional yard of clothing.

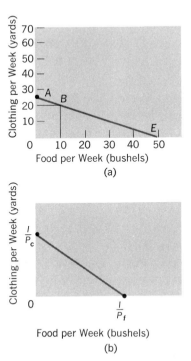

(a)

(b)

Figure 6–3
The line of attainable combinations.

A more general representation of the consumer's line of attainable combinations is shown in Figure 6–3(b). Dividing the consumer's income, I, by the price of clothing, P_c, we obtain the point marked $I/(P_c)$ on the clothing axis. This represents the amount of clothing he can buy if he takes no food. Dividing his income by the price of food, P_f, we obtain $I/(P_f)$, the amount of food he could buy if he purchases no clothing. The straight line joining the two points is the line of attainable combinations. Note that its slope,[4] showing how much clothing must be given up to get an additional bushel of food, is $(P_f)/(P_c)$.

ALLOCATION OF INCOME AMONG GOODS AND SERVICES

We assume that the consumer's objective is to maximize satisfaction; that is, to distribute his income among goods and services available to him in such a way that he obtains as high a level of satisfaction as possible. His indifference map and his line of attainable combinations provide the tools for uncovering the principles according to which this objective is accomplished. These are brought together in Figure 6–4. The consumer's income is fixed at I_1, while the prices of clothing and food are assumed to be P_{c_1} and P_{f_1}, respectively. These determine the position of his line of attainable combinations, AF. We have drawn only a few of the many indifference curves on his indifference map.

An Elementary Exposition

Imagine now that the consumer is at point A and is going to journey across his preference field along his line of attainable combinations. Any combination of clothing and food along that line or under it is available to him. As he moves from A toward B, giving up clothing purchases and increasing his food purchases, what happens to his satisfaction level? He is moving to higher indifference curves—to combinations of goods more and more highly preferred—or to higher and higher levels of satisfaction. But he can do even better if upon reaching B he continues to and through point C until he reaches combination D. If he goes beyond D toward E and F, he is moving to lower indifference curves; that is, to less preferred combinations.

He maximizes his satisfaction with combination D, taking f_1 bushels of food and c_1 yards of clothing per week. His line of attainable combina-

[4] The slope of the line is $[I/(P_c)]/[I/(P_f)]$, which reduces to $I/(P_c) \cdot (P_f)/I$, or $(P_f)/(P_c)$.

tions will not let him reach an indifference curve above *IV*. Note that on indifference curve *IV* only combination *D* is available to him. For monetary reasons all other combinations shown by it are out of his reach. The combination at which satisfaction is maximized is that at which the line of attainable combinations is tangent to an indifference curve, that indifference curve being the highest one the consumer can reach.

An Advanced Exposition

Although the preceding section explains the consumer's allocation of income well enough for most purposes in a beginning economics course, it may be desirable to probe further into the theory of consumer behavior. What motivates the consumer to move from *A* to *B*, from *B* to *C*, from *C* to *D*, and then to move no further down the line of attainable combinations? To be sure, the consumer seeks the most preferred of all the combinations available to him, but the explanation will be more thorough if we compare explicitly the market forces confronting the consumer with the consumer's preference patterns.

The slope of the line of attainable combinations indicates what the

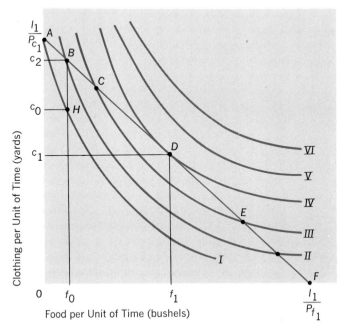

Figure 6–4
Consumer equilibrium.

consumer is able to do in the markets for clothing and food. The ratio of the price of food to the price of clothing states the number of yards of clothing the consumer is required by the market to forgo in order to obtain an extra bushel of food. In Figure 6–4 if the consumer is initially at A and is to move from A to B, he must give up c_2A yards of clothing in order to make the move. The increase in food purchased is measured by c_2B, so the slope of the line of attainable combinations is $(c_2A)/(c_2B)$, which is, of course, equal to $(P_{f_1})/(P_{c_1})$.[5]

If we were to consider the AH portion of indifference curve I to be linear, a straight line, what information would its slope convey to us? The slope would be measured by $(c_0A)/(c_0H)$, and, as we learned earlier, it is called the marginal rate of substitution of food for clothing—the consumer would be willing to give up c_0A yards of clothing to obtain c_0H bushels of food.

The market forces inducing the consumer to move from A to B down his line of attainable combinations now become apparent. In order to increase his food consumption by $O_{f_0}(= c_0H = c_2B)$ the consumer would *be willing* to give up c_0A of clothing, according to the marginal rate of substitution. But in the market he would *have* to forgo only c_2A of clothing, according to the ratio $(P_{f_1})/(P_{c_1})$. If he behaves as the market says he must, giving up only c_2A of clothing to obtain 0_{f_0} of food, and he is willing to give up c_0A of clothing, then c_0c_2, the extra amount he was willing but was not required to give up, is pure gain to the consumer. Whatever satisfaction c_0c_2 gives him is over and above what he was obtaining at A.

Now suppose that instead of looking at the slope of a curve between discrete points we think of it at one point only on the curve. In the case of the line of attainable combinations, nothing is changed conceptually. At point B in Figure 6–4 the slope of AF is still $(P_{f_1})/(P_{c_1})$ and it indicates at that point the rate at which the market will permit the substitution of food for clothing. The slope of indifference curve II at point B is still the marginal rate of substitution of food for clothing at that point—the rate at which the consumer is willing to substitute food for clothing.

We can reason at points B, C, and all other points from A to D precisely as we did for the movement from A to B. At the point B intersection of the line of attainable combinations and indifference curve II the slope of the indifference curve is greater than the slope of the line of attainable combinations. This means the consumer *is willing* to forgo more clothing than he *has to* in the market to obtain a small increase in food; consequently, he receives a net gain in satisfaction from a trade made on market terms. At every other point between A and D the same condition prevails. At point D the rate at which the consumer is willing to substitute food for clothing is the same as the rate specified by the market at which

---

[5] If $P_f = \$1$ and $P_c = \$1.50$, what will be the slope of the line of attainable combinations and what does it mean?

he would have to do so. Thus there is no reason for further substitution to occur. Why will the consumer not move from D to E?

Symbolically the conditions that must be met if the consumer is to maximize satisfaction are:

$$MRS_{xy} = \frac{P_x}{P_y}$$

where x and y are any two products with prices P_x and P_y, and

$$xP_x + yP_y = I$$

where x and y are the quantities of X and Y taken when income I is all being spent. These can be readily generalized to as many goods and services a consumer takes.

PRINCIPLES OF INDIVIDUAL CONSUMER DEMAND

The hard labor has been done; the use of indifference curve techniques to show the relations between the price of a product and the quantities of it a consumer will take per time unit is almost anticlimactic. Holding constant the consumer's preferences as pictured by his indifference map, his income, and the price of one product, we shall vary the price of the other product. At each such price, when the consumer is in equilibrium or is maximizing his satisfaction, we can read off the quantity taken.

If food is the product for which the demand curve is to be derived, suppose we check the impact of changes in its price on the line of attainable combinations. In Figure 6–5 let I_1 be the consumer's income, P_{c_1} the price of clothing, and P_{f_1} the initial price of food. These points determine the line of attainable combinations, EF. Let the price of food be lowered now to P_{f_2}. At the lower price, if the consumer were to spend his entire income on food, he could purchase a larger quantity, OG. His line of attainable combinations becomes EG. (Why does point E not change?) At a still lower price, P_{f_3}, it becomes EH.

Each of these three lines of attainable combinations will be tangent to certain indifference curves on the consumer's indifference map. Line EF is tangent to indifference curve I at point A; thus at price P_{f_1} the consumer would take quantity f_1 of food. Line EG is tangent to indifference curve II at point B, so the quantity of food the consumer would take at price P_{f_2} is f_2. At price P_{f_3} for food the line of attainable combinations, EH, is tangent to indifference curve III at point D and the quantity of food taken is f_3.

These price–quantity relationships form a part of the consumer's demand schedule or points on his demand curve. The demand schedule

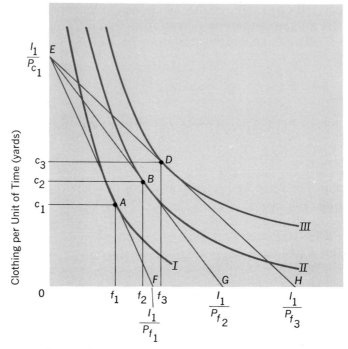

Food per Unit of Time (bushels)

Figure 6–5
Effects of price changes.

would be that of Table 6–1, which, when plotted, would yield an individual consumer demand curve like that of Figure 6–6. The relationships are such that the demand curve slopes downward to the right; that is, the lower the price of the product, the more of it the consumer will take.

The increase in quantity of food taken in response to the decrease in its price is attributable to a combination of *income effects* and *substitution effects*. With reference to Figure 6–5, the decrease in the price of food from P_{f_1} to P_{f_2} moves the line of attainable combinations from EF to EG.

TABLE 6–1
Individual Consumer Demand Schedule for Food

PRICE*	QUANTITY**
P_{f_1}	f_1
P_{f_2}	f_2
P_{f_3}	f_3

*$P_{f_1} > P_{f_2} > P_{f_3}$.
**$f_1 < f_2 < f_3$.

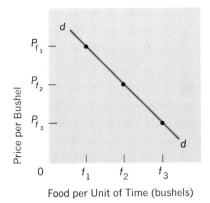

Figure 6-6
The individual consumer demand curve.

If the consumer had so desired, he could have continued to take c_1 of clothing *plus* a larger amount of food than f_1. This constitutes an increase in the consumer's *real income* or purchasing power. In the illustration only a part of this increase in the consumer's real income is spent on food; another part of it is used to increase his consumption of clothing as well.

The substitution effect is the inducement given the consumer to substitute food for clothing *because* the price of food has decreased relative to that of clothing. In Figure 6–5 note that since the slope of the line of attainable combinations is measured by $(P_f)/(P_c)$, when P_f decreases from P_{f_1} to P_{f_2} the slope is decreased also. A decrease in the slope of the line of attainable combinations causes the consumer to move around his indifference curves from a steeper point such as A on indifference curve *I* to a less steep point such as B on indifference curve *II*. The rate at which the consumer is able to substitute food for clothing in the market has been increased, thus providing a greater incentive for him to do so.

SUMMARY

Indifference curve analysis is used in this chapter to (1) show how a consumer tends to allocate his income among different goods and services and (2) explain the demand curve of a consumer for one product.

The consumer's preferences are represented by his indifference map, which is composed of his set of indifference curves. Any one indifference curve shows combinations of two goods for which the consumer shows equal preference. Indifference curves lying farther from the origin of his indifference map show combinations preferred to those on lower indifference curves.

Graphically the slope of an indifference curve at any point indicates the rate at which the consumer is willing to substitute one product for another at the combination of goods represented by the point. This is called his marginal rate of substitution of one good for the other. As the consumer moves from combination to combination around an indifference curve his marginal rate of substitution of the product being increased for the product being decreased is decreasing, thus indifference curves are convex to the origin of the indifference map.

The consumer is restrained in what he purchases per time period by his income and the prices of the goods and services he desires. Graphically the combinations available to him are separated from those not available to him by his line of attainable combinations. The slope of the line of attainable combinations is determined by the inverse of the ratio of the prices of the two products and shows the rate at which the market will permit the consumer to trade units of one good for units of the other.

The consumer's allocation of income between the products tends to be that at which his line of attainable combinations is tangent to one of his indifference curves. This is the highest indifference curve he can reach. At this point his marginal rate of substitution of one product for another is the same as the rate at which the market will permit him to trade one for the other, and he has no incentive to move away from it.

Points forming the consumer's demand curve for one product are obtained from his indifference map as we confront him with different prices of the product. Each different price generates a different line of attainable combinations that is tangent to a different indifference curve. Because of substitution effects, generally supplemented by income effects, the lower the product price, the greater will tend to be the consumer's level of consumption.

APPENDIX TO CHAPTER 6

The Basis of Exchange

Many people believe that when exchange of goods and services takes place one party is likely to gain at the expense of another. Ordinarily *both* parties to a voluntary exchange will gain; in fact, it is the expectation of gain by each party that generates the exchange in the first place. About the only way in which one party may be said to take advantage of the other is that his gains may exceed those of the other. The indifference apparatus lends itself well to a demonstration that this is the case.

Suppose in Figure 6–7 that two individuals obtain a total of OC yards of clothing and OF bushels of food per week. Mr. Smith's indifference map is rotated 180 degrees and is placed on that of Mr. Jones in such a position that Smith's food axis intersects Jones's clothing axis at point C and his clothing axis intersects Jones's food axis at point F. Further, Jones's and Smith's indifference map axes must form a rectangle so that the total amount of clothing received by both is measured by either OC on Jones's map or $O'F$ on Smith's map. The total amount of food is measured by either OF on Jones's map or by $O'C$ on Smith's. Any point inside the rectangle is a possible distribution of food and clothing between them. Consider point A, for example. If this were the distribution, it means that Jones receives OE yards of clothing per week and Smith receives EC yards. Jones receives OG bushels of food per week and Smith receives GF bushels.[1]

If point A in fact represents the initial distribution, both parties can gain from exchange. For GH bushels of food, Jones would be willing to exchange EJ yards of clothing. Smith would be willing to give up GH bushels of food for only EK yards of clothing.[2] Thus for GH bushels of food Jones is willing to give up more clothing than Smith would require for it. Suppose they divide the difference so that Jones gives Smith EL yards of clothing for GH bushels of food. Jones is better off by whatever JL yards of clothing are worth to him, and Smith is better off by whatever LK yards of clothing are worth to him. From a slightly different viewpoint, note that after the exchange the distribution is at point B—on higher indifference curves of both Jones and Smith.

---

[1] For convenience we shall use the axes of Jones's map for our measurements. If we so desired we could, of course, use those of Smith.

[2] If you have trouble understanding this point, rotate the diagram 180 degrees so that Smith's indifference map is in a familiar position.

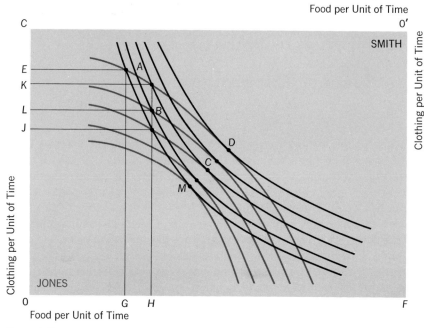

Figure 6–7
The gains from exchange.

The economic principle illustrated here is that if the marginal rate of substitution of one product for another is greater for one person than for another, both parties can gain from exchange. With reference to Jones's axes, the slope of Jones's indifference curve at point *B* is greater than that of Smith—Jones's marginal rate of substitution of food for clothing exceeds Smith's. Thus both can gain from further exchange, with Jones trading clothing to Smith for food.

If the distribution of food and clothing is that at point *C* or *D* or *M*, at which an indifference curve of Jones is tangent to an indifference curve of Smith, both parties cannot gain from exchange. The marginal rate of substitution of food for clothing is the same for both; Jones values a yard of clothing relative to a bushel of food exactly the same as Smith, so no voluntary exchange will occur.

The points of tangency between the indifference curves of Jones and those of Smith trace out a line *MCD*, called the *contract curve*. If the distribution of goods is represented by a point off the contract curve, both parties can gain from exchange, and any exchange that occurs will move the point toward the contract curve. Once the contract curve is reached, any further exchanges either on or away from the contract curve will make one or both of the parties worse off. Movements along the curve will make one party better off at the expense of the other; for example, exchanges that move the distribution point from *M* toward *D* will place Jones on higher and higher indifference curves while Smith is forced to lower and lower indifference curves. Movements away from the contract curve introduce the further possibility that both parties may be made worse off by the exchange.

EXERCISES AND QUESTIONS FOR DISCUSSION

1. Suppose you are at some point on the line of attainable combinations for two goods, *A* and *B*. The $MRS_{AB} = 5$ at this point. Suppose, further, that *A* sells for $2 per unit and *B* sells for $4 per unit. In which direction along the line of attainable combinations must you move in order to increase your satisfactions? What if the $MRS_{AB} = \frac{1}{8}$?
2. How do you think indifference curves for tennis rackets and tennis balls would look? for hamburgers and hot dogs?
3. Mr. Shadow enjoys spending his leisure time reading novels or watching movies. He has an "entertainment fund" of $30 a month which he uses for these purposes. Admission to a movie is $2 and the novels sell for $5 each. Draw his line of attainable combinations for these two items. Suppose the price of novels drops to $3. Draw the new line of attainable combinations on the same graph. Follow the same operation for a price of $2 per novel. Now arbitrarily draw in an indifference map for these two goods. (Be sure to make an indifference curve tangent to each of the lines of attainable combinations.) From the graph you have constructed, derive Mr. Shadow's demand curve for novels.
4. "Given a person's level of income and given that that level may not change, any combination of two goods not located on his budget line cannot be attained by the consumer." Evaluate.

SELECTED READINGS

Dorfman, R., *Prices and Markets.* Englewood Cliffs, N.J.: Prentice-Hall, Inc., 1967, Chap. 3.

Hicks, J. R., *Value and Capital,* 2d ed. Oxford: The Clarendon Press, 1946, Chaps. 1 and 2.

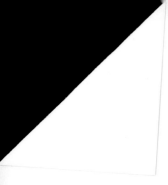

Principles of Production

CHAPTER 7

In this chapter and the next we turn to that group of economic units falling under the heading of business firms. They will be subjected to the same detailed examination as were households as consumers in the last two chapters, and we will note that there are many parallels between the behavior of a business firm and that of a consumer.

How does a business firm decide on the proportions in which it will use different kinds of resource inputs in producing a product? For example, in producing a product like an airstrip, why would a construction firm in India use vast quantities of workers who move earth with shovels, mix concrete in mud boxes, and carry it in baskets on their heads? Why would it not make more extensive use of earth-moving equipment and other kinds of advanced construction technology? The answer, of course, lies in the comparative costs of doing the job. It costs less in India to use relatively much of the abundant, inexpensive labor and relatively little of the scarce and very expensive capital than it does the other way around. The economics leading to the selection by a firm of the resource combinations that will minimize the costs of producing given amounts of product per unit of time are the subject matter of this chapter.

THE PRODUCTION FUNCTION

Schematically a firm can be thought of as a hopper into which resource inputs are poured to be stirred and mixed in special ways by special sticks —the whole process being known as technology—and from which product output emerges. If a firm were producing shirts, the resource inputs would be machinery and tools of specific kinds, buildings to house the machinery, land on which the whole complex rests, cloth, thread, buttons, zippers, snaps, and labor representing a wide range of skills. The quantity of product output obtained per month would be related to the quantities of resource inputs. This relation is called *the production function*, the term "function" being used in the mathematical sense to indicate the dependency of the output quantity on the quantities of inputs.

Nature of the Production Function

Probably the most obvious characteristic of the production function is that if all resource inputs are increased, the firm's product output will be increased also. Almost as obvious, the firm's output will depend upon the technology available to it.

The range of production techniques available to the firm together with the resources available to it determine its production function. The firm will not necessarily use the same techniques at different output levels. For small outputs of many products not much use can be made of large, complex machines, whereas large outputs of the same products may very well be produced most efficiently with resources of these kinds. A specific production function takes into account that of the techniques available the ones selected are those most suited to the firm's level of output. New technological discoveries that will enable the firm to produce more than before at given levels of resource inputs *shift* or *change* the production function itself.

Another often overlooked characteristic of the production function is that within the function resource inputs can be substituted for one another usually to some degree and frequently to a considerable degree. Consider your own production function for washing your car. You can, if you desire, use a bucket of plain water, rags, and quite a lot of labor. You can cut down on the labor if you add detergent to the water. Labor input can be decreased still more if you use a hose rather than a bucket and a sponge to wash off the detergent before using the chamois. And the labor input can be further decreased if you increase the capital input by running the automobile through a commercial car wash. In most production processes capital can be substituted for labor; one kind of capital can be substituted for another; and one kind of labor can be substituted for another.

The possibility of substituting resources for one another in the production process opens up still another possibility. Larger quantities of one resource used with constant quantities of others should increase a firm's output up to some point. A simplified production function demonstrating this characteristic is shown in Table 7–1 and Figure 7–1. Suppose we have

TABLE 7-1

Total Product and Marginal Physical Product of Labor

(1) LAND (ACRES)	(2) LABOR (MAN HOURS)	(3) TOTAL PRODUCT (BUSHELS)	(4) MARGINAL PHYSICAL PRODUCT OF LABOR (CHANGE IN PRODUCT/ CHANGE IN LABOR)
1	1	20	20
1	2	42	22
1	3	66	24
1	4	88	22
1	5	108	20
1	6	124	16
1	7	136	12
1	8	144	8
1	9	148	4
1	10	148	0

conducted a series of experiments using different quantities of labor per unit of time on an acre of land. The results of the experiment are recorded in the total product column of the table. The total product curve of labor, TP_l is plotted from columns (2) and (3) of the table.

The Law of Diminishing Returns

Everyone has heard of the celebrated law of diminishing returns and almost everyone confuses it with the principle of diminishing marginal utility. Diminishing returns is frequently said to have set in when a boy makes himself sick eating bananas or when after 40 years of marriage a woman is ready to divorce her husband.

The term is used in economics in a much more restricted and specialized sense. It should be kept apart from the principle of diminishing marginal utility. The concepts may be parallel but they are not the same. The *law of diminishing returns* states that if in a production process the input level of one resource is increased unit by unit while those of other resources are held constant, beyond some point the resulting increases in product output will become smaller and smaller.

The law is illustrated in Table 7-1 and Figure 7-1. It becomes effective when four man hours of labor are used with a unit of land. As the quantity of labor is increased beyond that point, the increases in total product diminish. When 9 or 10 man hours per acre are used the total product obtainable from an acre is maximum and the increases in total product have decreased to zero.

Instead of referring to the law in terms of diminishing increases in total product, it is easier to view it in terms of diminishing marginal physical product of the resource being increased. *Marginal physical prod-*

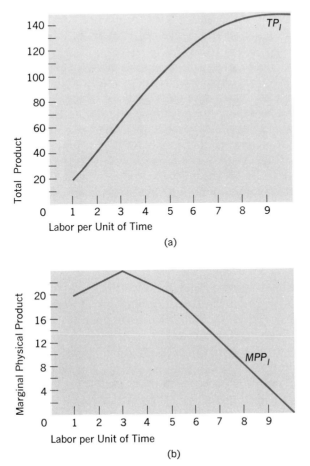

Figure 7-1
Total product and marginal physical product of a resource.

uct of a resource is defined as the change in total product resulting from a one-unit change in its level of use, the quantities of other resources remaining constant.[1] Thus when employment of labor is increased from one to two man hours the increase in total product—its marginal physical product—is 22 bushels of product. For an increase in labor from two to three man hours, the marginal physical product is 24 bushels. The rest of column (4) is derived from columns (2) and (3) in a like manner.

The marginal physical product curve for labor in Figure 7-1(b) is derived from the total product curve of Figure 7-1(a). At each level of labor employment we measure the increase in total product occurring when

[1] We call it *marginal physical product* instead of simply marginal product in order to distinguish it from the concept of *marginal revenue product*, which we shall encounter later. Frequently both concepts are referred to loosely as marginal product, a usage which often results in confusion.

employment is increased to that level from a level one man hour smaller. These increases, the marginal physical product of labor at different employment levels, are plotted in Table 7–1(b).

The law of diminishing returns is operative in production processes all around us. It rests ultimately on the proposition that there is an upper limit to the amount of product that can be obtained from any given complex of resources. Suppose, for example, that a resource complex consists of 1000 acres of wheat land, specific quantities of machinery to use on it, and a given complement of labor. Now if fertilizer were applied to the complex, the wheat output would increase. The larger the amount of fertilizer applied, the larger the output would be—up to a point. This point is simply the maximum output attainable from the original complex of land, machinery, and labor, and as it is approached the marginal physical product of fertilizer must be decreasing; that is, the law of diminishing returns with respect to fertilizer must be operative. At the point at which an increase in fertilizer will not increase output, the marginal physical product of fertilizer becomes zero.

Often for relatively small quantities of a resource applied to a given complex of other resources *increasing returns* will result from the first few increments in its level of use. This may happen because the resource is used too sparingly to be efficient. Consider, for example, a large steel mill in which all of the resources necessary for making steel are available in large quantities with the exception of labor. One man working the plant alone will not produce much steel. But if helpers are added they can divide up some tasks and cooperate on others. Equal increments in the labor resource up to some point will bring about larger and larger increases in steel output. However, as the quantity of labor relative to the quantities of other resources is further increased, diminishing returns will set in.

Diminishing returns for specific resources represent a far more important phenomenon than increasing returns. In the production process each resource used by a firm will ordinarily be utilized in the range of diminishing returns. We mention increasing returns in passing in order to make the analysis of resource use as complete as possible.

LEAST-COST COMBINATION OF RESOURCES

Hopefully, the discussion of a firm's production function puts us in a position to get at the main question raised in this chapter: What determines the proportions in which a firm utilizes different resources in the production process? We shall assume that the firm is motivated in this respect by efficiency objectives, or a desire to produce whatever output it produces at a total cost as low as possible. Stated another way, the firm strives to get as much output as possible from any given level of expenditure on resources. Suppose, for example, that the firm is a factory producing shirts and that it intends to produce 100 shirts per day. These can be produced at numerous different cost levels, depending upon the resource combinations and the techniques of production chosen by the firm. Assume that the least of these possible cost levels is 75 dollars. To say that 75 dollars is the least cost of producing 100 shirts is also to say that 100 shirts is the maximum number that can be produced for 75 dollars.

Suppose that the shirt factory makes a given cost outlay on two resources and the firm's intent is to secure the largest possible output of shirts with that cost outlay. We shall assume that the two resources are not directly related to one another; that is, that the quantity used of one does not directly affect the productivity of the other. Let the two resources be the labor of pressers and the labor of packers,[2] and that the quantities of each are represented by R and A, respectively. The marginal physical product schedules of both are listed in Table 7-2 as MPP_r and MPP_a; the cost outlay, TCO, is 16 dollars; the price or wage rate of pressers, p_r, is 2 dollars per unit; and the price or wage rate of packers, p_a, is 1 dollar per unit. Note that the law of diminishing returns becomes operative for pressers with the third unit and for packers with the fourth unit.

Suppose that initially the firm is spending the entire 16 dollar cost outlay on pressers. The quantity employed is eight and MPP_r is four shirts. Since the eighth presser costs 2 dollars, the marginal physical product per dollar's worth of this kind of labor, $(MPP_r)/(p_r)$, is two shirts. A dollar's worth of pressers' labor contributes two shirts to the

TABLE 7-2
Marginal Physical Product of Pressers and Packers

Pressers		Packers	
R	MPP_r (SHIRTS)	A	MPP_a (SHIRTS)
1	14	1	8
2	14	2	8
3	13	3	8
4	12	4	7
5	10	5	6
6	8	6	5
7	6	7	4
8	4	8	3
9	2	9	2
10	0	10	0

[2]As a matter of fact, these resources would undoubtedly be related in some degree, but for purposes of simplicity we shall assume that they are not. The conditions that must be met for a combination of resources to be a least-cost combination are not affected by this simplifying assumption.

firm's output—take a dollar's worth away and a two-shirt decrease in output occurs.

Is this the best the firm can do with its 16 dollar cost outlay? Consider packers' labor. Employment of a packer will add eight shirts, the MPP_a of a single packer, to the firm's total output. The packer costs a dollar, so $(MPP_a)/(p_a)$, the marginal physical product of a dollar's worth of packers' labor at the one-unit level of employment, is also eight shirts. Since $(MPP_r)/(p_r)$ is only two shirts, the transfer of a dollar from pressers to packers will bring about a net increase of six shirts in the firm's output. Transfer of a second dollar from pressers to packers will bring about another six-shirt increase in output—a loss of two shirts more than offset by a gain of eight as a second packer per unit of time is employed. A third dollar removed from expenditure on pressers reduces output by three shirts, and if spent on a third packer increases output by eight for a net gain of five shirts. A fourth dollar withdrawn from pressers and spent on packers yields a net increase of four shirts. The transfers of fifth and sixth dollars in the same direction yield net output increases of two shirts and one shirt, respectively.

The firm is now maximizing the output obtainable from a 16 dollar per unit of time outlay on pressers and packers. Five pressers and six packers are employed. The marginal physical product of both a dollar's worth of pressers' labor and a dollar's worth of packers' labor is five shirts. Transfer of a dollar in either direction will decrease output.

We have arrived at the fundamental proposition that if a firm is to get the greatest possible product output attainable from a given outlay on resources, it must combine the resources in such a way that the marginal physical product per dollar's worth of any one resource used must be equal to that of any other resource available to it. For any two resources, A and B, the combination must be such that $(MPP_a)/(p_a) = (MPP_b)/(p_b)$. If the marginal physical product of a dollar's worth of B is greater than that of A, then output can be increased *with no increase in cost* by transferring dollars from A to B until the equality is established. Maximum output from a given cost outlay means the same thing as minimum cost for a given amount of product output. Economists have generally but not exclusively preferred to put the proposition in this latter form and to refer to it as the *least-cost combination* of resources rather than the *maximum-output combination*, although one statement is just as correct as the other.

ISOQUANTS AND ISOCOSTS

Some people will prefer to use the more sophisticated isoquant-isocost approach to a firm's least-cost combination of resources, although the analysis in this book does not require it. The firm's production function is represented by an *isoquant map*, parallel in concept to a consumer's indifference map. Its cost restraints are represented by *isocost curves* that are similar mathematically to the consumer's line of attainable combinations. These are brought together to show how the firm's least-cost combination of resources is determined.

The Isoquant Map

A firm's isoquant map is composed of isoquant curves. The latter are similar to a consumer's indifference curves and any one isoquant shows the different combinations of resource inputs that will produce a given level of product output. The input combinations that will produce higher levels of output are shown by higher isoquants while those that can produce lower levels only are represented by lower isoquants.

Table 7–3 gives a typical isoquant schedule, and the corresponding isoquant curve is plotted in Figure 7–2. Suppose that the product being produced is shirts and the resource inputs are labor and capital. In Figure 7–2 units of labor are measured along the vertical axis while units of capital are shown by the horizontal axis. Both the output and the inputs are flows over time, or quantities per time period.

Let us assume that we have determined through experimentation the combinations of capital and labor that will yield a product output of 100 shirts per time period. These are combinations such as *A, B, C,* and *D,* listed in Table 7–3 and plotted in Figure 7–2. Still other combinations such as *E* and *F* could be determined also. All possible combinations of labor and capital that just yield 100 shirts trace out the curved line *AEBCFD,* which is an isoquant or equal-product curve.

The 100-shirt isoquant is a downward-sloping curved line, convex to the origin of the diagram. Is this the shape our everyday observations lead us to expect? Initially it seems correct. The higher the proportions of labor to capital used, the less capital each worker has to work with and the less productive a man will be. Under these circumstances an additional unit of capital may substitute for or do the work of several units of labor. A movement from *A* to *B* illustrates the case. As the firm moves to smaller ratios of labor to capital, from *B* to *C* and from *C* to *D,* additional units of capital are likely to substitute for smaller and smaller amounts of labor, because labor becomes more and more productive as each man has more and more capital with which to work. Yet these statements prove nothing; rather, they indicate simply that it seems reasonable to expect that an isoquant will take on the shape illustrated.

Other isoquants can be drawn at higher and lower production levels. A number of them are shown for output intervals of 10 shirts each. If we start at the origin of Figure 7–2 and move along a straight line to point *B,* the successive points along the line show combinations containing more

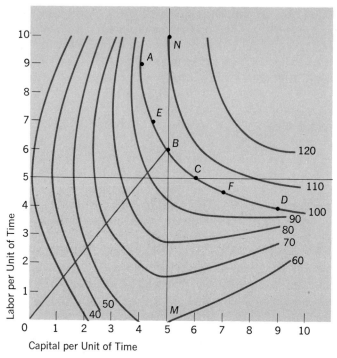

Figure 7–2
An isoquant map.

TABLE 7–3
Combinations of Labor and Capital Yielding 100 Shirts per Unit of Time

COMBINATION	LABOR	CAPITAL
A	9	4
B	6	5
C	5	6
D	4	9

and more of both resource inputs. Consequently, we would expect the isoquants lying farther from the origin to show resource combinations that will yield higher levels of product output. A set of isoquants makes up the firm's *isoquant map* and provides a graphic picture of its production function.

A total product schedule for one resource like that of Table 7–1 is easily obtained from the firm's isoquant map. Suppose that the input of capital per unit of time is held constant at five units and that the firm increases its labor input unit by unit. The path followed on the isoquant map of Figure 7–2 is line *MN*.

At one unit of labor (and five units of capital) we are between the 60-shirt and the 70-shirt isoquants. The isoquant going precisely through this resource combination is not drawn, but by interpolation it appears that it would be the 67-shirt isoquant. At two units of labor (and five units of capital) the firm should be on about the 74-shirt isoquant. Continuing these observations, we construct the total product columns—(2) and (3) in Table 7–4. (Check each total product quantity in the table with Figure 7–2 to make sure you understand how each such quantity in the table is obtained.)

The marginal physical product of labor is computed from columns (2) and (3) of Table 7–4 and is recorded in column (4) for each level of utilization of labor. When employment of labor is increased from one to two units the increase in total product—marginal physical product—is seven shirts. The increase from two to three units of labor increases total product by eight shirts, and the other quantities in the MPP_l column are found in the same way. The law of diminishing returns with respect to labor becomes effective with the fourth unit of labor used per time period.

TABLE 7–4
Total Product and Marginal Physical Product of Labor: Capital = 5 units

(1) CAPITAL	(2) LABOR	(3) TP$_l$ (SHIRTS)	(4) MPP$_l$ (CHANGE IN SHIRTS/ CHANGE IN LABOR)	
5	1	67	—	
5	2	74	7	
5	3	82	8	
5	4	89	7	Diminishing
5	5	95	6	returns
5	6	100	5	with
5	7	104	4	respect
5	8	107	3	to
5	9	109	2	labor
5	10	110	1	

The isoquant map provides a more general view of the firm's production function than we have been able to obtain heretofore. From it we can obtain a number of total product curves for labor. Instead of assuming that the quantity of capital used is constant at five units, we could have assumed that it was constant at three units. The total product schedule for labor would have been different; that is, it would have been lower at each level of labor input than the one of Table 7–4. Similarily, we could have assumed that the quantity of labor used is constant—say four units—and by considering larger and larger quantities of capital used with it we could have obtained a total product curve for capital. The isoquant map enables us to show the *dependency* of the productivity of labor on the quantity of capital used and the *dependency* of the productivity of capital on the quantity of labor used.

Isocosts

We turn now to the cost side of the picture. In Figure 7–3 suppose that the firm makes a cost outlay of O dollars on labor and capital. If all of it were spent on labor at a price of P_l per unit, $O/(P_l)$ units of labor could be purchased. On the other hand, if it were all spent on capital at a price of P_c per unit, $O/(P_c)$ units of capital could be purchased. Analogous to a consumer's line of attainable combinations, the straight line AB shows the combinations of labor and capital that the cost outlay O will purchase. Its slope is $(P_c)/(P_l)$, and it measures the amount of labor the firm would be required to give up if it were to purchase an additional unit of capital with no change in the cost outlay.[3] We call this line an *isocost curve*, meaning that all along its path the cost outlay of the firm is the same.

The Least-Cost Combination

If we put the firm's isoquant map on the same diagram with the isocost curve, we can readily determine the least-cost or maximum-product combination of labor and capital. The isoquant identified as X shows the combinations of labor and capital that will produce X units of product output, and the one marked X_1 shows those that will produce an output of X_1. Isoquants lying farther from the origin are for higher quantities of output than are the closer ones. In Figure 7–3, then, the least-cost or maximum-product combination of resources is that at which the isocost curve just touches or is tangent to an isoquant—combination E containing L_1 units of labor and C_1 units of capital. Quantity X_1 is the largest output that a cost outlay of O will produce. Or, looked at the other way around, cost outlay O is the least cost of producing output X_1. These propositions hold for resource combination E, at which point the isocost curve is just tangent to an isoquant. If the firm were to purchase another combination of labor and capital—D or G, for example—the product output obtained would be below X_1. Or if the firm were to purchase combination H or K a cost outlay larger than O would be required.

Since the least-cost or maximum-output resource combination is that

---

[3] Slope $AB = \dfrac{O}{P_l} \quad \dfrac{O}{P_c} = \dfrac{O}{P_l} \cdot \dfrac{P_c}{O} = \dfrac{P_c}{P_l}$

If $P_c = \$2$ and $P_l = \$1$, then slope $AB = 2/1$, meaning that, given the cost outlay, if the firm wants an additional unit of capital (costing \$2) it must give up two units of labor (costing \$1 each).

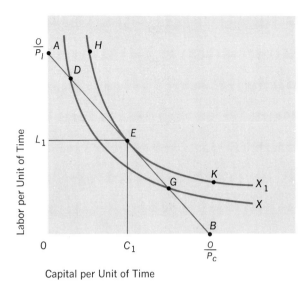

Figure 7–3
The least-cost combination.

at which an isocost curve is tangent to an isoquant, it is apparent that the tangency condition will bear additional scrutiny. At the point of tangency, point E, the two curves have identical slopes. We know already that the slope of the isocost is $(P_c)/(P_l)$ and that it indicates the amount of labor the firm must release in order to obtain an additional unit of capital, if the cost outlay is to remain unchanged.

What does the slope of an isoquant show? Suppose in Figure 7–4 that A and B are points very close together on a given isoquant and that we have this segment of the isoquant under a magnifying glass. If A and B

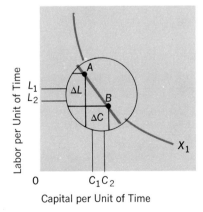

Figure 7–4
The marginal rate of technical substitution.

are close enough to each other we can think of the line segment AB as being a straight line. So conceived, the slope of AB or of that small segment of the isoquant is $(\Delta L)/(\Delta C)$, and this ratio is referred to as the *marginal rate of technical substitution* of capital for labor, or $MRTS_{cl}$. It measures the amount of labor for which a unit of capital will just substitute with no loss in product output.

The magnitude of the $MRTS_{cl}$ between A and B depends upon the marginal physical product of labor and the marginal physical product of capital when the firm is using a combination of L_1 units of labor and C_1 units of capital. If the firm gives up ΔL units of labor, the loss in product output will be $\Delta L \cdot MPP_l$. If the firm acquires ΔC units of capital, the gain in product output will be $\Delta C \cdot MPP_c$. For such a substitution of capital for labor, if the firm is to continue producing a product output of X_1, then

$$\Delta L \cdot MPP_l = \Delta C \cdot MPP_c$$

that is, the loss in product from giving up labor must equal the gain in product from acquiring more capital.

Restating this equality as

$$\frac{\Delta L}{\Delta C} = \frac{MPP_c}{MPP_l}$$

we see that at any given point on an isoquant

$$MRTS_{cl} = \frac{MPP_c}{MPP_l}$$

This logic is rather abstract; suppose we slip some numbers into the algebra and geometry of the marginal rate of technical substitution of capital for labor. If at point A the marginal physical product of capital is eight shirts and that of labor is four shirts, then

$$MRTS_{cl} = \frac{MPP_c}{MPP_l} = \frac{8}{4} = \frac{2}{1}$$

This means that a unit of capital will substitute for two units of labor in the firm's production function. This makes sense, since at combination A a unit of capital is twice as productive as a unit of labor.

The original purpose of this discourse was to examine the implications of tangency between an isocost curve and an isoquant. At the point of tangency—E in Figure 7–2—the slopes of the two curves are the same. The slope of the isoquant is the $MRTS_{cl}$ or $(MPP_c)/(MPP_l)$ at that point. The slope of an isocost curve is $(p_c)/(p_l)$. Therefore, at the point of tangency

$$\frac{MPP_c}{MPP_l} = \frac{p_c}{p_l}$$

or

$$\frac{MPP_c}{p_c} = \frac{MPP_l}{p_l}$$

For a resource combination to be a least-cost or maximum-output combination, the marginal rate of technical substitution of one resource for the other must be in the same ratio as their prices; or, to put it another way, the marginal physical product per dollar's worth of one resource must equal the marginal physical product per dollar's worth of any other available resource.

SUMMARY

This chapter examines how a business firm determines the proportions in which different resources will be used in the production process. The objective of business firms is assumed to be that of producing a given amount of product at the least possible cost or of producing the maximum amount of product for a given cost outlay.

The relation between the quantities of resource inputs and the technology that a firm uses on the one hand and the quantities of product output that it obtains on the other is called its production function. In general the production function shows how product output changes when the quantities of all resources used change in the same direction, and it indicates how resources may be substituted for one another in the production process. Additionally, it shows how output will change when any one resource input is changed in quantity, the quantities of the others being held constant. This latter relation is summed up in a total product schedule or a total product curve for the resource that is varied in quantity.

Marginal physical product of a resource is defined as the change in total product per unit change in the quantity used of a resource, the inputs of other resources being held constant in quantity. Except in some cases for the first few units of the variable resource applied to fixed amounts of other resources, marginal physical product of the variable resource will decrease as larger quantities of it are used. This phenomenon is known as the law of diminishing returns.

A least-cost or maximum-product combination of resource inputs for a firm is one at which the marginal physical product of a dollar's worth of any one resource is the same for the firm as the marginal physical product of a dollar's worth of any other resource available to it. A given cost outlay so made yields the maximum possible output. Or this output can be said to be produced at the least possible cost.

Isoquant–isocost techniques provide a more sophisticated look at least-cost or maximum-product resource combinations. An isoquant is a curve showing the various resource combinations that will produce a given level of product output. A set of isoquant curves makes up the firm's *isoquant map*, showing which resource combinations will produce larger quantities of product output and which will produce less. Isoquants also show the marginal rate of technical substitution of one resource for another in the firm's production processes—that is, the amount of one resource the firm can just give up to obtain an additional unit of another, the product output remaining constant. An isocost curve shows the combinations of resource inputs that a given total cost outlay on the resources will purchase for the firm.

Given the firm's isoquant map and the isocost curve for a specific cost outlay, the least-cost or maximum-product combination of resources is that at which the isocost curve is just tangent to an isoquant. At this point the slopes of the two curves are the same. Since the slope of the isocost is measured by the inverse ratio of the price of one resource to the price of the other, and since the marginal rate of technical substitution is measured by the inverse ratio of the marginal physical product of one to that of the other, for any two resources, A and B,

$$\frac{MPP_a}{MPP_b} = \frac{p_a}{p_b}$$

or,

$$\frac{MPP_a}{p_a} = \frac{MPP_b}{p_b}$$

EXERCISES AND QUESTIONS FOR DISCUSSION

1. Test your understanding of the method for finding the least-cost combination of resources by reference to the table given below. The quantities of labor and land and their respective marginal physical productivities are given. What is the least-cost combination of these two resources if the price of labor is $2, the price per unit of land is $1, and the total cost outlay is $12? Before you begin, what can you say about the relationship between the MPP_{labor} and the MPP_{land} at the least-cost combination?

LABOR	MPP$_{labor}$	LAND	MPP$_{land}$
1	9	1	14
2	10	2	12
3	9	3	10
4	8	4	8
5	7	5	6
6	6	6	4
7	5	7	2
8	4	8	0

2. Figure 7–1(a) is a production function showing both increasing and decreasing returns. Can you illustrate graphically a production function having only increasing returns? only decreasing returns? Can you give an example of each?
3. The $MRTS_{cl}$ (slope of an isoquant) shows us the amount of labor a producer is "willing" to give up to get an additional unit of capital and still produce the same output. The slope of an isocost curve shows the amount of labor that the market tells the producer he "must" give up to get an additional unit of capital and still spend the same amount of money. Using this terminology, can you explain why a rational producer would not use combinations D or G in Figure 7–3?
4. Suppose you are at some point on an isoquant showing the different amounts of labor and capital yielding the same output of lamps. You decide to decrease your use of labor by one unit and increase your use of capital by one-fourth unit. If the MPP_l at this point is two lamps, what must the MPP_c be in order for you to remain on the same isoquant?
5. We might think of a university as being a firm that produces knowledgeable persons. Within this firm we find workers (professors) working on the raw material (students). The professors often complain that after a certain point, if they continue to add to the number of students in a class, their effectiveness begins to fall off. Perhaps this is due to the fact that more students cause more distractions or that some students are farther away from the speaker or that the odds of being called on to answer a question are reduced. What important law in production theory have we illustrated?
6. What would you expect the effect to be on the total product curve for labor of the placement of a new labor-saving invention in the production process?

SELECTED READINGS

Ferguson, C. E., *Microeconomic Theory*. Homewood, Ill.: Richard D. Irwin, Inc., 1966, Chap. 7.
Watson, Donald S., *Price Theory and Its Uses*. 2d ed. Boston: Houghton Mifflin Company, 1968, Chaps. 9 and 10.

Costs of Production

CHAPTER 8

A steel mill has just modernized its plant and equipment. It has installed up-to-date furnaces and rolling mills and it specializes in the production of sheet steel used for making automobile bodies. But market demand for automobiles is in a slump. Orders for steel from automobile manufacturers have fallen off and the steel mill is operating at a fraction of its capacity. Among other things, management is concerned about the high costs of producing a ton of steel. Its members watch economic indicators constantly, hoping that steel orders will increase. They expect that at higher rates of utilization they can reduce substantially their production costs per ton. For plant and equipment already in place, with costs per ton high at low levels of utilization, why would they expect these costs to become lower as the level of utilization is increased? Further, is there some level of product output (plant utilization) beyond which per ton costs will increase?

A company that manufactures light aircraft has made an announcement that startles the rest of the industry. It plans to triple the plant and equipment necessary for producing the small two-place airplane at the bottom of its product line. A spokesman for the company states that lower production costs associated with the larger outputs will enable the firm to cut prices of the airplane substantially. Why is this the case? Are large plants always more efficient—that is, can they always produce at lower per unit costs than small ones? Can plants get too large to operate efficiently?

In this chapter we seek the answers to the questions just raised. The examples pose two distinct types of cost situations, the short run and the long run, that students frequently have difficulty in keeping separate. We shall examine each in detail, but first we must see what comprises costs of production.

NATURE OF COSTS

We usually think of a firm's costs of production as being the money obligations incurred in producing its output; yet costs involve more than these. To be sure, whatever the firm must pay for the resources it uses is a cost outlay or a cost obligation. But there are frequently some costs that a firm does not pay directly. Further, what determines the magnitude of a firm's costs?

The Alternative-Cost Principle

Where there are a number of alternative uses to which units of a given resource, say machinists' labor, can be put, any one firm must pay for a unit of it whatever that unit is worth to any alternative user. An aircraft manufacturer will pay for a man hour of machinists' labor whatever it is worth to him in the production of aircraft. An automobile manufacturer, desiring to hold his force of machinists intact or desiring to hire more, must pay at least as much as the aircraft manufacturer or machinists will work for the latter instead of for him. Generalizing from this, we see that the cost of a unit of any resource used by a firm is its value in its best alternative use. This principle is known sometimes as the *alternative-cost principle* and sometimes as the *opportunity-cost principle*.

The principle operates for society as a whole as well as for any single firm. Resource units used to produce one item cannot be used to produce another. Suppose that wood and nylon strings of certain types can be used to produce either guitars or violins. An increase in the production of guitars means a sacrifice in the production of violins, so the cost of a guitar to society is the value of violins sacrificed by using the materials to produce a guitar instead.

Implicit and Explicit Costs

Some of a firm's costs are obvious ones. The owner-operator of the corner grocery store must pay his rent, his utility bills, and the cost of his stocks of goods. These obvious outlays for resources bought or hired, and which any accountant would record as costs, are called *explicit costs.*

There are, however, other resources used in the production process for which the cost obligations are not so obvious. What about the labor that the owner-operator puts into his business? What about the furniture, fixtures, and equipment owned by him and used in the business? Frequently resources such as these are left out of account in determining a firm's costs. But the self-owned, self-employed resources of a business go into its production hopper and contribute to the firm's output just as do those that are bought and hired. These costs are called *implicit costs,* and to the economist, concerned with the costs of *all* resources used in production, they are just as important as the explicit costs.

How can the implicit money costs of self-owned, self-employed resources be determined if they are not currently bought or hired in resource markets? The alternative-cost principle provides the appropriate guide. An owner-operator's labor should be appraised at what he could earn if he were to work for someone else in his best earning capacity. For other such resources we determine what similar resources are worth hired out in their best alternative use.

THE SHORT RUN AND THE LONG RUN

The short run and the long run are not really calendar concepts at all. In planning their outputs and in estimating their costs, firms generally proceed along two lines. On the one hand, they consider the different outputs per time period that can be produced with their present complement of plant and equipment. This is called *short-run* planning. On the other hand, they consider the possibilities of changing the complement of plant and equipment or *scale of plant* that they use. They consider a wider range of outputs than any one scale of plant can produce. This is called *long-run* planning.

The Short Run

For economic analysis of short-run planning it is convenient to divide resources into two classifications, fixed and variable. *Fixed resources* are the ones that comprise the firm's scale of plant, and in short-run planning changes in the quantities used of these are not considered. We think of them as being fixed in quantity and as setting an upper limit to the amount of output per time period that the firm can produce. Stated another way, the short-run planning period is one in which changes in the firm's scale of plant are not possible. Some of the resources classified in the fixed category in the short run are the firm's land site, its buildings and heavy machinery, and its key management personnel.

The short-run *variable resources* are those that we think of as being run through the plant to produce product output. The greater the quantities of variable resources used, the larger the output will be—up to the limits imposed by the firm's current scale of plant. Typical variable resources for short-run planning purposes are labor (except for top management), raw and semifinished materials, power, and transportation services.

The Long Run

In long-run planning there are no fixed resources. The quantities of all resources used by the firm are thought of as subject to variation. The time horizon extends far enough to permit the incorporation into the firm's plans of depreciation and sale of existing plant and equipment. Similarly, the acquisition or construction of new plant facilities are possibilities open to the firm. Expansion, contraction, and reorganization of top management may occur. Thus, from the point of view of production possibilities, there are no significant limits to the range of outputs per unit of time that the firm may consider.

SHORT-RUN COSTS

The short-run costs of a firm consist of its cost obligations for all resources used, fixed and variable. Quantities of resources used differ at different output levels; consequently, costs will differ also, depending upon the firm's output level. First, suppose we look at the manner in which the firm's total costs vary with its output. We can then derive its per units costs for the range of outputs open to it. But as we do so there are two important conditions that we assume to be fixed for any given set of cost schedules or curves. These are (1) the prices of the resources used by the firm and (2) the technological possibilities for the scale of plant used. If either of these change, the entire set of schedules or curves will change also.

Total Costs

Since in the short run we classify resources into fixed and variable categories, we break up the firm's total costs of production in the same way. The costs of fixed resources are *total fixed costs* and those of variable resources are *total variable costs.*

Total Fixed Costs

The magnitude of a firm's total fixed costs depends upon its scale of plant and not upon the level of output produced with that scale of plant. The firm's scale of plant is defined in terms of given quantities of fixed resources, so the costs of these will not vary as output is varied. In the steel mill example the amortization costs of the furnaces and the other heavy equipment, the costs of the land site, and the salaries of top man-

TABLE 8–1

Short-Run Total Costs of a Hypothetical Firm

(1) QUANTITY OF X PER WEEK	(2) TFC	(3) TVC	(4) STC	(5) SMC
0	$100	$ 0	$100	$ —
1	100	15	115	15
2	100	25	125	10
3	100	46	146	21
4	100	. 79	179	33
5	100	124	224	45
6	100	182	282	58
7	100	254	354	72
8	100	341	441	87
9	100	444	544	103
10	100	564	664	120

agement do not depend upon what output is produced with the plant once it is in place. They depend only upon the quantities of resources that make up the plant. They will be the same whether the product output of the firm is zero or whether it is near the maximum output capacity of its given scale of plant.

The total fixed cost schedule and the total fixed cost curve, showing the typical relation of total fixed costs to the output of a hypothetical firm, are illustrated in Table 8–1, and Figure 8–1, respectively. Suppose that the firm's scale of plant—the quantities of fixed resources used— are such that it is obligated to pay 100 dollars a week for them. Whether the output is zero or 10 units per week, this obligation remains the same. The total fixed cost schedule is therefore illustrated by columns (1) and (2) of Table 8–1, and this schedule is plotted in Figure 8–1 as the TFC curve.

Total Variable Costs

Total variable costs show the relation between the firm's cost obligations for variable resources and its output of product. If the firm's output were zero, there would be no need to hire or buy variable resources, so at that output total variable costs are zero. But to produce product, variable resources must be run through the plant. The larger the output produced, the larger the quantities of variable resources used, and the larger total variable costs will be. This direct relation is illustrated by columns (1) and (3) of Table 8–1 and by its graphic counterpart TVC in Figure 8–1.

But in addition to its upward slope as the firm considers higher output levels, the TVC curve of Figure 8–1 exhibits a rather peculiar inverted S-shape. Is this the usual shape of a TVC curve or does it result from an accident of choice in setting up the example? The principles of produc-

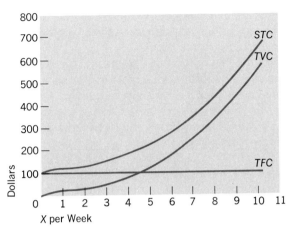

Figure 8–1
A firm's total cost curves.

tion, covered in the preceding chapter, will help us find the determinants of its shape and its position.

First, the total variable cost curve shows the least possible cost of producing each of the outputs that the firm may consider. The least total outlay on variable resources that will yield a product output of six units per week is 182 dollars. In the terms of the last chapter, at this output variable costs can be held down to 182 dollars only if the firm uses that outlay for a least-cost combination of variable resources; that is, so the marginal physical product per dollar's worth of one variable resource used is equal to that of every other variable resource available to the firm.[1] The same reasoning is applicable to all other output levels—each one has its own least-cost combination of variable resources.

Second, the inverted S-shape of the TVC curve stems from the operation of both the law of increasing returns and the law of diminishing returns. Where the law of increasing returns is effective, equal increases in product output are obtainable with smaller and smaller increases in the quantities of the variable resources used.[2] Translated into costs, this means that equal increases in the product output can be obtained with smaller and smaller increases in cost outlay on the variable resources. This reasoning applies to the whole complex of variable resources used by the firm. If increasing returns are effective for the complex of variable resources used in the firm's fixed scale of plant, equal increases in product output can be obtained with smaller and smaller increases in total vari-

---

[1] We can think either of 182 dollars as being the least total variable cost of producing six units of output per week or we can think of six units of output as being the maximum output attainable with a variable cost outlay of 182 dollars.

[2] This is the same as saying that equal increases in the quantities used will yield larger and larger increases in product output.

able costs. Consequently, the total variable cost curve is concave down-ward—it increases at a decreasing rate—where increasing returns to the complex of variable resources occur.

The effects of the law of diminishing returns on the shape of the total variable cost curve are much more important for economic analysis than are those of increasing returns. For some firms there may be no increasing returns to the variable resources at all; diminishing returns may exist for all quantities of variable resources used with the firm's fixed scale of plant. In any case, as we shall see, the firm will generally be operating at an output level at which diminishing returns to variable resources occurs: the quantities of variable resources used in relation to the fixed scale of plant will be large enough for this to be the case.

The effects of diminishing returns on the total variable cost curve are precisely the reverse of those brought about by increasing returns. Where diminishing returns occur to the complex of variable resources run through the fixed scale of plant, equal increases in output require larger and larger increases in the quantities of variable resources used.[3] This means that equal increases in output require larger and larger increases in the total cost obligations for variable resources; that is, the TVC curve is concave upward for output levels where diminishing returns to variable resources are effective.

Short-Run Total Costs

The firm's over-all short-run total costs of production, or STC, are simply the summation of total fixed costs and total variable costs at each output level. Thus in Table 8–1, column (4) is the sum of columns (2) and (3). In Figure 8–1, STC is found by adding the TFC curve vertically to the TVC curve. The total cost curve STC and the total variable cost curve TVC look alike. This is as it should be, since the STC curve *is* the TVC curve displaced upward by the amount of TFC.

Per Unit Costs

Each of the total cost curves discussed above has its per unit counter-part. If we divide total fixed costs by output at the various possible output levels, we get *average fixed costs*, or AFC. Similarly, *average variable costs*, or AVC, are found by dividing total variable costs by output, and over-all short-run average costs, or SAC, are over-all total costs divided by out-put. Columns (2), (3), and (4) in Table 8–2 are thus derived from columns (1), (2), (3), and (4) of Table 8–1. These are plotted in Figure 8–2 as AFC, AVC, and SAC. Each of these curves has a common sense meaning im-portant both to the economist and to the managers of the firm.

---

[3] Or, equal increases in the quantities of variable resources used bring about smaller and smaller increases in product output.

TABLE 8-2
Short-Run Per Unit Costs of a Hypothetical Firm

(1) QUANTITY OF X PER WEEK	(2) AFC (TFC/x)	(3) AVC (TVC/x)	(4) SAC (STC/x)	(5) SMC $(\Delta STC)/(\Delta x)$
0	$ —	$ —	$ —	$ —
1	100	15	115	15
2	50	$12\frac{1}{2}$	$62\frac{1}{2}$	10
3	$33\frac{1}{3}$	$15\frac{1}{3}$	$48\frac{2}{3}$	21
4	25	$19\frac{3}{4}$	$44\frac{3}{4}$	33
5	20	$24\frac{4}{5}$	$44\frac{4}{5}$	45
6	$16\frac{2}{3}$	$30\frac{1}{3}$	47	58
7	$14\frac{2}{7}$	$36\frac{2}{7}$	$50\frac{4}{7}$	72
8	$12\frac{1}{2}$	$42\frac{5}{8}$	$55\frac{1}{8}$	87
9	$11\frac{1}{9}$	$49\frac{1}{3}$	$60\frac{4}{9}$	103
10	10	$56\frac{2}{3}$	$66\frac{2}{3}$	120

Average Fixed Costs

The most obvious characteristic of the average fixed cost curve is that it decreases as the output level is increased. The greater the output, the smaller the costs of the fixed resources attributable to each unit of output. We interpret this to mean that the more output the firm can get out of its fixed scale of plant, *the more efficiently the fixed resources alone are used.*

Average Variable Costs

The average variable cost curve decreases with the increase in output, reaches a minimum, and then increases as the level of output is increased.

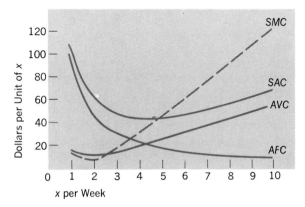

Figure 8-2
A firm's per unit cost curves.

Following the foregoing pattern of analysis, we see that this means that the efficiency of variable resources increases as output is increased up to the two unit per week level; then it decreases as the level of output is raised beyond that level.[4]

Average Costs

The short-run average cost curve, plotted as *SAC* in Figure 8–2, also exhibits a dish-shape, or a *U-shape,* as it is generally referred to by economists. Since the *SAC* curve is a combination of the *AFC* curve and the *AVC* curve, this is not altogether surprising. The shape of the *SAC* curve is a reflection of the efficiency of the firm's over-all operation in the short run. As the output level is increased from zero, average fixed costs fall as the fixed resources are used more efficiently. The output increases permit greater efficiency in the use of variable resources too if the law of increasing returns is operative for them. Increasing efficiency in the use of both fixed and variable resources means increasing efficiency for the entire operation of the firm. In Table 8–2 and Figure 8–2, from an output level of two units to four units per week average fixed costs decline and average variable costs increase. But the decreases in average fixed costs (increases in the efficiency of fixed resources) more than offset the increases in average variable costs (decreases in the efficiency of the variable resources), and short-run average costs continue to decline. Beyond the four-unit output level the decreasing efficiency in the use of variable resources becomes dominant.

The four-unit level of output for the hypothetical firm is the output of most efficient operation. This is the output level at which *SAC* is minimum. We call this output level the *optimum rate of output.* However, it is not necessarily the most profitable level of output for the firm. Profits depend upon revenues as well as upon costs, and so far we have not taken the firm's revenues into consideration.

Marginal Costs

If the management of the steel mill were contemplating an increase in the output level at which its fixed scale of plant is to be used, a very relevant question to ask is, What will the increase do to short-run total costs? Another relevant question is, What will the increase do to total receipts? Posing these two questions simultaneously, and looking at the answers concurrently, is still more relevant. If the contemplated increase in output

---

[4] Would increasing and decreasing returns to variable resources have anything to do with these happenings? What would the *AVC* curve look like if increasing returns to the variable resources did not occur?

will increase short-run total costs more than it will increase revenues, it obviously will not pay to make it. It is just as obvious that profits will be increased (or losses diminished) if the output increase raises total receipts more than it raises total costs.

With respect to costs (we shall look at revenues in the next chapter), the change in total costs resulting from a one-unit change in output by a firm is called *marginal cost.* If the change in output is Δx and the corresponding change in cost is ΔSTC, then marginal cost is $(\Delta STC)/(\Delta x)$. Short-run marginal costs, or *SMC* in column (5) of Table 8–1, are computed in this way for each output level.

A firm's marginal cost curve bears a unique relation to its average cost curve. Where average cost decreases as output is increased, marginal cost will be less than average cost. Where average cost increases as output is increased, marginal cost will be greater than average cost. It follows that if average cost were neither increasing nor decreasing with output changes, marginal cost and average cost would be the same. These relations are illustrated both in Table 8–2 and Figure 8–2.

The mathematical relation between marginal cost and average cost is a commonplace one that we encounter almost every day. Suppose that on an automobile trip at some point we compute our average speed. If we have covered 100 miles in two hours, our average speed is 50 miles per hour. Now we know that if we drop the rate of speed (marginal speed) below 50 miles per hour, average speed will fall, *but it will not fall to the level of our new rate of speed.* Similarly, if we increase our rate of speed to 60 miles per hour, average speed will rise *but not to the level of the new rate of speed.* If we hold our rate of speed constant at 50 miles per hour, average speed will be equal to the rate of speed and will not change.

In the same vein, suppose that we compute the average costs of production at a given output level. If output is increased by one unit and the resulting increase in total cost—marginal cost—is greater than the previous average cost, average cost is pulled to a higher level but will be less than marginal cost. If the increase in total cost is less than the previous average cost, average cost is pulled down but not to the level of marginal cost. If the amount added to total cost is equal to the previous average cost level, average cost will not change.[5]

The Steel Mill Case

The problems of the steel mill raised at the beginning of the chapter fall into proper perspective now. Total fixed costs are large. At low output levels average fixed costs are high, making over-all average costs high.

[5] These same relations hold for *SMC* and *AVC* for the same set of reasons: in the short run all changes in *STC* as output changes are really changes in *TVC*, since *TFC* cannot change.

Higher output levels would reduce average fixed costs and, up to an output level at which decreasing efficiency in the utilization of variable resources more than offsets increasing efficiency of the fixed resources, short-run average costs as well.

LONG-RUN COSTS

In long-run planning a firm has more possibilities open to it than in the short run. Increases or decreases in the scale of plant, that is, in the utilization of the resources that make up the firm's scale of plant, can be considered, and this greatly expands the range of outputs that are open to the firm. In fact, long-run planning encompasses the alternative short-run possibilities of all possible scales of plant. The meaning of this point will become clear in a moment.

Long-Run Average Costs

Suppose that technology in the light aircraft industry is such that only three alternative sizes of plant are possible—a little one, a medium-sized one, and a large one. For each of these a short-run average cost curve exists. In Figure 8–3 these are SAC_1, SAC_2, and SAC_3, respectively. For

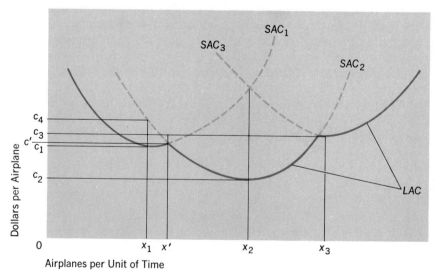

Figure 8–3
Construction of the long-run average cost curve.

long-run planning any one of the three can be built and used, and the firm can expand or contract from one scale to another. How would the firm go about choosing which one to construct and use?

The decision turns on the output to be produced. Presumably it would be desirable to produce whatever output is to be produced at an average cost as low as possible. If output were x_1, which of the three possible scales of plant would accomplish this objective? With SAC_1 average cost would be c_1 dollars per airplane, but with SAC_2 is would be c_4 dollars. The better choice would be SAC_1. Alternatively, suppose that output x' is the one to be produced. Either SAC_1 or SAC_2 could be chosen, since either will produce x_1 airplanes per unit of time at an average cost of c' dollars. Similarly, SAC_2 will produce output x_2 at the lowest possible average cost for that output, and SAC_3 is the choice for an output of x_3 airplanes.

The long-run average cost curve of a firm shows the least possible average costs at which all alternative output levels can be produced when the firm is free to make a choice among alternative scales of plant and the output ranges that can be produced with each possible scale of plant. Thus in Figure 8–3 we have already drawn the firm's long-run average cost or LAC curve. It is the solid-line portions of SAC_1, SAC_2, and SAC_3. (Can you explain why this is the case?)

Ordinarily, the long-run average cost curve of a firm would be much smoother than the one pictured in Figure 8–3. Most firms are faced with a choice among an infinite number of scales of plant rather than being restricted to three. It is almost always possible to increase or decrease the scale of plant infinitesimally, and where this is so the parts of the SAC curves that constitute portions of the LAC curve are so small that they are merely points such as A, B, and C in Figure 8–4. Thus the long-run

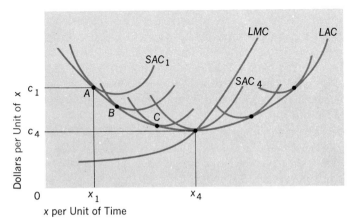

Figure 8–4
Relation of long- and short-run average costs.

average cost curve becomes the smooth *LAC* curve of Figure 8–4, lying tangent to the short-run average cost curves, some of which are drawn, of all possible scales of plant.

Economies and Diseconomies of Scale

We have drawn the long-run average cost curve as a U-shaped curve, first falling as output (and the scale of plant) is increased, then rising as output (and the scale of plant) is increased further beyond some certain level. Actually, there is some controversy among economists as to whether or not this is the prevailing shape of the *LAC* curve; some argue that it falls as output is increased, levels off, and does not turn up again. This controversy need not detain us here, but we shall inquire into the meaning of whatever shape the *LAC* curve takes and the forces that shape it. The U-shape provides a convenient framework for that inquiry.

If the *LAC* curve were U-shaped, as we have drawn it in Figure 8–4, what does the U-shape mean? Obviously it means that larger scales of plant up to some certain size have lower and lower *SAC* curves, and beyond that size they have higher and higher *SAC* curves. Since scales of plant with lower *SAC* curves are by definition more efficient than those with higher *SAC* curves, we must explain why efficiency increases as the scale increases and why—in some cases at least—beyond some critical size efficiency falls off.

The forces causing the long-run average cost curve to decrease as the scale of plant is increased are called *economies of scale.* Most of us are familiar with the two most important ones. First, larger scales of plant make possible the *specialization of labor* on particular parts of the production process. Greater efficiency results partly because workers can specialize on those things at which they are most adept and partly because with specialization less time is lost in moving from one task to another and from one set of tools or machines to another. Second, larger scales of plant enable the firm to use *cost-saving techniques of production* that are not possible or feasible for small scales of plant. The assembly line, automatic stamping machines, and the like can be used in the larger scales of plant, whereas their costs would be prohibitive in smaller scales of plant with low levels of output.

The forces causing long-run average costs to increase—if they increase—are called *diseconomies of scale.* These are said to consist of increasing difficulties in coordinating and controlling larger and larger scales of plant. Decision-making by top management becomes more complex. More coordination—and proliferation of red tape—among lower management officials becomes necessary. Management loses direct contact with line production workers and their problems. One thing is certain. In some industries, the automobile industry, for example, the scale of plant beyond which diseconomies occur may be extremely large.

The most efficient scale of plant of all the alternative possibilities is called the *optimum scale of plant*. It is the one lying at the bottom of the *LAC* curve—SAC_4 in Figure 8-4. It is large enough to take advantage of economies of scale but not large enough for diseconomies of scale to exert dominance over the economies. A firm will not necessarily build and use the optimum scale of plant in the long run; some other scale of plant may be more profitable. If in Figure 8-4 the market is small and the firm finds output x_1 to be the most profitable one, scale of plant SAC_1 will produce that output at a lower average cost than will any other. Scale of plant SAC_4 would be the best one to build and use only if the firm's desired output is x_4.

Long-Run Marginal Costs

For long-run as well as short-run planning purposes a firm is vitally concerned with what changes in output will do to its total costs and to its total receipts. In the long run changes in output entail changes in the quantities of scale of plant resources as well as other resources used. If the aircraft manufacturer intends to increase his output of two-place planes by 1000 per year, production facilities appropriate for the higher output must be built and put into service, and the increase in yearly costs attributable to amortization and/or depreciation of the extra facilities are a part of the extra costs of production. The increase in total costs per unit increase in output for the long run is called *long-run marginal cost*. If the 1000 unit per year increase in the production of airplanes brings about a $5 million increase in the company's yearly costs, long-run marginal cost for the increase is $5000 per airplane, although ordinarily we would compute marginal cost on a much smaller increment in output.

Long-run marginal costs bear the same relation to long-run average costs as short-run marginal costs bear to short-run average costs. Long-run marginal costs that are below long-run average costs pull the latter down. If long-run marginal costs exceed long-run average costs, they pull the latter up. At the output level at which long-run average costs are minimum—neither rising nor falling—long-run marginal costs are equal to the average. In Figure 8-4 the long-run marginal cost curve *LMC* is drawn in correct relation to the *LAC* curve.

The Aircraft Manufacturer Case

The decisions of the light aircraft manufacturing company considered at the beginning of the chapter make sense in terms of long-run planning by the firm. Apparently the firm's officials have established through engineering and cost studies that their present scale of plant is too small to effect all possible economies of scale. The present scale of plant could be represented by SAC_1 in Figure 8–4 and the output level may be x_1. Their studies indicate that if they increase the scale of plant to some such size as SAC_4 and output to some such level as x_4, per unit costs will fall[6] from c_1 to c_4. The larger scale of plant permits them to take advantage of economies of scale. A possibility exists that if the plant size is expanded far enough diseconomies of scale may become dominant.

SUMMARY

Costs of production are the obligations incurred by a firm for the resources it uses in turning out its product output. In order to obtain or to hold resources for its own use a firm must pay for them as much as they would be worth in their best alternative uses. This principle is known as the alternative-cost principle and also as the opportunity-cost principle. Explicit costs are the costs of resources bought or hired by the firm while implicit costs are the costs of self-owned, self-employed resources.

In the analysis of a firm's costs two time viewpoints are used, the short run and the long run. The short run represents a short enough planning period that the firm does not have time to alter the quantities of resources that constitute its scale of plant. The long run is a planning period reaching far enough ahead for the firm to consider, build, use, and change its scale of plant; that is, the quantities of all resources can be changed if the firm so desires. Short-run costs relate costs to the outputs obtainable with a given scale of plant. Long-run costs relate costs to outputs obtainable with all possible alternative scales of plant.

In short-run planning those resources making up the firm's scale of plant are called fixed resources and their costs are fixed costs. Resources that can be altered in quantity are called variable resources and their costs are variable costs. Total fixed costs are constant for all levels of output that the firm can produce with its fixed scale of plant. Total variable costs vary directly with output, but increasing returns and decreasing returns to the complex of variable resources run through the plant give the total variable cost curve a sort of inverted S-shape. The short-run total cost curve is identical to the total variable cost curve, except that it is displaced upward by the amount of total fixed costs.

When short-run total fixed costs, total variable costs, and over-all total

---

[6] There is nothing magic about these particular output levels. Nothing is said in the discussion about the size of profits made at either x_1 or x_4. All we try to demonstrate here is that *if* a decision were made to increase output from x_1 to x_4, long-run per unit costs would fall from c_1 to c_4.

costs at various output levels are divided by those output levels, we obtain the average fixed costs, average variable costs, and over-all average costs of the firm. The shapes of these curves reflect the efficiency with which they are used by the firm. The average fixed cost curve decreases as output is increased. The average variable cost curve has a U-shape because of increasing and diminishing returns. The average cost curve has a U-shape also, taking its shape from those of the average fixed and average variable cost curves.

Short-run marginal cost of the firm is defined as the change in total cost (total variable cost) per unit change in the firm's output level.

In long-run planning the firm can contemplate the average costs of production for all alternative scales of plant. For any given output the firm would be expected to choose the scale of plant that would produce that output at a lower cost than the other alternatives. A long-run average cost curve, showing the least average cost of producing alternative outputs when the firm is free to choose among alternative scales of plant, is made up of very small segments of the short-run average cost curves of those scales of plant. It is generally taken to be a U-shaped curve. Economies of scale, or forces that make larger scales of plant more efficient than smaller ones, underlie the decreasing portion of it. Diseconomies of scale that cause firms to become less efficient beyond some certain size cause the curve to turn up again—if it does indeed turn up. A long-run marginal cost curve shows the changes in the firm's long-run total costs per unit change in its output, and it bears the same relation to the long-run average cost curve as does a short-run marginal cost curve to its corresponding short-run average cost curve.

EXERCISES AND QUESTIONS FOR DISCUSSION

1. The cost schedules given below are those for a firm producing refrigerators. From these derive the STC, AFC, AVC, SAC, and SMC schedules for the firm. Also draw the total cost curves on one graph and the average and marginal curves on another, using the schedules you have derived.

Short-run Total Costs of Refrigerators		
REFRIGERATORS PER WEEK	TFC	TVC
0	$200	$ 0
1	200	90
2	200	170
3	200	240
4	200	300
5	200	370
6	200	450
7	200	540
8	200	650
9	200	780
10	200	930

2. On the graphs you drew in problem 1 point out the areas of increasing and decreasing returns. What is the optimum rate of output?

3. "Anytime a producer is operating at the optimum rate of output he is also operating at the optimum scale of plant." Evaluate.

4. An aged widow suffered heavy financial losses during the bank failures of the 1930s. Since that time she has kept her savings behind a loose brick in the fireplace, content with the thought that her savings are safe and that this safety is "not costing a thing." Is this latter statement correct?

5. To prove your understanding of different time horizons, determine which of the following decisions represent short-run and which represent long-run planning problems.

   a. Metropolitan Life decides to hire two more selling agents.

   b. Beechnut decides to increase its tobacco production by adding 30 more shaving and packing machines to its assembly line.

   c. U.S. Plywood decides to increase production by extending the working day from 5 P.M. to 7 P.M.

   d. Baldridge Bakery increases its pastry production by adding to its present cake plant.

   e. Your local bank changes from manual to electronic check processing.

SELECTED READINGS

Bain, Joe S., *Industrial Organization.* New York: John Wiley and Sons, Inc., 1959, pp. 145–169.

Dorfman, Robert, *Prices and Markets.* Englewood Cliffs, N.J.: Prentice-Hall, Inc., 1967, Chap. 3.

Weiss, Leonard W., *Economics and American Industry.* New York: John Wiley and Sons, Inc., 1961, pp. 347–350.

Competitive Pricing and Outputs

CHAPTER 9

If you were about to establish, or if you were actually operating, a baby-sitting service, a computerized dating bureau, a laundry, a grocery store, an automobile manufacturing concern, or any other kind of business enterprise, you would want to make a thorough analysis of the production function of the business and of its various cost components. But the analysis would be more meaningful if you were to take an additional step—if you also analyzed the market for your product and estimated the prices and the revenues that you would receive at different possible output levels. You could compare revenues and costs at alternative output levels and determine which, if any, would make it worth your while to be in business; if there were indeed a range of profitable outputs, you could choose the most profitable one.

Thousands of business firms engage in analyses of their cost and revenue positions, and it is upon these analyses that they base their pricing and output decisions. These are the decisions that organize production in the private, as distinguished from the government, sector of the economy. Pricing patterns are established and the composition of output is determined. In this and the following two chapters we shall be concerned with the organization of production at three levels of operation: (1) that of the individual firm, (2) that of the industry, and (3) that of the entire private sector of the economy.

COMPETITION IN SELLING MARKETS

Sellers of goods and services encounter a wide range of competitive conditions depending upon what they sell and where they sell it. The seller of wheat finds that there are *many firms selling a product identical to what he has to place on the market*—so many, in fact, that by himself he cannot affect the price of wheat. If there were no effective governmental price supports for wheat, *its price would rise or fall in response to changes in total demand of consumers and in total supply that sellers bring to market.* The seller of wheat is *free to sell wherever he desires to sell,* and this will usually be where he can receive the highest price. Any product market which sellers face in which the italicized conditions are present is said to be one of *pure competition.*

At the other end of the spectrum we find *pure monopoly.* In this market situation there is only *one seller of the product and no good substitute products exist.* Examples are provided by the seller of telephone services in a given region and by most other public utilities.

Between the extremes of pure competition and pure monopoly there are differing degrees of competitiveness. The whole in-between range of conditions is called *imperfect competition.* Sometimes in a specific market there is only a handful of sellers of a product, as is the case for automobiles. We call this situation *oligopoly,* meaning *few sellers.* Again there may be *many sellers* in a market, but the *product sold by each differs in some way from that sold by each of the others.* These are markets of *monopolistic competition.* Both oligopoly and monopolistic competition are subclassifications of imperfect competition.

Although most sellers of goods and services operate in markets of imperfect competition, situations of pure competition provide a convenient launching pad for the analysis of pricing and output. Purely competitive market models occupy about the same place in economic analysis as does frictionless mechanics in the study of physics. They provide us with rather simple cause and effect relationships that, appropriately modified, furnish much insight into the more complex conditions of monopoly and imperfect competition. Then, too, there are enough market situations reasonably close to pure competition to make purely competitive principles as such valuable tools of analysis. In this chapter we concentrate on purely competitive markets.

VERY SHORT-RUN PRICING

Suppose that there is a certain supply available of a product and that the time period during which the product must be sold is too short to permit additional quantities of it to be produced. For example, clothing stores have stocks of spring suits on hand that, because of style factors and costs of storage, cannot be carried over to next spring. Grocers have stocks of fresh fruits and vegetables that will spoil if kept on the shelves.

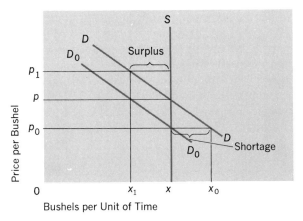

Figure 9–1
Very short-run price determination.

Following wheat harvest no more wheat can be grown until the next season. The planning period for sellers in this type of situation is called the *very short-run*—a planning period that limits opportunities open to sellers even more than the short-run period.

The main characteristic of the very short run for the sellers of any given product is the *fixed supply of the product*. The length of time for which this condition exists differs from product to product, being so short for some that it is of no importance at all. For other products, it may however, be a month, six months, a year, or even longer. Where it is a significant length of time, how does an economy determine how the fixed supply of the product is to be divided up or rationed?

The price system provides a rationing mechanism. Suppose that the year's apple harvest has been completed and that quantity x of apples in Figure 9–1 is the total supply available until the next harvest. The quantity cannot be increased no matter what price is offered to the sellers, so the supply curve is the vertical line xS. The demand curve, DD, shows the quantities per year that consumers are willing to take at alternative price levels. If the price were p_0 per bushel, there would be a shortage of apples amounting to xx_0 and consumers would bid against each other, driving the price up to p. At this price consumers would voluntarily ration themselves to the total supply available. On the other hand, if the price were p_1 per bushel, there would be a surplus of x_1x bushels that would induce sellers to undercut each other, driving price down to p. At this price consumers would be willing to take the entire supply off the market.[1]

In very short-run pricing situations costs of production play no part

---

[1] Do you see any resemblance between this situation and the end of season sales of clothing stores or to the low prices placed by bakers on day-old bread or pastries?

whatsoever in price determination. Once a given quantity of a product is in existence, the only important question with regard to price determination is how much buyers are willing to pay for that quantity. Buyers simply are not interested in what it cost at some past date to produce the item. If in Figure 9–1 demand were to decrease to $D_0 D_0$, price would fall to p_0 and the quantity exchanged would remain at x. The moral of this story is that when you want to sell your house you might as well forget what it cost to build it. Sunken costs are sunken costs; you can get only what buyers are willing to pay.

SHORT-RUN PRICING AND OUTPUT

If we extend the time horizon to the planning periods defined in the last chapter as the short run and the long run, costs of production play an important role in price determination. As we shall see, unless variable costs of production are covered in the short run and unless all costs are covered in the long run, a product will not be produced. In this section we shall be concerned with short-run pricing and output. We look at the operations of an individual firm first, and we then extend the analysis to the entire industry of which the firm is a part.

The Firm

Why are business firms established in the first place? What are the objectives of those who own and operate them? There are many reasons, of course. Someone has invented the wheel and wants to make the fruits of his knowledge available to the sliding, skidding, walking population of the world. Another sees himself becoming a captain of industry, the guiding genius of an industrial empire. Others find themselves in control of an already existing firm and seek to maintain its identity and position in its industry. But in all probability the most important objective is that of making money or profits. For most firms most of the time this objective is strong enough to provide the rationale for their economic activities, and we shall so accept it here.

The Firm's Profit

In economic analysis *profit* is the difference between a firm's total receipts and its total costs. It is not the same thing as the accounting "profits" of a firm that appear on its profit and loss statement. In accounting procedures all economic costs are not deducted from the firm's revenues in computing its "profits"; in particular, there are certain implicit costs that are not deducted. A corporation, for example, pays dividends to its stockholders out of its "profits" and does not classify those dividends as costs. But what are dividends from the point of view of economic analysis? Stockholders of a corportation are the owners of its assets and they let the corporation use those assets. In return, stockholders expect to receive dividends at least equal to what they could earn if they invested elsewhere in the economy. These are payments for the use of stockholders' resources, and to the economist they are costs.[2] Total costs, as the term has been defined already and as it is used throughout this book, include an average rate of return to investors on what they have invested in the business as well as all other implicit costs.

The Firm's Revenue

The costs of production of a firm were examined in detail in the last chapter, but we have said little up to this point about its revenues. The revenue side of the picture is a much simpler set of concepts and its description will require much less time and space.

Suppose there are 100 sellers of transistor radios and that all of these firms are of approximately equal size. Suppose, further, that there is no appreciable difference among the radios sold by the different firms. The market is one of pure competition—no one seller by himself can influence the product price. The market price of the product is 103 dollars per radio. What can we deduce about one firm's revenues?

Columns (1) and (2) of Table 9–1 represent demand as it looks to the firm. *Demand* to the firm means what the firm can sell at alternative possible prices. At a price above 103 dollars it can sell no radios at all. Buyers would turn to other sellers who are selling at the market price of 103 dollars. On the other hand, one firm in a purely competitive market sells such a small proportion of the total for the industry that its sales will not significantly affect price. It can sell all it desires to sell at the going market price, so there is no need to sell for less. The demand schedule, plotted as a demand curve, is shown as *dd* in Figure 9–3. Note that it is perfectly elastic.

The total revenue of a single firm at alternative output levels is shown in column (3) of Table 9–1. For whatever output the firm sells, a price of 103 dollars per radio is received. Consequently, at each output level, *total revenue* is simply price times quantity. The higher the sales level, the

---

[2] This is not to say that economists are "right" and accountants are "wrong." One of the purposes of accounting procedures is to determine what part of the firm's revenues are available to its owners. Economists seek something different. They want to know what is left after *all* costs, *including payments for the use of the self-owned, self-employed resources,* have been deducted.

TABLE 9-1

Revenues, Cost, and Profits of a Firm Selling Transistor Radios

(1) QUANTITY OF RADIOS PER DAY (x)	(2) PRICE PER RADIO [(TR)/x]	(3) TOTAL REVENUE (TR)	(4) MARGINAL REVENUE [(ΔTR)/(Δx)]	(5) TOTAL COSTS (STC)	(6) AVERAGE COSTS [(STC)/x]	(7) MARGINAL COSTS [(ΔSTC)/(Δx)]	(8) PROFITS (TR − STC)
0	$103	$ 0	$ —	$200	$ —	$ —	$ (−) 200
1	103	103	103	215	215	15	(−) 112
2	103	206	103	225	$112\frac{1}{2}$	10	(−) 19
3	103	309	103	240	80	15	69
4	103	412	103	261	$65\frac{1}{4}$	21	151
5	103	515	103	292	$58\frac{2}{5}$	31	223
6	103	618	103	340	$56\frac{2}{3}$	48	278
7	103	721	103	410	$58\frac{4}{7}$	70	311
8	103	824	103	513	$64\frac{1}{8}$	103	311
9	103	927	103	656	$72\frac{8}{9}$	143	271
10	103	1030	103	856	$85\frac{3}{5}$	200	174

$\dfrac{TC}{x} = A.C.$

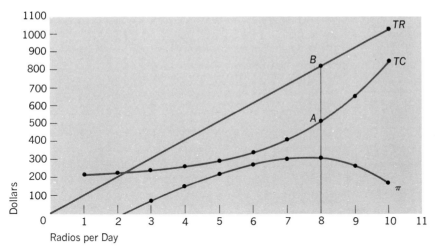

Figure 9–2
Profit maximization: total curves.

higher will be total revenue. The corresponding total revenue curve is shown as *TR* in Figure 9–2.

The change in the firm's total revenue per unit change in its sales level is called *marginal revenue*. Since the price of the product is 103 dollars per unit no matter how many units are sold, a one-unit change in the sales level will bring about a 103 dollar change in total revenue. For the purely

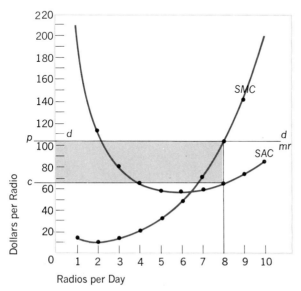

Figure 9–3
Profit maximization: per unit curves.

competitive seller of product marginal revenue will always be the same as the market price of the product. Marginal revenue, computed from columns (1) and (3), is shown in column (4) of Table 9–1 and as *mr* in Figure 9–3. The *mr* curve coincides with the *dd* curve.

Profit Maximization

If the costs to the firm of selling transistor radios are those of columns (5), (6), and (7) of Table 9–1, its profit-maximizing output is easily determined. Subtracting the total costs of column (5) from the total receipts of column (3), we obtain column (8), which shows the profits available at each alternative output and sales level. In Figure 9–2 we accomplish the same thing by subtracting the *TC* curve from the *TR* curve at each output and sales level. The differences are plotted as the π, or profits curve. The maximum profit obtainable occurs at either seven or eight radios per day and is 311 dollars.

The per unit cost and revenue curves also provide the information necessary for determining the firm's profit-maximizing output. The key concepts are marginal cost and marginal revenue. Since marginal cost and marginal revenue are the change in total cost and the change in total revenue, respectively, for a one-unit change in output, a comparison of the two for any change in output shows the effect of the change on profits. For example, in Table 9–1 and Figure 9–3 we note that for an increase in output from three to four radios per day the marginal cost is 21 dollars and the marginal revenue is 103 dollars, the former being the increase in total cost and the latter the increase in total revenue. Therefore, profits are increased by 82 dollars per day by the output increase. A glance at column (8) of Table 9–1 and a quick computation will verify this result.

Further increases in output will increase profits still more. If output is increased to five radios, marginal cost becomes 31 dollars and marginal revenue is 103 dollars. Profits are increased by 72 dollars. At an output level of six radios, marginal cost is 48 dollars, marginal revenue is 103 dollars, and profits are increased by 55 dollars by this one-unit addition to output. Similarly, an increase in output to seven radios will raise profits an additional 33 dollars.

For an increase from seven to eight radios marginal cost and marginal revenue are the same—103 dollars—and nothing is added to the firm's profits. But neither is anything lost. Marginal revenue is less than marginal cost for an increase from eight to nine radios as well as for an increase from nine to ten. These increments in sales levels would bring about decreases in profits.

We have uncovered an important set of principles with regard to profit maximization by a firm. Output increases for which marginal revenue is greater than marginal cost will increase the firm's profits while those for which marginal revenue is less than marginal cost will decrease profits. It follows then that *profits are maximum at the output level at which marginal cost equals marginal revenue.*[3]

The marginal cost equals marginal revenue relation shows the output level at which profits are maximum but tells us nothing about the magnitude of total profits. The per unit information from which total profits can be determined is average cost and average revenue or price at the profit-maximizing output. Consider Table 9–1 and Figure 9–3. At the eight-unit output level, price, p, is 103 dollars and average cost, c, is $64\frac{1}{8}$ dollars. The firm's profit per unit is $38\frac{7}{8}$ dollars, the difference between the two. Total profit for the entire eight-unit output level is $38\frac{7}{8}$ dollars multiplied by 8, or 311 dollars This result checks with the computation of profit at that level of output in Table 9–1.

The Firm's Short-Run Supply Curve

Every firm selling in a purely competitive market has a *short-run supply curve* showing the amounts of the product that it is willing to place on the market at alternative price levels, other things being equal. The "other things being equal" are the fixed conditions underlying a given set of short-run cost curves—the prices of the resources used and the technological possibilities open with the firm's fixed scale of plant.

In Figure 9–4 we show the cost curves of a soft coal mine. If the price of coal were p_3 dollars per ton, what output would the firm produce? If its objective is profit maximization, and we assume it is, its output would be

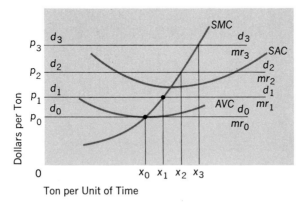

Figure 9–4
A firm's short-run supply curve.

---

[3] Profits are also maximum at an output level one unit less than that for which marginal revenue equals marginal cost. However, it is convenient—and still correct—to state the profit-maximizing conditions as we have in the text.

x_3. If the price is p_3, both the demand curve facing the firm and its marginal revenue curve are horizontal at that level. Output x_3 is the one at which marginal cost and marginal revenue are the same. (Can you determine the level of average cost and show geometrically what the firm's total profits are at this price and output level?) If price were p_2, profits would be maximized by an output of x_2.

If the price of coal were p_1, the firm would incur losses, since there is no output at which that price exceeds average costs. If the firm were to reduce its output to zero, its losses would be its total fixed costs, or those that are incurred in the short run whether or not the firm produces and regardless of the output it produces. However, if it produces an output of x_1, its total receipts will be greater than its total variable costs (since the price exceeds average variable costs at that output). The excess of total receipts over total variable costs covers a part of the fixed costs, thus making the firm's losses less than total fixed cost. At price p_1 it pays to produce rather than shut down the plant; losses are minimized by producing output x_1, that at which marginal cost equals marginal revenue.

If the price of coal is p_0 in Figure 9–4 and output is x_0, total receipts and total variable costs are the same; total receipts cover total variable costs but not total fixed costs. Whether the firm produces x_0 or nothing is unimportant, since in either case losses are equal to total fixed costs.

If the market price is so low that total variable costs are not covered by total receipts (price is less than average variable costs), the firm keeps its losses at a minimum by producing no output. If price is less than p_0 and the firm does produce, a part of the variable costs are not covered nor are any of the fixed costs, so losses exceed total fixed costs. Losses are lower, therefore, if output is zero.

The firm's *short-run supply curve* is that part of its short-run marginal cost curve lying above its average variable cost curve. At any price below minimum average variable costs the firm will produce nothing. At any price above minimum average variable costs it minimizes losses or maximizes profits, as the case may be, by producing the output at which short-run marginal cost equals marginal revenue or price of the product.

The Market or the Industry

We have explained how the output of a single firm is determined when the market price of the product it produces is known. But what determines the market price? It is not determined by any one single firm; in a purely competitive selling market no one firm by itself has any influence on price. Rather, it is determined by the interaction of sellers with buyers in the market for the product. This interaction, described in Chapter 4, is examined here in more detail.

The Market Supply Curve

The market supply curve for a product is built up from the supply curves of individual firms that produce the product. Suppose that in Figure 9–5 we look at the short-run marginal cost curves, SMC_1 and SMC_2, of two coal-mining firms. We are concerned with and we show only the parts lying above the respective average variable cost curves of the firms. If product price were p_0, firm 1 would maximize profits by producing output x_0. Firm 2 would produce output x'_0. Together they would produce an output of $X_0 (= x_0 + x'_0)$ at that price. If price were p_1, firm 1 would produce x_1; firm 2 would produce x'_1; and together they would produce $X_1 (= x_1 + x'_1)$. The curve SS is located in this manner and shows the combined outputs of the two firms for alternative price levels; it is the combined supply curve of the two firms. By extending this sort of *horizontal summation* of individual-firm short-run marginal cost curves to all of the firms producing and selling in this soft-coal market we obtain the *short-run market supply curve* for the product.

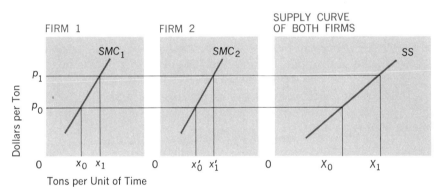

Figure 9–5
The market supply curve.

Price and Output

Both the market demand and the market supply curves for soft coal are pictured in Figure 9–6, together with the short-run average cost and the marginal cost curves of one of the many firms in the industry. The market demand curve, *DD,* is the horizontal summation of the demand curves of consumers of the product, and the supply curve, *SS,* is the horizontal summation of the marginal cost curves of all sellers. The vertical scales of the two diagrams are identical, but the horizontal scale of the market diagram is greatly compressed as compared with that of the firm.

The equilibrium, or market, price of coal will be *p* dollars per ton— determined by the interactions of *all* buyers and sellers. Consequently,

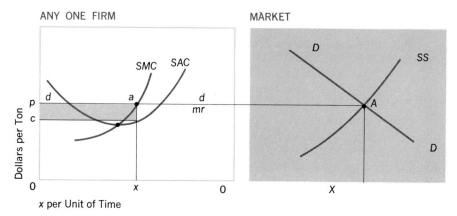

Figure 9–6
Market price, individual firm output, and market output determination.

the demand curve facing any one firm will be *dd*, and its marginal revenue, *mr*, will be the same. To maximize profits the firm shown, and every other firm in the industry, will produce an output at which marginal cost equals that marginal revenue. For the firm pictured the output is *x* and for all firms together the output level is *X*, the sum of the outputs of the individual firms.

The firm for which we show cost curves is making profits. At output *x* average cost is *c*. Profit per ton of coal is *cp*, and total profits are *cp* dollars multiplied by *x* tons.

Effects of Demand Changes

Suppose that the price of fuel oil goes up and that consumers switch to coal for heating purposes. What are the short-run effects of the change in demand for coal? The analytical apparatus that we have just put together is useful in sorting out these effects.

With reference to Figure 9–7, the increase in the price of fuel oil causes an increase in market demand for coal from DD to D_1D_1. When demand was at DD the market price was p; the market output was X; the individual firm output was x; the average cost for the firm was c; and the profits for the firm were cp times x. With the increase in demand to D_1D_1, the market price rises to p_1, shifting the demand curve facing the firm and the marginal revenue curve to d_1d_1 and mr_1, respectively. To maximize profits the single firm increases its output to x_1, at which marginal cost is equal to the higher level of marginal revenue. Profits increase to c_1p_1 times x_1. Since all firms in the industry do the same thing, market output expands to X_1. Thus, in the short run, an increase in demand for a product increases the price as well as the quantity of the product that is produced

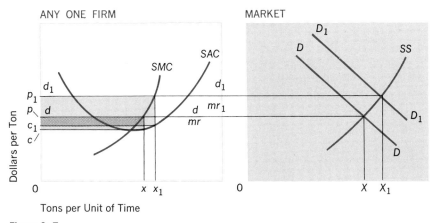

Figure 9-7
Effects of a change in demand.

and sold. Profits provide an incentive for individual firms to work their given scales of plant more intensively. A decrease in demand brings about the opposite results.

Changes in Costs

The effects of a change in costs are as easily handled as are those of a change in demand. In Figure 9–8 suppose that in the market for soft coal the initial demand is DD. The cost curves of any one firm are SAC and SMC. Individual firm output is x and market output is X. Profits of the firm are cp times x.

Suppose now that the United Mine Workers obtain a substantial pay

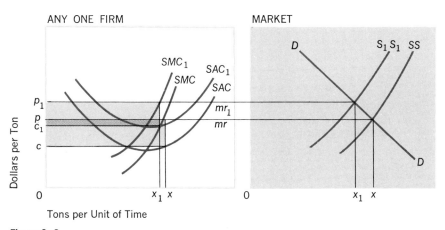

Figure 9-8
Effects of a change in costs.

increase across the board. The cost curves of each firm will be shifted upward to SAC_1 and SMC_1. An upward shift in a firm's SMC curve is also a shift to the left, so the market supply curve, obtained from the horizontal summation of individual-firm SMC curves, is shifted to the left to S_1S_1. Price rises to p_1. Individual firm output falls to x_1, where SMC_1 is equal to mr_1. Profits for the firm are now c_1p_1 times x_1. Market output and sales are X_1. Thus forces causing short-run cost increases for a product will increase the market price of the product and reduce the amount produced and sold. Individual-firm output and profits will be reduced. Forces that decrease short-run costs will have the opposite effects.

LONG-RUN PRICING AND OUTPUT

In the long run there is much greater flexibility in the possible quantities of a product that can be put on the market than in the short run. In the short run the productive capacity of an industry is fixed by the plant size of individual firms and by the number of firms in the industry; however, this fixed over-all capacity can be operated at alternative levels of output within the limits that existing plant facilities impose. In the long run there are no fixed capacity limits to production for the industry as a whole. Individual firms can increase or decrease their investments in plant and equipment. It is also possible for new firms to enter the industry and for existing firms to leave if they so desire.

Individual-Firm Scale of Plant Adjustments

The principles involved in long-run profit maximization are no different from those established for the short run, except that the long-run average cost and the long-run marginal cost curves are the relevant ones rather than the short-run average cost and the short-run marginal cost curves. Long-run profit maximization is illustrated in Figure 9–9. The firm's long-run average cost curve is LAC and its long-run marginal cost curve is LMC. Initially we will suppose that the market price of coal is p_1 per ton. Consequently, the demand curve facing the firm and the firm's marginal revenue curve are d_1d_1 and mr_1, respectively. Long-run profits will be maximum at output level x_1 at which long-run marginal cost equals marginal revenue.

The scale of plant that will minimize cost for output x_1 is the one represented by the short-run average cost curve SAC_1. If either a larger or a smaller scale of plant, say SAC_0 or SAC_2, were used, average cost for that output level would be greater than c_1. Only scale of plant SAC can produce output x_1 at a cost per ton as low as c_1.

Entry or Exit of Firms

The firm in Figure 9–9 is making profits of c_1p_1 times x_1. Profit has been defined previously as total revenues of the firm minus *all* costs, both implicit and explicit. We include as a part of costs returns to investors in the industry equal to what they could have earned on the average elsewhere in the economy. Thus when profits occur, this means that the owners of the business earn a higher than average return on their investment in the business. Even if a firm makes no profit, as we define and use the term, it is doing all right. The owners of all resources used in making the product are receiving as much for their resources as they would had they placed them elsewhere in the economy.

The industry of which the firm in Figure 9–9 is a part is a good one in which to invest. Investors receive returns higher than they can make on the average elsewhere in the economy, as evidenced by the firm's profits. Investors go where opportunities exist, so new firms would be established in the industry.

What is the impact of the entry of new firms? One thing is certain: the market supply of the product will increase, and this will force down the price per ton of coal. As the market price falls both the demand and the marginal revenue curves facing the firm shift downward. The individual firm output level at which marginal cost equals marginal revenue becomes

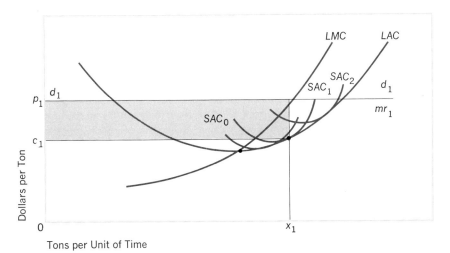

Figure 9–9
Long-run profit maximization.

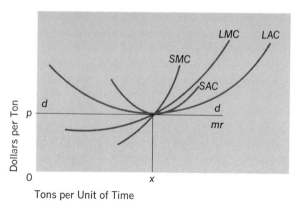

Figure 9–10
The conditions of long-run equilibrium.

smaller and smaller. However, as long as profits are made there still exists an incentive for new firms to enter the industry.

Eventually the entry of new firms will force the price down to p per ton, the level of minimum long-run average costs, as illustrated in Figure 9–10. Long-run marginal cost equals marginal revenue at output x. Profits are zero, since price and long-run average cost at output level x are the same.

When enough firms have entered the profit-making industry to reduce profits to zero, the industry is in long-run equilibrium. Whenever the price is above p there is a range of outputs in the neighborhood of x at which profits can be made. New firms are attracted in, forcing the price back to p. Whenever the price is below p there is no output level at which the firm can avoid losses. Firms begin to leave the industry, reducing supply and causing the price to rise toward p. At price p neither profits nor losses are made. Investors in the industry earn an average return on investment. There is no incentive for new firms to enter or for existing firms to leave.

Individual firms are also in long-run equilibrium. At the market price p long-run marginal cost is equal to marginal revenue at output level x. This is the firm's best output level, for at any other losses would occur. The firm builds and uses scale of plant SAC in order to hold its costs for output x as low as possible. Once the firm is at that output with a scale of plant such as SAC, it has no incentive to change either the scale of plant or its output.

Note carefully a unique characteristic of long-run equilibrium under conditions of pure competition. The individual firm is induced to build an optimum scale of plant. Only with an optimum scale of plant can the firm avoid losses. Any scale of plant other than SAC cannot produce at an average cost as low as p. Further, the optimum scale of plant SAC

must be operated at its optimum rate of output. Any output level other than x will raise average costs above p. To put it another way, the firm is induced to build and use the most efficient scale of plant and to use it at its most efficient output level.

Changes in Demand

If an industry were initially in long-run equilibrium, what sort of chain of events would be set off by a change in demand for the product? What would be the short-run effects on the price and the output of the product and on costs of production? Then, in the long run, what further adjustments in price, output, and costs would occur? The nature of the short-run effects of a change in demand were examined earlier and will be passed over quickly here. The long-run effects depend upon whether the industry is one of increasing costs, constant costs, or decreasing costs. These different types of cost conditions are described in the following sections.

Increasing-Cost Case

Suppose that the wheat-growing industry is initially in long-run equilibrium. In Figure 9–11 the market demand curve is DD. For any one firm long-run average costs are shown by LAC. The scale of plant currently in operation is SAC, and the short-run marginal cost curve is SMC. The horizontal summation of the SMC curves of all firms in the industry establishes the market short-run supply curve, SS. Market price of the product is p, individual firm output is x, and market output is X. Product

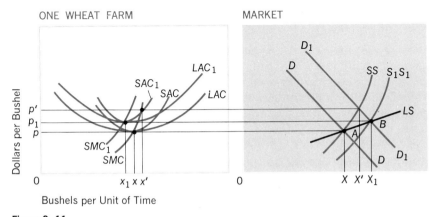

Figure 9–11
Effects of a change in demand: increasing-cost case.

price and average cost are equal, so no profits are made nor are losses incurred.[4]

Suppose now that television commercials cause the tastes of children—young and old—to shift toward wheat products, moving the demand curve to D_1D_1. We use SAC and SMC to trace out the short-run effects of the demand change. Market price will rise to p'. Individual-firm output will rise to x', the level at which short-run marginal cost equals marginal revenue and at which profits are maximized after the increase in demand. Short-run profits are made by the individual firm and will be equal to the difference between price and short-run average cost at output x' multiplied by that output. Industry output will be X'. This is the extent of the short-run effects.

The long-run effects of the demand change are more complex. In the long run the profits made by individual firms in the industry provide an incentive for new firms to enter. Land formerly used for growing other crops is converted into wheat farms, and some land that might not have been cultivated at all may be brought into production. The entrance of new firms moves the market short-run supply curve to the right, since there are more and more individual-firm SMC curves to add together horizontally. Consequently, market price declines, and as this occurs the demand and marginal revenue curves facing the individual firm shift downward.

In industries of increasing costs the cost curves of individual firms are shifted upward by the entry of new firms into the industry. This situation will occur where an industry uses substantial parts of the total supplies available of the resources necessary for making its product. The entry of new firms into the industry increases demand for those resources, which in turn causes resource prices to rise. In the example at hand we would expect land prices and the prices of machinery used in producing wheat to rise along with the prices of fertilizer and labor. Since the position of a given set of cost curves for a firm, LAC, SAC, and SMC, is determined by a given set of resource prices, changes in those resource prices cause shifts in the whole set of cost curves. Therefore, increases in the prices of resources shift the cost curves upward. It follows, of course, that decreases in resource prices would shift the cost curves downward.

Individual-firm profits decline as new firms enter. The more firms that enter the industry, the greater will be the supply of the product and the lower will be the product price. Also, the more firms that enter, the higher will be the level of each firm's costs. Profits are squeezed from above and from below until enough firms have entered to reduce profits to zero. As long as profits are positive, new firms enter. When enough firms have

---

[4] The firm's long-run marginal cost curve is not needed for the analysis at hand, and in the interests of keeping an already cluttered diagram as clear as possible it is omitted from Figure 9–11. If it were drawn in, it would intersect the marginal revenue curve of the firm at output x.

entered to reduce profits to zero, entrance into the industry will cease and long-run equilibrium will be re-established.

The new long-run equilibrium position of a single firm and of the industry is also illustrated in Figure 9–11. The entrance of new firms increases the short-run supply curve to S_1S_1, driving price down from p' to p_1. The firm's long-run average cost curve shifts upward to LAC_1. It uses the optimum scale of plant, SAC_1, which has the short-run marginal cost curve SMC_1. Individual-firm output will be x_1.[5]

The preceding analysis provides information for tracing out the long-run supply curve for the product. The *long-run supply curve* shows the alternative quantities of the product that would be placed on the market by all firms together at all possible prices, assuming that ample time is allowed at each possible price for long-run equilibrium to be reached. It joins such points as A and B in the market diagram. Point A shows the quantity of wheat that would be placed on the market by all firms together at price p when long-run equilibrium prevails for the industry at that price. Point B shows the same thing at price p_1. The long-run supply curve is more elastic than either of the short-run supply curves shown. Both of the latter show the quantity response of the industry to different possible prices when the number of firms and the productive capacity of the industry is fixed. The long-run supply curve allows for the entrance or exit of firms to or from the industry; that is, for variability in the productive capacity of the industry.

Constant-Cost Case

The short-run analysis of the constant-cost case is the same as that of the increasing-cost case. Suppose that the industry under consideration manufactures pins. In Figure 9–12 the initial demand is DD, and that the firm's cost curves are LAC, SAC, and SMC. The industry is in long-run equilibrium at price p, individual firm output is x, and industry output is X. If an increase in the birth rate increases the demand for pins to D_1D_1, the market price will rise to p', the firm's output will increase to x', and industry output will increase to X'. The firm will be making short-run profits. (Can you measure them in Figure 9–12? The profit rectangle has *not* been drawn on the diagram.)

The profits will attract new firms into the industry, and it is at this point that the constant-cost case exhibits its unique characteristics. For an industry to be one of constant costs there must be no upward or downward shifts in the cost curves of its firms as new firms enter the industry

---

[5] The new individual-firm output may be equal to, greater than, or less than the output it was producing before the change in demand occurred, depending upon whether the cost curves shift straight up, upward to the right, or upward to the left. Any one of these possibilities may occur.

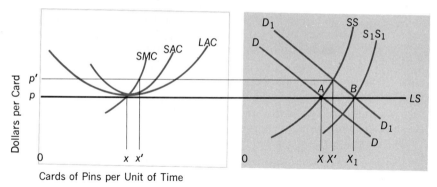

Cards of Pins per Unit of Time

Figure 9–12
Effects of a change in demand: constant-cost case.

or as existing firms leave. All firms together must take such insignificant proportions of the total supplies of the resources used in the industry that increases or decreases in the amounts they use have no effect on the prices. For example, it is hardly conceivable that increases or decreases in the manufacture of pins could affect total demand for steel enough to cause changes in the price of this resource.

Thus as new firms enter the short-run supply curve is pushed to the right and product price declines from the high short-run level of p'. But as long as market price exceeds minimum possible average costs for the firm (found at output level x), it is possible for profits to be made and firms will continue to enter. Eventually enough firms will enter the industry to increase short-run supply to S_1S_1. The price will be forced back to p, the individual firm's output will be reduced again to x, and industry output will be at X_1.

In the constant-cost case the industry's long-run supply curve, LS, joins such long-run equilibrium price–output combinations as A and B. It shows how much of the product all firms together would place on the market at various possible prices when there is ample time for all desired long-run adjustments to be made. But price p, at the level of minimum possible long-run average costs, is the only long-run equilibrium price level. The quantity placed on the market will be adjusted to whatever quantity is demanded at that price; that is, the long-run supply curve is perfectly elastic. Demand governs the quantity placed on the market.

Decreasing-Cost Case

Some industries may experience decreasing costs in the long run during periods of substantial industry growth. For this to be so the cost curves of individual firms in the industry must shift downward as new firms enter, a situation that seems to fly in the face of common sense. It appears that when new firms enter an industry the consequent increase in demand for resources used in producing the product will ordinarily increase the prices of those resources, giving rise to the increasing-cost case. It would seem that the constant-cost case would be the very least that one could expect, the entry of new firms having an insignificant effect on resource prices. Are there circumstances in which increases in the number of firms in an industry and consequent increases in demand for resources cause resource prices to fall?

Suppose that an industry takes root in a geographic area where large supplies of some of the essential resources used in producing the product are found but that demand for the product is not great. Now suppose that demand increases and it becomes highly profitable to produce the product. New firms enter the industry, locating in the area. Heretofore it has not been worthwhile for a branch-line railroad or an airport to be built, but with the increasing economic activity in the area transportation facilities are improved. Firms in other industries that utilize by-products of the original industry begin to locate in the area. Still other firms that are suppliers of resources to the original industry also move nearby. Warehousing facilities come into existence. An industrial complex far larger than that of the original industry is developed that provides the latter with cost-reduction opportunities. Thus decreasing costs may be possible for an industry during a period of expansion. However, the case does not appear to be reversible. Once the industry has taken advantage of the cost reductions it will become one of constant or increasing costs.

The decreasing-cost case is shown diagrammatically in Figure 9–13. Using the short- and long-run patterns of analysis developed for the increasing- and constant-cost cases, can you trace through the effects of the increase in demand on the price, individual firm output, and market output of the product?

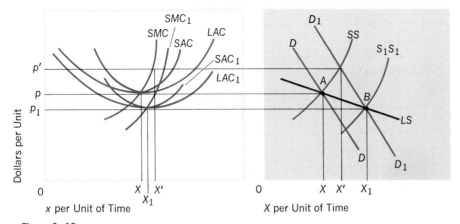

Figure 9–13
Effects of a change in demand: decreasing-cost case.

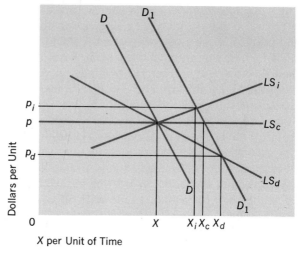

Figure 9–14
Comparison of output effects of an increase in demand.

Comparison of the Quantity Responses

How do the increasing-cost, constant-cost, and decreasing-cost cases compare with one another with respect to the long-run quantity response to an increase in demand? These various situations are summarized in Figure 9–14, in which the initial equilibrium price for all three cases is assumed to be p and the initial equilibrium output is assumed to be X. The long-run supply curves are LS_i, LS_c, and LS_d for the increasing-cost, decreasing-cost, and constant-cost cases, respectively. The comparative effects of the increase in demand to D_1D_1 are clear. In the increasing-cost case quantity increases only to X_i, a part of the increase in demand being siphoned off by an increase in price. In the constant-cost case the quantity increase to X_c absorbs the entire demand increase. In the decreasing-cost case the quantity response to X_d exceeds the demand increase, the decrease in costs furnishing an impetus for an increase in output beyond that provided by the increase in demand.

SUMMARY

The forces that determine the prices and the outputs of products produced by sellers in purely competitive selling markets are examined in this chapter. Pure competition in selling is a situation in which (1) there are enough sellers of a product that no one seller by himself can appreciably affect product price; (2) the product sold by one of the many sellers is identical to that sold by the rest; (3) prices are free to move in response to changes in demand and supply; and (4) sellers are free to sell wherever they desire to sell.

The very short run in the market for any specific product is a planning period so short that the quantity of the product available for sale cannot be changed. The price system performs the function of rationing the available supply among consumers and of clearing the market of the supply on hand. Costs of production play no part in determining the price of the product.

The short run in the market for a product is a time period too short for firms to have time to increase or decrease their scales of plant, but long enough for them to be able to increase or decrease the outputs they produce with their given scales of plant. The objective of the firm in the short run is to produce the output level that will maximize its profits, with profits defined as the difference between the firm's total revenues and its total costs.

The firm can choose its output level but not its price when selling in a purely competitive market. It accepts the market price as given and adjusts output to the profit-maximizing level. Marginal revenue, defined as the change in total revenue per unit change in output, under these circumstances is constant at all levels of output and sales and is equal to the market price of the product. Profits are maximized at the output level at which the firm's marginal cost equals the marginal revenue from its sales.

Market price of the product is determined by the interactions of all buyers and all sellers of the product. These activities are summed up in the market demand and market supply curves for the product. The short-run market supply curve is found by summing horizontally those parts of individual firm short-run marginal cost curves that lie above the firms' respective average variable cost curves and it shows the amounts that all firms together, with their given scales of plant, will place on the market at different possible product price levels. Changes in demand or changes in costs of production will change both the short-run output and the short-run price of the product.

The long run in a product market is a time period long enough for individual firms to increase or decrease their scales of plant to any desired size, as well as for new firms to enter or for existing firms to leave the industry. To maximize profits in the long run a firm selects the output at which its long-run marginal cost is equal to its marginal revenue. But if profits can be made, new firms are attracted into the industry, increasing supply and decreasing the product price until the profit level is zero. When the industry is in long-run equilibrium, with firms at a zero profit level, each firm is induced to build an optimum scale of plant and use it at the optimum rate of output.

Purely competitive industries are classified as increasing-cost, constant-cost, or decreasing-cost cases, depending upon their long-run cost responses to changes in demand. Following an increase in demand and profits, in the increasing-cost case the entry of new firms into the industry increases the prices of resources used in producing the product, thus shifting the cost curves of all firms upward. In the constant-cost case the cost curves of individual firms do not shift because the entry of new firms does not perceptibly increase resource prices. In the decreasing-cost case the entry of new firms, the expansion of the industry, the expansion of complementary industries, and better organization of resource markets cause the cost curves of individual firms to shift downward. The quantity response to an increase in demand is the greatest in the decreasing-cost case, next greatest in the constant-cost case, and least in the increasing-cost case.

EXERCISES AND QUESTIONS FOR DISCUSSION

1. A prerequisite for pure competition is that there must be many sellers of the product. Since no one seller is actually aware of what another is doing, this would seem to imply a lack of competition rather than an abundance of it. Discuss.
2. Explain and show how a purely competitive firm determines the output it will produce and the price it will charge in the short run. What assumptions have you made? Why are these assumptions necessary?
3. List several firms in your area that you think approximate purely competitive ones. From the information you can gather, is the industry of each firm an increasing-, decreasing-, or constant-cost industry? After you have established this, discuss the firm's effect on pricing and output decisions in each industry.
4. "In pricing a product a firm considers the costs incurred in producing a unit of that product and then adds a margin of profit above those costs. If this amount is not covered, a firm will not produce." Evaluate this statement.
5. "Costs of production play no part whatsoever in price determination." Under what circumstances is this so? not so?
6. A firm maximizes profits at the output level for which total revenue is the farthest above total cost. Yet the economist says that the firm maximizes profits at the output level for which marginal revenue equals marginal cost. Can both of these statements be correct at the same time? Explain.

SELECTED READINGS

Bilas, R. A., *Microeconomic Theory: A Graphical Analysis.* New York: McGraw-Hill Book Company, Inc., 1967, pp. 159–173.
Colberg, M., D. R. Forbush, and G. R. Whitaker, Jr., *Business Economics,* 3d ed. Homewood, Ill.: Richard D. Irwin, Inc., 1964, Chap. 5 and Cases 5–1, 5–2, and 5–3.
Ferguson, C. E., *Microeconomic Theory.* Homewood, Ill.: Richard D. Irwin, Inc., 1966, Chap. 9.
Robinson, J., *The Economics of Imperfect Competition.* London: Macmillan and Company, Ltd., 1948, Chap. 17.
Stigler, G., *The Theory of Price,* 3d ed. New York: Crowell-Collier and Macmillan, Inc., 1966, Chap. 10.

Pricing and Output under Pure Monopoly

CHAPTER 10

Pure monopoly, at the other end of the spectrum, is a market situation in which there is only one seller of a product for which there are no good substitutes. The monopolist has no competitors but has the market all to himself.

Monopoly is common in public utilities. Your local telephone company, or in most cases your local branch of the Bell Telephone System, is an example. There are no good substitutes for telephone service nor are there competing companies that supply the same service in your community. This is a market that does not lend itself well to competition. Imagine what it would be like if there were a half dozen competing exchanges, each operating independently of the others. How would you establish telephone contact with people having phones on exchanges other than your own? Other utilities that usually operate as monopolies are power and light companies, gas companies, and public transportation companies.

Outside the public utility field pure monopoly is harder to find, although historically this market situation has been approached in several industries.[1] For example, between 1870, when Standard Oil of Ohio was first organized, and 1899, when Standard Oil of New Jersey was set up as a holding company to control the entire Standard Oil empire, this oil company is said to have gained control of some 90 percent of the petroleum industry; between 1912 and 1940 the Aluminum Company of America is said to have controlled over 90 percent of the aluminum ingot market; and it was alleged that in 1953 the United Shoe Machinery Cor-

---

[1] See Irwin M. Stelzer, *Selected Antitrust Cases* (Homewood, Ill.: Richard D. Irwin, Inc., 1955), pp. 4, 16, 45.

poration supplied over 75 and probably as much as 85 percent of the U.S. shoe machinery market. In the latter case this was estimated to be a smaller share of the market than the company supplied in 1915. These have been among the more famous near-monopoly cases.

Even though firms that represent pure monopoly do not embrace a very large proportion of the productive capacity of the United States, the principles governing their economic behavior form an invaluable part of the general body of economic theory. They are, of course, essential for analyzing cases where pure monopoly, or situations approaching it, exist. Equally important, these principles help us to analyze and understand cases of oligopoly and, in addition, serve to deepen our understanding of competitive markets.

REVENUE DIFFERENCES IN PURE MONOPOLY

As we consider how the prices and outputs of products are determined in selling markets of pure monopoly we shall find that some of the principles established for the purely competitive case can be carried over intact. A monopolist's profit-maximizing output is that at which marginal cost is equal to marginal revenue. Too, the costs of a monopolistic firm have the same characteristics as those of a purely competitive one. Further, in the short run, if the total receipts of the monopolist are not sufficient to cover total variable costs, losses will be minimized by producing nothing. But the revenue concepts look different to the pure monopolist than to the pure competitor.

The Demand Curve Facing the Firm

Since the monopolist is the only seller of the product or service in which he deals, the market demand curve for the product is the demand curve that he faces. He *is* the industry on the selling side of the market; consequently, the quantities of his product that he can sell at alternative possible prices are precisely those that buyers in the market are willing to take at those prices. Instead of seeing demand as a prevailing market price at which he can sell all he wants to place on the market, the monopolist recognizes—or soon discovers—that there are limits to the quantities he can sell. In order to increase his sales volume he must lower the price that he charges. If he raises the price, sales will fall as the product becomes too expensive to fit into the expenditure patterns of some consumers and as other consumers reduce the quantities they purchase. He simply faces the market demand curve that we have discussed previously in some detail and that in most cases slopes downward to the right.

TABLE 10-1
Hypothetical Demand and Revenue Schedules for Mineral Water

(1) PRICE PER PINT (p)	(2) QUANTITY PER DAY (x)	(3) TOTAL REVENUE (px)	(4) MARGINAL REVENUE $[(\Delta px)/(\Delta x)]$
$122	1	$122	$122
117	2	234	112
112	3	336	102
107	4	428	92
102	5	510	82
97	6	582	72
92	7	644	62
87	8	696	52
82	9	738	42
77	10	770	32
72	11	792	22
67	12	804	12
62	13	806	2
57	14	798	(−) 8
52	15	780	(−) 18

The Revenue Concepts

A nineteenth-century French economist provided a classic example of what it means to a monopolist to face a demand curve sloping downward to the right.[2] Suppose that an individual has discovered on his property a mineral spring with remarkable curing properties. Suppose further that the costs of selling pints of the water are negligible. If there are no costs, the monopolist's problem in maximizing profits is greatly simplified: maximization of total receipts also amounts to maximization of profits.[3] Suppose that the market demand schedule for pints of mineral water is that of columns (1) and (2) in Table 10–1. The corresponding demand curve is *DD* in Figure 10–1(a).

Total Revenue

The relation of the monopolist's total revenue to his sales level differs from that of the pure competitor. For the latter the larger the output level, the greater the total revenue. Further, the total revenue curve for the pure competitor is a straight line from the origin sloping upward to the right. Note in column (3) of Table 10–1 what happens to the monopolist's total

---

[2] See Augustine Cournot, *Mathematical Principles of the Theory of Wealth* (New York: The Macmillan Company, 1897), pp. 56 ff.

[3] A warning note is in order here. Only if the monopolist has no variable costs will profit maximization and revenue maximization occur at the same output level. If variable costs are associated with production and sales, as they usually are, the output of profit maximization will be smaller than the output of revenue maximization.

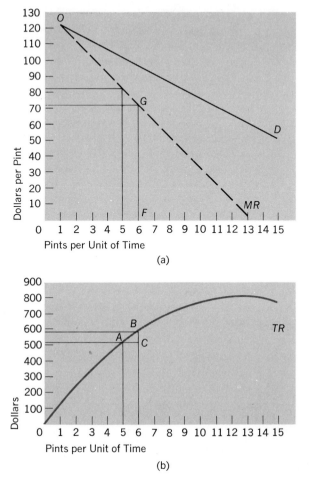

Figure 10–1
A monopolist's total and marginal revenue.

revenue as the sales level is increased: it increases to a maximum of 806 dollars at a sales level of 13 pints and then decreases for higher sales levels. This situation is also illustrated by the *TR* curve in Figure 10–1(b). The concave downward shape of the curve reflects the fact that higher sales levels, given the demand for the product, can be achieved only by lowering the asking price for the product. Beyond some point—13 pints in the illustration—the effects of lower prices more than offset the effects of higher sales levels.

Marginal Revenue

When we look at marginal revenue for the monopolist at different sales levels we discover that it is not equal to product price, as it was for the purely competitive firm. To be sure, marginal revenue for the monopolist is defined just as it was for the pure competitor: it is the change in total revenue per unit change in the level of sales $[(\Delta TR)/(\Delta x)$ or $(\Delta px/\Delta x)]$. But when we compute marginal revenue in Table 10–1, listing the results of the computations in column (4), and when we plot the relation of marginal revenue to the sales level in Figure 10–1(a), at each sales level above 1 it is less than the corresponding price of the product.[4]

Actually, it should come as no surprise to find that when a firm faces a downward-sloping demand curve marginal revenue is less than price. The demand curve is the firm's *average revenue curve*—price is revenue per unit of sales at any given sales level. Consequently, we should expect the relation between marginal revenue and average revenue (price) to be the same as that between any average curve and marginal curve derived from the same *total* curve, for example, average cost and marginal cost.[5]

To demonstrate arithmetically why the difference occurs, suppose that the firm is selling four pints of water per day at 107 dollars per pint. Sales are now expanded to five pints per day, a decrease in price to 102 dollars per pint being required in order to induce customers to make the increase in their purchases. The extra pint of sales per day by itself yields 102 dollars in revenue; but whereas the original volume of four pints formerly sold for 107 dollars each, they now sell for only 102 dollars each, a decrease in the revenue yield from them of 5 dollars each, or a total of 20 dollars. The net increase in total revenue from the one-unit increase in the sales level is thus 102 dollars minus 20 dollars, or 82 dollars, as is indicated in Table 10–1 and Figure 10–1(a).

The transition from diagrams such as Figure 10–1, on which the axes are actually scaled numerically, to representative diagrams on which numerical scales are not shown will be easier if we look at Figure 10–1 from both points of view. In Figure 10–1(b) consider an increase in the sales level from five to six pints per day. Total revenue rises from 510 dollars, or by 72 dollars—the marginal revenue of the sixth unit of sales. In representative terms marginal revenue is the vertical distance CB in Figure 10–1(b). Moving up to Figure 10–1(a), we see that marginal revenue at a sales level of six pints is plotted as 72 dollars. In representative terms FG is marginal revenue at that sales level.

---

[4] In Figure 10–1(a) the DD curve and the MR curve are the same at the one-unit sales level and spread apart at higher sales levels. Ordinarily, on representative diagrams, they are shown starting from a common intercept on the price axis. This apparent discrepancy comes from our use of a relatively large distance along the quantity axis to represent one unit of product. If in the diagram we had used the distance measuring 10 pints of water to measure 100 pints of water, the one-unit level would be so close to zero that we could hardly distinguish it from zero. So, for most purposes, it is quite in order to show both curves originating at a common point on the price axis.

[5] See pp. 130–131.

Maximization of Revenue

Have you ever heard it said that a monopolist will charge the highest price he can get? The example of the mineral spring monopolist indicates that this is not likely to be so. The highest price the monopolist can get in this example is 122 dollars per pint, the price at which he sells only one pint per day. Similarly, the highest prices that can be charged by any monopolist for his product will be that at which the sales level is only one unit.

The seller of mineral water can increase his total revenue by increasing his sales beyond one pint per day, and if revenue maximization is his aim, he will sell 13 pints. The price that he can obtain at this volume is 62 dollars per pint. An increase or a decrease in the sales volume will lower his total revenue.

Revenue is maximized at the sales level at which marginal revenue is zero, or is as close to zero as it can be for discrete sales intervals. If marginal revenue is positive, increases in the volume of sales must increase total revenue. In Table 10–1 and Figure 10–1 this is the case for sales levels up to and through 13 pints per day. Beyond that point marginal revenue is negative, meaning that increases in the sales level will decrease total revenue.

THE SHORT RUN

Suppose now that the water sold by the mineral spring monopolist is not a free good, for costs are incurred in bottling and selling. For short-run decision-making the monopolist operates with his existing scale of plant and contemplates the alternative outputs possible with that scale of plant. He will have both fixed and variable costs, with the former independent of the output level and the latter dependent upon how much he bottles and sells.

Profit Maximization: Total Costs and Total Revenues

Hypothetical cost data for the monopolist are presented in Table 10–2. Total fixed costs are assumed to be 100 dollars per day. Total variable costs increase with the output level. Over-all total costs are the sum of the two at each possible output level. The total cost curve is plotted as *TC* in Figure 10–2(b).

Revenues of the monopolist are assumed to be the same as they were in the preceding section. Total revenue at the different levels of output is

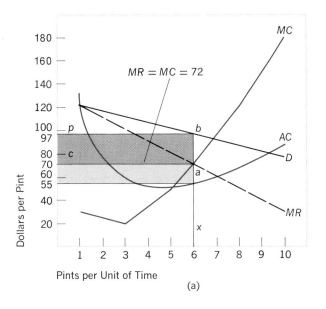

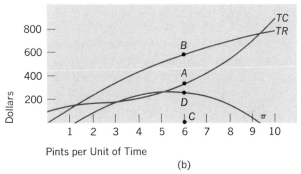

Figure 10–2
Profit maximization by a monopolist.

TABLE 10–2
Hypothetical Total Cost, Revenue, and Profit Schedules for Mineral Water

(1) QUANTITY PER DAY	(2) TOTAL FIXED COSTS	(3) TOTAL VARIABLE COSTS	(4) TOTAL COSTS	(5) TOTAL REVENUE	(6) PROFITS
1	$100	$ 30	$130	$122	$(−) 12
2	100	55	155	234	79
3	100	75	175	336	161
4	100	110	210	428	218
5	100	160	260	510	250
6	100	232	332	582	250
7	100	328	428	644	216
8	100	450	550	696	146
9	100	600	700	738	38
10	100	780	880	770	(−)110

repeated in column (5) of Table 10–2 and is plotted as *TR* in Figure 10–2(b).

Profit at each level of output is the difference between total revenue and total cost. These levels are listed in column (6) of Table 10–2 and are plotted as π in Figure 10–2(b). The greatest vertical spread between the *TR* and the *TC* curve is at either five or six units of sales, and total profit is 250 dollars per day. This is measured geometrically by *AB* in Figure 10–2(b). The distance *CD* in the figure is, of course, also equal to 250 dollars, or the distance *AB*.

Profit Maximization: Per Unit Curves

Table 10–3 and Figure 10–2(a) illustrate the profit-maximization principles that apply to the monopolist in terms of per unit costs and revenues. For output levels below six pints per day, marginal revenue is greater than marginal cost, meaning that additions to output will add more to total receipts than to total costs and will therefore increase profits. An increase in output from four to five pints per day increases total receipts by 82 dollars, total costs by 50 dollars, and profits by 32 dollars. A further increase in output from five pints to six pints per day generates equal additions to both total revenue and total cost, neither adding to nor reducing profits. At this output level, where marginal revenue is equal to marginal cost, profits are maximum.[6] For further increases in output, marginal revenue is less than marginal cost, and if these increases are made total profits will be reduced.

TABLE 10–3
Hypothetical per Unit Cost, Revenue, and Profit Schedules for Mineral Water

(1) QUANTITY PER DAY	(2) AVERAGE COSTS	(3) MARGINAL COSTS	(4) MARGINAL REVENUE	(5) PRICE PER PINT	(6) ADDITIONS TO PROFITS
1	$130	$ 30	$122	$122	$ 92
2	$77\frac{1}{4}$	25	112	117	87
3	$58\frac{1}{3}$	20	102	112	82
4	$52\frac{1}{2}$	35	92	107	57
5	52	50	82	102	32
6	$55\frac{1}{3}$	72	72	97	0
7	$61\frac{1}{7}$	96	62	92	(−) 38
8	$68\frac{3}{4}$	120	52	87	(−) 68
9	$77\frac{7}{9}$	150	42	82	(−)108
10	88	180	32	77	(−)148

[6] Profits are also maximum at one unit less than that at which *MC* equals *MR;* but this is because we are using discrete number intervals to measure output.

In Figure 10–2(a) we use the demand curve facing the firm and the average cost curve to complete profits. At the profit-maximizing output of six pints per day the monopolist can charge 97 dollars per pint for the mineral water. At that output average cost is $55\frac{1}{3}$ dollars. Profit per unit is $41\frac{2}{3}$ dollars. Multiplying the latter by six we find that total profit is 250 dollars.

Geometrically, profit is the shaded rectangle in Figure 10–2(a). Price at output $0x$ is measured by xb (or $0p$) and average cost is xa (or $0c$). Profit per unit is ab (or cp), and total profit is ab times $0x$ (or cp times $0x$), the area of rectangle $cpba$. (Can you find the rectangles measuring total receipts and total costs at output x?)

Effects of Monopoly on Price and Output

Monopoly is thought by many champions of the free enterprise system to constitute economic sin. The sinful acts are restrictions of outputs and increases in prices as compared with what outputs and prices would be under competitive conditions. We shall look first at why such restrictions may occur and then at whether they are always disadvantageous to the public.

Suppose that Figure 10–3 illustrates an industry of pure competition. The market demand curve is DD and the market short-run supply curve is SS—the horizontal summation of individual-firm short-run marginal

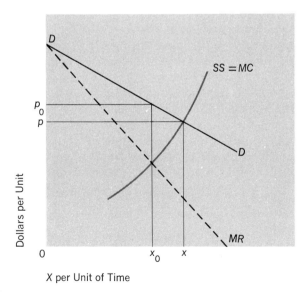

Figure 10–3
Monopolistic restriction of output.

cost curves. Market price is p and market output is x. The short-run supply curve is the industry marginal cost curve, and industry output is that at which the industry marginal cost curve cuts the industry demand curve.

Now suppose that one firm buys up all the others and the industry becomes one of pure monopoly. The plant capacity of each of the former firms is unchanged and is used as a branch plant of the monopolist. To present the monopolist in the best possible light, suppose that no economies or diseconomies of scale are involved in the process of monopolization. What was the short-run supply curve of the purely competitive industry is now the marginal cost curve of the monopolist.

Profit maximization for the monopolist occurs at output x_0 sold at price p_0. Output is smaller and price is higher than it was for the purely competitive market. Why does this restriction occur? Individual-firm diagrams for the purely competitive case are not drawn in Figure 10–3; however, we learned in the previous chapter that each firm faces a horizontal demand curve at the level of market price. Marginal revenue for the purely competitive firm is the same as price; consequently, each firm maximizes profits at an output at which marginal cost is equal to marginal revenue *and to price*. But when an industry is monopolized the monopolist faces a downward-sloping market demand curve, and at each possible sales level marginal revenue is *less than price*. Thus, since he maximizes profits at the output at which his marginal cost equals his marginal revenue, he stops short of that output at which the marginal cost curve cuts the demand curve, or at which marginal cost is equal to price.

This illustration is not intended as an argument that all markets should be purely competitive; rather, it is meant to demonstrate the restrictive characteristics inherent in monopoly. Even though the markets facing U.S. producers are the largest in the world, in a large proportion of these markets pure competition is not possible. For pure competition to be possible in an industry the product market must be large enough and the optimum scale of plant for any one firm must be small enough so that there can be many firms—each with an optimum scale of plant—producing and selling the product. By *many firms* is meant enough so that no one firm acting by itself can increase or decrease market supply sufficiently to influence price perceptibly. Industries where this is so represent a small proportion of the total productive capacity of the economy.

THE LONG RUN

For long-run planning purposes the monopolist is not married to any particular scale of plant. Like the pure competitor, he has ample time to increase or decrease his scale of plant to whatever size he desires. And, as in the competitive case, there is time for the monopolist to withdraw from the market and time for new firms to enter. We shall consider these possibilities in turn.

Scale of Plant Adjustments

Suppose that a monopolist in the field of electric power generation presently operates the scale of plant SAC_0 in Figure 10–4. Demand for electricity has settled at DD and the marginal revenue curve corresponding to that demand curve[7] is MR. The short-run profit-maximizing output is x_0, since this is the price at which short-run marginal cost equals marginal revenue. The price is p_0 and the short-run profits are $c_0 p_0$ times x_b.

But as a long-run proposition the monopolist can improve his profit position. At output x_0 marginal revenue exceeds long-run marginal cost. An increase in output through an increase in the scale of plant will add more to total receipts than to total costs and, therefore, will increase profits. This will be so up to output level x, at which long-run marginal cost is equal to marginal revenue. At output x long-run profits are maximized.

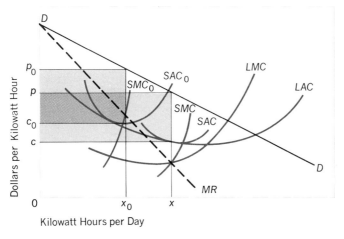

Figure 10–4
Long-run equilibrium.

[7] The demand curves thus far have been drawn as straight lines because their corresponding marginal revenue curves are then easier to draw. The marginal revenue curve for a straight line demand curve lies halfway between the demand curve and the price axis, while that for a nonlinear curve does not. If the demand curve is convex to the origin, the marginal revenue curve will lie to the left of a line drawn midway between the demand curve and the price axis. If it is concave to the origin, the marginal revenue curve will lie to the right of such a line. See Joan Robinson, *The Economics of Imperfect Competition* (New York: The Macmillan Company, 1933), Chap. 2.

The scale of plant that minimizes cost for output x is SAC, the scale of plant for which the short-run average cost curve is tangent to, or forms a part of, the long-run average cost curve at that output. With either a larger or a smaller scale of plant, average costs at output x would be higher than c. Price is p and profits are cp times x. The monopolist is in long-run equilibrium, since he has no further incentive to change either his scale of plant or his output.

Entry Possibilities[8]

Now what about the possibilities of new firms entering a monopolized industry in which profits are made? One thing is certain: it is difficult to keep firms from entering any profitable line of endeavor. This is undoubtedly why monopoly is rarely found outside the area of public utilities. *If a profit-making monopoly is to remain a monopoly in the long run it must be able to block potential entrants from the field.* This is attempted in several different ways.

Probably the most effective barrier to the entrance of firms into a profit-making area is *governmental decree and legislation.* Exclusive franchises granted by governmental units protect most public utilities from competition. These may be extended to such quasi-public utilities as taxicab companies. Patents have served to block potential entrants in some cases, although in many instances they have not been completely effective. Tariffs and import prohibitions may protect a domestic firm from foreign competition. There are a number of governmental obstacles to entry, though many of these impede and limit entry rather than blocking it completely.

Firms already in an industry may block the entry of potential newcomers by *securing and maintaining control of resources* needed to produce the product. In the nineteenth century, for example, Standard Oil attempted to secure control of the means of transporting petroleum and petroleum products; and prior to World War II, the Aluminum Company of America owned virtually all of the world's known bauxite supplies. The concentration of resources, say of ore deposits, greatly facilitates the use of barriers of this type. On the other hand, where such resources as ore deposits or petroleum reserves are scattered throughout the world it is difficult for any one company to secure control of them.

Entry into a monopolized market may be blocked in some instances by the *size of the product market relative to the amount of output that a firm can produce* when it is using a scale of plant large enough to take ad-

---

[8] This section is equally applicable to long-run conditions in oligopolistic markets and we shall return to it in our study of oligopoly.

vantage of economies of scale. In some cases the total market for the product may be large enough for one or two such firms to make profits, but if another firm were to enter the consequent increase in output and decrease in price might be great enough to cause all to incur losses. A potential entrant recognizing this possibility would have little incentive to move in.

Output Restriction

The output restriction stemming from the difference between price and marginal revenue for a monopolist is compounded by blocked entry in the long run. Under conditions of open entry into an industry the appearance of profits attracts firms into the profit-making areas, increasing supplies and driving prices down (and costs up in some instances) until prices are equal to average costs and the profits disappear. In the absence of profits consumers are paying for goods and services what it costs to produce them. Profits, where they occur, indicate that consumers value resources used in producing the profitable products relatively more than they value them used in producing other products; the evidence of this is that they are willing to pay more for resources so used than the resources cost, that is, more than they are worth in their other uses. But blocked entry prevents resources from moving out of the less valuable uses where no profits occur and into the more valuable uses where profits are made.

A dilemma may arise here with respect to whether governmental action against monopoly is appropriate, and, if so, what directions it should take. We often hear it said that a specific monopoly should be broken up into a number of smaller firms. The advocate of this line of action thinks that if there are a number of firms, the market situation is closer to pure competition. This, however, is not necessarily so. Consider the entry barrier case in which the monopolist has a scale of plant somewhere in the neighborhood of optimum size and the market is not large enough to support two firms of this size. Breaking a monopoly up into several firms with smaller scales of plant may very well mean that each firm now must have a less than optimum scale of plant; that is, none is large enough to take advantage of significant economies of scale. The short-run average cost curves of all of the firms may lie at considerably higher levels than did that of the monopolist, and in order to cover costs they may produce even less than did the monopolist and charge an even higher price for the product.[9]

---

[9] And what would prevent one of these pseudocompetitive firms from enlarging its scale of plant, undercutting the prices of the others, and securing all of the market for itself?

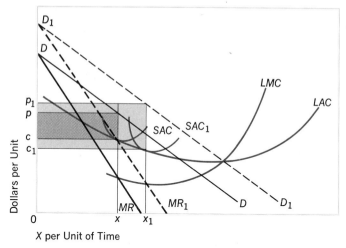

Figure 10–5
Effects of a change in demand.

A more positive line of action may be to attack barriers to entry. Government-supported entry barriers, particularly, may need careful scrutiny to determine which ones can and should be eliminated. Where profits are made, incentives to enter are strong and monopoly positions in the absence of governmental support are difficult to maintain. Some economists go so far as to argue that in the absence of governmental support these incentives will prevent monopoly from seriously disrupting the organization of the economy's productive capacity.

Changes in Demand

What will be the effects of an increase in demand on the long-run price and output of a monopolistic firm? In Figure 10–5 the monopolist's long-run cost curves are LAC and LMC. Suppose he is confronted initially with the demand DD and its marginal revenue curve MR. The profit-maximizing output is x and the price is p. Scale of plant SAC is appropriate for producing that output. Profits are cp times x.

If consumer preferences shift toward product X, the demand curve shifts to the right to some position such as D_1D_1. Marginal revenue is now shown by MR_1 and at output x exceeds long-run marginal cost. An expansion of output to x_1, at which marginal cost is equal to marginal revenue, is necessary if profits are to be maximized. The scale of plant will be increased to SAC_1. Product price increases to p_1 and average cost becomes c_1. Profits increase to c_1p_1 times x_1.

The increase in demand does indeed bring about some expansion in the monopolist's productive capacity and output. However, the more striking effect is the increase in profits. With the entry of additional firms blocked, the only increase in the industry's productive capacity that can occur is the increase in the scale of plant of the monopolist alone.

Changes in Costs

What effects on product price and output can we expect from a change in a monopolist's costs? Again, the response to such a change is internal, that is, within the monopolistic firm itself, since there can be no entry of firms into the market if the monopolist is to remain a monopolist. Suppose that the monopolist's costs are LAC and LMC in Figure 10–6 and that demand and marginal revenue are DD and MR, respectively. The level of maximum profits is cp times x at output x and price p.

If the change that occurs is a technological breakthrough of some kind, the cost curves will shift downward to positions such as LAC_1 and LMC_1. The profit-maximizing output becomes x_1 and price decreases to p_1 because of the increase in output. Profits increase to c_1p_1 times x_1.

The output response of the monopolist is limited. To be sure, output rises and price declines, but only the output of the single firm is changed. Other firms cannot enter to expand output still more and erode away the extra profits arising from the change in costs. The difference between closed- and open-entry cases is simply that in the open-entry case any change that increases profits for the firm provides an incentive for new firms to enter, increasing output and decreasing price, until the profits disappear; in the closed-entry case, however, any change that increases profits induces the firm already in the industry to increase output just

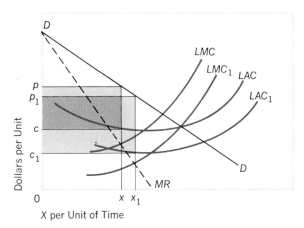

Figure 10–6
Effects of a change in costs.

enough to maximize those profits. Instead of the change being mostly absorbed by an output response, a part of it is siphoned off in increased profits.

SUMMARY

Pure monopoly is a market situation in which there is only one seller of a product for which there are no good substitutes. It is rarely encountered in the United States outside the public utility field, but as a limiting case, at the opposite extreme from pure competition in the selling market spectrum, it provides principles useful in analyzing all selling market situations.

Monopoly differs from pure competition in that the monopolistic firm faces the market demand curve for the product. This means that the firm sees the demand curve as sloping downward to the right rather than as a horizontal, perfectly elastic curve. Consequently, total revenue for the monopolist does not increase indefinitely as sales increase, but reaches a maximum at some sales level and then decreases as sales are increased still more. For the monopolist marginal revenue at different sales levels is not equal to product price but is less than the price at which any given amount of product can be sold.

Short-run profit maximization by a monopolist occurs at the output at which his marginal cost is equal to his marginal revenue. This point will be short of the output at which marginal cost is equal to product price, since the marginal revenue curve lies below the demand curve. Thus a monopolist, because of this difference, restricts output below and raises price above what would prevail if the industry were competitive.

In the long run an additional difference between pure monopoly and pure competition is evidenced. In a profitable industry operated by a monopolistic firm, the firm must have entry into the industry blocked in order to maintain its monopolist position. Increases in the productive capacity of the industry via the entry of new firms—such as that which occurs in a profitable purely competitive industry—is not possible. Adjustments in the monopolized industry's productive capacity are limited to the changes in scale of plant that the monopolist is able and willing to make. Changes in demand for a monopolist's product tend to have greater effects on profits and less effects on productive capacity than would be the case for a product produced and sold under conditions of pure competition. The same may be said for the effects of changes in cost conditions.

Monopolists may block entry of new firms in one or more of several ways. They may be able to enlist the aid of governmental units; they may own or control sources of essential raw materials; or, in some cases, technological conditions may require that for efficient operation a firm be large enough to supply the entire market for the product.

EXERCISES AND QUESTIONS FOR DISCUSSION

1. A monopolist restricts output in order to raise the price of his product and thereby increase his profits. Evaluate this statement.
2. What would be the effects of patent laws on the operation of a purely competitive economy?
3. According to recent periodicals, profits in 1966 soared to record highs. Does this indicate that the United States is becoming characterized by more firms with monopoly power? Why or why not?
4. Many large corporations in the United States have acquired other corporations producing different lines of products. How might this situation affect the extent of monopolization by the original firm?
5. Would a monopolist ever operate in the inelastic portion of his demand curve? if so, when? if not, why not?

SELECTED READINGS

Ferguson, C. E., *Microeconomic Theory*. Homewood, Ill.: Richard D. Irwin, Inc., 1966, Chap. 10.

Lanzilotti, R. F., "The Aluminum Industry," *The Structure of American Industry*, 3d ed., Walter Adams, ed. New York: Crowell-Collier and Macmillan, Inc., 1961.

Robinson, J., *The Economics of Imperfect Competition*. London: Macmillan and Company, Ltd., 1948. Chaps. 3, 4, and 5.

Imperfect Competition

CHAPTER 11

Most markets are not the white or black of pure competition or pure monopoly but fall into the grey area of *imperfect competition.* In this market classification we usually find that more than one firm is engaged in selling a product or service; in most cases, however, there will not be enough such firms to make the market one of pure competition. Even in markets where there are many sellers, what any one firm sells is likely to differ in some respects from that sold by the others; that is, the product units sold by different firms in an industry will not be homogeneous. Nevertheless, the principles developed for markets of pure competition and pure monopoly—the least complex of all selling market structures—will prove helpful in the analysis of markets of imperfect competition. Markets of imperfect competition are ordinarily classified in two categories, oligopoly and monopolistic competition.

OLIGOPOLY

Oligopoly embraces a wide range of selling market situations rather than the single type of situation of the pure competition or the pure monopoly classification. Consequently, unlike for pure competition or pure monopoly, we cannot construct for it a neat precise theory of pricing and output; there are a number of overlapping theories and many of these are imprecise. We shall initially discuss what oligipoly is and what it is not, and we shall consider demand as it looks to an oligopolistic seller. Next we shall examine pricing and output in the short run and in the long run, and finally, we shall turn to one of the most distinctive features of oligopolistic behavior—nonprice competition.

Nature of Oligopoly

Oligopolistic markets are more easily described than defined. "Oligopoly" comes from the Greek words meaning "few sellers", and this is the essential characteristic of this market situation. If more than one seller and less than many sellers of a product or a service are operating in a given market, the market is one of oligopoly.[1] In Chapter 9 we define many sellers as a situation in which no one seller acting alone can exert an influence on the market as a whole. Few sellers, then, implies that the number is small enough for one seller acting alone to be able to affect the market for the product. What are the implications of this for the behavior of oligopolistic firms?

The fact that there are few sellers in a given product market makes the sellers interdependent or rivalrous. If what one seller does, for example, if he advertises or increases his output or changes the quality of his product, can affect the market price or prices of the product, then what he does also affects what the other sellers are able to do; and the market behavior of any one of the others will also affect what the first seller is able to do. Consequently, in taking any specific action that affects the market, an oligopolist tries to assess the impact of his actions on other sellers and in turn the effects of their reactions on him. Frequently this cannot be done with a high degree of accuracy, since it is difficult to predict how rivals will react to the behavior of any one firm. We call this *oligopolistic uncertainty*.

In a given oligopolistic industry different firms may or may not sell homogeneous products. Where different firms sell identical products, the situation is one of *pure oligopoly*. The basic steel industry comes very close to product homogeneity. The different forms in which basic steel is produced conform to certain specifications and a particular form produced by one company will be the same as that produced by another.

Many industries fall into the category of *differentiated oligopoly*. In this situation the product sold by the different firms will differ in some respects, although not in any basic way. Sunbeam toasters are slightly different from Westinghouse toasters; Firestone and Goodrich tires have different tread designs. The outstanding example of differentiated oligopoly, however, is the automobile industry. Certainly most of us believe

[1] See Fritz Machlup, *The Economics of Sellers' Competition* (Baltimore, Md.: The Johns Hopkins Press, 1952), pp. 79–125. This book contains excellent discussions of the different types of markets.

that Fords differ from Chevrolets and that both differ from Chryslers. Where product differentiation occurs, consumers tend to become attached in some degree to favorite brands.

The fact that a firm sells its product as an oligopolist has nothing to do with its costs of production. Oligopoly, like pure monopoly and pure competition, refers to the situation the firm finds itself in as a seller. The firm's cost curves are of the same nature as those described in Chapter 8, 9, and 10.

Demand

The Demand Curve Facing the Firm

Oligopolistic behavior differs from that in the other types of selling markets because of differences in demand as individual sellers see it. The demand concepts to oligopolistic firms are less precise than in other market situations and hence the demand curve facing the firm cannot be located with as much precision as it can in pure competition or pure monopoly. The problem stems from the interdependence of the sellers in any given oligopolistic industry.

The demand curve facing any one firm depends upon the behavior of the other firms in the industry, that is, how they react to changes on the part of the one. Suppose, for example, that a firm selling 14 cubic foot refrigerators is attempting to locate the demand curve it faces. If it is able to sell currently 3000 units monthly at a price of 400 dollars each, point A in Figure 11-1 is on its demand curve. If the firm cuts its price to 375 dollars, how much can it expect to sell at the lower price? This depends on whether and how rival firms react to the price cut. If rival firms react by holding their prices constant, the one firm can expect to pick up sales not only because the market for refrigerators is larger at the lower price but also because it cuts into the sales of its rivals. Sales will increase to some such figure as 5000 refrigerators monthly and point B on its demand curve is established. Apparently the demand curve follows a path such as AB.[2]

How will the demand curve look to the firm if rival firms react to the price cut by reducing their prices by a matching amount? Total sales for all firms increase, and the one gets only a roughly proportionate share of the increase. It does not encroach on the sales of rivals. Quantity sold increases to some such figure as 4000 refrigerators monthly, and the resulting demand curve AC is less elastic for the price change than is AB.

---

[2] We do not know for certain that AB would be a straight line. To determine its shape with greater precision the firm must test the market at a number of price levels between 400 and 375 dollars.

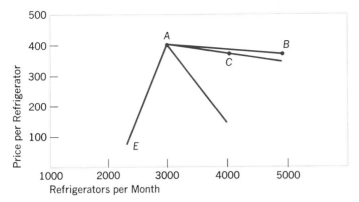

Figure 11-1
Alternative demand curves facing an oligopolist.

Rivals may do more than match the price cuts of the one firm. They may decide to teach the price cutter a lesson by undercutting the price of 375 dollars. In this case the original price cutter does not even retain the share of the market that he has been getting, since the prices quoted by his rivals are relatively more attractive to customers after the price cuts than they were before. The firm faces a demand curve such as AD or, perhaps, even AE in Figure 11-1. It is possible that rivals may undercut the original firm to the extent that the original firm actually *loses* sales.

The accuracy with which an oligopolistic firm can locate the demand curve that it faces varies directly with the degree of certainty with which the firm can predict how rivals will react to its price changes. If the firm cannot accurately predict the reactions of rivals, neither can it locate the position and shape of its demand curve. Complete ignorance of the probable reactions of rivals will not ordinarily be the case, and at least reasonable estimates can be made of the neighborhood in which the demand curve lies. There are, however, many possible variations in the position and shape of the curve.

Most oligopolists would expect to face demand curves that slope downward to the right even though there is uncertainty regarding their exact positions and shapes. A firm will expect that a price cut will lead to an increase in its sales volume. It will also anticipate that an increase in its sales volume will cause the product price to fall. The open questions are, how stable and how elastic is the demand curve that the firm faces?

Market Demand

Under conditions of differentiated oligopoly it may be difficult or impossible to locate and draw the market demand curve because the production units sold by one firm are not the same as those sold by others. A 14-ounce box of powdered detergent differs from a 14-ounce bottle of liquid detergent. Similarly, in the automobile industry a Cadillac does not represent the same unit as a Volkswagen. What do we measure on the quantity scales for market demand curves in these cases? The indicated difficulties do not rule out the use of the concept of market demand, although they inform us that the market demand curve for a differentiated oligopolistic industry is often a fuzzy and imprecise concept and one that it is easier to discuss than to use with mathematical precision.

Short-Run Pricing and Output

In oligopolistic selling situations firms face two opposed sets of incentives. One consists of incentives among the firms of an industry to act jointly or collusively in the market while the other consists of incentives for an individual firm to act independently of the other firms in its industry. To obtain some feel for the wide range of oligopolistic policies and practices that are followed, suppose we consider several typical situations.

Cartel Arrangements

To illustrate the incentive to collude we shall consider a *cartel*. Cartel arrangements represent the most complete form of collusion possible among the firms of an industry. In an arrangement of this type the firms jointly establish a central organization to make price and output decisions, to establish production quotas for each firm, and to supervise the market activities of the firms in the industry. Firms seek to collude in this manner for two reasons. First, through joint market activities they eliminate the uncertainty that surrounds each when each operates independently. Second, through collusion and restraints of competition among the firms monopoly gains can accrue to the firms as a group.

A case of cartel pricing and output is illustrated in Figure 11–2. Suppose that light bulbs are produced and sold by only a few firms. The market demand curve is DD and the short-run average and marginal cost curves of one of the firms are SAC and SMC, respectively. The price scales of the firm and the market diagrams are the same; however, the quantity scale of the market diagram is compressed as compared with that of the firm.

The primary objective of the cartel is assumed to be profit maximization. The profit-maximizing principles applicable to the cartel are the same as those that apply to purely competitive or purely monopolistic

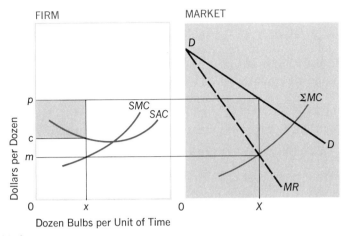

FIRM   MARKET

Figure 11–2
Cartel price, output, and quota allocation.

firms. The output for the market as a whole should be that at which market marginal revenue equals market marginal cost. How can market marginal revenue and market marginal cost be determined?

Since the cartel is making price and output decisions for all firms of the industry, the demand curve that it faces is the market demand curve. Individual-firm demand curves are irrelevant, since they have delegated price-making authority to the central agency of the cartel. The marginal revenue curve for the cartel, then, will be that derived from the market demand curve DD and is shown in Figure 11–2 as MR. It will bear the same relation to DD as any marginal curve bears to its companion average curve. For a decreasing average curve, the marginl curve lies below the average curve.

The industry marginal cost curve is constructed from individual-firm marginal cost curves. If we add the short-run marginal cost curves together horizontally we obtain a market curve similar to the industry short-run supply curve of a purely competitive industry. This curve, shown as ΣMC in Figure 11–2, is the industry marginal cost curve. It shows what the level of marginal cost will be for each firm at alternative industry output levels if the central agency always allocates quotas to the firms so that the level of marginal cost for each of the firms is the same,[3] and it also shows the level of marginal cost for the entire industry at each of those outputs.

---

[3] If the central agency allocates any given output among the firms so that marginal cost for any one firm is equal to that of any other firm, the industry cost for that output will be minimized. Can you explain why this is so?

The central cartel agency will maximize industry profits by setting the output of the industry at X—the output at which industry marginal revenue is equal to industry marginal cost. The cartel can obtain a price of p per dozen light bulbs at that output. The level of industry marginal cost (and marginal revenue) is m, so each firm will be allocated a production quota sufficient to bring its marginal cost up to that level—output x for the firm in Figure 11–2. The total of such quotas will just be equal to the industry output X. From Figure 11–2 we can also determine how much profit one firm contributes to total industry profits. For the firm pictured, average cost at output x is c per dozen light bulbs. Since the bulbs are sold at p per dozen, the profit contributed by the one firm is cp times x. If the other firms were included in the diagram, their profits could be computed in the same way.

Cartels as formal private organizations are generally illegal in the United States. The core of federal antimonopoly legislation is the Sherman Act of 1890 and its amendments which forbid price-fixing arrangements by firms that operate in interstate commerce. Most states have similar legislation for firms operating within their boundaries. But governments are somewhat ambivalent toward collusion and in a number of instances they permit and even promote cartel-like associations. Government antimonopoly policy and regulation of business are the subject matter of Chapter 13.

Price Leadership

Since most formal collusive price-fixing arrangements are illegal in the United States, firms in some oligopolistic industries use other means of acting jointly. A favorite device is *price leadership*, with one firm setting product price and the others following its lead. The arrangement is usually an informal one and is not illegal as such as long as no explicit collusion can be proved.

The price leader is typically one of the larger firms in the industry.[4] As such it is likely to be more active in market research and to have a greater knowledge of the industry and its potentialities than its smaller competitors. It may also be in a lower cost position because of economies of scale. The smaller firms frequently find the arrangement advantageous. They are spared the costs of extensive marketing research and, equally important, they are sheltered from the effects of competition among one another—competition which would surely make their profits smaller and which might very well lead to price wars.

---

[4] U.S. Steel has been a price leader in the steel industry since World War II. See Leonard W. Weiss, *Economics and American Industry* (New York: John Wiley & Sons, Inc., 1962). Chap. 7 and esp. pp. 293–295.

The Incentive for Independent Action

Although the firms of an oligopolistic industry feel the incentives of monopoly gains and reduction of uncertainty in pricing pulling them toward some kind of collusive activity, another incentive pulls them in the other direction toward independent action by the single firm. A single firm of the industry, if it can break away from the others, might find that it can increase its profits by doing so, *provided the other firms continue to operate collusively and ignore what the one firm is doing.* This incentive is illustrated in Figure 11–3.

Suppose initially that we have a cartel operating in the automobile tire industry. Following the principles advanced above, the central agency of the cartel maximizes industry profits by establishing a market output of X tires, selling them at price p per tire. The quota of the one firm would be x, the quantity at which its marginal cost is equal to industry marginal revenue. The *dd* and *mr* curves for the firm are irrelevant at this point and should be ignored for the moment. Individual firm profits are cp times x.

Now suppose that the one firm contemplates breaking away from the others. By charging a slightly lower price for tires it can expand its sales considerably *if no other firm does the same thing and if the cartel price is held at p.* Many consumers will switch from the other sellers to the price-cutting firm because of the latter's lower price; the price-cutting firm thus takes over a part of the other firms' markets. The resulting demand curve facing the firm, represented by *dd*, will be highly elastic, more elastic than the market demand curve for the product at price p. (Why is this the

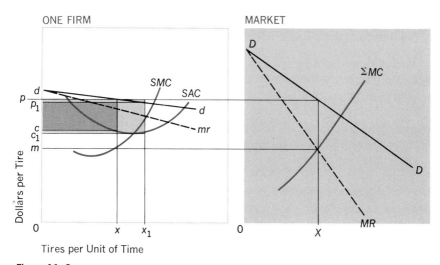

Figure 11–3
The incentive for independent action: oligopoly.

case?) Because the elasticity of demand for the sales of the one firm is greater than that of the market demand curve, marginal revenue for the one firm at price p is greater than is marginal revenue for the industry as a whole.[5] Consequently, for the firm acting independently, marginal revenue at output level x is greater than its marginal cost. Additions to its output will add more to total receipts than to total costs and will therefore increase profits. Under these circumstances the firm would maximize its profits by producing an output of x_1, selling it at a price of p_1. Profits would be c_1p_1 times x_1, greater than they would have been had the firm stayed in the cartel.

If all firms producing tires cut their prices simultaneously, the gains just mentioned would not be available to any of them. Each firm tends to hold only its own share of the market. It does not cut into the markets of others because they have also reduced their prices. In this case the firm does not face a demand curve more elastic than that for the market as a whole and has nothing to gain from price reductions. In fact, all firms will find their profits reduced by simultaneous price-cutting, output-increasing activities, since industry profits are maximum at price p and output level X.

The constant temptation to individual firms to act independently makes collusive arrangements hard to maintain over time. Successful collusion usually requires policing efforts by the colluding firms to prevent individual firms from breaking away from the group. Frequently they turn to the government to do their policing for them, securing the passage of such legislation as resale price maintenance, minimum barber prices, and minimum dry cleaning prices to make price cutting illegal.

The Results of Independent Action

It should not be inferred from the preceding discussion that collusion is characteristic of most oligopolistic market behavior. It may or it may not be. There is not enough evidence available to determine conclusively the extent of collusive activity or the extent to which oligopolistic firms make independent price and/or output decisions. Certainly there must be a large number of oligopolistic firms that make their own market decisions.

An oligopolistic firm that makes its own market strategy decisions estimate as best it can how rivals will react to its market behavior and what effects those reactions will have on its own actions. In effect, the firm attempts to determine the demand curve that it faces—or at least the neighborhood in which it lies. Once the firm has done this, short-run

[5] The more elastic the demand curve at each of different alternative prices, the closer to the demand curve the marginal revenue curve will be. Consider the perfectly elastic demand curve facing and purely competitive seller. Where does the marginal revenue curve lie?

pricing and output to maximize profits is a matter of determining the output at which marginal cost and marginal revenue are equal. The principle is as applicable here as it is in any other market situation.

Independent action by the sellers in an industry sometimes results in *price wars* in which firms undercut each other as they vie for market shares or as they seek to unload what they consider to be excess inventories. One seller lowers his price in order to attract more customers and to increase his sales. But this takes sales away from rival sellers. One or more of the latter may undercut the first firm in order to regain sales volume and to teach the original price cutter a lesson. Undercutting may spread rapidly through the market—to the delight of customers and to the distress of sellers. Among the best-known examples of price wars are those occurring in the retail gasoline trade.

Price wars are more frequently potentialities rather than realities, but in the absence of collusive activity the possibility that they may occur is difficult to ignore. For this reason oligopolists may be rather slow to make downward price changes in response to decreases in demand or to reductions in costs. The extent to which price decreases can be postponed or avoided when demand has fallen depends, in part at least, on how easy it is to reduce the quantities brought to market. Where a few large firms dominate a selling market decreases in demand are more easily (and safely) met by reductions in quantity produced and sold. Where the number of firms is larger, however, and each believes that its own output is not of great significance in the market as a whole, price cutting rather than quantity reductions may well be the response on the part of sellers to a decrease in demand or a reduction in costs.

Price increases in response to increased demand or increased costs are much less dangerous for an individual oligopolist than are the price decreases discussed above, since a price increase by one firm does no damage to a rival firm. Nevertheless, an oligopolist that raises the price of his product will find that his customers tend to give their business to rival firms that do not raise their prices. In addition, as we have witnessed in recent years, oligopolistic firms that raise prices may find themselves subjected to strong governmental pressure to avoid such action.

Long-Run Pricing and Output

The long run for oligopolistic sellers is defined in the same way as for sellers in other types of markets. It is a planning period long enough for the firm to execute any changes it desires in its scale of plant and also long enough for new firms to enter the industry, if they are permitted to do so.

Scale of Plant Adjustments

What questions confront the firm in the long run from the point of view of production? Assuming that the firm has made its conjectures about how rival firms will react to its output and pricing policies and that it has decided on its long-run rate of output, it would be expected to produce that output at the least possible cost. This means that it chooses from among the scales of plant available to it the one that forms that small part of its long-run average cost curve at the selected output level. In Figure 11–4, for example, if the firm's long-run output were to be x_0 units per month, scale of plant SAC_0 would produce it at the least cost per unit. If the output were to be x_1, then SAC_1 would be the appropriate scale of plant. But if it were to be x_2, the firm should build and use scale of plant SAC_2.

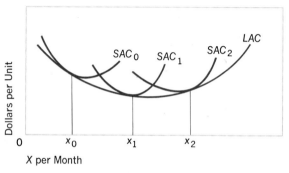

Figure 11–4
Long-run scale of plant adjustments: oligopoly.

How the long-run output is determined is an important and interesting question. It is also one that an oligopolist finds difficult to answer with any degree of precision. If the firm can make a reasonably good estimate of its demand curve, it can maximize profits at the output at which its estimated marginal revenue. If it cannot estimate the position and shape of its demand curve, the long-run output may be one that is simply at a "satisfactory" level. If the firm belongs to a cartel or some other kind of colluding group, the output may be determined for it by the group.

Entry into the Industry

If profits can be made in an oligopolistic industry, new firms will have an inducement to enter. Consider the color television field in 1964 and 1965. Very few firms had access to the patents and the know-how for making receivers. But their processes were good enough and a sufficient number of programs were being broadcast in color to make them extremely profitable. By the end of 1966 a number of additional firms had entered the field, substantially increasing the productive capacity and the output of the industry.

Entry into some oligopolistic industries may be completely open; for others it may be completely blocked; and for still others it may be somewhere between the two extremes. If there were no barriers to entry and profits were being made, new firms would be attracted in. Individual firms and groups of firms already in the industry would find the demand curves they face shifting to the left or downward as the new firms encroached upon their shares of the market. Cost curves would remain constant or shift upward or downward, depending upon whether the industry were one of constant, increasing, or decreasing costs. Entry would continue until profit possibilities were squeezed out. Long-run profits are not possible where there are no barriers to the entry of new firms.

Long-run profits become a possibility when entry into an industry is partially or completely blocked. If entry is completely blocked the "in" group of firms may be in a position similar to that of a pure monopolist. This situation sometimes results from collusion among the "in" group to control particular patents, to control sources of raw materials, to freeze out potential entrants, and so on. Complete control over entry is difficult to maintain over time, however. Patents expire or similar products and processes are developed and new or substitute sources of raw materials are found. Innumerable, and in many cases ingenious, ways are found to enter potentially profitable fields of production.

Nonprice Competition

Individual firms in an oligopolistic industry are rivalrous and, in most cases, each firm seeks a larger share of the market for its output than it currently enjoys.[6] An obvious way to attempt to gain a larger market share is to cut the product price below that charged by other firms. This is a dangerous tactic, however, for it often starts a price war. Other firms can meet price cuts immediately and what was originally a satisfactory situation for most firms may become a very unsatisfactory one.

What alternatives are open to the firm to increase its market share? It can launch an advertising campaign or it can change the design or quality of its product. Through these methods, either singly or together, the firm may succeed in enlarging its share of the market. A successful

[6] Exceptions occur in specific industries at different points in time. There is some question as to whether General Motors at the present time seeks a larger share of the automobile market. If it were able to increase its share substantially above its current share it might run the risk of antitrust action being taken against it.

advertising campaign may be hard to duplicate, and the same may be true of an innovation in product quality or design, particularly if it is patented. A firm that increases its profits by these means may find that it can hold its advantage for some time.

Advertising

When an individual firm advertises it expects that the demand curve that it faces will shift to the right. It hopes also that it will make the demand curve less elastic by convincing consumers that there is a gap between the desirability of its brand and that produced by competitors. If the advertising campaign is successful, the firm will be able to increase its output, it price, and its profits. (But what is likely to happen to the other firms in the industry or even to other firms in the economy as consumers shift more of their purchasing power toward the advertised brand?)

How much should an oligopolist spend on advertising? The economic criteria are the familiar ones. Advertising is expected to generate additional revenue, and the change in revenue per dollar change in advertising is the *marginal revenue* from advertising. Similarly, each one dollar change in advertising outlay is a one dollar change in cost; that is, the marginal cost of a dollar's worth of advertising is one dollar and is constant for all levels of outlay. It pays to expand advertising outlays as long as the marginal revenue from it exceeds its marginal cost. But this is easier said than done. It is very difficult to determine in advance what the public reaction to and, consequently, the marginal revenue from, advertising will be.

A firm does not always expect that advertising will *expand* its particular share of the market, since frequently it must advertise merely to *hold* its market share. Suppose, for example, that the total market for cigarettes can be increased very little by the advertising of the different tobacco companies. Does this mean that advertising on the part of a single firm should cease? Any company that stops sponsoring television shows and running ads in the various news media will likely *lose* some of its market share. All sellers are forced to advertise because no one can quit with impunity. This situation is good for advertising agencies but costly to the general public, since product prices must be higher than they would otherwise be in order to cover the advertising expense. Advertising of this kind that increases the costs of all firms without increasing the market share of any and that does not expand the total market for the product[7] is called *competitive advertising*.

---

[7] And even if it does, the expansion may very well be at the expense of some other producing sector of the economy.

Not all of the resources used in competitive advertising are lost to the economy as a whole. Whether or not the "art work" of billboards contributes to consumer well-being is questionable. However, news media are heavily subsidized by advertising and as consumers we enjoy "free" radio and television programs. Actually, consumers as a group pay the full costs of all these benefits in the form of higher prices for the advertised goods, yet the functions of determining the kinds and quantities of newspapers, magazines, and radio and television shows that will be produced is taken away from consumers and placed in the hands of the advertisers. In addition, the consumers who pay for particular programs through their purchases of the advertised products may not be the ones who listen to or watch them. Thus the "free" goods and services furnished the consumer in this way are not "free" at all. The system is simply an inefficient way of choosing what entertainment and how much entertainment the economy's resources will be used to provide.

The advertising picture is not completely black, however. Some advertising is of an informative nature, letting consumers know what products are available, what their qualities are, and where they can be obtained. Advertising of this kind can help consumers make intelligent choices among the goods available to them. In any case, be it good, bad, or indifferent, there is much economic activity generated by, and dependent upon, the advertising outlays of oligopolists.

Product Design and Quality

Changes in product design are well illustrated by the annual model changes in automobiles, television receivers, and a host of other products. Such changes may or may not be accompanied by changes in the quality of the product. If from one year to the next only the design of the grill and the placement of chrome strips are changed, the quality of the automobile may very well be unaffected. On the other hand, the introduction of the self-starter and of individual front wheel suspension undoubtedly represented improvements in quality as well as changes in design.

The firm that implements changes in the design and quality of its product expects to increase the size of the market that it serves; that is, to shift the demand curve facing it to the right. The firm that accomplishes this objective does so at the expense of other firms in the industry and/or of other firms in the economy. Additional expenditures by consumers on the product in question represent a diversion of purchasing power from the products sold by others. These changes are not effected without cost, although changes in design may be relatively inexpensive to make. From the firm's point of view whenever such changes add more to total receipts than to total costs, or whenever marginal revenue as a result of the changes is greater than the marginal cost of making them, profits will be increased.

It is difficult to assess with accuracy the impact of design and quality changes on the level of consumer want satisfaction over time. Few people would question that over time, in the aggregate, such changes have made tremendous contributions to consumer well-being. Technological progress consists of making alterations in the design and quality of the product together with introducing new or modified production processes and new goods and services. But what are the prime movers of invention and innovation? Certainly a large incentive is the prospects of obtaining a profit advantage over rival firms; yet this is not the whole story. Such factors as the quest for knowledge, creativity, and even accident play important roles too, and how does one determine how much progress is attributable to each?

Whether or not design changes alone contribute to consumer well-being is often questionable. A design change can, of course, make a product more appealing esthetically, and the importance of this for consumer satisfaction should not be overlooked. However, where the introduction of a new model serves only to make the old model obsolete and to bring about a switch in demand from the old style to the new, there may be no net gain in consumer satisfaction levels.

MONOPOLISTIC COMPETITION

There is not much to distinguish *monopolistic competition* as the term is now used from pure competition.[8] It refers to a market situation in which there are many sellers of a product, and, although all sell the same general type of product, that of each seller is in some way differentiated from that of the others. The basic distinction between monopolistic competition and pure competition is that in the former the products of the various sellers in an industry are differentiated, while in the latter they are homogeneous.

The retail and service industries in medium-sized and large cities probably offer the best examples of monopolistic competition. In these areas there are many grocery stores selling many brands of each of a wide variety of products. Each store has its group of steady customers who

---

[8] Monopolistic competition was introduced into the discipline of economics in Edward H. Chamberlin, *The Theory of Monopolistic Competition*, (Cambridge, Mass.: Harvard University Press, 1933). The term as used by Chamberlin included oligopoly as well as what is here called monopolistic competition. The case of few sellers was later put into a separate category called oligopoly, while the case of many sellers selling differentiated products retained the designation monopolistic competition.

like its convenience, its special kinds of service, its credit arrangements, or other features. Each one also has a fringe group of customers just on the verge of trading elsewhere. Because of the number of stores in the city, however, most are not affected if one store goes out of business or if a new store is established. The same general situation is true of restaurants and bars, dry cleaners and laundries, medical service establishments, and others.

To illustrate the slight differences and the great similarities between monopolistic competition and pure competition we shall look first at demand, then at short-run pricing and output, and finally at long-run pricing and output in markets characterized by monopolistic competition.

Demand

Market Demand

Market demand curves for a firm characterized by monopolistic competition, like those for differentiated oligopoly, cannot be drawn neatly and precisely. Where products of different sellers belong generically to the same industry but are differentiated, common units in which to measure quantities along the quantity axis may not exist. What kinds of quantity units can we use to combine fluid milk from some sellers and powdered milk from others on the same quantity axis? A further complication is that firms selling in the same market may be charging different prices for units of product that are very similar, for example, aspirin. All is not lost, however, if we are willing to think of market demand in a somewhat less precise way than we have thus far. We can think of a cluster of prices existing at any given time and a corresponding cluster of product quantities at those prices. Certainly we would expect that the quantities demanded would vary inversely with the prices. Graphic precision is lost, but the concept of market demand is still available for us to use.

The Demand Curve Facing the Firm

How does the demand curve facing a single firm in monopolistic competition look? A convenient starting point is the demand curve facing a purely competitive firm. Since the primary difference between the two types of markets is product differentiation, our main task is to examine the effects of this factor. Toward this end suppose we start in Figure 11–5 with dd, a hypothetical demand curve facing a purely competitive firm. Now consider the impact of product differentiation on it.

Where product differentiation occurs, different consumers tend to become attached to or develop preferences for the kind or brand of product

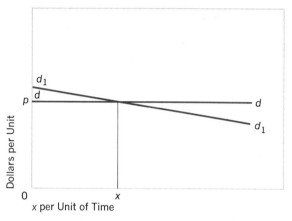

Figure 11-5
Demand curve facing the firm: monopolistic competition.

sold by particular sellers. Some consumers have a stronger preference than others for a particular seller's product or service. Still, in an industry of monopolistic competition, the products sold by the different sellers are good substitutes for one another—and there are many of these—and at any given time any one seller will have fringe customers just on the verge of turning to other sellers. Small relative price changes will tip the scales.

How does this affect the demand curve dd in Figure 11-5? Suppose a firm is selling quantity x at price p and that product differentiation exists between what is sold by this firm and what is sold by other firms in the industry. If the price is increased slightly, fringe customers find the products sold by other firms in the industry more attractive because of their now relatively lower prices. They desert the firm and sales fall off rapidly. Some of the more loyal customers hang on, but with so many good substitutes available it will not take a very large relative price rise for the firm to price itself completely out of the market. If the firm decreases rather than increases its price, it will pick up fringe customers of many other sellers and its sales will expand rapidly. The price decrease necessary to attract all the customers it can handle will not be large. Product differentiation, with its different degrees of consumer loyalties to individual sellers, tips the demand curve from the horizontal dd of Figure 11-5 to the downward-sloping but highly elastic d_1d_1. What factor is at work that makes d_1d_1 highly elastic?

Short-Run Pricing and Output

The analysis of short-run pricing and output of the products sold by individual firms in an industry of monopolistic competition requires the use of no new principles at all. Since the firm faces a downward-sloping demand curve—*dd* in Figure 11–6—the marginal revenue curve, *mr*, will be below *dd* rather than coinciding with it. The firm's cost curves are of the same type as those we have discussed previously. If *SAC* and *SMC* are the short-run average and marginal cost curves, respectively, the firm maximizes profits at output level *x*, where *SMC* is equal to *mr*. Average costs at that output are *c*, profits per unit of product are *cp*, and total profits per unit of time are *cp* times *x*.

For an industry characterized by monopolistic competition the short-run productive capacity, like that of the other types of markets, is fixed. Individual firms do not have time to change their scales of plant. Neither is there time for new firms to enter or for existing firms to leave the industry. Individual-firm outputs, as well as that of the industry, can be changed, of course, by utilizing the existing plant capacity to a greater or lesser degree.

Product prices will not be the same for all sellers in the industry because of product differentiation. But price differentials are not likely to be great. The single price of the purely competitive market is replaced with a cluster of prices for the differentiated items of the monopolistically competitive industry. The small price differentials reflect differences in consumer evaluations of what the different sellers of the industry place on the market.

Long-Run Pricing and Output

The long-run adjustment mechanisms are basically the same in monopolistic competition as they are in pure competition. The individual

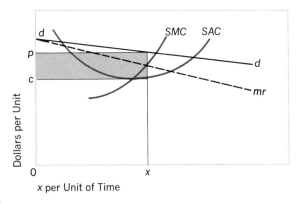

Figure 11–6
Short-run price and output: monopolistic competition.

firm seeks the scale of plant that will minimize its costs at its estimated long-run profit-maximizing output. If profits occur in an industry, new firms have an incentive to enter, and if losses are incurred firms are pressured into leaving.

Scale of Plant Adjustments

In Figure 11–7 if a single firm is confronted with demand curve *dd* and marginal revenue curve *mr* for its product, and if its long-run average and marginal cost curves are *LAC* and *LMC*, respectively, what should be its scale of plant? Maximum profits are made at output level *x*, where *LMC* is equal to *mr*. The appropriate scale of plant for producing output *x* is *SAC*, which forms the miniscule part of the *LAC* curve for that output level. The selling price is *p* and profits are *cp* times *x*.

Entry or Exit of Firms

The entry of new firms or the exit of existing firms in response to profit or loss incentives is not usually difficult in an industry of monopolistic competition in the long run. In a situation like that of Figure 11–7, profits can be made at any output level at which *dd* lies above *LAC*—although they are maximum at *x*. At this level new firms would enter as investors seek higher than average returns on what they invest.

The entry of new firms puts pressure on profits. The productive capacity and the total output of the industry are expanding; consequently, the demand curves facing the individual firms are shifting downward or to the left as the market share of each is reduced. The cost curves, too,

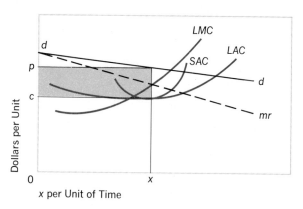

Figure 11–7
Incentives for entry: monopolistic competition.

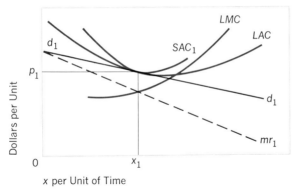

Figure 11–8
Long-run equilibrium: monopolistic competition.

may be shifting as new firms enter, the nature of the shifts depending upon whether the industry is one of increasing, constant, or decreasing costs.[9] If the firms of the industry ever reach a position like that of Figure 11–8, long-run equilibrium for the industry will exist. Note that the LAC curve nowhere lies below the d_1d_1 curve, but at output level x_1 the two curves are tangent. At this output level and at price p_1 all costs of production are covered but no profits are made. At any other output losses would be incurred.[10]

The entry of new firms will surely make further scale of plant adjustments necessary for the individual firm. Suppose a representative firm of the industry is initially using such a scale of plant as SAC in Figure 11–7 and is making profits. The entry of new firms causes the demand curve facing the firm and the marginal revenue curve to shift to the left. This provides the firm with an inducement to reduce its long-run output and its scale of plant until, in the long-run equilibrium situation of Figure 11–8, the scale of plant is reduced to SAC_1.

Again there is no reason to expect that all firms in the industry will charge identical prices. Product differentiation almost provides assurance that they will not.[11] Differences in what consumers think about comparative qualities of the products or services sold by the different firms will be reflected in price differentials.

---

[9] See pp. 155–160.

[10] At output x_1, long-run marginal cost and marginal revenue are equal. Why is this so? The tangency of LAC and d_1d_1 at output x_1 means that they coincide or are the same curve at that output. Since both are average curves, their corresponding marginal curves must be equal at that output level.

[11] In some cases, notably barbering and dry cleaning in some states, identical prices are required by law. But this is not a free market phenomenon.

SUMMARY

This chapter examines the selling market situations lying between the limiting cases of pure competition and pure monopoly. These are markets of oligopoly and of monopolistic competition. An oligopolistic industry is one in which there are few enough sellers of a product or service that the behavior of one firm affects what the others are able to do. If the product units sold by the different sellers are homogeneous, we call the situation pure oligopoly. But if consumers think that each seller in the industry sells a product that is different from those sold by every other seller, we have what is called differentiated oligopoly. An industry of monopolistic competition is one in which there are many sellers who sell differentiated products.

The analysis of oligopolistic pricing and output tends to be imprecise because it is frequently difficult to locate accurately the demand curve facing any one firm. This situation, in turn, stems from the interdependence of the sellers in the industry: what one seller does affects what others are able to do and their reactions then affect the first firm. In different oligopolistic industries there will be differing degrees of uncertainty for any one firm with respect to how this interdependence will affect it.

Oligopolists in an industry are subjected to two opposing sets of incentives. First, they have an incentive to collude or to act in concert to reduce uncertainties stemming from interdependence and to reap monopoly gains from their selling market. Second, any one firm has an incentive to break away from a collusive arrangement provided other firms in the industry do not do so and, further, do not retaliate. The most rigorous form of collusion is that of a cartel arrangement, in which the firms of the industry surrender certain managerial functions, particularly pricing and output decisions, to a central cartel board acting for the industry. The illegality of many cartel arrangements induces firms to resort to other, lesser means of collusion such as price leadership, in which a dominant or a low-cost firm establishes a price for the product, initiates changes, and is followed by the other firms in the industry.

In many oligopolistic industries firms pursue independent pricing and output policies. In some cases they expect to do better alone than they could in concert. In others a pattern of concerted action has never been initiated or built up. In still other industries fear of government antimonopoly action discourages collusion. Independent action may touch off price wars or rivalrous price undercutting among the firms of an industry.

Short-run pricing and output analysis for oligopolistic industries centers around profit-maximizing objectives. Any firm, in order to maximize profits, attempts to produce the output at which its short-run marginal cost is equal to marginal revenue—if it can determine where the demand curve it faces and its marginal revenue curve lie.

In the long run the productive capacity of an oligopolistic industry can be altered by scale of plant adjustments of individual firms and by the entry or exit of firms. Once a firm has determined what its long-run output is to be, it minimizes costs by constructing and using that scale of plant for which the SAC curve is tangent to the LAC curve at that output. Profits or losses provide the incentives for entry or exit of firms.

Entry conditions into oligopolistic industries may vary from completely open to completely closed. Under open-entry conditions new firms will be attracted in by profits until the output levels are sufficiently increased and prices are sufficiently reduced to eliminate the profits. Under closed or partially blocked entry conditions long-run profits are a possibility.

The possibility that price changes to gain a greater share of the market will be followed by others, together with the persistent possibility of touching off price wars, induce oligopolists to engage in nonprice competition, or rivalry on a basis other than price. Nonprice competition takes the forms of (1) advertising and/or (2) changes in product design and/or quality. To maximize profits a firm should make such changes to the point at which the marginal revenue resulting from them is equal to the marginal cost of implementing them. Some advertising is informative and assists consumers in making choices among alternative spending possibilities. Competitive advertising, on the other hand, or the kind that firms must engage in to hold their respective places in the market, adds unnecessarily to costs of production. Some design and quality changes are of dubious value to consumers; but others are the essence of technological progress.

Monopolistic competition differs from pure competition in a minor way: it is a many-seller case with product differentiation. Product differentiation and some attachment of consumers to specific sellers' products or services make the demand curve facing the firm slope downward to the right to some small extent. In the short run a monopolistically competitive firm maximizes profits at the output at which its marginal costs equal its marginal revenue. In the long run, if profits are made, new firms may enter until the profits are squeezed out.

EXERCISES AND QUESTIONS FOR DISCUSSION

1. List a few of the advertisements you have heard and/or seen lately. Under what type of market structure would you classify each of the firms producing the advertised products? Why do you think each was advertising?
2. Why is rivalry among firms peculiar to oligopoly? What effects has this fact had on oligopolistic pricing and output policies?

3. Cite as many examples as you can of price leadership. Why is one firm able to set prices? How would it determine what price to charge?
4. If a monopolistic competitor advertises, he may influence fringe buyers and increase the demand for his product. However, with an increase in demand price will rise and he may lose more customers than he gained by advertising. Evaluate this statement.
5. Could long-run profits ever exist in a market of monopolistic competition? Why or why not?
6. Under what circumstances is advertising beneficial to the consumer? When is it not?

SELECTED READINGS

Bain, J. S., *Industrial Organization.* New York: John Wiley and Sons, Inc., 1959, Chap. 7.

Brehm, C., "The Residential Construction Industry," and Hendey, J. B., "The Bituminous Coal Industry," *The Structure of American Industry,* 3d ed., Walter Adams, ed. New York: Crowell-Collier, Macmillan, Inc., 1961.

Chamberlin, E. H., *The Theory of Monopolistic Competition,* 8th ed. Cambridge, Mass.: Harvard University Press, 1962, Chaps. 3, 4, and 5.

Colberg, M. R., D R. Forbush, and G. R. Whitaker, Jr., *Business Economics,* 3d ed. Homewood, Ill.: Richard D. Irwin, Inc., 1964, Chap. 6.

Nicholls, W. H., *Price Policies in the Cigarette Industry.* Nashville, Tenn.: Vanderbilt University Press, 1951, Part II.

Market Structures and the Operation of the Economic System

CHAPTER 12

Why classify selling markets as we have in the preceding three chapters? Elegant though it may be, the classification is of no particular value in and of itself. Rather, its merit lies in the fact that it can aid us in assessing how well the economy operates and in determining what government policy measures should be implemented to make it work better. Our goal in this chapter is to piece together the relation between market structure and economic performance.

How do we measure the performance of an economic system? What do we expect it to do for us? As we noted earlier, we look to our economic system to provide us with high and rising standards of living. Additionally we expect our economic system to help us achieve the following sub-goals (1) efficiency in production, so that our resources and our existing state of technology are used in ways that contribute a maximum value of goods and services to the economy; and (2) innovation and economic progress in the sense of continual development of new products and modifications of old ones to fulfill more accurately consumer desires, and in the sense of continual discovery of new resources, resource modifications, and new technologies to permit continual expansion of output; (3) responsiveness of the productive capacity of the economy to an ever-changing structure of consumer demand and cost conditions; and (4) the availability of a broad range of choices in the quality and style of specific products and services. What are the implications of the different market classifications with respect to the degree to which these goals are attained?

EFFICIENCY

The market classifications provide clues to the efficiency with which the firms comprising an industry operate. *Efficiency* refers to the value of output produced in relation to the value of resource inputs used to produce that output. The greater the value of output obtained per dollar of cost, the greater the efficiency of the productive process used. To put it the other way around, the smaller the cost per dollar's worth of product output, the more efficient the productive process used.

Efficiency Criteria

Some rough notions of the comparative efficiency of firms in the different market classifications can be obtained by examining their cost curves. For example, of the scales of plant available to the firm in the long run, which are most efficient? An optimum scale of plant is the logical choice, since the firm's short-run average cost curve lies at the lowest possible level—at the bottom of the long-run average cost curve. Further, of the possible output levels that can be produced with an optimum scale of plant, the optimum rate of output is produced more efficiently than the others, or at the lowest per unit cost for that scale of plant. A firm achieves maximum efficiency in production, then, when it uses an optimum scale of plant at the optimum rate of output.

We must ask ourselves, too, whether resources are more likely to be used wastefully in some selling markets than in others. For example, is there rivalry among firms that leads to wasteful advertising in some kinds of markets but not in others? Does rivalry lead to wasteful changes in product quality and design in some but not in others?

Cost Comparisons

Suppose we compare firms operating in the different market classifications on the basis of the scale of plant they would tend to build and operate in the long run. It should be emphasized that we can speak only of *tendencies*. We cannot compare with complete validity long-run equilibrium *positions* under pure competition, pure monopoly, oligopoly, and monopolistic competition because these are situations that are seldom if ever reached in the real world. Firms *tend* to move toward long-run equilibrium positions, but before they reach that point changes occur in demand or in costs, thus altering long-run equilibrium positions. They chase, but never catch, long-run equilibrium. These qualifications should be kept in mind as the comparisons are made.

The scale of plant of a pure monopolist will be of optimum size only by accident or chance. Three possibilities exist for such a firm, all illustrated in Figure 12–1, and which of the three we find in any given monopolized market depends upon the cost possibilities faced by the firm together with the size of the market (the position of the demand curve) for the product being sold. In Figure 12–1(a) the technology available to the monopolist is such that his cost curves lie well to the right as compared with demand for the product. His long-run profit-maximizing output is x_a sold at price p_a, and the scale of plant that will minimize cost for that output is SAC_a—a less than optimum scale of plant operated at less

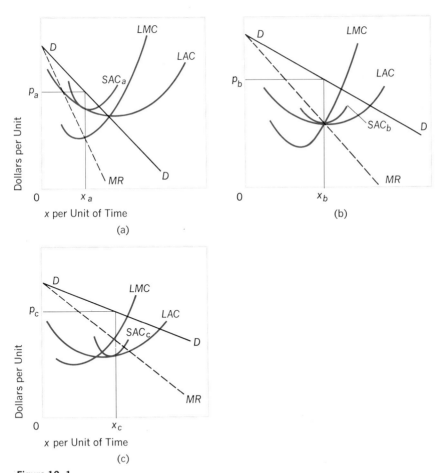

Figure 12–1
Alternative scales of plant for a monopolist in long-run equilibrium.

than the optimum rate of output. In Figure 12–1(b) the monopolist finds the conditions of cost and demand that he faces such that his profit-maximizing output is x_b sold at price p_b. Scale of plant SAC_b—the optimum scale of plant—is the appropriate one for him to use, and he will use it at its optimum rate of output. The monopolist will push toward a larger than optimum scale of plant operated at more than the optimum rate of output if the situation of Figure 12–1(c) prevails. Profits are maximized at output x_c sold at price p_c, and scale of plant SAC_c minimizes costs at that output.

In contrast, as a purely competitive industry moves toward long-run equilibrium, the individual firm is *forced* to move toward the use of an optimum scale of plant. Consider Figure 12–2. If the firm uses any scale of plant other than SAC, its average cost will exceed the price of the product and losses will occur. If the price of the product is high enough for some part of the (horizontal) demand curve facing the firm to lie above some part of the LAC curve, profits can be made. New firms are attracted into the industry until profits are squeezed out; that is, until the LAC curve for each firm is tangent to the dd curve faced by it. Since the demand curve facing the firm is horizontal, it can only be tangent to the LAC curve at the minimum point of the latter, or when the firm is using an optimum scale of plant at the optimum rate of output. Thus in the long run the purely competitive firm is forced toward an optimum scale of plant used at the optimum rate of output by the horizontal position of the demand curve that it faces and by the entry of new firms into the industry whenever profit possibilities exist.

Monopolistic competition is not much different from pure monopoly in this respect. The individual firm under full long-run equilibrium con-

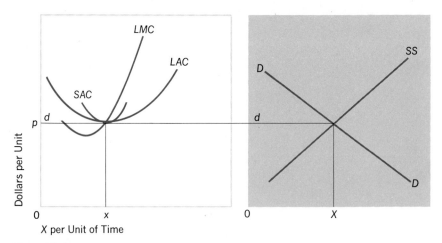

Figure 12–2
Scale of plant for a purely competitive firm in long-run equilibrium for the industry.

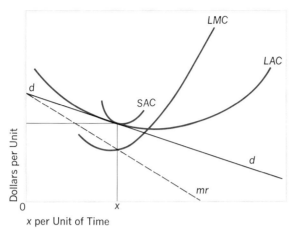

Figure 12–3
Scale of plant for a monopolistic competitor in long-run equilibrium for the industry.

ditions for the industry would be somewhat less efficient than a purely competitive firm under the same conditions. Where profits occur new firms enter until the demand curve faced by each firm is tangent to its long-run average cost curve. Since under monopolistic competition the demand curve facing the firm slopes slightly downward to the right, this tangency must occur to the *left* of the minimum point of the *LAC* curve, as Figure 12–3 demonstrates. Therefore, the firm is forced toward a less than optimum scale of plant operated at less than the optimum rate of output.[1] The more elastic the demand curve facing the firm, the less will be the deviation of the scale of plant used from that which is optimum. Since monopolistically competitive firms face highly elastic demand curves, and since full long-run equilibrium conditions are seldom achieved, the decrease in efficiency attributable to this type of market structure is not likely to be large.

With respect to the efficiency of its plant over the long run, the oligopolistic firm is closer to the purely monopolistic firm than to the competitive one. If entry into an oligopolistic industry is open, individual firms are forced toward a situation in which the demand curves they face are tangent to their long-run average cost curves. This situation leads toward a less than optimum scale of plant similar to that of monopolistic competition: the less elastic the demand curve, the greater will be the deviation from the optimum scale. If entry into the industry is blocked or obstructed, so that firms are not forced into a no-profit situation, the scale

[1] On this basis economists frequently argue that industries characterized by monopolistic competition will have excess productive capacity; that is, that individual firms are not induced to make full use of their plants.

of plant that firms tend to use may be optimum, less than optimum, or greater than optimum, depending upon the characteristics of the firms' cost curves and on the output they expect to produce over the long run. We would expect that whatever outputs they choose to produce in the long run, they will build and use those scales of plants that will minimize costs for those outputs.

Evaluation of Comparative Productive Efficiencies

The preceding discussion seems to imply that on grounds of productive efficiency pure competition and monopolistic competition are the superior types of selling markets, with oligopoly and pure monopoly bringing up the rear. Yet these surface manifestations are somewhat misleading; the more important implications of each of these market situations are more subtle.

In the private sector of the economy what conditions must be present for an industry to be one of pure competition? By definition there must be many firms producing a homogeneous product. This situation can exist only if the market for the product is large enough to support many firms *each operating an optimum scale of plant.* If the market for the product is not large enough to support many firms, each with an optimum scale of plant, then the first firm or firms to enlarge their plants to optimum size will have cost advantages over other firms. They will fill the market for the product at prices equal to or above their average costs, and either oligopoly or, in the most extreme case, monopoly must prevail.

When we consider how large the optimum scale of plant must be in many leading industries, it becomes apparent that pure and monopolistic competition cannot be the predominant types of selling markets. As extensive as the automobile market is, it cannot support a large number of firms each with an optimum scale of plant. In this industry modern technology and the requirements of product distribution and servicing make the optimum scale of plant for a firm such that pure or monopolistic competition is out of the question. An optimum scale of plant in the auto industry seems to be one on the order of that of General Motors or of Ford.[2]

Let us examine the problem from another angle. Suppose that the government were to break up the automobile industry into many firms. Each firm would likely be too small to take advantage of certain significant economies of scale, and each would probably have a scale of plant like *SAC* in Figure 12–4. The resulting higher cost levels—higher than those

---

[2] It is possible, of course, that the scales of plant of General Motors or Ford are larger than optimum. Still, the fragmentary evidence available indicates that the average costs of these firms lie at lower levels than those of Chrysler or American Motors.

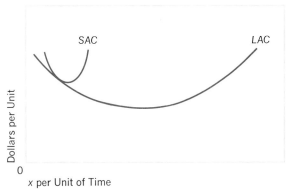

Figure 12–4
Possible effects on costs of breaking up a large firm.

that would prevail with fewer firms, each with a larger scale of plant—could well lead to higher prices and lower outputs than those possible in the current oligopolistic market structure.

The market structure postulated above is frequently thought to be one of enforced pure or monopolistic competition. Yet this is erroneous thinking, since in this case we would have a situation of *pseudo* pure or monopolistic competition. The scale of plant of each of the many firms in an industry must be of almost optimum size if the market is to be one of *real* pure or monopolistic competition.

From the point of view of market realism there is no avoiding oligopolistic market structures in many segments of the economy and monopoly in most of the public utility industries. But if entry into oligopolistic industries is kept open, the resulting scales of plant may not be significantly far from optimum, especially if there are enough firms in the industry and if there is sufficient absence of collusion for the demand curves facing individual firms to be highly elastic.[3]

Wastes from Nonprice Competition

Whenever resources are employed in such a way as to contribute nothing to consumer well-being or to contribute less than they would in alternative uses, the economic system is operating at a lower level of efficiency than it is possible to achieve. What do we learn from theories of

---

[3] It would be worthwhile to diagram this case. Show an oligopolistic firm with a highly elastic demand curve making economic profits. Now let new firms enter until the profits disappear; that is, the demand curve shifts to the left (or downward) until it is tangent to the firm's *LAC* curve. Is the scale of plant at the point of tangency significantly far from an optimum scale?

market structure about the possibilities of waste in the use of resources? Consider the likelihood of competitive or rivalrous advertising and/or of changes in product design and quality in the different kinds of selling markets.

Waste of this kind is most likely to occur under differentiated oligopoly. At first glance it appears that monopolistic competition, too, could be responsible for the same thing, the culprit here being product differentiation. However, there is an important difference between differentiated oligopoly and monopolistic competition; namely, the numbers of sellers in the industry. In monopolistic competition the fact that there are many sellers precludes rivalrous nonprice competition among the firms, since no single firm believes that the activities of any other firm will affect it nor that its activities will affect others. Only in industries of *few* firms will the kind of rivalry exist that may lead to significant wasteful nonprice competition.

We must at this point sound a warning whistle. Nonprice competition is a major avenue for innovation and economic progress. Therefore, how can we minimize its wastes while at the same time we take advantage of its merits?

INNOVATION

Nature of Innovation

The term "innovation" covers at least five basic kinds of contributions to economic progress. First, it means the discovery and the development of new kinds of resources. Second, it refers to modifications of existing resources. Third, and closely related to the first two, the development of new technologies is a type of innovating activity. All three of these forms of innovation must be cost reducing in nature if they are to contribute to economic progress or to consumer well-being. The other two kinds of innovation are, fourth, modifications of existing products and, fifth, the development of new products. Again for the latter two to represent economic progress they must enable the resources used in carrying them on to satisfy wants more fully than if the innovations had not been made.

What are the circumstances under which innovations are most likely to occur? The well-known U.S. economist J. M. Clark distinguishes among (1) underlying conditions, (2) enabling conditions, and (3) incentives or inducements to innovate.[4] *Underlying conditions* conducive to innovation

---

[4] John M. Clark, *Competition as a Dynamic Process* (Washington, D.C.: The Brookings Institution, 1961), pp. 195–211.

are those in which people are not tradition or culture bound but are willing to depart from the usual ways of doing things; that is, they are cultural conditions that foster a spirit of innovation. *Enabling conditions* refer to the institutional arrangements of the society within which innovation takes place. Are firms of sufficient size financially to be able to put substantial funds into research? Are there agencies apart from private firms that either accomplish or facilitate research? *Incentives* or *inducements* are the financial rewards for innovation—that is, whether innovating firms can expect innovating activity to be profitable.

Impact of Market Structures on Innovation

So far research has yielded no clear-cut answers concerning the relation between market structure and the amount of innovating activity that is carried on in a free enterprise economy. An examination of the effects of different market structures on the conditions conducive to innovation may indicate why definitive answers have not been forthcoming.

Enterprises that operate in oligopolistic markets are usually thought to provide superior enabling conditions and superior incentives for innovation. It is argued that on the average such firms are larger than those in purely competitive and monopolistically competitive markets and, therefore, can afford to devote larger amounts of resources to research. It is pointed out further that oligopolistic rivalries spur individual firms to seek ways and means of reducing costs and of expanding their individual product markets. Under pure competition, and usually under monopolistic competition, it is argued that profits made in this manner are soon eroded away by the entrance of new firms, whereas in an oligopolistic industry the fact that new firms are blocked or impeded from entering makes it possible for a firm to enjoy the profits from its innovations for a longer period of time, the length of the period depending upon how strong the entry barriers are.

Many people believe that monopolies provide excellent enabling conditions for innovation. Size is the important ingredient here, and American Telephone and Telegraph Company is the prime example. On the other hand, monopolists are not subjected to the rivalry that exists in oligopolistic industries and may lack incentives to innovate; that is, they may not be forced to innovate to hold their market share or their profits. Further, many monopolies, public utilities in small and medium-sized towns, for example, are not gigantic enterprises at all but can be classified as small businesses.

Markets of pure and monopolistic competition are generally populated by small firms among whom there is no rivalry. There may be a spirit of freedom and initiative associated with these market structures—

although not necessarily greater than under monopoly and oligopoly—that provides the underlying conditions for innovation. But a problem of incentives may occur. Easy entry of new firms would be expected to erode away the profits resulting from innovating activity.

RESPONSIVENESS

The responsiveness of the productive capacity of an economy to changes in both consumer demand and cost conditions is, of course, a part of the general issue of economic efficiency. To be efficient over time an economy must have flexibility—it must be able to take in stride changes in consumer preferences as well as the discovery and development of new resources, new products, and new technology, for these are integral aspects of economic progress.

Profits and losses are the signals provided by the price mechanism to show that shifts in productive capacity from some goods and services to others are in order. Profits made by the firms in any one industry indicate that consumers place a higher value on what the resources can produce in that industry than on other products that the same resources could have been used to produce. The alternative or opportunity cost principle is the basis of this observation. The cost of producing any product is the value (to consumers) of the resources used in their best alternative uses. Similarly, where a product is produced at a loss, it is evident that consumers prefer alternative products which the resources could be used to produce.

It seems clear enough that monopoly provides serious obstructions to the responsiveness of the productive capacity of the economy to dynamic change. Contraction of productive capacity in the long run where losses are incurred is not really a problem: a monopolist who is incurring losses will go out of business as readily as a pure competitor. The problem lies in the amount of expansion of productive capacity that will occur in a monopolized industry when profits are made. The monopolist can be expected to expand his productive capacity, or his scale of plant, only to the extent necessary to maximize his profits. Further expansion of the industry's productive capacity through the entry of new firms seeking profits is ruled out. The monopolist has entry blocked.

What can we say about the responsiveness of productive capacity in oligopolistic markets? The answer depends on the conditions of entry into the industries and will differ from one oligopolistic industry to another. Where entry is relatively unrestricted, for example, in the case of filling stations in a small city, profits attract new firms and new capacity grows readily. Where entry is blocked or highly restricted, as in commercial air transport, profits may persist over a long period of time, indicating that consumers get less of the product than they would like to have relative to other goods and services that are produced.

Responsiveness would be expected to be optimum under conditions of pure and monopolistic competition. Any single firm in one of these markets tends to adjust its productive capacity to maximize its profits, as does a monopolist or an oligopolist. But where profits are made new firms are attracted in, further expanding productive capacity until profits disappear. Examples are provided in the retail grocery field, in the textile industries, and in the manufacture of men's and women's clothing. The larger part of the economy's output comes from oligopolistic industries. Modern technology precludes the existence of an economic system composed entirely of purely and monopolistically competitive industries. What then can we advocate in the way of economic policy to insure that the economy's productive capacity will respond readily to dynamic change?

We are not likely to achieve perfection. Yet in the absence of perfection there seem to be two possible avenues that policy-makers can follow in the interests of making productive capacity as responsive as market and technological circumstances will permit. The first is the establishment of price ceilings or maximum prices for the limited number of goods and services produced under conditions of monopoly or near-monopoly. Rate regulation in public utilities provides an example. This possibility is explored in some detail in the following chapter. The other is a systematic elimination of barriers to entry into oligopolistic and into some monopolized industries. As we noted earlier, many such barriers are government made and government enforced and as such can be reduced or eliminated.

Generally speaking, the economy of the United States seems to be surprisingly responsive to dynamic change, providing testimony that in the long run monopoly and strong oligopoly positions are difficult to maintain. Where profits are made and there are incentives for new firms to enter, enter they will in one way or another. If direct entry through the front door with a competing brand of the same product is closed, entry through the back door with a reasonably good substitute for the product is likely to take place.[5]

RANGE OF CHOICES AMONG QUALITIES AND STYLES

How do you react to a housing development where all of the dwelling units on a given block are identical in style and design? What would you

---

[5] See Joseph Schumpeter, *Capitalism, Socialism, and Democracy*, 3d ed. (New York: Harper & Row Publishers, Inc., 1950), Chap. VIII.

think of an economy that produced only Volkswagens in the automotive field? Would you prefer that neckties came in brown only and that all shirts have button-down collars?

Consumers are widely diverse in their tastes. Some prefer elaborate houses and yards while others are primarily interested in keeping out the cold and the rain and in minimizing their yard work. To some people an automobile is a prized possession and the more elegant it is the better it satisfies their desires. For other people an automobile simply represents a means of getting from here to there. Since people differ for a variety of reasons, an economy that produces many styles and qualities is likely to provide higher levels of consumer well-being than one that does not. For example, for one whose tastes run to Cadillacs, a dollar's worth of Opel will yield less satisfaction than will a dollar's worth of Cadillac. For one interested in economy of operation and ease of handling in traffic, the Opel may well yield greater satisfaction per dollar's worth than the Cadillac.

In providing a wide range of choices in product quality and style oligopolistic market structures receive a high score. As such firms jockey for market shares they make available a broad array of variations through product differentiation. In purchasing a washing machine one has a choice between agitator types and tumbler types, among several different wash and rinse cycles, and among a number of other features, the presence or absence of which makes the machine more or less expensive and even more or less useful. The consumer can choose the make and model that best suits his desires and his pocketbook. The automotive field offers an even better example. No longer are consumers given a choice of "any color they want as long as it is black," as Henry Ford was credited with saying about his famous Model T. There are literally hundreds of possible variations in automobiles among which consumers may choose. The Ford Mustang, for example, has well over one hundred different options available. Such examples abound in oligopolistic industries.

Monopolistic competition, like oligopoly, offers consumers a wide range of variations on any given product. It should be noted, however, that too much product differentiation may occur in some cases. Consumers may be so overwhelmed with the shapes, sizes, qualities, and packaging of clothing, detergents, floor waxes, cameras, and the like that comparison, evaluation, and choice is difficult. In some cases confusion stemming from this sort of thing may make consumers susceptible to fraud. There are, of course, certain guides available to aid in evaluating product design and quality, the best known being the testing services of Consumers Union and of Consumers' Research.

Monopolists may or may not provide a multiplicity of design and quality in their products since they are under no competitive or rivalrous pressures to do so. A monopolist may find that he can expand his market by producing several qualities—say good, better, and best—and/or several different designs, but he will expand his costs of production, too. If an expansion in the range of qualities offered promises to add more to total receipts than to total costs, we would expect it to be made.

Purely competitive market structures may limit the consumer in his range of choices, since the firms in a purely competitive industry produce homogeneous units of product. The production of several qualities, designs, or styles is not precluded, but if the market structure is to remain one of pure competition there must be enough sellers of *each* variant of the product so that no one seller can influence the total market for it. *Incentives* for product variation—expansion of the market faced by a single firm—are missing in purely competitive markets.

SUMMARY

We conclude in this chapter that no one of the different market structures is clearly *the* market structure in terms of economic performance. Purely competitive firms, and to a slightly lesser extent monopolistically competitive firms, tend in the long run to be pushed toward the most efficient scale of plant and rate of output, but technology, together with limited market size, will not permit either to exist in the industries that produce the bulk of the economy's output. Oligopolistic markets appear to be the type most conducive to innovation. Pure competition and monopolistic competition provide the greatest measure of responsiveness of productive capacity to dynamic changes. Oligopoly and monopolistic competition are the structures that make possible a wide variety of choice in product design, style, and quality.

Surely we are looking for too much if we expect all monopoly to be eliminated. In most public utility fields monopoly probably performs better than the other types of market situations. But we should always ask whether monopoly is necessary as we look at any given industry, for unregulated monopoly will generally restrict the outputs of the monopolized items below what the public desires as compared with those of nonmonopolized goods and services.

Apart from the public utility fields the key to satisfactory performance of the private sector of the economy seems to lie in minimizing the restrictive effects of monopoly and oligopoly. This means that in both types of markets every effort should be made to remove barriers to entry so that productive capacity can expand in response to profit signals. It also means that collusion among oligopolists—activity that makes them behave in a monopolistic fashion—must be minimized. In other words, to secure the best possible performance the economic system must be kept workably competitive. Policy measures aimed at achieving this objective are examined in the next chapter.

EXERCISES AND QUESTIONS FOR DISCUSSION

1. List a few of the manufacturing concerns in your area. In what type of market structure do they participate? What kinds of product differentiation do they have? To your knowledge, what innovations have they made?
2. Under what circumstances is advertising considered to be a wasteful form of nonprice competition?
3. Monopoly is always inferior to the other types of market structures. Evaluate this statement.
4. Discuss the effects you think yearly model changes have on costs and outputs in differentiated oligopolistic and monopolistically competitive industries.
5. Government grants for research in the United States have usually gone to large firms. How do you think this situation affects the profit incentive for innovation?

SELECTED READINGS

Clark, J. M., *Competition as a Dynamic Process.* Washington, D.C.: The Brookings Institution, 1961.

Loucks, William N., *Comparative Economic Systems,* 6th ed. New York: Harper & Row, Publishers, Inc., 1961, Chaps. 3 and 4.

Mansfield, Edwin, *Monopoly Power and Economic Performance.* New York: W. W. Norton and Company, Inc., 1964, Part I.

Monsen, R. Joseph, Jr., *Modern American Capitalism.* Boston: Houghton Mifflin Company, 1963, Chap. 3.

Schumpeter, Joseph, *Capitalism, Socialism, and Democracy.* New York: Harper & Brothers Publishers, 1947, Part II.

Weintraub, Sidney, *Intermediate Price Theory.* Philadelphia: Chilton Company, 1964, Chap. 13.

Government and Business   CHAPTER 13

The impact of different market structures on economic performance poses a set of perplexing problems for government policy-makers. Monopolized markets are characterized by output restriction below that at which marginal costs are equal to product prices and, where profits are made, blocked entry prevents the desired (by consumers) expansion of productive capacity and output. The same effects may be found in oligopolistic industries, particularly where collusion occurs and where entry is either blocked or made difficult. Yet the large scales of plant that are made possible by our present level of technology, together with the limited sizes of the markets served, make monopoly in some industries and oligopoly in others inevitable. In view of these and other points made in the preceding chapter, what constitutes appropriate public policy?

Government policy-making in this area has been somewhat piecemeal; consequently, it has been neither uniform nor completely consistent. As it has emerged over time, three general approaches to policy-making can be discerned. First, the inevitability of "natural" monopoly and oligopoly in public utility and in some transportation industries has been recognized and accepted. Thus in many instances policy-makers have sought to impose government regulation. Second, efforts have been made to restrain collusive and monopolizing activities in other industries through anti-monopoly legislation. Third, in still other industries legislators have indicated that they think the public interest is best served by reducing or restraining competition.

REGULATION OF "NATURAL" MONOPOLY

In some industries cost structure and market size simply make competition not feasible. Consider, for example, the sale of electrical services in a medium-sized city. Economies of scale in the generation and distribution of electricity are so marked that if several companies were in competition in the market, costs would be substantially higher than they are with a single firm. Further, in the distribution of electricity and gas, consider the construction chaos that would result if several competing companies laid lines and took them up again as customers switched from one seller to another. Or consider the inconvenience of having half a dozen competing telephone companies in a given community. For each customer to be able to communicate with every other customer, a half dozen phones would be necessary; or, alternatively, the companies would have to have some sort of operating agreement among themselves and thus any advantages of competition would be lost. The inevitability of monopoly in public utility cases has been generally accepted, and in many instances government, both state and local, has attempted to regulate their operations.

Other industries, in which only a limited number of firms can operate, have also been subjected to government regulation as public utilities. These include the railroads, the airlines, radio and television, and nationwide transmission of electricity and natural gas. These industries operate in interstate commerce and are therefore regulated by the federal government. In radio and television broadcasting individual firms are allocated exclusive frequencies on which they can broadcast in given geographic areas. The consequences of competing stations broadcasting on the same frequency in the same area are apparent—some would not be able to get through to consumers. Limits to the number of frequencies available, for example, 12 VHF channels, for assignment may therefore limit the number of firms that can operate in an area.[1] But apart from these assignments of exclusive frequencies some economists question whether regulation in the oligopolistic areas mentioned is either necessary or desirable.

Regulation may take several forms, all presumably designed to prevent natural monopolists or oligopolists from taking undue advantage of their position. Accounting and financial practices are frequently scrutinized by government agencies. Specifications are often set with respect to the quantity and quality of a product or service. But above all else, regulatory agencies have concerned themselves with price fixing.

The Theory of Price Regulation

If you were serving on a commission charged with regulating the price charged by a natural monopoly, how would you approach your task? The theory of monopoly and of oligopoly pricing should provide a framework

---

[1] The limiting influence of a given number of frequencies can easily be overestimated. No practical limits are imposed by these in low frequency commercial broadcasting or in UHF television broadcasting.

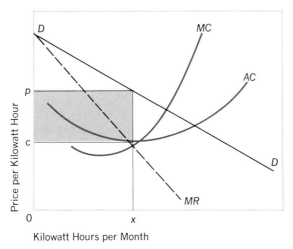

Figure 13-1
Profit maximization by a monopolist.

for action, but you would inevitably run into a number of serious practical problems. From the point of view of theory, two alternative approaches to the problem suggest themselves. These are (1) a marginal cost approach and (2) an average cost approach.

The simple individual firm diagram of Figure 13-1 is basic to both approaches. Suppose that the firm produces and sells electricity. The market demand curve for its service is DD and the corresponding marginal revenue curve is MR. Its average cost and marginal cost curves are AC and MC, respectively. In the absence of regulation the profit-maximizing output is x kilowatt hours per month and the price is p per kilowatt hour. Profits are $cp \cdot x$. The problem is to improve the firm's market performance. How can the firm be induced to lower its price and increase its output; that is, how can monopolistic restriction of output be mitigated in some degree?

Marginal Cost Pricing

Suppose that a commission is empowered to set a maximum limit on what the company can charge for electricity. Suppose further that it decides to set the limit at p_1 in Figure 13-2, the level at which the marginal cost curve of the firm intersects the market demand curve. The company is permitted to charge less than p_1 but not more. Carefully compare Figures 13-1 and 13-2.

The shape of the demand curve facing the firm is changed by the ceiling price. Since the firm cannot charge more than p_1, and since at that price consumers are willing to take up to x_1 kilowatt hours, the demand

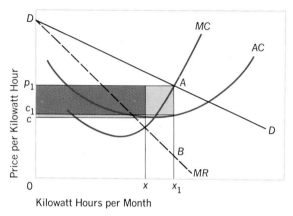

Figure 13–2
The effects of marginal-cost pricing.

curve facing the firm is horizontal at level p_1 for all sales levels between zero and x_1. Sales levels greater than x_1 can be obtained only if lower prices are charged—the demand curve facing the firm for these coincides with the market demand curve.

The marginal revenue curve, too, has a different shape. Since the firm faces the horizontal demand curve p_1A for output levels from zero to x_1, marginal revenue is equal to the product price and coincides with p_1A. Beyond output level x_1, where the demand curve facing the firm is also the market demand curve, the marginal revenue curve is the same as it was before the maximum price was established. At output x_1 it is discontinuous, jumping from point A down to point B.

The profit-maximizing output of the firm under the new set of circumstances will be greater than it was before. If output were held at the previous level, x, profit would be measured by the area $cp_1 \cdot x$. But at this output marginal revenue is greater than marginal cost, that is, additions to the output level increase total receipts more than they increase total costs, and an expansion of output will increase profits. The new profit-maximizing output is x_1 kilowatt hours per month. Profit at this output level is $c_1p_1 \cdot x_1$. Although profit still exists, it is smaller than it was before the maximum price was established, and the restrictive effects of the original monopoly position are partially offset.

Average Cost Pricing

Average costs of the power company may be easier to find than marginal costs. In Figure 13–3, suppose a maximum price of p_2 per kilowatt hour is established and is at the level at which the firm's average cost curve intersects the market demand curve. What will be the firm's response to the price ceiling?

If left to respond to the usual profit incentives, the price ceiling will induce the firm to increase its output to x_1 kilowatt hours. The firm faces a horizontal demand curve, p_2A_2, for output levels from zero to x_2 and a marginal revenue curve that coincides with it. Consequently, x_1, at which marginal cost is equal to the new marginal revenue, is the profit-maximizing output after the imposition of the ceiling price.

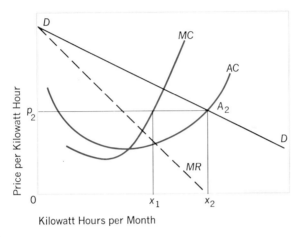

Figure 13–3
The effects of average-cost pricing.

But all is not quite as it should be. At output x_1 there is a shortage of x_1x_2. Consumers want more electricity at price p_2 than the company is inclined to produce. If a shortage is to be avoided, the commission will find it necessary to *require* that the firm produce as much as consumers demand. The firm can, of course, produce x_2 without incurring losses, but if it were permitted to reduce the output level below x_2 it could not only avoid losses but could make profits as well.

Price Regulation in Practice

Regulation of natural monopoly and oligopoly prices in the public utility field has not met with unqualified success for several reasons. One is that those who serve on regulatory commissions are often inadequately trained and usually lack the information necessary to carry out what they are supposed to do. Another is that the tasks given such commissions are ill defined conceptually.

Regulatory Commissions

Commissions empowered to regulate the rates of natural monopolies or oligopolies are appointed at the government level appropriate to the market the industry serves. Utilities with state and local markets are usually regulated by state public utility or corporation commissions, although in some instances local or city commissions may have jurisdiction. Those with regional, national, and international markets are regulated by federal commissions.

At the state and local level personnel appointed to or elected to the regulatory agency seldom have specialized training for the task at hand, and as in many government positions, salaries are not sufficient to attract the most capable people. Those on the commissions usually come from law or business and in some cases may have some background in the industries that are to be regulated. In their day-to-day operations commission personnel are continually subjected to the viewpoint of the utilities that they are to regulate, and it becomes difficult to maintain detached judgments on the issues coming before them. A major drawback to the effective operation of such commissions is that they seldom have access to detailed information in the businesses they regulate, or if such information is available to them they seldom have the staff necessary to analyze it. Members of federal regulatory commissions generally have been better qualified for the positions they fill than members of state commissions. Moreover, federal commissions have funds available for hiring professionals in key staff positions.

The most important federal commissions of this kind are the Interstate Commerce Commission, the Federal Power Commission, the Federal Communications Commission, and the Civil Aeronautics Board. The industries they regulate are oligopolies, primarily, that in some cases border on being monopolistically competitive or even purely competitive. The Federal Power Commission, for example, is responsible for regulating the prices charged by natural gas producers in the field, and some 16,000 cases have come before the Commission since the Natural Gas Act was passed in 1938. Similarly, there are a great many trucking companies whose status as common carriers subjects them to regulation by the Interstate Commerce Commission. The Federal Communications Commission is responsible for the regulation of a very large number of broadcasters, and a number of airlines are subject to the Civil Aeronautics

Board. The number of firms in industries such as these and the degree of competition present in them has led many people to question whether they ought to be regulated at all.

Problems of Rate Regulation

Available evidence seems to indicate that most regulatory commissions follow an average cost pricing approach to rate regulation. This approach stems from an 1898 Supreme Court decision made in the case of *Smith v. Ames,* in which the rather vague principle was handed down that maximum regulated rates should allow a "fair return on a fair value." Presumably this means that in setting maximum prices regulatory commissions should aim at permitting the regulated firms to earn a rate of return on their investment equal to the average that is earned throughout the economy. This could be accomplished if, as in Figure 13–3, the maximum price were set at p_2 and the firm were required to serve all comers at that price; that is, place quantity x_2 on the market.[2] But there is many a slip between the cup and the lip. The rate of return on investment is computed arithmetically by dividing the yearly net income of a business by the value of investment in the business. The obvious problems are (1) what constitutes a "fair" value of investment in a business, and (2) what price and quantity of the services rendered by the business will yield a net income that provides a "fair" return on investment?

Regulatory agencies have found it difficult to compute the "fair" value of investment in a business. The data available to an agency on investment in a specific firm will usually be incomplete, and agency personnel, far removed from active management of the business, may not be able to evaluate accurately the data they have. Nevertheless, evaluate it they must. In so doing, at different times and in different cases, two methods of evaluation have been developed. One is known as the *original cost method* while the other is called the *replacement cost method.*

Roughly, to value investment in a business using the *original cost method,* we start with the initial costs of the firm's assets—its land, buildings, equipment, and so on. To these costs we add those of additions to assets made from time to time, in each case valuing the additions at what they cost when they were made. Depreciation must be deducted in order to arrive at a valuation figure.

If, however, there has been inflation between the time that assets were acquired and the time they are valued, does the original cost of the firm's

---

[2] A prime example of a situation in which a regulated industry is required to produce more than it wants to produce is commercial air transport. Airlines frequently desire to cut off certain routes and to reduce service on others but are prevented from doing so by the Civil Aeronautics Board.

assets accurately reflect their present value? A machine that cost $20,000 two years ago may still be worth $20,000 today simply because prices have risen, even though the firm has charged off $8000 in depreciation for the two years. The original cost valuation would be only $12,000, so inflation causes the assets of the firm to be *undervalued* when this method is used. (Can you carry the effects of deflation through to their logical conclusions?)

The replacement cost method of determining the value of investment in a business asks, essentially, what it would cost at the present time to replace the assets of the firm. This method is in line with the type of cost reasoning generally used in economic analysis—the alternative cost principle. It does not tell us what amount of investment has been made in the business but rather what investment in the business is currently worth, based on the value of the best alternative uses of the resources that would be required to recreate the firm's assets. This method of computing the amount of investment in the business avoids the difficulties created by inflation and deflation in the original cost method. However, it may be difficult to arrive at replacement cost figures for some parts of the firm's assets.

No completely satisfactory method of determining the amount of investment in a business has been found as yet. Regulatory agencies find the mechanical simplicity of the original cost method convenient and recent court decisions appear to lend support to the use of this approach. But economic analysis would point to the replacement cost method as involving fewer logical pitfalls.

The difficulties involved in regulating public utility prices do not end when the regulatory agency arrives at a valuation figure for investment in the business. The problem remains of determining a price that will yield a "fair" return on that investment. What should be considered a "fair" return on investment? Is it 6 percent, 8 percent, 10 percent, or some other figure? Some general guidelines are offered by the alternative cost doctrine. We ask what the average return on investment is over the economy as a whole. Yet this is a difficult question to answer with precision. Return on investment varies a great deal from industry to industry and from firm to firm, depending upon the length of time for which investments are made, the degree of risk associated with different investments, and the like.

Further, can a regulatory commission determine a product price that will yield the firm a net income permitting, say, a 6 percent return on investment? It seems highly unlikely that it can, for its ability to do so presupposes economic knowledge that the commission does not have—indeed, that the firm itself usually does not have. It presupposes that the demand curve for the product is known, or that the sales volume and total revenue for each of several feasible prices can be predicted accurately. It presupposes, in addition, that average costs of the firm for each of those sales volumes are known.

The difficulties inherent in public utility rate regulation have led many economists to argue that economic performance would be at least as good without it. In some state and local areas where public utility rates are not regulated prices do not appear to be significantly different from those in which rates are regulated. Regulatory agencies become involved in all sorts of auxiliary activities—for example, regulating entry into the industry or specifying qualities and quantities of services—that effect the efficiency with which the firm operates. Regulation by commissions is far from a perfect answer to the problems of natural monopoly and oligopoly.

ANTIMONOPOLY LEGISLATION

Court decisions in the early part of U.S. history reflected a general public aversion to monopoly. A body of common law was built up that tended to prohibit unreasonable restraints of trade, but the determination of what was or was not unreasonable was left in the hands of judges. Large business empires were built up in such industries as oil, steel, and tobacco in the last half of the nineteenth century, accomplished largely through mergers and consolidations of companies in an atmosphere of rapid economic expansion. Public reaction to the developing forms and practices of business was expressed in legislation for the first time in 1890 with the passage of the Sherman Antitrust Act. The Sherman Act was later amended by the Clayton Act of 1914 and the Celler Antimerger Act of 1950. A supplementary piece of legislation, the Federal Trade Commission Act, was passed in 1914.

The Sherman Antitrust Act, 1890

The basic provisions of the Sherman Act are as follows:

> Sec. 1. Every contract, combination in the form of trust or otherwise, or conspiracy, in restraint of trade or commerce among the several states, or with foreign nations, is hereby declared to be illegal. Every person who shall make any such contract or engage in any such combination or conspiracy, shall be deemed guilty of a misdemeanor, and, on conviction thereof, shall be punished by fine not exceeding five thousand dollars, or by imprisonment not exceeding one year, or by both said punishments, in the discretion of the court.

Sec. 2. Every person who shall monopolize, or attempt to monopolize, or combine or conspire with any other person or persons, to monopolize any part of the trade or commerce among the several states, or with foreign nations, shall be deemed guilty of a misdemeanor, and, on conviction thereof, shall be punished by fine not exceeding five thousand dollars, or by imprisonment not exceeding one year, or by both said punishments, in the discretion of the court.[3]

Although opinions vary with respect to how sections 1 and 2 differ, the meaning of both is clear. Conspiracies, combinations, and activities of persons and firms to monopolize or to restrain trade in interstate commerce is made illegal. But it is left to the courts to decide what constitutes monopolization or restraint of trade. Both civil and criminal legal actions can be taken against alleged violators of the act, and these can be initiated either by injured parties or by the government.

Several remedies may be ordered by the courts against violators of the act. *Injunctions* may be issued against alleged violators where the activities enjoined may be of irreparable harm to the party claiming injury even though violation of the act has not been proved. *Cease and desist orders* may be issued directing companies or persons found guilty of violating the act to stop the illegal practices. The courts may even order dissolution of a company found guilty of violating the act; that is, order that the company be broken up into several firms of smaller size.

In addition to the court actions listed above, the *consent decree* is a device widely used to remedy alleged violations of the Sherman Act. The alleged violator admits neither guilt nor innocence. He simply enters into an agreement with the government to stop engaging in the activities that are supposedly illegal. If the terms of the decree are broken, contempt of court proceedings are brought against the firm or person.

Fines and *prison sentences* can be levied on those found guilty of illegal restraint of trade or monopolization. A business enterprise as such can only be fined, but individual officers who are found responsible for the illegal activities can be both fined and sentenced to jail as individuals.

The crowning civil action that can be taken against convicted violators of the act is the *triple damage suit.* If the party or parties injured in the course of the violation can prove in court the amount of the financial damage suffered because of the illegal activities, they can collect three times that amount from the guilty party. Thus if proved monopolistic restraint of trade causes a buyer to pay $100,000 more for products than he would have had to pay had the restraint not occurred, he can recover $300,000 from the violator.

[3] 26 U.S. Statutes at Large, 209 (1890).

Amendments and Supplements

The Sherman Act came out foursquare against economic sin but was vague about what kinds of activities were actually sinful. This vagueness, together with mounting public interest in antimonopoly activities of the government, led to the Clayton Act of 1914 and the Celler Antimerger Act of 1950. Both of these were amendments to the Sherman Act. A piece of supplementary legislation, the Federal Trade Commission Act, was passed in 1914.

The Clayton Act spelled out kinds of arrangements and activities that are illegal when their effects are to decrease competition substantially or to tend to create monopoly. First, *price discrimination,* or sale of a product at lower prices to certain customers, was forbidden. Second, *exclusive dealerships,* in which a firm must agree to handle the products of one producer only, were made illegal. Third, *interlocking directorates,* in which one individual sits simultaneously on the boards of directors of competing companies, were prohibited. Fourth, the *acquisition of stock* of competing companies by one or a group of other companies was ruled out. There were prohibitions of other less flagrant monopolizing activities, but those just listed were most commonly used at the time.

A loophole in that clause of the Clayton Act relating to the acquisition of stock of competing companies led to the Celler Act of 1950. The Clayton Act said nothing about one or more firms acquiring the *assets* of competing companies, and a number of mergers were effected in this way. The Celler Act made merger by *acquisition of the assets* of competing companies illegal as well when the effect is to lessen competition substantially.

The Federal Trade Commission Act of 1914 established the Federal Trade Commission to conduct investigations of anticompetitive practices by firms operating in interstate commerce. The five-man Commission can on its own initiative undertake investigations or act in response to complaints made to it. When the evidence indicates that it should do so, the Commission issues orders intended to correct the undersirable practices. If such orders are not followed, the Commission can petition the appropriate courts to enforce them. On the other hand, businesses subjected to Commission orders may go to the courts to protest if they believe the Commission has erred.

Court Interpretation of Antimonopoly Laws

The antimonopoly laws leave much discretion to the courts to determine what activities are in violation of the law. Prior to the Clayton Act this discretion was abundantly evident, for no illegal practices as such were named. The Clayton Act provided some help in the form of specific kinds of practices that were suspect, but it was still the courts' prerogative to determine whether or not the practices were in restraint of trade.

Through the first 20 years of the Sherman Act there was little change in the judicial attitude toward monopolization. Certain obviously collusive price-fixing and other arrangements were held to be illegal, but no major barriers to the combining of firms were raised. Business went on much as usual.

Two Supreme Court decisions handed down in 1911 provided guidelines for antimonopoly policy.[4] The Standard Oil Company of New Jersey and the American Tobacco Company had both been convicted of unreasonable restraint of trade by lower courts. The Supreme Court upheld these convictions, and the logic through which its decisions were reached came to be known as the *rule of reason*. The Supreme Court made it plain that it was not condemning the size of the firms in relation to the markets they served. Rather, it was the behavior of the firms in their respective markets that the Court found objectionable, behavior that constituted unreasonable restraint of trade.

The rule of reason was sharpened by a 1920 Supreme Court decision involving the U.S. Steel Corporation.[5] The suit was initiated by the federal government, which charged that informal agreements, pricing practices, and other activities in which U.S. Steel was the leader were combinations in restraint of trade. The Court's decision was favorable to the corporation. The Court held that although the company was large in size, size alone or the existence of unexerted power does not constitute an offense under the law. Rather, the Court maintained, it is how bigness is used that determines whether or not a violation has occurred and, according to the Court, the government had not proved that restraint of trade had actually taken place.

The economic expansion of the 1920s coupled with the rule of reason interpretation of the Sherman Act triggered a substantial merger movement in that period. But in the 1930s vigorous pursuit of antimonopoly activities by the Department of Justice under the leadership of Thurman Arnold brought with it a retreat from the 1920 interpretation.

Decisions rendered by the Supreme Court now began to hold that combinations formed for the *purpose* of affecting the price of a product are illegal regardless of whether or not the *effects* are reasonable; that is, *market structure* itself as well as the *market conduct* of monopolizing firms determines whether or not they are in violation of the act. Following World War II, in a case involving the Aluminum Company of America,[6]

---

[4] *U.S. v. Standard Oil Co. of New Jersey*, 221 U.S. 1 (1911), and *U.S. v. American Tobacco Co.*, 221 U.S. 106 (1911).
[5] *U.S. v. U.S. Steel Corporation*, 251 U.S. 417 (1920).
[6] *U.S. v. Aluminum Company of America*, 148 F 2d 416 (2d Cir., 1945).

the Supreme Court held that intentional monopolization of an industry is prohibited regardless of what the firm does with its monopoly powers. The Court position was not entirely clear, however. In the late 1940s it allowed U.S. Steel to purchase a war surplus plant owned by the government in Utah and to acquire by merger a fabricating plant on the West Coast. These acquisitions made the company the largest producer in the West. In ruling against the Department of Justice in this case the Court held that the acquisitions were not large enough to constitute monopoly of the industry by the corporation.

There is some evidence that since 1950 antitrust legislation has been more stringently interpreted and enforced. A lengthy case lasting from 1949 through 1957 found the Antitrust Division of the Department of Justice charging that ownership of large amounts of General Motors stock by the duPont Company gave the latter undue advantage over other firms in selling fabrics and paints to General Motors.[7] The duPont Company was required to divest itself of its General Motors stock. A Celler Act injunction issued by a lower court against a proposed merger of Bethlehem Steel and Youngstown Sheet and Tube, on the grounds that it would substantially lessen competition, was allowed to stand without being appealed by the companies. In 1960 several suppliers of electrical equipment were convicted of price fixing. Fines were levied, company executives were sentenced to prison terms, and a rash of successful triple damage suits were filed.

We cannot assess the effects of antimonopoly laws and their enforcement solely on the basis of the cases that have come to court. The actual number of cases tried has been relatively limited. Many people believe that the laws have their greatest impact as deterrents to those who would otherwise engage in monopolizing practices.

The Federal Trade Commission

A word should be said about the work of the Federal Trade Commission, since it engages in activities that complement those of the Antitrust Division of the Department of Justice. The Commission has worked closely with the Department of Justice in the reviewing of evidence and the consequent determination of whether proposed mergers, if consummated, would restrain trade. It has also worked with business groups and trade associations in the establishment of acceptable standards of competition or of business practices within specific industries. Still another task of the Commission is the investigation of the validity of advertising claims of business firms. Where it finds objectionable practices it may issue cease and desist orders.

[7] *U.S. v. E. I. duPont de Nemours & Co.,* 353 U.S. 586 (1967).

Much of the Commission's work goes unsung and is not apparent to the general public. In many cases it never reaches the stage of an order. Upon receiving a complaint from one firm about the practices of another, the Commission may be able to assist in working out a satisfactory solution short of a cease and desist order. Questionable practices coming to the attention of the Commission may be discussed with the firms responsible for them and an agreement may be reached on whether or not they are legal and proper. Much of the Commission's work is of a preventive nature.

MEASURES TO DECREASE COMPETITION

Those who comprise the general public, sometimes in their roles as consumers but more often in their roles as producers, have not always been happy with the results of competition. Through their elected representatives they have sometimes seen fit to curb competition. Legislation restricting competition has been enacted at both the state and federal level.

State Regulation of Competition

Licensing Laws

Suppose that you are a barber struggling to make a living. You try to run a clean, sanitary shop and to give good haircuts. It seems, however, that there are entirely too many people wanting to be barbers. New shops are being set up in your territory, many by inferior workmen who cut corners on sanitation. It becomes difficult for decent craftsmen like yourself to make a living.

You and others like you become concerned about your profession. You get together to discuss your problems, and your chief complaints are that (1) the unsanitary shop conditions of some of your competitors are likely to endanger the public health, and (2) the public is getting inferior service in these shops.[8] In the interest of protecting the public you talk to your legislators and eventually you get a state licensing law passed and a state barbering board appointed composed of your fellow-barbers. To become

---

[8] On the first point, the writer spent two and one-half years in Asia and one year in South America where sanitary conditions in barber shops were far inferior to those in the United States and appears to be suffering no ill effects.

On the second point, some portion of the public obviously believes that a dollar's worth of the inferior service is worth more to it than a dollar's worth of better barbering.

licensed, barbers must pass examinations given by the board, and new barbers coming into the profession must, in addition, have attended approved barber colleges. Presumably, standards are elevated in the craft. Certainly numbers plying the trade are reduced below what they would be otherwise because it has become more costly to enter and to operate. The public will also pay a higher price for a haircut since the supply of barbering services has been reduced.

Licensing laws for a host of occupations have been established in a number of states. The professions covered vary from state to state but common ones include medicine, law, real estate, plumbing, undertaking, barbering, dry cleaning, architecture, and even watch repairing. For some of these licensing is based on public health arguments while for others it must rest on a "protect the public from its own ignorance" justification. All such licensing has one feature in common: it tends to hold down the number of persons in the occupation and, consequently, the price of the service is higher than it would otherwise be.

Price Fixing

In some states legislators have been persuaded to take an additional step and to permit state boards for some occupations to set prices. The typical cases in point are barbering and dry cleaning. In Oklahoma, for example, the licensed barbers in each county may meet and jointly determine the minimum price to be charged for services in the county. Once the price is approved by the state barbering board, it has the force of law. Violators may have their licenses revoked and be subjected to fines.

What is the economic rationale of this price-fixing case? If barbers are allowed to compete, the demand curve for haircuts facing any single shop will be highly elastic. Other barbers, as well as a Sears home barbering set, provide good substitutes for the services of the one. If any single barber raises the price in this sort of situation above an equilibrium level, he will lose customers and find his total receipts falling. But the *market demand* for haircuts in the neighborhood of an equilibrium price level is likely to be inelastic—the rate at which hair grows seems to be more or less fixed. Thus all barbers, acting together, can raise the price and *increase* the total receipts of the group and of individual members of the group.

Fair Trade Laws

A number of state legislatures have or have had so called "fair trade" laws on their statute books. These usually fall into one or another of two categories. The first is a *minimum mark-up* type of law while the second is generally referred to as a *resale price maintenance* law.

Minimum mark-up laws were largely a response to the growth of retail chain stores during and following the 1920s. It was thought, with some justification, that chains would drive small independent retailers out of business. With much less justification it was also thought that chains were doing so by selling goods below costs—that is, economies of scale were largely overlooked. To protect the small independents from the chain stores many states enacted laws specifying the minimum mark up over costs that retailers of certain kinds of products could charge. Anyone who cut product prices enough to drop the mark up below the specified minimum would be in violation of the law. Exceptions were permitted for liquidation or clearance sales. (What impact would you expect laws such as these to have on economic efficiency?)

Resale price maintenance laws were spawned in the Great Depression of the 1930s when there was much concern over maintaining price levels. Such laws provide that a manufacturer may make a contract with a retailer who handles his product specifying the price at which that product may be sold. Some legislation goes farther and provides that such a contract made by a manufacturer with *one* retailer binds *all* retailers handling that product to the specified price. The impact on competition among retailers is self-evident.

Federal Restraints of Competition

Fair Trade Laws

The federal government joined the states in passing legislation to restrain competition at the retail level. In 1937 Congress passed the Miller-Tydings Act to permit resale price maintenance contracts for goods moving in interstate commerce. Its intent was to exempt parties making such contracts from prosecution under the Sherman Act. The range of cases to which it is applicable was severely restricted by a Supreme Court decision in 1951. This act was followed by the McGuire Act in 1952 which lends federal support to state resale price maintenance laws.

The anti-chain store movement of the 1920s gave rise to the Robinson-Patman Act, passed by Congress in 1936. The objective of the act was to prevent large buyers of products, particularly chain stores, from obtaining price concessions from sellers, both manufacturers and wholesalers, that were not available to small buyers. Large buyers are frequently in a position to obtain favorable treatment simply because of the quantities that they purchase, although, from the sellers' point of view, per unit costs of selling large orders are in many cases lower than for small orders.

Court support for fair trade laws has been spotty. Many state statutes have been declared unconstitutional for one reason or another and the Supreme Court pulled a large part of the teeth from the Miller-Tydings Act. On the other hand, enforcement of the Robinson-Patman Act has rested with the Federal Trade Commission and has been quite effective.[9]

Patent Laws

Another federal anticompetitive measure is the law governing patents. One who discovers a new product or process can apply for and receive a patent on it granting him the exclusive right of the use and the sale or lease of it for a period of 17 years. The purpose of this monopoly privilege is to encourage invention and economic progress.

There is much controversy concerning whether the patent laws accomplish their objective. Some people argue that in reinforcing monopoly and near-monopoly conditions their adverse effects on the use of the economy's resources more than offset any contributions to progress that they might make. Others argue that without them innovative activity would be significantly lower. The validity of these arguments is hard to assess. How important are they in fostering innovation and economic progress? Do they contribute markedly to the extent of monopoly in the economy? These are questions that need to be but have not been answered in determining whether or not the patent laws in and of themselves are an important economic issue.

Other Restraints

There are several other, more significant ways in which the federal government operates to diminish competition. These are so important, in fact, that we shall devote separate chapters to them at appropriate places in the book. They include policies having to do with agriculture, labor, and international trade.

SUMMARY

Over the years government policies with respect to market structure and the economic performance of business enterprises have evolved in three general forms: (1) regulation of natural monopoly and oligopoly in

---

[9] See Corwin D. Edwards, *The Price Discrimination Law: A Review of Experience* (Washington, D.C.: The Brookings Institution, 1959).

public utility and transportation fields, (2) promotion of competition through antimonopoly legislation, and (3) reduction of competition in some areas where such reductions are thought to be in the public interest.

Regulation of public utilities and transportation generally takes the form of maximum price setting; however, regulatory commissions may also concern themselves with the qualities and quantities of services produced and sold. Two approaches to price setting that are suggested by our discussion of pricing are the marginal cost pricing approach and the average cost pricing approach, with the latter more commonly used in practice.

The objective posed by the courts for price or rate regulation is to permit a "fair return on a fair value" of investment in the business being regulated. This stated objective poses important difficulties for regulatory commissions. A "fair return" on investment is difficult to determine. Further, the net investment in a business is not easily computed. Finally, it is almost impossible to determine a price that will yield income and cost figures such that the rate of return on investment will be some specified "fair" rate. Regulation by commissions has not enjoyed unqualified success.

Antimonopoly legislation in the United States consists basically of the Sherman Act of 1890, the Clayton Act of 1914, the Federal Trade Commission Act of 1914, and the Celler Antimerger Act of 1950. The Sherman Act made restraint and monopolization of trade in interstate commerce illegal but left determination of what constitutes such acts to the courts. The Clayton Act specifies certain specific acts that are illegal, and the Celler Act plugs one of the loopholes of the Clayton Act. The Federal Trade Commission Act provides machinery for the policing of business practices and the preventing of anticompetitive practices.

A definitive court interpretation of the antimonopoly laws began to take shape in 1911 with the initial enunciation of the rule of reason doctrine, which holds that a firm's size is not in itself evidence of violation of the laws, but rather what is important is how the firm behaves in the market it serves. In the 1930s the Supreme Court's attitude was modified toward the position that firm size as well as behavior can be in violation of the law. But it is still within the power of the Supreme Court to determine how large a market share must be to be declared illegal.

Both state and federal governments have enacted legislation aimed at decreasing competition in the economy. At the state level we find licensing laws, price-fixing, and so-called fair trade laws. At the federal level fair trade laws have been enacted also, although enforcement of them, except for the Robinson-Patman Act, has been difficult. Patent laws have been enacted at the federal level, giving rise to debate over their effectiveness in stimulating innovation. Other restraints to competition that will be considered later include policies with regard to agriculture, labor, and international trade.

EXERCISES AND QUESTIONS FOR DISCUSSION

1. "If all the antitrust laws currently in existence were strictly enforced, the growth of monopoly would be sufficiently curbed." What do you think about this statement? What suggestions can you make for improvement in regard to our current laws?
2. Is large firm size in itself a hindrance to competition? Discuss instances when it might and when it might not be.
3. Suppose your city is served by a privately owned, publicly regulated electric company. Discuss the merits and lack of merit as well as the possible difficulties involved in setting a maximum price per kilowatt hour that the company may charge.
4. Describe the economic effects of the following developments:
   a. The movie theater owners of your city collusively set a minimum admission price.
   b. A large chain store undercuts the price of local competitors on brand-name products.
   c. A fair trade law is enacted in your state.
5. Some people have recommended that the U.S. steel industry be placed under public regulation. What arguments do you think could be used both for and against this proposal?
6. Should co-operative associations be placed under antimonopoly legislation? Discuss.

SELECTED READINGS

Adams, Walter, *The Structure of American Industry*, 3d ed. New York: Crowell-Collier and Macmillan, Inc., 1961, Chap. 15.

Lindahl, Martin L., and William A. Carter, *Corporate Concentration and Public Policy*, 3d ed. Englewood Cliffs, N.J.: Prentice-Hall, Inc., 1959, Chaps. 10 and 26.

National Bureau of Economic Research, *The Rate and Direction of Inventive Activity: Economic and Social Factors.* Princeton, N.J.: Princeton University Press, 1962.

Wilcox, Clair, *Public Policies Toward Business*, 3d ed. Homewood, Ill.: Richard D. Irwin, Inc., 1966, Chaps. 3, 5, 11, 12, and 19.

Government and Agriculture

CHAPTER 14

The agricultural sector of the U.S. economy represents another major area in which there has been wholesale government intervention in the operation of the price system. Much debate has centered on "the farm problem," and "solutions" to it have been advanced in the political arena and in the press. Emotions run high on this issue and, as is so often the case, they tend to obscure a great many facts. We shall attempt in this chapter (1) to determine what the major economic problems are in agriculture, (2) to indicate how the government has responded to these problems, and (3) to consider directions that long-run solutions to the problems should take.

AGRICULTURAL PROBLEMS

Two conditions in particular that have characterized economic activity in agriculture have generated concern on the part of Congress and the public. The first is *low average incomes or poverty,* and the second is *instability of farm prices and farm incomes over time.* The two are intertwined —indeed, each may be partly responsible for the other—but there is an analytical advantage in treating them separately.

Poverty and instability are not problems unique to the agricultural sector. Both occur in other sectors of the economy. Yet a large number of people are affected by these conditions in the farming sector, and the people so affected in turn have had a disproportionately large representation in Congress. Consequently, agricultural programs, presumably

TABLE 14-1
Per Capita Disposable Personal Income, Farm and Nonfarm,
Selected Years, 1935–1967

YEAR	FARM FROM ALL SOURCES[1] (DOLLARS)	NONFARM FROM ALL SOURCES (DOLLARS)	FARM AS A PERCENTAGE OF NONFARM
1935	237	533	44.5
1940	246	675	36.4
1945	655	1,162	56.4
1950	841	1,459	57.7
1955	893	1,772	48.2
1960	1,100	2,017	54.5
1961	1,226	2,050	59.8
1962	1,308	2,127	61.5
1963	1,410	2,191	64.4
1964	1,462	2,340	62.5
1965	1,772	2,477	71.5
1966	1,976	2,637	74.9
1967	2,037	2,784	73.2

[1] Includes all income received by farm residents from nonfarm sources, such as wages and salaries from nonfarm employment, nonfarm business and professional income, rents from nonfarm real estate, dividends, interests, royalties, unemployment compensation, and Social Security payments.
SOURCE: *Farm Income Situation*, July, 1968, U.S. Department of Agriculture, Economic Research Service, p. 50.

intended to alleviate the problems, have been given a high place on the legislative agenda.

The Low-Income Problem

Available data indicate that average incomes among the farm population are lower than those in other areas of the economy. Table 14–1 compares the disposable income[1] per person for farm and nonfarm individuals for selected years from 1935 to 1967. Although per capita farm income has been much greater relative to nonfarm income in the 1960s than it was in the 1930s, it is still far below nonfarm income in both relative and absolute terms.

Distribution of Income within Agriculture

Are all farm families poor? A drive through the corn belt of Iowa or the large wheat farms of Kansas and Oklahoma will reveal large modern homes, color television sets, Cadillacs in garages, and even private air-

[1] Disposable income is essentially the income available to be spent or to be disposed of per year after all personal taxes have been paid.

TABLE 14-2

Classification of Farm Operators by Value of Farm Products Sold, 1967

CLASSIFICATION by VALUE OF SALES (DOLLARS)	NUMBER OF FARMS (THOUSANDS)	PERCENT OF FARMS	CASH RECEIPTS FROM FARMING[1] (MILLIONS OF DOLLARS)	PERCENT OF RECEIPTS	REALIZED NET INCOME PER FARM (DOLLARS)
2500 or less	1,347	42.8	1,599	3.5	1,018
2500–4999	360	11.5	1,533	3.4	2,019
5000–9999	446	14.2	3,724	8.1	3,585
10,000–19,999	492	15.6	7,921	17.3	6,266
20,000–39,999	318	10.1	9,542	20.8	9,792
40,000 and over	183	5.8	21,548	46.9	23,754
All farms	3,146	100.0	45,867	100.0	4,526

[1] Includes government payments. SOURCE: *Farm Income Situation,* July, 1968, U.S. Department of Agriculture, Economic Research Service, pp. 70–75.

planes on a good many farms. At the same time, a drive through parts of rural Mississippi or Arkansas or Oklahoma will show tumbled-down shacks and poverty of the bleakest kind. The data of Table 14-1 fall far short of providing all the information we need to analyze the low-income problem of agriculture, for we must also know how income is distributed among agricultural families.

Some idea of the way families in the agricultural sector fare with respect to each other can be inferred from the data presented in Table 14-2. In 1967 only 31.5 percent of farms had cash receipts of $10,000 or more per year, leaving 68.5 percent of farms with cash receipts of less than $10,000. Suppose we call the former group "good" farms and the latter group "poor" farms. Support for this classification is provided by the column showing realized net income[2] per farm for each value of sales classification.

These data indicate that poverty is not typical of all farms. It does not reside to any significant degree with the good farms. Most of the latter are reasonably well-operated commercial enterprises and some are outstandingly successful business firms. The good farms take advantage of the latest developments in farm technology—equipment, plant and animal genetics, fertilization, and soil care—with their resulting economies of scale. The poverty problem rests with the poor farms. This 68.5 percent of all farm units consists mostly of small, infertile, poorly run farms that provide little beyond subsistence for their operators.

[2] Realized net income per farm includes more than cash receipts from farming; it includes nonmoney income in the form of the value of farm products consumed directly in farm households and the value of housing provided by farm dwellings. See *Farm Income Situation* (U.S. Department of Agriculture, Economic Research Service, July, 1967) pp. 74, 75.

Causes of Poverty

Why do we find so many small-scale, low-income-producing farm units in the United States? The answer turns to a large extent on what has happened over time to demand for and supply of a good many agricultural products. It also turns on the slowness of the rural population to adjust to the changing economic climate of the country as a whole.

Over time demand for agricultural products in the United States has not kept pace with the rapidly rising demand for other products. This pattern is typical in an economy that has reached a relatively high level of economic development. The demand for agricultural products—for food, feed, and fiber—is more closely geared to the physical needs of the population than is that for manufactured goods and for services. Once an economy reaches the stage at which most of the population is reasonably well fed and clothed, for further increases in per capita income the portions that are spent on agricultural products diminish while the portions spent on automobiles, houses, appliances, medical care, government services, and so on, increase. In terms of demand for its output, agriculture is a *relatively declining industry;* that is, demand for its output is increasing more slowly than demand for the output of the nonagricultural sector of the economy.

On the supply side, tremendous advances have occurred in farm technology over the last 50 years. Until the 1940s it was not at all uncommon to see plows, cultivators, grain binders, and other farm machinery pulled by horses. But beginning in the late 1920s, the horse was in the process of being replaced by the tractor. Further, more intensive use was being made of crop rotation and of fertilizers. Advances in plant and animal genetics were increasing the yields of plant and animal products. Since World War II there have been spectacular increases in the efficiency of agricultural production, and ours is indeed an era of scientific farming.

The slowly rising demand for agricultural products, coupled with the rapidly increasing supply, have caused prices of farm products to lag behind those in other areas of the economy. That is, farm prices have been decreasing relative to the prices of manufactured goods and services. These effects are illustrated in Figure 14-1, in which we let automobiles represent manufactured products and wheat represents farm products. Suppose that in 1920 the demand for automobiles was D_aD_a and the supply was S_aS_a. In the same year suppose that the demand for wheat was D_wD_w and the supply was S_wS_w. By 1970 suppose that the demand for automobiles has increased to $D_{a_1}D_{a_1}$. Automobile supply has also increased markedly to $S_{a_1}S_{a_1}$, but the demand increase has outstripped the supply increase by enough to bring about a large relative increase in both automobile prices and the quantities sold. For the same time period, suppose that the demand for wheat increased from D_wD_w to $D_{w_1}D_{w_1}$—

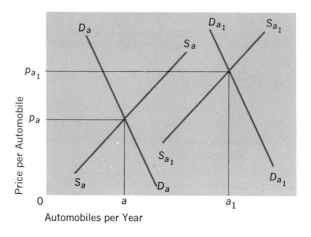

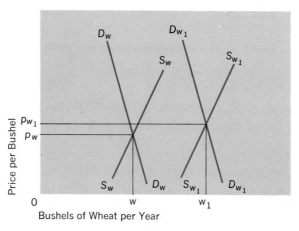

Figure 14–1

The impact of increases in demand on prices of agricultural products as compared with manufactured products.

much less, relatively, than for automobiles. Improvements in farm technology have increased wheat yields and dramatically lowered costs per bushel of producing specific quantities, increasing the supply from $S_w S_w$ to $S_{w_1} S_{w_1}$. The much smaller increase in the demand for wheat relative to the increase in its supply brought about a much smaller relative increase in its price and in the quantity sold than was the case for automobiles. The slower increase, or the relative decrease, in farm prices as compared with nonfarm prices has been accompanied by a slower increase in the total income earned from agriculture than from other sectors of the economy. This situation, however, has not affected all farmers adversely. The more progressive ones, or those on the good farms, have adjusted very well. By taking advantage of the latest technological developments and by increasing their scales of operations they have been able to keep pace with, or even to exceed, the rate of increase of average family income in the United States. Farming for this group is no longer simply a way of life. It has become a business proposition, conducted in every respect as any other well-run business.

On the other hand, the 68.1 percent of farm units run by small, marginal operators, sharecroppers, and the like have failed to adjust to the changing economic facts of farm life. These people are usually poorly educated and lack the business acumen that characterizes their more progressive brethren. They have not been able to compensate for lower relative farm prices by increasing their outputs and sales volumes. Cultural and social forces, together with an absence of training for other pursuits, conspire against the economic incentives that would pull them into more lucrative employments and they tend to remain on the farm. This part of the farm population constitutes the real problem area from the income point of view.

The Instability Problem

Instability of farm prices and income, the second major farm problem, arises primarily from two sources. One is such natural phenomena as the uncertainties of the weather. The other is the peculiar vulnerability of agriculture to recession, depression, and inflation.

Natural Causes of Instability

Agricultural production is more dependent on natural phenomena than is that in most other sectors of the economy. For example, the amount of rainfall in an agricultural area may vary from year to year. Droughts may occur over a wide section of the wheat belt in some years, or, as it happened in the 1930s, for a succession of years. In other years rainfall may be more than ample, resulting in flooding and washing out of crops. Too, excessive rainfall may seriously delay harvests or make grain recovery difficult. In addition, crops are subject to damage from wind and hail, and insect invasions have occasionally cut yields substantially. All of these factors may create uncertainties and instability in farm businesses, particularly where entire farms are dependent on a single crop.

External Economic Causes of Instability

Economic fluctuations are generally thought to bear more heavily on farm prices and farm incomes than on average price and income levels. Farm prices tend to fall more than do average prices during periods of

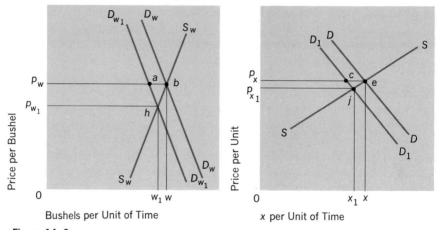

Figure 14–2
Comparative responses of agricultural and manufacturing prices and incomes to economic fluctuations.

recession, while in periods of prosperity and expansion farm prices tend to rise more rapidly than do prices in general. This is so because the demand for and the supply of most farm products tend to be less elastic than for most nonfarm products. These circumstances are illustrated in Figure 14–2. Suppose that product X is some nonfarm product and that in the neighborhood of the initial equilibrium price, p_x, both demand and supply, DD and SS, are fairly elastic. Suppose that demand and supply of wheat, D_wD_w and S_wS_w, are much less elastic in the neighborhood of the equilibrium price, p_w. Consider now a recession that decreases the demand for wheat and the demand for X in about the same proportion in the neighborhood of their respective original equilibrium prices; that is, ab is to p_wb as ce is to p_xe. The decrease in the price of X is from p_x to p_{x_1} only. It is cushioned by the high elasticity of both demand and supply. The decrease in the price of wheat from p_w to p_{w_1} is much greater because demand and supply are much less elastic. The income from wheat sales before demand decreased is represented by the area of the rectangle $0p_wbw$. After the decrease in demand, it is represented by the area of rectangle $0p_{w_1}hw_1$. Income from X decreases from area $0p_xex$ to area $0p_{x_1}jx_1$.

GOVERNMENT RESPONSES

Volumes have been written on the agricultural programs of the federal government. We shall not attempt to cover them in detail here, for they have undergone substantial changes over time. Rather, we shall focus on the basic economic principles underlying farm legislation as it has developed over the last 40 years.

Large-scale government intervention in the agricultural sector of the economy has its roots in the Great Depression of the 1930s. Until the Depression federal aid to agriculture had been quite limited. For example, agricultural research, together with the development and dissemination of new farm technology, was encouraged by the establishment of a nationwide system of land-grant colleges, and limited amounts of low-cost credit was made available to farmers. But agricultural programs as we see them in operation today grew largely out of the Depression experience.

Parity Prices

Permeating New Deal thinking in the 1930s was the idea that the key to recovery lay in raising prices. The ill-fated National Industrial Recovery Act of 1933 was based on this philosophy, as was the Agricultural Adjustment Act of 1933. Subsequent agricultural legislation has been in keeping with the view that farm incomes can best be maintained by supporting farm prices. The concept of "parity" prices for farmers has occupied a central position in the thinking of legislators.

The Concept of Parity

Parity prices refer to "fair" prices received by farmers for what they sell relative to the prices they must pay for nonfarm products. Prices of farm products fell more rapidly than did those of most nonfarm products during the downswing of the Depression from 1929 to 1933. Many people, including Congressmen and officials of the Roosevelt Administration, thought this situation "unfair" to farmers. Parity prices for farm products, then, would seem to be a set of prices bearing a higher ratio to the set of nonfarm prices than existed at the depths of the Depression: presumably they should be as high, relatively, as those existing in the immediate pre-Depression period.

Congress did even better in defining parity. Instead of considering the ratio of prices received to prices paid in the pre-Depression 1920s as "fair," it went back to the 1910–1914 period, a period in which the ratio of prices received to prices paid was still more favorable to farmers. Thus the parity price for wheat in 1937 was the price that had the same relation to prices paid by farmers in that year as the price of wheat bore to prices paid by farmers on the average during the 1910–1914 period.

Is a parity price for a farm product really the same thing as a fair price? Many people seem to think so. Political campaigns and newspaper editorials frequently dwell on the inequities done the farmer by the price system as farm prices fall over time relative to nonfarm prices. But if a parity price today is actually to be considered a "fair" price, two conditions must be met. First, the ratio of prices paid to prices received must have been fair in the 1910–1914 period. But what constitutes fairness as far as relative prices are concerned? Second, nothing must have occurred since the 1910–1914 period to change what would be a fair ratio.

In an economy that relies on a price system to indicate the relative value of different goods to consumers and to organize production accordingly, there are no "fair" relations among prices that are unchanging over time. As we noted previously, demand for many farm products has not been increasing as rapidly as has demand for many nonfarm products. Farm technology, on the other hand, has advanced as rapidly on the average as technology in other sectors of the economy. This means that increases in the supply of many farm products has kept pace with those of other products. Under circumstances such as these we would expect prices for many farm products to decline relative to those for many other products. As a matter of fact, the structure of prices of *all* products is constantly changing as conditions of demand and of supply of specific products change. Such changes are the mark of a viable, dynamic economy in which the price system is operating as it should.

The Applications of Parity

Although parity prices for many farm products have been defined in legislation and computed each year by the Department of Agriculture, government support has not aimed at providing full parity for any product. Some discretion has been left to the Secretary of Agriculture as to what prices would be supported and as to the level of support. The Agricultural Adjustment Act of 1933 made supports mandatory for corn and cotton at prices between 53 and 76 percent of parity. Subsequent legislation changed, but generally extended, the list for which supports were mandatory while at the same time changing the limits of the support levels. Support levels as a percentage of parity were generally raised, until from 1942 to 1954 they were fixed at 90 percent. Since 1954, support levels as a percentage of parity have been decreasing.

A new parity formula was introduced in 1948. Instead of using the ratios of prices received to prices paid during the 1910–1914 period, moving ratios over the most recent 10-year period were to be used for computations of parity prices. The new formula yielded lower parity prices for some products and higher ones for others, but from 1948 to 1956 the

Secretary of Agriculture was required to use for each crop whichever formula, the new or the old, would provide the higher price. Since 1956, the new formula has been used across the board.

Price Supports

One of the most important features of government agricultural policy since 1933 has been price support for certain farm products. Almost all nonperishable farm products have come under a price-support program of some type; however, well over half of the total value of farm products is generated outside the supported areas. Two general methods of supporting prices have occupied the attention of economists and policymakers. These are (1) the establishment of a fixed support price for both sellers and buyers, accomplished in practice by *a storage and loan program*, and (2) the establishment of a fixed support price for sellers, letting buyers pay whatever they are willing to pay for the amounts brought to market— in short, *support through subsidies.*

Storage and Loan

A storage and loan program has provided the primary means of supporting prices. Under this program the Commodity Credit Corporation, established as an independent agency by the federal government in 1933, has stood ready to make loans to farmers, secured by crops eligible for price supports that are placed in approved storage facilities. For example, on a price-supported crop such as wheat, a farmer could obtain a loan at harvest time amounting to the announced support price multiplied by the number of bushels of wheat he has placed in approved storage bins.[3]

Loans of this sort are called nonrecourse loans, meaning that if during the year the market price of the product goes far enough above the support price to more than pay storage costs, the farmer may sell the crop and pay off the loan and storage costs. Any excess of receipts over the loan and storage costs is his. On the other hand, if the market price is not high enough to make it worthwhile for the farmer to sell the product, he simply keeps the loan and lets the government have the crop. Thus the market price stays near the support level. In effect the government buys any quantities of the crop that the market will not take at support price levels.

The economics of the storage and loan program are illustrated in Fig-

[3] Most farm legislation has placed certain eligibility requirements on the farmer for obtaining loans. The primary requirement has been compliance with acreage quotas. These will be discussed later in connection with supply restrictions.

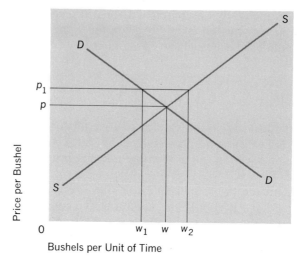

Figure 14-3
A storage and loan program.

ure 14–3. In the absence of the program, the market price would be p and the quantity produced and sold would be w. Suppose now that a support price level is established at p_1. At that price consumers will take only w_1 of the product, but farmers will produce quantity w_2. The quantity w_1w_2 is a surplus that cannot be sold at that price, and therefore it is turned over to the government.

We can deduce from simple demand and supply analysis that when support prices are effective, that is, when they are above what equilibrium market prices would be, the government will accumulate surpluses. When market prices are above support prices the government can sell off some of its accumulated surpluses without jeopardizing the support price. This is precisely what has occurred historically. When price supports were made mandatory for basic crops in 1938, government stocks of these began to accumulate. From 1942 to 1948 market prices exceeded support prices and government stocks of surplus products were gradually worked off. From 1948 to the early 1960s (1956 for cotton) support prices generally exceeded equilibrium prices for cotton and wheat in particular and government stocks of these commodities reached embarrassing as well as costly proportions. Since 1962, disposal of wheat to famine-threatened countries, particularly India, has reduced government stocks to more comfortable levels. Surplus cotton continues to present a problem.

We can identify at least three types of costs associated with the storage and loan method of supporting prices. First, consumers receive smaller quantities of the price-supported goods and pay higher prices for them whenever the price supports are effective than they would if the supports were not effective or were absent. Second, the handling, storing, and disposal of surplus goods is costly.[4] Resources used for these purposes could have been used to produce other goods and services. Third, taxpayers must provide the funds used by the government to purchase surpluses. Apart from such direct costs as restrictions in the quantities available of supported products and the resource costs of handling, storing, and disposing of surpluses, the storage and loan program transfers purchasing power from consumers and taxpayers to farmers. From a policy point of view we must ask ourselves whether or not this is desirable. We shall have more to say about this in a later section of this chapter.

Direct Subsidies

The federal government through the Commodity Credit Corporation supports the prices of some products, notably wool and mohair, by means of direct subsidy payments to producers. Some people have argued that if prices are to be supported, this method should be used generally in lieu of the storage and loan method. President Truman's post-World War II Secretary of Agriculture was one of the foremost proponents of this program, and after him the method is usually referred to as the Brannan plan. Its major feature is that at the support price level for any one product the producer is permitted to market as much as he desires at whatever price the product will bring. The government makes up the difference between the market price and the support price.

The mechanics of the subsidy plan are illustrated in Figure 14–4. Suppose again that the product is wheat. Given demand and supply as DD and SS, the equilibrium price is p. But suppose a support price is set at p_1. Producers will place quantity w_2 on the market and consumers will be willing to pay p_2 for that amount. The subsidy per bushel that the government must pay is thus p_2p_1. The total cost to the government of the support operation is $p_2p_1 \cdot w_2$.

Proponents of the subsidy method claim three advantages for it over the storage and loan approach. First, with a subsidy no surpluses occur, so storage and disposal costs are eliminated. Second, consumers get larger amounts of the product at lower prices, thus increasing what their incomes will buy. Third, the subsidy is in the open for everyone to see. Under a storage and loan program neither consumers nor producers know what the market price would be in the absence of the price support,

---

[4] The Commodity Credit Corporation estimates that wheat storage has cost about $13\frac{1}{2}$ cents per bushel annually since 1960, and prior to that it was $16\frac{1}{4}$ cents per bushel. Cotton storage costs have been between 41 and 46 cents per bale. See *Summary of 30 Years' Operations of the Commodity Credit Corporation* (Washington, D.C.: Department of Agriculture, 1964), pp. 30–31.

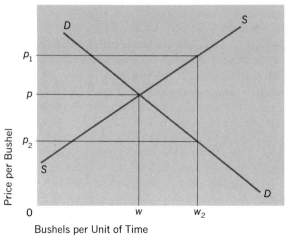

Figure 14–4
A subsidy program.

nor do they know what it would be for the quantities actually produced at the support price level. The total costs of such a program can be computed, however.

Recent Support Measures

Recent price support legislation utilizes both of the basic techniques discussed above. Support for wheat has become a rather complex three-level system in which wheat for domestic consumption is supported at the highest level, that for export at the next highest level, and the remainder at the lowest level. Only farmers who comply with acreage allotments[5] set by the Department of Agriculture are eligible for the support prices. Of a complying farmer's normal production, 45 percent receives the domestic consumption support, 45 percent receives the export support price, and the remainder is supported at the low level.

In general, support operations provide—as does the simple storage and loan program—that the government will relieve the farmer of any surpluses that cannot be sold at support prices. The lowest level of support is the basic support price, and this is set as a storage and loan rate. A complying farmer then receives free from the Department of Agriculture marketing certificates valued at the difference between the storage and loan price and the domestic consumption support price for that portion of his crop eligible for domestic consumption support. He receives similar certificates for the export portion of his crop, which are redeemed

[5] See pp. 251–252.

by the Commodity Credit Corporation at their face value. Domestic processors of wheat and exporters of wheat normally pay the storage and loan price for it. In addition, domestic processors must buy domestic marketing certificates from the Commodity Credit Corporation at a face value equal to the difference between the basic loan support price and the domestic consumption support price, and for every bushel of wheat they purchase from farmers they must surrender to the CCC one such certificate. Exporters must purchase export marketing certificates with face values equal to the difference between the export support price and the loan support price and surrender these in amounts equal to the number of bushels of wheat they export. Thus wheat farmers in effect receive the specified support prices for their wheat and wheat purchasers in effect pay those support prices for what they buy from farmers. Any surpluses that occur will accumulate in CCC storage facilities.

Supply Restrictions

Another important feature of government agricultural policy has been the restriction of supplies of basic farm products; that is, attempts to move the supply curves of certain products to the left. The intent of the Agricultural Adjustment Act of 1933 was to raise prices toward parity levels through reductions in supply. The subsequent pegging of support prices above equilibrium levels, the introduction of nonrecourse loans to farmers, secured by crops placed in storage, and the resulting surpluses accumulating in government hands led to supply restriction features as integral parts of farm legislation in order to hold down or to reduce those surpluses.

Supply Restriction, Prices, and Receipts

Will supply restriction for a specific product in and of itself raise the receipts of the producers of that product? We know that a decrease in supply, given the demand for the product, will raise the price. It will also decrease the quantity exchanged. What are the effects on the producers' receipts? In Figure 14–5 suppose DD and SS are the demand and supply curves, respectively, for cotton. The price is p_c and the quantity sold is c. The total receipts of cotton producers are $c \cdot p_c$, or the area of the rectangle op_cec.

If the government now enacts measures that succeed in moving the supply curve to the left to S_1S_1, the price will rise to p_{c1} and the quantity sold will fall to c_1. Consumers are moved up and to the left on DD to position f. What happens to consumer expenditures, or, what amounts to the

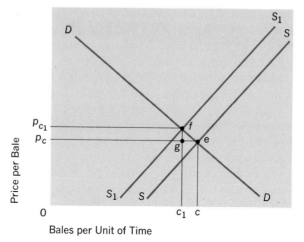

Figure 14–5
A supply restriction program.

same thing, to producers' receipts? A review of demand analysis indicates that the answer turns on the elacticity of demand for cotton. If demand for cotton is inelastic for the increase in price, as it is in Figure 14–5, the total receipts of cotton farmers will increase. The area of the rectangle $op_{c1}fc_1$ represents total receipts after the change in supply, and by inspection we can determine that it is larger than that of $op_cec.$[6] However, if the elasticity of demand were unitary for the price increase, there would be no change in the total receipts of cotton farmers. If demand were elastic, total receipts would actually decrease. Supply restriction by itself, then, can always raise the price of a product, but it can increase the total receipts of sellers *only if demand for the product is inelastic.*

Supply Restriction and Surpluses

As the federal agricultural program has developed since 1933, supply restrictions have not really been used directly for the purpose of increasing receipts of sellers, except for a short period in 1933. Rather, they have been aimed at reducing yearly surpluses and at holding down the total costs of price-support operations. In Figure 14–6, given the demand curve DD and the supply curve SS, if the price of wheat were to be supported by the storage and loan method at p_1, surpluses of w_1w_1' per time period would accrue. These would build up a surplus stock of the product that would present problems with respect to storage costs and what to do with it.

---

[6] The reduction in supply chops c_1gec off the original total receipts rectangle and adds $p_cp_{c1}fg$ to it.

If supply could be decreased toward S_1S_1, the periodic additions to the stockpile of the product would be smaller. If it could be decreased even more to S_2S_2, the stockpile could be diminished by an amount w_2w_1 per time period. Restriction of supply to S_1S_1 would make it unnecessary for farmers to seek government loans and this very substantial cost of the program would be eliminated. The only remaining costs would be those of storing and disposing of any existing stock that has been accumulated in past years.

Methods of Restricting Supply

The federal government has employed two primary methods to reduce supplies of price-supported products. Farm legislation has included *acreage allotments* for reducing acres planted for some crops. In some instances the "stick" technique has been used to secure compliance with acreage allotments—that is, penalties have been placed on noncomplying farmers. In other cases the government has used the "carrot," or payments to farmers for placing land in a soil bank; that is, for diverting land to soil-building uses or for leaving it idle altogether. For other crops it has used *marketing quotas* specifying the amounts that individual farmers can market at support prices. For still others acreage allotments and marketing quotas have both been employed.

Marketing quotas are generally more effective than acreage controls

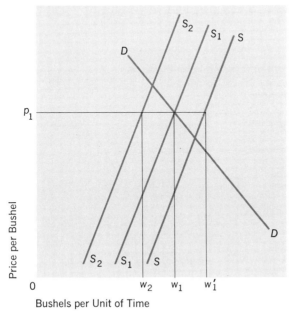

Figure 14–6
A combination of price support and supply restriction.

in reducing supplies. The effectiveness of acreage allotments is reduced by at least two reactions on the part of farmers. First, farmers withdraw their most infertile acres from cultivation. Second, they tend to farm more intensively those acres left in cultivation by working the ground better and using better fertilizing techniques. Consequently, the reductions in the total outputs of a farmer are likely to be proportionally much less than the reductions in the acreage that he plants.

Surplus Disposal

Supply restrictions have not been stringent enough to prevent the stockpiling of very substantial surpluses of a number of farm commodities. Table 14–3 indicates the peak investment of the Commodity Credit Corporation in various farm products and the year in which the peak was reached. Note that investment in three commodities alone—corn, cotton, and wheat—each exceeded two billion dollars. Some inroads have been made on the surpluses since the peak years indicated in the table.

The CCC has made every effort to sell from its surplus stocks domestically, but it is handicapped, since by law it cannot sell commercially at less than 5 percent above the support price of the product. Commercial sales can be effected, then, only when the market price exceeds the support price by 5 percent. The CCC is permitted, however, to donate from its stocks for a number of charitable or welfare purposes. These include nonprofit school lunch programs, assistance to the needy, disaster relief,

TABLE 14–3
Peak Investment in Selected Farm Products
by the Commodity Credit Corporation
(millions of dollars)

Product	Investment	Year of peak Investment
Wheat and products	3,096.6	1960
Corn and products	2,733.7	1961
Cotton, upland	2,352.2	1956
Grain sorghum	844.3	1962
Tobacco	673.6	1956
Butter and products	327.0	1954
Soybeans	277.6	1959
Rice	238.6	1956
Cottonseed oil	178.2	1954
Cheese	174.0	1954
Barley	155.4	1959
Milk, dried	115.1	1962

Source: *Summary of 30 Years' Operation of the CCC* (Washington, D.C.: U.S. Department of Agriculture, 1964), p. 27.

emergency livestock feed, grain for migratory waterfowl and game birds, and others.

By far the most important outlet for surplus disposal has been exports to foreign countries. Exports of surplus stocks by the CCC have been primarily of two kinds: (1) export sales for dollars and (2) exports made under Public Law 480, the Agricultural Trade Development and Assistance Act of 1954, as amended from time to time. Export sales by the CCC differ from domestic sales in that there is no requirement that they be made at prices exceeding support prices. In fact, they are usually made at less than support prices, that is, at a loss to the CCC. Export disposals under the provisions of Public Law 480 are made to dollar-short countries for their own currencies rather than for dollars, for relief and economic assistance abroad, to nonprofit volunteer relief agencies for distribution abroad, and for long-term dollar credit sales to foreign countries. These, too, involve the CCC in losses. Nevertheless, surplus disposal in recent years has succeeded in reducing the once embarrassingly large surpluses to relatively modest proportions.

AN APPRAISAL OF THE FARM PROGRAM

What can we say about the effectiveness of the federal farm program in alleviating agriculture's twin problems of instability and relatively low incomes? Now that we have some grasp of the nature of farm legislation, we should be able to make a tentative appraisal of what it has accomplished in these areas.

The Impact on Instability

To begin with, we can ask ourselves how a price-support program, particularly a storage and loan program, might be expected to contribute toward stability of farm incomes. Many proponents of this sort of plan argue that accumulated stocks of farm commodities act as a buffer against the exaggerated effects of fluctuations in economic activity in general on farm prices and farm incomes, as well as against irregularities in supply caused by natural phenomena. The argument runs to the effect that in periods of recession and depression the government should support prices above their equilibrium levels and thus accumulate surpluses. This would serve to hold farm incomes above what they would be if equilibrium or free market prices were to prevail. During periods of boom and inflation, the government's stocks of goods should be placed on the market, depressing prices below the equilibrium or free market levels that would otherwise prevail. This would curb the disproportionately large rise in farm incomes that ordinarily occurs in times such as these. The average level of farm incomes would be neither increased nor decreased by the government's purchase and sale operations. It would simply be leveled out over the range of business fluctuations.

The main fly in the ointment in the practice of storage and loan operations has been that in periods of prosperity and inflation the government has not been willing to depress domestic prices of farm products enough to sell off its surpluses. Support prices since World War II have, with some exceptions, been above equilibrium levels and the surpluses discussed in the preceding section were accumulated. Only by disposing of these—at substantial losses—to other countries has the CCC been able to relieve itself of impossible surplus problems. To put all of this another way, stabilization of farm incomes over the course of economic fluctuations has been subordinated to the goal of supporting farm prices.

The Impact on Poverty

The farm program has undoubtedly served to increase average farm income, but there is considerable room for doubting that it has decreased farm poverty. Table 14–1 provides supporting evidence for the first part of this seeming paradox, while Table 14–2 furnishes us material for the doubting expressed in the second part.

The methods used for distributing funds to farmers simply have not been geared to alleviating poverty. In fact, they have tended to increase the differences between the incomes of large and small farmers. Price supports, representing a very large share of the total payments made to farmers, reward farmers in direct proportion to the amounts they produce. Similarly, soil bank payments are greater for those owning large amounts of land than for those owning smaller amounts or none at all. Those farmers who need government assistance the least are precisely those who receive the largest amounts of it. These are the operators of the large, efficient farm businesses. The poor farmers, the small, inefficient operators, who should receive relief if relief is to be based on any kind of an income test, receive very small amounts of help. What kind of a welfare program is this?

Some Modest Proposals

Destructive criticism is easier to offer than constructive recommendations. We have been critical of farm legislation as it has developed in the

United States. What can we say of a positive nature? If the farm problems were tossed in our laps, how would we go about trying to alleviate them?

Toward Stability

The problem of inherent instability of farm incomes during fluctuations in economic activity is only one piece of the larger problem of instability of the economy as a whole. If economic fluctuations for the entire economy can be controlled, then we will have gone far toward achieving stability in farm incomes. The last half of this book is largely devoted to the causes and consequences of economic instability and to its control.

Instability of farm incomes stemming from natural phenomena is a less serious problem and is being attacked in a number of ways. The present crop insurance program goes far toward providing protection from hail, flood, and insect invasion. Much research done under the auspices of the Department of Agriculture is aimed toward pest and insect control. In many areas irrigation techniques have been developed that materially decreases farmers' dependence on uncertain rainfall. Thus, much is being done to mitigate instability of this kind.

Toward Alleviating Poverty

We have already discussed the causes of farm poverty. The relatively slow increase in demand for agricultural products, together with the rapid rise in agricultural technology, has caused the proportion of the economy's resources used in the production of agricultural products to become too large compared with that used for nonagricultural goods and services. Further, on a large number of farms resources are used inefficiently. The great many small farms, producing under $10,000 worth of product per year, are too small to take advantage of some very important economies of scale.

In terms of cold, hard logic, there appear to be two key elements necessary for alleviating farm poverty. One is the movement of resources, particularly human resources, out of agriculture and into nonagricultural uses. The fact that consumers are willing to pay less for what those resources can produce in agriculture than for what they could produce in other sectors of the economy[7] points toward this sort of movement as a solution. The other is the consolidation of small, inefficient farm units into larger, businesslike operations.

Changes of both types are occurring. From 1935 to 1966 the farm

[7] This, in turn, is evidenced by the lower earnings of resources used in agricultural pursuits.

population decreased from 32.2 million to 11.6 million persons, and the exodus from the farm continues. Average acreage per farm in the United States increased from 155 acres in 1935 to 359 acres in 1967.[8] These data reflect a decreasing number of small farms, or those under 500 acres, and an increasing number of large farms. But these changes have not yet progressed rapidly enough nor gone far enough to solve the low income problem.

Agricultural legislation appears to have done little or nothing toward eliminating the causes of poverty. Rather, it has been directed at the symptoms of the problem—relatively declining agricultural prices. To some extent, by rewarding large-scale farmers more handsomely than small-scale farmers, it may have accelerated the trend toward larger numbers of large farms and smaller numbers of small farms. But on the other hand, in paying extra amounts per unit of product produced, such legislation has made farming in general relatively more attractive than it would otherwise be, and thus to some extent it impedes the flow of resources out of agriculture.

Government agricultural policies should facilitate the structural readjustment now going on. The requisite background is a stable prosperous economy with low levels of unemployment. Instead of paying out large sums of money to the already prosperous segments of the farm population, large sums of money could be paid to the poor segments, retraining them for nonfarm occupations and subsidizing their migration out of agriculture. To some extent these objectives are being accomplished through the Great Society legislation of the middle 1960's. Further, government and quasi-government programs designed to encourage young people to enter agriculture should receive less emphasis. This is not to say that those who want to be farmers should not be trained to be efficient farmers. But young people, particularly in rural areas, should be made aware of alternative occupational and earning opportunities.

SUMMARY

The economic problems in agriculture that have evoked wholesale government intervention in that sector of the economy are (1) low average incomes and (2) instability of prices and incomes.

Not all farmers are poor. The largest part of farm product output and

[8] *Statistical Abstract of the United States,* 1967 (88th edition) (Washington, D.C.: U.S. Bureau of the Census, 1967), p. 605.

farm income—over 85 percent of the latter—is generated by less than one-third of all farm units. Most of these are well-run business enterprises. The poverty problem occurs in the other two thirds of the total number of farm units that generate less than 15 percent of total farm income.

Farm poverty comes about because a large sector of the farm population has not been willing or able to adapt to changing conditions of demand for and supply of agricultural products. Over time, demand for these has increased at a slower pace than it has for industrial products and for services. At the same time, farm technology has advanced rapidly, creating relatively large increases in supply. Thus farm prices have risen more slowly than prices in general. These circumstances call for a shift of population out of agriculture—a shift that has been taking place at a pace too slow to solve the income problem. They also call for an increase in the acreage size of farms in order that advantage can be taken of economies of scale.

Instability of farm prices and incomes stems from two sources. One is the peculiar dependence of agriculture on the forces of nature. The other is the sensitivity of agriculture to instability in the economy as a whole.

The massive response of government to agricultural problems has centered on maintaining farm prices above what they would be in a free market. Parity prices are prices of farm products that bear the same relation to nonfarm prices as existed in some base period. These serve as reference points for price supports but have themselves always been above support levels.

Price supports for nonperishable key farm commodities have been instituted for the most part through a storage and loan program. In essence, farmers sell what they can at support prices and the government buys and stores the remainder. When price supports are above equilibrium price levels, surpluses accumulate.

Subsidies are also used to support some farm prices. These permit farmers to sell their entire supplies at whatever the market will pay, with the government making up the difference between the support price and the market price. Subsidies have the virtues of avoiding surpluses and of being easily and directly seen for what they are.

Surpluses are troublesome as well as costly and have resulted in legislation to restrict supplies of the price-supported products through acreage controls and market quotas for individual farms. They have also induced the government to search for as many outlets for disposal as possible. To date, disposal of surplus products to underdeveloped economies have had the most success in keeping surplus stocks manageable.

The farm program has not been an unqualified success in attacking the problems of instability and poverty. The former has been subordinated to the latter to some extent, but in any case stability of farm incomes is to a large extent dependent on stability of the economy as a whole. Undoubtedly, the price-support program has increased average farm incomes, but it has done so by giving much more to larger, higher-income farmers than to smaller, lower-income farmers. It is a sort of topsy-turvy relief program.

From the point of view of economic analysis, the alleviation of farm poverty calls for two things: (1) the movement of resources, human resources in particular, out of agriculture and into other sectors of the economy and (2) a movement toward more and more large farms together with fewer and fewer small farms. Both of these shifts are taking place. It would appear desirable that farm programs be geared to facilitating them.

EXERCISES AND QUESTIONS FOR DISCUSSION

1. What would be the consequences if the present price-support programs were suddenly eliminated?
2. "Agricultural incomes are low because the farmer is paid less than a 'fair' price for his produce." Evaluate this statement.
3. If you were in a position to make decisions regarding the current "farm problem," how would you modify the present approach?
4. Under what type of market structure would you classify the agricultural industry? Is there a need for government intervention? Give reasons.
5. Why might foreign countries complain about the U.S. government selling its surplus in their market? How might this affect U.S. private producers' exports of agricultural products?

SELECTED READINGS

Committee for Economic Development, *An Adaptive Program for Agriculture,* 3d printing. New York, The Committee, 1963.

Higbee, Edward, *Farms and Farmers in an Urban Age.* New York: The Twentieth Century Fund, 1963.

Rasmussen, Wayne D., and Gladys L. Baker, "A Short History of Price Support and Adjustment Legislation and Programs for Agriculture, 1933–1965," *Agricultural Economics Research,* Vol. XVIII, July 1966, pp. 69–78.

U.S. Department of Agriculture, *Report of the President of the Commodity Credit Corporation.* Washington, D.C., yearly.

———, *Summary of 30 Years' Operations of the Commodity Credit Corporation.* Washington, D.C., 1964.

PART 3 Microeconomics: Markets for Resources

In Part 3 we turn the microscope from the upper half of the circular flow model of Figure 2–1 to the lower half. We shall examine in detail the markets for resources—the ingredients used by business firms to produce the goods and services they sell. The participants in resource markets are the business firms that use them on the demand side and the resource owners who place them in employment on the supply side.

Since we earn our incomes by selling or hiring out the resources we own, it is small wonder that we evidence great individual and collective interest in the operations of resource markets. We worry about the opportunities for the employment of our resources—and rightly so. The Great Depression of the 1930s, with its massive unemployment of both labor and capital, must rank among the major economic disasters of modern times. In more recent times—in the late 1950s and early 1960s—many economists thought that unemployment rates of from 4 to 7 percent of the labor force were unduly high and policy measures were enacted by the federal government to reduce them.

Many people believe that incomes in the United States are not distributed equitably. They think that some—usually the other fellows—make too much, while others—usually themselves—make too little. Thus we have legislation that superimposes redistribution schemes on the market mechanism. The best examples are the progressive income tax, social welfare legislation, including War on Poverty measures and Medicare, minimum wage laws, and agricultural legislation. Additionally, we have labor unions dedicated to income redistribution among other things.

The debates that turn on these issues in the newspapers, in periodicals, on television, and from soap boxes are generally marked by a lack of understanding of elementary economic principles. What are the relations between resource prices and their levels of employment? How do resource prices affect their allocations among different employments? Does it matter whether the firms that use resources sell their outputs in competitive or in monopolized markets? What do resource prices have to do with the distribution of income and of the economy's output? How do unions affect all this? These are the kinds of questions that Part III should help us to answer.

Resource Pricing and Employment in Competitive Markets

CHAPTER 15

A competitive model provides the simplified framework for establishing the principles of resource pricing and employment. Using such a framework in this chapter, we shall review first the nature and objectives of competitive firms. Next, we shall examine the conditions of demand for and of supply of specific resources. The determination of prices and quantities exchanged follows. Finally, we shall take another look at a subject we met in Chapter 7—least-cost combinations of resources for a single firm.

COMPETITIVE FIRMS

Competition in Resource Purchases

Competition in the sale of products has already been explored, but we have not said much about competition in purchasing. We noted that the essential ingredient for competition among sellers is that no one seller of a product can place a large enough proportion of the total supply of the product on the market to influence its price. The seller faces a horizontal demand curve for his output at whatever the going market price happens to be. He cannot, by himself, influence market price of the product.

Competition in purchasing is very similar. *Pure competition* in the purchasing of an item or a service can occur only if each purchaser demands such a small part of the total amount demanded that by himself he cannot influence the market price. Any single purchaser can take as much or as little as he desires at the going price. As we shall see, this makes the supply curve of whatever he is purchasing appear to him to be at a constant level, or horizontal at the going market price. This, together with pure competition in the selling of products, is the kind of situation that we assume exists in the analysis presented in this chapter.

OBJECTIVES IN RESOURCE PURCHASES

Business firms are usually established to make money, and the people who operate them are usually interested in making more money rather than less. Technically, we say the objective is to make profits. Generally we suppose that, given the economic climate within which business firms must operate, they attempt to maximize profits. We have already discussed the behavior of firms as product sellers, based on the postulate of profit maximization. Firms tend to produce at the output levels at which their marginal costs equal their marginal revenues.

Consider now a profit-maximizing firm contemplating the quantities of variable resources that it ought to use per unit of time. Since by itself the firm has no control over the prices of the resources it buys, it can adjust only the quantities employed. Consider specifically such a resource as common labor. How much of it should the firm employ? The answer is found by increasing or decreasing slightly the quantity employed and by observing the resulting effects on the firm's total revenues and total costs. If a one-unit increase in the level of employment increases the firm's total receipts by more than it increases its total costs, then the increase in the employment level brings about a *net addition* to the firm's profits. It pays to make the increase. If a one-unit decrease in the employment of labor decreases total receipts by less than it decreases total costs, then profits are increased by the decrease in the employment level.

No new principles were introduced in the preceding paragraph; we simply placed familiar principles in a new setting. Instead of looking at marginal cost and marginal revenue in terms of one-unit increases or decreases in the firm's *output,* we view the same concepts in terms of one-unit increases or decreases in the firm's *resource inputs.* In this latter context the fundamental principles still hold. If the marginal revenue of a resource input exceeds its marginal cost, it pays to increase its employment. If its marginal revenue is less than its marginal cost, its employment should be contracted. Profits are maximized at the employment level at which the marginal revenue of the input is equal to its marginal cost. This concept will be examined in detail in the following sections.

DEMAND FOR A RESOURCE

Do you believe that the quantity demanded of a resource varies inversely with its price? Do you expect that farmers will purchase less fertilizer per year at higher prices than at lower prices? Do you believe that higher beef prices will induce your student union or dormitory cafeteria to put less meat in the stew? If wage rates rise, will the amount of labor employed in the supermarket decrease? Most of us intuitively would answer these questions in the affirmative, yet in our everyday discussions with others we frequently deny their validity. Suppose we look into the nature of demand for a resource. The first step is to get a firm grasp of a concept called *marginal revenue product* of a resource. This will enable us to define and construct an individual firm's demand curve for the resource. We shall then consider the forces that cause changes in demand and, finally, how individual firm demand curves are put together to form the market demand curve.

Marginal Revenue Product

The *marginal revenue product* of a resource is defined as the change in a firm's total receipts resulting from a one-unit change in the quantity of the resource employed. How is it computed and how does it behave as the firm increases or decreases the employment level of the resource? The answers to these questions are constructed from the analytical framework established in Chapters 7 and 9. In Chapter 7 we observed how changes occur in a firm's product output for one-unit changes in the quantities of its resource inputs. We related this *marginal physical product* of a resource to the quantity of it employed and we noted that, because of the law of diminishing returns, it declines as the quantity of the resource employed is increased. In Chapter 9 we found that a firm selling its output under conditions of pure competition sells as much or as little as it desires at a constant price—the market price—per unit, and that marginal revenue from a one-unit increase or decrease in sales is equal to that price. Putting these together, we see that a one-unit change in the employment level of a resource changes the firm's output by some certain amount—the marginal physical product of a resource. This change in the firm's output multiplied by the change in its total receipts per unit change in output—the marginal revenue—is the marginal revenue product of the resource. If we compute the marginal revenue product for each possible level of employment, we obtain a marginal revenue product schedule that slopes downward to the right.

Table 15-1 presents a marginal revenue product schedule for common labor in a hypothetical brick factory. The total daily outputs of bricks at different employment levels are given in columns (1) and (2). Marginal physical product of labor at different employment levels in column (3) is computed from the total product schedule. The price of bricks is assumed to be given at 25 cents each, so marginal revenue from the firm's sales will also be 25 cents. This is shown in column (4). The marginal revenue product schedule is found by multiplying the marginal physical product of labor at each level of employment by marginal revenue from the sale of bricks. For example, when the employment level is increased from three to four workers, marginal physical product is 110 bricks. Since each brick sells for 25 cents, the increase in the employment level increases the firm's total receipts by 110 times 25 cents, or by $27.50. Similarly, a further increase in the employment level to five workers would increase total receipts by another $25. When this is done for all levels of employment, we obtain the marginal revenue product schedule of column (5), which indicates at each level of employment how much a one-unit change in employment will change the firm's total receipts. The schedule is plotted as marginal revenue product curve MRP_l in Figure 15-1.

Demand Schedules and Demand Curves

The firm's marginal revenue product schedule or curve for a resource is really its demand schedule or curve for the resource, although this may not be readily apparent. The demand schedule should show quantities of the resource that the firm will take at alternative prices, other things being equal. When the firm is a purely competitive purchaser of the resource, the marginal revenue product schedule shows just that.

What about the impact of changes in the employment level on costs? Suppose the price per unit of labor for the brick factory is $15. Since it purchases labor under conditions of pure competition, it can get all it wants at that price, so a one-unit change in the quantity of labor employed changes the firm's total costs by $15, an amount equal to the price. We call the change in total cost per unit change in the employment level the *marginal resource cost* of whatever resource we are considering. Thus the marginal resource cost of labor is $15 at all employment levels, as indicated in column (6) in Table 15-1.

We now have all the information we need to determine the firm's profit-maximizing level of employment. Referring to Table 15-1, we see that the employment of one unit rather than none increases total receipts by $35 ($MRP_l$) while it increases total costs by $15 ($MRC_l$). Thus $20 is added to the firm's profits by this move. We call the change in profit per unit change in the employment level the *marginal profit* from employment

TABLE 15-1
Profit Maximization with Respect to Common Labor
in a Hypothetical Brick Factory[a]
(outputs and inputs are rates per day)

(1) QUANTITY OF LABOR (L)	(2) TOTAL PRODUCT (X)	(3) MARGINAL PHYSICAL PRODUCT $\left(\dfrac{\Delta X}{\Delta L} = MPP_l\right)$	(4) MARGINAL REVENUE $\left(\dfrac{\Delta TR}{\Delta X} = MR_x\right)$	(5) MARGINAL REVENUE PRODUCT $(MPP_l \cdot MR_x$ $= MRP_l)$	(6) MARGINAL RESOURCE COST $\left(\dfrac{\Delta TC}{\Delta L} = MRC_l\right)$	(7) MARGINAL PROFIT $\left(\dfrac{\Delta \pi}{\Delta L}\right)$
1	140	140	$0.25	$35.00	$15.00	$20.00
2	270	130	0.25	32.50	15.00	17.50
3	390	120	0.25	30.00	15.00	15.00
4	500	110	0.25	27.50	15.00	12.50
5	600	100	0.25	25.00	15.00	10.00
6	680	80	0.25	20.00	15.00	5.00
7	740	60	0.25	15.00	15.00	0.00
8	780	40	0.25	10.00	15.00	(−) 5.00
9	800	20	0.25	5.00	15.00	(−) 10.00
10	800	0	0.25	0.00	15.00	(−) 15.00

[a] Let X represent quantities of bricks and L quantities of common labor.

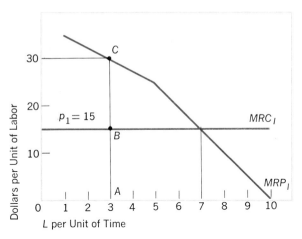

Figure 15-1
The profit-maximizing level of employment of a resource.

of the resource. A further increase in employment to two units per day
yields a $17.50 increase in profits. Third, fourth, fifth, and sixth units per
day also yield profit increases. But now, consider a move to the seven-unit
level of employment. It adds $15 to total receipts and the same amount
to total costs; therefore, it adds nothing to profits. Neither does it decrease them. However, pressing the employment level to eight units
causes profits to fall by $5. If profits increase up to the seven-unit level of

employment and fall with the eight-unit level, they must be maximum at seven units, or where the *marginal revenue product of labor* (MRP_l) is equal to the *marginal resource cost of labor* (MRC_l). Thus if the price of labor were $15, the brick factory would be in equilibrium—that is, would be maximizing its profits with respect to labor—by taking seven units of labor.[1] This price–quantity combination is one point on the firm's demand curve for labor.

The marginal revenue product column, column (5) in Table 15–1, also indicates the other quantities that the firm would take at alternative possible prices of labor. If the price (and marginal resource cost) were $30, the firm would employ three units per day. If it were $10, the firm would take eight units per day. Whatever the price of labor happens to be, profits are maximized with respect to it by adjusting the quantity employed to the point at which MRP_l is equal to MRC_l. In other words, the marginal revenue product schedule is the firm's demand schedule for the resource.

All of the data for the preceding analysis can be presented graphically. In Figure 15–1, the MRP_l curve is simply column (5) of Table 15–1 plotted against column (1). The MRC_l line represents column (6). If the employment level were less than seven units—say three units—marginal resource cost is *AB*, or $15; and the marginal profit of labor is *BC*, or $15. At the seven-unit employment level MRP_l is equal to MRC_l and marginal profit is zero; that is, profits have reached their maximum. At higher employment levels marginal profit is negative and total profit could be increased by decreasing the level of employment.

If we step back now and look at the firm's demand curve for a resource —that is, the marginal revenue product curve—we note that it slopes downward to the right because of the law of diminishing returns. Marginal revenue product is composed of two elements: (1) the marginal physical product of the resource and (2) the marginal revenue of the product being produced and sold. Letting MPP_a be the marginal physical product of resource A and MR_x be the marginal revenue from the sale of product X, we can define the marginal revenue product of A as

$$MRP_a = MPP_a \times MR_x$$

The law of diminishing returns assures us that as the employment of A is increased, MPP_a will decline, causing MRP_a to decline also. (What happens to MR_x as the purely competitive seller of X increases its sales?) The downward slope of the resource demand curve indicates, too, that

---

[1] Actually, with the discrete—as opposed to a continuous—set of quantity numbers used in Table 15–1, profits are maximum at the six- as well as at the seven-unit level of employment. It is more convenient and not incorrect to consider the $MRP_1 = MRC_1$ quantity, or the one as close to it as one can get, as the profit-maximizing quantity.

an increase in the price of a resource, other things being equal, will reduce the firm's level of employment of it.

Changes in Demand

Changes in a firm's demand curve for a resource may occur when "other things being equal" change. The three most important of these other things are (1) the quantities of those resources used by the firm that are related to the resource under consideration, (2) the marginal revenue from the product that the resource is used to produce, and (3) the techniques of production available to the firm. Let us examine the significance of each of these factors.

Quantities of Related Resources

The resources used by a firm in making a product may be related to one another in either of two ways. Some of them may be *complementary*—the more of one such resource used, the more productive those complementary to it will be. Other resources may be *substitutes*—the more of one that is used, the less productive the substitutes will be.

Consider, for example, the production of men's suits. Labor used in the production process is, in general, complementary to the capital comprising the plant in which production takes place. Given the work space, tables, thimbles, and needles, the quantity of labor can be varied, and a marginal physical product curve such as MPP_{l_1} in Figure 15–2(a) is determined. Given the price at which men's suits are sold, the marginal physical product at each level of employment can be multiplied by the marginal revenue (equals price) per suit, and the marginal revenue product curve, MRP_{l_1}, of Figure 15–2(b) is thus established. Now suppose that the amount of capital is increased through the addition of sewing machines. At each of the alternative employment levels the marginal physical product of labor will now be greater, shifting the curve to the right to MPP_{l_2}. This in turn shifts the marginal revenue product curve in Figure 15–2(b) to the right to MRP_{l_2}—that is, *an increase in the quantity of one of two complementary resources utilized will increase the demand for the other. A decrease in the quantity of one such resource will decrease the demand for the other.*

Consider another example, one that has now become history. In the 1920s and 1930s horses and tractors were substitute sources of power for farming operations. Given the tractor power available to a wheat farm, the marginal physical product curve for alternative numbers of horses can be determined. Then, given the price per bushel of wheat, the mar-

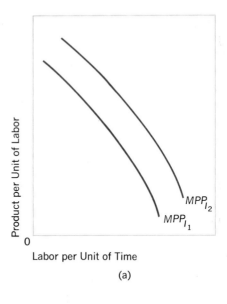

(a)

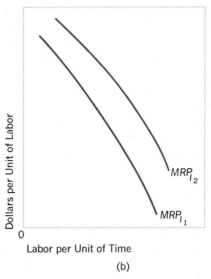

(b)

Figure 15-2
The effects on *MPP* and *MRP* of a resource of changes in quantities employed of related resources.

ginal revenue product curve of horses can be computed. Suppose now that the tractor power available increases. The marginal physical product of horses at each of the possible employment levels will now be less than before, or, as we usually put it, there is "less for the horses to do now." The marginal revenue product curve for horses—that is, the demand curve for them—will now have shifted to the left. (Can you show this situation diagrammatically?) *An increase in the employment level of one of two substitute resources will decrease the demand for the other. A decrease in the employment level of one will increase the demand for the other.*

Changes in Marginal Revenue

Anything that changes the price or marginal revenue that a firm receives from the sale of the product it produces will change the firm's demand curve for any resource that it uses. Price and marginal revenue changes come from changes in the conditions of market supply of and demand for the product. The latter were discussed in Chapters 4 and 9.

Table 15–2 illustrates the effects of changes in the firm's marginal revenue on its demand for a resource. Suppose that columns (1) and (2) represent the marginal physical product schedule of 100-pound bags of fertilizer on a wheat farm. The price of wheat and the marginal revenue from its sale are given in column (3) as $2 per bushel. The resulting marginal revenue product schedule, or the demand schedule for fertilizer, is given in column (4). Now suppose that in the economy the demand for wheat increases, raising the price to $3 per bushel, as indicated in column (3a). The marginal revenue product schedule or the demand schedule for fertilizer becomes that of column (4a). *An increase in the marginal revenue received from the sale of its output will increase a firm's demand for the resources that it uses.* A decrease in marginal revenue will have the opposite effect.

TABLE 15–2
Effects of Alternative Marginal Revenue
Levels for Wheat on the Demand for Fertilizer[a]

(1) FERTILIZER (F IN 100-LB. SACKS)	(2) MARGINAL PHYSICAL PRODUCT $\left(\frac{\Delta W}{\Delta F} = MPP_f\right)$	(3) MARGINAL REVENUE $(MR_w = P_w)$	(4) MARGINAL REVENUE PRODUCT $(MRP_f = MPP_f \cdot MR_w)$	(3a) MARGINAL REVENUE (MR_w)	(4a) MARGINAL REVENUE PRODUCT $(MRP_f = MPP_f \cdot MR_w)$
1	15	$2.00	$30.00	$3.00	$45.00
2	14	2.00	28.00	3.00	42.00
3	13	2.00	26.00	3.00	39.00
4	12	2.00	24.00	3.00	36.00
5	11	2.00	22.00	3.00	33.00
6	9.5	2.00	19.00	3.00	28.50
7	7.5	2.00	15.00	3.00	22.50
8	5.5	2.00	11.00	3.00	16.50
9	3	2.00	6.00	3.00	9.00
10	0	2.00	0.00	3.00	0.00

[a] Let F represent quantities of fertilizer in 100-pound sacks and W quantities of wheat in bushels.

Changes in Technology

Demands for resources are affected by changes in the technology used by a firm. Technological improvements will increase the demand for some resources while for others demand will fall as new technology makes them obsolete.

Many examples exist of increased demand for resources generated by technological changes. How have improvements in automobile technology affected General Motors' demand for steel? What impact has the development of atomic energy plants had on the demand for uranium? How has the advent of computers affected the demand for keypunch machines?

Similarly, an abundance of examples can be found in which new technology has decreased the demand for certain resources. Physicians and traveling salesmen no longer demand horses and buggies. Cigar rolling machines decreased the demand for human cigar rollers (but increased the demand for machine tenders). The development of television teaching techniques may reduce the demand for instructors in economics.

Market Demand Curves

Now that we understand individual firm demand curves for a resource, how do we move on to the total market demand curve? We can learn a lesson here from Chapter 5. The construction of the market demand curve for a resource from individual firm demand curves is similar to the construction of the market demand curve for a product from those of individual consumers.

In Figure 15–3, suppose that firm I and firm II are two of the many firms using some certain resource A. At a price of p_a, firm I wants quantity a and firm II wants quantity a'. Quantities desired by other firms at that price are similarly determined, and the sum of all of these quantities will be the market quantity A. Quantity A at price p_a is one point on the market demand curve, the point labeled H in the market diagram. Similarly, at a price of p_{a_0}, firm I would take a_0; firm II would take a'_0; and other firms would also take those quantities at which their MRP_a curves are equal to p_{a_0}. Together, firms will take quantity A_0, which, when plotted against the price, locates point J in the market diagram. The quantities that will be taken by all firms at other price levels can be determined in this way and they trace out the market demand curve $D_a D_a$. Thus the market demand curve is found by summing at each possible price level the quantities that individual firms will take.

The firms using resource A need not all be in the same industry, and, as a matter of fact, probably will not be. Any given resource is likely to be used in making a number of different products. Common labor, for

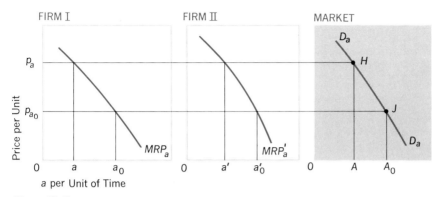

Figure 15-3
Construction of market demand for a resource.

example, is used in the making of almost all goods and services. Thus in Figure 15-3, firm I may very well be producing one product while firm II produces another. Each has its own demand curve for *A,* and these can be used to construct the market demand curve, or the quantities that all firms together will take at different possible price levels.

SUPPLY OF A RESOURCE

Turning now to the supply side of the picture, we need to discover what determines the market supply of any given resource. First, we must determine who resource owners are, and these include a wide variety of persons and institutions. Labor resources are owned and placed in employment by almost every family in the economy. Government units own some resources, or at least control the services of them; electricity sold to businesses by a municipally owned power plant is a case in point. The outputs of some firms, for example, those in the basic steel industry, are resource inputs to others. Even churches may own land and buildings that they rent out to others to be used in production processes.

Individual resource owners have their own individual supply curves for whatever it is that they own. The shape of one such curve depends upon the response that the owner would make to alternative price offers. Owners of a given kind of labor may be willing to work more hours per day at good wage rates than at lower wage rates; for example, desire for a higher salary may well induce a professor to spend nights in his office in hopes that he can improve his publication record and earn more money. At higher wage rates leisure time is made more expensive and people may thus be willing to do with less of it. Business enterprises, the outputs of which are resource inputs for other firms, are motivated by higher prices to expand the quantities they place on the market because they can make more profits by doing so.[2] In general, then, we expect the supply curves of individual suppliers of resources to slope upward to the right; that is, more of a resource will be placed on the market at higher prices than at lower prices.[3]

What about market supply curves? We construct them from the supply curves of individual owners in the same manner as we construct market demand curves. In Figure 15–4, if the price of resource A were p_a, owner I would place quantity a on the market; owner II would place a' on the market; other owners would do likewise, and the total quantity forthcoming at that price would be A. Point L on the market supply curve would thus be determined. By similar additions of quantities at other prices, other points tracing out the supply curve S_aS_a are found. Since supply curves of individual owners generally slope upward to the right, we expect market supply curves to do so too.

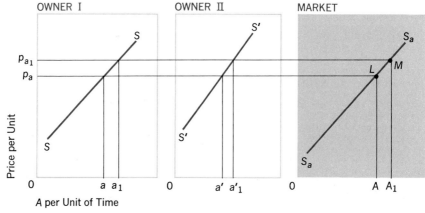

Figure 15–4
Construction of market supply of a resource.

At higher price levels more resource owners may be pulled into the market for any given resource. A workman may have talents as a carpenter, as a bricklayer, and as a plumber, and his choice of trade will depend upon the comparative earning possibilities in the three. If there are a number of workers with several such arrows for their bows, a relative increase in carpenters' wages will draw additional workers into that occupation, whereas a relative decrease will cause workers to choose one of the other occupations.

[2] See Chapters 9, 10, and 11.
[3] Sometimes the opposite seems to occur. A man may "moonlight" because his primary employment pays too little to provide the consumption level desired by him and his family.

RESOURCE PRICING AND EMPLOYMENT

The remaining problem of how the price and employment levels of a resource are determined in a purely competitive market is a familiar one. When we bring market demand and market supply together, the pricing problem is identical to the one we met in Chapter 4. We shall add to it a discussion of a persistent problem that recurs in our economy—the use of minimum pricing in an attempt to secure greater equity in income distribution.

The Equilibrium Price and Employment Level

Suppose in Figure 15–5 that the market demand and supply curves for common labor are D_lD_l and S_lS_l, respectively, and that MRP_l is the demand curve of one of the many firms that employ this resource. Although the vertical scales of the two diagrams are identical, the quantity scale of the market diagram is greatly compressed as compared with that of the firm.

The equilibrium price or wage is p_l. It is determined by the forces of demand and supply in the same fashion as any other price is determined under conditions of pure competition. If the wage rate were above p_l, surpluses or unemployment of some units of labor would occur and, in the interest of obtaining employment, some workers would shade their asking prices, moving the wage rate downward toward p_l. If the wage rate

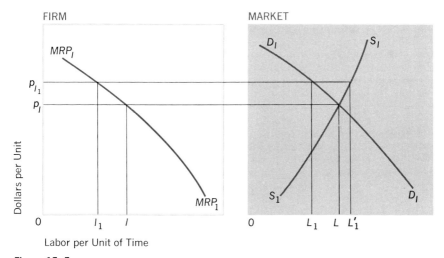

Figure 15–5
Resource pricing and employment.

were below p_l, the labor market would be plagued by shortages. Employers would bid against each other for the available supply, driving the wage rate toward p_l. The quantity of labor that employers want to employ is equal to the quantity of labor desiring employment at wage rate p_l.

The equilibrium employment level is L units of labor for the market as a whole. For any one firm using the resource, the employment level is some quantity at which the marginal revenue product of the resource is equal to its marginal resource cost; that is, the firm employs the quantity of the resource that maximizes its profits. The quantity L in the market diagram is the sum of such quantities as l for the individual firm at wage rate p_l.

Minimum Prices

Many people expect that firms will employ as much of a given resource at higher prices as they will at lower prices. Indeed, there is wide support for laws or policies that establish minimum prices for certain resources, and the advocates of such measures insist that there will be no adverse effects on employment levels. Cases in point are minimum wage laws and legislative and other government support of labor union activities in the wage-setting sphere. In certain imperfectly competitive markets, which we shall discuss in the next chapter, these advocates may be correct; but in competitive markets, a minimum price that is effective—that is, that lies above the equilibrium level—will result in unemployment.

Suppose in Figure 15–5 that a minimum wage level is set at p_{l_1}, either through collective bargaining between unions and employers or by means of a minimum wage law. The individual firm pictured there will reduce this employment level from l to l_1 units of labor. Other firms in the market for this kind of labor will do the same thing, and altogether the market level of employment will be reduced from L to L_1. But at the higher wage level more labor units are placed on the market and unemployment is measured by L_1L_1'.

That unemployment is the ordinary consequence of minimum price fixing in competitive markets should elicit no surprise. Given the price it must pay for a resource, an individual firm maximizes its profits by adjusting the quantity of the resource taken to that level at which its marginal revenue product is equal to its marginal resource cost (and price). The higher the price, the smaller the profit-maximizing quantity. In Figure 15–5, if the firm were taking quantity l at price p_{l_1}, it could increase its profits by reducing employment toward l_1. Each one-unit reduction in the employment level would reduce total costs more than it would reduce total receipts until employment level l_1 is reached.

Have the minimum wage provisions of the Fair Labor Standards Act of 1938 and its amendments brought on large-scale unemployment of labor? The answer to this question, at least to the mid-1960s, is clearly negative. Although there may have been unemployment effects in certain low-paying areas of the economy—southern sawmilling, clam picking, pecan shelling, and the like—the numbers involved have not been large. But this in no way negates the analysis of this section. By and large the minimum wage has not been effective in any significant proportion of the economy. Many small businesses not engaged in interstate commerce have been exempt from its provisions. Further, demand for labor has increased greatly since the 1930s, pressing most equilibrium wage levels well above the minimums established by the act, thus leaving the minimum levels largely ineffective.

The Value of a Resource

A question frequently raised by resource owners concerned with whether their incomes are as high as they ought to be is what the resources they place in employment are really worth. We should push the question one step further and ask what their resources are worth *to whom*. In economic analysis we distinguish between (1) the value of a resource to the firm that employs it and (2) the value of the resource to society.

To the Firm

How can we measure the value of units of a given resource to any one firm that employs them? Actually, we have solved this problem already. A unit of a resource is worth to the firm what it adds to the firm's total receipts—its marginal revenue product. This is why the firm will expand the employment level of the resource if the marginal revenue product of the resource exceeds its marginal resource cost; that is, if the resource is worth more to the firm than it costs. This is also why the firm will contract the employment level of the resource if the marginal revenue product of the resource is less than its marginal resource cost; that is, if the resource is not worth what it costs. In order to maximize profits the firm adjusts employment to that level at which the resource is just worth its marginal resource cost, or to the level at which marginal revenue product equals marginal resource cost. Thus, in general, in competitive markets resource units are worth to the firm just about what they are paid.

To Society

Although the value of a unit of any given resource to society as a whole is the same in dollar terms as it is to the firm where resource markets are competitive, its measurement is different, conceptually. Suppose we add one unit of common labor that had previously been unemployed to a firm's level of employment of that resource. The firm *and* society gain a certain amount of product—the MPP_l. If X is the product being produced, then $MPP_l \cdot MR_x$ represents the *marginal revenue product,* or the worth to the firm of the increase in employment. Note carefully that this is marginal physical product of the resource multiplied by the *marginal revenue* to the firm of the increment in product output and sales. The value placed by society on the extra product produced is measured by the price, p_x, that society is willing to pay for each unit of product. Thus the worth of a unit of labor to society is measured by $MPP_l \cdot p_x$, or the marginal physical product of the resource multiplied by the *price* of the product. This measure of the value of a unit of resource to society is appropriately called the *value of marginal product of the resource,* or in this case, VMP_l. To repeat, the value of a unit of any given resource to the firm is the marginal revenue product of the resource, while its value to society is its value of marginal product.

The marginal revenue product of a resource and its value of marginal product will not always be identical. Only where the resource users sell in competitive product markets are they the same. This statement can be easily understood with the following symbolic definitions:

$$MRP_l = MPP_l \cdot MR_x$$
$$VMP_l = MPP_l \cdot p_x$$

A one-unit change in the employment level of labor or any other resource will change product output by MPP_l, but only in purely competitive selling markets will MR_x and p_x be the same. What if the firm were selling its product under conditions of pure monopoly?

COMBINATIONS OF VARIABLE RESOURCES

The analysis of resource pricing and employment contained in the preceding sections enables us now to round out the discussion, introduced in Chapter 7, of least-cost combinations of variable resources used by a firm. Two points can be readily demonstrated. First, when a firm using two or more variable resources is using the profit-maximizing quantity of each, it is also using them in least-cost proportions. Second, when the profit-maximizing quantity of each variable resource is employed, the firm is producing the profit-maximizing quantity of output.

Suppose that a firm uses two variable resources, A and B, to produce product X. The profit-maximizing employment level of A is that quantity at which the marginal revenue product of A is equal to its marginal resource cost. For a firm that buys resource A under conditions of pure competition, marginal resource cost and the price of the resource are the same. All of these statements are equally valid for resource B. Consequently, we can express the profit-maximizing conditions for the employment of A and B as follows:

$$MPP_a \cdot MR_x = MRC_a = p_a \qquad (15.1)$$

and

$$MPP_b \cdot MR_x = MRC_b = p_b \qquad (15.2)$$

Least-Cost Combinations

Equations 15.1 and 15.2 look differently from the least-cost conditions expressed in Chapter 7, but appearances are sometimes deceiving. Dividing through equation 15.1 by MR_x and p_a, and dividing through equation 15.2 by MR_x and p_b, we obtain the following statements:

$$\frac{MPP_a}{p_a} = \frac{1}{MR_x} \qquad (15.3)$$

and

$$\frac{MPP_b}{p_b} = \frac{1}{MR_x} \qquad (15.4)$$

It now becomes apparent that since both $(MPP_a)/(p_a)$ and $(MPP_b)/(p_b)$ are equal to $1/(MR_x)$, they are also equal to each other; thus we can write

$$\frac{MPP_a}{p_a} = \frac{MPP_b}{p_b} = \frac{1}{MR_x} \qquad (15.5)$$

or, for our present purposes, simply

$$\frac{MPP_a}{p_a} = \frac{MPP_b}{p_b} \qquad (15.5a)$$

Equation 15.5a is, of course, the familiar statement of the conditions that must be met if resources are to be used in a least-cost combination. The last dollar spent on resource A must yield the same increment in the total output of the firm as the last dollar spent on resource B.

The Profit-Maximizing Product Output

We learned in Chapters 9 and 10 that a firm maximizes its profits by producing the product output at which its marginal cost is equal to its marginal revenue. We can state these conditions as

$$MC_x = MR_x \tag{15.6}$$

Suppose now that we work with equation 15.5. If we invert each term we have

$$\frac{p_a}{MPP_a} = \frac{p_b}{MPP_b} = MR_x \tag{15.7}$$

If we can show that $(p_a)/(MPP_a)$ and $(p_b)/(MPP_b)$ are each the same thing as MC_x—that is, the marginal cost of producing product X—we are home. We will have shown that employment of the profit-maximizing quantity of each variable resource results in the profit-maximizing product output for the firm.

Consider now a one-unit increment in the employment of resource A. It adds an amount to the total cost of the firm equal to its price, or p_a. It contributes an addition to the firm's output of MPP_a. Thus the expression $(p_a)/(MPP_a)$ means the increase in the firm's total cost per unit increase in its output of product, and this is nothing more nor less than the marginal cost, or MC_x, at whatever output level the firm is producing. Similarly, $(p_b)/(MPP_b)$ also defines MC_x. Therefore,

$$\frac{p_a}{MPP_a} = \frac{p_b}{MPP_b} = MC_x = MR_x \tag{15.8}$$

In order to maximize its profits a purely competitive firm must employ those quantities of variable resources at which their marginal revenue products are equal to their respective prices, and this in turn means that the firm will be using a least-cost combination of resources and that the marginal cost of its output is equal to marginal revenue.

SUMMARY

The principles governing profit maximization by a firm with respect to its purchases of resources are no different fundamentally from those we studied with respect to a firm's sales of product. If a one-unit increase in the firm's employment level of a resource adds more to total receipts than to total costs, it pays to make the increase. If a one-unit decrease in the employment level decreases total costs more than it decreases total receipts, then the move adds to profits. Profits are maximized at that employment level at which a one-unit change in the quantity of a resource used has the same effects on total costs and total receipts.

A firm's demand curve for a resource is the same thing as its marginal revenue product curve for the resource. Marginal revenue product is defined as the change in the firm's total receipts per unit change in the employment level of the resource. It is found by multiplying the marginal physical product of the resource at each possible employment level by the marginal revenue from the firm's sales of product at the corresponding output levels; that is, for a given resource A used in making product X.

$$MRP_a = MPP_a \cdot MR_x$$

Profits are maximized with respect to resource A when the employment level is such that its marginal revenue product is equal to its marginal resource cost. Marginal resource cost is defined as the change in the firm's total costs per unit change in its employment level of the resource. For the purely competitive purchaser of the resource, marginal resource cost is the same as the resource price. Thus for profit maximization by the firm,

$$MRP_a = MRC_a = p_a$$

Changes in the firm's demand curve for the resource occur when there are changes in one of the "other things being equal." These are (1) the the quantities of related resources used, (2) the marginal revenue from the products that the resource is used to produce, and (3) the techniques of production used by the firm.

The forces of market demand and supply determine the equilibrium price of a resource under competitive conditions. Market demand is found by summing the quantities that all firms will take at alternative prices, the horizontal summation of the marginal revenue product curves. Market supply indicates what all owners of the resource are collectively willing to place on the market at each alternative price. The equilibrium price is that price at which users of the resource are willing to take the quantity that suppliers are willing to place on the market.

The normal downward slope of the demand curve for a resource means that firms are willing, generally, to employ more of the resource at lower prices than at higher prices. Consequently, if minimum prices are set above equilibrium levels, the result will be unemployment for some units of the resource. We distinguish between the value of a resource to the firm that uses it and its value to society as a whole. The value of a unit of any given resource to the firm that uses it is measured by the marginal revenue product of the resource, or marginal physical product of the resource multiplied by the marginal revenue from the sale of that product. Its value to society is measured by the value of the marginal product of the resource, or its marginal physical product multiplied by the price paid by consumers for that product. These values are the same when the firms using resources buy and sell as pure competitors; but, as we shall see in the next chapter, they differ where there is monopoly in the sale of products.

When a firm uses several variable resources to produce a product it would be expected to use the profit-maximizing quantity of each, under ordinary circumstances. This would mean that the firm would also use the least-cost combination of those resources. It means, too, that the firm will be producing the profit-maximizing level of output.

EXERCISES AND QUESTIONS FOR DISCUSSION

1. For a minimum wage law to be effective, is it necessary that it be passed and enforced by the federal government?
2. "The coming of the computer age will cause human employment to decline rapidly as men are replaced by machines." Evaluate this statement critically.
3. In a competitive society could there be individuals who are being paid less than they are worth? Why or why not?
4. "If labor unions succeed in getting wages raised, the result will be higher incomes for those employed." Is this statement true? What additional statement could be made?
5. If a firm is using a least-cost combination of resources, is it automatically using those amounts of resources that will maximize its profits? Explain.

SELECTED READINGS

Cartter, Allan M., *Theory of Wages and Employment.* Homewood, Ill.: Richard D. Irwin, Inc., 1959, Chaps. 2–5.
Chamberlain, Neil W., *The Labor Sector.* New York: McGraw-Hill Book Company, Inc., 1965, Chaps. 17 and 18.
Friedman, Milton, "Minimum Wage Rates," *Newsweek,* September 26, 1966.
Hicks, John R., *The Theory of Wages,* 2d American ed. New York: St. Martins Press, 1963, Chaps. 1 and 5.

Resource Pricing and Employment in Monopolistic and Monopsonistic Markets

CHAPTER 16

Although purely competitive markets provide a convenient base on which the principles of resource pricing and employment can be constructed, as we look around us we find that many, if not most, markets are of different types. In the sale of automobiles and television sets we know that the selling markets are oligopolistic. The telephone company sells as a monopolist. On the buying side, too, many markets are not purely competitive. For example, are there enough buyers of the services of baseball players or of opera stars so that no one buyer can influence the purchase prices? Clearly the answer is no. Just as sellers in many product markets exercise some degree of monopoly power, buyers in many resource markets also exercise some degree of monopsony power, or monopoly in buying. We must take both sets of forces into account and as we do so we must draw a clear distinction between the selling side and the buying side of markets.

THE EFFECTS OF MONOPOLY IN SELLING

We use the term "monopoly" in a broader sense in this chapter than we did in Chapter 10. For present purposes it is not necessary that we distinguish pure monopoly from oligopoly and from monopolistic competition, so "monopoly" will be used to cover all three of these types of markets. The important implication of the term is that the seller of a good or service faces a downward-sloping demand curve for whatever he sells, with the result that the marginal revenue curve for his sales lies below the demand curve.

We shall continue to suppose in this section that pure competition prevails in the buying of resources; in other words, that there are enough buyers of any given resource and that each takes a small enough proportion of the total supply available to prevent one firm through its own actions from influencing the price. Pure competition in resource purchasing means exactly the same thing here as it did in Chapter 15. By proceeding in this manner we can isolate the effects of monopoly in product sales on resource pricing and employment.

Demand for a Resource

What determines the demand curve of a monopolistic seller for a resource that the firm purchases under conditions of pure competition? It seems reasonable to expect that the marginal revenue product curve for the resource is the firm's demand curve, just as it is in the case of a purely competitive seller. This is indeed so, but because of monopoly in the product market, the construction of the curve is somewhat more complex.

Marginal Revenue Product

Suppose that Chrysler Corporation wants to find its demand curve for machinists. The first step is to increase or decrease the level of employment by one-unit changes and to record the consequent changes in the firm's output. The result is a marginal physical product schedule or curve like that of Figure 16-1(b).

Given the quantities of other resources used by the firm, each employment level of machinists will correspond to a specific level of product output. Measuring product output along the X axis in Figure 16-1(a), suppose that employment level m_1 yields an output level X_1; employment level m_2 yields an output level X_2; and so on. There will not be, of course, a one-to-one correspondence between the employment level of machinists and the output of automobiles because of the operation of the law of diminishing returns. Equal increases in the input of machinists' labor will eventually yield smaller and smaller increments in the output of automobiles.

The marginal revenue product of machinists or of any resource was defined in the last chapter as the change in the firm's total receipts per unit change in its level of employment of that resource. At any given employment level the marginal revenue product is found by multiplying the marginal physical product of the resource by the marginal revenue at the corresponding level of product output. With reference to Figure 16-1, when m_1 units of machinists are employed, the marginal physical product

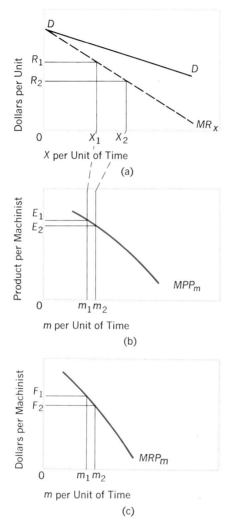

Figure 16-1
A monopolistic seller's demand curve for a resource.

of machinists is E_1 automobiles.[1] At output level X_1 for automobiles, marginal revenue is R_1. Thus marginal revenue product of machinists at employment level m_1 is found by multiplying E_1 automobiles—the change in output from increasing employment from one less than m_1 to m_1—by R_1. The result is recorded as F_1 in Figure 16–1(c). Similarly, at employment level m_2, we find F_2 by multiplying E_2 by R_2.

The marginal revenue product curve for machinists is a downward-

---

[1] This may well be only a fraction of an automobile.

sloping curve, meaning that the greater the level of employment of machinists, given the quantities of other resources used, the smaller will be the increase in the firm's total receipts per one-unit increase in the employment level. This downward slope occurs for two reasons. First, because of the law of diminishing returns the marginal physical product of machinists decreases as the quantity employed increases. Second, as the output of automobiles increases with increases in the employment level of machinists, marginal revenue from the sale of automobiles declines.

The Firm's Demand Curve

The marginal revenue product curve is the firm's demand curve for the resource, since it shows the quantities of the resource that the firm will take at alternative possible prices. Like the purely competitive seller, the monopolistic seller will maximize profits with respect to any specific resource by employing that quantity of the resource at which its marginal revenue product is equal to its marginal resource cost. Since the monopolistic seller in this case is assumed to be a pure competitor in the purchase of the resource, he cannot influence resource price, and marginal resource cost is therefore the same as the price. In Figure 16–2, if the wage rate or price of machinists were p_{m_1}, the firm would maximize profits by employing quantity m_1. If the wage rate were p_{m_2}, the profit-maximizing level of employment would be m_2.

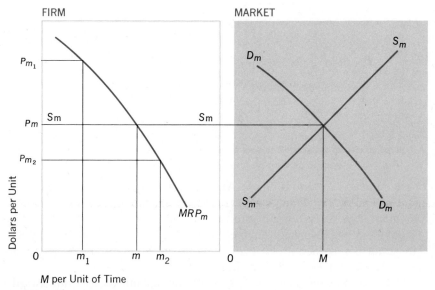

Figure 16–2
Equilibrium price and employment level of a resource.

Pricing and Employment

The determination of the equilibrium price and employment level of a resource, where its buyer exercises monopoly in *product selling* but is a pure competitor in *resource buying*, is no different from that of the thoroughgoing purely competitive case of the last chapter. In Figure 16–2, the market demand curve, $D_m D_m$, is found by summing horizontally the MRP_m curves of the firms that use machinists—that is, at each alternative price level the quantities taken by each of the firms are added to find the corresponding total market quantities. The market supply curve, $S_m S_m$ indicates the quantities of machinists' labor that would be placed on the market at alternative wage or resource price levels. The equilibrium price is p_m. At this price any one firm maximizes profits at an employment level such as m. The market level of employment is M.

Monopolistic Exploitation

Monopolistic sellers of product are said to *exploit* resources that they employ, which implies that resource units are worth more than they are paid. Again we must ask, Worth more to whom? The terms *value of marginal product,* introduced in Chapter 15, and *marginal revenue product,* as we have used it in both Chapter 15 and in this one, are the key concepts for discussing the issue. It should be clear by now that the marginal revenue product of a resource is the measure of its worth to the firm that employs it and that firms operating as purely competitive buyers adjust the quantity employed so that the marginal revenue product is equal to the marginal resource cost and to the resource price. Units of the resource are paid what they are worth to the firm.[2]

The value of marginal product of the resource measures the worth of any one unit of it to society and, where firms are monopolistic sellers of product, it will differ from the marginal revenue product. The difference is illustrated in Figure 16–3, which builds on Figure 16–1. Suppose now that the firm employs m_1 units of machinists' services and that the product output corresponding to this level of employment is X_1. Marginal physical product is E_1. To the firm the resource is worth E_1 times R_1, or marginal revenue product F_1—that is, what it will add to the firm's total receipts. Society values the resource at E_1 times p_{x_1}, or by the value of its marginal product, V_1. In general, at any specific level of employment of a given resource A used in making some product X, the marginal physical product of the resource and, consequently, any one unit of the

---

[2] Note that what they are worth to the firm, marginal revenue product, is brought into line with the market price of the resource by the adjustments in the quantity employed.

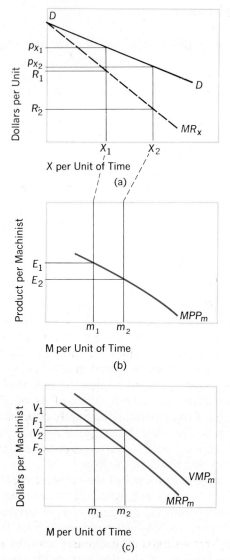

Figure 16–3
The difference between marginal revenue product and value of marginal product.

resource, is worth to the firm what it will add to the firm's total receipts; that is,

$$MRP_a = MPP_a \cdot MR_x$$

The value of a unit of the resource to society is whatever society is willing to pay for the marginal physical product of it; that is,

$$VMP_a = MPP_a \cdot p_x$$

Where product sellers are monopolistic, product price is greater than marginal revenue from it; therefore the value of marginal product exceeds marginal revenue product. This situation is shown at all levels of employment in Figure 16–3(c).

Monopolistic exploitation of a resource is the difference between what a unit of the resource is worth to society as a whole and its marginal resource cost when this difference results from monopoly in the sale of the product. In Figure 16–4, suppose that the equilibrium price for machinists is p_m. The profit-maximizing employment level is m; however, the value of any one unit to society is v_m. Exploitation amounts to $p_m v_m$ per unit of machinists' services. If exploitation is to be avoided, the employment level should be m', but if the firm is to increase employment from m to m', more will be added to the firm's total costs than to its total revenues and profits will fall. Exploitation is not a malicious act on the part of the firm; it is simply the natural consequence of monopoly in selling.

Monopolistic Restriction of Employment

Suppose now that among the many users of a specific kind of resource some sell their product outputs monopolistically and others sell competitively. The monopolistic sellers will restrict their individual levels of employment below that which is economically desirable, while at the same time the competitive sellers will employ too much.

We shall use a construction company to illustrate a monopolistic seller of product and a farm operation to illustrate a competitive seller. Both use common labor to produce their products. There are, of course,

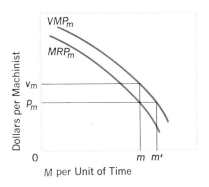

Figure 16–4
Monopolistic exploitation of a resource.

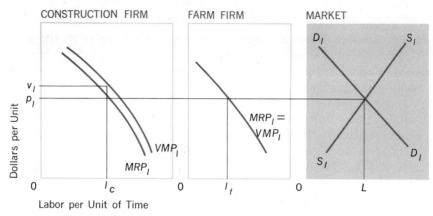

Figure 16–5
Monopolistic restriction of employment.

many other users of common labor, but we are concerned here only with these two. The appropriate diagrams are given in Figure 16–5. At the equilibrium price p_l for labor, the construction firm will employ l_c workers while the farm employs l_f.

How do we know that, from the point of view of consumers, the construction firm's employment level is too small while that of the farm is too large? How much value do consumers attach to a unit of labor employed in construction? How much worth do they ascribe to a unit of labor used on the farm? The answers are provided by the value of marginal product of labor in each of its uses. In the construction operation the value of marginal product is v_l while on the farm it is only p_l. The greater value that society places on a unit of labor used in construction indicates the desirability to society of expanding employment in construction while contracting it in farming. The market provides no incentives for this to take place. Each firm is employing precisely the quantity of the labor resource that it desires to employ. Each is maximizing profits with respect to the employment of labor. This is what we mean when we say that monopolistic sellers of product restrict the employment of the resources that they use below that which society considers desirable.

THE EFFECTS OF MONOPSONY IN BUYING

Monopsony in buying is a market situation that we have not yet met. We have assumed heretofore that pure competition among buyers exists —that no one buyer of anything takes a large enough proportion of the total supply to be able to influence the price. *Monopsony*, on the other hand, implies that an individual buyer does take a large enough part of the total supply to exercise an influence on the price. Essentially it is in buying what monopoly is in selling.

The Firm's View of Supply

Suppose that General Motors uses large quantities of a unique kind of bearing in the manufacture of its automobiles that none of the other manufacturers uses. Specifications for the bearing have been given to a number of machine shops in the Detroit area and these constitute General Motors' source of supply. How does the supply curve for bearings appear to the company? What will be the pattern of its marginal resource cost?

The Supply Curve Facing the Firm

Because it is the only purchaser of the bearings, General Motors faces the market supply curve for them. The machine shops producing and selling bearings would be willing to place more on the market at higher prices than at lower prices, so we would expect the supply curve to be upward-sloping to the right.[3] This is the distinguishing feature of monopsony in resource buying.

As an illustration of the difference between pure competition and monopsony in resource buying, consider Figure 16–2. The firm in that diagram is a purely competitive buyer of machinsts' labor and as such faces the horizontal supply curve $s_m s_m$ at the going market price p_m. But now suppose that only one firm in the economy has a need for machinists. The firm would face the market supply curve $S_m S_m$ and the price that must be paid for machinists' labor would depend upon the quantity per unit of time that it desires to employ.

Marginal Resource Cost

The fact that the monopsonistic buyer faces a nonhorizontal supply curve has important implications for the marginal resource cost to the firm of the resource so purchased. In the usual case, in which the buyer sees an upward-sloping supply curve, marginal resource cost will be greater than the resource price rather than equal to it. Why is this so?

Suppose that the supply situation for bearings purchased by General Motors is that of Table 16–1. Columns (1) and (2) comprise the supply

[3] The bearing supply curve is, of course, the output supply curve of all the machine shops together, and as such it is determined in the same way as any other output or product supply curve (see p. 149).

TABLE 16–1

Hypothetical Supply Situation for Bearings for General Motors Corporation

(1) Quantity (A)	(2) Price (p_a)	(3) Total Cost (TC_a)	(4) Marginal Resource Cost (MRC_a)
200	$1.00	$200.00	
201	1.00	201.00	$1.00
202	1.01	204.02	3.02
203	1.02	207.06	3.04
204	1.03	210.12	3.06

schedule. For any given quantity purchased, the total cost in column (3) is found by multiplying quantity purchased by the price necessary to obtain that quantity. Marginal resource cost, listed in column (4), is found at any given level of employment by reducing the level of employment one unit and observing the resulting change in total costs. Where higher resource prices are necessary to draw out larger quantities supplied of the resource, simple arithmetic demonstrates that marginal resource cost exceeds resource price.

This unique relation occurs because the resource supply schedule or curve is really the average cost schedule or curve of the resource to the firm. The marginal resource cost curve bears the same relation to the average resource cost curve as any marginal curve bears to its average curve.[4] If the supply schedule of Table 16–1 were plotted, it would be horizontal from 200 to 201 bearings. Note that for the increase in quantity purchased the marginal resource cost and the price of bearings are the same. But for an increase in the quantity purchased per unit of time from 201 to 202, the price must rise to $1.01 per bearing. The additional bearing costs the firm $1.01. Each of the other 201 bearings that had previously cost $1.00 each now cost $1.01, thus adding $2.01 more to the firm's total costs. The entire change in total costs to the firm from the one-unit increase in the employment level of bearings is $1.01 plus $2.01, or $3.02. Similarly, if the level of employment is raised from 202 to 203 bearings, the extra bearing by itself costs $1.02. The other 202 now cost $1.02 rather than $1.01 each, so the additional cost of all of these together is $2.02. Thus the marginal resource cost becomes $3.04. (You should be able to compute the marginal resource cost of bearings at the 204-bearing employment level.)

A representative marginal resource cost curve, MRC_b, for bearings is

---

[4] Compare the relation between average revenue and marginal revenue (see pp. 166–167) and average cost and marginal cost (see pp. 130–131).

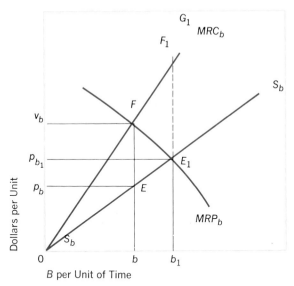

Figure 16–6
Monopsony pricing and employment of a resource.

drawn in Figure 16–6 in proper relation to the supply curve, S_bS_b, in that diagram. If the level of purchase or employment were b, the marginal resource cost would be bF and the price would be bE. At a purchase level of b_1, the marginal resource cost would be b_1F_1 and the price would be b_1E_1.

Resource Pricing and Employment

The Profit-Maximizing Price and Employment Level

What are the effects of monopsony on the price and employment level of a resource? Suppose in Figure 16–6 that the marginal revenue product curve of this particular kind of bearing is MRP_b.[5] The profit-maximizing level of utilization by General Motors must be that at which the marginal revenue product is equal to the marginal resource cost. The appropriate level of utilization is b, at which marginal revenue product and marginal resource cost are both at F. At a lower level of employment marginal revenue product exceeds marginal resource cost and an expansion of employment to b will increase profits. If employment is expanded beyond b, the additions to the firm's total receipts are smaller than the additions to its

[5] Other kinds of bearings may be substitutes for it.

total costs and profits will contract. The equilibrium price of the resource is p_b even though marginal revenue product is v_b. Price p_b is all that is necessary to attract the machine shops into supplying b bearings per unit of time.

Monopsonistic Exploitation

Monopsony in the purchase of resources, like monopoly in the sale of products, causes units of the resource to be exploited. We define *monopsonistic exploitation* of a resource as the difference between what the resource is worth to the firm and what is paid for the resource when this difference is brought about by monopsony in its purchase. In Figure 16–6, when General Motors is buying b bearings per unit of time the marginal revenue product of a bearing is v_b. The price paid is p_b per bearing, so exploitation amounts to $p_b v_b$ for each one purchased.

Monopsonistic exploitation does not arise from any malicious act on the part of the monopsonist. The monopsonist, like any other business firm, including the pure competitor, is simply trying to maximize his profits and he does this at the level of purchase at which marginal revenue product is equal to marginal resource cost. It does not pay—in fact it will make him worse off—to expand employment beyond b. Yet this is what society wants. If a resource is worth more than it is paid in some certain use, this is positive proof that society desires its employment level in this use to be expanded.[6] But it is not maliciousness that is responsible for this situation; it is the mathematical fact that the supply curve facing the firm is upward sloping to the right, and, therefore, marginal resource cost exceeds the price of the resource.

Nevertheless, monopsonistic as well as monopolistic exploitation have adverse effects on the efficient use of resources. We shall explore the matter further in the next chapter, but an explicit statement of the nature of the problem is warranted here. Wherever monopoly in product selling and monopsony in resource purchasing occur, it is likely that the value of marginal product of any one resource used by different firms will differ from one firm to another, even if units of the resource were paid the same price by each firm. This would mean that consumers place a higher value on units of the resource in some uses than in others. It also means that from the point of view of consumers too little of the resource is employed in the higher value of marginal product uses and too much is employed in lower value of marginal product uses.

---

[6] If marginal revenue product of the resource is greater than the price paid for the resource, then certainly value of marginal product must be also. Can you explain why this is so? Can you draw a diagram showing a resource being exploited both monopolistically *and* monopsonistically, indicating exactly the magnitude of each? Check the definition of monopolistic exploitation again.

Sources of Monopsony

How many employment alternatives are open to operatic tenors? How many hospitals in the United States can utilize effectively the talents of a skilled brain surgeon? How many major league ball clubs are bidding for the talents of gifted young players? How many major motion picture studios or television networks bid for the services of topflight entertainers? How many large-volume users of Bendix magnetos are there in the United States?

These questions point up one of the main sources of monopsonistic buying or hiring of resources, to the extent that it occurs. Whether the resource is labor or magnetos or bearings or something else, *if it is specialized to one user or to a small group of users* monopsony is likely to occur. The number of alternative employment opportunities are limited in number, so that any one user faces an upward-sloping supply curve for his purchases. If he wants a larger number of units or a better quality, he must pay a higher price.

A second source of monopsony is *immobility of resources among geographic areas.* The classic example of this was the one-company mining town of the central and southern Appalachian area where the town's population was dependent on the company for employment. Communications with the rest of the country were limited and the labor force was not well informed as to alternative earning opportunities elsewhere. Many youngsters growing up in the area remained as permanent residents. The town constituted a self-contained labor market and the company faced the market supply curve.

Both of the sources of monopsony discussed above are forms of immobility, but they arise from different circumstances. The first, specialization to particular uses, arises from economic activity of a dynamic, inventive, and progressive kind and as such is not likely to cause us great concern. The second, fortunately, is much less common today than it was 50 to 75 years ago. Some geographic immobility of labor undoubtedly still exists, but with modern methods of travel, mass communication, and rising educational levels its importance is diminishing.

Methods of Counteracting Monopsony

Although it is by no means certain that monopsony creates problems of significant magnitude, certain kinds of preventive types of action, like preventive medicine or preventive maintenance on an automobile may be worthwhile. Of course, the best way of avoiding monopsonistic exploitation and restriction of employment of resources in certain uses is to eliminate or control the factors responsible. Failing in this, minimum prices set on a resource may possibly be of some benefit.

Control of the Causes

Few people would argue that there is a pressing need to prevent monopsonistic exploitation of television stars, big league baseball players, and brain surgeons. Monopsony in the purchase of highly specialized resources may very well be one of the prices we must pay for economic progress. In any case, the owners of high-paid, specialized resources are not likely to get a sympathetic ear when they complain that they are paid less than they are worth.[7] The resource owners we are concerned with are those whose incomes are low because their resources are purchased monopsonistically.[8] Ordinarily we would expect these to be workers who for some reason or another are immobile. Conceivably they can be or are being helped by government policies aimed at increasing mobility. These include the operation of a nation-wide system of federal employment exchanges, War on Poverty legislation aimed at retraining and relocating workers from poverty areas, and the upgrading and improving of educational facilities.

Employment exchanges can and should perform several important tasks. They should collect and disseminate data on the kinds of job openings available and where they are located. They should also gather and publicize information on occupational and geographic wage structures; that is, on what occupations pay the highest wages and on what geographic areas are high-wage areas. In addition, they should perform the more perfunctory job of matching those desiring employment with the job opportunities that are available. Some of these tasks are now being performed by the Office of Employment Security, but the information made available is by no means complete nor does it always reach those in need of it.

Most of the War on Poverty legislation is aimed at making labor more mobile among occupations and geographic areas. It is not aimed specifically at monopsony situations but at increasing the productivity, and consequently, the incomes of low-income workers, whatever the cause of their low-income situations. Nevertheless, through the retraining of workers whose skills have become obsolete or through training those

---

[7] On grounds of economic efficiency, however, where there is monopsonistic exploitation of high-paid resources, the argument for expanding employment of the resources in those uses is as strong as it is in the case of monopsonistic exploitation of low-paid resources.

[8] We are usually concerned with these people on grounds of inequities in income distribution rather than of economic inefficiencies. Nothing said here should be taken to imply that monopsony is a major cause of poverty. It may be one small contributing factor but there is no evidence available to indicate that it is of prime importance.

who have never developed skills in the first place not only may workers be made more productive but at the same time a blow may be struck at monopsony.

There is a high correlation between the educational levels attained by individuals and their mobility. High school graduates are much less likely to remain in their home towns and follow their fathers' occupations than are grade school graduates and high school dropouts. University graduates are even less likely to remain in the environment in which they were raised. How many of your present class will return to their home towns upon graduation? Will you? Educational opportunities promote mobility upward from occupations requiring lower to those requiring higher skill levels. Adult education may enable those in declining occupations to move into other areas that show greater promise. Counseling services may do much to steer those entering the labor force toward more remunerative jobs.

Minimum Pricing

Monopsonistic exploitation of a resource can be offset by the establishment of a minimum price for it—provided the minimum is "correctly" set. Suppose in Figure 16–6 that B refers to bricklayers and that in the market under surveillance they are hired by only one large construction company. The supply curve is S_bS_b and the marginal resource cost curve is MRC_b. The marginal revenue product curve for bricklayers to the firm is MRP_b. The profit-maximizing level of employment is b and the wage rate necessary to secure that quantity is p_b. Monopsonistic exploitation amounts to p_bv_b per unit of labor.

If a minimum wage rate were fixed at p_{b_1}, how would the supply curve facing the firm appear?[9] Since the firm is not permitted to purchase labor at a price below p_{b_1}, that part of the supply curve below E_1 is no longer relevant. At p_{b_1} the firm can get any quantity of labor it desires up to b_1. But if more were desired, higher wage rates would be necessary to attract the larger quantities into employment. For quantities of labor greater than b_1, that part of the market supply curve lying above E_1 is relevant.

The change in the supply curve facing the firm changes in turn the marginal resource cost curve. The horizontal part of the supply curve— the $p_{b_1}E_1$ part—is now like that facing a purely competitive firm; consequently, the marginal resource cost curve for that part coincides with the line $p_{b_1}E_1$. At employment level b_1 the marginal resource cost curve is discontinuous, jumping from point E_1 to point F_1. For employment levels greater than b_1 the marginal resource cost curve follows its original path.

---

[9] The minimum wage rate could be set by law or by collective bargaining between a bricklayers' union and the firm. The method of setting it is of no consequence at this point; all that matters is that no labor is sold at a price below that minimum.

Now that the marginal resource cost curve is $p_{b_1}E_1F_1G_1$, employment level b no longer maximizes the firm's profits. At employment level b marginal revenue product is v_b but marginal resource cost is p_{b_1}. Profits will be increased by an increase in the employment level to b_1. At that point marginal revenue product and marginal resource cost are equal at p_{b_1} and profits are maximum. The resource is paid p_{b_1} also, so monopsonistic exploitation has been eliminated. Note that the employment level is higher than it was before.

The correct minimum price is much easier to establish on paper than in practice. Presumably the devices used to set it would be either minimum wage laws or collective bargaining, and there is little evidence to indicate that either legislators or union leaders try consciously to offset monopsony by these means. As a matter of fact, most of them have never even heard of the term.

A general minimum wage like those set under the Fair Labor Standards Act of 1938, as amended, is clearly not appropriate for this purpose. The number of workers affected by it has been small. Further, to the extent that monopsony in labor markets occurs, it is a set of different situations, each calling for a different minimum to offset exploitation, rather than a general situation embracing all labor. The single rate of the minimum wage law may accidentally be correct for some situations but certainly it will not be for all.

Minimum wages set through collective bargaining could be more nearly tailored to differing monopsony situations. However, even if the two parties in collective bargaining knew the correct minimum to set, do you think they would settle on that wage level? Is it likely that business firms, purchasing labor monopsonistically, would be willing to raise wage rates up to that level? If the union were able to force it that high, would it then be content to force it no higher?

COMBINATIONS OF VARIABLE RESOURCES

When we introduce the possibility of monopoly and monopsony into the principles of resource pricing and employment we come up with some slight modifications of the analysis of least-cost combinations and profit-maximizing levels of employment presented in the preceding chapter. Suppose a firm producing and selling product X uses two variable resources, A and B. Suppose, further, that X is sold monopolistically and A and B are purchased monopsonistically. To maximize profits with respect to these resources the employment levels must be such that the marginal revenue product of each is equal to its marginal resource cost; that is,

$$MPP_a \cdot MR_x = MRC_a \qquad (16.1)$$

and

$$MPP_b \cdot MR_x = MRC_b \qquad (16.2)$$

Least-Cost Combinations

Equations 16.1 and 16.2 together show the conditions for a least-cost combination of resources A and B. We divide through equation 16.1 by MR_x and by MRC_a. We divide through equation 16.2 by MR_x and MRC_b. These operations yield

$$\frac{MPP_a}{MRC_a} = \frac{1}{MR_x} \qquad (16.3)$$

and

$$\frac{MPP_b}{MRC_b} = \frac{1}{MR_x} \qquad (16.4)$$

so

$$\frac{MPP_a}{MRC_a} = \frac{MPP_b}{MRC_b} = \frac{1}{MR_x} \qquad (16.5)$$

Keeping in mind the definitions of marginal physical product and marginal resource cost of a resource, we know that $(MPP_a)/(MRC_a)$ means *the change in product per dollar change in expenditure on A*. Similarly, $(MPP_b)/(MRC_b)$ means *the change in product per dollar change in expenditure on B*. Thus equation 16.5 means that the last dollar spent on A yields the same increase in the firm's product output as the last dollar spent on B. This, of course, means that equation 16.5, ignoring $1/(MR_x)$ for the moment, states the conditions that must be met for variable resources to be used in a least-cost combination.

Equation 16.5 also expresses the profit-maximizing conditions for the firm with respect to its output of product X. If we examine $(MRC_a)/(MPP_a)$ and $(MRC_b)/(MPP_b)$, we find that each of these is an expression of the marginal cost of product X—the change in total cost per unit change in the level of the firm's output. Consequently, equation 16.5 can be rewritten as

$$\frac{MPP_a}{MRC_a} = \frac{MPP_b}{MRC_b} = \frac{1}{MC_x} = \frac{1}{MR_x} \qquad (16.5a)$$

or, inverting the two equalities on the right,

$$MC_x = MR_x \qquad (16.6)$$

If a firm employs those quantities of variable resources at which their respective marginal revenue products are equal to respective marginal resource costs, it will be using those resources in a least-cost combination and will at the same time be producing the profit-maximizing quantity of product.

SUMMARY

In this chapter we examine the effects of monopoly in product selling and monopsony in resource purchasing on the pricing and employment of resources. The term "monopoly" is used broadly to mean any market situation in which the seller faces a downward-sloping demand curve for his product. "Monopsony" means any market situation in which a resource buyer faces an upward-sloping supply curve for the resource.

The principles of resource pricing and employment are basically the same where firms are monopolistic sellers as they are where firms are purely competitive sellers. The firm's demand curve for a resource is its marginal revenue product curve for it. The market demand curve is the sum of the quantities that individual firms will take at each price. Market demand and market supply determine the equilibrium price and employment level. Each firm employs that quantity at which the marginal revenue product of the resource is equal to the marginal resource cost or price—provided the firm is a purely competitive purchaser of the resource.

Monopolistic sellers of product are said to exploit the resources they purchase. Monopolistic exploitation of a resource means that resource units are paid less than their value of marginal product—what they are worth to society—because of monopoly. They are paid a price equal to their marginal revenue product—what they are worth to the firm. For monopolistic sellers of product the value of marginal product of a resource exceeds the marginal revenue product because the price of the product sold exceeds the marginal revenue from its sale. Where the resource is used by both monopolistic and competitive sellers of product the monopolistic users will restrict the employment of the resource below the amounts that society desires used in the production of those products.

The monopsonist in the purchase of a resource, like any other resource purchaser, maximizes profits by employing that amount at which marginal revenue product is equal to marginal resource cost. But since the monopsonist faces a resource supply curve (average cost curve) that slopes upward to the right, the marginal resource cost curve lies above the supply curve. Consequently, at the profit-maximizing level of employment the price paid for each unit of the resource is less than either its marginal revenue product to the firm or the value of its marginal product to society.

Monopsonists also exploit resources and restrict the levels of their employment as compared with purely competitive resource purchasers. Monopsonistic exploitation of a given resource is measured by the difference between its marginal revenue product to the firm and the price paid for it and is the consequence of the difference between the resource supply curve facing the firm and the marginal resource cost curve. In the absence of monopsony, the resource would be employed up to the level at which its marginal revenue product is equal to the resource price.

If we are to attempt to counteract monopsony, we should understand its causes. These are (1) specialization of the resource to a particular user and (2) geographic or occupational immobility of the resource. Measures to increase resource mobility are of primary importance in controlling the impact of this factor on the economy. The alternative is minimum pricing techniques.

Where monopoly in selling products and monopsony in the purchase of resources occur, the conditions of least-cost resource combinations and profit-maximizing levels of employment of several variable resources must be modified slightly. Monopsonistic purchases of the resources requires for a least-cost combination that

$$\frac{MPP_a}{MRC_a} = \frac{MPP_b}{MRC_b} = \cdots = \frac{MPP_n}{MRC_n}$$

for as many variable resources as are so purchased. For profit maximization, we extend the conditions to

$$\frac{MPP_a}{MRC_a} = \frac{MPP_b}{MRC_b} = \cdots = \frac{MPP_n}{MRC_n} = \frac{1}{MC_x} = \frac{1}{MR_x}$$

EXERCISES AND QUESTIONS FOR DISCUSSION

1. In the orchards of California the average wage of migratory workers is comparatively low. What are some possible bases of this problem? Could the organization of a labor union improve the situation? What other methods might be used?
2. Are monopoly and monopsony equally adverse in their effects on labor? Explain.
3. The American and National football leagues recently merged and will have a common draft of players. Discuss with the help of graphs what the effects of the merger are likely to be.
4. "Labor unions have perhaps done as much as the Justice Department, with their enforcement of antimonopoly laws, in curbing monopoly power." Evaluate this statement.
5. Labor unions often argue that because of the workers' increased productivity, wages should be increased. Is this a legitimate argument? Elaborate.
6. In the absence of monopsony, is there any justification for the establishment of a minimum price for a resource? Why or why not?

SELECTED READINGS

Bloom, G. F., and Herbert R. Northrup, *Economics of Labor Relations,* 5th ed. Homewood, Ill.: Richard D. Irwin, Inc., 1965, Chaps. 9 and 10.

Cartter, A. M., and F. R. Marshall, *Labor Economics.* Homewood, Ill.: Richard D. Irwin, Inc., 1967, Chap. 10.

Chamberlin, E. H., *The Theory of Monopolistic Competition,* 8th ed. Cambridge, Mass.: Harvard University Press, 1962, Chap. 8.

Colberg, M., D. R. Forbush, and G. R. Whitaker, Jr., *Business Economics,* 3d ed. Homewood, Ill.: Richard D. Irwin, Inc., 1964, Chap. 12, Cases 12–1, 12–2, 12–3.

Resource
Allocation
CHAPTER 17

New discoveries, new inventions, and new knowledge make these years exciting ones in which to live. During your lifetime you have seen color television come into its own as a standard item of household consumption. You have witnessed the advent of supersonic airplanes, flights into space, utilization of atomic energy, and the computer. You have seen polio and other dread diseases brought under control. Synthetic fabrics, TV dinners, and cake mixes are commonplace to you. So are tape recorders, transistor radios, and high-fidelity stereo sets. Much less obvious to most of us have been the tremendous changes accomplished in production methods for a wide variety of goods and services. New discoveries, new inventions, and new knowledge change the supplies of resources available to be used in the economy. They also bring about changes in consumer tastes and demand. If in the face of these dynamic changes the economy is to use its resources efficiently, there must be flexibility in where and how resources are to be used. Continuous reallocation of resources must occur from areas that are becoming less important to consumers to those that are increasing in importance.

In this chapter we are interested primarily in the mechanism employed in a free enterprise type of economic system to bring about the desired reallocation of resources. We can understand it best if we discuss it initially as though it worked almost perfectly. Toward this end, in the first part of the chapter we shall assume that the economy is purely competitive. Later, monopoly, monopsony, and other problems will be introduced.

ALLOCATION AMONG GEOGRAPHIC AREAS

As a vast oversimplification, think of the eastern half of the United States as being divided into two areas, the North and the South. Over a short period of time, say one year, suppose that resources are not mobile between the two areas but that over a longer period the owners of both labor and capital are willing to migrate from one to the other to seek employment for their resources, wherever it appears to be to their advantage. To put this in technical economic language, we assume that in the short run the North and the South are separate resource markets. In the long run they are interconnected.

We shall make two further simplifying assumptions. First, think of all units of labor as being homogeneous. Second, assume that pure competition in the sale of products and in the purchase of resources prevails in both areas. Neither of these fits the facts of the real world. With regard to the first, there are thousands of different kinds of labor—the Department of Labor lists over 25,000 different occupational classifications. On the second point, although pure competition is approached in some markets, it is by no means a universal market condition. Nevertheless, together these assumptions enable us to get at the most important principles that are at work and that often tend to be obscured in the much more complex real world.

Allocation of Labor

Suppose now that there are differences in the amounts of capital that labor has to work with in the North and in the South. It may be, for example, that machines, factory buildings, mineral deposits, transportation facilities, and other capital resources have been more abundantly developed and accumulated relative to the labor supply in the North than in the South. These are the circumstances depicted in Figure 17–1.

Evidence of Misallocation

What can we say about the demand for and the supply of labor in the North and in the South? What about the wage rates and the productivity of labor in the two areas? Do these provide any clues as to whether labor is correctly or incorrectly allocated between the North and the South?[1] Because of the larger ratio of capital to labor, the demand curve for labor in the North lies farther to the right with respect to its supply curve than does that of the South. Or, in the South, the supply curve for labor lies farther to the right with respect to the demand curve than does that of the North.

---

[1] The correct allocation of a resource is that in which the resource makes its maximum contribution to the value of the economy's output, or to national income. If a resource were correctly allocated the transfer of a unit of it from one use to any other use would cause national income to fall. We shall take a closer look at the correct allocation shortly.

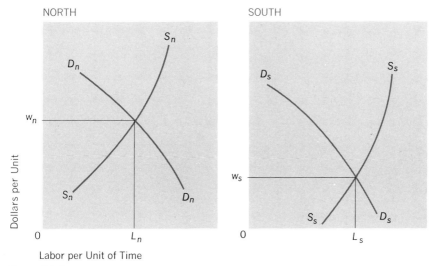

NORTH   SOUTH

Figure 17-1
Misallocation of labor between the North and the South.

Basic demand–supply analysis informs us that the price of labor, or the wage rate, will be higher in the North than in the South. The difference in the wage rate makes us suspicious that labor may not be correctly allocated. The lower wage rate in the South leads us to believe that there may be too much labor in the South as compared with the North.[2] Can we support this view with the analysis we developed in Chapter 15? Can we show that any one unit of northern labor is more productive than any one unit of southern labor?

If we compare the value of marginal product of southern labor with that of northern labor, we obtain the information required to answer the questions just raised. Because of pure competition in resource purchases in the North and in the South, the marginal resource cost in each area is the same as the respective wage rates, w_n and w_s. In the North we expect each firm to be employing that quantity of labor at which the marginal revenue product is equal to the marginal resource cost. Thus in the North the marginal revenue product of labor is also w_n. In the South we expect the same thing, so the marginal revenue product of labor in that area will be w_s. Since w_n is greater than w_s, the marginal revenue product of labor used by northern firms is greater than that used by southern firms. Because of pure competition in the sale of products, the marginal revenue product of the resource in each area is equal to its value of marginal product in that area. Thus the value of marginal product of labor is greater in the North than in the South; that is, the last one-unit

---

[2] Some people seem to believe that low wage rates wherever they appear are indicative of exploitation. What do you think about this?

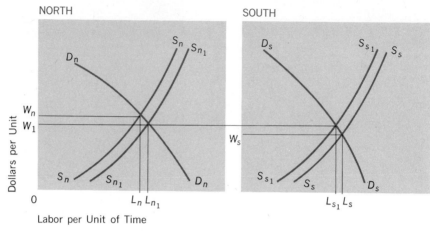

Figure 17-2
Reallocation of labor from the South to the North.

increase in the level of employment in the North is valued more highly by consumers than is the last one-unit increase in the level of employment in the South. This difference in the value of marginal product of labor in its different uses is the evidence that labor is not correctly allocated. Consumers would like more labor used in northern employments and less in southern employments.

The Mechanism of Reallocation

The incorrect allocation of labor brings about differences in the wage rates, and these differences provide the motivating force for the desired reallocation. Given sufficient time, workers will tend to migrate from the low-wage area to the high-wage area, since the latter provides the prospect of higher incomes. This situation is illustrated in Figure 17-2. The movement of labor from the South to the North shifts the supply curve in the North to the right, toward $S_{n_1}S_{n_1}$. It shifts the supply curve in the South to the left, toward $S_{s_1}S_{s_1}$. The price of labor in the North falls toward w_1, while in the South it rises toward the same level. When enough labor has moved North so that the wage rate is w_1 in both areas, the incentive for migration is no longer present. The marginal revenue product of labor is the same in both the North and the South, and so is the value of marginal product.

Effects on National Income

What will be the effects of the reallocation of labor on national income, or the value of the economy's output? Look again at the original situation pictured by Figure 17-1. As we determined above, the value of marginal product of labor is greater in the North than in the South. Now, if a unit of labor is withdrawn from employment in the South, by how much does national income fall? It falls by w_s dollars—the value of marginal product of labor in the South. If the unit of labor goes to work in the North, by how much does national income (after the decrease just described) rise? The increase is equal to slightly less than w_n. Putting these two results together, we see that the transfer of a unit of resource from the lower value of marginal product area to the higher value of marginal product area will increase national income: the increase in national income when the unit of labor goes to work in the North is larger than the decrease in national income occasioned by its withdrawal from the South. The following is a valid general principle: *whenever units of a resource are moved from lower value of marginal product uses to higher value of marginal product uses, national income is increased.*

Suppose we restate this very important proposition numerically. Let w_s be $10, meaning that any one unit of labor employed in the South yields a value of marginal product of $10. Take away a unit of labor and the economy loses $10 worth of product or services. Let w_n represent $16. Any one unit of labor employed in the North yields a value of marginal product of $16. Take away a unit of labor and the economy would lose $16 worth of product. But if instead of taking away a unit of labor in the North one unit more than L_n is employed, the economy would gain almost $16 worth of goods and services. (Why almost $16 worth?) The transfer of a unit of labor from the South to the North under these circumstances would increase national income by almost $6 worth of goods and services.

The Correct Allocation

Homogeneous units of labor or of any other resource are correctly allocated when the value of marginal product of the resource is the same in all of the alternative uses of the resource and when there are no higher value of marginal product possibilities available to the resource. Once the resource is so allocated, any further transfers from one use to another will bring about a net decline in national income. The law of diminishing returns, which makes the value of marginal product curve of the resource slope downward to the right for any firm that uses it, assures us that this will be the case.

It is useful to look at this proposition the other way around. Units of a resource are misallocated when its value of marginal product differs in different uses. In the labor example, the first indication of misallocation between the North and the South is the difference in the wage rate between the two areas. On closer examination we find that the wage rate differences in this case are also value of marginal product differences and, hence, represent actual misallocation.

The operation of the price mechanism as it continually reallocates resources under purely competitive conditions is summed up in a few sentences. First, an incorrect allocation of a resource causes different prices to be paid for it in different areas or uses. Second, these prices provide the incentive for reallocation in the correct direction. Third, the price differences decrease as the reallocation takes place—when the resource is correctly allocated they will have disappeared. Fourth, the reallocation increases national income.

Capital Allocation

In the North-South example, capital as well as labor may have been poorly allocated initially. If the ratio of labor to capital was lower in the North than in the South, then the ratio of capital to labor must have been higher. This opens up the possibility that, if capital in the South is not inferior to that in the North, the marginal revenue product and the price of capital may be greater in the South than in the North.[3] If this were so, then investors (resource owners) seeking the greatest possible earnings or return on their investment, would have an incentive to reduce the dollars invested in the North and to increase the dollars invested in the South. What this amounts to, of course, is a transfer of plant, equipment, and other capital resources from the North to the South.

The transfer of capital from the North to the South would decrease the demand for labor in the North and increase it in the South, thus reducing the extent to which labor should be reallocated from the South to the North. This situation is illustrated by Figures 17–1 through 17–3. Let the initial situation be that of Figure 17–1. There is relatively too much labor and relatively too little capital in the South. In the North these circumstances are reversed. Figure 17–2 indicates what we would expect to happen if reallocation of labor but not of capital were possible. Figure 17–3 completes the picture. An out migration of capital from the North reduces the demand for labor in the North toward $D_{n_2}D_{n_2}$. An in migration of capital to the South increases demand for labor in that area toward $D_{s_2}D_{s_2}$. The achievement of a correct reallocation of labor requires only that the southern supply curve shift left to $S_{s_2}S_{s_2}$, while

---

[3] Capital is made up of so many different items that it is difficult to conceive of a "quantity" of capital in such a way that we can compare the quantity in the North with that in the South. The best procedure probably is to think of the quantity of capital in the North (or the South) as the investment in buildings, machinery, tools, and other items measured in dollar terms. The marginal revenue product and the "price" of capital will then be the yield, or return, on each dollar invested.

that for the North shifts to the right to $S_{n_2}S_{n_2}$, and these are smaller shifts than those pictured in Figure 17–2.

Any reallocation of capital that occurs will also increase national income. Under conditions of pure competition, movement of capital from the North to the South would occur only if the value of marginal product of capital were greater in the South than in the North. Thus a unit of capital leaving the North would decrease national income by less than the increase in national income brought about by its employment in the South. As is the case for any resource, units of homogeneous capital are correctly allocated when the value of marginal product is the same in all its uses.

We cannot determine from Figures 17–1 through 17–3 whether the allocation of capital is correct. None of the figures shows the return per unit of capital or the value of marginal product of capital. All we can say is that if, in Figure 17–1, capital as well as labor is incorrectly allocated, the resulting economic events would be those described.

The North-South Historical Record

The historical record indicates that a pattern of resource reallocation very much like that just discussed has, in fact, been taking place over the last 50 years. In the nineteenth century the South was predominantly agricultural, while industry grew up around coal and iron deposits, waterways, and population centers of the North. In the present century, as demand for industrial goods and services has far outstripped demand

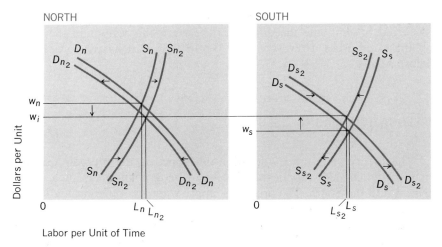

Figure 17–3
Reallocation of labor and capital.

for agricultural products and as capital has accumulated more rapidly in the North, we find the South left with too much labor and too little capital as compared with the North. This situation has been evidenced by the well-known North-South wage differential.

The actual North-South differential is only partly explained by differences in the amount of capital each worker has to work with, although, to be sure, this has been much smaller in the South. The average southern worker differs in several respects from the average northern worker. He is more agriculturally oriented, less skilled, and he is not as well educated as his northern counterpart. For these reasons southern labor has been less productive and, consequently, less well paid. To a very large extent the North-South differential in wage rates and productivities is an urban-rural differential. Most of what has just been said about the South compared with the North could also be said in almost any rural-urban comparison.

The differential apparently has provided a continuing incentive for migration of labor to the North and of capital to the South. These shifts have been particularly in evidence since the 1920s as the means of transportation and communication have been improved. This does not mean that the South as a whole has lost population, although certainly some areas have experienced a net loss. Net out migration merely requires that the number of people leaving an area be greater than the number of people coming into it from outside. If it is more than offset by an excess of births over deaths, the population of the area continues to grow. Similarly, migration of capital from the North to the South does not necessarily imply a reduction in the total amount of capital in the North. Rather, it means that the rate of capital formation is greater in the South than in the North. Not enough reallocation of labor and capital has occurred to eliminate the differential between the regions in the prices of these resources. However, since World War II it has narrowed them substantially.

ALLOCATION AMONG USES

The theory of resource allocation developed in the preceding section is not limited in its application to broad geographic areas such as the North and the South. The principles apply wherever different markets or different uses for a resource can be distinguished—among counties, metropolitan areas, rural areas and adjacent metropolitan areas, industries, firms, and so on. The North and the South in the previous example are simply replaced by the appropriate different uses among which units of the resource can move over time. As an illustration, suppose we look at a hypothetical allocation of accountants' services between the oil industry and the construction industry.

We shall take as our starting point an equilibrium situation, although this is not strictly necessary. Assume that both the oil industry and the construction industry sell their products and services under conditions of pure competition. Initially accountants are correctly allocated between them—the value of marginal product of accountants' services used in the oil industry is the same as it is in the construction industry. Marginal revenue product will also be the same in both industries and, if pure competition prevails in the employment of accountants, the marginal resource cost and the price per unit of accountants' labor will be equal. If firms in both industries are employing profit-maximizing quantities, the marginal resource cost of accountants will be equal to their marginal revenue product in each industry. If we put all of this together symbolically—and it is extremely convenient to do so—we can state the equilibrium conditions as:

$$VMP_{ao} = VMP_{ac} = MRP_{ao} = MRP_{ac} = MRC_a = P_a \quad (17.1)$$

Be sure that you understand what each of these symbols means and why equilibrium is implied by equation 17.1.

What economic forces, bearing on accountants, would be set in motion by a shift in consumer demand away from petroleum products and toward construction services? We would expect the lower demand for petroleum products to bring about a decrease in their price level, p_o. The increase in demand for construction services would increase the per unit price, p_c, of these. Thus the value of marginal product of accountants used in the construction industry would be higher while that of accountants used in the oil industry would be lower. We can express the result symbolically as:

$$VMP_{ac} > VMP_{ao} \quad (17.2)$$

or, breaking each of these terms down into its component parts, we can write

$$MPP_{ac} \cdot p_c > MPP_{ao} \cdot p_o \quad (17.2a)$$

in which MPP_{ac} is the marginal physical product of accountants used in construction and MPP_{ao} is their marginal physical product in the oil industry. Equations 17.2 and 17.2a simply mean that consumers now value the services of accountants (and other resources) more highly in the construction industry than in the oil industry.

Accountants are now incorrectly allocated, but the market mechanism moves to correct the situation. Firms in the oil industry find that the value of marginal product of accountants (and other resources) is less than the price they must pay to employ them, or

$$VMP_{ao} < p_a \qquad\qquad (17.3)$$

Consequently, they reduce the quantity of accountants that they employ. At the same time, firms in the construction industry find that the value of marginal product of accountants (and of other resources) is greater than the resource price, or

$$VMP_{ac} > p_a \qquad\qquad (17.4)$$

They thus have an incentive to increase the quantity of accountants that they employ.

Accountants will have an income incentive to transfer from the oil industry to the construction industry. The reduction in the oil industry's demand for accountants will reduce the price paid for them in that industry slightly below p_a. At the same time, the increase in the construction industry's demand for them will advance the price offered to slightly more than p_a. In other words, the incorrect allocation causes a resource price differential between the two uses to develop.

The reallocation of accountants will continue until the correct allocation is achieved. As more and more accountants (and other resources) are employed in the construction industry and as its output expands, the price of construction services will fall. So, too, will the value of marginal product of accountants in that industry. The exit of accountants (and other resources) from the oil industry reduces the supply of petroleum products, causing their prices to rise. This will raise the value of marginal product of accountants in that industry. When the prices of construction services have fallen far enough—with the increase in the industry's output —and the prices of oil products have risen enough—with the contraction of the industry's output—to make the value of marginal product of accountants once more the same in both industries, the incentives for transfer will have disappeared. The appropriate adjustment to the change in consumer demand will have been made in the economy's productive capacity. The conditions of equilibrium stated in equation 17.1 will again prevail.

Thus, as changes constantly are occurring in consumer demand, technology, and resource supplies, the price mechanism operates to correct the resulting misallocation of resources. Value of marginal product and price differentials in different uses appear for the misallocated resource, providing the incentives for the resource owners to transfer what they own from the lower-paying to the higher-paying uses. Often, or probably generally, before the reallocation of such a resource is completed other changes take place, calling for a still different allocation pattern. To achieve high efficiency, the economic system must operate so that resources can make the necessary movements rapidly and smoothly.

IMPEDIMENTS TO CORRECT RESOURCE ALLOCATION

The price mechanism does not always work as smoothly as we have just described it as it goes about the job of reallocating resources. Sand from several different sources clogs the gears. Two come to mind immediately. The economy is not one of thoroughgoing, pure competition. Monopoly in product sales and monopsony in resource purchases are troublesome. Price-fixing by the government or by private organizations as well as certain social and cultural factors may also impede movements toward correct allocations.

Monopoly

What effect does some degree of monopoly in the sale of products—such as duPont with nylon or Xerox with copying machines—have on the allocation of resources? One effect can be deduced from the fact that entry into monopolistic and oligopolistic industries is obstructed or blocked, permitting profits to be made over a period of years. Thus even though the value of marginal product of resources used by a monopolistic or an oligopolist may be higher in those industries than in others, the entry barriers prevent the movement in of additional quantities of them. As long as the entry barriers remain, the resources used by the firms that maintain the barriers are likely to remain incorrectly allocated.

For any given resource used by a monopolist, there is a more subtle reason why a correct allocation is not likely to be achieved. This is the difference that always exists between the value of marginal product and the marginal revenue product of a resource used by a firm that faces a downward-sloping demand curve for its output.[4] The difference will not be the same for different monopolists that use the resource. In Figure 17–4, for example, monopolist I and monopolist II are two of many users of resource A. The market price of the resource is p_a and, assuming that it is purchased competitively, so is its marginal resource cost. To maximize profits, each of the firms will employ that quantity of A at which its marginal revenue product is equal to its marginal resource cost. For monopolist I this is quantity a_1 and for monopolist II it is quantity a_2. Will any further reallocation of the resource occur? Is resource A correctly allocated?

The price system is through with its allocation job. The price of the resource is the same in both employments, so resource owners have no

[4] See pp. 285–287 for a review of the difference.

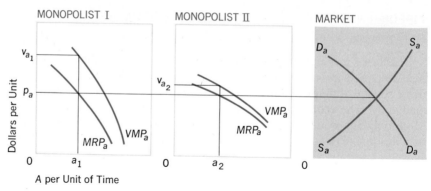

Figure 17-4
Monopolistic misallocation of a resource.   .

incentive to transfer resource units from one to the other. Since each firm is obtaining the quantity it wants at the market price, p_a, neither has an incentive to bid for additional units nor to reduce the current employment level.

The resource is not correctly allocated even though the price system will bring about no changes in its present allocation. The value of marginal product of A is higher in the use to which monopolist I puts it than it is for monopolist II and differences of this kind would be expected to prevail among its different uses—except as among purely competitive sellers of product. Thus monopoly in product selling tends to cause distortions in the allocation of resources among different uses.

Monopsony

Distortions in the allocation of resources similar to those just discussed are caused by monopsony in resource purchases. In a situation of pure monopsony there is only one user of a given kind of resource, so no allocation problem exists. But if there are four or five buyers of the resource, each one large enough to influence its price, then each has some degree of monopsony and an allocation problem among the different users may exist. This is the situation that we analyze here.

We would expect the owners of the resource to seek employment where they can obtain the highest price. This means that units of the resource will be allocated among the monopsonists so that the resource price, p_a, is the same to all. This situation is illustrated in Figure 17–5 for two monopsonists, employing quantities a_1 and a_2, respectively. At price p_a, each monopsonist faces an upward-sloping supply curve for the resource, meaning that if either wants to employ larger amounts it must increase the offering price to obtain them. But at price p_a the supply

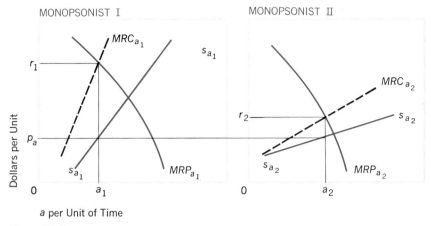

Figure 17–5
Monopsonistic misallocation of a resource.

curves facing the two firms are not likely to have the same elasticity and, consequently, for one—monopsonist I in this case—at price p_a the marginal resource cost will be higher than for the other. The price system has completed its job. The price of the resource is the same wherever it is used. But among the monopsonists marginal resource costs differ, and if each monopsonist is in equilibrium—maximizing profits—marginal revenue products of the resource will differ, too. With marginal revenue products of A differing for the different firms, it is highly unlikely that values of marginal product will be the same in all uses.

Price-Fixing

Incorrect allocations sometimes may be caused in whole or in part or may be maintained over time by price-fixing on the part of the government or by private organizations. There are two general classes of price-fixing cases. First, minimum prices may be placed on resources; second, prices of products may be fixed.

Resource Price-Fixing

Collective bargaining between business enterprises and labor unions provides by far the most common case of resource price-fixing. Suppose that common labor is used both in the construction industry and in agriculture. The demand and supply curves for the resource used in agriculture have become D_aD_a and S_aS_a in Figure 17–6, while in construction they have become D_cD_c and S_cS_c. Labor is not correctly allocated.[5] The incorrect allocation will cause wage rate differences to develop between the two types of employment—in agriculture it will be p_a and in construction it will be p_c. If there were no impediments to movement, labor would migrate from agriculture into construction until the wage differential is eliminated. The labor supply curve in construction will have shifted to the right to $S_{c_1}S_{c_1}$, while in agriculture it will have shifted to the left to $S_{a_1}S_{a_1}$. Wage rate p would prevail in both markets.

What would happen if before the migration of labor has time to occur a union of construction workers through collective bargaining with an association of contractors establishes a minimum wage rate for labor at level p_c in the construction industry? The minimum would prevent the desired reallocation from occurring. At wage rate p_c, employers in the construction industry will employ only L_c workers. Each firm is employing that quantity at which the marginal revenue product of the resource is equal to the wage rate. For any firm the employment of a larger quantity will decrease its profits. If workers leave agriculture, where are they to go? Who will employ them? The minimum wage rate in construction bars them from that industry. If these were the only two industries employing common labor, those in agriculture would be forced to remain in that sector. The supply curve would remain at S_aS_a and the wage rate would remain at p_a. The resource would be chronically misallocated and national income would be below its potential maximum.

Minimum wage laws are another means of establishing minimum prices for labor resources. In the foregoing example, suppose that Congress decides that any wage rate below p_c is substandard and, consequently, that it is illegal for any employer to pay less. In Figure 17–6, with the original demand and supply situation, employers in agriculture would be willing to hire only L'_a workers at that wage rate. Quantity L_{a_2} will be seeking employment, so there will be $L'_aL_{a_2}$ workers made unemployed by the enforcement of the minimum. These cannot be absorbed by any industry such as construction that currently pays the minimum wage rate.

An argument frequently made by proponents of minimum wage laws is that workers who lose their jobs because of the minimum—some of the agricultural workers in this case—will be forced to seek employment in higher-paying areas. In the above example, uses that currently pay more than the minimum—more than the construction industry pays—must be available if the unemployed are to be "kicked upstairs." Unemployment may well provide an incentive to workers to move. But so may a differential in the wage rate. The argument for the minimum wage rests on a

---

[5] This may have come about because product demand relative to supply has risen faster in construction than in agriculture.

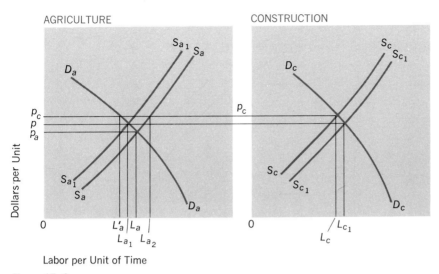

AGRICULTURE

CONSTRUCTION

Figure 17–6
Misallocation through resource price-fixing.

value judgment that unemployment is the more effective and the more desirable incentive. An argument against the minimum wage rests on a value judgment that the more desirable—but possibly not the more effective—incentive is the wage differential.

Product Price-Fixing

Misallocation of specific resources can be caused when product prices are fixed by the government, although in some cases such price-fixing may improve the allocation rather than make it worse. Resource allocation is likely to be made worse when the price-fixing is done in competitive product markets, in which the value of marginal product and the marginal revenue produce of the resource or resources in question are not far apart. A case in point is agricultural price supports.

What is likely to be the impact of a support price for wheat that is above the equilibrium wheat price level? The demand curves for resources used in the production of wheat will be shifted to the right. For any given resource, say labor, the marginal revenue product curve of a firm prior to the imposition of the support price will lie to the left of the position it will take after a support price is put into effect. In Figure 17–7, MRP_l represents the presupport marginal revenue product curve for labor and, since a wheat farmer acts as a purely competitive seller of product, the value of marginal product curve for labor coincides with it. Since the curve shows the marginal physical product of labor at different employ-

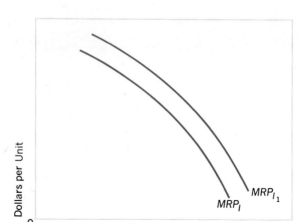

Figure 17–7
Effects of product price-fixing on *MRP* of a resource.

ment levels multiplied by the price of wheat, it also shows the value that consumers attach to labor used by the firm at each of those employment levels.

The implementation of a support price for wheat shifts the marginal revenue product curve and the value of marginal product curve to the right to MRP_{l_1}. At each level of employment the marginal physical product of labor is now multiplied by the (higher) supported price of wheat. The curve no longer reflects consumers' valuation of the labor used by the firm. It reflects an arbitrary higher valuation that will attract units of labor away from other employments into this one. That which we expect for the one wheat farmer we would expect for all, thus larger quantities of resources will be attracted into wheat farming relative to other employments than consumers desire.

Other Impediments

A number of other factors may impede the price system in its task of reallocating resources in response to dynamic changes occurring in the economy. Some, in fact, may circumvent it altogether. We might characterize these as sociocultural and as educational and training factors.

In the sociocultural area we frequently find obstacles to geographic mobility of resources. Workers may be reluctant to move from one area to another even though the latter promises higher earning opportunities. There are several reasons why this may be so. Social ties to family and friends may be strong. They may be reluctant to go into a new and unknown community. The older the workers, the stronger such forces seem to operate on them. Thus we see pockets of unemployed or underemployed persons in Appalachia, the Ozarks region, and in other areas depending heavily on welfare payments to make ends meet.

Educational and training factors tend to block upward mobility of labor resources. The higher earnings available to more skilled workers provide the economic incentive to acquire those skills, or for upward mobility, but the opportunities for developing them are not always available to everyone. Blacks in particular have not had the educational opportunities open to them that most whites have had. Consequently, they have not been able to respond to such incentives. For some occupations training facilities are not available to all who desire to enter and who have the necessary ability. Medicine provides an outstanding example.

Economic policy-making with respect to persons earning low incomes must center around making such individuals more productive. Particularly, it should work toward removing impediments to geographic and to upward mobility. This is, of course, the aim of much recent antipoverty legislation. As impediments are removed, the price system should become more effective in performing its reallocation functions.

SUMMARY

New inventions and new discoveries create continual changes in consumer wants, in resource supplies, and in techniques of production. These call for corresponding changes in the productive capacity of the economy, or in the allocation of resources among different uses. This chapter sets out the principles that guide resource allocation in a free enterprise economy—how the price system signals that misallocation is occurring and how it goes about correcting the misallocation.

If pure competition prevails in product selling and in resource buying, the price system will tend to correct any misallocation of a given resource. Misallocation will result in different prices being paid for the resource in its different uses. Where its marginal revenue product and value of marginal product are higher, the price or prices paid for the resource will also be higher. These are the uses in which consumers want more of the resource employed; that is, in which they value it more highly. The different prices provide the incentive to resource owners to transfer units of the resource from lower-paying, lower-value uses to higher-paying, higher-value uses. Every such transfer increases national income. As the process of reallocation takes place, the differences in prices paid for the resource become less and less, and when the malallocation has been entirely corrected—if it ever is—the price of the resource and its value of marginal product will be the same in all its uses.

Monopoly in product selling prevents the price system from allocating units of a given resource in an entirely correct way. The price system tends to allocate the resource so that its price and its marginal revenue product are everywhere the same. But monopoly causes the value of marginal product of a resource to be higher than its marginal revenue product for the monopolistic firm. For different monopolists the difference between value of marginal product and marginal revenue product will vary, causing the latter to be different even though the former are the same. Firms in which the value of marginal product is higher are using less of the resource than consumers wish to have employed in producing that product or service.

Some degree of monopsony in resource purchasing also prevents the price system from fulfilling its allocation functions completely. The price system tends to allocate a given resource so that its price is the same in all uses. However, because of differing elasticities of supply for different monopsonists, marginal resource cost will differ among them. So, too, will marginal revenue product and value of marginal product.

Price-fixing by private organizations or by government agencies may prevent resources from being correctly allocated. Collective bargaining, for example, may establish a high minimum price for labor in high value of marginal product, high-paying uses. This will preclude the transfer of labor from lower value of marginal product lower-paying uses. If the minimum is extended to the lower-paying uses, raising the wage rate above the equilibrium level, unemployment will result.

Product price-fixing may also cause resources to be allocated incorrectly. A product price support, above the equilibrium level, shifts the demand curves for resources used in producing the product to the right of where consumer desires indicate they should be. Thus larger quantities of resources will be drawn into production, leaving smaller quantities in uses other than those consumers' desire.

Sociocultural together with educational and training factors may interfere with or negate the operation of the price system in reallocating resources. Family and community ties may impede the geographic mobility of labor resources. Lack of educational and training opportunities may also impede the upward mobility of workers.

EXERCISES AND QUESTIONS FOR DISCUSSION

1. List several groups or kinds of labor in your community within which units of labor seem to be homogeneous. For each group is the wage the same in the different employments of its labor? If it is not, why do you think it is different?

2. Under what circumstances would a minimum price for a product or resource improve the allocation of resources? in what situations would it not?
3. "If all agricultural price supports were abruptly removed, many farmers would become unemployed. Since unemployment is a forceful incentive for resources to find other employment, the allocation of the economy's resources would be improved." What do you think about this statement? What might impede the correct reallocation of these resources?
4. If its marginal revenue product is higher in one employment than in another, will national income be increased if units of a resource move from the lower marginal revenue product use to the higher marginal revenue product use? What assumptions did you make? What if one industry is purely competitive and another is monopolistic in product selling (both are purely competitive in resource purchasing)?
5. Suppose that the government sets the price of a product produced by a purely competitive industry below the equilbrium level. What would be the impact of this action on the allocation of those resources of which this industry uses a part?
6. What methods are currently being used in your community to improve the mobility (horizontal or vertical) of resources? How would you modify the current program?

SELECTED READINGS

Bloom, G. F., and H. R. Northrup, *Economics of Labor Relations,* 5th ed. Homewood, Ill.: Richard D. Irwin, Inc., 1965, pp. 417–432.

Boulding, K. E., *Economic Analysis,* Vol. I, *Microeconomic Analysis.* New York: Harper & Row, Publishers, Inc., 1966, Chap. 6.

Ginzberg, E., *The Development of Human Resources.* New York: McGraw-Hill Book Company, Inc., 1966, Chap. 17.

Stigler, G. J., "The Economics of Minimum Wage Legislation," *American Economic Review,* June 1946, 36:3, 358–361.

Distribution of the Product

CHAPTER 18

Why is it that Henry Ford II can claim a much larger share of the economy's yearly output than can a southern sharecropper? We know, of course, that the distribution of the economy's output among consuming units depends primarily on how income is distributed among them. Each can obtain a share approximately in the same proportion as his income bears to total income earned in the economy per year. During any given year individuals also have the alternative of either not spending a part of their income or of spending more than their income, if they are willing to use up a part of their past accumulated wealth. Thus, basically, the distribution of the economy's output depends upon the distribution of income. To rephrase the question, why is it that Henry Ford II has a large income while a southern sharecropper has a small one?

The price system plays a key role in the distribution of income or product, the third major function of an economic system. It is not the only factor at work and it does not necessarily lead toward the distribution that we would consider most desirable. After we have surveyed briefly what the actual distribution of income has been, we shall turn to the principles of income distribution, with emphasis on the functions of resource prices in the accomplishment of the distribution process. Next, we shall seek out the causes of income differences, and, finally, we shall examine the possibilities of income redistribution.

THE FACTS OF INCOME DISTRIBUTION

Income differences among consuming units of an economy have been an age-old source of conflict. In the United States they have been a major issue in many political campaigns and they have provided much of the basis for support of socialistic and communistic activities in the less developed countries of the world. Our purpose here is to get away from the more emotion-laden aspects of income distribution and to get at some of the facts.

The Functional Distribution of Income

The Department of Commerce functional distribution of income is the breakdown of income distribution that we see most often. It classifies income earned according to the types of resources placed in the productive process—almost. For example, it separates out most of the wages and salaries earned by labor resources. These are called *compensation of employees*. It also separates out most of the income earned by capital resources in the forms of *corporate profits, net interest income,* and *rental income of persons*. It contains still another classification, *proprietors' income,* which it does not break down between labor resources and capital resources.

Table 18–1 gives the functional distribution of income for 1947, 1955, 1964, and 1967. The most pronounced characteristic of earned income that is reflected in the table is that between 65 and 72 percent of it is compensation of employees, clearly earned by *labor resources*. The portion clearly earned by *capital resources*—rental income, corporate profits, and net interest—varies between 17 and 19.5 percent of the total. The 10–18 percent allocated as proprietors' income is a combination of earnings by labor resources and capital resources.

Suppose we make a rough division of proprietors' income between the labor and capital resource classifications in order to get some idea of the total shares of each over time. For example, for 1964, suppose we divide the amount between labor income and capital income in the same proportion as the rest of income earned was divided between those two classifications. The 1964 percentage figure of 9.9 would be split, allocating 2.1 percent of total income to capital and 7.8 percent to labor.[1] Total

---

[1] Labor income (compensation of employees) exclusive of proprietors' income is 71.0 percent of total income. Capital income (rental income + corporate profits + net interest) exclusive of proprietors' income is 19.1 percent of the total. Proprietors' income is 9.9 percent of the total and is to be divided between capital and labor in the ratio 19.1/71.0. Letting C represent the part of proprietors' income to be allocated to capital and L the part to be allocated to labor, we have the following equations:

$$\frac{19.1}{71.0} = \frac{C}{L} \tag{18.1}$$

$$C + L = 9.9 \tag{18.2}$$

Solving these simultaneously for C and L, we obtain

$$C = 2.1 \text{ percent of total income}$$
$$L = 7.8 \text{ percent of total income}$$

TABLE 18-1
National Income by Source, 1947, 1955, 1964, 1967

Source of Income	1947 Income (billions)	1947 Percent of Total	1955 Income (billions)	1955 Percent of Total	1964 Income (billions)	1964 Percent of Total	1967 Income (billions)	1967 Percent of Total
Compensation of employees	$128.8	65.0	$223.9	67.8	$365.3	71.0	$468.2	71.7
Proprietors' income	35.5	17.9	42.1	12.7	51.1	9.9	60.7	9.3
Rental income	6.5	3.3	10.7	3.3	18.2	3.6	20.3	3.1
Corporate profits	23.6	11.9	43.1	13.1	64.5	12.5	80.4	12.3
Net interest income	3.8	1.9	10.4	3.1	15.2	3.0	23.3	3.6
Total	$198.2	100.0	$330.2	100.0	$514.3	100.0	$652.9	100.0

Source: U.S. Department of Commerce, Survey of Current Business, April 1965, 6, and September 1968, 8; and U.S. Department of Commerce, Business Statistics 1963 Edition, 1–2.

TABLE 18–2
Distribution of National Income by Source

	1947 (PERCENT)	1955 (PERCENT)	1964 (PERCENT)	1967 (PERCENT)
Labor	78.2	77.7	78.8	79.1
Capital	21.8	22.3	21.2	20.9
Total	100.0	100.0	100.0	100.0

SOURCE: Computed from Table 18–1.

labor income for 1964, then, is 78.8 percent of total income. Total capital income is 21.2 percent of total income. These results are recorded in the 1964 column of Table 18–2. For 1955, the allocation of proprietors' income is 2.8 percent of total income to capital and 9.9 percent to capital. The allocation of total income earned for that year is 77.7 percent earned by labor and 22.3 percent earned by capital. Using the same procedures for 1947 and 1967, we obtain the results shown in the appropriate columns of Table 18–2.

The functional distribution of income tells us nothing about why some consuming units are rich and others are poor. It is commonly believed that the rich live mostly on income from capital while the poor live on income from labor. This is not entirely so. According to data collected by the Bureau of the Census in 1960,[2] only one family in every one hundred in the top 5 percent of income receivers depended entirely on income from interest, dividends, rents, and royalties. The rest were generally dependent on incomes received from professions or from self-employment. One-third of the top income-receiving families reported no income at all from investments. On the other hand, about one third of the families in the lowest 20 percent of income receivers were over 65 years of age, in retirement, and living on Social Security benefits. Still others were families with no workers who were living on private pensions, welfare payments, or income other than earnings from labor.

The Personal Distribution of Income

The *personal distribution of income* provides us with more useful information than the functional distribution. The term refers to how families

[2] U.S. Bureau of the Census, *How Our Income Is Divided* (Washington, D.C., 1963), Graphic Pamphlets GP 60–2.

TABLE 18-3

Percentage Distribution of Families and Unrelated Individuals by Size of Income, Selected Years, 1947–1966 (1966 dollars)

MONEY INCOME BEFORE TAXES	1947	1955	1960	1966
Families				
Under $3000	28.9	22.8	19.5	14.3
$3000–$4999	30.6	22.5	18.0	13.9
$5000–$6999	19.7	23.3	21.6	17.8
$7000–$9999	13.0	19.7	22.5	24.4
$10,000–$14,999	8.1	8.8	13.3	20.4
$15,000 and over		2.9	5.3	9.2
Percent	100.3[1]	100.0	100.2[1]	100.0
Number (thousands)	37,237	42,889	45,456	48,922
Median income	$4,401	$5,377	$6,174	$7,436
Unrelated individuals				
Under $1,500	51.6	48.0	43.2	36.7
$1500–$3000	23.8	22.5	20.6	22.2
$3000–$4999	17.1	18.5	18.9	18.2
$5000–$6999	4.3	7.1	10.8	11.5
$7000–$9999	1.6	2.8	4.7	6.9
$10,000 and over	1.6	1.2	1.8	4.4
Percent	100.0	100.1[1]	100.0	99.9[1]
Number (thousands)	8,165	9,889	11,081	12,368
Median Income	$1,437	$1,610	$1,908	$2,270

[1] Data as reported do not total 100 percent.

SOURCE: U.S. Bureau of the Census, *Current Population Reports*, Series P–60, No. 53, "Income in 1966 of Families and Persons in the United States," (Washington, D.C.: Government Printing Office 1967), p. 2.

and unrelated individuals[3] share in the total income or total value of output of the economy. It lets us know the number of rich people, the number of poor people, and how wide the gaps are between them. It also helps us to understand what is happening to economic well-being over time.

Shortly after assuming office in November 1963, President Johnson announced his intent to wage an all-out war on poverty. The President's Council of Economic Advisors defined poverty as an annual income of less than $3000 per year. This rather arbitrary dividing line was later refined, reaching from $1080 for an unrelated individual living on a farm to over $5000 for an urban family of seven. The two definitions arrive at similar results, so in the interest of simplicity we shall use a (in 1966 prices) $3000 dividing line in this section.

[3] Unrelated individuals are those living alone, unattached to any family group.

How does the current distribution of personal income look? How has it changed over the last 25 years? What further changes appear likely? Tables 18–3 and 18–4 provide relevant information. Looking first at 1966 data, we find that 14.3 percent of the nation's families were below the $3000 per year line. At the other end of the scale, 29.6 percent of the families earned $10,000 or over per year. Another 24.4 percent earned yearly incomes of $7000–$10,000. Median family income was $7436.

Over the last 25 years there has been a sizable shift upward in family income levels. In 1947 some 29 percent of U.S. families were living in what the Council of Economic Advisors has defined as poverty. Only 8.1 percent of all families earned $10,000 or more. There were sharp drops in the poverty category from 1947 to 1955 and from 1960 to 1966, with a somewhat less spectacular decrease from 1960 to 1965. Median family income rose steadily throughout the period.

Some projections by Martin Gainsbrugh, chief economist of the National Industrial Conference Board, for 1970 and 1975 are given in Table 18–4. Gainsbrugh estimates that by 1975, if present trends continue, only 11 percent of families will be under the poverty line. In the higher-income brackets almost 43 percent of families are expected to earn incomes of $10,000 or more per year.

Trends for unrelated individuals have been similar to those for families, but annual income levels have been much lower. Most of those so classified were in age groups 14 to 24 and 65 and over, in which earnings are typically low. In addition, in 1966 approximately 63 percent of the total were women.

TABLE 18–4
Distribution of Families by Size of Income, 1965, 1970*, 1975* (1965 dollars)

	1965		1970		1975	
MONEY INCOME BEFORE TAXES	NUMBER OF FAMILIES	PERCENT OF FAMILIES	NUMBER OF FAMILIES	PERCENT OF FAMILIES	NUMBER OF FAMILIES	PERCENT OF FAMILIES
Under $3000	8.0	16.6	7.2	13.8	6.4	11.2
$3000–$4999	7.7	15.8	7.0	13.5	6.5	11.4
$5000–$6999	9.0	18.6	7.7	14.7	7.2	12.6
$7000–$9999	11.6	24.1	13.0	24.9	12.6	22.1
$10,000–$14,999	8.3	17.3	11.2	21.5	14.3	25.2
$15,000 and over	3.7	7.6	6.1	11.6	9.9	17.5
Total	48.3	100.0	52.2	100.0	56.9	100.0

*Estimated

SOURCE: Martin R. Gainsbrugh, "Some Notes on the Distribution of Income in the United States and the Relationship to Poverty," Joint Council on Economic Education *Newsletter*, May 1967.

CAUSES OF INCOME DIFFERENCES

We return now to the fundamental question of *why* some people are rich while others are poor. We shall look first at the determinants of individual or family income. Then we shall examine the specific causes in income differences—differences in labor resources owned, in capital resources owned, and in prices received in different employments of the same resource.

Income Determination

The principles governing income determination are relatively simple and will not detain us long. They follow directly from those that govern resource pricing and employment. The income of an individual or a family depends upon two factors: (1) the quantities of resources owned and (2) the prices received for them.

Quantities of Resources Owned

Some families own labor resources only, but most own both labor and capital. Given the prices of different kinds of labor and different kinds of capital, the more the family is able to place on the market, the larger its income will be. Consider the resources owned by a university professor. His full-time work—teaching, research, and counseling students—may be all that he cares to do, and his university salary may represent the entire family income. It is quite possible, however, that he has the energy and the desire to do additional work, so he spends evenings, weekends, and holidays writing a textbook. Hopefully, he receives additional income from its sale. If he still has energy to burn he can take on consulting work for business or for government and earn still more from his labor resources.

The professor seeks investment possibilities for that part of his income that he saves, so he begins to accumulate capital resources. He may invest in real estate—buying apartment houses, farm land, or other kinds of real property. He may invest in stocks and bonds; that is, acquire titles or claims to capital resources used by corporations in producing goods and services. As he acquires larger quantities of capital resources, his income becomes correspondingly higher.

Resource Prices

The forces that determine the market price of a resource were examined in Chapters 15 and 16 and need not be repeated here in any detail. When a resource is purchased competitively its market price is determined by the demand for and the supply of it. A firm will employ that quantity of the resource at which the marginal revenue product of the resource is equal to its market price. Thus any unit of the resource is paid a price approximately equal to what it is worth to its employer—its marginal revenue product. Yet even though units of the resource are paid what they are worth to the employer, they may or may not be paid what they are worth to society. If the firm is a purely competitive seller of product, the value of marginal product of the resource will tend to be the same as the price paid for it, but if the firm is a monopolist, the value of marginal product of the resource will exceed its price. Only under conditions of monopsony will the value of a resource to its employer be greater than its price.

Differences in Labor Resources Owned

There are large differences in the earnings received from labor resources among different individuals. Why is this so? The labor resource classification does not really contain one unique kind of resource. There are a great many different resources within the classification. Suppose we subclassify these, differentiating among different *skill levels*. We obtain *vertical* groupings ranging from the lowest type of unskilled labor to the highest skill levels in existence. Garbage collectors are in one resource group. Ordinary carpenters are in another. Ordinary economics professors are in still a different group. Further, suppose that at each skill level we differentiate among occupations, obtaining a number of *horizontal* groupings. At any one level—say a professional level—we place lawyers in one group, physicians in another, university professors in another, and so on. These classifications are useful in explaining income differences stemming from differences in labor resources owned.

Vertical Differences

Most of the large differences in individual incomes earned from labor resources spring from differences in skill levels. Unskilled workers—common laborers—usually receive comparatively low wages. Highly skilled workers—entertainers, physicians, business executives—usually command high fees or salaries for the labor services they perform. The technical reason for this pattern is not hard to find. The demand for the services in the higher-skill occupations is greater relative to the supply available than is the case in the lower-skill occupations.

As we move upward from the lower- to the higher-skill occupational categories, we find that to a considerable extent each occupation constitutes a separate labor market. Opera singers operate in one market. Television and movie actors operate in another. Business executives are in another. Mathematics professors are in still another. Machinists, carpenters, and plumbers each have their own markets, and so does common labor. These separate groups of workers are sometimes referred to as *noncompeting* groups, but this is probably putting it too strongly. Interrelationships occur among groups at any given skill level and among groups at adjacent skill levels. Elvis Presley moved from truck driving into the entertainment field. Albert Schweitzer was a musician and a theologian before becoming a physician. Plumbers and carpenters can learn to be machinists. Common laborers can develop higher skills.

On the demand side, highly skilled workers, per man hour exerted, generally produce goods or services more urgently desired than those produced by workers with lesser skills. To put it another way, the value of marginal product curves for workers with high skill levels ordinarily are higher than those for unskilled workers. Compare, for example, the value of marginal product of a heart surgeon with that of a bricklayer, measuring man hours of labor on the horizontal axis and value of marginal product on the vertical axis.

On the supply side, the higher the skill level, the smaller the supply of labor seems to be. The number of persons eligible for top-management jobs in General Motors, Radio Corporation of America, or International Business Machines is rather limited. There is a scarcity of airline pilots. Topflight history professors can be rather easily counted. Several factors contribute to this pattern.

The higher the skill level required for an occupation, the fewer persons there will be with the physical and mental characteristics necessary to qualify for it. There are more mediocre minds than there are outstanding ones. And the number of people with the physical dexterity necessary for accomplishing certain complex processes varies inversely with the level of physical skill required. These differing capacities of individuals to attain specific skill levels result from myriad possible combinations of mental and physical characteristics. They have nothing to do with merit but are accidents of birth or inheritance.

Even if individuals have the physical and mental capacities to move up to high skill levels, there is no assurance that they can do so. The opportunities for developing inherited characteristics differ widely for different individuals. *Social obstacles* may block higher education—or even secondary education—for individuals who are inherently capable. The attitudes of family, friends, and community have much to do with an individual's desires to develop his capabilities. For verification of the point one needs only to look at the slum areas of New York City, Chicago, or Los Angeles. Some people may find that training facilities are not open to them because of *racial obstacles*. Certainly this has been the case in the past in many communities of the South; however, it has occurred and still occurs on a nation-wide basis. *Financial obstacles* also tend to limit the supplies of high-level man power. The tuition at law schools, medical schools, and engineering schools is high—particularly at universities that offer outstanding programs. These are more easily available to persons with wealthy parents than to the children of the poor.

Obstacles notwithstanding, many individuals from underprivileged backgrounds have been able to move into high-skill occupations. It has been no easy task, but a number of blacks have been able to enter and succeed in the entertainment field and in other occupations as well. So, too, have individuals from white urban and rural slum areas. University training is becoming increasingly available to the children of the poor. Scholarship and fellowship aids as well as low-cost loans are providing more and more opportunities for students who are long on ability and short on means.

Not all of those who have opportunities for training take advantage of them. The development of one's physical and mental capacities requires more than the mere existence of opportunities. It requires initiative and drive on the part of the individual himself, and these traits differ considerably from person to person. But the fact remains that those born to parents farther up the income and social scale not only have more opportunities open to them but also grow up in an environment that is more likely to foster taking advantage of those opportunities.

Horizontal Differences

Within particular skill levels there are also income differences. These occur because of differences in the resource demand and supply conditions existing for different occupations. Engineering professors, for example, are generally paid higher salaries than professors of history. This is not because engineering professors are better trained or more highly skilled in their particular field but because there is a wider demand throughout the economy for engineers than there is for historians relative to their respective supplies.

There are at least two reasons why the supply of historians may have remained relatively large over time. First, personal preferences to work in the field of history rather than in the field of engineering may have induced many individuals to become historians even though they were well aware that their remuneration as historians would be lower. We can think of the historian in this case as taking a part of his pay in the form of on-the-job satisfaction.[4] Differences in pay attributable to differences in the desirability of jobs are referred to as *equalizing differences* and play a recognized role in the over-all pattern of wage and salary differences. Second, as individuals were in the process of choosing their professional field they

---

[4]Another example of this principle is provided by the individual who sacrifices several thousand dollars per year in order to work for a university rather than for a private business or a government agency.

may not have had complete information on comparative remuneration. Thus earnings possibilities may not have played a major role in their choice. Information of this kind is rapidly becoming more a part of common knowledge than it has been in the past. For example, it may have influenced your choice of what field to study.

Another common cause of income differences within a given profession has to do with experience or length of time in the field. Physicians, lawyers, and even schoolteachers find that their annual earnings rise as their experience increases, reaching a maximum some 20 or 30 years after entering the profession. Frequently the new entrant is as skilled as the old-timer—indeed on certain newly developed techniques he may be better. Yet the old-timer commands the premium. The difference here, of course, is on the demand side. Consumers place a premium on experience.

Differences in Capital Resources Owned

Differences in capital resources owned account for substantial differences in individual incomes. Some people own vast amounts of land, including the mineral deposits contained in it. Others own large amounts of corporate stocks and bonds. Still others own buildings or are direct owners of the plant and equipment of businesses. Some people own small amounts of the tools used in their regular occupations. What are the factors that bring about wide disparities in the capital resources owned by different individuals? A list of the more prominent ones must include inheritance, luck, and the psychological propensity or will to accumulate.

Inheritance

If you want to be wealthy you will have made giant strides toward the achievement of your goal if you chose your parents wisely. Most people who own large amounts of capital—and who receive large incomes from capital—inherited much of what they have. Survey the wealthy families in your home community and you will find that by and large this is the case. Would the present generation of the Rockefellers, the Fords, or the Kennedys be as wealthy today as they are if they had been born in the Watts area of Los Angeles? No one can say for sure, but it is highly unlikely that their capital holdings would approach their present magnitudes if this had been their lot.

Luck

Sometimes plain, old-fashioned luck brings about differences in the quantities of resources owned. A person may have purchased a piece of land for agricultural purposes, the price of the land based on its expected net yield in producing farm products. Then the discovery of oil transforms the nature of the capital resource and makes its owner rich. Another familiar example of the same thing occurs from such things as a legislative decision to build a lake adjoining the property. To turn the example around, consider the initial impact of the relation between smoking and lung cancer on the value of capital used in cigarette production. In all of these examples there is an unexpected change in demand or marginal revenue product of the capital resources in question.

Propensities To Accumulate

Both of the factors just described attribute differences in quantities of capital owned to accidents of birth or chance; yet this is misleading. Many people with sizable holdings of capital resources built up most of their stocks over their own lifetimes. The starting point may have been a healthy endowment of labor resources—physical or mental or both. Many big-league baseball players have parleyed their initial salary earnings into bowling alleys, restaurants, sporting goods companies, real estate, insurance companies, and other kinds of capital. The original Henry Ford turned an idea into a fine stock of capital resources. Professional people often find it possible to set aside income from the use of their labor resources and to use what they have set aside to accumulate capital.

The personal characteristics that lead to capital accumulation vary widely among different individuals. Some who would like to accumulate capital are never able to do so because they have neither the requisite abilities nor the funds necessary for getting the whole thing started. Some whose incomes are large enough to permit some saving and investment in additional capital resources have no inclination to do so. Others have demonstrated marked capabilities of using up stocks of capital resources that they have inherited. Of one thing we can be sure, it is easier for people whose incomes are already large to accumulate additional capital resources than for those whose incomes are low. But a large income does not guarantee further capital accumulation.

Differences in Prices Paid for a Resource

Units of a given kind of resource are not always paid the same price, even when their qualities are more or less equal. These differences in price cause differences in the income earned by their owners. This may be so for several reasons. First, the differences may occur in the short run, before forces inducing reallocation from lower-paying to higher-paying uses have had time to work themselves out. Second, the differences may be the consequences of price-fixing in some employments of the resource. Third, they may arise from supply restrictions or limitations on the quantity of the resource that can be used in certain employments of it. We met all of these phenomena in the three preceding chapters; nevertheless, they should be reviewed again in the context of their impact on income distribution.

Short-Run Differences

The conditions of demand for and supply of a resource in its different employments or in different geographic areas are constantly changing. With a shift in consumer demand from radios to television sets we expect that electronics technicians will be better paid in the latter field temporarily. Aircraft maintenance and repair shops catering to general aviation have experienced difficulty in retaining mechanics in recent years. With the relatively rapid growth of commercial air travel, rates of pay offered by the airlines have increased relative to those offered by the smaller general aviation shops.

Income differences of this kind are an integral and necessary feature of the price mechanism in the performance of its function of continually reallocating resources from uses where they contribute less to what consumers want to those where they contribute more. The income differences ordinarily indicate or reflect such differences. These provide the incentive for reallocation toward the higher-paying uses, and, in turn, the reallocation tends to wipe out the difference.

Price-Fixing

In Figure 18–1 we have a hypothetical free market demand for and supply of milk-wagon drivers in Chicago. The equilibrium wage rate is w and the level of employment is M. If all drivers work the same number of hours weekly, they will earn equal incomes.[5] Now suppose that through unionization and collective bargaining a wage rate of w_1 is put into effect. The employment level drops to M_1 and, of the number formerly employed, M_1M workers are now unemployed. The incomes of those who retain employment will be higher, but those made unemployed have no income at all from their labor resources.

The picture probably will not be as dark as it has just been painted. The M_1M drivers who no longer are employed on the milk trucks will seek employment elsewhere, perhaps as light truck drivers or perhaps in other occupations. But it is almost certain that their incomes will be lower in

[5]Since milk-wagon drivers are essentially light truck drivers, their wage rates and incomes should be very close to those of other light truck drivers.

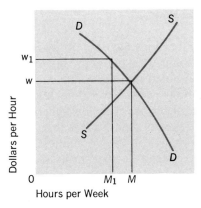

Figure 18-1
Effects of minimum price-fixing on income distribution.

the new occupations than they were originally. Wherever else they go they increase the supply of labor in those employments, pressing those wage rates downward. And in most instances the occupations or employments into which they move were paying less than milk-wagon driving—otherwise they would have been in them before rather than on the milk trucks.

In general, we would expect minimum price-fixing, whenever it is effective, to create and to maintain income differences over time. Monopsony situations provide an exception to this statement for in these, if minimum prices are correctly set, not only will the wage rates and incomes of those originally employed be increased but the employment level will be increased as well.

Supply Control

Differences in incomes earned by units of a given resource are sometimes created or perpetuated through control of the supply that can be used in any specific employment. Supply controls may be imposed by organizations of suppliers or by the government. Where a union is able to restrict the number of members enrolled and is at the same time able to negotiate agreements with the major part of the employers using that specific kind of labor in which union membership must be a condition of employment, differences in earnings between union and nonunion members in the trade may develop. Or, if the government limits the number of acres that can be planted to cotton, causing land that would otherwise have been planted to cotton to be put to some other use, differences in earnings between the land used for the former purpose and that used for the latter will occur. Analytically the case is very much the same as that of minimum price-fixing.

Measures To Help the Poor

No one seriously questions the desirability of alleviating poverty; the important consideration is what methods should be used toward this end. The preceding section noted that the whole structure of family and individual incomes is shifting upward over time, leaving fewer and fewer persons in the poverty category as it is now officially defined. The upward trend has been made possible by the fact that growth in the economy's output has exceeded growth in the population. But what are the policy measures that either concentrate specifically on the special problems of the poor at the present time or could do so in the future if we were inclined to move in that direction?

The Poor

Before we can look intelligently at possible antipoverty policies we must answer another question. Who are the poor? Table 18–5 provides some answers to the question for the year 1967. A large proportion of households—in which the head of the household was 65 years of age and over are poor. In this general category of families over 20 percent were poor. Clearly, age brings with it a strong possibility of poverty. Among households with a female head the incidence of poverty was high. A much greater proportion of households with nonwhite female heads was poor than was the case for those with white female heads, but the poor house-

TABLE 18–5
Incidence of Poverty Among Families
by Selected Characteristics, 1967

FAMILY CHARACTERISTICS	PERCENT BELOW POVERTY LEVEL		
	TOTAL	WHITE	NONWHITE
Male head	8.0	6.7	22.2
65 years and over	19.2	17.8	43.3
Female head	32.3	25.1	54.1
65 years and over	26.5	24.6	43.4
Nonfarm: all families	10.3	8.1	29.8
Male head	7.6	6.3	20.8
Female head	32.6	25.4	54.3
Farm: all families	15.0	12.0	48.6
Male head	14.5	11.8	48.6
Female head	23.7	16.2	N.A.

SOURCE: U.S. Bureau of the Census, Current Population Reports, Series P-60, No. 55, "Family Income Advances, Poverty Reduced in 1967," (Washington, D.C.: Government Printing Office, 1968), p. 7.

holds among the latter outnumbered those among the former. Being non-white, whether the household head is male or female, increases the likelihood that the household will be poor. Further, we find that the incidence of poverty is heavier on farm than on nonfarm families.

There are, of course, other characteristics contributing to poverty that are not indicated by Table 18–5. From 1965 data, not strictly comparable with that of the table, we can elicit some additional information on education that seems to be important.[6] Of families earning under $3000 per year, 58 percent of the heads had eight years or less of education and another 32 percent had one to four years of high school.

Other characteristics also contribute to the chances of a household being poor, but we have identified the most important ones. To summarize, the chances are greatest if the household head is *65 years of age or over* or is *female* or is *nonwhite* or is *lacking in education*. The last three characteristics are frequently found either separately or together in slum areas.

Policies To Increase Earning Power

Armed with some idea of the characteristics of the poor we can examine the general types of actual and possible policy measures that may serve to alleviate poverty. Such measures fall into two broad, and overlapping, categories. One includes those intended to increase the earning power of the poor. The other includes income supplements. We shall look at the first category in this subsection and at the second category in the next.

One of the most important sets of policy measures is that of providing *education* for the poor. Specifically, it is of prime importance in getting at the poor households in which the household head is under 65 years of age. The economic benefits to be derived are obvious. Education should enable its recipients to move upward into occupations more in demand by society. It should increase the quality of the labor resources owned by the poor and, consequently, their income levels.

The federal government has moved extensively into the area of education since the mid-1960s. The Elementary and Secondary Education Act of 1965, among other things, provides grants to school districts in which a fairly large proportion of the children come from poor families. The Higher Education Act of 1965 provides grants to a limited number of high school graduates coming from low-income families. Additional legislation has established Project Headstart for preschoolers and the Work-Study Program at higher levels.

---

[6] Martin R. Gainsbrugh, "Some Notes on the Distribution of Income in the United States and the Relationship to Poverty," Joint-Council on Economic Education *Newsletter*, May 1967, p. 6.

The strengthening of conventional educational programs is intended to break down the social and economic barriers that the children from poor families face, but parents, adolescents, and young adults in poor families may not be reachable by conventional educational programs. Technical training programs such as the Job Corps for high school dropouts is a move toward meeting the needs of this group.

The Manpower Training and Development Act represents a further step intended to provide basic literacy for unemployed persons, or persons in very low-income jobs, and to develop or upgrade their skill levels. Retraining programs have not enjoyed an unqualified success. The task of retraining older persons compared with that of providing a sound educational foundation for young people is a formidable one.

Other policy measures to increase the earning power of the poor are directed at increasing *economic* (and social) *mobility*. If we are to alleviate poverty, we need to eliminate the barriers that prevent the poor from moving to higher-paying occupations. Racial discrimination has been a particularly pernicious barrier to mobility for blacks, Mexicans, Puerto Ricans, and Orientals. The Civil Rights Act of 1964 was intended to outlaw racial discrimination in hiring, firing, conditions of work apprenticeship, and training as well as to accomplish other nondiscrimination objectives. In addition to policy measures intended to eliminate racial discrimination, others should point toward keeping occupations open to all qualified or potentially qualified persons interested in pursuing them. This means that, among other things, licensing laws, apprenticeship rules, resource price-fixing practices, and other devices that may lead to controlled resource supplies should be continually evaluated to determine whether or not they inhibit mobility.

Policies To Maintain Income

Not all of the poor can take advantage of measures to increase their earning power. As we have seen, over a third of the poor families are headed by individuals over 65 years of age. Another 20 percent are headed by females, some of whom find the double task of raising a family and being the family breadwinner impossible. Still others are ill or disabled. These who are necessarily outside the labor force must either be provided with income supplements or starve to death.

The underlying purpose of the Social Security System is to provide income supplements to those no longer participating actively in the labor force. To a considerable extent, through payroll deductions while they are in the labor force, individuals are expected to help foot the bill for benefits that they will receive later—Old Age, Survivors', and Dependents' Insurance benefits; Medicare; and Unemployment Compensation are illustrative of these. But these supplements are not restricted to the poor—they are available to all who meet the eligibility requirements, and poverty as such is not one of them.

Public assistance, in which individual states pay almost half of the costs and establish the standards of eligibility, is the major income maintenance program specifically for the poor. Under public assistance cash payments are made to unemployable persons upon proof of need. Recipients usually include the aged, the blind, the disabled, and families with no male breadwinner. In order to hold down costs, however, states have generally set up rather stringent eligibility requirements, so that not more than an estimated 22 percent of the poor receive aid through this channel.[7]

Other government policies are aimed at raising and/or maintaining incomes of certain groups. These groups are not always the poor, although in some cases they may be. Minimum wage laws and agricultural income supplements provide examples. The former are intended to help the poor, but it is questionable whether or not they really accomplish this objective. The latter, developed over time in the name of increasing the incomes of poor farmers, miss the mark almost entirely, as we indicated earlier. To press still further, what is the purpose of tariffs and import duties, government support of labor unions and collective bargaining, and other policies of a similar nature?

Some Questions and Problems

The cost of bringing every household above the poverty line as now defined would not impose an impossible burden on the economy. The continuing problem is that of *how* it should be done. The existing system has done much toward alleviating poverty, but at the same time it has raised many problems and questions. Aid to dependent families, for example, has been said to encourage the breaking up of families by requiring that there be no employable male as a member of an eligible household. Are there cases in which income supplements are so high that incentives for recipients to seek employment are reduced significantly? Do we want cradle-to-the-grave social security coverage for *all* members of our society or are we concerned primarily with assistance to poor families? Are there alternatives to the present methods of making payments to the poor (and sometimes to those who are not poor) that promise to be superior to present methods? For example, is it possible—or desirable—to reduce the many programs that now exist to one simplified program? Certainly at this point in time we do not have all the answers!

[7] *Economic Report of the President,* 1967 (Washington D.C.: Government Printing Office, 1967), p. 141.

Within the framework of a free enterprise economic system, we can alter the distribution of income however we as a society wish. We can tax the wealthy to support programs to increase earning power and to maintain the incomes of the poor. Income transfers of this kind need not interfere with the *operation* of the price mechanism at all. They will, of course, decrease the purchasing power of those who are taxed and increase the purchasing power of those who benefit from the program, and these alterations in purchasing power may in turn change the structure of priorities that consumers as a group place on the range of goods and services available. And this is as it should be—unless we who pay the taxes are certain that we know more about what is good for the poor than they themselves know.

SUMMARY

In a free enterprise economy the distribution of the economy's output among families and unrelated individuals depends basically upon the distribution of income earned. Income earned is frequently classified in two different ways. The functional distribution of income classifies it according to the amounts earned by capital resources and by labor resources. The personal distribution of income classifies families and unrelated individuals according to the size of their incomes regardless of whether the source is labor or capital. Over the last 20 years there has been little change in the share of income earned by labor resources and that earned by capital resources; the figures have been, roughly, 78 and 22 percent, respectively. The trend in personal income has been one of continual movement upward in family income size.

Differences in family or individual incomes may arise from differences in labor resources owned. Vertical differences in labor resources owned refer to differences in skill levels. These account for the major differences in incomes at any given skill level. Horizontal differences refer to occupational differences at any given skill level. When labor is classified vertically and horizontally a number of labor markets emerge and differences in demand for and supply of labor among these markets result in differences in wages and salaries (prices) paid them.

Differences in capital resources owned may also account for substantial differences in family and individual income levels. These differences arise to a considerable extent as a result of inheritance. They result partly from luck on the part of capital owners, but they also arise from differences in the opportunities and in the propensities of people to accumulate.

In addition, income differences may be the result of differences in prices paid for different blocks of units of the same kind of resource. These differences in price may be short run in character, stemming from changes in demand for the resource in its different employments. They may also be of a more permanent nature when a minimum price is fixed by private organizations or by the government in some uses of the resource but not in others. The same effect may be obtained when the supply of the resource that can be employed in some of its uses is controlled or fixed.

The major problem with respect to income distribution appears to be that of how to alleviate poverty, or how to get everyone up to some minimum income level. According to current definitions of poverty, some 12–15 percent of households in the economy are poor. In a large proportion of these the household head is 65 years of age or older. The incidence of poverty is also high when the family head is nonwhite or female or has less than a high school education.

One category of policy measures to maintain incomes consists of attempts to increase the earning power of the poor. In this category we find measures to provide and improve conventional educational facilities at all levels. Additional special educational measures are aimed at high school dropouts and at those in need of or desiring to upgrade their skills or learn new ones. In addition to educational measures, positive programs to eliminate barriers to the economic mobility of the poor are essential.

The other major category of policy measures designed to maintain income includes supplements to the incomes of families or individuals. Social Security programs are in part intended for this purpose, as are minimum wage laws. Some programs to supplement incomes help the poor very little. These include payments to those in agriculture, tariffs to protect special groups of producers against foreign competition, and subsidies or other price-maintenance devices.

EXERCISES AND QUESTIONS FOR DISCUSSION

1. Why does labor receive a larger portion of national income than capital? Can this disparity be related to the productivity of each resource? Explain.
2. Incomes of families and of unrelated individuals have been moving upward over the past few years. What factors account for this rise? Explain how you think each has contributed.
3. "Since the higher the price paid for a resource the greater the income will be for the owner of that resource, minimum prices for resources will increase income in the economy." Is this statement correct? Elaborate.
4. What measures are currently being used to alleviate poverty? What would you do to improve these policies? Be specific.

5. List the job opportunities that will be open to you upon graduation from college. What equalizing differences are there among the occupations? Is prospective income the major reason you have chosen the field in which you are now studying?

SELECTED READINGS

Boulding, Kenneth E., *Economic Analysis,* Vol. I, *Microeconomics,* 4th ed. New York: Harper & Row, Publishers, Inc., 1966 pp. 90–105.
Tobin, James, "On Improving the Economic Status of the Negro," *Daedalus Journal of the American Academy of Arts and Sciences,* Fall 1965, pp. 878–898.
U.S. Bureau of the Census, *Current Population Reports,* Series P-60, No. 53, "Income in 1966 of Families and Persons in the United States." Washington, D.C.: Government Printing Office, 1967.
Will, Robert E., and Harold G. Vatter, eds., *Poverty in Affluence.* New York: Harcourt, Brace & World, Inc., 1965, Section 8.

The Economics of Organized Labor

CHAPTER 19

Any discussion of resource pricing, resource employment, resource allocation, and income distribution would be seriously incomplete if organized labor were left out of the picture. Unionism as a movement has stirred emotions, both pro and con, and around its struggles a sort of folklore has been built up. Our purpose here is in no sense to provide a complete resume of a fascinating area of study but rather to separate out those aspects of labor union activities that have important implications for the operation of the economy. We shall discuss in turn the structure of organized labor, unions and the government, the objectives of organized labor, the weapons used by unions, and the extent and effects of unionism.

THE STRUCTURE OF ORGANIZED LABOR

Labor unions are organizations of workers, usually below the supervisory level, that attempt to improve the well-being of their members. Their activities are intended to enhance the social and political well-being of their members as well as their economic status; however, since the latter has taken precedence in the United States, we shall be primarily concerned with it. We shall classify labor organizations in two ways— (1) according to the kinds of workers they enroll and (2) according to their positions in the organizational hierarchy.

Classification by Kinds of Workers

In classifying unions by kinds of workers we distinguish between craft unions and industrial unions. *Craft unions* enroll members of a particular skill or occupation, for example, plumbers. Other examples are furnished by carpenters' unions, bricklayers' unions, and printers' unions. Typically, but not exclusively, craft unions operate in industries characterized by small firms. Historically the craft type of organization was predominant until the 1930s.

Industrial unions include workers in a particular industry or in some cases a group of industries, regardless of skill levels or specific occupations. The United Auto Workers or the United Steelworkers are outstanding examples. As big business developed in the late 1800s and through the first half of the 1900s the craft type of organization in many ways became inadequate to serve the purposes of many workers. Large numbers of workers in each of several occupations working for a single employer, conflicting claims to specific kinds of work, and the difficulties inherent in securing coordination among several different unions in dealing with an employer or an employer group favored the development of industrial unions in the mass-production industries typically populated by larger firms.

All unions in the United States do not fit neatly into one classification or the other. Some contain elements of both craft and industrial unionism but may be oriented toward one or the other pure type. The Teamsters Union, a case in point, consists predominantly of drivers but it also includes shipping clerks, mail room employees, retail clerks, and others.

Classification by Organizational Level

From the standpoint of the organizational hierarchy, there are three levels of unionism. These are local unions, national or international unions, and federations of unions. Their relations to one another are illustrated in Figure 19–1.

Local Unions

Local unions are the building blocks of organized labor. They are the organizations in which workers hold their memberships, and, as the name implies, they ordinarily embrace workers of a local geographic area. The local may be either craft or industrially oriented. A craft-oriented local frequently cuts across individual firm lines, having as members as many of those who ply the trade in the community as it can induce, or that it finds advantageous, to enroll, regardless of the firm for which they work. The plumbers of half a dozen or more plumbing establishments in your home community undoubtedly belong to a single plumbers' local. The same is very probably true of the carpenters employed by most of your local builders. Frequently, though not necessarily, locals with an indus-

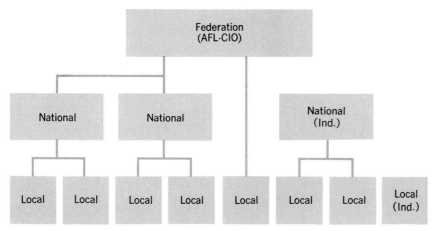

Figure 19–1
The organizational structure of labor unions.

trial orientation have as members the employees of a single company in a particular locality—for example, a General Motors Detroit local of the United Auto Workers. But wide differences exist from union to union and from area to area with respect to the precise coverage of any local union.

The officers of a local union are not ordinarily full-time union officials. Usually they are workers in the plant or craft where the local is located. In most cases they are not even paid as union officials, but frequently they are permitted time off for union duties although they are paid by the employer as full-time employees. The roster of officials includes at least a president, a secretary-treasurer, and shop or job stewards.

National or International Unions

National or international unions occupy the next level in the hierarchy. They are made up of groups of local unions, usually from the same craft or from the same industry, but sometimes they include locals from several related industries. The difference between national and international unions is a technical one only. Some locals of international unions are located in other countries, while all those of national unions are located in the United States. The United Auto Workers union is an international, since it has Canadian locals. We shall refer to both as national unions, since for our purposes the terms can be used interchangeably.

A national union is governed ultimately by a convention of delegates from its locals who meet in most cases annually or biennially. National officers are elected by the convention to carry on the business of the union throughout the year. The officers are full-time, paid union officials and they exercise leadership of the national and of the locals comprising it. As full-time, paid officials they are specialists in union business. Add to this the superior financial strength of the national as compared with most locals and it becomes apparent that much of the power of organized labor lies in the national unions. Normally the national receives its financial support from a designated portion of the dues that members of the locals must pay.

The Federation

At the top level of the organizational structure in the United States is a *federation of national unions*—the American Federation of Labor and Congress of Industrial Organizations. There were two such federations from 1937 to 1955. One was the American Federation of Labor, dating from 1886, while the other was the Congress of Industrial Organizations, which split off from the AFL in 1937, with the craft versus the industrial type of union organization being a key issue in dispute. The CIO at the time of the split was composed of young, growing unions highly oriented toward industrial unionism, while the old-guard AFL unions were predominantly craft oriented. The two federations merged as the AFL-CIO in 1955.

Not all national unions belong to the Federation. Some, such as the railway brotherhoods, have never seen fit to join, while others, such as the Teamsters Union, have been expelled from the Federation. These nationals operate independently. Some local unions are also independent, belonging neither to a national nor to the Federation. Still other locals may belong to the Federation but not to a national union.

The Federation engages primarily in education, promotion, and research in matters affecting unionism. Its headquarters are in Washington, D.C., and its officers and employees devote much time to lobbying for favorable legislation and to discussing with public officials the issues of concern to organized labor. It plays a role in setting standards of ethics in the labor movement and in settling jurisdictional disputes among member unions; that is, disputes with regard to which unions should have jurisdiction in organizing particular groups of workers. By and large the Federation's power is limited by the fact that most large national unions can withdraw from it and operate effectively on their own.

The Federation, like nationals, is governed by a convention. In the case of the AFL-CIO, the Convention meets every other year. The convention is made up of representatives from member nationals, and officers of the Federation are elected by the convention. They, like national union officers, are full-time, paid union employees and are ordinarily highly skilled in the performance of their duties.

UNIONS AND THE GOVERNMENT

The attitude of the public as reflected by government policy toward unions has changed over time from one of hostility to one of positive encouragement. In recent years the policy of encouragement has been tempered in some degree by government regulation of unions (and employers) and their affairs. Government policy is expressed through court decisions and through legislation. A brief history of the relations between government and organized labor will go far toward explaining the development of unionism in the United States.

Pre-1935 Policies

Labor unions in the nineteenth century faced adverse public opinion, hostile courts, and legislation inimical to their growth and development. In the early 1800s they were treated under common law as criminal conspiracies. However, toward the middle and later 1800s modifications in common law led to their treatment not as criminal organizations but as organizations subject to civil suits by parties they were alleged to have injured. This change in the courts' method of attack marks some improvement in the status accorded unions, but the attitude of the courts toward them was still far from favorable.

The Sherman Antitrust Act of 1890, although intended by Congress as an antimonopoly act applying to business firms, was used against unions in the early 1900s. In the latter part of the nineteenth century unions found themselves subjected increasingly to court *injunctions*, or orders forbidding them from carrying out some of their most effective tactics—strikes and boycotts—on the grounds that these might do irreparable harm to those against whom they were directed. The Sherman Act added a legislative kicker to common law—it reinforced the use of the injunction and it added the possibility of triple-damage suits against unions by parties that unions were alleged to have injured.

During the second decade of the twentieth century a slight turn became evident in the policy of government toward unions. Among other things, the *Clayton Act of 1914* contained provisions intended to remove unions from the scope of the Sherman Act and to free them from subjection to most injunctions issued by federal courts. But the respite of unions was short. A series of Supreme Court decisions interpreted the act as merely restating existing law and the application of injunctions and Sherman Act penalties to unions was reaffirmed.

The *Railway Labor Act of 1926*, as amended in 1934, marked a positive change in the policy of the federal government toward a small segment of the labor movement. It accomplished two important objectives for the railway brotherhoods. First, it stated positively that railway unions have the right to engage in collective bargaining with their employers. Second, it established a procedure for settling any disputes in which unions and the railroad operators became deadlocked.

The *Norris-LaGuardia Act of 1932*, applying to the whole of organized labor, followed on the heels of the Railway Labor Act. *"Yellow-dog contracts"* had become widely used by employers. These were agreements that employees were induced to sign stating that they would not join a union while employed by a specific firm, and they were enforceable in the courts. Under the Norris-LaGuardia Act such agreements were no longer enforceable in federal courts. A second, and equally important, feature of the act was that it severely restricted the used of court injunctions against unions.

Post-1935 Policies

The real turning point for organized labor came with the passage of the *National Labor Relations Act of 1935*, commonly known as the Wagner Act. This piece of legislation threw the full support of the government behind the right of labor unions to engage in collective bargaining with their employers. Workers were guaranteed the right to form and join unions of their own choosing for this purpose. To prevent the kind of employer interference that had historically almost stopped unionism in its tracks, certain employer practices were designated as *unfair labor practices*. These included (1) failure of the employer to bargain with the union in good faith; (2) attempts to coerce workers to join or not join a union and with regard to what union to join if they chose to join one; and (3) discrimination against any worker for union activities.

A National Labor Relations Board was created as a quasi-judicial agency to carry out the provisions of the act. The Board heard complaints of unfair labor practices and prescribed the appropriate remedies. It was also responsible for seeing to it that workers could form unions if they so desired and for certifying those unions as the *bargaining agent* for employees. Toward this end the Board had the power to determine what constitutes an appropriate employee bargaining unit—a department of a plant, an entire plant, all the machinists of a given employer, all the plumbers of a specific city, or some other unit. Once the appropriate bargaining unit was designated, the Board conducted an election, if necessary, among employees to determine whether or not they wanted to be represented by a union and, if so, by what union. If a majority of employees of a designated bargaining unit indicated through an election a desire to be represented by a given union, that union was so certified by the Board and had to be so recognized by the employer.

The impact of the Wagner Act on union membership from 1933 to 1950, as we shall see later, was little short of spectacular. However, through the 1940s some disenchantment with certain union activities was becoming evident. In 1947 Congress passed the *Labor Management Relations Act*, better known as the Taft-Hartley Act, as an amendment to the Wagner Act. Under it the labor policy of the federal government was still one of positive encouragement to the organizing of workers into unions for collective bargaining purposes, but at the same time it marked the beginning of government control of collective bargaining relations. A set of unfair labor practices on the part of unions was listed, the most important one being the use of secondary boycotts.[1] Further, the act made the *closed shop* illegal, but it authorized the *union shop*[2] in cases in which an employer and a union agree to it. Still another important provision established a national emergency strike procedure, in which an 80-day injunction can be issued against a union to postpone a strike that threatens the national health, welfare, or safety. During the 80-day interim a fact-finding board investigates the dispute and makes public its findings. It has no real power to settle the issues, but the hope is that its findings will influence the parties to reach an agreement.

Still another amendment to the National Labor Relations Act was passed by Congress in 1959. This amendment, the *Landrum-Griffin Act*, has two objectives. One is to protect union members and the public from certain undesirable practices on the part of union leaders. It requires that unions use prescribed democratic voting procedures in elections if they are to take advantage of other provisions of the National Labor Relations Act. The other objective is to further limit unions in their use of the secondary boycott and picketing for organizational purposes. The act represents the first attempt on the part of the federal government to regulate the internal affairs of unions.

THE OBJECTIVES OF ORGANIZED LABOR

To say that unions try to increase the well-being of their members is not very helpful in describing the range of their activities. As one reads through the voluminous literature on the labor movement in the United States, it appears that unions have four areas of more concrete objectives. These are (1) to redistribute income, (2) to establish a system of job

[1] See p. 355 for a definition and example of a secondary boycott.
[2] See p. 352 for definitions of these terms.

rights and to improve working conditions, (3) to preserve and extend the union as an organization, and (4) to focus the political power of workers, that is, to serve as a political pressure group. The specific objectives stressed by individual unions differ from union to union, but in the United States most can be considered *business unions*. They are more concerned with economic action centering around the first three objectives than with political and social action.

In the pursuit of the first three objectives listed above, union officials negotiate with employers over the terms and conditions of employment. The negotiation process is known as *collective bargaining*. Through collective bargaining a *collective agreement* or *contract* is reached by the negotiating parties, with the terms of agreement put into writing and signed by the responsible representatives of each party. Agreements may be negotiated to run for one year, two years, or even longer. Ordinarily the longer-term agreements provide that certain key issues—particularly wage rates—will be negotiated annually.

Redistribution of Income

Probably the most important objective of unions is to redistribute income. The common argument made is that business firms earn too much and workers earn too little. The union desires to make the owners of business share their earnings with workers. Collective bargaining with respect to wages covers a whole range of issues—whether rates will be hourly or by the piece, the size of differentials for different skill levels, whether wage increases will be based on seniority, the extent of fringe benefits, and others—but above all else the union seeks wage increases for its members. To the extent that it is successful in raising wages, a transfer of income from others in the economy to employed union members occurs. But does it really come from the business firm with which the union bargains?

Employment and Transfer Effects

Under any market conditions other than monopsony in the purchase of labor, if a union succeeds in obtaining wage rates *above what their equilibrium levels would be* there will be a reduction in the number of union members employed.[3] Those excluded from the unionized employment will either be unemployed or will work in employments not covered by the union in question. Their exclusion from the unionized employment

[3] See pp. 331–332.

means that they are added to the labor supply in other employments, forcing wage rates down somewhat in the latter labor markets. They and other workers would thus earn less than they would earn had the union been less successful. The union in this case receives income gains at the expense of those excluded from the unionized employment.

Consumers also contribute to the higher income of the employed union members. Higher wage rates increase production costs, leading to a lower level of output of the product produced, and reduced supplies cause the prices paid by consumers to be higher than they would otherwise be.

Total Income of Union Members

We frequently hear it said that if a union secures a wage increase, its purchasing power will be increased. This is not necessarily the case, unless the wage increase follows or accompanies an increase in demand for the labor of the union members. If there is no such increase in demand and a union succeeds in obtaining a wage increase, placing the wage rate above the equilibrium level, the total income (purchasing power) of union members may increase, decrease, or remain the same, the direction depending upon the elasticity of demand for labor. If demand is inelastic, the total income of the union workers will increase. However, if demand is elastic, their total income will decrease. If demand elasticity is unitary, the total income of the union members will not change.

Monopsony

The consequences of wage levels set above equilibrium levels will be different when the labor in question is purchased under conditions of monopsony. Under these circumstances the union may be able to increase simultaneously wage rates and the level of employment. There are no adverse effects on the economy's output or price level nor on the earnings of other workers in the economy. The effect of a wage level arrived at through collective bargaining carefully set above the equilibrium monopsony wage level, will be to increase the employment level as well as the wage rate.[4]

Establishment of Job Rights

The establishment of job rights, or of a system of "industrial jurisprudence," has been one of the important objectives of labor unions. Unions have long sought to protect their members from arbitrary or

[4] See p. 295.

capricious actions on the part of supervisory personnel. They have also sought to retain for their members what those members consider to be their vested rights in particular jobs or in opportunities for promotion. A system of job rights ordinarily consists of a grievance procedure, a seniority system, and a set of working rules.

The Grievance Procedure

The collective agreement negotiated between union and employer usually establishes the formal outlines of a *grievance procedure*. By means of the grievance procedure all sorts of problems, complaints, and alleged unfair treatment of individual workers can be brought into the open and discussed by union and management officials. Collective bargaining on grievance matters is not limited to the period of the contract negotiation; only the procedure itself is established at that time. Rather, it is a continuous process that takes place throughout the year. Typically a worker complaint is handled first at the lowest possible administrative level. Discussion takes place between a union shop steward and the worker's foreman, and frequently the matter can be cleared up at this point. Otherwise the case is referred upward to a department superintendent and a higher union official, or eventually to top management and top union officials. A smoothly functioning grievance procedure can do much to promote good worker-employer relations.

Seniority Systems

Seniority systems are more narrowly centered around individual rights to particular jobs. They establish the order, based primarily on length of service, in which workers will be laid off in slack times, rehired, promoted, and so on. The intent of the union is to eliminate arbitrary actions in these matters on the part of supervisory personnel. Usually management objects to a strict seniority system, claiming that it does not permit putting the best man on a particular job, since length of service and efficiency are not necessarily coincidental. The union counterclaim is that in the absence of a seniority system, favoritism rather than efficiency is likely to be the main criterion for the actions of supervisors. They also argue that length of service and efficiency are likely to be closely related even if they are not precisely coincident in specific workers.

Working Rules

Working rules, too, are an attempt on the part of workers to protect what they consider to be their rights to specific jobs. Frequently their purpose is to lessen the impact of technological change, and usually their purpose is to increase the number of workers needed to perform a certain job above the number thought necessary by the employer. Work rules take several forms. Some require unnecessary work to be done. The International Typographical Union, for example, used for many years the famous "bogus work rule," requiring that the same advertisement in several newspapers be set into type separately for each newspaper even though a mat can be made from the first setting and used for subsequent runs. In the case of railroads, larger crews than are necessary have been required by the unions to operate diesel locomotives. In the construction trades work rules have often forbidden the use of prefabricated materials. Such practices are generally referred to as *featherbedding*.

Preservation and Extension of Unionization

All unions devote much effort to keeping their organizations intact. Most, but not all, are interested in organizing the unorganized. What are the reasons for activities of this sort? What forms do these activities take?

The Reasons

Unions have a direct economic interest in keeping their organizations strong and in most cases in extending membership to the unorganized workers of their particular occupational or industrial jurisdictions. Suppose that the workers of a garment factory are organized but that a great many of those in the trade are not organized. The union is thus limited in the pressure it can exert on the employer for higher wages or for other benefits for its members. The existence of good substitutes for the labor of the union members makes the demand curve for union labor highly elastic. Rather than submit to union pressure, the employer can seek out nonunion employees. If the union can extend membership to cover other workers in the trade, the employer is denied access to nonunion competitive sources of labor and the union can be successful in bringing much more pressure to bear on him.

Some craft unions, rather than desiring to extend their membership, prefer to keep their organizations small and strong. Their objective is to maintain control of all the jobs available in their occupation and to limit the number who can enter it. Again, the economic rationale of the union is to make the demand for the union members as inelastic as possible. Further, limits to the number of workers who can ply the trade mean higher wages and larger incomes for those in the occupation. (Can you show this using a simple demand and supply diagram for labor?)

Another factor inducing most unions to try to extend their membership is the valid principle that there is strength or power in numbers. The larger the proportion of the work force that unions can count as members, the greater will be their abilities to accomplish other objectives as well as to obtain higher wage rates. If unions contain 100 percent of the labor force below supervisory levels, there will be no alternative nonunion sources of labor open to any one employer. Neither would there be nonunion territory to which employers can move or where nonunion competitors to unionized business can operate. Any employer attempting to resist union demands finds a very important alternative closed off.

There is still another reason why unions work continuously to preserve and extend their organizations. In the labor movement there are many individuals—union officers as well as union employees—whose present jobs and whose future positions depend upon the preservation of their organizations. A sort of bureaucracy has been built up with vested interests at stake. In this respect the union is no different from other organizations that have paid officers and paid employees.

The Methods

Union efforts at preservation and extension of unionism are carried on primarily in two ways. The most obvious one consists of drives to organize the unorganized. Most national unions have or have had paid organizers who go into nonunion plants and nonunion territories to convince workers of the benefits of unionism and to enroll them in new locals. These efforts have met with varying degrees of success. From 1935 through World War II union membership grew by leaps and bounds, but following World War II growth was slow. Since 1957 union membership has declined despite intensive organizing efforts.

The second activity consists of *union security* clauses which ordinarily form an important part of any collective bargaining contract. The term "union security" refers to the degree to which union membership is to be required among the workers in any given bargaining unit. There are four primary types of arrangements between the union and the employer, any one of which may be established. These are the closed shop, the union shop, maintenance of membership, and the open shop.

Under the *closed-shop* arrangement the employer agrees to hire no one who is not a member of the union. Expulsion from the union constitutes grounds for dismissal by the employer of any employee. A closed-shop arrangement places much power in the hands of the union and, of course, places a premium on union membership. The closed shop was legal under the Wagner Act but was outlawed for unions and employers operating in interstate commerce by the Taft-Hartley Act. Nevertheless, closed-shop arrangements, while not written into agreements as such, continue to be the practice in many collective bargaining relations. They have been common in the building, printing, and transportation trades.

The *union shop* is a somewhat less exclusive type of arrangement. Under the union shop the employer may hire whomever he pleases, but within a certain short, specified time period, say 30 days, the employee must join the union. Union-shop arrangements are legal under the Taft-Hartley Act provided the employer and the union agree to it in collective bargaining. Individual states are, however, permitted by the Taft-Hartley Act to pass so-called "right-to-work laws," making the union shop as well as the closed shop illegal in their particular jurisdictions.

A third type of union security arrangement is called *maintenance of membership*. Maintenance of membership provides that employees who are union members in good standing at the time the collective agreement is made must remain so during the life of the agreement in order to remain employed. The practice came into being during World War I as a compromise arrangement recommended by the War Labor Board between unions pressing for the closed or union shop and employers pressing for no union security arrangement at all.

Most, but not all, employers have traditionally sought the *open shop*. Under the open shop employers are free to employ either union workers or nonunion workers as they see fit. Collective bargaining relations are ordinarily maintained under open-shop conditions only if the union is able to keep a majority of the employees of a particular bargaining group in the union; that is, if it is able to keep the union certified by the National Labor Relations Board.

Political Objectives

Labor unions in the United States have been somewhat restrained in their political activities, concentrating for the most part on matters pertaining to wages and employment. Still, organized labor is generally conceded to be a rather potent force in the political arena, and most major political decisions take it into account. Unions have attempted to provide a focal point for marshaling worker support for or against particular issues and candidates. Their political policy has been called one of "rewarding friends and punishing enemies." Toward this end labor has worked within the framework of the major political parties rather than attempting to set up a party of its own.

Class consciousness has been weak in the United States. For the most part labor union members are not unionists first and foremost. As well as being unionists they are Methodists, Baptists, Catholics, and so on. They are members of the PTA. They go fishing, boating, and water skiing. They play softball, tennis, poker, and bridge. Their sons and daughters have opportunities to complete high school and to attend universities. The union is not the sole source of economic, social, or political opportunities. It is viewed by most workers as one of many sources.

The political activities of organized labor have centered around the support of legislation and candidates favorable to its objectives. It has pressed for legislation that will promote the existence and extension of unionism and that will increase the union's power in collective bargaining. It has lent strong support to social legislation—minimum wages, maximum hours, and the whole gamut of social security measures. However, only the former can be considered a uniquely union program. Social legislation was not of union origin.

THE WEAPONS OF ORGANIZED LABOR

Except for its political activities, organized labor pursues its objectives through collective bargaining with employers. However, employers are not usually inclined to make extensive concessions to union negotiators just for the asking—or vice versa for that matter. In support of its collective bargaining demands unions have traditionally used three methods of inducing employers to yield ground. These are strikes, boycotts, and the force of public opinion.

The Strike

A *strike*, or a work stoppage, on the part of employees is the main weapon in the union's arsenal. If it is to be effective, the union must be able to block the employer from obtaining an alternative supply of labor. Picket lines are thrown up around the premises to advertise that a strike is in progress and to prevent—sometimes forcibly—nonunion workers from coming on the job. Members of other unions almost always honor the picket lines in any given industrial dispute and, to a very large extent, so do nonunion workers. The delightful name "scab" is applied to those who work as strikebreakers.

Strikes are costly to an employer. His revenue from sales will be cut off unless he has accumulated substantial inventories that he can sell while the strike is in progress; this has sometimes been the case in strikes against automobile manufacturers. Variable costs of the firm are reduced to zero, but fixed costs continue, thereby involving the firm in losses if sales revenue is insufficient to cover fixed costs. Further, the strike may cost the firm the customers who must turn to competitors while the strike is in progress. Thus the demand curve facing the firm, even after the strike has ended, may be shifted to the left.

Union members also bear the burdens of a strike since they usually lose their pay checks for the duration of the work stoppage. Most large national unions have accumulated strike funds that they use to offset partially the pay check loss, but few are able to pay strike benefits to a large number of strikers over a long period of time.

The duration of a strike depends upon each party's evaluation of what it has to gain or lose from continuing it. The employer must weigh the costs of prolonging the strike against the costs of a settlement that will be acceptable to the union. The union must weigh pay check losses against possible gains to be obtained. Each must attempt to evaluate the other's position. All of these calculations are quite nebulous, for immediate gains or losses are not the only ones involved. If the employer makes concessions, what effect will this have on future union demands, or if the union makes concessions, what effect will this have on future employer resistance? Further, emotions or "principles" enter into the picture. Unions have on occasion prolonged strikes to the point at which pay check losses were greater than any possible gains that could be obtained, and employers have refused settlements that would be less costly than permitting the strike to continue. All of these factors lend uncertainty to a strike's duration, but the mounting losses on both sides provide an increasing incentive for a compromise arrangement to be worked out.

The Boycott

Boycotts are another means used by unions to put pressure on employers. A *primary boycott* refers to a situation in which members of the union refrain from using or consuming the product of the employer with which there is a dispute. Through picketing union members may attempt to persuade others not to buy the product. In this manner the union hopes to inflict costs on the employer sufficient to induce him to meet the union's requests.

A *secondary boycott* is a more complex activity. In its usual form it means that the union boycotts and pickets an employer not a party to the dispute in the expectation that this third party will in turn bring pressure to bear on the employer from whom the union hopes to gain concessions. Suppose, for example, that a union of bakery workers is seeking higher wages or other benefits for its members. It throws up picket lines around supermarkets or other grocery stores through which the bakery markets its products. The hope is that these third parties will be hurt enough to exert pressure on the bakery to settle the dispute. This technique has been highly effective in a variety of circumstances. The presumed injustice of economic injury to parties outside the labor dispute is the basis for the Taft-Hartley Act and the Landrum-Griffin Act prohibitions of most secondary activities of this kind.

Public Opinion

The third major weapon used by organized labor is the force of public opinion. This can be thought of in two contexts: (1) in terms of building a favorable public attitude toward labor organizations in general and (2) in terms of securing public support in any given dispute between a union and an employer.

Unions, like other organizations, thrive best in an atmosphere of public support. As we shall see in the next section, this has been the historical experience in the United States. Although there were bitter labor disputes of paramount importance to the parties concerned prior to 1935, unions had no widespread impact on economic activity before that time. Their greatest gains followed public and governmental acceptance of them as legitimate organizations. The fact that this turnabout in attitudes occurred is indicative of the abilities of organized labor to influence public opinion over time.

THE EFFECTS AND THE EXTENT OF UNIONISM

How have labor organizations affected the growth of the U.S. economy and the participation of workers in that development? It is impossible to answer the question with any degree of completeness or finality. As much information as there is available on the labor movement, wages and labor productivity, and on the economy's performance over time, there are no good measures of what impact the labor movement has had or now has on economic activity. In the absence of objective measurements, we can only infer from economic theory and from the information that is available what the impact has been.

Economic Effects of Unions

To the extent that unions are successful in the pursuit of their objectives, it appears likely that their impact on the performance of the economy is adverse. If they succeed in obtaining and holding wage rates for union members above what the equilibrium levels would be, the result will be either unemployment or a persistent misallocation of labor resources, with too much of it being blocked out of unionized employment. We would expect, also, that their interference with the introduction of new productive techniques, to the extent that it is successful, would increase costs and hold down output in the affected industries. It appears likely, since it is the more highly skilled and better-paid workers that are unionized, that rather than decreasing income inequality unions increase it.

But are these adverse economic effects of great consequence in our economy? We hear much debate pro and con containing generous portions of emotion and opinion and uncomfortably little factual information. Against the adverse economic effects, social and psychological benefits, if any, should be weighed. But beyond these it appears likely that the effects of unions are overstated both by their advocates and by their adversaries. For example, ask almost any noneconomist to identify the most important factor responsible for bringing about the tremendous increase in wage rates since the middle 1800s and unions will be named. Yet the facts of union membership indicate that this cannot be so. The proportion of the labor force that has been unionized over time has not been sufficient for unions to be able to exert this kind of pressure or influence.

Total Union Membership

Although unions have been a part of the labor scene since colonial days, they have made up a significant part of the labor force only since the mid-1930s. Table 19–1 and Figures 19–2 and 19–3 show total union membership and membership as a percentage of the total labor force for selected years from 1900 to 1964. The irregular year intervals are included to show extraordinary changes that occurred.

Good data are not available for the nineteenth century, but from what we have it appears that unions were not an important force in the economy during that period. Certainly union membership did not exceed 3–4 percent of the labor force at any time. Still, the groundwork was being laid for the increase in union power and prestige during the twentieth century. Several national craft unions, notably the railway brotherhoods, trace their origins to the last half of the 1800s. A forerunner of industrial unionism—and indeed an attempt to enroll all workers in one big union —rose and fell between 1869 and 1886. This organization, the Knights of Labor, had over 700,000 members when it reached its peak in 1886 and represented the bulk of organized labor. But following that date it quickly collapsed and passed out of the picture. The year 1886 marks the advent of the American Federation of Labor, the first real federation of national unions.

The union influence on the economy has been markedly greater in the twentieth century. Membership rose from 1900 to 1920, sparked partly by World War I and friendly administrations in the White House, but these gains were lost in the "return to normalcy" of the 1920s and the

TABLE 19–1

Total Union Membership, Selected Years, 1900–1966

YEAR	TOTAL MEMBERSHIP[1]	PERCENT OF LABOR FORCE[2]
1900	791,000	2.8
1910	2,116,000	4.0
1920	5,034,000	12.5
1930	3,632,000	4.1
1933	2,857,000	5.2
1935	3,728,000	6.7
1937	7,218,000	7.4
1938	8,265,000	14.6
1940	8,944,000	15.5
1950	15,000,000	22.0
1953	17,860,000	25.2
1956	18,477,000	24.8
1960	18,117,000	23.3
1961	17,328,000	22.0
1962	17,630,000	22.2
1963	17,586,000	21.8
1964	17,976,000	21.9
1965	18,519,000	23.9
1966	19,181,000	24.3

[1] Includes Canadian members of labor unions with headquarters in the United States.

[2] Canadian members excluded in computing percentages except for 1900 and 1920.

SOURCE: U.S. Bureau of the Census, *Statistical Abstract of the United States: 1968,* 89th ed. Washington, D.C., 1968, p. 239; 87th ed., p. 246; 83d ed., 1962, p. 241; 80th ed., 1959, p. 238.

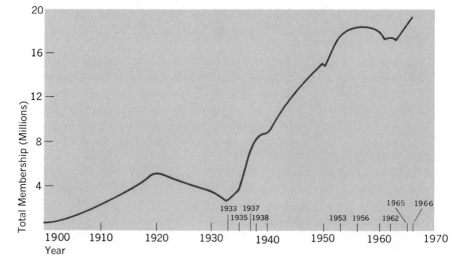

Figure 19–2
Union membership, 1900–1966.

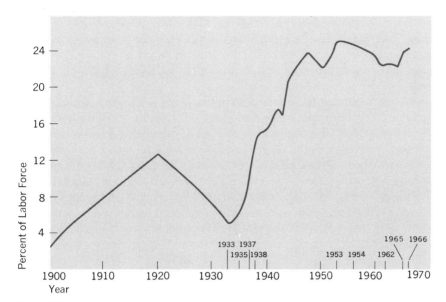

Figure 19-3
Union membership as a percentage of the labor force, 1900–1966.

Great Depression beginning in 1929. A low point was reached in 1933 at the depths of the depression.

Government support and encouragement of unionism and collective bargaining came to full fruition under the Roosevelt Administration, which came to power in 1933. It was expressed through the National Labor Relations Act of 1935. The ensuing surge in union membership is shown in Table 19-1 and in Figure 19-2. Union membership reached a peak in absolute numbers in 1966. As a proportion of the total labor force, a peak of 24.8 percent was reached in 1953. This percentage has since declined, although since 1943 it has been above the 20 percent mark. Looked at the other way around, the nonunion segment of the labor force has never been less than three fourths of the total, and it has generally been greater than this.

Distribution of Union Membership

Although, relative to the total labor force, the significance of the union as reflected by union membership appears to be rather limited, are there areas in the economy that show relatively heavy concentrations of unionized workers? Certain broad trends in the distribution of union membership among sectors of the economy are shown in Table 19-2. The bulk of the membership has been split fairly evenly between the manufacturing sector and the nonmanufacturing sector for the years shown, and a small fraction of it has been found in government employments. Both large sectors have experienced slight losses relative to total union membership, while the proportion of union members working for the government has been increasing.

We gain a somewhat better perspective by concentrating on the manufacturing and the nonmanufacturing sectors separately. A study made in 1965, using 1962 data, shows that in 1962 in the manufacturing sector the workers employed in making transportation equipment—automobiles, locomotives, airplanes, and so on—were the most highly unionized.[5] Some 83 percent of them belonged to such unions as the United Automobile Workers and the International Brotherhood of Machinists. Almost as large a proportion of workers in primary metals manufacturing— steel, lead, zinc, copper, aluminum, and others—were union members. Workers in pulp and paper were also about 80 percent union members. Others over the average of 62 percent for all manufacturing were rubber; stone, clay and glass; electrical equipment; fabricated metals; and tobacco. Others below the average for all manufacturing were food, printing, leather, machinery, apparel, furniture, instruments, and lumber. At the low end of the scale were textile manufacturing workers who were only about 27 percent unionized.

In the nonmanufacturing sector the largest numbers of union members were found in contract construction and in transportation. In 1962 these two groups accounted for 13.8 and 14.6 percent, respectively, of total union membership. Wholesale and retail trade, services, and mining and quarrying followed in that order.[6] Those subsectors with the largest proportions of workers belonging to unions were contract construction, transportation, and mining and quarrying. In wholesale and retail trade and in services not more than 5–10 percent of the workers were unionized. In agriculture unionization was virtually nonexistent.

Geographically, union membership tends to be concentrated rather heavily in a few states, the largest numbers being found in New York, California, Pennsylvania, Illinois, and Ohio. The states with the highest proportions of their work forces unionized are Washington, West Virginia, New York, Michigan, and Missouri.[7]

In some areas of the economy, then, the bulk of the workers are organized. Where this is the case, one very astute student of labor economics estimates that the unions may be able to raise and hold the wage rates

[5] Arnold Strasser, "Factory Workers under Bargaining Agreements," *Monthly Labor Review,* Vol. 88 (February 1965), pp. 164–167.

[6] H. James Neary, "American Trade Union Membership in 1962," *Monthly Labor Review,* Vol. 87 (May 1964), pp. 501–507.

[7] Harry P. Cohany, "Trends and Changes in Union Membership," *Monthly Labor Review,* Vol. 89 (May 1966), pp. 510–513.

TABLE 19-2
Union Membership by Sector of the Economy, Selected Years, 1956–1964

YEAR	MANUFACTURING		NONMANUFACTURING		GOVERNMENT		TOTAL	
	NUMBER (THOUSANDS)	PERCENT	NUMBER (THOUSANDS)	PERCENT	NUMBER (THOUSANDS)	PERCENT	NUMBER (THOUSANDS)	PERCENT
1956	8,839	48.8	8,350	46.1	915	5.1	18,104	100.0
1958	8,359	46.5	8,574	47.7	1,035	5.8	17,968	100.0
1960	8,591	47.7	8,375	46.4	1,070	5.9	18,036	100.0
1962	8,050	45.8	8,289	47.2	1,225	7.0	17,564	100.0
1964	8,342	46.6	8,125	45.3	1,453	8.1	17,920	100.0

SOURCE: Harry P. Cohany, "Trends and Changes in Union Membership," *Monthly Labor Review*, Vol. 89 (May 1966), pp. 510–513.

of their members by as much as 15–25 percent above what they would be in the absence of unions.[8] He suggests that this may be the case for the craft unions of the building and printing trades, railroads, and the entertainment industry. He also suggests that the strong industrial unions in such industries as steel or autos may be able to do the same thing. Another able economist who has studied the labor movement extensively estimates that on the average the effect of unions on the wages of union members is no more than 4 percent, although in a very small group of industries it may be as high as 20 percent.[9]

SUMMARY

Labor unions are organizations of workers that attempt to improve the well-being of their members, concentrating for the most part on economic well-being. Craft unions enroll workers of a given skill or occupation. Industrial unions enroll workers in a given industry or in related industries regardless of occupation or skill level. Union members hold their membership in local unions, whose jurisdiction is ordinarily a local firm, a local industry, or a local craft or occupation. Local unions from the same craft or industry or related industries usually band together to form a national union, these being the power centers of the labor movement. Most national unions, in turn, are joined together in a federation of unions, the AFL-CIO.

Government policy toward labor unions is expressed in court decisions and in legislation. In the 1800s it was adverse to unions, treating them first as common law criminal conspiracies and later as organizations subject to such civil actions as injunctions and damage suits. Under the Sherman Act of 1890 unions were often on the wrong side of triple-damage suits. In the early 1900s there was some softening on the part of the federal government. The Clayton Act of 1914 was intended to remove unions from Sherman Act jurisdiction, but court interpretations of it made it ineffective in so doing. The Railway Labor Act of 1926 declared the right of unions in the railroad industry to engage in collective bargaining with employers and also established a procedure for settling disputes over which the two parties became deadlocked. The Norris-LaGuardia Act of 1932 made "yellow-dog" contracts nonenforceable in federal courts and severely restricted the use of injunctions against union activities. With the National Labor Relations Act of 1935 the federal

---

[8] Albert Rees. *The Economics of Trade Unions* (Chicago: University of Chicago Press, 1962), pp. 77–80.

[9] H. G. Lewis, *Unionism and Relative Wages in the United States* (Chicago: University of Chicago Press, 1963), pp. 7–9.

government completed a 180-degree turn in policy by declaring its active support of unions and collective bargaining, and for a decade and a half union membership climbed rapidly. The Labor-Management Relations Act of 1947 placed control of union activities and regulation of collective bargaining relations on top of the government's support of unions and collective bargaining. The Landrum-Griffin Act of 1959 supplements the Labor-Management Relations Act, regulating the internal affairs of unions and placing further restrictions on the permissible range of their activities.

The activities of labor unions are aimed toward four general objectives: (1) a redistribution or transfer of income toward union members, (2) the establishment of job rights for union members, (3) preservation and extension of the union as an organization, and (4) the focusing of the political power of union members. They work toward the first three by negotiating with the employers for whom their members or prospective members work; the negotiating process is called collective bargaining. Terms and conditions of employment successfully negotiated form a collective agreement or contract.

To the extent that unions are successful in raising wage rates for their members above equilibrium levels, a transfer of income to union members from those excluded from the unionized employment and from consumers occurs, except in the case of monopsony. Whether or not the total wage bill or purchasing power of union members increases or decreases depends upon the elasticity of demand for union labor.

Unions attempt to protect the job rights and working conditions of their members through a grievance procedure, a seniority system, and working rules. These are important parts of any collective agreement. Working rules that require the employer to hire more men than are necessary for the job at hand are generally referred to as featherbedding.

Preservation and extension of the union as an organization has a firm economic rationale. If it is successful, it denies employers substitute sources of labor, thus making the demand curve for union labor less elastic. Further, the greater strength of greater numbers induces most unions to attempt to bring additional workers under the union mantle. Also, paid union officials have a vested interest—their jobs—in maintaining the organization intact and in expanding it. In order to obtain and hold workers as members, unions attempt to organize the unorganized and they bargain with employers for union security clauses for their agreements. The closed shop, in which only union members may be hired, is the strongest form of union security. Next is the union shop, in which the employer may hire whom he pleases but the employees must join the union within a specified time period. We sometimes find maintenance of membership arrangements, in which those who are union members at the time an agreement is reached must remain so for the duration of the agreement. Under an open-shop agreement the workers of a given employer may or may not be union members, depending upon their individual desires.

Politically, organized labor has taken the position of "rewarding friends and punishing enemies." Candidates for office often woo the labor "vote," but they can never be sure that union leaders can deliver it for them.

Unions make use of three weapons in attempting to secure their collective bargaining objectives. These are strikes, or work stoppages; boycotts, or refusals to buy from the employer; and the force of public opinion. In all of these the union makes extensive use of picketing.

The impact of unions on economic activity is probably over-rated by most people. Union members made up less than 4 percent of the labor force until the early 1900s. With the favorable climate brought about by the National Labor Relations Act, membership rose rapidly from 1935 to the early 1950s and has since tapered off slightly. At its relative peak in 1953 union membership was 24.8 percent of the labor force and has since declined. Although unions are strong in certain sectors of the economy, the fact remains that almost four fifths of the labor force is nonunion.

EXERCISES AND QUESTIONS FOR DISCUSSION

1. Suppose that in a certain city all public school teachers are encouraged to form and join a union. If this were accomplished, what would be the probable economic impact on the number of teachers hired and the salary level? on the quality of public education?
2. Earlier in the text it was stated that technological improvements increase employment. Unions, however, resist technological change because it will cause some of their members to become unemployed. Can these two statements be reconciled? Explain.
3. Discuss the pros and cons of unionism. Is the redistribution of income, as a result of unionization, equitable? Defend your answer.
4. Define the following: strike, primary boycott, secondary boycott. Under what circumstances do you think unions should be allowed to use each? When should they not?

SELECTED READINGS

Bloom, Gordon F., and Hubert R. Northrup, *Government and Labor*. Homewood, Ill.: Richard D. Irwin, Inc., 1965, Chaps. 2–6.

Cartter, Allan M., and F. Ray Marshall, *Labor Economics*. Homewood, Ill.: Richard D. Irwin, Inc., 1967, Chaps. 15 and 18.

Friedman, Milton, "Labor Unions and Economic Policy," *Labor and the National Economy*, William G. Bowen, ed. New York: W. W. Norton & Company, 1965, pp. 23–34.

Rees, Albert, *The Economics of Trade Unions*. Chicago: University of Chicago Press, 1962, Chaps. 2, 8, 9, and 12.

PART 4

The Economy as a Whole

We turn now from the study of the parts of the economy to the study of the economy as a whole, or, from *microecononics* to *macroeconomics.* The microeconomic analysis of Parts 2 and 3 presupposed a given state of affairs from the macroeconomic point of view. It was assumed that unemployment of resources was negligible and that the economy would, if its resources were correctly allocated, produce almost as much as it is capable of producing. We largely ignored the fact that economic fluctuations occur and that these generate an additional set of problems.

In our study of the economy as a whole we examine the range of issues that surround economic instability. The exposition moves from a simple to a progressively more complex and more complete treatment of the nature of instability, the problems created by it, and its control.

In Chapter 20 we focus on the measurement of economic instability and the

effects of instability on economic well-being.
In Chapter 21 we introduce a monetary
analytical framework that is developed further
in Chapters 22 and 23. Chapters 24 and 25
bring government spending and taxation
into the picture. These chapters set the stage
for the national income analysis of Chapters
26 through 29.

Economic
Instability

CHAPTER 20

What was your reaction to the recent increase in tuition and fees at your university? What did you think when university housing costs and the food prices at the cafeterias went up? Were you concerned because the money available to you for your education would not go as far after the price increases as it would before? But on the other hand, hasn't your family income risen also? Isn't your family, or at least the average family, able to purchase more goods and services today than it could five years ago? Despite increasing price levels, our levels of living have moved persistently upward because family incomes have been increasing at an even more rapid rate.

We worry about inflation, recession, unemployment, and economic growth without a very clear idea of how or whether these things are related. Our purpose in the next few chapters is to pinpoint the nature of economic fluctuations and their implications for economic well-being and to discuss government policy aimed at controlling them. In this chapter we look specifically at what economic fluctuations are and how they affect us.

INDICATORS OF ECONOMIC PERFORMANCE

We know that the economy does not always run smoothly, but which aspects of its over-all performance are of particular importance to us? From the discussion of economic activity in Chapter 1, it is apparent that the *total output* of the economy is of paramount concern. Along with total output, the *level of employment* of resources, particularly labor resources, must rank as a major dimension of economic performance. For less obvious reasons that will be developed as we move through the ensuing chapters, *price level stability* is a third item of crucial importance.[1]

Total Output

We refer to the value of the economy's total output as *gross national product,* or GNP. Ordinarily the term is used to mean *all* goods and services produced in final form in a year's time valued at their market prices where they are bought and sold in markets or at the cost of the resources used to produce them where they are not.[2] GNP of the United States since 1929 is presented in Table 20–1 and is shown graphically in Figure 20–1. Note carefully that there are two different kinds of measurements shown on the vertical axis. In reading GNP for different years we interpret the vertical scale as showing billions of dollars. The use of the other kind of measurement, percent, will be explained shortly.

Looking first at column (1) of the table, or at GNP (current dollars)[3] in the graph, we note two things. First, there appears to have been a tremendous growth in GNP over the 38-year period—an increase from $103.1 billion to $763.7 billion. Second, if we look carefully, we can discern that the growth pattern was not smooth. There was a sharp decrease from 1929 to 1933, followed by a gradual increase to 1937. This period was, of course, the infamous Great Depression of the 1930s. From 1937 to 1938 a substantial dip occurred, but then as we moved into and through World War II GNP doubled in monetary value terms.[4] There was a slight decrease from 1945 to 1946 and another from 1948 to 1949. From 1953 to 1954 and again from 1957 to 1958 the increases were much smaller than the average year-to-year increase. These dips and interruptions in the growth of GNP are indications of what we have come to call *recessions,* and which we shall define more precisely after we have gained more background information.

GNP data alone do not furnish as sensitive or as comprehensive an index of the economy's performance as we might like. They may show a consistent pattern of economic growth and yet tell us nothing about whether or not the economy is producing up to its potential. Further,

---

[1] The term "stability" is used here to mean an absence of large or violent changes and not a complete absence of changes.

[2] National defense is an example of services furnished us that we do not purchase in markets. National income statisticians, as they compute GNP, value it at what it costs.

[3] GNP (current dollars) means that for each year the goods and services produced that year are valued at that year's prices—1929 output is valued at 1929 prices; 1930 output is valued at 1930 prices; and so on.

[4] As we shall see later, GNP in terms of volume of goods and services did not double. A part of the increase in value terms was due to a rising price level.

TABLE 20-1

Gross National Product, Price Levels, and Unemployment Rates in the United States, 1929–1967

Year	(1) GNP (Billions of Current Dollars)	(2) Implicit Price Deflator (1958 = 100)	(3) GNP (Billions of 1958 Dollars)	(4) Unemployment Rate (Percent of the Labor Force)
1929	103.1	50.6	303.6	3.2
1930	90.4	49.3	183.5	8.7
1931	75.8	44.8	169.3	15.9
1932	58.0	40.2	144.2	23.6
1933	55.6	39.3	141.5	24.9
1934	65.1	42.2	154.3	21.7
1935	72.2	42.6	169.5	20.1
1936	82.5	42.7	193.0	16.9
1937	90.4	44.5	203.2	14.3
1938	84.7	43.9	192.9	19.0
1939	90.5	43.2	209.4	17.2
1940	99.7	43.9	227.2	14.6
1941	124.5	47.2	263.7	9.9
1942	157.9	53.0	297.8	4.7
1943	191.6	56.8	337.1	1.9
1944	210.1	58.2	361.3	1.2
1945	211.9	59.7	355.2	1.9
1946	208.5	66.7	312.6	3.9
1947	231.3	74.6	309.9	3.6
1948	257.6	79.6	323.7	3.4
1949	256.5	79.1	324.1	5.5
1950	355.3	80.2	284.8	5.0
1951	328.4	85.6	383.4	3.0
1952	345.5	87.5	395.1	2.7
1953	364.6	88.3	412.8	2.5
1954	368.8	89.6	407.0	5.0
1955	398.0	90.9	438.0	4.0
1956	419.2	94.0	446.1	3.8
1957	441.1	97.5	452.5	4.3
1958	447.3	100.0	447.3	6.8
1959	483.7	101.6	475.9	5.5
1960	503.7	103.3	487.7	5.6
1961	520.1	104.6	497.2	6.7
1962	560.3	105.8	529.8	5.6
1963	590.5	107.2	551.0	5.7
1964	631.7	108.9	580.0	5.2
1965	681.2	110.9	614.4	4.6
1966	739.6	114.2	647.8	3.8
1967	789.7	117.3	673.1	3.8
1968	852.9*	121.2*	703.4*	3.8**

* Second quarter, 1968.
** June, 1968.
Sources: U.S. Department of Commerce, *The National Income and Product Accounts, 1929-1965* (Washington, D.C., 1966), pp. 2–5. U.S. Bureau of the Census, *Historical Series of the United States* (Washington, D.C., 1960), p. 73. U.S. Bureau of the Census, *Statistical Abstract, 1962,* and *Statistical Abstract, 1966.* Washington, D.C. Council of Economic Advisors, *Economic Indicators* (Washington, D.C., July 1968); U.S. Department of Commerce, *Survey of Current Business,* September 1968, pp. 7–10.

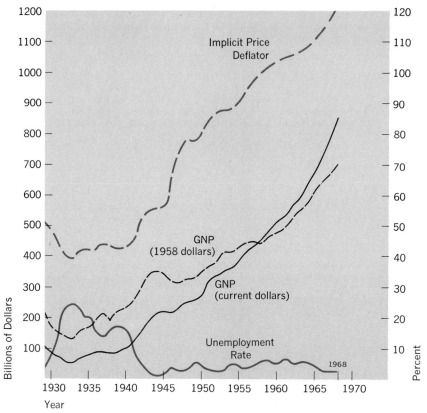

Figure 20–1
GNP, price levels, and unemployment rates in the United States, 1929–1967.

we sometimes have trouble determining from GNP data alone whether or not a recession or a serious slowdown in economic activity is occurring; the 1953–1954 and 1957–1958 periods are cases in point. We shall return to these points later.

Employment

Economic fluctuations show up more vividly in the level of unemployment. Indeed, it is here that the impact of depressions and recessions hits hardest. Consumers postpone their purchases of automobiles, homes, refrigerators, and other goods and the dwindling profits induce producers to lay workers off. Imagine, if you can, the situation in 1933 when almost 25 percent of the labor force was unemployed.

Consider for a moment the concepts associated with employment. According to the Bureau of the Census and the Bureau of Labor Statistics, the *labor force* of the economy consists of all persons 14 years of age or over who are employed, who are looking for work, or who are on layoff from a job. It includes those in the armed forces. Out of our total population of roughly 200 million, about 79 million persons comprise the labor force. The *employed* at any given time are those who did any work for pay during the week that an employment survey is made or who worked without pay for 15 hours or more in a family enterprise or who had a job or business from which they were temporarily absent when the survey was made. The *unemployed* are those who did not work during the week or who were on layoff.

Looking now at the unemployment rate column of Table 20–1 and the unemployment rate curve of Figure 20–1, economic fluctuations stand out more clearly. In Figure 20–1, to read off the unemployment rate for each year we use the vertical axis to measure percentages. The very large unemployment rates of the Great Depression were not really alleviated until we were well into World War II. The increases in unemployment in 1948–1949, 1953–1954, 1957–1958, and 1960–1961 clearly indicate that all was not well in those periods.

We cannot expect the entire labor force to be employed at any given time. Some part of it is always in the process of moving from one job to another and is therefore listed as unemployed at the time an employment survey is made. Unemployment of this kind is called *frictional unemployment*. Its magnitude is hard to pinpoint, but in general the more affluent an economy, the more time off people can take for job changes and the larger the percentage figure for this kind of unemployment will tend to be. Unemployment of a nonfrictional nature—*involuntary unemployment* —is the difficult and the serious problem that we must face. In general, we seem to think at the present time that an unemployment rate somewhere between 3 and 4 percent, including frictional unemployment, is tolerable.

The Price Level

We are reminded constantly by business columnists in newspapers and periodicals, by television newscasters, by the milkman, and by university professors that the value of the dollar is "going to pot," meaning really that it is decreasing in purchasing power. This latter part of the statement is, of course, correct. The purchasing power of the dollar in 1967 was about 43 percent of what it was in 1929. But this does not mean that we are worse off now than we were then; in fact, we know full well that we are much better off.

Price Index Numbers

We measure the changes that occur in the general level of some complex of prices by means of a *price index number*. There are several of these in current use, the most common ones being the consumer price index and the wholesale price index. Within each of these broad groups indexes are computed for more narrow classifications of goods and services—for example, for agricultural products or for consumer durable goods. A broader price index than either that for consumer goods or that for wholesale goods is the *implicit price deflator* of Table 20–1. This is a composite price index intended to measure price level changes for the entire complex of goods and services produced in the economy.

If we construct a simple set of price index numbers for a hypothetical group of goods, we shall understand better what the concept implies. We shall do this in four easy steps. First, from the entire group of goods for which we want to construct the index we choose a representative sample composed of a more limited number. Second, we attach appropriate weightings to each of the representative goods. Third, we make price observations and compute the weighted value of the sample for the years for which we want to construct the index. Fourth, we select a base period and compute the index.

Consider the first two steps. Suppose that goods *X*, *Y*, and *Z* are representative of the group for which we want to compute the index and that we choose these as our sample. To weight each one we compare their respective sales volumes. Suppose that three units of *Y* are purchased for every unit of *X* that is taken and that two units of *Z* are purchased for every such unit of *X*. We attach a weight of 1 to *X*, 2 to *Z*, and 3 to *Y*. These are listed in the "weight" column of Table 20–2.

Suppose now that we make the step-three price observations for *X*, *Y*, and *Z* for the years 1966, 1967, and 1968 and that these are duly recorded in the "price" columns of the table. For each of the three years the price of each product is multiplied by the appropriate weight, giving

TABLE 20–2

Construction of Price Index Numbers for a Hypothetical Group of Goods
(1967 = 100)

PRODUCT	WEIGHT	PRICE 1966	PRICE 1967	PRICE 1968	WEIGHTED VALUE 1966	WEIGHTED VALUE 1967	WEIGHTED VALUE 1968	PRICE INDEX 1966	PRICE INDEX 1967	PRICE INDEX 1968
X	1	$2	$3	$3	$ 2	$ 3	$ 3			
Y	3	4	5	6	12	15	18			
Z	2	6	6	5	12	12	10			
Total					$26	$30	$31	86.7	100	103.3

us the weighted values of each good for each of the three years. Now for the year 1966 we sum the weighted values of the three goods. We do the same thing for 1967 and 1968. These weighted values of the entire sample are recorded at totals of $26, $30, and $31 for the three years, respectively.

The fourth and final step is the computation of the index. Any one of the years may be selected as the base year; suppose we select 1967. Now we simply express the weighted value of the entire sample for each year as a percentage of that for the base year, and these percentage numbers are the index numbers. For the 1967 base year, $30 is 100 percent of $30, so the index number for that year is 100. For 1966, $26 is 86.7 percent of $30, so the price index number is 86.7. For 1968, $31 is 103.3 percent of $30, so the price index number is 103.3.

Any one set of price index numbers is intended to reflect the general price movement—both the direction and the magnitude of the movement —of the complex or group of goods for which it is designed. Prices of individual goods making up the complex ordinarily will not all vary in the same proportion. They may even change in different directions over time. In the example of Table 20–2 the movement of the general price level is upward, as is indicated by the set of price index numbers; however, only commodity X increased in price over all three years. The price of commodity X increased from 1966 to 1967 but remained constant from 1967 to 1968. There was actually a decline in the price of Z from 1967 to 1968.

Changes in the general level of prices of a group of goods, say consumer good, as reflected by a set of price index numbers must always be regarded as approximations. Over time goods change in nature and in quality—an automobile of the mid-1920s was not the same thing as this year's. Weights to be attached to different items in a sample change over time also. A modern consumer price index number sample would attach less relative weight to food prices than one of 50 years ago, since food today occupies a position of less importance relative to other goods than it did at that time. More faith can be put in an index covering a few years, say five, than in one covering a span of 40 to 50 years, since changes in product quality and patterns of purchase would not be as great during the shorter time span. A price index is no better than the samples and weights selected allow it to be, and these are selected by people who just may on occasion be fallible.

Inflation and Deflation

Changes in the general price level are known as inflation and deflation. *Inflation* is a period in which the general price level is rising and is illustrated by all of the upward movements of the implicit price deflator of Table 20–1. *Deflation* is a period in which the general price level is falling, or is the opposite of inflation. The best illustration of deflation is the downward movement of the implicit price deflator from 1929 to 1933. Newspaper references to inflation or deflation generally imply a less broadly defined price index, usually the consumer price index.

It should be noted carefully that inflation and deflation refer to price levels in the process of changing. If for a period of three years there were no changes in the price level, there would be neither inflation nor deflation regardless of the absolute level of prices. If prices were then to rise during one year to a higher level, remaining at the new level for three more years, we would say that inflation occurred during the year of rising prices only. During the ensuing three years there is no inflation.

In fact, reference to high or to low prices can be made in relative terms only. What is a high price level? What is a low price level? We can say that prices are high compared with those of some previous time period. Or, alternatively, we can say that prices were low in the previous period as compared with present prices. However, there are no absolute criteria of what is high and what is low.

Economic Fluctuations and the Price Level

Until the 1930s economists concerned with economic fluctuations looked to changes in the general price level as a primary bellweather of economic activity. Recession and depression were expected to be accompanied by—indeed heralded by—falling prices or deflation. Prosperity was expected to be accompanied by either a stable price level or mild inflation. Although these expectations have not been abandoned entirely, they have been considerably modified since the Great Depression.

The trouble with the old theory is that a slowdown in economic activity no longer seems to be accompanied by deflation. Table 20–1 shows the change that seems to have taken place in the relation between economic activity and the price level. The drop in economic activity in the early years of the Great Depression—1929–1933—was accompanied by a decline of some 20 percent in the price level, as the old theory would lead us to expect. As economic activity increased from 1933 to 1937 there was mild inflation. In the 1937–1938 recession the price level fell, as the old theory says it should. Inflation was the order of the day through World War II and up to the recession of 1948–1949, and the latter event brought with it the expected slight drop in prices. But from here on the picture changes. The increase in the unemployment rate of 1954 provides evidence of the decline in economic activity that we call the recession of 1953–1954, *but the price level continued to increase*. The same thing happened in the 1957–1958 recession and again in that of 1960–1961. Either the recessions were not severe or prolonged enough to force prices down or prices have come to be too rigid in a downward direction—that is, not responsive enough to a decrease in demand—for deflation to be a running mate of recession.

Real GNP

Is there any way that we can determine what part of the changes in GNP in current dollars from year to year are actually changes in the output of the economy and what part are merely the result of deflation or inflation? Consider GNP in current dollars for 1956—the $419.2 billion is the value of output for that year measured in terms of 1956 prices. Now consider GNP in current dollars for 1958—the $447.3 billion is the value of output for that year measured in terms of 1958 prices. If we could "correct" the 1956 GNP for changes in the price level, that is, if we could build the 1956–1958 inflation into it, then a comparison of the "corrected" 1956 GNP and the actual 1958 GNP would be a comparison of actual or *real* outputs. We would have eliminated, or rather would have taken into account, for comparative purposes the effects of inflation on GNP from 1956 to 1958.

The set of price index numbers in the form of the implicit price deflators enables us to accomplish what we want to do. Since 1958 serves as the base year, the index of the price level for 1956 means, then, that the 1956 price level was 94 percent of that for 1958, or GNP for 1956 in terms of the 1956 price level is 94 percent of what it would be in terms of the 1958 price level. Consequently, if we divide $419.2 billion by 0.94, the $446.1 billion result is 1956 GNP in terms of 1958 prices. The entire GNP (1958 dollars) column is computed in this way. It shows GNP for the entire series of years in terms of 1958 dollars; thus a comparison of the values for different years is a comparison of real outputs and is called *real GNP*.

Potential and Actual GNP

The Council of Economic Advisors to the President of the United States[5] in recent years has made estimates of the economy's *potential GNP*, defined as the volume of goods and services that the economy

---

[5]This Council was established by the Employment Act of 1946. Its functions are to keep the President informed of economic developments and problems, to conduct appropriate studies, and to recommend appropriate economic programs and policies.

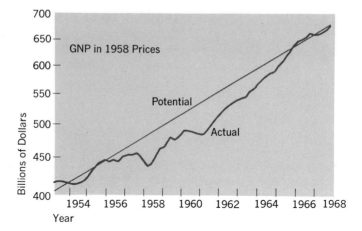

Figure 20-2
Potential and actual GNP, 1952–1966.

would ordinarily produce if the unemployment rate were no higher than 4 percent. These estimates, which reach back only to 1953, are plotted in Figure 20-2, along with actual GNP for the same series of years. Though the range of years covered is not great and though the estimates of potential GNP are not infallible, the comparison between the two over time provides an excellent base for the study of economic fluctuations.

The gap between potential and actual GNP measures the goods and services lost to the economy because of fluctuations in economic activity. The average gap for any one year measures the loss for that year; for example, in 1961 the loss approached $50 billion. Over a series of years losses approaching this magnitude add up to a rather staggering total that we could have had—if.

NATURE AND EFFECTS OF ECONOMIC FLUCTUATIONS

Why are we so concerned about economic fluctuations? A part of the answer is obvious. When actual GNP is below potential GNP we have fewer goods and services than we could have to consume or to use to add to the productive capacity of the economy. But the answer extends beyond that. In this section we shall dissect and examine fluctuations in order to obtain a more complete picture of how they affect us and to lay the groundwork for analysis in the chapters to come of their causes and how they might be controlled.

Full-Employment Equilibrium

The circular flow diagram of Figure 2–1 provides a convenient starting point. Suppose that initially actual GNP and potential GNP are equal and that the economic system is in equilibrium. Households are spending all of their incomes and business firms are paying out their entire business receipts to households as resource owners. For all practical purposes there is no involuntary unemployment.

Two additional concepts that will be useful to us are aggregate demand and aggregate supply. In Figure 20–3 suppose that the total output of the economy is measured along the horizontal axis in some sort of homogeneous physical units—identical baskets of goods. Suppose also that the price level in terms of a set of price index numbers is measured along the vertical axis. *Aggregate demand* refers to the quantities per time period of all goods and services that will be purchased at alternative price levels. *Aggregate supply* means the quantities per unit of time that will be placed on the market at different price levels.

Figure 20–3 represents the full-employment equilibrium situation described above. The general price level is p and the full-employment output level is X. From Table 20–1 we know that output level X is not fixed for all time. Aggregate supply and aggregate demand ordinarily are moving to the right as the economy's productive capacity expands and as more purchasing power comes into the hands of resource owners. Output X moves to the right and it appears too that the price level tends to rise

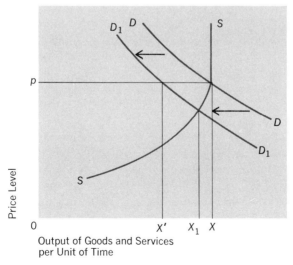

Figure 20–3
Full-employment equilibrium and the effects of a decrease in aggregate demand.

on the average over time. But these dynamic changes are rather complex; we can show what we want to get across at this point with the simple diagram of Figure 20–3, ignoring for the moment the increases in the full-employment level of GNP over time.

Recession, Depression, and Deflation

Suppose now that total spending in the economy decreases (or fails to increase as fast as it has in the recent past). This can result from any one or a combination of reasons. Political or economic uncertainties may cause people to become more cautious in their spending habits. The government may have taken actions that cause the decline to occur. Or, perhaps, stock market activity generates a wave of pessimism. We shall add to the list of possible causes through the next few chapters.

The change in total spending is reflected in Figure 20–3 by a decrease in aggregate demand (or a failure of aggregate demand to increase as much from year to year as it has in the recent past) to D_1D_1. GNP declines (or fails to increase as much as it has in the recent past), but the amount of the decline depends upon what happens to the price level. If the price level is completely rigid downward at level p—that is, will not decline at all—the volume of goods and services falls off to X'. However, if prices decline as aggregate demand declines, the decrease in real GNP will be smaller—it may decrease to only X_1. (Can you find illustrations of each of these alternatives in the historical data of Table 20–1?)

The level of employment is tied rather closely to the level of real GNP. We refer to X as the full-employment level of output for the economy. This is the best it can do with its present quantities of resources and its present level of technology, and for this reason the aggregate supply curve goes only very slightly to the right of X.[6] The employment level for output X' will be smaller than for output X_1— and both will be less than full-employment levels.

We have described a *recession* in the preceding paragraphs. It is ordinarily characterized by an increase in unemployment and by either a substantial decline in the rate of increase of GNP or an absolute decline in GNP. The price level may or may not decrease, but to the extent that it does the effects of the recession on real GNP and employment will tend to be smaller.

The difference between a recession and a depression is one of degree. Even though every depression starts as a recession, a recession may or

[6]It is possible to have more than a full-employment level of output, temporarily at least, when people for some reason—say patriotism—go to work when they would really prefer not to as a permanent thing. This was illustrated during World War II in 1943, 1944, and 1945.

may not turn into a full-blown depression.[7] A *depression* is a sharp reduction in economic activity, in GNP and in the employment level, that persists for several years.

Although *deflation* may not occur during a recession, it is almost sure to be present in a depression. The decline into depression from 1929 to 1933 is the latest evidence available on this point; however, the surplus goods and unemployment that would persist over a long depression period would surely exert tremendous downward pressure on the price level. An exception may occur in the case of a country experiencing very rapid inflation. The inflation may engender so much economic uncertainty and loss of confidence that it becomes a proximate cause of depression. This seems to occur rather frequently in the underdeveloped countries of Asia, Africa, and South America.

Economic Effects of Recession, Depression, and Deflation

What are the effects of recession, depression, and deflation on the well-being of the general public? A part of the answer is so obvious that it seems almost silly to ask the question, but some subtle effects are often overlooked. To systematize our thinking, we can divide the effects into two groups: (1) output effects and (2) redistributive effects.

Output Effects

The obvious effects of recession and depression are on the economy's output. In recession the unemployment rate typically rises to some 5–7 percent of the labor force and in depression it rises even more—to approximately 25 percent in the Great Depression of the 1930s. Additionally, capital of different kinds will be underutilized. There will be idle machines and unused plant capacity, more pronounced, of course, in depression than in recession. Actual GNP falls below potential GNP and this means that levels of living are lower than they need to be. Although recession does not *necessarily* mean that levels of living decline, depression certainly implies that they do.

Redistributive Effects

As output shrinks during depression and deflation, changes take place in the distribution of income among families and in the portion of the

[7]As a matter of fact, most economists believe that we have the knowledge, the techniques, and the necessary sophistication in economic matters on the part of the government to prevent a depression from ever again occurring. We shall develop this line of thought in the next four chapters.

economy's output that each can claim. The incomes of some families decline more rapidly than those of others; consequently, the former will lose relatively more than the latter from depression. It is even possible that some may gain from depression if the prices they must pay for what they buy decrease in greater proportion than their money incomes. However, there are not likely to be many people in this fortunate position.

One group that loses relatively more from depression than others can be identified immediately. These are *the unemployed*—those who have lost their jobs because of the decline in economic activity.

Another group for whom income declines relatively more when economic activity slows down are *those who furnish resources to durable goods industries and to capital goods industries.*[8] The old car or the old refrigerator can always be replaced later rather than now, so demand for durable goods decreases relatively more than demand for such goods as food. Similarly, business firms can always postpone additions to their plant and equipment, or even replacement of present equipment; consequently, demand for capital goods falls relatively more than demand for most consumer goods. The resource owners hurt most are the owners of the affected businesses and the workers laid off because of the decline in production. Wage rates tend to be quite sticky in a downward direction, especially where unions are strong, and those who remain employed may not be hurt as much, relatively.

During deflation, *salaried employees* frequently find that their incomes decline relatively less than do average incomes. This is particularly the case for the employees of such nonprofit institutions as governments, educational institutions, churches, and those of an eleemosynary nature. They find that as prices move downward the decreases in their incomes are relatively smaller than the decreases in the price level. It is in this group that we find some of those who may gain from depression, although it is by no means certain that any substantial proportion of them will be so affected. Most will simply lose less, relatively, than the average.

Fixed-income receivers stand to gain from deflation. These include persons who receive their incomes in the form of interest, annuity payments, old-age pensions, disability pensions, or other payments of a similar kind. These generally are fixed in terms of dollars per month, so as the price level falls the recipients find that their fixed dollar incomes will buy more and more goods and services.

Debtors are hurt and *creditors gain* from deflation. Suppose that the loans made to a debtor were obtained before deflation occurs and that subsequently the price level declines. When repayment of the loan is made, the number of dollars repaid is equal to the number of dollars bor-

---

[8] Durable goods industries are those producing products that are expected to last for several years—automobiles, refrigerators, television sets, and other such items. The capital goods industries produce such goods as basic steel, machines, and tools for industry.

rowed, plus the interest. But since the price level has declined, each dollar repaid will purchase more than each dollar borrowed. So the debtor must repay more purchasing power than he borrowed and the creditor receives back more purchasing power than he loaned out.[9]

Expansion and Inflation

Aggregate demand can increase as well as decrease, leading to an expansion in economic activity or inflation or both. The causes of increases in total spending or in aggregate demand, like the causes of decreases, are varied in nature and will come to light in the next few chapters. For the moment, suppose that both households and business firms have become more optimistic about the future and increase their spending.

What are the effects of the increase in aggregate demand? The effects differ depending upon whether or not the gap between actual and potential GNP is large or small. The size of the gap, together with the rate at which aggregate demand increases, will also determine the amount of inflation that occurs. Again we shall consider in turn (1) the output effects and (2) the redistributive effects.

Output Effects

When the actual GNP of the economy is well below the potential GNP some inflation ordinarily accompanies, and may be a necessary part of, the process of recovery and expansion. Consider, for example, the U.S. economy in 1933 and the years immediately following. Unemployment of labor resources amounted to almost 25 percent of the labor force. There was much unused plant capacity and other capital equipment. In Figure 20–4, suppose we represent the 1933 state of affairs by an aggregate demand of DD and an actual GNP of X, well below the full-employment or potential GNP of X_3. An increase in aggregate demand to D_1D_1 now occurs, and at the 1933 output level of goods and services some shortages will arise. These shortages cause prices to rise and business to become somewhat more profitable, providing incentives for expansion in productive activity. Unemployed resources are drawn into production and the

[9]As an illustration, suppose that Mr. A obtains a standard bank loan of $120 for one year, with interest at 6 percent paid in advance on the entire principle and with the principle plus interest ($127.20) to be repaid in 12 equal monthly installments of $10.60 each. If the price level falls by 50 percent, the purchasing power represented by each monthly installment is twice what it would have been if deflation had not taken place. To the debtor, the $10.60 monthly installment is twice what it would have been had there been no deflation—that is, it is as though he must repay $21.20 for every $10.60 that he originally owed. To the creditor, the situation is just the reverse—every $10.60 payment he receives will purchase as much for him as $21.20 would have had there been no deflation.

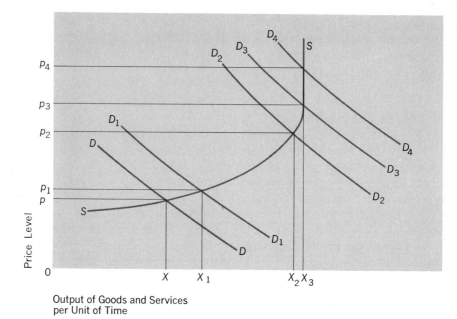

Output of Goods and Services
per Unit of Time

Figure 20–4
The effects of increases in aggregate demand.

subsequent increase in consumer incomes tends to bring about a further increase in aggregate demand, and the process repeats itself as recovery progresses.

Though the expansion and recovery process is led by inflation, the increases in the price level will tend to be small when the actual-potential GNP gap is large. Note in Table 20–1 the small price level increases from 1933 to 1937. It takes very little in the way of price increases to stimulate business expansion under these circumstances. When large amounts of resources are unemployed, job opportunities rather than higher resource prices are the important factors in the expansion of employment levels, so expansion can take place with only a very small increase in production costs. In Figure 20–4 we represent this situation with a very flat segment of the aggregate supply curve for the increase in aggregate demand from DD to D_1D_1.

The smaller the actual-potential GNP gap becomes, the more effect increases in aggregate demand will have on the price level and the less they will have on output. As aggregate demand increases toward D_2D_2 and then toward D_3D_3 the economy is moving closer and closer to the full-employment level of GNP. But before the full-employment level of *all* resources is reached, full employment will have been reached for *many* resources, particularly those that are most efficient in producing the goods and services most urgently desired. As full-employment levels of the most efficient resources are reached, firms must turn to those that are less and less productive. At the same time, they will bid the prices of the more productive resources higher and higher. When the full-employment level is reached for *all* resources, further increases in aggregate demand can only increase the price level. The economy's output can increase no more.

The distribution of the effects of increases in aggregate demand between the economy's level of output and the price level is illustrated in Figure 20-4. When unemployment is great and there is a large gap between actual and potential GNP, an increase in aggregate demand is absorbed almost entirely by an increase in output and employment. As unemployment diminishes and the gap becomes smaller, increases in aggregate demand have more and more of an impact on the price level and less and less influence on output. Finally, when full employment is reached, any further increases in aggregate demand must be absorbed entirely by increases in the price level. These effects give the aggregate supply curve its unique curvature.

Redistributive Effects

Economic expansion and inflation, like contraction and deflation, bring about a redistribution of income. When less than full-employment levels of economic activity prevail both redistributive and output effects occur at the same time, but once the economy has reached a full-employment level of output, inflation brings about redistributive effects only. Suppose we consider the redistributive effects, starting from an initial situation in which actual GNP is substantially below potential GNP.

As expansion and inflation occur, the incomes of some groups will increase relatively more than those of others. The most obviously favored group is made up of those whose resources have been unemployed and which are now put back to work. Another group favored by expansion includes those who furnish resources to durable goods and capital goods industries. While these industries undergo more severe contractions during recession and depression, they also experience more vigorous expansion in prosperity and inflation than do other consumer goods industries.

Debtors gain from inflation while *creditors lose*, relatively. An increase in the price level in the interim between obtaining a loan and repaying it works in the debtor's favor. Because of the rising price level the dollars that he must repay have less purchasing power than those that he borrowed. The creditor, on the other hand, receives back less purchasing power than he loaned out.

Fixed-income receivers lose when inflation occurs. Those whose money incomes consist of fixed amounts of interest, pensions, annuities, and the like find that they can buy less and less as the price level rises. Salaried employees of the government, of educational institutions, and of eleemosynary institutions ordinarily find that their incomes lag behind rising prices. They lose in terms of purchasing power, but to a lesser degree than do those who receive fixed incomes.

SUMMARY

Three major indicators of economic performance have been used in evaluating the seriousness of economic fluctuations. One is the behavior of GNP, the value of the economy's entire yearly output of goods and services in final form. Another is the movement in the general price level or average level of all prices over time. The third is the unemployment rate or the percentage of the economy's labor force classified as unemployed. The unemployment rate is probably the most sensitive of the three as an indicator of economic fluctuations in a downward direction. The price level tends to be the most sensitive indicator of rapid economic expansion. GNP over time is indicative of the pattern of economic growth.

Movements in the general price level are measured by means of price index numbers, which show percentage deviations in average price levels for specific years from some year selected as the base year. A set of price index numbers can be computed for any given complex of product prices, for example, wholesale prices, retail prices, agricultural prices, or others. The implicit price deflator of Table 20–1 provides the broadest possible complex, since it is intended to cover all goods and services making up GNP. With the implicit price deflators, GNP in current dollar terms can be converted into GNP in real terms. Movements in the general price level are called inflation and deflation. Inflation refers to a period of rising prices while deflation means a period of falling prices.

Comparisons of actual GNP with potential GNP provide a meaningful basis for examining economic fluctuations. Potential GNP is defined as the level of GNP that could be attained if the unemployment rate were no more than 4 percent. Economic fluctuations in a downward direction —recession and depression—are reflected in a widening gap between actual and potential GNP, while those in an upward direction—periods of rapid expansion—bring about a decreasing gap or, in some cases, even a negative gap. Although a recession may or may not be accompanied by deflation, a depression almost certainly will be because of its greater severity. Rapid expansion is almost always accompanied by inflation; the closer the economy is to a full-employment level of GNP, the greater will be the inflation associated with a given increase in the economy's output.

The effects of recession, depression, and deflation can be classified in two categories, (1) output effects and (2) redistributive effects. Output effects are obvious; actual GNP is below potential GNP and the public has less to consume than it could have. Redistributive effects refer to relative changes in incomes among families and individuals that stem solely from the downturn in economic activity. Those whose net incomes fall relatively more than average incomes fall will be those made unemployed by the decline, those who furnish resources to durable goods and capital goods industries, and debtors. Those whose net incomes fall relatively less than average incomes fall include salaried persons, those living on fixed incomes, and creditors.

Similarly, rapid expansion and inflation will have output effects and redistributive effects. Output affects can occur only if there are unemployed resources in the economy. Expansion occurring from an increase in aggregate demand under full-employment conditions can result in inflation only. Redistributive effects occur as the net incomes of some groups increase more rapidly than those of others. Favored groups are those who have been unemployed and who obtain employment, those who furnish resources to durable goods and capital goods industries, and debtors. Those who lose relatively are salaried personnel, fixed-income receivers, and creditors.

EXERCISES AND QUESTIONS FOR DISCUSSION

1. "Since unemployment was at a high level during the Great Depression, there was a scarcity of goods. This implies that prices should have been relatively higher in this period, not lower." Evaluate this statement.
2. Why are some economists not concerned about a moderate amount of inflation? Explain.
3. Give several possible reasons why recessions are no longer necessarily accompanied by deflation. Explain each one carefully.
4. How is real GNP computed? What useful purposes can this concept serve? Explain.
5. Contrast a recession and a depression with an economic expansion. Consider in your discussion the movements of the level of unemployment and the general price level in each. Illustrate each situation graphically.

SELECTED READINGS

Economic Report of the President. Washington, D.C.: Government Printing Office, January 1965, pp. 81–83.
———. Washington, D.C.: Government Printing Office, January 1967, pp. 37–50.
Lee, Maurice W., *Macroeconomics: Fluctuations, Growth, and Stability,* 3d ed. Homewood, Ill.: Richard D. Irwin, Inc. 1963, Part 3 and Chap. 20.
Ross, Arthur M., "How Good Are Government Statistics?" *Challenge,* May–June 1966, pp. 14 ff.
Slichter, Summer H., "How Bad Is Inflation?" *Harper's Magazine,* August 1952, pp. 53–57.

Money

CHAPTER 21

What are the causes of recession, depression, deflation, expansion, and inflation? Can they be brought under control so that year in and year out actual GNP is somewhere in the neighborhood of potential GNP and so that their arbitrary redistributive effects are largely eliminated? We hear and read conflicting opinions on what the government ought or ought not to be doing if we are to avoid the Scylla of inflation on the one hand and the Charybdis of recession on the other. In this and the following chapters we try to sort out the main causes of instability and to find the appropriate means of controlling them. In doing so we shall make a detailed study of the monetary system, of the government's expenditure and tax structure and policies, and of the body of economic principles generally referred to as national income analysis. The order of exposition is not necessarily the order of importance of these three subject areas. Rather, it is in an ascending order of complexity.

We concentrate on money in this chapter—stuff that we are so accustomed to handling that we accept it and its uses automatically and unquestioningly. In so doing we may very well miss or lose sight of the important role that it plays in the exchange of goods and services and in economic fluctuations. We shall start by defining the term and then we shall identify the functions of money. Third, we shall examine the determinants of the value of money and then outline a simple framework of monetary theory.

WHAT IS MONEY?

A Definition

Money can be easily and simply defined as a medium of exchange that is generally accepted as such by the public. It is anything that we are willing to accept from others in return for giving up to them items that we possess and that in turn other people are willing to accept in return for items that they give up to us. It is something whose units the community has by custom come to adopt and use as a means of measuring and expressing relative values of different goods and services.

Historically, a rich variety of tangible objects and intangible debts have served as money. These include cloth in Samoa, in parts of Africa, and in parts of China; whales' teeth in the Fiji islands; shells and animals' teeth in a number of Pacific islands; animals such as pigs, buffalos, reindeer, and cattle in almost every continent of the globe; beads in Africa and among American Indians; rice and other grains in Japan, the Philippines, India, Babylonia, Europe, and other agricultural areas; tobacco in Colonial North America; fur in Alaska and Canada; tea bricks in China; salt in Ethiopia and China; bronze in ancient Italy and Rome; slaves in Africa and Ireland; silver and gold throughout the world; and, in the modern world, paper and evidences of debt.[1]

Modern Money

The money in circulation today in most countries is classified into two categories: (1) demand deposits in banks and (2) currency in the form of bills and coins. Frequently we think of money as consisting of currency only, but a little reflection on our use of the checkbook and on the definition of money given above will convince us that deposits are not only money but constitute the most important part of the total money supply of the economy. Note in Table 21–1 that in July 1968 they represented almost 75 percent of the total.

Demand Deposits

Suppose we look more carefully at *demand deposits,* or checking accounts in banks, and consider how we use them in economic transactions. When we make a deposit we turn over to the bank assets of ours—currency or checks made out to us by other people—and these become bank assets. But in accepting our assets the bank incurs liabilities or debts to us that we call *demand deposits,* or checking accounts. Our demand deposits carry with them a special privilege. If we so desire we can transfer a part of what the bank owes us to other persons by writing checks in their favor. When they deposit the checks the bank owes them that much more and owes us that much less. Bank debts transferred in this manner from one person to another are widely used as a medium of exchange and

[1] Probably the most extensive historical account of items used as money is that of Paul Einzig, *Primitive Money* (London: Eyre and Spottiswoode, 1949).

TABLE 21-1

Kinds of Money in Circulation
in the United States, July 1968
(millions of dollars)

Demand deposits[1]		147,200
Currency[2]		
Federal Reserve notes	41,982	
Silver dollars	482	
United States notes	302	
Fractional Coins	4,904	
Treasury currency (in process of		
retirement)	309	47,979
Total money supply		195,179

[1] Seasonally adjusted
[2] Includes currency held in commercial bank vaults and outside
the U.S.
SOURCE: *Federal Reserve Bulletin,* September 1968, pp. A-16,
A-17.

are well accepted by the public as such. They fulfill all of the requirements
necessary to be designated as money.

Currency

The major part of the *currency* component of the U.S. money supply
consists of paper bills, almost all of which are Federal Reserve notes, as
is indicated in Table 21–1. *Federal Reserve notes,* like demand deposits,
represent debt. They are certificates of indebtedness of the Federal Reserve banks[2] to those who have possession of them, but since they are
declared by the U.S. government to be "legal tender for all debts, public
and private," what would you exchange them for if you went to a Federal
Reserve bank to claim what is owed you? The rest of the paper currency
is hardly worth bothering about. Until 1964 most one dollar bills were
silver certificates, sort of warehouse receipts for silver held in the U.S.
Treasury that could be exchanged for silver at a fixed price. But this has
been done away with and silver certificates have been entirely replaced
in circulation by Federal Reserve notes. U.S. notes are debt certificates,
too, issued by the Treasury under an authorization dating back to Civil
War days. It will be a rare occasion when you find one of these in your
billfold; they have almost all been retired from circulation.

Coins, the remaining part of the currency component, are circulated
by the Treasury and are for convenience in making change and in operating coin machines. The values of the metals that they contain must always be less than or equal to their value as money. If this were not so

[2] Federal Reserve banks are quasi-governmental institutions. They are examined in detail
in Chapter 23.

they would not remain in circulation, since it would pay people to obtain them at their money value, melt them down, and sell the metal at the higher commercial value.[3]

FUNCTIONS OF MONEY

Money performs three major functions in an economic system. First, it serves as a *medium of exchange*. Second, it serves as a *unit of account*, or as the unit in terms of which economic values are measured. Third, it serves as a *liquid store of value*. These functions are closely related and they overlap, as we shall see as we examine each in detail.

Medium of Exchange

Money as a *medium of exchange* is a great technological convenience in any society in which exchanges commonly occur. The alternative is a *barter system*, in which goods and services are exchanged for goods and services. The inconvenience of such a system is well illustrated by the example of the traveler in Africa who wanted a boat. A boat owner was found who was willing to trade a boat for a certain amount of ivory. The traveler had no ivory but through inquiry a man with ivory was found who wanted cloth for the ivory. Unfortunately, the traveler had no cloth; all he had was a quantity of wire. But luck was with him. He found a trader who had cloth and wanted wire in exchange. The traveler traded wire for cloth and cloth for ivory. He then exchanged the ivory for the boat, finally fulfilling his original desire.

Barter arrangements would be even more inconvenient in a complex, modern economy in which most of us complete only a small part of any specific productive process. Who, for example, would be willing to trade groceries or housing or clothing directly to an economist in exchange for a few lectures on how the economic system works? However, in a money economy the economist is able to gather together groups of persons either desiring or forced to learn economics. He sells his services to them for money and in turn uses the money to purchase the things he wants. The

---

[3] This is why silver dollars have gone out of circulation. The price of silver has risen so much since the government ceased fixing the price that a silver dollar now contains much more silver than a dollar's worth. It is illegal to melt down the coin at the present time; however, there is a general expectation that the prohibition will be removed in the near future. In the face of this expectation people in possession of silver dollars will not use them as currency; rather, they will sell them or hold them as though they were silver bullion—the form in which they are the most valuable.

greater the degree of specialization in an economy, the more convenient money is for exchange purposes.

Measure of Value

The units of a monetary system are used as a measure of value for goods, services, and resources. The value of a loaf of bread is measured as 35 cents; that of an automobile as $4500; that of a haircut as $2.50; and that of an hour of skilled labor as $5. We use such measurements for purposes of comparing values and as a means of keeping accounting records. Comparative values expressed in monetary units provide the basis for most of our economic decision-making and exchange. As consumers we compare the market values (prices) of the different goods and services available and we make our choices as to how to allocate our incomes among them. As resource owners we compare the values placed on units of the resources we own in their various alternative uses and we sell or hire them out accordingly. The decisions of businessmen with respect to what products to sell and what resources to purchase are based on comparative values. Revenues expressed in money terms compared with money costs indicate what output levels yield the greatest profits.

Unfortunately, monetary units are not perfect for measuring values. During periods of inflation the dollar represents smaller and smaller physical quantities of goods and services, and during periods of deflation it represents larger and larger quantities. Thus we often find ourselves using a rubber yardstick for economic and accounting measurements. However, we can and do make use of price index number techniques to compensate for the variations that occur.

Liquid Store of Value

Most people find it desirable to accumulate and hold a stock of assets over time. The stock is held in many different forms—real estate, business assets, common stocks, bonds, homes, and personal property of different kinds. Ordinarily a part of it will be held in the form of money.

We speak of different kinds of assets as having different degrees of *liquidity,* the term "liquidity" referring to the ease with which one kind can be converted into another. Anyone who has tried to sell a house knows that it is rather illiquid; it takes time to find the buyer willing to pay what the house is worth. Common stocks or bonds are much more liquid. But money is the most liquid of all assets, since it can be converted immediately into other desired forms.

We hold money as a *liquid store of value* for several reasons. We need to keep enough on hand to see us through from one pay check to another, to take care of our ordinary day to day *exchange transactions*. We like to keep a little more than that on hand in order to take advantage of any special opportunities that may come our way. Further, we like to be in a position to meet *unforeseen emergencies and contingencies*. Once we have reached an income level that enables us to hold a stock of money that we consider sufficient for these purposes, we begin to think in terms of *investment* and to keep a stock of money on hand to invest at propitious times in promising stocks and bonds or other properties.

THE VALUE OF MONEY

What gives money its value? Is it the gold that the government has stored away in Fort Knox? Most people think that gold "backing" provides the key to the value of our money. Almost every financial and business writer in the country tells us that this is so, and at one time, they may have been right. When we had gold and silver coins circulating freely along with gold and silver certificates[4] the commercial value and the money value of the metals could never be far apart. But *the value per unit of our present money supply is independent of any gold or silver backing.* For example, can you exchange a five dollar bill, a five dollar demand deposit, or five dollars in coin for five dollars worth of gold or silver?

In any sort of meaningful sense the *value of money* is the goods and services that a unit of money will purchase; that is, its purchasing power. Whether money is "backed" by gold or silver is immaterial. If the general price level rises, the purchasing power or the value of the dollar falls; and if the price level falls, the purchasing power or the value of the dollar rises. Since the value of money varies inversely with the price level, we must pursue the question of what determines the price level.

The Equation of Exchange

Everything about our study of economics thus far suggests that the prices of goods and services depend upon the demands for them on the one hand and on the quantities of them made available on the other. In the preceding chapter, for the economy as a whole we put this in terms of aggregate demand and aggregate supply. We shall be concerned with a

[4] These were "warehouse receipts" for gold and silver stored by the government.

slightly different form in this section, but the underlying aggregate demand and aggregate supply analysis will be evident.

The main determinants of the value of money or of the general price level can be demonstrated readily with an old expository device known as *the equation of exchange*. In its simplest form it states

$$MV = PT$$

Let the time period under consideration be one year. M is the average stock of money in circulation—demand deposits plus currency; V is the velocity of circulation, or the number of times the average dollar is spent per year; and T represents the physical volume of goods and services traded per year. Since pairs of socks, automobiles, hamburgers, and the like cannot be added to form any kind of meaningful total, it is the same kind of abstraction as is the measurement along the output axis in Figure 20–3. We can think of it as homogeneous baskets of all kinds of goods and services, a basketful being the quantity that will sell for, say, $100 in a year that we choose as a base year. P is the price level, or the price of a basket of goods—or, in reality, it is a price index number.

The equation of exchange is a truism saying that

Total Spending = Value of Goods and Services Sold

The average stock of money, M, multiplied by the velocity of circulation, V, is the total spending that occurs per year. The physical volume of trade, T, multiplied by the price level, P, is the value of goods and services sold per year. The equation is a truism, since what people spend as purchasers (MV) must equal the value of goods sold, or what people receive as sellers (PT). But it brings together in the proper relation the determinants of the value of money.

The value of money is shown by the price level, which depends upon the relation between total spending on the one hand and the physical volume of trade on the other. Suppose, for example, that M increases but that V and T remain constant.[5] The increase in the money supply means an increase in the total spending side of the equation of exchange. Both mathematics and common sense let us know that if the left-hand side of the equation increases, so must the right-hand side; an increase in total spending necessarily means an increase in the value of goods sold. Since we have assumed that T is constant, the rise in the value of goods sold can occur only through an increase in the price level, P. To put it another way, the increase in the money supply increases spending in the economy.

---

[5] This does not imply that V and T must always remain constant when M increases. We are simply following the procedure of changing one independent variable at a time in order to determine the impact of each such change on a dependent variable.

With more dollars chasing the same volume of goods and services, shortages occur at the original price level. These, in turn, cause the price level to rise as purchasers bid against one another for the short supplies.

In a similar way the impact of changes in V and in T on the price level and, therefore, on the value of money is easily determined. If V falls, with M and T remaining constant, P must fall and the value of money rises. If M and V remain constant and T rises, then P must fall and the value of money increases. In fact, M, V, and T may all be changing simultaneously, with the net effect on P depending upon the directions and the comparative magnitudes of the changes.

Inflation

Suppose we examine inflation, or a period in which the value of money is declining, in terms of the equation of exchange. At the outset it is apparent that if P is to rise, MV, or total spending, must be increasing relative to T. An absolute increase in total spending may ensue from an increase in the stock of money, from an increase in velocity, or from both. Also, M may increase while V declines, but if total spending is to increase, the rise in M must more than offset the decline in V. This may work the other way. Total spending may be increased by a rise in V even though a decrease in M occurs simultaneously, provided the proportional rise in V is greater than the proportional decline in M.

Ordinarily there will be some direct response of both T and P to an increase in total spending, the amount of the response depending upon the extent to which the economy's resources are employed. The closer the economy is to full employment, the less will be the relative response of T to an increase in total spending and the greater will be the relative response of P.

Historically, the United States experienced its last period of significant inflation from August 1939 to August 1948. This period embraced World War II and its aftermath and provides an excellent example of the points discussed in the preceding paragraph.[6] Letting P refer to the wholesale price level, there was an increase of 118 percent for the entire period, or, alternatively, the value of money at the end of the period was roughly one half what it was at the beginning of the period. What were the causes of the change? In order to finance World War II the stock of money (M) was almost tripled during the period, being increased by 197 percent.

---

[6] See Milton Friedman and Anna J. Schwartz, *A Monetary History of the United States, 1867–1960* (Princeton, N.J.: Princeton University Press, 1963), Chapter 10, for a detailed discussion of this period.

Direct data on the physical volume of trade (T) are hard to come by; however, industrial production in the economy almost doubled. If we can assume that industrial production was representative of the economy's entire output of goods and services, then T can be said to have doubled also. The velocity of circulation (V) was lower at the end of the period than at the beginning, falling by slightly less than 15 percent. For the period as a whole, then, there was a large increase in total spending stemming from a very large increase in M tempered somewhat by a decrease in V. The increase in T was much less proportionally than was the increase in total spending; consequently, there was a very large rise in P and a correspondingly large decrease in the value of money.

Recession and Depression

Recession and, perhaps, depression occur when total spending declines relative to the volume of goods and services available to be purchased. Reductions in total spending may result from reductions in M, in V, or in both. As total spending declines, sellers of goods find that they cannot sell as much as before at the previous price level and T declines also. During a recession the entire impact of a relative decline in total spending may rest on T, with no decline in the price level; however, during a depression P will fall also because of surpluses in sellers' inventories over a prolonged period of time. For reasons that we will discover later, declining economic activity usually causes further decreases in M, thus making matters worse. To compound the problem, further reductions in V are likely to be induced, too, by declining economic activity, for as recession, depression, and deflation occur people become more reluctant to spend what they have. Why buy now when prices are likely to be lower next week? Besides, it's necessary to save now for when times get worse, isn't it? Thus dollars are held longer than before and V falls.

The king-sized Great Depression of the 1930s was ushered in by a contraction lasting from August 1929 to March 1933.[7] Over this period the stock of money, M, declined by about one third and the velocity of circulation fell by approximately the same amount. The physical volume of trade fell by something like one third; thus the relatively greater decline in total spending pulled the price level, P, down by about one third also. That all of these magnitudes decreased in more or less the same proportion is a little on the coincidental side; however, the main point illustrated is that the fall in aggregate demand or total spending pulled both the volume of trade and the price level down. The value of money, of course, increased.

[7] See Friedman and Schwartz, Chapter 7, for an excellent discussion of the period.

QUANTITY THEORY OF MONEY

It is apparent from the foregoing analysis that the stock of money plays a key role in economic fluctuations or economic instability. The monetary theory that attributes prime importance to the average quantity of money in circulation and to changes in its magnitude has become known as the *quantity theory of money*. Put succinctly, the theory states that the price level and the level of economic activity tend to move in the same direction as the quantity of money in circulation. Special note should be taken of the word "tend," which indicates that exceptions may occur. It is possible, for example, for the volume of trade to increase at a slightly greater rate than total spending and, even though M may be increasing, for the price level to be falling. This occurred in the United States from 1923 to 1929.

The velocity of circulation further loosens the link between the quantity of money and the price level. As a matter of fact, changes in velocity can themselves change the price level with no help from changes in M. Suppose, for example, that the general public comes to expect or to believe that inflation will occur. Money, which decreases in value as the price level rises, becomes less attractive as a part of people's asset holdings than goods of various kinds; consequently, they are more inclined to exchange dollars for goods. The increase in total spending is accomplished through an increase in velocity and will have its effects on the price level—and, perhaps, the volume of trade—even though M has not increased. (Can you explain the effects of expectations on the part of the public that a recession is imminent?)

Usually in the course of economic fluctuations M and V change in the same direction; however, it is possible for a change in M to be nullified in whole or in part by a change in V in the opposite direction. When both change in the same direction, the quantity theory prediction that the price level will also change in the same direction will hold, except in the unusual case in which T changes relatively more than does total spending. Even when a change in M is accompanied by a change in V in the opposite direction, we usually expect that the former will outweigh the latter and that total spending will change in the same direction as does M. Ordinarily, the more stable the quantity of money, the more stable velocity will be.

If we are to press further into the causes of economic instability and the means of controlling it, the quantity theory of money indicates that we should inquire into the determinants of the money supply and especially into the forces that cause it to change up or down over time. Referring to Table 21–1, we see that the currency component of the money supply can be fairly easily explained. The bulk of the currency consists of

Federal Reserve notes, with the total dollar amount of these determined by Federal Reserve authorities. The coin component is under the control of the U.S. Treasury. Thus the total currency component, representing a small part of the total money supply, is under the control of government agencies and has not in the recent past been subject to marked manipulation. It has grown rather steadily over time. The checking account or demand deposit component of the money supply is much more important and more complex. An explanation of it will require that we examine the structure and operation of the banking system. This is done in the following two chapters.

SUMMARY

Money is anything used as a medium of exchange that is generally accepted by the public as such. In the United States it consists of demand deposits and currency. Demand deposits are bank liabilities or debt to depositors and are freely transferable from one person to another. Currency consists of coins and paper bills. The main functions of money in an economic system are to serve (1) as a medium of exchange, (2) as a measure of value, and (3) as a liquid store of value.

The value of money refers to what money will buy—that is, what it is worth as a medium of exchange—and does not depend on the value of the substance of which it is made. The value of money varies inversely with the general price level of what is purchased in the economy. Determinants of the price level and of the value of money are total spending on the one hand and the physical volume of goods to be purchased on the other. These factors are brought together conveniently in the equation of exchange. Increases in total spending may result from increases in the stock of money in circulation, from increases in its velocity of circulation, or from both. Decreases in total spending stem from decreases in the same magnitudes. When the rate of increase in total spending exceeds the rate of increase in the volume of goods to be purchased, inflation occurs and the value of money declines. Similarly, when total spending declines at a more rapid rate than the volume of goods and services to be purchased there will be deflation and a rise in the value of money. Deflation may or may not take place during recession but it will most surely occur during depression.

The quantity theory of money assigns a key role to money in both the cause of economic fluctuations and their control. It states that the price level and the level of economic activity tend to move in the same direction as the quantity of money in circulation. Thus it becomes important to inquire into the determinants of the money supply. The currency component of the money supply is determined by the primary monetary agencies of the federal government, Federal Reserve and Treasury authorities. Determinants of the demand deposit component come under scrutiny in the next two chapters.

EXERCISES AND QUESTIONS FOR DISCUSSION

1. "If monetary authorities increase the money supply, production in the economy will increase." Evaluate this statement.
2. Today Federal Reserve notes comprise almost our entire supply of one dollar bills, whereas in the past silver dollars served this function. Which was worth more in early 1966 when silver dollars, silver certificates, and Federal Reserve notes were circulating side by side? Which is worth more today? Explain.
3. The U.S. dollar now is worth less than it was several years ago. What changes in the variables making up the equation of exchange could account for this? What might have caused each variable to change?
4. In the recession of the late 1950s prices continued to rise. What are the possible determinants of this phenomenon?

SELECTED READINGS

Boulding, K. E., *Economic Analysis,* Vol. II, *Macroeconomics,* 4th ed. New York: Harper & Row Publishers, Inc., 1966, pp. 68–78.

Chandler, L. V., *The Economics of Money and Banking,* 4th ed. New York: Harper & Row Publishers, Inc., 1964, Chap. 1.

Friedman, M., and A. J. Schwartz, *A Monetary History of the United States, 1867–1960.* Princeton, N.J.: Princeton University Press, 1963, Chap. 10.

Radford, R. A., "The Economic Organization of a P.O.W. Camp," *Economica,* November 1945, pp. 189–201.

Banks and the Money Supply

CHAPTER 22

When you paid your tuition and your room and board, you wrote a check on the bank in which you have a checking account. You write checks for other sizable expenditures and from time to time when you need currency you cash a check. You may even have borrowed from a bank in order to buy an automobile or some other costly item that you could not do without and that your immediate liquid assets would not cover. But as indispensable as banks are to your personal economic activities, it probably never crossed your mind that banks create the major part of our money supply and that they play an important role in the ups and downs of the economy. In this chapter we shall study the banking system as a creator and destroyer of money. We shall then relate these activities to economic fluctuations.

DEMAND DEPOSITS AS MONEY

What kinds of business enterprises are banks that they can create and destroy money? What are the mechanics of demand deposit transfers from individual to individual? These are the questions to which we address ourselves in this section.

Banks as Business Enterprises

An ordinary commercial bank is a business enterprise, usually a corporation, established, like any other business, for the purpose of earning income for its owners. Banks sell two major kinds of services to the general public. They provide money to business firms and individuals that are good credit risks and in need of purchasing power as well as to the government. This is effected through bank lending, although banks may also purchase relatively small amounts of corporate stock. The interest that banks charge on the loans they make constitutes their main source of revenue. The second kind of service that the bank provides to the public is the provision of facilities for making payments through the transfer of ownership of demand deposits, or banks' debts to individuals. All of us use these instruments consistently. Some banks absorb the cost of these operations from their other income, but most levy a service charge of a specified amount per check.

The Balance Sheet

In analyzing the monetary activities of banks we shall be concerned with changes in their assets and liabilities; consequently, we shall find a T-account or balance sheet framework indispensable. This device is illustrated in Figure 22–1 and is based on the bookkeeping identity:

$$\text{Assets} = \text{Liabilities} + \text{Net Worth}$$

Assets are listed on the left-hand side of the balance sheet while liability and net worth items appear on the right. Suppose now that the State Bank of Perkins has just been formed with an initial issue and sale of $50,000 worth of common stock, the stock being paid for in currency. This transaction is represented by (1) in Figure 22–1. The currency or cash becomes the property of the bank and is listed as an asset. The bank does not yet have liabilities. The owners' equity in the business, or the net worth, is represented by $50,000 worth of capital stock.

Changes in the balance sheet will occur as the bank prepares itself for business. Suppose that it spends the $50,000 in cash for a building and for the necessary banking equipment. The purchase is recorded as trans-

STATE BANK OF PERKINS

BALANCE SHEET

ASSETS			LIABILITIES AND NET WORTH		
Cash	(1)	+ $50,000	Demand deposits		
	(2)	− $50,000	Smith	(3)	+ $10,000
	(3)	+ $20,000	Wilson	(3)	+ $10,000
Building and					
equipment	(2)	+ $50,000	Capital stock	(1)	+ $50,000

Figure 22–1
The balance sheet of a bank.

action (2) in Figure 22–1. Cash is decreased by $50,000 and a new asset account, Building and Equipment, amounting to $50,000, comes into being. The State Bank of Perkins is ready for business.

Primary Deposits

Further changes in the balance sheet of the bank will occur as it begins to carry on its banking operations. Two persons, Mr. Wilson and Mr. Smith, decide to make use of the bank's facilities and each makes a cash deposit of $10,000. The changes are shown in Figure 22–1 as transaction (3). Cash rises by $20,000 and a $10,000 demand deposit is established for each man. The cash has become the property of the bank and is therefore an asset. In return for the cash the bank incurs a liability of $10,000 to Smith and of $10,000 to Wilson. These liabilities are called *demand deposits,* because within the limits of the amount on deposit the bank is obligated to pay out cash to the appropriate depositor upon demand or to any third party designated in writing by the depositor. Such written instruments of demand are, of course, the checks that we write.

The deposits of Wilson and of Smith were made in cash and, as such, are called *primary deposits.* When these are established the money supply of the economy is not affected. The cash turned over to the bank is withdrawn from circulation and is replaced by an equivalent amount of demand deposits. The process of money creation by banks will appear shortly.

Transfer of Deposit Ownership

When one person writes a check to another, certain bookkeeping mechanics on the part of banks are involved. To illustrate these, the simplest possible example, a *monopoly-bank system,* will be used first. We shall then build up a more complex example in which the economy uses a *multibank system.*

The Monopoly-Bank System

If the State Bank of Perkins is the only bank in the economy, the transfers of deposit ownership associated with the use of demand deposits as a medium of exchange are accomplished through bookkeeping entries on the part of the bank. This is illustrated in Figure 22–2. The bank initially has cash assets of $20,000 resulting from the deposits of Smith and Wilson. The deposit liabilities of the bank are, correspondingly, $10,000 for each of them. The Building and Equipment asset account is $50,000 and the bank's Net Worth account is also $50,000.

STATE BANK OF PERKINS

BALANCE SHEET

ASSETS		LIABILITIES AND NET WORTH	
Cash	+ $20,000	Deposits	
		Smith	$10,000
			(1) + $ 1,000
		Wilson	$10,000
			(1) − $ 1,000
Building and equipment	$50,000	Capital stock	$50,000

Figure 22–2
Deposits as money: the single-bank case.

If Wilson buys some article from Smith priced at $1000 and writes a check to him for that amount, Smith will take the check to the bank for deposit in his account. The check informs the bank that Wilson "demands" that $1000 of its debt to him be transferred to Smith, and this is precisely what the bank does. It reduces on its books the amount owed Wilson by $1000 and increases the amount it owes Smith by the same amount. These changes are shown in Figure 22–2 by transaction (1), and this is the end of the matter.

The Multibank System

Payments made by means of deposit transfers become more complex when more than one bank serves the economy. Suppose that in addition to the State Bank of Perkins the National Bank of Ripley is in operation. Wilson has deposited $10,000 in cash in the State Bank of Perkins and Smith has deposited the same amount in the National Bank of Ripley. The appropriate balance sheets are shown in Figure 22–3.[1]

Again Wilson buys a $1000 item from Smith and pays for it with a check drawn on the State Bank of Perkins. Smith takes the check to the National Bank of Ripley, endorses it, and deposits it in his account. The Ripley bank increases its debt to Smith by $1000 and sends the check to the Perkins bank for collection. The State Bank of Perkins interprets the check as a request to pay $1000 of what it owes Wilson to Smith and to mean that Smith, by his endorsement has turned over his claim to the National Bank of Ripley. The State Bank of Perkins therefore pays $1000 in cash to the National Bank of Ripley, and in so doing it discharges $1000 of its deposit obligation to Wilson. Transaction (1) in Figure 22–3 illustrates the appropriate balance sheet changes.

[1] We have omitted both the Building and Equipment and the Net Worth accounts, since these are not necessary for our purposes.

STATE BANK OF PERKINS

BALANCE SHEET

ASSETS		LIABILITIES	
Cash	$10,000	Deposits	
	(1) − $ 1,000	Wilson	$10,000
			(1) − $ 1,000

NATIONAL BANK OF RIPLEY

BALANCE SHEET

ASSETS		LIABILITIES	
Cash	$10,000	Deposits	
	(1) + $ 1,000	Smith	$10,000
			(1) + $ 1,000

Figure 22–3
Deposits as money: the multi-bank case.

In an economy in which there are many banks, each with many depositors, cash transfers among banks can be minimized by *clearing operations*. Individuals with accounts at bank A will be writing checks to individuals who maintain accounts at other banks. Individuals who maintain accounts at other banks will be making payments by check to individuals who maintain accounts in bank A. Instead of sending out currency immediately for every check returned to it for collection, bank A waits until the end of the day (or some other appropriate time period) and totals up the amount it owes other banks. Other banks do the same thing. It may develop that bank A owes bank B $10,000, that bank B owes bank C $10,000, and that bank C owes bank A $10,000. If this is the case, when all three banks become aware of who owes what to whom they simply cancel out their debts to each other and no cash transfers are necessary.

In practice, a group of banks among which many interbank transactions occur may designate one bank as a *clearing house* to facilitate clearing payments. Each bank maintains a deposit at the clearing house bank for this purpose. In Figure 22–4, the State Bank of Perkins and the National Bank of Ripley are assumed to have each deposited $5000 in cash with the First National Bank of Tulsa, which serves as the clearing house. These deposits are liabilities for the Tulsa bank, but for the Ripley and Perkins banks—the depositors—they are assets; that is, they are amounts that the Tulsa bank owes them. Now suppose that Wilson, who banks with the State Bank of Perkins, writes a $1000 check to Smith, who banks with the National Bank of Ripley. Smith takes the check to the Ripley bank for deposit. The Ripley bank increases Smith's deposit by $1000 and at the same time increases on its books its Deposit at Tulsa account by $1000. It then sends the check to the First National Bank of Tulsa for clearance. The Tulsa bank decreases the Perkins bank's deposit with it by $1000 and increases the Ripley bank's deposit with it by $1000. It then sends the check to the Perkins bank, which reduces Smith's deposit by $1000 and at the same time reduces on its books its Deposit at Tulsa account by the same amount. The whole series of changes is shown by transaction (1). The State Bank of Perkins in this case is said to have an *adverse clearing balance*. This example can be easily expanded to include many banks using the clearing house facilities.

A careful reexamination of the foregoing examples will reveal that none of them has changed the amount of money in circulation. In every case a total of $20,000 in cash was withdrawn from circulation, placed in the banks' vaults, and there it stayed throughout the transactions illus-

---

FIRST NATIONAL BANK OF TULSA — BALANCE SHEET

ASSETS		LIABILITIES		
Cash	$10,000	Deposits		
		Perkins		$5,000
			(1) −	$1,000
		Ripley		$5,000
			(1) +	$1,000

STATE BANK OF PERKINS — BALANCE SHEET

ASSETS		LIABILITIES		
Cash	$5,000	Deposits		
		Wilson		$10,000
Deposit at Tulsa	$5,000		(1) −	$ 1,000
	(1) − $1,000			

NATIONAL BANK OF RIPLEY — BALANCE SHEET

ASSETS		LIABILITIES		
Cash	$5,000	Deposits		
		Smith		$10,000
Deposit at Tulsa	$5,000		(1) +	$ 1,000
	(1) + $1,000			

Figure 22–4
Clearing operations.

trated. In lieu of the cash, $20,000 in demand deposits was placed in circulation. Primary deposits simply result in an exchange of cash or currency for an equivalent amount of demand deposits for use as a medium of exchange.

Advantages of Deposits as Money

The use of demand deposits for exchange purposes has several advantages. In the first place, a canceled check, endorsed by the person to whom it is made out, provides a convenient, though not in all cases legal, receipt for a payment made. Second, demand deposits are not as easily misplaced, lost, or stolen as is currency. Can you imagine sending a $100 bill through the mail? Third, checks can be written for exact amounts of transactions, thereby doing away with the necessity of making change. Fourth, demand deposits are convenient for making large payments—a satchel full of bills and coins is awkward to carry around.

DEPOSIT CREATION AND DEPOSIT DESTRUCTION

Banks can go beyond the mere placing of primary demand deposits in circulation in lieu of currency; they are able to create additional or *secondary deposits* that do not require the withdrawal of an equivalent amount of currency from circulation, and they can also destroy these deposits. This means that banks can create and destroy money. If banks are not regulated, the possibility is introduced that they may expand or contract the money supply in a way that will contribute to economic instability. Throughout the remainder of this chapter we shall assume that banks are not regulated. This will enable us to see more clearly the economic forces affecting banking operations and the effects of banking practices on economic activity. It will also give us a greater appreciation of the need for and the problems associated with the regulation of the system. We shall look first at a monopoly-bank system and then at a multibank system.

The Monopoly-Bank System

Money creation and destruction for a monopoly-bank system is essentially the same as for an entire multibank system except that it is simpler because adverse clearing balances do not occur. Consequently, we assume here that the monopoly bank carries out all the banking operations of the economy.

One Hundred Percent Reserves

The monopoly bank of Figure 22–5 initially has had $100,000 in cash deposited in it, giving rise to $100,000 in cash assets and $100,000 in deposit liabilities. The cash is available to the bank for any contingency, but principally it is available as a reserve to meet depositors' claims against it. As such, it is ordinarily called *reserves* rather than *cash*. Actually, the *reserves* of a bank consist of more than the cash it has on hand; the deposits that it has at Federal Reserve banks, to be discussed in the next chapter, are also a part of its reserves.

The ratio of a bank's reserves to its deposits is called the *reserve ratio* and is ordinarily expressed as a percent. In all the cases that we have considered thus far the reserve ratio has been 100 percent. As long as the reserve ratio of the monopoly bank is 100 percent, no money is created. But 100 percent reserves are not likely to be found in practice.

Fractional Reserves and Deposit Creation

The managers of the monopoly bank soon discover that there is no need to maintain a reserve ratio of 100 percent. When one depositor writes a check to another the bank simply makes a bookkeeping entry, decreasing the deposit of the former and increasing that of the latter, and reserves are undisturbed. Occasionally a depositor writes a check to "cash" when he needs currency for some specific purpose. Such a check, say for $100, will decrease its writer's deposit by $100 and the bank's cash by the same amount. But when the individual spends the currency, those who receive it are likely to redeposit it in the bank, increasing their deposits and the bank's reserves by $100. Only if people are expected to turn completely away from the use of demand deposits as money is it important that the bank have reserves of 100 percent. For the monopoly bank the $100,000 in reserves is far more than enough to take care of depositors' requests for currency.

MONOPOLY BANK					
					BALANCE SHEET
ASSETS			LIABILITIES		
Reserves		$100,000	Deposits		$100,000
	(1) − $ 5,000			(2) + $ 5,000	
	(2) + $ 5,000				
L & I	(1) + $ 5,000				

Figure 22–5
Money creation by a monopoly bank.

It seems possible—and profitable—that some of the $100,000 can be put to work earning interest. There are always businesses or individuals desirous of obtaining loans and willing to pay interest for them. Here is a ready-made source of loans. A local clothing store wants to order its fall suits and needs $5000 for a three-month period. A loan officer of the bank assures himself that the clothier is a good credit risk and approves the loan at 7 percent interest.[2] The borrower signs a promissory note to the bank for this amount and, for the moment, let us suppose he takes the loan in cash. In Figure 22–5, the balance sheet changes are shown by transaction (1). Reserves are decreased by $5000 and in their place the promissory note becomes a $5000 asset. The account in which assets of this type are carried is called *Loans and Investments,* or *L & I* for short.

The loan increases the money supply of the economy by $5000. Demand deposits remain at $100,000, but the net amount of currency that has been withdrawn from circulation and that is resting in the bank's vaults is now only $95,000. There is now $100,000 in demand deposits in circulation in lieu of the $95,000 in currency that makes up the bank's reserves. When the bank increases the money supply its reserve ratio drops below 100 percent and it is said to be operating on *fractional reserves.*

The money supply increase generated by a bank loan may take place through an increase in the volume of demand deposits rather than through a return of currency to circulation. Suppose the clothier pays out the $5000 in currency to a wholesaler for fall suits. Since there is only one bank in existence, the wholesaler also uses the bank. He sacks the currency, takes it to the bank, and deposits it to his account, thereby increasing the cash of the bank by $5000, bringing total cash of the latter back to $100,000—and increasing the bank's deposits by $5000—bringing its total deposits up to $105,000. These changes are represented by transaction (2) in Figure 22–5. In lieu of $100,000 in currency, $105,000 in demand deposits is now in circulation.

In the usual case loans are not made in currency at all. When the clothier or anyone else borrows from a bank the loan is usually taken directly in the form of an increase in a deposit account, or an increase in the bank's liability to the borrower. In return the borrower signs a promissory note to the bank increasing the bank's L & I account. Transaction (1) in Figure 22–6 illustrates the point. The borrower incurs a debt to the bank in exchange for a bank debt to him. The borrower's

---

[2] Simple interest at 7 percent on a $5000 loan for a three-month period amounts to

$$\$5000 \times \tfrac{3}{12} \times .07 = \$87.50$$

This sum of money is *income* to the bank, used to pay expenses and, hopefully, dividends to stockholders. As such, it need not enter into the balance sheet transactions with which we are primarily concerned.

MONOPOLY BANK

BALANCE SHEET

ASSETS		LIABILITIES	
Reserves	$100,000	Deposits	$100,000
L & I	(1) + $ 5,000		(1) + $ 5,000
	(2) + $395,000		(2) + $395,000

Figure 22-6
Deposit creation by a monopoly bank.

debt to the bank is not generally acceptable to the public as a means of payment and is therefore not money; however, the bank's debt to the borrower is transferable and is acceptable as a means of payment, and thus it is a part of the economy's money supply.

Additional loans made by the bank will generate additional deposits. If the bank were to make additional loans to other businesses and to private individuals totaling $395,000, the results would be as shown by transaction (2) in Figure 22-6. L & I is increased by that amount and the loans are given to the borrowers in the form of demand deposits. The monopoly bank has now created $400,000 in money that did not exist before it began its lending activities. The deposits arising from lending activities—the $400,000—are called *secondary* or *derivative deposits*.

Deposit Contraction

Deposit contraction or the destruction of demand deposits is the opposite of deposit creation. Figure 22-7 shows the monopoly bank with reserves of $100,000, loans and investments of $400,000, and deposits of $500,000. (Can you break the $500,000 in deposits up into primary deposits and secondary deposits and explain the basis of the distribution?) The clothing store's note for $5000 is due. In anticipation of paying off the note, the clothier has accumulated more than this in his account and he writes a check for $5000 to the bank. The bank marks the note "paid,"

MONOPOLY BANK

BALANCE SHEET

ASSETS		LIABILITIES	
Reserves	$100,000	Deposits	$500,000
			(1) − $ 5,000
L & I	$400,000		
	(1) − $ 5,000		

Figure 22-7
Deposit contraction by a monopoly bank.

turns it over to him, reduces its L & I account by $5000, and reduces the deposit account of the clothier by $5000 (see transaction (1) in Figure 22–7). Further repayment of other loans that were made by the bank will bring about a further reduction in demand deposits or the money supply.

One of the rights of depositors is to demand and receive currency for their deposits whenever they so desire. If a bank is operating on fractional reserves, as is the monopoly bank of Figure 22–7, it is obvious that if all depositors go to the bank and insist on exchanging their deposits for currency, the bank cannot meet their demands. Once it has paid out $100,000 in currency its reserves are exhausted and the rest of its depositors are left high and dry. Mass behavior of this kind on the part of depositors is called a *run on the bank*. In periods of economic stability it is unlikely to occur, but if the public loses confidence in the bank's capacity to meet its demands for currency, as it did between 1929 and 1933, a run may develop.

Capacity for Money Creation

The rules governing money creation and destruction by the bank can be summed up briefly. If the dollar amount of new loans and investments being made exceeds the dollar amount of those being paid off or liquidated, new money is being created. If, on the other hand, the dollar amount of new loans and investments being made is less than the dollar amount of those being paid off or liquidated, money is being destroyed. Are there any limits to the volume of demand deposits that can be created?

Business prudence will determine how far the bank will go in creating money, and the reserve ratio turns out to be the critical factor. The larger the dollar volume of the bank's loans, the more income it can earn, interest on loans being the bank's main source of income. But given the amount of the bank's reserves, the larger the dollar volume of its loans and, consequently, its deposits, the smaller its reserve ratio will be. The smaller its reserve ratio, the more vulnerable the bank becomes to depositors' demands for currency. In the absence of governmental determination of what the minimum reserve ratio will be,[3] the bank must strike some sort of balance between the income incentive on the one hand and prudence on the other. As long as people have as much confidence in demand deposits as in currency as a medium of exchange, the limits on deposit creation are extremely high, or, put the other way around, the reserve ratio can be extremely low. A reserve ratio as low as

[3] As we shall see in the next chapter, minimum reserve ratios for the larger part of the banking system are set by law.

1 percent may be sufficient to take care of day-to-day demands for currency. But in periods when public confidence in the banking system is shattered, such as at the onset of the Great Depression, 50 percent reserve ratios may be too low. Traditionally, unregulated banks seem to have kept their reserve ratios somewhere between 8 and 20 percent, depending on the state of the economy.

Once we know the reserve ratio desired by the monopoly bank, its present level of deposits, and the amount of reserves that it has, we can easily determine the amount of *additional* money that it can create. Suppose, for example, that the bank desires to maintain a *reserve ratio* of not less than R percent. Suppose, further, that the *present level of deposits* is D dollars and that *total reserves* are C dollars. If the bank's deposits are all primary deposits, then

$$C = D$$

The *required reserves* for the present level of deposits is only $R \cdot D$, so, letting X represent excess reserves, we find that

$$X = C - R \cdot D \tag{22.1}$$

These excess reserves are available to support the creation of secondary deposits through loans and investments by the bank. Letting ΔD represent the total possible *deposit expansion* or *creation*, we obtain

$$\Delta D \cdot R = X$$

or

$$\Delta D = \frac{X}{R} \tag{22.2}$$

This is a perfectly general principle for a monopoly-bank system which states that if the bank has excess reserves, it can create additional deposits in the amount of the excess reserves times the reciprocal of the reserve ratio. The formula holds also for the computation of the necessary deposit contraction for a *reserve deficiency* of X dollars.

As an illustration of how to use the deposit-change formula, consider Figure 22–8. Reserves of the monoply bank, or C, are \$10,000. Total deposits, or D, are \$40,000. Suppose the desired reserve ratio, R, is 20 percent. First, we compute the excess reserves, and since

$$X = C - R \cdot D$$

then

$$X = \$10,000 - 0.2 \cdot \$40,000 = \$2000$$

The possible deposit expansion is

$$\Delta D = \frac{X}{R}$$

MONOPOLY BANK			BALANCE SHEET	
ASSETS			LIABILITIES	
Reserves L & I	$10,000 $30,000		Deposits	$40,000

Figure 22–8
The limits of deposit creation by a monopoly bank.

so

$$\Delta D = \frac{\$2000}{0.2} = \$10,000$$

The monopoly bank can create an additional $10,000 in demand deposits.

The Multibank System

The principles of deposit creation and destruction developed for the monopoly-bank system are applicable to the multibank system generally found in modern economies. They are applicable only to the system as a whole, however, rather than to individual or single banks in the system. In the multibank system, individual banks are subject to *adverse clearing balances*, a phenomenon not possible in the monopoly-bank system.

Single-Bank Expansion

By how much can a single bank of a multibank system expand its deposits when it has excess reserves? The question can be best answered by an example. Suppose that bank A in Figure 22–9 is only one of many banks in a multibank system and that initially it has reserves of $100,000, loans and investments of $400,000, and total deposits of $500,000. Now suppose that someone makes a primary deposit of $10,000 in the bank, increasing both reserves and deposits by $10,000, as shown by transaction (1) in the figure. Using equation 22.1, we find that if bank A desires to maintain a reserve ratio of at least 20 percent, its excess reserves are $8000.[4] According to equation 22.2, these should support the deposit expansion of $40,000 shown by transaction (2). After the expansion, reserves of $110,000 are supporting deposits of $550,000, the reserve ratio is 20 percent, and everything seems to be in order.

---
[4] There is nothing magic about the 20 percent figure for the desired reserve ratio in either this or the monopoly bank examples. We use 20 percent in order to make computations easy. At the same time, it is not too far from actual reserve ratios of banks.

BANK A

BALANCE SHEET

ASSETS		LIABILITIES	
Reserves	$100,000	Deposits	$500,000
	(1) + $ 10,000		(1) + $ 10,000
	(3) − $ 40,000		(2) + $ 40,000
L & I	$400,000		(3) − $ 40,000
	(2) + $ 40,000		

Figure 22–9
Adverse clearing balances and deposit creation in a multi-bank system.

But we have not yet taken into account the possibility that one bank of a multibank system may have adverse clearing balances. The people who have borrowed the extra $40,000 from bank A may use their deposits to make payments to people who keep their accounts in other banks. If the entire $40,000 were paid to people who keep their accounts in other banks, those banks would have claims against bank A's reserves amounting to $40,000, thus reducing the reserves of bank A to $70,000. The reserve ratio would be 7/51, or 13.7 percent. This situation is represented in Figure 22–9 as transaction (3). Obviously, one bank of a multibank system cannot expand as much on the basis of given excess reserves as can a monopoly bank that does all the banking for the entire economy.

When we allow for all possible adverse clearing balances, the maximum expansion of deposits that a bank's excess reserves will permit is an amount equal to its excess reserves. Any expansion beyond that amount leaves the bank open to adverse clearing balances that will reduce its reserve ratio below the desired level. In Figure 22–10, for example, we show again the same initial balance sheet for bank A. Transaction (1) shows a primary deposit of $10,000, leading to excess reserves of $8000. Suppose now that loans and deposits are both increased only by the amount of the excess reserves, as shown by transaction (2). If these bor-

BANK A

BALANCE SHEET

ASSETS		LIABILITIES	
Reserves	$100,000	Deposits	$500,000
	(1) $ 10,000		(1) $ 10,000
	(3) − $ 8,000		(2) + $ 8,000
L & I	$400,000		(3) − $ 8,000
	(2) + $ 8,000		

Figure 22–10
The limits of deposit expansion by one bank of a multi-bank system.

rowers pay out all they have borrowed to individuals who keep their accounts in other banks, clearing operations will reduce bank A's deposits as well as its reserves by $8000, as transaction (3) indicates. The reserves remaining are $102,000, supporting $510,000 in deposits. This time bank A is able to meet the adverse clearing balances *and* to maintain a reserve ratio of 20 percent. As a general principle, then, we can state that *when a single bank in a multibank system has excess reserves, its loans and deposits can be expanded by an amount equal to the excess reserves.*

Deposit Expansion by the System

By how much can deposits for the banking system as a whole be expanded when excess reserves appear? To keep the analysis as simple as possible we shall use an example in which deposit expansion takes place in one bank at a time serially. We shall assume that all who borrow from one bank make payments to individuals who maintain their deposits in only one other bank; for example, those who borrow from bank A make payments to people who keep their accounts in bank B; those who borrow from bank B make payments to individuals who keep their accounts in bank C; and so on. All banks are assumed to desire a 20 percent reserve ratio.

Consider now in Figure 22–11 the effects of a primary deposit of $10,-000 at bank A on possible loan and deposit expansion. The bank designates $2000 of the $10,000 in currency as desired reserves, leaving it with excess reserves of $8000. As a single bank of a multibank system, bank A, then, may make loans, thereby creating new deposits, of $8000. The expansion is illustrated by the plus transactions for bank A in Figure 22–11. Now let those who borrowed from bank A make payments to individuals who keep their deposit accounts at bank B. When the latter deposit their checks, bank B's deposits increase by $8000. Bank B sends the checks to bank A for collection. Bank A's deposits (of those who wrote the checks) are reduced by $8000, and when it sends bank B $8000 in currency its reserves are reduced by that amount also. Correspondingly, bank B's reserves are increased by the same amount. These changes are shown by the minus $8000 entries in bank A's balance sheet and by the plus $8000 entries in bank B's balance sheet.

Bank B now finds itself with an $8000 increase in both its reserves and its demand deposits. Its position is just as it would be if an $8000 primary deposit had been made. Of the $8000 increase in reserves, 20 percent, or $1600, will be designated as desired reserves for the $8000 increase in deposits, leaving $6400 as excess reserves. The excess reserves permit bank B as a single bank of a multibank system to expand its loans and therefore its deposits by $6400. This situation is shown in Figure 22–11

BANK A

BALANCE SHEET

ASSETS		LIABILITIES	
Reserves	$10,000	Deposits	$10,000
	− $ 8,000		+ $ 8,000
L & I	+ $ 8,000		− $ 8,000

BANK B

BALANCE SHEET

ASSETS		LIABILITIES	
Reserves	+ $8,000	Deposits	+ $8,000
	− $6,400		+ $6,400
L & I	+ $6,400		− $6,400

BANK C

BALANCE SHEET

ASSETS		LIABILITIES	
Reserves	+ $6,400	Deposits	+ $6,400
	− $5,120		+ $5,120
L & I	+ $5,120		− $5,120

BANK D

BALANCE SHEET

ASSETS		LIABILITIES	
Reserves	+ $5,120	Deposits	+ $5,120

BANK E

BALANCE SHEET

ASSETS		LIABILITIES	

Figure 22–11
The limits of deposit expansion by a multi-bank system as a whole.

by the plus $6400 items in bank B's balance sheet. Suppose that the borrowers from bank B make payments to people who maintain deposit accounts as bank C. The checks are deposited at bank C, thereby increasing deposits by $6400. Bank B will now experience adverse clearing balances. Collection by bank C from bank B increases the former's reserves by $6400 and decreases the latter's reserves and deposits by the same amount. Bank B's decreases and bank C's increases are shown on their balance sheets by the appropriate minus and plus designations.

The impact of bank A's initial $8000 in excess reserves is becoming apparent. Bank A expanded loans and deposits by the amount of its excess reserves. Bank B expanded loans and deposits by an additional $6400—bank B's excess reserves. Bank C expands loans and deposits by $5120—the amount of its excess reserves—and can expect to lose this amount of reserves to bank D. Bank D expands loans and deposits by $4096. The process continues through bank after bank. Each successive bank, upon acquiring additional reserves and deposits, retains 20 percent (or whatever the desired reserve ratio is) of the newly acquired reserves as desired reserves against the newly acquired deposits. This enables each to make loans equal to its excess reserves, or 80 percent of its newly acquired reserves, and to expand deposits by the same amount. Thus the lending and deposit-creating ability of each successive bank is equal to 80 percent of that of the preceding bank, and eventually it approaches zero.

The total increase in deposits that can originate from the original $8000 in excess reserves approaches $40,000. This is the sum of the deposit increases of all banks. Mathematically, it is a converging geometric progression, and as the increases approach zero the sum of the increases can be expressed as:

$$\$8000 + 8000 \cdot \tfrac{4}{5} + 8000 \cdot (\tfrac{4}{5})^2 + 8000 \cdot (\tfrac{4}{5})^3 + \cdots$$
$$= \$8000 \cdot \frac{1}{1 - \tfrac{4}{5}} = 8000 \cdot 5 = \$40,000$$

We have taken a long and complex, but necessary, route to show that the multibank system as a whole behaves according to the same principles as the monopoly bank. Given excess reserves in the system, the possible deposit expansion for the system as a whole is found by using the equation

$$\Delta D = \frac{X}{R} \tag{22.2}$$

No one individual bank of the system can expand by this amount—one bank can expand only by the amount of its excess reserves—but the sum of individual bank expansion triggered by excess reserves is equal to the excess reserves multiplied by the reciprocal of the reserve ratio.

Deposit Contraction by the System

Deposit contraction is the opposite of deposit expansion for the multi-bank system. If the banks of the system decide that higher reserve ratios than they currently hold are in order, or if withdrawals of cash by depositors leave them with reserve deficiencies, they will contract their deposits. As was explained earlier, this is accomplished by letting the dollar volume of old loans being paid off exceed the dollar volume of new loans being made. This reduces the deposits of banks, but it does not reduce their reserves. Equation 22.2 is also the formula for deposit contraction for the system as a whole. If X is a reserve deficiency, deposits must be contracted by X times $1/R$.

MULTIBANK SYSTEM		CONSOLIDATED BALANCE SHEET	
ASSETS		LIABILITIES	
Reserves	$100,000	Deposits	$500,000
	− $ 10,000		− $ 10,000
L & I	$400,000		− $ 40,000
	− $ 40,000		

Figure 22–12
Deposit contraction by a multi-bank system.

Suppose that Figure 22–12 depicts a consolidated balance sheet for all banks of a multibank system. Initially it shows reserves of $100,000, loans and investments of $400,000, and deposits of $500,000. The desired reserve ratio is assumed to be 20 percent. Depositors now withdraw a net amount of $10,000 in currency from the banks. Reserves decrease by $10,000 and so do deposits; consequently, the reserve ratio drops below the desired 20 percent level. The reserves required to support $490,000 in deposits would be $98,000, but the reserve account stands at only $90,-000. The $8000 reserve deficiency will induce the banking system to contract loans and deposits by an additional $40,000, bringing total deposits down to $450,000 and the reserve ratio up to the desired 20 percent.

ECONOMIC FLUCTUATIONS AND THE BANKING SYSTEM

The principles of deposit expansion and contraction by the banking system shed additional light on economic fluctuations. They provide an explanation of why an increase in total spending may feed on itself and may lead to serious inflation, as occurred from 1946 through 1948. They also help to explain a recession-depression spiral like that of 1929–1933.

Expansion and Inflation

Whatever it is that triggers the increase in total spending that ushers in an expansion, whether it is an increase in M or an increase in V, the expansion itself induces the banking system to increase the money supply, generating still further increases in total spending, in the money supply, and so on. Both the banking system and the public are responsible for this self-generating upward spiral. When banks are increasing the amounts of their loans outstanding they are increasing the money supply—and the economic climate during expansion encourages increases in lending activities. During periods of expansion and prosperity, the public desires to increase its volume of borrowing for at least two reasons. First, expanding business activity calls for an expanding volume of loans to finance larger inventories and the other expenses associated with it. Second, consumers are less reluctant to go into debt during an expansion period, since expansion and inflation work in favor of debtors. On the supply of loans side, banks worry less about defaults on loans during periods of expansion. They are willing to expand loans and increase deposits, letting the reserve ratio fall, in order to increase their interest income.

Recession and Depression

The shoe is on the other foot during periods of recession and depression. On the demand for loans side, business firms and individuals are less eager to borrow as business activity contracts. Business firms desire to cut back their inventories and have less need for loans to finance these and other expenses. Individuals fear the burden of a large debt during recession and depression and are generally more reluctant to borrow. On the loan supply side, banks are seeking safety when economic activity is contracting and want to increase their reserve ratios to achieve a greater measure of it. Thus as old loans are paid off new loans will not be made in sufficient quantities to offset them. The money supply shrinks, decreasing total spending still further, which may lead to further decreases in the money supply, and so on into a depression spiral.

An uncontrolled, unregulated banking system operates in a *destabilizing* manner over the course of business fluctuations. When total spending tends to decrease, the banking system decreases the money supply, thus accelerating the rate of decline. When total spending begins to increase, the banking system increases the money supply, thus augmenting the rate of increase. This is not to accuse bankers of diabolical intent; they operate their businesses like the managers of other types of enterprises operate theirs—to make profits. But because of the very special nature of the banking business, the production of its services—the extension of loans or credit—brings about significant changes in the money supply of the economy. There are very few other types of businesses where this is the case, and, at the present time at least, none is as important in this respect as banks.

SUMMARY

Commercial banks are business enterprises engaged in providing two major kinds of services to the public: (1) they sell loans for which they are paid interest and (2) they provide the mechanism for transferring ownership of demand deposits from one person to another, for which they are usually paid service charges.

Demand deposits are bank liabilities or debts to individuals or organizations and they serve as a medium of exchange when the ownership of them is transferred from one to another by means of checks. When deposits are transferred between persons using the same bank no currency changes hands—only a bookkeeping transfer is required. When deposits are transferred between persons using different banks, the bank from which the deposit is transferred has an adverse clearing balance and must transfer assets to the bank receiving the deposit. To minimize and to facilitate clearing payments, banks utilize a clearing house, one bank in which the others maintain deposits primarily for clearing purposes.

Banks create deposits or money when they make loans and investments. Deposits arising from loans and investments are called secondary deposits. Deposits made in currency are called primary deposits. The latter do not affect the total quantity of money in circulation: they simply substitute demand deposits for currency. The cash assets of a bank plus the deposits it has at other banks are called its reserves. The ratio of its reserves to its total deposits is its reserve ratio. If all deposits were primary deposits, the bank's reserve ratio would be 100 percent, but when the bank makes loans, extending them to the borrower in the form of additional or secondary deposits, the reserve ratio is less than 100 percent and the bank is said to be operating with fractional reserves. The difference between the actual reserves that a bank has and the reserves it needs to maintain some desired reserve ratio is called its excess reserves. The amount of money that the banking system can create is equal to its excess reserves multiplied by the reciprocal of the average desired reserve ratio in the system. The banking system is increasing the money supply whenever the volume of new loans and investments being made exceeds the volume of old loans and investments being paid off or sold.

Contraction of the money supply by the banking system is the opposite of money creation. It occurs whenever the volume of old loans and investments being paid off or sold exceeds the volume of new ones being made by banks in the system. A reserve deficiency in the banking system will bring about a contraction of deposits amounting to the deficiency multiplied by the reciprocal of the reserve ratio.

When viewed in relation to business fluctuations, the banking system left uncontrolled and unregulated operates in a destabliizing way. During expansion and inflation the system creates additional money, thus increasing the rate of expansion. During recession and depression the system contracts the money supply, increasing the rate at which total spending falls.

EXERCISES AND QUESTIONS FOR DISCUSSION

1. "The banking system does not actually create money, since loans are not considered as part of the money supply. The only way money can actually be created is for the government to print new paper money." Evaluate this statement.
2. If a banking system did not have clearing houses, would it still be possible for the system to create demand deposits? Explain.
3. What would be the seasonal (for example, Christmas) effects on the banking system's ability to create money? Elaborate.
4. If you were asked to tell banks what reserve ratio to maintain, on what economic factors would you base your decision? Under what circumstances would it be higher? lower?
5. "During the depression of the 1930s there were many 'runs' on banks. This resulted from a lack of prudence on the part of bankers during this period." Analyze this statement critically.

SELECTED READINGS

Barger, Harold, *Money, Banking, and Public Policy.* Chicago: Rand McNally and Company, 1962, Chap. 7.

Chandler, Lester V., *The Economics of Money and Banking,* 4th ed. New York: Harper & Row, Publishers, Inc., 1964, Chap. 5.

Ludtke, James B., *The American Financial System: Markets and Institutions.* Boston: Allyn and Bacon, Inc., 1961, pp. 102–117.

The
United States
Banking
System

CHAPTER 23

Until comparatively recent times the money-creating and destroying activities of U.S. banks were not widely appreciated and, therefore were not subjected to quantitative regulation. There is little doubt that in the absence of such regulation expansion and contraction of the money supply by the banking system contributed in an important way to the economic fluctuations that recurred so persistently until the early 1950s. In passing the Federal Reserve Act in 1913 the federal government recognized some responsibility for pursuing policies that would contribute to stability, but not until the early 1950s, following the Employment Act of 1946, was this responsibility assumed explicitly. At the present time stabilization policies are pursued through the Federal Reserve System on the one hand and through the tax-expenditure measures enacted by the Congress on the other. Under the Federal Reserve System the banking system can be directed in a positive way toward combating economic fluctuations.

In order to understand the contributions of the Federal Reserve System to economic stability we shall look first at the structure of the U.S. banking system. Next, we shall discuss the functions of a central bank, particularly as they are performed by Federal Reserve banks. Third, the role of gold in the U.S. monetary system will be examined. Fourth, we shall consider the tools available to Federal Reserve authorities for controlling the money supply. Finally, we shall see how the latter are coordinated to combat instability.

STRUCTURE OF THE BANKING SYSTEM

Since the Federal Reserve Act was passed in 1913 the United States has had a *central banking system.* The public comes into contact with the system at the commercial bank level. Most commercial banks are in turn subjected to regulation by Federal Reserve authorities acting through the medium of *Federal Reserve banks,* which make up the *central bank* element of the banking structure.

Commercial Banks

Commercial banks are the familiar banks that carry on the banking activities of the general public. They make loans and in so doing create the demand deposits that form the major part of the economy's money supply. They also provide the mechanism for the transfer of deposits from one individual or business to another. There are approximately 13,800 commercial banks operating in the United States at the present time.

Some commercial banks are national banks while others are state banks. *National banks* are corporations chartered by the federal government under the provisions of the National Bank Act of 1863. *State banks* are corporations chartered under the laws of a state and are subject to the banking laws of the state or states in which they operate. There are approximately 4800 national banks and 9000 state banks in the United States.

The Federal Reserve System

Not all commercial banks are *member banks* of the Federal Reserve System. All national banks are required to be members while for state banks membership is optional. A member bank may take advantage of all of the facilities of the System, but at the same time it has an obligation to follow the rules, regulations, and procedures established by the Federal Reserve Act and the Board of Governors of the Federal Reserve System acting under the law. Of the state banks, some 1300 are members; the other 7700 operate outside the System. Since member banks tend to be larger than nonmember banks, between 80 and 85 percent of total demand deposits of the banking system is held in member banks.

Federal Reserve Banks

The Federal Reserve Act divides the United States into 12 Federal Reserve districts and provides for a Federal Reserve bank in each district, as illustrated in Figure 23–1. The Federal Reserve bank in any given district is owned by the member banks of that district—they are its stockholders. Each Federal Reserve bank has its own board of directors and

— Boundaries of Federal Reserve Districts
＊ Board of Governors of the Federal Reserve System
○ Federal Reserve Bank Cities
· Federal Reserve Branch Cities

Figure 23-1
The Federal Reserve Districts and their branch territories. From *Federal Reserve Bulletin*, September, 1967.

its own officers who are responsible for coordinating the bank's activities with Federal Reserve policies and for conducting the day-to-day operations of the bank.

Federal Reserve banks are not necessarily profit-making organizations. When the net income of a bank permits, dividends up to a maximum of 6 percent of the face value of their stock holdings may be paid to member banks. Net income over and above this amount is paid into the U.S. Treasury. On the other hand, if losses occur they are absorbed by the Treasury. These provisions make it possible for Federal Reserve banks to operate in the interest of the public rather than in their private interest.

Administration of the System

A seven-member *Board of Governors* sets Federal Reserve policies and exercises general control over the System. The President of the United States appoints Board members subject to Senate confirmation. Each member is appointed for a 14-year term, with the terms staggered so that an appointment expires and a new one is made every two years. No two members may come from the same Federal Reserve district. One of the seven is appointed by the President to be Chairman of the Board.

The other important administrative entity in the Federal Reserve System is the *Open Market Committee*. The Committee consists of 12 members, including all seven members of the Board of Governors. The other 5 are elected by the 12 Federal Reserve banks; however, the Board of Governors is obviously in a position to dominate the activities of the Committee. These activities will be examined shortly.

Of less importance in the System's administrative hierarchy is the *Federal Advisory Council*. It is made up of one representative from each of the 12 Federal Reserve districts, the selection being made by the board of directors of the appropriate Federal Reserve bank. The Council meets at least four times a year and serves as a liaison between the Board of Governors and the administrators of the individual Federal Reserve banks.

CENTRAL BANK FUNCTIONS OF THE FEDERAL RESERVE SYSTEM

Although the 12 Federal Reserve banks are privately owned and each has its own identity, the activities are coordinated by the Board of Governors of the Federal Reserve System in such a way that they operate essentially as a single central bank. Since the concept of a central bank is more easily described than defined, we shall explain it by discussing the main central bank functions performed through the Federal Reserve banks. These are: (1) to serve as a bankers' bank, (2) to operate as a clearing house for commercial banks, (3) to operate as a bank for the federal government, (4) to exercise control over the volume of demand deposits created by the banking system, and (5) to furnish the economy with the supply of currency (but not total money supply) that it desires. For convenience we shall use a combined balance for the 12 Federal Reserve banks, treating them as a single unit, and shall refer to the unit as the FRB.

A Bankers' Bank

In its role of the commercial banks' bank the FRB serves commercial banks that are members of the System in much the same way that commercial banks serve the public. Member banks may obtain deposits both by turning currency over to the FRB and by borrowing from it. Except for the vault cash necessary to carry on day-to-day operations, member banks carry their reserves on deposit at the Federal Reserve banks of the

BANK A

BALANCE SHEET

| Reserves | $100,000 | Deposits | $500,000 |
| L & I | $400,000 | | |

BANK B

BALANCE SHEET

| Reserves | $100,000 | Deposits | $500,000 |
| L & I | $400,000 | | |

FRB

BALANCE SHEET

Cash	+ $200,000	Deposits	
		Bank A	+ $100,000
		Bank B	+ $100,000

Figure 23–2
Member-bank deposits at the FRB.

districts in which they are located. Reciprocally, a member bank's reserves consist of whatever it has on deposit at the FRB plus its vault cash.

Member-bank *cash deposits* at the FRB are illustrated in Figure 23–2. Member banks A and B each have cash reserves of $100,000 initially and the FRB balance sheet is initially blank. Both banks now deposit their reserves at the FRB, increasing its cash asset account by $200,000, in return for which the FRB sets up a liability or deposit account of $100,000 for each member bank. For the FRB what is owed bank A is a liability, while for bank A it is an asset. In fact, bank A is entitled by law to consider its deposit at the FRB as reserves. The same applies for bank B and other member banks. All that has happened in the balance sheets of banks A and B is that cash reserves are replaced by reserves in the form of deposits owed them by the FRB. Reserves of member banks are unchanged by the deposits of cash in the FRB.

When a member bank borrows from the FRB, *reserves that did not exist before are created by the borrowing.* There are two methods used for borrowing. First, and by far the more important, the member bank simply gives its promissory note to the FRB for the amount borrowed, using

MEMBER BANKS

BALANCE SHEET

Reserves	$100,000	Deposits	$500,000
	+ $ 10,000		
L & I	$400,000	Borrowings	+ $ 10,000

FRB

BALANCE SHEET

Cash	$100,000	Deposits	
		Member banks	$100,000
			+ $ 10,000
Discounts and			
advances	+ $ 10,000		

Figure 23–3
Member-bank borrowing from the FRB.

government bonds and notes due it as security. Loans made to member banks in this way are called *advances.* Second, the member bank may take some of the notes due it[1] and endorse them to the FRB, making the notes the property of the latter but leaving the member bank liable for them if payment is not met when the notes fall due. This process is called *discounting.* Interest charged the member banks for loans by the FRB is called the *discount rate,* regardless of which process is used.

Member-bank borrowing by means of advances is illustrated in Figure 23–3. A consolidated balance sheet for member banks is shown along with that of the FRB. The initial positions of both are represented by the figures without plus signs, while the plus figures indicate the changes brought about through the borrowing process. The borrowing of $10,000 by member banks creates a $10,000 liability account (due the FRB) for them; this account is called *Borrowings.* The $10,000 in promissory notes made out to the FRB by the commercial banks in the process are FRB assets and are listed under the heading *Discounts and Advances.* The FRB makes the loans by increasing the amount it owes the member banks by $10,000; that is, by increasing member-bank deposits at the FRB by that amount. The $10,000 increase in member-bank deposits in the Federal Reserve bank is, of course, a $10,000 increase in member-bank reserves and is so listed on their balance sheets. The borrowing transaction has increased the assets and the liabilities of both member banks and the FRB

[1] The FRB specifies which of these are eligible and which are not.

by $10,000. Of great importance, as we shall see later, is the fact that $10,000 in *additional reserves* has been created for member banks.

Clearing House Functions

Since member banks carry their reserves as deposits at the FRB, the latter is in a natural position to perform clearing operations. These are illustrated in Figure 23-4. Banks A and B are member banks with reserves deposited at the FRB. Again the initial positions of all three banks are shown without plus or minus indications, with the plus and minus figures denoting the changes that occur. We will employ this procedure throughout our discussion. Now suppose that someone with a deposit at bank A makes a $1000 payment by check to someone who deposits the check at bank B. Bank B's deposits and reserves are both increased by $1000 and the check is sent to the FRB. The latter transfers $1000 on its

FRB   BALANCE SHEET

Cash	$200,000	Deposits	
		Bank A	$100,000
			− $ 1,000
		Bank B	$100,000
			+ $ 1,000

BANK A   BALANCE SHEET

Reserves	$100,000	Deposits	$400,000
	− $ 1,000		− $ 1,000
L & I	$300,000		

BANK B   BALANCE SHEET

Reserves	$100,000	Deposits	$400,000
	+ $ 1,000		+ $ 1,000

Figure 23-4
The FRB as a clearing house.

books from bank A's deposits to bank B's, then sends the check to bank A. Bank A must decrease its deposits and reserves by $1000 each and the clearing operation is complete.

Banking Functions for the Government

The Federal Reserve banks function as a fiscal agent for the federal government, or as the government's banker, carrying out in this role two principal types of banking operations. First, government deposits on which government checks are drawn are maintained at the FRB, and, second, the government borrows from the FRB from time to time.

One method by which the government acquires deposits at the FRB is illustrated in Figure 23–5. Suppose that the U.S. Treasury collects $10,000 in taxes from the general public. Taxpayers write checks to the government for that amount and the Treasury deposits the checks at the FRB. The latter transfers $10,000 from the deposit accounts of the member banks on which the checks were written to the deposit account of the Treasury—member banks and the Treasury are customers of the FRB just as businesses and individuals are customers of member banks. The checks are sent to the appropriate member banks, and member-bank reserves as well as deposits (those of the taxpayers) are reduced by $10,-000. The net effect of the whole set of transactions is a deposit transfer at the FRB from member banks to the Treasury, along with a corresponding decrease in member-bank reserves and the deposits at member banks.

MEMBER BANKS			BALANCE SHEET	
Reserves	$100,000	Deposits	$400,000	
	− $ 10,000		− $ 10,000	
L & I	$300,000			

FRB			BALANCE SHEET	
Cash	$100,000	Deposits		
		Member banks	$100,000	
			− $ 10,000	
		U.S. Treasury	+ $ 10,000	

Figure 23–5
Government deposits at the FRB acquired through tax collections.

Figure 23-6
Government deposits at the FRB acquired through borrowing.

The government borrows from the FRB by selling government bonds or Treasury bills to it, and this process enables the FRB to *create* deposits for the government. The amount of government securities acquired directly from the Treasury that the FRB can hold is limited by law to $5 billion, but through the acquisition of such securities from other sources —the securities having been sold previously to those other sources by the Treasury—it can and does hold much larger amounts. Direct government borrowing from the FRB is illustrated in Figure 23–6. If $10,000 in government securities is acquired by the FRB, a government securities asset account of that amount is established. The FRB pays for the securities by increasing its deposit liabilities to the government (that is, by creating new government deposits) in the amount of $10,000. (If the government were now to spend what it has borrowed, what would be the possible impact on the total amount of money that the banking system could create?)

Money Supply Control Functions

Control of the economy's supply of money is without question the most important of the FRB's functions. It is so important that we shall examine it in considerable detail later in the chapter. At this juncture it will be given brief mention in very general terms only. This is not to say that the functions already discussed are unimportant; rather, it means that in performing its other functions the FRB is in a unique position to control the volume of demand deposits of member banks and, hence, the money supply. Control of the money supply is important because it provides a partial means of controlling economic fluctuations.

In considering the instruments of control we shall argue frequently as though FRB officials can determine precisely when the money supply should be expanded and when it should be contracted and that the appropriate expansion or contraction follows immediately. This is not entirely so—it is not always easy to determine when and by how much the money supply should be changed. Further, control is not always direct nor is it complete. Lags occur between the initiation of action on the part of the FRB and the resulting changes in demand deposits. Further, demand deposits of member banks do not constitute the entire money supply. Finally, Treasury operations may make it extremely difficult for Federal Reserve authorities to change the money supply in the direction and magnitudes that they desire—Treasury operations and FRB operations are not always mutually consistent.

Currency Supply Functions

We noted previously that the major part of the currency supply in the United States consists of Federal Reserve notes. What are Federal Reserve notes and how do they get into circulation?

A Federal Reserve note is just what the name implies. It is a certificate of indebtedness of the issuing Federal Reserve bank to the bearer of the note, a kind of promissory note payable to the bearer instead of to a specific person. It is payable in whatever form of money the bearer desires. He can convert it into demand deposits or coins of any kind.

The amount of Federal Reserve notes in circulation depends upon the proportion of the total money supply that the general public desires to hold in that form. Suppose, for example, that an individual goes to his bank to cash a check for $1000 and that the bank has no Federal Reserve

MEMBER BANKS

BALANCE SHEET

Reserves	$100,000	Deposits	$500,000
	−$ 1,000		− $ 1,000
L & I	$400,000		

FRB

BALANCE SHEET

Currency	$100,000	Deposits	
		Member bank	$100,000
			− $ 1,000
		Federal	
		Reserve notes	+ $ 1,000

Figure 23–7
How Federal Reserve notes are put into circulation.

notes—or, as is more likely, the withdrawal will pull the amount that it holds in its vaults below the amount that it desires to hold. As Figure 23–7 shows, the member bank goes to the FRB and exchanges $1000 of its deposits there for Federal Reserve notes. Member-bank deposits at the FRB are decreased by $1000. The FRB can either turn over to the member bank $1000 in Federal Reserve notes that it is holding idle in its currency asset account or it can print $1000 in new Federal Reserve notes, turning these over to the member bank. If the FRB follows the latter course, a $1000 liability account, *Federal Reserve Notes,* is created. The member bank turns the $1000 in notes over to its customer, reducing his account by $1000 and its reserves by the same amount. (Can you construct an example illustrating the opposite of this process—the retirement of Federal Reserve notes?) If the banking system were fully loaned out, that is, if there were no excess reserves in the system before the process was started, a multiple contraction of deposits would be generated because the conversion of reserves to Federal Reserve notes results in a deficiency in member-bank reserves.

GOLD IN THE MONETARY SYSTEM

When the U.S. government in March 1968 removed a long-standing requirement of the Federal Reserve Act that Federal Reserve banks maintain a 25 percent gold certificate reserve against the total of Federal Reserve notes that they had issued, it cut the last attachment of the U.S. money supply to gold.[2] However, the attachments were weak prior to the government's action. A before and after look will help us assess what role, if any, gold has played in our monetary system in recent years.

The Old System

Prior to March 1968 the United States was on what might be called a modified gold standard. The price of gold was fixed by the government at $35 an ounce and it stood ready to buy or sell to foreign countries or to industrial users of gold at that price. Gold had not been circulated as money since 1933—in fact, private parties in the United States were not permitted to hold gold except for industrial uses and licenses were re-

---

[2] This move was one part of the government's response to a developing shortage of gold for monetary uses. Since 1950, the United States has been losing gold to other countries to pay for yearly excesses of what we owe them over what they owe us. The international aspects of the gold crisis of 1968 will be considered in Chapter 31.

quired for these users. Gold producers were required to sell their outputs to the government at the fixed price. However, Federal Reserve banks were required by law to maintain a 25 percent gold certificate reserve against their Federal Reserve notes outstanding. A similar reserve for their deposits had also been required but was eliminated in March 1965.

Gold certificates came into the hands of the FRB via the U.S. Treasury. Suppose, for example, that a gold-mining company sells $100,000 worth of gold to the Treasury. The Treasury writes a check on its FRB account for $100,000 and the mining company deposits the check in its member-bank account. Deposits and reserves of member banks are increased by $100,000. On the FRB balance sheet Treasury deposits are decreased by $100,000 and member-bank deposits at the FRB are increased by the same amount. All of these changes are illustrated by transaction (1) in Figure 23–8. The Treasury stores the gold in its warehouse and prints $100,000 worth of gold certificates, or receipts for the gold. These are deposited at the FRB, increasing the latter's *Gold Certificate* asset account and replenishing Treasury deposits by $100,000, as illustrated by transaction (2) in Figure 23–8. The net result of the entire set of events is a $100,000 increase in member-bank reserves and deposits, along with a $100,000 increase in the gold certificate reserves of the FRB.

Under these circumstances it looks as though a purchase of gold by the Treasury will increase total demand deposits and that gold sales will

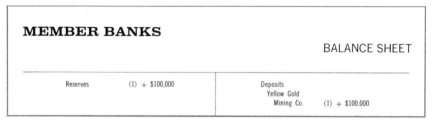

FRB

BALANCE SHEET

Currency	$200,000	Deposits	
Gold certificates	(2) + $100,000	Member banks	$100,000
			(1) + $100,000
		U.S. Treasury	$100,000
			(1) − $100,000
			(2) + $100,000

MEMBER BANKS

BALANCE SHEET

Reserves	(1) + $100,000	Deposits	
		Yellow Gold	
		Mining Co.	(1) + $100,000

Figure 23–8
The effects of a domestic sale of gold to the government.

reduce them. If the FRB were to take no action to counteract the effects of gold sales and purchases, these would indeed affect the money supply and the value of the dollar. But by using its powers to control the total volume of demand deposits in the banking system, the FRB could and did offset the effects of gold movements into and out of the U.S. Treasury. So, in fact, gold had no real influence on the value of money.

The Present System

Under the new rules, not only has the gold certificate reserve requirement for Federal Reserve banks been eliminated but the Treasury no longer freely buys and sells gold at $35 an ounce. As a matter of fact, it will not buy from gold producers and other private parties at all, nor will it sell to industrial users. It will buy from and sell to other governments, only, at $35 an ounce, and these must be governments that agree not to deal in private gold markets. Gold producers, industrial users, and other private parties now operate outside this official government market, and in their private markets the price of gold is free to move wherever it will in response to demands for and supplies of gold.

The new rules have no significant direct implications for the money supply in the United States and for the value of the dollar. Federal Reserve authorities have not been constrained by the gold certificate reserve requirement. It has never prevented them from exercising whatever control over the volume of demand deposits and, consequently, over the money supply that they deemed appropriate. Neither are they constrained by the new rules. One point of minor importance might be mentioned. Since the Treasury no longer buys gold from private producers or sells to industrial users, it is not now necessary for Federal Reserve authorities to offset the minor effects of such purchases and sales on the money supply.

INSTRUMENTS OF CONTROL

Federal Reserve authorities have three major instruments available for controlling the volume of demand deposits: (1) changes in the required reserve ratio of member banks; (2) changes in the discount rate; and (3) open-market operations. A supplementary tool is control of stock market margin requirements for the special purpose of attempting to avoid excess speculation in the stock market.

The three major tools go to the heart of the money-creating and destroying capabilities of banks operating on fractional reserves. They either change the *minimum reserve ratio* that member banks must hold or they change the *quantity of reserves* available to the banking system. Changes in either of these lead to changes in the permissible level of bank lending and to consequent changes in the volume of demand deposits in the system. Use of the tools to contract or to restrict the expansion of demand deposits is known as a *tight money policy*. When they are used to encourage expansion of demand deposits an *easy money policy* is said to be in effect.

Changes in the Required Reserve Ratio

The Banking Act of 1935 provides that the Board of Governors of the Federal Reserve System at its discretion can set and change within limits the minimum reserve ratios that member banks of the system must maintain. Member banks are classified in two categories for this purpose, reserve-city banks and country banks, the basis of the classification being the size of the city in which the banks are located. *Reserve-city banks* include all banks in medium-sized and large metropolitan areas designated by the Federal Reserve Board as reserve cities, while *country banks* are all other banks. For each classification the limits within which the minimum reserve ratio can be adjusted are shown in Table 23–1. But in examining the use of reserve ratio variation it will be more convenient to disregard the above classification and to work with reserve ratios that are multiples of five. This will in no way affect the validity of the analysis and it will greatly simplify the arithmetic.

Suppose now that member banks are initially in the position shown in Figure 23–9, with reserves of $100,000, loans and investments of $400,000, and total deposits of $500,000. Suppose that the limits within which the minimum reserve ratio can be varied by the Board are from 10 to 25 percent and that the present ratio is 20 percent. As long as reserves remain

TABLE 23–1
Reserve Requirements of Member Banks

	RESERVE-CITY BANKS (PERCENT)	COUNTRY BANKS (PERCENT)
Maximum	22	14
Minimum	10	7

SOURCE: *Federal Reserve Bulletin*, September 1968, p. A-10.

MEMBER BANKS

BALANCE SHEET

Reserves	$100,000	Deposits	$500,000
L & I	$400,000		− $100,000
	− $100,000		

REQUIRED RESERVE RATIO
Initial 20%
Raised to 25%

Figure 23-9
Effects on demand deposits of an increase in the required-reserve ratio.

at $100,000, member banks have created as much money as they are capable of creating.

To effect a tight money policy using this instrument by itself, the Board can raise the required reserve ratio as high as 25 percent. If it does this the $100,000 of member-bank reserves will no longer support $500,000 in deposits; only $400,000 in deposits can be supported. Banks must let old loans be paid off faster than new loans are made until a net amount of $100,000 in old loans has been liquidated. This will have the effect of reducing deposits by the same amount, as is indicated in Figure 23–9.

An easy money policy via reserve ratio changes is put into effect by the Board through decreases in the minimum reserve ratio requirement. In Figure 23–10 we start from the same initial position as before, with a designated reserve ratio of 20 percent, $100,000 in reserves, $400,000 in loans and investments, and $500,000 in demand deposits. If the required reserve ratio were now reduced to 10 percent, reserves required to support $500,000 in deposits would be only $50,000, leaving $50,000 as excess reserves.

MEMBER BANKS

BALANCE SHEET

Reserves	$100,000	Deposits	$500,000
L & I	$400,000		+ $500,000
	+ $500,000		

REQUIRED RESERVE RATIO
Initial 20%
Reduced to 10%

Figure 23-10
Effects on demand deposits of a decrease in the required-reserve ratio.

Using the formula developed in the last chapter, we find that excess reserves of $50,000 will permit an expansion in loans and investments and in demand deposits of $500,000—that is, $50,000 multiplied by the reciprocal of 10 percent. Thus total reserves of $100,000 will support $1,000,000 in demand deposits: cutting the reserve ratio in half doubles the potential demand deposit expansion.

This tool of control, along with those yet to be discussed, contains a fundamental weakness with respect to an easy money policy. When the Board decreases the required reserve ratio member banks are under no obligation to increase their loans and investments and their deposits. When the required reserve ratio for member banks is reduced, reserves may simply be shifted from required reserves to excess reserves with no increase in the money supply. The required reserve ratio is a legal minimum below which member banks cannot go. However, there is no legal maximum. Member banks can, if they so desire, let their reserve ratios stand at 100 percent.

Changes in the Discount Rate

The Federal Reserve Act provides that *discount rates,* or interest charged member banks when they borrow from Federal Reserve banks, are to be set by the individual Federal Reserve banks for the member banks in their districts with the approval of the Board of Governors of the System. This makes it appear that the initiative for any changes in the discount rate rests with the 12 Federal Reserve banks. But appearances are not altogether reliable; the Board of Governors can and does exercise influence over individual Federal Reserve banks in this matter and, from an operational standpoint, is in control of the discount rate.

Some part of member-bank reserves consist of reserves borrowed from Federal Reserve banks. As some member banks that have borrowed in the past repay their loans other member banks are in the process of securing new ones; thus we can expect that there will always be some fraction of member-bank reserves that are obtained in this way. For example, Figure 23–11 shows member banks initially with reserves of $100,000, loans and investments of $450,000, deposits of $500,000, and borrowings from the Reserve bank of $50,000. Of the $100,000 in member-bank reserves, $50,000 was obtained by the borrowing. The minimum reserve ratio is assumed to be 20 percent and will remain so throughout the analysis. The discount rate is assumed to be 4 percent initially.

Suppose now that discount rate changes are used to put a tight money policy into effect. An increase in the discount rate to 5 percent makes borrowing more costly to member banks and, presumably, induces them to contract the average amount of their borrowing. If it induces them to reduce their level of borrowing by $10,000, then $10,000 of member-bank deposits at the FRB are used to pay off $10,000 in the latter's discounts and advances. On the balance sheet of member banks borrowings are reduced by $10,000 and so are member-bank reserves, since the decrease in member-bank deposits at the FRB is a decrease in member-bank reserves. Member banks now have only $90,000 in reserves supporting $500,000 in deposits. The reserve deficiency of $10,000 calls for a $50,000 contraction in member-bank loans and investments and in deposits, thus putting the tight money policy into operation.

For an easy money policy the FRB lowers the discount rate. Member-bank borrowing from the Federal Reserve becomes less costly, presumably bringing about an increase in the average level of such borrowing. An increase in member-bank borrowing means an increase in member-bank deposits at the Reserve bank, and this in turn means an increase in member-bank reserves. Excess reserves acquired in this way permit an increase in member-bank deposits (via an increase in loans and investments) equal to the increase in reserves multiplied by the reciprocal of the reserve ratio.

Changes in the discount rate have not proved to be the most powerful tool available to the FRB for controlling the volume of demand deposits. Traditionally, member banks have been reluctant to borrow except to meet temporary reserve deficiencies, and once borrowing has occurred

MEMBER BANKS

BALANCE SHEET

Reserves	$100,000	Deposits	$500,000
	− $ 10,000		− $ 50,000
L & I	$450,000	Borrowings	$ 50,000
	− $ 50,000		− $ 10,000

FRB

BALANCE SHEET

Reserves	$50,000	Deposits	
		Member banks	$100,000
Discounts and advances	$50,000		− $ 10,000
	− $10,000		

Figure 23–11
Effects on demand deposits of an increase in the discount rate.

there is a strong tendency on the part of member banks to repay promptly. Consequently, although changes in the discount rate may have some impact on member-bank borrowing, the effect has not been a major one.

Open-Market Operations

Open-market operations represent the FRB's most important means of controlling the volume of demand deposits in the economy. The term refers to the purchase and sale of marketable government bonds and Treasury bills by the FRB as directed by the Open Market Committee. Marketable bonds and Treasury bills, representing the bulk of the U.S. government debt of approximately $360 billion, are bought and sold in securities markets among institutions and individuals at whatever prices they will bring, much in the same manner as are corporation bonds. If persons or institutions wish to sell their holdings of government securities, they can sell them for whatever they (or their brokers) can get someone to pay. The existence of this large supply of government securities, issued and originally sold by the Treasury at past dates, makes open-market operations possible.

Both the FRB and member banks at any given time hold government securities as a part of their assets. In the FRB balance sheet of Figure 23–12 it is assumed that the FRB holds $200,000 worth of government securities initially. Member banks have invested $200,000 in government securities also, and in this and subsequent diagrams we break government securities away from the loans and investments account, showing each category of assets separately. Previously we have included member-bank holdings of government securities as a part of their loans and investments accounts.

If Federal Reserve authorities want to implement a tight money policy, the Open Market Committee directs the FRB to engage in *open-market sales* of government securities.[3] The impact of sales amounting to $10,000 are recorded in Figure 23–12. We assume that the required reserve ratio is 20 percent. The government securities asset account of member banks is increased by $10,000. Member banks pay for the securities by writing checks on their accounts at the FRB, thus decreasing their deposits at the latter along with their reserves by $10,000. The government secu-

---

[3] To simplify the analysis we shall assume that open-market transactions of the FRB are made with member banks only; however, open-market sales are in fact made to the public, *including member banks,* and open-market purchases are made from the public, *including member banks.* When transactions are made with the nonbank public the end results are approximately the same as they would be had they been made with member banks, except that the routes for getting to those results are more devious.

MEMBER BANKS

BALANCE SHEET

Reserves	$100,000	Deposits	$500,000
	− $ 10,000		− $ 50,000
L & I	$200,000		
	− $ 50,000		
Government securities	$200,000		
	+$ 10,000		

FRB

BALANCE SHEET

Reserves	$100,000	Deposits Member banks	$100,000
			− $ 10,000
Government securities	$200,000	Government	$200,000
	− $ 10,000		

Figure 23–12
Effects on demand deposits of open-market sales of government securities.

rities account of the FRB is decreased by $10,000. The purchase leaves member banks with a reserve deficiency of $10,000; consequently, in order to re-establish a reserve ratio of 20 percent, member banks must reduce the volume of their loans outstanding and their demand deposits by $50,000. *Thus open-market sales lead to a contraction of the money supply that is a multiple of the amount of the sales.*

An easy money policy is implemented through *open-market purchases* of government securities by the FRB, as illustrated in Figure 23–13. Again let the required reserve ratio be 20 percent and the initial positions of member banks and the FRB be represented by the figures without plus and minus signs. A $10,000 purchase of government securities from member banks by the FRB decreases the member-banks' government securities account and increases that of the FRB by that amount. The latter pays for the bonds by increasing member-bank deposits by $10,000. This, of course, increases member-bank reserves by $10,000 and permits a $50,000 increase in member-bank loans and deposits. *Open-market purchases make possible an increase in the money supply that is a multiple of the amount of purchases.*

How can the Federal Reserve induce member banks to buy or sell government securities at the appropriate time? Member banks typically desire to maintain some sort of balance between earning assets that produce higher income yields but that may be somewhat more risky and those that produce lower yields but are more secure. Loans to private in-

MEMBER BANKS

BALANCE SHEET

Reserves	$100,000	Deposits	$500,000
	+ $ 10,000		+ $ 50,000
L & I	$200,000		
	+ $ 50,000		
Government			
securities	$200,000		
	− $ 10,000		

FRB

BALANCE SHEET

Reserves	$100,000	Deposits	
		Member banks	$100,000
Government			+ $ 10,000
securities	$100,000	Government	$100,000
	+ $ 10,000		

Figure 23–13
Effects on demand of open-market purchases of government securities.

dividuals illustrate the first type and holdings of government bonds or other government securities the latter. An increase in the yield on government securities relative to that on commercial loans will change the relative attractiveness of the two types of assets, inducing banks to make adjustments in favor of larger amounts of government securities. The process also works in reverse.

The FRB will increase the yield obtainable on the bonds it offers for sale in order to induce member banks to purchase them. This is accomplished by a reduction in the asking price for the bonds. Suppose that a bond with a face value of $100 carries an interest rate of 4 percent, that is, it pays interest of $4 per year, and it matures in one more year. As this bond is bought and sold, its market price may fluctuate, but it pays interest of $4 per year and at the end of one more year the government will redeem it at its face value of $100. If government bonds now owned by member banks are currently yielding 4 percent on what the banks have invested in them, and if the FRB offers $100 face value bonds like the one described above at $99 each, purchases of such bonds will yield member banks 5.05 percent on their investment.[4] This is obviously

---

[4] Investment in the bond yields interest of $4 plus appreciation of $1 in the price of the bond for a total of $5. The $5 yield divided by the $99 investment in the bond is the rate of return on the investment; that is, 5.05 percent.

an attractive offer and will induce member banks to increase their holdings of government securities.

Member banks can be induced to sell government securities to the Federal Reserve by the opposite technique. The Federal Reserve will increase its offering price for the bonds until it becomes attractive enough for member banks to sell. By appropriate price manipulations the Federal Reserve can get member banks either to buy or sell whatever quantities of government securities are deemed desirable.

It looks as though open-market operations are a losing proposition for the FRB, since it appears to buy at high prices and sell at low prices. Although this may be the case, it does not necessarily happen in precisely this way. To sell bonds, the FRB needs only to sell below the current market price, and this says nothing about the prices at which the bonds were originally acquired. They may have been acquired originally for less. The same reasoning applies to purchases. But even if the Federal Reserve were to lose on open-market transactions, this would be of no consequence. Control over the money supply is its most important objective. Profit-making is secondary.

Open-market operations seem to be the most effective or the most important of the three instruments of control. The FRB uses it as the leading or primary means of control, coordinating it with changes in the discount rate and, in the long run, changes in required reserve ratios. One of the strong points of open-market operations is that it brings about definite changes in member-bank reserves and, if carried far enough, can bring about increases or decreases of almost any desired magnitude.[5] Fine adjustments or changes in the amount of member-bank reserves can be easily and quickly induced through changes in the selling or purchase prices of government securities. A second point in its favor is that it is not disruptive of member-bank expectations—they are not forced or coerced by Federal Reserve authorities to do anything. The FRB *makes it attractive* for member banks to buy or sell government securities, whichever is desirable, on a *voluntary* basis.[6]

Control of Margin Requirements

An additional control function exercised by the Board of Governors of the Federal Reserve System is the *regulation of margin requirements* for

[5] The limiting factor here is the amounts of government securities held by the FRB available to be sold. Since open-market operations have come to the foreground as an instrument of control this limit has never been approached in practice.

[6] Compare this with the legal *compulsion* to comply with an increase in reserve ratio requirements.

purchases of securities on the stock exchanges. This authority, established by the Securities Exchange Act of 1934, permits the Board of Governors to limit the amount of funds that can be borrowed for the purpose of buying stocks, bonds, or other securities. For example, if margin requirements are set at 70 percent, brokers and others who lend to securities purchasers are permitted to lend only 30 percent of the value of a stock transaction and the purchaser must put up the other 70 percent. This instrument of control is an outgrowth of the 1929 stock market crash, believed by many to have been caused by excessive speculation. The intent is to limit such speculation through the control of borrowing for stock purchase purposes.

MONETARY POLICY FOR STABILITY

The tools of monetary control should be used in a coordinated way to combat economic fluctuations. Federal Reserve activities of this kind are referred to as *monetary policy.* A tight money policy is appropriate for controlling inflation, while recession and depression call for an easy money policy. But things are not always so simple. Though monetary policy can contribute to economic stability, it is not likely to be sufficient in and of itself to bring about simultaneously full employment, economic growth, and price-level stability. As we shall see later, monetary policy must be coordinated with fiscal policy and other appropriate measures to reach an acceptable measure of success in achieving those goals. But for the present we are concerned primarily with monetary policy.

Combating Inflation

The implementation of a tight money policy to control inflation starts logically with open-market operations. The Federal Reserve can engage in the sale of government securities, thus reducing reserves of member banks. If member banks have excess reserves, open-market sales will reduce them, curtailing the potential ability of the banking system to expand its loans and its deposits. Once all excess reserves have been absorbed, further open-market sales will induce contraction of the money supply.

Concurrently with open-market sales, an increase in the discount rate serves as a second order or back up control measure. Conceivably, member banks as they lose reserves through their purchases of bonds can replenish those reserves by borrowing from the FRB. An increase in the discount rate will reduce their incentive to increase their level of borrowing and will thus reinforce the effectiveness of open-market sales.

Direct action to reduce member-bank excess reserves and to create reserve deficiencies can, of course, be taken via increases in the required reserve ratio, but this tool should be used sparingly. If banks were confronted with frequent changes in the reserve ratio, the effectiveness of the device would soon be lost. It would be necessary for banks to hold adequate reserves to meet the highest anticipated reserve ratio, and this would mean that the level of loans and of deposits would no longer be responsive to (frequent) changes in the ratio.

Combating Recession and Depression

The order in which the control instruments should be used to implement an easy money policy during recession and depression are the same as for the tight money policy. The first line of defense is open-market purchases of government securities by the Federal Reserve from member banks to increase the volume of member-bank reserves and to make deposit expansion more attractive to them. Additionally, the discount rate could be lowered and so could the required reserve ratio, but neither of these is likely to be as effective in inducing member banks to increase their lending, or even to halt their contraction of loans and of deposits, as an increase in member-bank reserves via open-market purchases.

Monetary policy aimed at combating recession and depression has certain fundamental weaknesses. The difficulty lies in securing an expansion of loans and of deposits by member banks during a period of recession or depression. Banks are reluctant to lend because of the repayment risks when economic activity is declining. In the interests of safety banks desire to increase their reserve ratios and, given the volume of their reserves, to do so they must contract the volume of their loans outstanding as well as their total deposits. Since the pace of business activity is slowing down, the public has less desire to borrow. Open-market purchases by the FRB offer the greatest possibility of combating these tendencies, but even in this case member banks may simply hold the excess reserves they acquire and do nothing to expand loans and deposits.

The chances of stemming recession by means of monetary policy will be enhanced if it is put to work promptly. The more serious the recession is allowed to become, the greater the barriers to preventing monetary contraction. The sooner the FRB acts, the less opportunity there is for public confidence to be shaken, and the easier it will be to prevent a contraction in loans and deposits and, perhaps, to encourage some expansion.

Recent Monetary Policy in the United States

Our experience with monetary policy as a means of stabilizing the economy is still rather limited. The Federal Reserve Act is now a little over 50 years old, but effective monetary policy has been slow in developing. Immediately after the act was passed World War I brought inflationary pressures that the fledgling system could not resist. On the heels of the war a misguided tight money policy helped to precipitate the recession of 1921–1922. Then through the prosperous 1920s there was little for the Federal Reserve to do. The mild recession of 1924 and 1927 were met appropriately by open-market purchases and by lowered discount rates.

But the FRB either could not or did not stop the Great Depression from getting underway in 1929. It has been frequently criticized for coming in too late with too little action. To be sure, discount rates were lowered and government securities were purchased, so the initial actions were in the right direction. The question arises over the magnitude of the actions taken in the early months of the recession. Various forces, combined with easy money policies, brought about large excess reserve accumulations in the middle 1930s, and the FRB, fearing the inflationary potential of these excess reserves, raised the required reserve ratio in 1937 to the maximum permissible level. A sharp decline in economic activity followed, and in retrospect the action taken appears to have been wrong.

During World War II and its aftermath the Federal Reserve was severely handicapped in pursuing sensible monetary policy. The Treasury was engaged in large-scale borrowing to finance the war. Desiring to maintain a good market for government bonds without increasing the interest rates yielded by them, the Treasury induced the Federal Reserve to agree to engage in open-market purchases of these securities in sufficient quantities to prevent their prices from falling (and their yields from rising). As larger and larger quantities were placed on the market by the Treasury this amounted to an easy money policy throughout the war. After the war the policy was continued at the insistence of the Treasury. The Federal Reserve authorities found themselves unable to do anything about the rapidly mounting inflation, and they became increasingly disturbed by the policy of supporting bond prices. Finally, in 1951, an "accord" was reached, with the Treasury freeing the FRB from the agreement and again placing it in a position to pursue monetary policy directed toward economic stabilization.

On the whole, since the 1951 Accord, monetary policy appears to have contributed to economic stability. On the heels of the Accord came a tight money policy to combat the inflation generated by the Korean War. Then with the 1953–1954 recession a switch was made to an easy money policy via open-market purchases, discount rate cuts, and reductions in the required reserve ratio. The inflationary pressures of 1956 and 1957 were met with a tightening of money—open-market sales and an increase in the discount rate. The recession of 1958 precipitated a reversal to easy money in that year and in 1959. Policy changes, first intended to stimulate and then to restrain economic activity in order to promote stability, have followed these patterns to date.

Though working in the proper direction for economic stability, monetary policy has exhibited certain shortcomings. In the first place, economic fluctuations still have a way of slipping up on us. Economic forecasting techniques seem to be improving, but they are not yet infallible. It is difficult for the Board of Governors to determine precisely when a tight money policy or an easy money policy ought to be inaugurated. Once a recession or an inflation is underway, the proper course of action becomes obvious, but precisely when should it be started and precisely when should it be terminated? Second, monetary policy by itself may not be able to accomplish the job of stabilization. Fiscal policy, to be discussed in the following chapters, may be needed to supplement it.

A third dilemma for those responsible for monetary policy (and for fiscal policy-makers as well) is whether full employment and price stability are compatible objectives. The unemployment rate exceeded 5 percent of the labor force in 1958, 1959, and 1960, and in 1961 it was approaching 7 percent. At the same time, a slight inflation of approximately $1\frac{1}{2}$ percent annually, was occurring in the consumer price index. Can policies designed to increase total spending and thereby to increase employment bring unemployment rates down to acceptable levels without generating an unacceptable rate in inflation? We shall return to this question after we have studied government finance and fiscal policy.

SUMMARY

The banking system of the United States consists of two levels of banks, commercial banks and Federal Reserve banks. Commercial banks are the national banks and state banks with which the general public does its banking business. Federal Reserve banks collectively serve as the central bank of the system. There are 12 of these, one for each of the 12 Federal Reserve districts into which the United States is divided, all under the general control of the seven-member Board of Governors of the Federal Reserve System.

The Federal Reserve System in its role as a central bank carries out five closely related functions. It serves as a bankers' bank, as a clearing house for member commercial banks, as the government's banker, and as a control agency over the demand deposit and the paper currency components of the money supply. Gold certificates issued by the U.S. Treasury and deposited at the FRB serve as reserves for the latter. Although these could and have affected the money supply in the economy, they do not now do so.

In carrying out monetary policy, or controlling the volume of demand deposits in a way intended to promote economic stability, Federal Reserve authorities employ three primary tools. These are changes in the required reserve ratios of member banks, changes in the discount rate, and open-market operations. The latter appear to be the most effective of the three and represent the first line of defense against recession or inflation. Raising or lowering the discount rate is a companion tool to open-market operations. Both devices affect the total volume of demand deposits through their impacts on the quantities of reserves available to member banks. The third instrument, changing the required reserve ratio, should in all probability be used sparingly. The Federal Reserve authorities are also empowered to set margin requirements in order to prevent excessive speculation in the stock market.

Effective use of Federal Reserve monetary policy has been rather limited, dating essentially from the early 1950s. From enactment of the Federal Reserve Act in 1913 to the Accord with the Treasury in 1951, the Federal Reserve was confronted with crisis after crisis while the system was short on experience. First came the inflation of World War I, then came the recession of 1921–1922. Next was the Great Depression of the 1930s, followed by World War II and the bond price-support program. Only in the last 20 years has the U.S. government taken on the full responsibility for providing economic stability. Monetary policy represents one avenue toward this end. Fiscal policy, yet to be studied, represents the other.

EXERCISES AND QUESTIONS FOR DISCUSSION

1. If each of the 12 Federal Reserve banks sets a different discount rate for its district, what do you think would be the net effect on the level of demand deposits in the entire system?
2. Under what circumstances might each of the tools of monetary policy be ineffective?
3. If inflation is occurring, are there ever any arguments that might be made against restrictive monetary policy? Elaborate.
4. Discuss the "proper" use of the reserve ratio, the discount rate, and open-market operations during (a) a recession; (b) an inflation, and (c) an inflation with high unemployment. Consider in your discussion the effects of each policy.
5. Why does the current market price of government securities fluctuate? What is the relevance of this fact to monetary policy?

SELECTED READINGS

Barger, Harold, *Money, Banking, and Public Policy.* Chicago: Rand McNally and Company, 1962, Chap. 9.

Board of Governors of the Federal Reserve System, *The Federal Reserve System,* 5th ed. Washington, D.C., 1963, Chaps. 2, 3, and 9.

Chandler, Lester V., *The Economics of Money and Banking,* 4th ed. New York: Harper & Row, Publishers, Inc., 1964, Section VI.

Smith, Warren L., "The Effects of Monetary Policy on the Major Sectors of the Economy," in *Money and Economic Activity,* 2d ed., Lawrence S. Ritter, ed. Boston: Houghton Mifflin Company, 1961, pp. 178–195.

Government Economic Activities: The Expenditures Side

CHAPTER 24

In his 1960 campaign for the Presidency, Senator John F. Kennedy's major theme was to "get this country moving again." Immediately after he assumed office in 1961 he proposed a "Program for Economic Recovery and Growth" that had been developed by a task force of economists headed by Professor Paul A. Samuelson of the Massachusetts Institute of Technology. Like most of his fellow-countrymen, President Kennedy was concerned about the high unemployment rates that had developed since 1958 and that had been accentuated by the recession of 1960–1961. He proposed to put government tax and expenditure policies to work to stimulate total spending, to increase output, and to reduce unemployment.

The ideas he expressed were not new. Economists have long advocated that governments use tax and expenditure policies—or fiscal policies—in such a way that they promote economic stability and growth.[1] But with the exception of the large-scale (for that time) "pump-priming" expenditures of the Roosevelt Administration in the middle 1930s to speed recovery from the Great Depression, those in control of governmental policy-making have been cool to proposals that taxes and expenditures be deliberately manipulated for this purpose. Both the Kennedy and the Johnson administrations were able in some measure to overcome that coolness and to succeed in using fiscal policy in limited doses for growth and stabilization ends.

---

[1] The brilliant British economist John Maynard Keynes was a leading exponent of this point of view. His classic work, *The General Theory of Employment, Interest and Money* (New York: Harcourt, Brace & World, Inc., 1936), widely heralded as creating a revolution in economic thinking, was instrumental in making it an acceptable part of the general body of economic theory.

In order to understand how fiscal policy operates we need to develop as clear a picture as we can of the economic operations of the various levels of government. In this chapter we shall concentrate on expenditures and in the next on receipts.

RATIONALE OF GOVERNMENT ECONOMIC ACTIVITIES

Almost all of the activities of government have economic aspects. These activities have evolved over time in any given society in response to needs felt either by the general public or by the group in control of the government. In our own society we say that governments should "promote the general welfare." This conveys the very important idea that acting through governments people should be able to obtain certain benefits that they either cannot obtain or can obtain less efficiently as individuals.

In an economic sense governments provide certain of the goods and services that we consume. As a matter of fact, in the United States government-provided goods and services, measured by the government expenditures made to put them in the hands of the public, account for almost 30 percent of GNP. This is the *public sector* of the economy as contrasted with the *private sector*, in which private enterprise produces goods and services. One important issue debated today both in the United States and throughout the world is that of how large, relatively, the public sector of an economy should be. The goods and services provided by government are frequently classified into three categories: (1) those collectively consumed; (2) those individually consumed; and (3) those semicollectively consumed. In addition to producing goods and services, governments also act to transfer purchasing power among individuals and families. A discussion of the three classifications of goods and of *transfer* expenditures will not resolve the debate, but it should clarify some of the issues involved in it.

Collectively Consumed Goods and Services

One service provided by all national governments to their citizens is national defense. How much is it worth to you as an individual? If you were asked to contribute to national defense on a yearly volunteer basis, what would your contribution be? Is there any way of determining for each individual in the economy the value of national defense to him? Another government service provided for the general public is space exploration—or have you ever thought of this activity as being a service to the public? The new technological knowledge gained from the development of space hardware and the knowledge gained from space exploration are expected to benefit the general public. But how valuable is the yearly effort to you personally?

Characteristics

The prime characteristic of *collectively consumed goods* is that their benefits are not divisible among the private economic units that consume them. A good or service provided for a group of consumers is collectively consumed if it is not possible to exclude one of the group from receiving its benefits. Can the protection afforded U.S. citizens by the armed forces be denied you? Can anyone be arbitrarily denied the benefits of space exploration? This principle of nonexclusion is brought home even more effectively by the classic example of the Bahamian fishermen who joined together and built a lighthouse on a coral reef where many had been shipwrecked. Once the lighthouse was in operation, anyone sailing those waters had access to its services—there was no way of restricting its light to those who planned it and built it.

It is possible for collectively consumed goods and services to be provided by private groups operating on a voluntary basis, but such groups are limited in an important way. A vigilante group organized to hunt down and hang all the cattle rustlers in Oklahoma provides benefits for all the cattlemen in the state. But suppose that one cattleman decides that he will not pay his share of the costs. Can he be denied the benefits that arise from an absence of cattle rustlers? Or suppose that a gigantic private concern were to furnish national defense with a mercenary army; could it deny you protection if you fail to pay your share of the cost? The problem encountered by private businesses in producing collectively consumed goods is that they face a "free rider" problem. It cannot coerce individuals into paying for them if those individuals do not wish to do so.

The Major Examples

Governmental units with their powers of coercion, are in a unique position to provide collective goods and services; it can force everyone in the group to pay a share of the costs. People can be "free riders" only by evading taxes, a practice that can lead to unsettling if not disastrous results for those who attempt it. The major government services that fit squarely ino this category are national defense, the whole system of law and order, and regulatory services of various kinds.

From the standpoint of costs, national defense (or its counterpart, armed aggression) is the most important collectively consumed item in most countries of the world. Historically, the provision of this service was a primary reason why people banded together in the first place. In primitive societies tribes came into being because people thought they could protect themselves—or prey on others—more effectively as a group than they could as individuals. And so it has been down through the ages.

As the individuals of a society engage in their daily activities they inevitably encroach upon the rights and privileges of others, giving rise to a desire on the part of most people for a system of law and order. Much of this encroachment is intentional as some people attempt to take advantage of others or to advance their own well-being at the expense of others. Robbery and murder—or, more generally, force and fraud—are cases in point. Other encroachments are accidental, as, for example, when street or highway traffic becomes congested enough to interfere with its free flow. In protecting themselves from both types of encroachments people have found that governments with their coercive powers are particularly well suited to provide the services of law and order. Laws are established against the unrestricted use of force and fraud by individuals. They are also established to provide for an orderly flow of traffic and for other purposes in which it is thought that the common interest is served. These laws provide the fabric of the social order and in most countries they are enforced by the police and by the courts. Their benefits are available to all whether or not all are willing voluntarily to contribute to their support.

As we have noted already, an economic system left to its own devices is likely to perform less than perfectly, giving rise to the possibility that certain regulatory services will be in the interests of the general public. Among the more obvious flaws of an unregulated free enterprise economic system are (1) the tendency for economic units to monopolize and (2) the tendency for economic fluctuations to occur. In an attempt to minimize the damage wrought by these, people—ordinarily through government—provide themselves with regulatory services, the benefits of which are available to all; for example, the government attempts to curtail monopoly by means of antitrust laws. With such agencies as the Interstate Commerce Commission, the Civil Aeronautics Board, the Federal Communications Commission, and state corporation commissions, governmental units regulate the operations of so-called natural monopolies, presumably in the public interest. By means of the monetary policies discussed previously and the fiscal measures now under consideration, the federal government attempts to promote economic stability.

In a very fundamental sense the system of law and order and the regulatory activities engaged in by government can be viewed as the rules of a game. Without a set of rules some mayhem is likely to result. The application of judiciously selected laws and regulations may increase the efficiency with which resources devoted to the economic game are used. But, as in any game, it is possible to make the rules so complex and so burdensome that they hinder rather than facilitate the attainment of the desired objectives.

Individually Consumed Goods and Services

Goods and services provided by governments are by no means confined to those that are collectively consumed. Governments at one time or another or in one place or another have actively operated almost every type of business, and all present-day governments provide a host of goods and services that are consumed individually. An *individually consumed good or service* is one that can be divided among consumers and the benefit received by each can be separated out and measured. Most goods and services produced in the private sector of the economy are of this nature. For example, hamburger consumption benefits consumers as individuals only. Nonconsumers are excluded from sharing in this particular gastronomical delight.

We can make a sizable list of individually consumed goods and services produced by governmental units. Postal services are a clear-cut example, as are transit services, electrical services, and garbage collection services owned and operated by municipalities. By and large, in the United States government activity in this area is confined to industries ordinarily thought of as public utilities—industries thought to be natural monopolies—and public or government ownership and operation of them is an alternative to private ownership and operation, subject to government regulation. However, it is by no means necessary that governments confine their activities as producers of individually consumed goods to public utility or natural-monopoly industries. In any society inclined toward socialism the list will extend well beyond these. Steel production, oil production, and hotel services in many countries provide examples, and in the Soviet Union the list includes almost all industries in the economy.

Semicollectively Consumed Goods and Services

Many goods and services provided consumers through governmental units lie somewhere between the purely collective and the purely individual categories, and we refer to these as being *semicollectively consumed.* Consider the nation's highway network. Certainly persons benefit individually from their use of the system. But what of the little old lady living in the middle of the city who owns no automobile and who never ventures beyond the neighborhood shopping center? Is the highway system of any significance to her? As a matter of fact, she has access to many things at the shopping center that would be denied her if the highway system did not exist.

The little old lady is said to receive *social* or *spill-over* benefits from the highway system. These are benefits that accrue to other persons over and above the direct benefits received by those who consume the product or use the service individually. The satisfaction levels of the former are influenced by the consumption levels of the good or service by the latter.

Another important example of a semicollective service produced by governmental units is education. The prime beneficiary of this service is the individual who goes through the prescribed curricula and who receives the appropriate diploma. The greater part of the benefits redound separately to individuals. Yet, there are social benefits for the entire society. An educated populace is essential for the existence of a smooth-working political democracy; crime rates are generally lowest where educational levels are highest; an educated labor force is a more productive work force; and the list can be extended. To those who doubt the social benefits of education, a visit to those parts of the world where literacy rates are below the 50–60 percent level would prove enlightening.

Semicollectively produced goods and services are not provided exclusively by government. Many are produced privately. The railroads and the airlines are privately owned and operated and so are the trucking companies that move goods over the highways. Yet all of these provide social benefits. Are there any significant differences between the benefits derived from government-owned and operated highways and those from privately owned and operated railroads to the little old lady in the middle of the city?

THE PUBLIC VERSUS THE PRIVATE SECTOR

What part of GNP should be produced by the public sector and what part by the private sector of the economy? We are not likely to resolve this question here, but suppose we look at some of the implications of the foregoing classification of goods for it.

The case for governmental units to engage in production is strongest for collectively consumed goods and services. Many of these would not be produced at all if they were not produced by government, even though their value to society as a whole may exceed their costs. A private producer faces the "free rider" problem and may lack the coercive power to extract payments from the public sufficient to cover costs of production. The government, on the other hand, can coerce all who stand to gain into paying taxes. In fact, through its coercive powers, the government is in a position to force taxpayers to pay for services that are worth less to them than they cost.

Individually consumed goods and services are at the other end of the spectrum. Whether or not these should be produced by the government or by private producers depends upon (1) the comparative efficiency of the two alternatives, and (2) the value judgments of the general public. These determinants are difficult to separate in fact. Those whose value judgments favor leaving the bulk of productive activity to the private sector of the economy argue that this sector utilizes resources more efficiently than the public sector. Those with socialistic value judgments argue that the private sector tends to waste resources and that through government ownership and operation of production facilities a greater measure of efficiency is achieved. If we could actually run tests and determine which sector does a given job with the greater efficiency, the allocation of individually consumed items to the public sector or to the private sector would be much easier. But no one has been able to establish measures of comparative efficiencies to everyone's satisfaction, and so the classic debate continues. In the United States our value judgments have favored leaving the production of most individually consumed goods and services to the private sector. In the Soviet Union value judgments are such that most goods and services are produced in the public sector.

In an economy oriented toward free enterprise, there is much controversy over whether goods and services semicollectively consumed should be produced by the private sector or by the public sector. The greater the social benefits yielded by an economic activity, the better the case that can be made for the socialization of it. But again, the real problem is that of measuring the social benefits. Some activities—primary and secondary education, for example—we have chosen to socialize; but it is by no means clear that this choice is the best among the possible alternatives.

The general economic principle for determining whether specific goods or services should be produced by the government—or the extent to which they should be produced by the government—is easy enough to state but difficult to use as an operating rule. Resources used by the government to provide goods and services have alternative uses in the private sector of the economy. Thus the government should use resources to provide goods and services only to the extent that at the margin the resources will contribute more to consumer well-being than they would if they were used by the private sector. The difficulty lies in determining the value to consumers of the resources used by the government.

Transfer Expenditures

Not all government economic activities and expenditures create goods and services consumed by the citizenry; that is, governments may make payments to persons who render or provide no goods or services in return. Welfare expenditures fall into this category, as do interest payments on government debt. Some individuals either cannot or will not accumulate sufficient stocks of resources to provide income during such periods of economic adversity as old age, mental and physical incapacity, sickness, unemployment, and the like. In many cases the fault is thought to lie with society as a whole rather than with the individual, but whether or not this is so, all advanced nations call on those who are more affluent to help those who are needy. Governments simply transfer purchasing power from taxpayers to those to whom payments are made. Interest payments on government debt, similarly, represent transfers of purchasing power from taxpayers to bond-holders (interest receivers). Through *transfer expenditures* of this kind consumer demand for privately produced goods and services may be redirected—say away from mink coats toward shoes; however, there is no transfer of production processes from the private to the government sector of the economy.

EXPENDITURES OF THE FEDERAL GOVERNMENT BY FUNCTION

We turn now to the public sector of the economy in order to get some feel for the vast array of economic activities in which our government is involved. The expenditures of the federal government are examined in this section. The expenditure format used in Table 24–1 is that employed by the President in his yearly budget proposals to the Congress. The

TABLE 24–1
Federal Expenditures by Function, 1967, 1968[2], 1969[2]
(billions of dollars)[1]

FUNCTION	1967	1968	1969
National defense	70.1	76.5	79.8
Health, labor, and welfare	40.1	46.4	51.4
Interest	12.5	13.5	14.4
Commerce and transportation	7.4	7.9	8.1
Veterans' benefits and services	6.9	7.2	7.3
Space research and technology	5.4	4.8	4.6
International affairs and finance	4.6	5.0	5.1
Agriculture and agricultural resources	4.4	5.3	5.6
Natural resources	2.1	2.4	2.5
Education	4.0	4.5	4.7
General government	2.5	2.6	2.8
Housing and community development	2.3	4.0	2.8
Adjustments	−4.0	−4.5	−3.1
Total	158.4	175.6	186.1

[1] Columns may not total due to rounding
[2] Estimated
SOURCE: *Budget of the United States Government: 1969* (Washington, D.C.: Government Printing Office, 1968), p. 52.

amounts of the proposed expenditures are intended to show as accurately as possible all cash payments made to the public by the government and all cash receipts of the government from the public.[2]

National Defense

It should come as no surprise that military expenditures[3] account for almost 45 percent of total estimated expenditures for fiscal 1969. Neither should it be a surprise that these expenditures increased rapidly with the escalation of the war in Vietnam. A large part of the total was for men and materiel for the current operations of the Army, the Air Force, the Navy, and the Marine Corps. Sizable chunks went for research and development of equipment and weapons systems. Other important military expenditures were for military construction and for the program of the Atomic Energy Commission. Lesser amounts were earmarked for military assistance to friendly countries, family housing for military personnel, civil defense, operation of the Selective Service System, and a host of administrative items.

Health, Welfare, and Labor

Expenditures for health, welfare, and labor—most of them of a transfer rather than of a direct income-creating nature—made up the second largest group of federal government expenditures. Included here is the bulk of the Johnson Administration's controversial Great Society program, reflected by the dramatic increase in the total expenditures from $33.2 billion in fiscal 1966 to an estimated $51.4 billion in fiscal 1969. Of this latter figure, approximately $33.8 billion is from Social Security trust funds in their various forms; that is, old age, survivors, and disability benefits. Still another $7.9 billion is in the form of payments for Medicare and Medicaid. These have exhibited a sharp increase over the three-

[2] A "new unified comprehensive" budget presentation was utilized for the first time for 1967 actual expenditure. Those interested in comparing it with the older "administrative budget" and "consolidated case budget" see *The Budget of the United States Government: 1969* (Washington, D.C., 1967), pp. 464–472.

[3] Since collectively consumed goods and services provided the public by governments are not sold to the public through markets, there is no objective way of determining their total value to the public. The standard procedure is to value them at what they cost. Thus national defense services are assumed to be worth what they cost—total military expenditures.

year period which will continue for many years to come. Also, apart from trust fund expenditures, direct expenditures of over $3 billion dollars were for public assistance to the indigent, vocational rehabilitation, and special food programs for school children and for the needy.

In addition to Social Security programs, other expenditures of considerably smaller amounts were for health services, labor and man-power training, economic opportunity programs, and other welfare services. Health expenditures were for health research, training for the health professions, hospital construction, attacks on such health hazards as air and water pollution and impure foods and drugs, maternal and child health care of indigents, and mental health programs. Labor and man-power expenditures were largely aimed at upgrading worker skills, particularly those of the economically disadvantaged, along with employment services for placement purposes. Economic opportunity programs, arising from the Economic Opportunity Act of 1964, included community action activities to fight poverty, the Job Corps to provide remedial education and vocational training for teenagers, work-training programs for both youth and adults, and support of VISTA volunteers.

Interest

How many times have you heard it said that the interest cost of the federal debt is a great burden on the economy? You will recall that the primary reason for the Federal Reserve policy of supporting the price of government securities from the end of World War II until the Accord with the Treasury in 1951 was to hold down interest payments on the debt.[4] In dollar terms this is the third largest category of federal expenditures. Like Social Security expenditures, these are transfer payments; new income does not come into being at the time they are made. Rather, dollars of purchasing power are transferred from taxpayers to bondholders. (What would be the impact of interest payments on the federal debt if taxes were levied on the general public in exactly the same distributive pattern as that of the interest payments made to the public?) Almost one fifth of the total yearly interest paid on the federal debt goes to government trust funds and to government agencies that have invested funds in government securities. This $3 billion in interest is an intergovernmental transfer of funds rather than a cash payment to the public.

[4] See p. 442.

Commerce and Transportation

The fourth-ranking commerce and transportation classification brings together a heterogeneous collection of expenditures. A number of them relate to the conduct of business. Activities that once centered around the issuance of patents have now become "promotion of technology." The regulatory activities of the Interstate Commerce Commission, the Federal Communications Commission, and the Civil Aeronautics Board are supposed to promote business activity and make it conform to the public interest. The financial services of the Small Business Administration are included in this expenditure group, as are the services of the Bureau of Standards and the Bureau of the Census. The expenditures here also include federal efforts to further area and regional development. In the transportation area are the services of the Federal Aviation Agency, the Coast Guard, the Alaska Railroad, and the Interoceanic Canal Commission. Further, the federal contributions to the Interstate Highway System and the Maritime Administration services to ocean shipping fall under this general expenditure classification. The expenditures of the Environmental Sciences Services Administration, that is, the Weather Bureau and related activities, are also included. The operation of postal services represent about one fifth of the total expenditures in this category.

Veterans Benefits and Services

Expenditures for veterans' benefits and services are estimated at almost the same level as those for commerce and transportation for fiscal 1969. A part of these are in the form of transfer expenditures, with the rest consisting of services to veterans and their families. The largest single item is service-connected death and disability compensation payments and pensions, separate and apart from national service life insurance payments. This item is followed closely by pensions for nonservice-connected deaths and disabilities. Adding insurance benefits to both of these brings their total to over $5 billion. All of these are transfer-type expenditures. Additionally, the government provided hospital and medical services to veterans costing slightly over $1.4 billion for the year.

Space Research and Technology

Most of the $4.6 billion set apart for space research and technology is for manned space flights in preparation for a manned landing on the moon by 1970. The rest is largely for unmanned exploratory probes of Mars and Venus and for meteorological and communications purposes.

Agriculture and Agricultural Resources

The federal government will spend some $5.6 billion in 1969 for services to the agricultural sector of the economy. The bulk of this amount could legitimately be called welfare expenditures for both the poor and the well-to-do segments of the rural population, with the latter obtaining the greater part of the support. These expenditures include income support to farmers and the provision of low-cost rural electricity and telephone services. (Can you defend special low-cost electricity and telephone rates for the rural as compared with the urban population?) Almost $1 billion was for soil conservation and agricultural research programs combined.

International Affairs and Finance

Do you get the impression from Congressional debate and from the newspapers and television that the foreign aid program is taking the United States straight down the road to bankruptcy, whatever that means for a nation? Yet consider the amount earmarked for international affairs, including foreign aid, for fiscal 1969—$5.1 billion out of a total federal budget of $186.1 billion and out of a GNP of $850.0 billion. Viewed in this light, the amount we devote to these purposes is a small drop in a rather large bucket. The major items are expenditures for the Agency for International Development and Food for Freedom. The former makes developmental loans to low-income nations and provides technical assistance in areas ranging from agriculture to tax collections. The latter program is a double-edged sword, making food available to countries where famine threatens and at the same time taking embarrassingly large agricultural surpluses off the hands of the Commodity Credit Corporation. In addition to foreign aid, expenditures for the conduct of international affairs fall under this heading—for the operations of the State Department, the U.S. Arms Control and Disarmament Agency, international financial institutions, the U.S. Information Agency, the Peace Corps, and others.

Natural Resources

The 1969 budget calls for $2.5 billion to be spent on further developing and using such natural resources as land, water, forests, minerals,

and wildlife. Most of this is spent for the development of land
and water resources. The Corps of Engineers is responsible for the construction and operation of projects providing navigational and irrigation
facilities. The Tennessee Valley Authority operates an enormous power-
generating project, and other power projects are in the planning stages.
Funds were provided for research in desalting water, for the development
of some 175 million acres of public lands in the western United States
and in Alaska, for the conservation of forests and wildlife, and, oddly
enough, for Indian education, vocational training, housing, and industrial development. Many of the expenditures of this classification are
associated with political "log-rolling," in which Congressmen vote for
each other's pet projects with an eye on the next election. Hopefully,
most are aimed at providing for better utilization of natural resources.

Education

Federal aid to education is estimated at $4.7 billion for 1969. Aid
is to be supplied at all educational levels from preschool to graduate
school. It includes grants for the construction of buildings, the purchase
of books and equipment, fellowships for training educational personnel,
the provision of counseling services, support of science education and
basic educational research, and other items. At the elementary and
secondary school levels special emphasis is placed on the education of
the disadvantaged.

General Government

General government expenditures support the legislative, judicial, and
executive branches of the government. The salaries of the President and
of Congressmen form a part of the bill, along with the expenses of operating their offices. General government expenditures include the costs
of operating the federal courts; the Internal Revenue Service; and the
Civil Service Commission which is responsible for the procurement and
management of government personnel. Also covered by this item are the
costs of constructing and maintaining government and public buildings
as well as a number of minor miscellaneous housekeeping expenses.

Housing and Community Development

One of the smaller categories of federal government expenditures is
represented by housing and community development. Most federal expenditures in this category consist of matching grants and insurance on

loans obtained from private sources for housing and development purposes. Projects for which these are made available range from urban renewal and urban mass transportation facilities to public housing programs for the elderly.

EXPENDITURES OF STATE AND LOCAL GOVERNMENTS BY FUNCTION

The economic activities of governments are by no means limited to those of the federal government. State and local government expenditures in 1966 amounted to $94.9 billion. If it were not for national defense, state and local expenditures would exceed total federal government outlays. Herein lies a major difference between the type of expenditures made by state and local governments and those made by the federal government. Federal government expenditures generally, though not exclusively, are for services devolving upon the population of the United States as a whole, whereas those of state and local governments are confined more narrowly to serving smaller groups or individuals falling within their respective jurisdictions. Many state and local government expenditures are in the area of semicollectively and even privately consumed goods and services, while the bulk of federal expenditures provide collectively consumed goods and services.[5]

Education

State and local government expenditures for education are more than twice those for any other item. Table 24–2 indicates that over $33 billion was spent for education in fiscal year 1966. The responsibility for producing primary and secondary education rests largely with local governments, while higher education is generally the province of state governments. Both receive financial assistance through federal grants, but aside from attempting to enforce desegregation the federal government has not participated actively in the operation of schools.

Highways

The construction and maintenance of streets, roads, and highways has long been considered a basic function of government. In the United

[5] See James M. Buchanan, *The Public Finances*, rev. ed. (Homewood, Ill.: Richard D. Irwin, Inc., 1965), pp. 417–420.

TABLE 24-2
State and Local Government Expenditures by Function, Fiscal Year 1966
(millions of dollars)

FUNCTION	EXPENDITURES
Education	33,287
Highways	12,770
Public welfare, unemployment compensation, and employee retirement	11,539
Health, hospitals, and sanitation	8,481
Utilities and liquor stores	7,281
Police and fire protection	4,152
General government	2,974
Interest on debt	2,690
Natural resources	2,039
Housing and urban renewal	1,406
Parks and recreation	1,187
Other	7,100
Total	94,906

SOURCE: U.S. Bureau of the Census, *Government Finances in 1965–66, Series GF-No. 13.* (Washington, D.C., 1967), pp. 18–19.

States state and local governments have shouldered the bulk of the burden, receiving some help from the federal government through a system of matching grants-in-aid. Federal participation in road building was increased greatly following the enactment by Congress of legislation in 1956 establishing an interstate highway system. State and local expenditures for the building and maintenance of roads totaled over $12 billion in 1966.

Public Welfare, Unemployment Compensation, and Employee Retirement

Public welfare, unemployment compensation, and employee retirement expenditures of state and local governments are transfer expenditures; that is, no direct productive service is performed by the recipients of the funds at the time the expenditures are made. In the years since the enactment of the Social Security Act of 1935, public welfare activities of state and local governments have consisted of caring for old people not eligible for Social Security, aid to dependent children, and aid to the blind or otherwise disabled. The Social Security Act provides for federal grants-in-aid to the states for this purpose. It also places the responsibility for the operation of a system of unemployment compensation on individual states, and for this purpose each state has established a trust fund into which payroll taxes are paid. Expenditures for employee retirement are self-explanatory. The total transfer expenditures of the three programs combined were over $11 billion in 1966, and it is likely that this item will increase significantly in the next few years, especially in the area of medical care.

Health, Hospitals, and Sanitation

In 1966 state and local governments spent some $8.4 billion on health, hospitals, and sanitation, making such services the fourth most important from the point of view of amounts spent. Most of the health and hospital expenditures were for the construction and operation of hospitals—over 2000 of them[6]—by cities, counties, and states. These hospitals do not ordinarily provide free services except to those who are too poor to pay. Their provision by governmental units rather than by the private sector of the economy presumes that the general public obtains social benefits from higher standards of public health and that private facilities would not be built in adequate quantities. Similarly, the assumption of responsibility for sanitation and for sewage disposal by state and local governments is based on the belief that these services would be inadequately supplied by private producers.

Other Expenditures

In addition to the services discussed above, Table 24–2 indicates that state and local governments carry on a number of economic activities of a smaller magnitude. The construction and operation of utilities and liquor stores—provision of privately consumed goods and services—required quantitatively a little over $7 billion dollars in 1966. Other functions are police and fire protection; housing and urban renewal projects; conservation of natural resources, including minerals, wildlife, and timber; and development of parks and recreational facilities. Expenditures are also made to pay interest on state debt and for general legislative, judicial, and administrative functions.

TRENDS IN GOVERNMENT EXPENDITURES

Total expenditures of federal, state, and local governments in 1966 were in the neighborhood of $220 billion. GNP in 1966 was in the neighborhood of $745 billion. This means that total government expenditures

[6] *Fiscal Outlook for State and Local Government to 1975* (New York: Tax Foundation, Inc., 1966), p. 14.

amounted to almost 30 percent of the value of the economy's gross output of goods and services in that year. It will be of interest to trace briefly the history of government participation in economic activity as indicated by its expenditures.

Changes in Magnitude

The major historical data for the twentieth century are presented in Table 24–3. We notice immediately the inexorable upward movement of government expenditures. Over the 65-year period covered in the table total expenditures rose from approximately $1.7 billion to slightly over $219 billion. What are the causes of the upward trend?

Inflation

Among the several possible causes *inflation* is an obvious one. When we examine the changes in the price level from 1902 to 1966 we find that an increase of slightly over 400 percent has occurred, or in terms of 1966 dollars, the 1902 level of government expenditures is somewhat in excess of $6.65 billion dollars. Although inflation has been a factor in increasing the level of government expenditures, clearly it has not been the major factor.

Population Growth

Another possible cause of rising government expenditures is *population growth*. The population of the United States rose from 79.1 million persons in 1902 to 196.9 million in 1966, an increase of approximately 250 percent. This factor too has had important effects on total expenditures, but it is far from being the complete explanation. Government expenditures per capita during the period have risen several times over.

War

A significant cause of increasing government expenditures has been for the provision and expansion of *military strength*. The rapid technological developments of the twentieth century have caused huge increases in the costs of military equipment and weapons systems and in the costs of training personnel to operate them. Further, each war has generated its own set of extra, continuing expenditures, veterans benefits and interest on a larger federal debt being the principle items.

Government Services

A growing population, an advancing technology, increasing urbaniza-tion, greater affluence, and other factors have generated a growing de-mand over time for *government services.* Until 1935 Social Security programs did not reach beyond limited amounts of public assistance and workmen's compensation for disabilities. Social Security expendi-tures now run in excess of $40 billion annually for all levels of govern-ment combined, and as Medicare and Medicaid get into full swing further large increases are inevitable. Expenditures on economic opportunity or War on Poverty programs have been increasing in recent years, and, with the focusing of more and more attention on the problems arising in the ghettos of our cities, we can expect these to increase even more rapidly in the future.

Apart from welfare and economic opportunity programs, governments are being called upon to improve and expand still other services. Intracity

TABLE 24-3
Total Federal, State, and Local Government Expenditures,[1]
Selected Years, 1902–1966

YEAR	STATE AND LOCAL[2]		FEDERAL		TOTAL		
	MILLIONS OF DOLLARS	PERCENT OF TOTAL	MILLIONS OF DOLLARS	PERCENT OF TOTAL	MILLIONS OF DOLLARS	PERCENT OF GNP	GNP
1902	1,088	65.5	572	34.5	1,660	6.9	24,200[4]
1913	2,245	68.8	970	30.2	3,215	8.1	39,600
1922	4,423	58.5	2,762	40.5	9,297	12.5	74,100
1932	8,171	65.7	4,266	34.3	12,437	21.4	58,000
1942	10,027	22.0	35,549	78.0	45,576	28.9	157,900
1944	9,427	8.6	100,547	91.4	109,974	52.3	210,100
1948	19,490	35.4	35,592	64.6	55,081	21.4	257,600
1952	28,279	28.3	71,568	71.7	99,847	28.9	345,500
1958	48,876	36.2	86,054	63.8	134,931	30.2	447,300
1962	62,377	35.6	113,428	64.4	175,805	31.4	560,300
1963	65,438	35.8	118,805	64.2	185,233	31.4	590,500
1964	70,483	35.9	125,949	64.1	196,431	31.1	632,400
1965	75,899	36.9	130,059	63.1	205,958	30.1	683,900
1966	81,700[3]	37.2	137,800	62.8	219,500	29.5	743,300

[1] Current dollars.
[2] Adjusted downward by federal grants to states that appear in the federal column.
[3] Estimate of the Tax Foundation, Inc.
[4] Annual average, 1902–1906.
SOURCES: *Facts and Figures on Government Finance: 1967* (New York: Tax Foundation, Inc., 1967), pp. 19, 20, 41; Bureau of the Census, *Historical Statistics of the United States, Colonial Times to 1957* (Washington, D.C., 1960), p. 139; U.S. Department of Commerce, *Survey of Current Business,* July 1967, p. 13.

and intercity transportation problems have become more and more pressing; street and highway expenditures are rising; increasing crime rates call for expanded police protection; and so it goes through a long list of services for which government at all levels has come to assume responsibility. Yet, it is interesting to note from Table 24–3 that from 1963 through 1966, even though government expenditures were increasing in absolute terms, they were decreasing as a percentage of GNP.

Federal versus State Expenditures

The second major fact evidenced in Table 24–3 is that federal expenditures have become larger relative to state and local expenditures. The shift in relative importance occurred in the latter part of the 1930s, but since World War II the situation has changed little. The shift is largely accounted for by the federal government's assumption of the responsibility of providing greater economic security through the Social Security program and by the increased costs of national defense during and since World War II. Both sets of expenditures have been increasing over the last 20 years, but so have state and local expenditures.

SUMMARY

Government expenditures and receipts exert a significant impact on the level of economic activity, and by appropriate manipulation of them, that is, through fiscal policy, governments can make positive contributions to economic stability.

Government-produced goods and services consumed by the general public are said to come from the public sector of the economy while goods and services produced and sold by private businesses are said to come from the private sector. There is much debate over the appropriate relative sizes of the two sectors. Generally speaking, from the point of view of economics, whether or not any specific good or service should be produced by the public sector or by the private sector depends upon which can do the job more efficiently. But this is often difficult to determine, and value judgments rather than objective facts tend to establish one's position in the debate.

Goods and services may be classified as (1) those that are collectively consumed, (2) those that are individually consumed, and (3) those that are semicollectively consumed. Collectively consumed goods and services include national defense, law and order, regulatory services, and the like, that once provided for a group of consumers, cannot be denied to any one in the group. If these were not produced by government, it is possible—and in many instances likely—that they would not be produced at all. Individually consumed goods and services, on the other hand, are enjoyed separately by consumers and are produced in the main by the private sector of the economy; however, in some instances government units produce and sell them, postal services and municipally owned utilities being cases in point. Semicollectively consumed goods and services, which are partly of an individually consumed nature but from which substantial social benefits are obtained by persons who do not consume them directly, form a great gray area about which the debate takes place.

Not all government expenditures are for the provision of goods and services for the citizenry. Some represent transfer expenditures for which the recipients provide no current services, the leading examples being Social Security and welfare payments along with interest payments on government debt to those who hold U.S. government securities.

The budget proposed by the President provides an overview of federal expenditures for various functions. The largest expenditure category is national defense. Health, welfare and labor expenditures rank second. Other functions in their order of magnitude for fiscal 1968 were commerce and transportation; veterans' benefits and services; space research and technology; international affairs and finance; agriculture and agricultural resources; natural resources; education; general government; and housing and community development.

State and local expenditures are largely for goods and services benefiting those in a particular jurisdiction. Those for education comprise the largest category, followed by highway construction and maintenance; public welfare, unemployment compensation, and employee retirement; and health, hospitals, and sanitation. There are a great many other state and local expenditures of smaller magnitudes.

In the twentieth century two major trends may be discerned in government spending in the United States. First, expenditures have increased rapidly. Second, an upward shift in the relative importance of federal versus state and local spending has occurred. The first trend is attributable to inflation, population growth, war, and to a broadening and deepening of the range of services provided as society has become more affluent. The second reflects the heavy entry of the federal government into social security and antipoverty programs along with the enormous increases in the costs of war and national defense.

EXERCISES AND QUESTIONS FOR DISCUSSION

1. Suppose your local government owns and operates the electric company that serves you. Do you think the government should involve itself in this sort of productive activity? Defend your answer.

2. "Semicollectively consumed goods and services must be provided by government, since the private sector would be less efficient in providing them." Evaluate this statement.
3. Are all transfer expenditures based on value judgments? Discuss.
4. "Government expenditures since the early twentieth century have increased tremendously. This is direct evidence that control of the U.S. economy has gone from private hands to those of big government." Analyze this statement critically.
5. List the expenditure categories of the federal and local governments.
   a. Which expenditures must be borne by government? Why?
   b. Which are for things that might be provided by the private sector of the economy? Why?
6. What is the present role of the federal government in providing funds for education? Do you think it should be larger or smaller? Give your reasons.

SELECTED READINGS

Buchanan, J. M., *The Public Finances,* rev. ed. Homewood, Ill: Richard D. Irwin, Inc., 1965, Chaps. 3–5.

Budget of the United States Government: 1969. Washington, D.C.: Government Printing Office, 1968, pp. 77–173.

Fiscal Outlook for State and Local Government to 1975. New York: Tax Foundation, Inc., 1966, p. 14.

Musgrave, R. A., *The Theory of Public Finance.* New York: McGraw-Hill Book Company, Inc., 1959, Chap. 1.

Sharp, A. M., and B. F. Sliger, *Public Finance.* Homewood, Ill.: The Dorsey Press, 1964, Chaps. 2, 3, and 5.

Government
Economic
Activities:
The Revenue
Side
CHAPTER 25

The goods and services that governments provide are not costless—and neither are their transfer expenditures. Most of us are aware that as a society we pay for them in one way or another, although we frequently expect that an expansion of some service that will benefit us will be paid for by others. The economics of financing government expenditures is developed in the first two sections of the chapter, while the last two sections examine the tax structures of both the federal government and of state and local governments.

THE ECONOMICS OF FINANCING GOVERNMENTS

Government versus Private Use of Resources

Where do governments obtain the resources necessary for producing such services as national defense and education or such capital goods as highways and airports? In a market economy governments bid, along with private producers, for most of the resources that they use. However, some resources, for example, man power for the military, are not always available in the desired quantities at the prices that the government is willing to pay. For these the government uses its coercive powers to requisition whatever amounts it wants. Resources used by governments are not available for use by the private sector of the economy, or, alternatively, resources used by the private sector are not available for government use. The real costs of governmental production of goods and services are the values of the foregone alternative products that could have been produced had the resources used by the government been left in private hands. Government-produced goods and services are costless only if the resources used to produce them would have been unemployed otherwise.

Even government transfer expenditures cause resources to be allocated differently from the way they would had the transfer expenditures not been made. The reallocation occasioned by them occurs *within* the private sector rather than *from* the private to the public sector of the economy. The people who are made better off by the transfer expenditures now have a greater influence on demands for goods and services, while those made worse off have less influence. These changes in private demand patterns touch off a corresponding reallocation of resources.

All government expenditures influence the allocation of resources, and the mechanism through which resources are released from one employment and reallocated to another depends upon how those expenditures are financed. The most important methods of financing them are through taxation, through the creation of new money, and through borrowing. An additional method, used particularly for government-produced individually consumed goods and services, is the direct sale of those goods and services to the public.

Taxation

If the federal government decides to expand its activities in the area of national defense, how can it obtain the necessary resources to meet the increase? One way to accomplish the reallocation is to increase the taxes levied on the general public, say through a surtax on individual and corporate incomes. The more the public pays in taxes, the less it has available to spend for goods and services produced and sold in the private sector of the economy. The decrease in demand for privately produced goods and services reduces the demand of private producers for resources. The additional spending power placed in the hands of the government puts the latter in a position to bid the desired resources away from the private sector. In summary, then, through the exercise of its taxing power the government can substitute its demand for resources for that of the private sector and thus bring about a reallocation from the private sector to the public sector.

Taxation can also aid in the process of diverting resources from one group of consumers in the economy to others through government transfer expenditures. Suppose that government officials decide that larger monthly payments should be made to the unemployed—that is, that the unemployed should be given relatively more command over what the resources of the economy are used to produce. Through taxation the demands for privately produced goods and services of those taxed are decreased, and when the corresponding transfer expenditures to the unemployed are put in the hands of the unemployed, the demands of the latter for privately produced goods and services are increased. To the extent that the new demand pattern differs from the old, forces are set in motion to reallocate resources correspondingly.

The use of taxation to finance government expenditures acts as a lubricant to ease the reallocation of resources that government officials intend to bring about. The demands of those taxed are reduced while the demands of government and of those who receive transfer expenditures are increased correspondingly. (When government expenditures are just met by tax collections, would you expect the impact on the level of total economic activity to be positive, negative, or neutral?)

The Creation of New Money

All national governments have found it expedient at some time or another to finance some part of their expenditures by creating new money directly; that is, by printing and spending new currency. Generally speaking, the "solid" citizens of the world tend to frown on this practice in the belief that it is inflationary. Suppose we look first at the diversion of resources from private to public uses and the impact of transfer expenditures when this method of financing is used. We shall then turn to the question of inflation.

The economic processes of resource reallocation vary only slightly from those of the taxation case. To secure resources for government productive processes the government creates money that it then uses to bid for resources. The increase in government demand relative to private demand enables the government to bid resources away from private producers, even though the absolute dollar demand of the latter has not been decreased. Similarly, transfer expenditures financed through the creation of money increase the demand of those to whom the expenditures go relative to the demands of others in the economy, although the absolute dollar demand of the latter has not been decreased. The former are given access to some resources that otherwise would have been controlled by the latter.

But will money creation of this kind be inflationary? If it is used extensively to finance large proportions of government expenditures, it probably will be. Carefully used in a growing economy, it need not be. Larger government demands not offset by smaller private demands will drive price levels up unless at the same time both the productive capacity and the output of the economy are growing. If, however, the economy's available supplies of resources are increasing, or if its techniques of production are improving, leading to an increasing volume of goods and services produced, a larger money supply is in order if price levels are to remain stable. The inflationary danger occurs only if total spending, government plus private, is made to increase at a more rapid rate than the volume of goods and services made available for purchase. If there is a significant amount of unemployment in the economy, mild inflation may be necessary in order to reduce it.

The financing of some part of government expenditures by means of money creation is not necessarily harmful and may even be desirable in a growing economy *if done judiciously*. It will not cause inflation unless it is carried to the point at which total spending *(MV)* is increasing more rapidly than the volume of trade *(T)*. In the aggregate, this method of financing expenditures differs from taxation in that it does not reduce private demands as an offset to the increase in government demands.

Borrowing

Governments also frequently resort to borrowing as a means of financing expenditures. Borrowing by the federal government is accomplished through the sale of government bonds and Treasury bills to the general public, to businesses, particularly financial enterprises, and to such government trust funds as that for Old Age, Survivors', and Disability Insurance. The economic effects of borrowing may be similar either to those of taxation or to those of creating new money, depending upon how lenders would have disposed of their funds had they not bought government securities. Government borrowing may, in fact, be the avenue through which new money is created.

Borrowing to finance government expenditures will have the same economic effects as the use of taxation when those who buy the securities do so in lieu of spending their available purchasing power on goods and services. If they elect to purchase government securities instead of goods and services, private demand is decreased by the value of the securities purchased and government demand is increased by the same amount. Further, if banks purchase government securities when their reserve ratios are as low as they want them to be, they can do so only at the expense of loans to the general public, thus substituting government purchasing power for private purchasing power.

Borrowing by the government to finance expenditures has effects equivalent to money creation when it brings about increased government spending with no corresponding decrease in private spending. Suppose, for example, that the public buys bonds with money that would have been hoarded or held idle otherwise. The rate of total spending in the economy is increased as idle money is put to work.[1] The same occurs when bonds are sold to government trust funds. Money balances that would have been held idle otherwise are put into circulation.

Direct money creation may result when government bonds are sold by the Treasury to Federal Reserve banks. In this case a Federal Reserve bank pays for the bonds by creating government deposits for the amounts involved. As these deposits are spent by the government, their recipients deposit them at their own banks, thus increasing commercial bank reserves and deposits. The increases in commercial bank deposits represent, of course, newly created money. Additionally, the set of transactions just described makes excess reserves available to commercial banks, and these can serve as a basis for further money creation.

The Predominance of Taxation

In the mix of taxation, money creation, and borrowing that governments use to finance their expenditures, we find that taxation is by far the most important. There may be greater resort to money creation and borrowing when recession occurs and depression is threatening. During inflationary periods there may be no money creation or borrowing at all—tax receipts may even exceed expenditures. Choices among the methods used, then, are made ideally, if not always in practice, according to the fiscal policies needed to promote economic stability. In keeping with its major role in fiscal policy, taxation will occupy us through the remainder of the chapter.

PRINCIPLES OF TAXATION

Writers in the field of public finance have traditionally been concerned with, among other things, the requisites of a "good" tax. What distinguishes a "good" tax from a "bad" one—that is, what makes some taxes more acceptable than others? Among the characteristics frequently listed, the most important ones are (1) adequacy, (2) simplicity, (3) certainty, and (4) equity. As we shall see, these characteristics are not entirely independent of one another.

---

[1] Actually, no new money is created, but the velocity of circulation is increased. The effects are essentially the same as they would be if new money were created while the velocity of circulation were constant.

Adequacy

The characteristic of *adequacy* requires little explanation: Does the tax do what it is supposed to do? The function of most taxes is to raise revenue, although some, those on tobacco and alcohol, for example, are for the additional purpose of suppressing consumption. If the purpose of a tax is to raise revenue, does it do so in the desired amounts? A tax on caviar is not likely to raise much revenue; a tax on all consumer goods will be much more lucrative.

Simplicity

A *simple tax* is one that can be easily understood by taxpayers and easily administered by the government. Examples of simple taxes are poll taxes and sales taxes. A *poll tax* is a tax of some set amount per year per person. Historically some state governments have employed it as a device to keep the poor, particularly blacks, from voting by denying them the franchise as a penalty for not paying the tax and, at the same time, denying them the opportunity to pay it. *Sales taxes* are levied in two ways. They may be levied on particular goods on the basis of product unit's measured in weight or volume—alcohol taxes, for example—or on the basis of product value, say a certain percentage of the sales price. The former are called *specific taxes* while the latter are referred to as *ad valorem taxes*. Sales taxes are easily collected by the government from the sellers of goods and services, and for this reason they have often been recommended as appropriate taxes for underdeveloped countries to levy. On the other side, probably few people in the United States who have wrestled with Form 1040 will deny either the complexity of the personal income tax or the desirability of simplicity in tax construction.

Certainty

The *certainty* of taxes implies several things, the most important being the consistency of the revenue over time, the impossibility of avoiding or evading the tax, and a knowledge on the part of the taxpayer of the amount of the tax that rests on him. Consistency over time does not mean that the tax structure or the tax rates must remain unchanged. Rather, it means that over time there is stability and orderly change so that both taxpayers and the government know where they stand from year to year. The *avoidance* of a tax refers to the success on the part of taxpayers of finding legal loopholes in the tax that enable them to avoid paying it.

Evasion is an illegal attempt not to pay the tax. Knowledge on the part of the taxpayer of the amount that he pays seems almost a foregone conclusion, but as we shall see, this is frequently not the case.

Equity

Above all else we want the taxes levied to meet public expenditures to be equitable in terms of the relative loads imposed upon different persons in the economy. But what constitutes equity in taxation? We can say easily and with impunity that persons in like circumstances should be subjected to like taxation, but once we depart from identical circumstances we are in trouble. How can we evaluate and compare the economic circumstances of widely diverse persons engaged in widely diverse activities in widely diverse parts of the country? Satisfactory answers are not easy to find; however, when we observe closely the tax laws enacted by legislatures we find that two rather different equity theories emerge. These are the benefits-received theory and the ability-to-pay theory.

Benefits-Received Theory

Taxation according to *benefits received* means that taxes are levied on individuals according to the benefits each obtains from government expenditures. To apply the theory it is necessary to evaluate the benefits received from government services for every person in the economy. Those receiving equal benefits from government expenditures would be required to pay equal amounts of taxes; those receiving the greatest benefits would pay the largest amounts of taxes; and those receiving the least benefits would pay the least.

There are two major arguments against the widespread use of the benefits-received theory. First, the calculation of the value of the benefits received for every individual in the economy is an impossible task. We need only consider the nature of government-provided collectively consumed goods and services to establish this point. Their very nature precludes determination of their values to particular individuals. Second, general use of the theory would preclude the use of transfer expenditures to redistribute income, thus violating the concepts of equity held by a great many people. Its use in providing welfare services would mean that the poor would be required to pay for their own relief—a result that is patently absurd.

Nevertheless, there are some special areas in which application of the theory leads to results that most people consider to be reasonably equitable. These are the areas in which the goods and services provided by government are to a large extent individually consumed. Highway-user taxes, or taxes on motor fuel, provide an example. Those who use the highways the most buy the most gasoline and thus pay larger shares of these taxes, which are generally earmarked for building and maintaining highways.

Ability-to-Pay Theory

Ordinarily when we think of equity in taxation we think in terms of ability to pay. Roughly, this means that those most able to pay taxes should pay larger amounts than those least able to pay. As we attempt to put the theory into practice two questions arise. First, what constitutes ability to pay? Second, what distribution of the tax load among people of differing ability to pay is equitable?

On the first question, comparative property holdings are sometimes thought to measure comparative abilities to pay. Personal property taxes illustrate this point of view. But this measure is not without shortcomings. Suppose, for example, that one individual owns large amounts of property or capital resources and not much in the way of labor power while another owns much in the form of labor power and not much in the form of property. If both earn the same yearly income, which has the greater ability to pay?

Comparative incomes are likely to provide a better criterion of ability to pay than are comparative property holdings. Both property and labor have value because of their capacities to generate income when they are used in the productive processes. Or, putting it the other way around, comparative incomes take into account the comparative holdings of both property and labor of different persons. Among the problems of using the income measure, the determination of what should and what should not be considered income is undoubtedly the most important. In any case, the topic provokes continuing controversy among economists and among accountants.

Even if incomes could be accurately defined and determined and arrayed according to size, the second question, the assignment of the appropriate tax load to each person, remains. In approaching this question economists classify taxes into three groups: (1) those that are proportional, (2) those that are progressive, and (3) those that are regressive. A *proportional tax* is one that takes the same percentage or proportion of everyone's income. A *progressive tax* is one that takes larger proportions of the income of the rich than it does of the poor. A *regressive tax* is one that takes larger proportions of the income of the poor than it does of the rich. Even in the case of a regressive tax, it is possible that the rich may have larger tax bills than the poor, although this is not necessarily so.

Some disagreement arises with regard to whether greater equity is achieved through the use of proportional taxes or through the use of progressive taxes. No one argues for regressive taxes on the basis of equity. The argument for progressive taxes is that any given proportion of a rich man's income is less important to him than is the same proportion of a poor man's income to the poor man. According to this argument, a man with a $50,000 per year income will miss $20,000 in taxes less than a man with a $5000 per year income will miss $2000 in taxes. This is a difficult proposition to prove; however, it does represent a generally held value judgment. Most people believe that in order to equalize tax loads among different income groups, the tax structure should be progressive.

The Shifting and Incidence of Taxation

What do we know about how much of the tax load each individual in the economy carries? Undoubtedly the correct answer is that we do not know as much as we think we know. Why pays the corporation income tax? If a sales tax is collected by the government from sellers, does this mean that sellers carry the burden or the *incidence* of the tax or are they able to *shift* it in whole or in part to someone else, say to purchasers, by charging higher prices for the product? Where is the incidence of a sales tax collected from purchasers instead of from sellers? The answers to these questions are not easily found.

One of the first points that we must get clearly in mind is that *things* do not pay taxes—people do. Yet many taxes are levied on things, partly because of convenience but partly, too, because some people believe that if things, corporations, for example, are taxed, people will somehow escape. Taxes levied directly on persons, individual income taxes and poll taxes, for example, are called *direct taxes.* Taxes levied on things, sales taxes or corporation income taxes, for example, are called *indirect taxes.*

The shifting and incidence of taxes are tricky matters, as is illustrated by the sales tax. In Figure 25–1(a) the initial equilibrium price of cigarettes is p per pack and the original quantity exchanged is X. A sales tax of t cents per pack is placed on the product. Who pays the tax? Where does its incidence lie?

Suppose that the sales tax law specifies that purchasers or consumers must pay the tax. Consumers' incomes and tastes are no different than they were before the tax, so the demand curve, DD, shows the price per pack *including the tax* that consumers are willing to pay for various quantities of cigarettes. Consequently, the price per pack that sellers can receive for each and every one of those quantities will be D_tD_t, the prices that consumers will pay *minus* the tax. At the original equilibrium price, *including tax,* consumers want quantity X. At that price, once the tax is

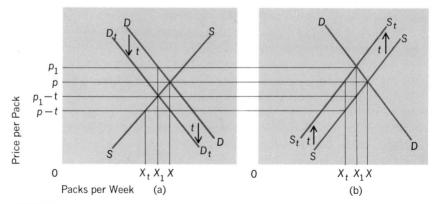

Figure 25–1
The incidence of an excise tax.

levied, sellers would receive $p - t$ and therefore would be willing to place only X_t on the market. A shortage of X_tX packs per week occurs and consumers will bid up the price. When the price *including the tax* reaches p_1, consumers want quantity X_1. At the price $p_1 - t$ that sellers are receiving, they are just willing to place quantity X_1 on the market. So, when the tax is collected from consumers, the new equiiibrium price level is p_1 *including the tax* or $p_1 - t$ *not including the tax.* But note that consumers and sellers share the tax. Consumers pay a higher price and sellers receive a lower price for the product than before. An amount pp_1 of the tax is borne by consumers, while the difference between p and $p_1 - t$ is borne by sellers. The incidence is on both. (Suppose that the supply curve in the neighborhood of the equilibrium price and quantity becomes more and more elastic. What happens to the amount of the tax borne by sellers and buyers respectively? If the demand curve instead of the supply curve becomes more and more elastic, what happens?)

The results would be exactly the same if the law were to state that the tax must be paid by sellers. The initial demand curve, supply curve, equilibrium price, and quantity exchanged are the same in Figure 25–1(b) as they are in Figure 25–1(a). If sellers must turn a tax of t cents per pack sold over to the government, they must still receive for themselves the prices shown by the supply curve in order to be induced to bring the various quantities to market. This means that they must collect the prices shown by S_tS_t, which lies above SS by an amount t, from consumers for those quantities. If consumers were to pay the equilibrium price, p, for the product, sellers would receive an amount $p - t$ for themselves; consequently, they would bring only X_t to market. A shortage would exist and consumers would bid up the price. At price p_1, consumers would take quantity X_1 while at price $p_1 - t$ received by sellers, the same quantity would be placed on the market. The new equilibrium price is p_1 for consumers and $p_1 - t$ for sellers. Again the incidence of the tax is on both consumers and sellers, with pp_1 being borne by consumers and with the difference between p and $p_1 - t$ resting on sellers. The reasoning, prices, and quantities in this paragraph are identical to those of the preceding one.

What conclusions can we draw from this discussion of tax shifting and incidence? Some taxes are more likely to be shifted than others. To whom can one shift a poll tax or a personal income tax, for example? Where shifting occurs, the public generally is not well informed as to the incidence of the tax or taxes in question. Taxes for which shifting occurs and for which the incidence is not generally known cannot meet the certainty criterion of a "good" tax. The other features of the tax may, however, be such as to override the importance of the certainty factor.

THE FEDERAL TAX STRUCTURE

What are the major taxes levied by the federal government and what is the relative importance of each in the over-all tax structure? How do they measure up with respect to the adequacy, simplicity, certainty, and equity criteria? The data contained in Table 25–1 will help us attack these questions.

TABLE 25–1
Federal Receipts from the Public, Fiscal Years 1967–1969 (billions of dollars)

SOURCE	1967	AMOUNT[1] 1968[2]	1969[2]
Individual income taxes	61.5	67.8	80.9
Corporation income taxes	33.8	31.3	34.3
Employment taxes	27.8	29.7	34.2
Excise taxes	13.7	13.8	14.7
Estate and gift taxes	3.0	3.1	3.4
Unemployment tax deposits by states	3.7	3.7	3.6
Customs	1.9	2.0	2.1
Other	4.0	4.5	4.9
Total	149.6	155.8	178.1

[1] Columns may not total due to rounding.
[2] Estimated.
SOURCE: *The Budget of the United States, 1969* (Washington, D.C. 1968), p. 52.

The Individual Income Tax

The federal government relies heavily on the *individual income tax* as a source of revenue. Almost 45 percent of the total estimated cash budget receipts of $178.1 billion are expected to come from this source. Its adequacy as a revenue source is hardly questionable; therefore, we shall appraise the tax in the light of the other requisites of a "good" tax.

Simplicity

The individual income tax is simple in concept and in practice for those with incomes under $10,000 consisting of wages subject to withholding tax and not more than $200 total of other wages, interest, and dividends and who wish to take the standard deduction. Those with larger incomes or with incomes that are generated from several sources run into myriad definitions, exemptions, and deductions so complex that it is usually necessary for them to seek the advice and services of an experienced tax specialist. Problems arise over the definition of income—what is and what is not to be counted. A variety of confusing criteria are used to determine the legitimacy of various deductions and complex formulas are established for computing deductions—depreciation and medical expenses provide examples—and for income averaging. Complexity arises in part from the way in which the individual income tax provisions of the Internal Revenue Code have evolved, for over time Congress has added to the law in a rather piecemeal way. Periodically there are discussions in Congress of simplifying the law, but to date there has been much talk and little action.

Certainty

The individual income tax measures up fairly well against the test of certainty. Provisions of the tax have been consistent enough over time so that taxpayers know generally what to expect from year to year. Changes, when introduced, have been minor enough, each considered separately, to avoid undue problems in this respect. Further, the individual income tax is a difficult one to shift, as are most direct taxes. The incidence of the tax is largely on the persons taxed.

Equity

A tax is difficult to evaluate accurately on the basis of its equitability because the value judgments of different people concerning what constitutes equity are likely to differ in degree if not in kind. The individual income tax is levied according to ability to pay, thus moving in the direction of what many people consider to be equity.

The individual income tax is progressive—the higher the taxable income of the taxpayer, the higher his tax rate. The tax rate is graduated according to the taxpayer's level of taxable income. For example, for 1967, that part of the taxable income of a single taxpayer up to $500 per year was taxed at a rate of 14 percent; that part between $500 and $1000 at 15 percent; that part between $1000 and $1500 at 16 percent; and so on, up to a level of $100,000 per year. The entire part of a taxpayer's taxable income in excess of $100,000 per year was taxed at the maximum rate of 70 percent. The rate applicable to the highest bracket of the taxpayer's income is called the *marginal rate of taxation,* and it is worth noting that with a rising marginal rate, the *average rate* rises but lies below the marginal rate. Differences of opinion arise as to the degree of progression that is most equitable—and even as to whether there should be progression. However, there is no great opposition to the general rate structure as it now exists, and this in itself indicates that many people believe it to be a reasonably equitable tax.

The Corporation Income Tax

The second largest revenue source for the federal government is the *corporation income tax,* accounting for almost 20 percent of its estimated 1969 receipts. The tax is based on the net income of the corporation, or income left after deducting expenses, including depreciation and interest payments, state and local taxes, and charitable contributions. The tax rate is presently set at 22 percent on the first $25,000 of net income per year and 48 percent on all income in excess of $25,000. The average rate structure is thus slightly progressive. As in the case of the individual income tax, the yield of the corporation income tax is high, so it may be judged adequate.

Simplicity

On simplicity grounds the corporation income tax is subject to the same criticisms as the individual income tax. There are ambiguities in the definition of what constitutes taxable income and with respect to what deductions are legitimate. There are complexities in computing allowable depreciation deductions, depletion allowances, and investment credits. But these may be of less consequence to the corporation than to an individual, since the former ordinarily has professional advice readily available and usually keeps a much better set of financial records than the latter.

Certainty

The corporation income tax does not come off very well with respect to certainty. It has been and is likely to continue to be a consistent tax over time, but there is much uncertainty, or lack of knowledge, on the part of the public with respect to its incidence, which is probably one of the important reasons for the popularity of the tax. The public has the impression that it is an impersonal "thing"—the corporation—that pays the tax and is quite willing that the "thing" rather than the public itself be taxed. Legislators do not appear to be averse to this line of thought, for corporations have no vote. Although the corporation is treated under law as if it were a person, it is ultimately owned by its stockholders, and these are the ones who pay the bulk of the tax. Stockholders receive the net income of a corporation after expenses have been met and they have little opportunity to shift the tax to others.

Equity

From the point of view of equity, many people believe that the corporation income tax leaves much to be desired. If equity requires that individuals in like income circumstances be treated alike, the tax does not meet the test. If equity requires that the tax structure be progressive with respect to those on whom the incidence of the tax rests, it also has shortcomings.

Suppose that all individuals in an economy earn equal taxable incomes and that initially there is no corporation income tax. Some individuals have invested in corporation stocks and receive a part of their incomes from this source. Others have invested in partnerships and receive their shares of partnership earnings. Still others receive income from their own sole proprietorships. With equal taxable incomes, all will pay equal individual income taxes. Now suppose that a corporation income tax is imposed. Will the income tax load still bear equally on all individuals in the economy?

Suppose now that incomes are not equal but that a general belief prevails that the tax structure should be progressive if it is to be equitable. The corporation income tax treats all stockholders of a given corporation alike regardless of their individual incomes. The corporation income tax on that part of their incomes earned through the corporate device is proportional. The millionaire stockholder is taxed by it at the same rate on the income that his stock earns as the widow who is barely able to live on the dividends earned by her stock.

Not everyone agrees that the corporation income tax has shortcomings on the equity basis. Some people argue that the tax is equitable on the grounds of benefits received. The corporation has certain legal advantages not available to partnerships and sole proprietorships, and the argument runs that the tax is simply payment for the privileges conferred on corporations—but at 22 to almost 48 percent of net income?

Employment Taxes and Unemployment Tax Deposits

At an estimated $34.2 billion for 1969, employment taxes are the third largest category collected by the federal government and have been increasing rapidly in amount. Most of these taxes are paid into the Old Age, Survivors', Disability, and Hospital Insurance trust funds from which retirements, disability, medical, and survivors benefits are paid to covered individuals or their families. At this writing, *Social Security* taxes were based on the first $7800 per year earned by employees in covered employments and by the self-employed under certain circumstances. The total tax rate at the time of writing was 8.8 percent of the employee's salary up to the $7800 maximum, with 4.4 percent being deducted from the employee's salary and matched by the employer. The rate is scheduled to move up to 9.6 percent on January 1, 1969. The tax rate on the self-employed was 6.4 percent in 1968 and is scheduled to be increased to 7.1 percent on January 1, 1969.

An additional $3.6 billion annually is collected from employers for unemployment compensation. The unemployment compensation part of the Social Security Act requires that on a state-by-state basis payroll taxes be remitted to the federal government, where, after deduction of a small "administrative" charge, they are placed in individual state unemployment compensation trust funds. Tax rates vary among employers, but the maximum rate in most states is 3.1 percent on the first $3000 of wages for each employee. Lower rates are obtainable by employers with favorable experience ratings; that is, by those for whom unemployment has been low.

These two sets of payroll taxes are simple but they are not certain from the viewpoint of taxpayer knowledge of their incidence. As a percentage of income up to the maximum taxable level, they are easily understood. They are also easy for the government to administer and collect. They are reasonably certain with respect to their consistency over time, but the public is in general mistaken with respect to their incidence. Although employment taxes are believed to be shared by employers and employees and unemployment taxes are believed to be paid by employers, the incidence of both is primarily on employees. To employers the taxes paid per unit of labor employed is simply a part of labor costs and does not differ in any significant way from the rest of wages paid. At any given employment level employers would be willing to pay workers a wage rate in the absence of the tax equal to the wage rate actually paid plus the tax. Costs per unit of labor to the employer would be the same either way.

Are payroll taxes, based on the first $7800 of income earned per year, equitable? They violate generally held views of what constitutes ability to pay. They are proportional up to the $7800 per year level and are regressive to the extent that some people earn incomes in covered employments reaching farther above $7800 than others. This regressivity is rationalized by some on the basis of the benefits-received theory—they call the tax insurance, but by no stretch of the imagination can it be made to fit into the actuarial pattern of private insurance. Instead, it resembles a situation in which the disadvantaged are asked to pay for their own relief.

Excise Taxes

Estimated excise tax receipts totaled $14.7 billion for 1969, thus amounting to slightly over 8 percent of the total estimated budget receipts for that year. These included excise taxes on alcohol, tobacco, certain kinds of documents, various manufactured products, and a number of miscellaneous items. Some, such as taxes on gasoline, trucks and buses, tires, and diesel fuel, go into a highway trust fund, earmarked for use in the construction of the interstate highway system.

In appraising excise taxes, we find that they meet the test of simplicity. Taxpayers generally understand clearly what is and what is not taxed and, at the federal level at least, such taxes are relatively easy to administer. Generally the government collects them from the seller of the item taxed.

Certainty is another matter. From the point of view of consistency over time, excise taxes may be certain, although it is by no means a foregone conclusion that they always will be. Legislators and the public are frequently mistaken with regard to the incidence of any given excise tax. It is generally assumed that the party from whom the collection is actually made bears the incidence of the tax, but, as noted earlier, this is not likely to be the case. Generally the tax is shared in some way by buyers and sellers, depending upon the elasticities of demand and supply.

Are excise taxes equitable? The highway trust fund receipts are in a large measure payments for the construction of the interstate highway system. Those using highways the most tend to pay the largest amounts of these highway-user taxes. The benefits-received theory of taxation would seem to justify excise taxes of this sort. But when we look at the heterogeneous items taxed to provide general revenue, the circumstances are different. For the most part these excise taxes exist because they are good revenue producers, but they are regressive in nature. By and large higher-income groups are likely to spend smaller proportions of their income on the taxed goods than are lower-income groups, since the proportion of income saved by higher-income groups is larger. Consequently, the tax load of the higher-income groups will be less proportionally than that of lower-income groups.

Estate and Gift Taxes

Estate and gift taxes are levied on transfers of resources or claims to resources from an individual to his beneficiaries. They are not very important as revenue measures but they raise some interesting issues. Federal estate taxes are levied on that part of estates exceeding $60,000 and the rate structure of the tax is highly progressive. Gift taxes are levied on gifts of over $3000 per year from one person to another, and for such gifts the receiver is allowed a lifetime exemption limited to $30,000. The rate on the taxable portion of gifts is highly progressive. The gift tax serves in part to prevent the avoidance of inheritance taxes through gifts made to beneficiaries while the giver is still living.

Estate and gift taxes are not simple, since extensive and expensive legal determinations are usually required to establish the tax base. Gift taxes are not certain with respect to incidence, since they seem to fall on both the giver and the receiver, the exact amount on each being difficult to determine. They are consistent over time.

The most interesting aspect of these taxes is equity. The controversial issue is whether an individual should be free to bequeath his entire estate to his heirs, thus in many cases placing those heirs in an advantageous economic position, or whether greater equality of opportunity among resource owners should be sought. There is, of course, no clear-cut answer to this question. As in most equity questions, value judgments reign supreme. However, any thoroughgoing program for equality of opportunity must contain provisions that prevent certain individuals from being placed by inheritance in especially favored positions.

THE STATE AND LOCAL REVENUE STRUCTURE

The revenue patterns of state and local governments are widely diverse. Rather than attempting to explain each of them we shall aggregate the totals from different revenue sources in this section. Data are not as readily available for state and local revenues as they are for federal reve-

TABLE 25-2
Estimated State and Local Revenues, Fiscal Years 1963–1966 (millions of dollars)

	Amount		
SOURCE	1964	1965	1966
Property taxes	21,241	22,583	24,670
Sales and gross receipts taxes	15,762	17,118	19,085
Individual income taxes	3,791	4,090	4,760
Corporation income taxes	1,695	1,929	2,038
Revenue from federal government	10,002	11,029	13,120
Liquor stores and utilities	5,975	6,355	6,619
Insurance trust fund	7,038	7,422	7,964
Other	15,951	17,251	19,363
Total	81,455	87,777	97,619

SOURCE: U.S. Bureau of the Census, Governmental Finances in 1965–66, Series GF No. 13, (Washington, D.C., 1967), p. 18.

nues because of problems of compilation. Neither are they as accurate. In Table 25–2 the major sources of state and local revenue are listed together with the latest available data on the amounts in each category.

Property Taxes

The largest single source of state and local revenue is the property tax. For purposes of taxation, property is divided into two classifications, tangible and intangible property. *Tangible property* is defined as physical assets, as distinct from claims to assets. The latter—bonds, mortgages, money, stock shares, and the like—are *intangible property*. Tangible property is further subdivided into *real property* and *personal property*, with the former consisting of land, buildings, and improvements on these, while the latter is made up of such things as automobiles, jewelry, and business inventories. These different property classifications frequently are taxed at different rates.

Property taxes are simple in that they are easily understood; however, they are difficult to administer. The key administrative agent is the county assessor, whose job it is to assess the property in his county for property tax purposes. The evasion that takes place through failure of taxpayers to declare property and of assessors to locate and evaluate property on a continuing basis is notorious.

Property taxes are reasonably certain taxes. They can be and generally are consistent over time. Further, even though they are indirect, the incidence seems to rest on the owners of the property assessed and taxed. In the short run, particularly, the tax is difficult to pass along to others, except to property renters.

Much could be said about the equity of property taxes—or, rather, the lack of it. Significant inequities stem from assessment shortcomings, such as the difficulty or the unwillingness of the assessor to find, classify, and value property correctly. But even if this were done perfectly, another serious inequity would exist. The property tax discriminations against investment in property as compared with investment in human beings. Suppose that upon finishing high school an individual faces a choice of investing $10,000 in a business or the same amount in a university education. If the annual dollar income yield from both investments were the same, investment in the university education would provide the individual with the greater net return because of property taxes. In both cases the annual income would be subjected to the same personal income tax. But an investment in property would subject the individual to property taxes as well, while an investment in education would not.

Other State and Local Revenues

Other state and local revenues include income taxes on both individuals and corporations, sales and gross receipts taxes, and government liquor store and public utility revenues. Of these, sales and gross receipts taxes are by far the most important.

Whereas federal excise taxes are levied on a limited number of products, state taxes of this sort are imposed on such a wide range of commodities and services that they are called appropriately *general sales taxes*. Almost four fifths of the states impose such taxes and these provide the largest part of state (but not local) government revenues. In their usual form, general sales taxes are *ad valorem* in nature, are imposed on retail sales, and are collected from sellers. But as we noted in the case of federal excise taxes, it is not at all certain that the incidence will rest on sellers. Ordinarily we would expect the incidence to be distributed between buyers and sellers.

In addition to general sales taxes, states frequently place specific excise taxes on particular products, partly for regulatory and control purposes and partly for purposes of financing particular kinds of state expenditures that benefit consumers of the product being taxed. State excise taxes on alcohol and tobacco illustrate the former. Motor fuel taxes illustrate the second.

All states charge registration and license fees for motor vehicles and for motor vehicle operators. These are included in the "other" classification in Table 25–2. They represent a special kind of taxes, providing revenues ordinarily earmarked for highway construction and maintenance and for highway safety. Motor vehicle license fees are more or less the same as property taxes with respect to the primary impact of the tax itself, while operator license fees resemble poll taxes. In both cases the incidence is generally on the one who pays the fee. Both of these taxes, like motor fuel excise taxes, are generally justified by the benefits-received theory. Those who use the highways the most provide the largest amounts of the revenue necessary for their construction and maintenance.

Revenue from the Federal Government

As Table 25–2 indicates, the federal government is a major source of funds for state and local governments. The federal government makes *grants-in-aid* for specific purposes, and in many cases the grant is conditional upon matching or pro rata funds being put up for the same purpose by the state or local entity to which it is made. The two major purposes of grants-in-aid are highway construction and public assistance to the needy, these purposes absorbing approximately half of the total. Grants-in-aid for education make up the third largest category and are expanding rapidly. The total list includes over 60 separate items.

Grants-in-aid specify the uses to which funds will be put by state and local governments and on this count they are often criticized. Some people argue that the primary rationale of transfers of funds from the federal government to the states is to bring about some sort of equity among states of different income-generating capacities. They maintain, further, that this purpose is best attained through grants to the poorer states to be used in any way they see fit. The counterargument is that if the federal government is to put up the funds, it is properly concerned with how those funds should be used. Should, for example, a federal grant to a state be used to aid segregated schools when integrated schools are mandatory under federal law?

SUMMARY

Government expenditures serve to reallocate resources from the private to the public sector of the economy and, within the private sector, away from the rest of the economy toward those receiving transfer expenditures. Determination of who in the private sector must give up resources, and the impact of government expenditures on economic activity, depend upon how those expenditures are financed.

The primary methods of financing expenditures are through taxation, the creation of new money, and borrowing. Most expenditures are financed by tax receipts, but in the interests of economic stability, judicious use of money creation and borrowing are in order. Financing by means of taxation substitutes government demand for private demand. Financing by money creation increases government demand without decreasing private demand. Borrowing may have effects like those of taxation or money creation, depending upon what would have been done with the money had it not been loaned to the government.

Several criteria may be used in selecting the kinds of taxes to use to raise government revenue. Most experts in public finance agree that taxes should be adequate, simple, certain, and equitable. Adequate taxes are those that provide good revenue yields. By simple it is meant that the taxes are easily understood and easily administered. Taxes are certain when taxpayers can expect consistency over time from them and when they have knowledge of the incidence of the tax. The incidence of a tax refers to who ultimately pays it. Those from whom a tax is collected are frequently able to shift the tax or some part of it to others. Equity in taxation is difficult to define. For some kinds of government expenditure financing is thought to be equitable when taxes are levied according to benefits received. But, in general, equity is thought to lie in the direction of taxation according to ability to pay.

The federal government relies most heavily on income taxes for its revenues, but in addition it levies employment taxes, excise taxes, and estate and gift taxes. Income taxes are levied on both individual and corporation incomes. Those imposed on the latter raise some questions as to whether the corporate form of business organization is discriminated against as compared with other forms. Employment taxes are to raise revenues for the various Social Security trust funds and for state unemployment compensation trust funds. Excise taxes are levied on a hodgepodge of items. Estate and gift taxes are not especially good revenue raisers but they bring up some interesting equity issues.

State and local governments obtain the bulk of their revenues from property taxes and from general excise or sales taxes. Property taxes are the principal revenue source for local governments, while sales taxes provide most of the receipts of state governments. Additionally, substantial federal grants-in-aid are made available for special types of projects, and these appear to be on the increase.

EXERCISES AND QUESTIONS FOR DISCUSSION

1. "Through money creation the government may increase its expenditures with no decrease in private expenditures. This practice is obviously superior to taxation as a method of financing expenditures, since the government via this method can pursue its activities at no expense to the private sector." Is this argument correct? Explain.

2. In each of the following situations which of the three methods of financing government expenditures would you deem most appropriate? Explain why you recommend the method you have chosen.
   a. Inflation.
   b. Unemployment.
   c. Inflation with unemployment.
3. Suppose that the sales tax in your state is earmarked for welfare expenditures. Can this be justified in the light of either the benefits-received or the ability-to-pay theory? Discuss.
4. "If a retailer is taxed at the rate of 2 cents for every loaf of bread he sells, he merely adds this amount to the price of each loaf; therefore, the incidence of the tax is clearly on the consumer." Evaluate this statement verbally and graphically.
5. "The most sensible way for the government to finance its expenditures is to have those who benefit from government-provided goods and services to pay accordingly, as is the case for toll roads and toll bridges." Evaluate this statement.

SELECTED BIBLIOGRAPHY

Buchanan, J. M., *The Public Finances,* rev. ed. Homewood, Ill.: Richard D. Irwin, Inc., 1965, Chaps. 21, 22, 24, 25, and 26.

Due, J. F., *Government Finance,* 3d. ed. Homewood, Ill.: Richard D. Irwin, Inc., 1963, Chaps. 5 and 6.

Sharp, A. M., and B. F. Sliger, *Public Finance.* Homewood, Ill.: The Dorsey Press, 1964, Chap. 14.

Simons, H. C., *Personal Income Taxation.* Chicago: The University of Chicago Press, 1938.

Fiscal Policy and the National Debt

CHAPTER 26

The vast amounts of money spent and collected by government units are eloquent testimony of the impact of government on economic activity. Both government spending and revenue collection—primarily tax collections—not only affect what goods and services resources are used to produce but they also affect in a very significant way the *level* of economic activity. Government expenditures and tax receipts are not closely tied to one another. In any given year expenditures and tax revenues may be the same, in which case the government is said to have a *balanced budget*. But it is entirely possible, and indeed quite likely, that expenditures will exceed tax collections, thereby creating a *budget deficit* or *deficit spending*, or that expenditures will be less than tax collections, creating a *budget surplus*. The use of budget deficits, surpluses, and the balanced budget in order to affect the level of economic activity, or for economic stability, is the essence of *fiscal policy*.

FISCAL POLICY FOR STABILIZATION

Federal government fiscal policy as a companion tool to monetary policy for achieving economic stability and growth has been discussed seriously by economists only since the Great Depression. The deliberate application of fiscal policy for this purpose has been quite limited. The so-called "pump-priming" expenditures of the Roosevelt Administration in the middle 1930s provides one example. To find another of major proportions one must search in vain up to the tax cut made by the Johnson Administration in 1964. The powerful stimulus of government spending to economic activity, although it was not intended for this purpose, was amply demonstrated during both world wars, the Korean War, and the Vietnam conflict after 1963. Thus, although fiscal policy as a tool for stimulating economic activity has not been extensively tested, its potential for this purpose is certainly clear.

In this section we shall examine the impact of fiscal policy on the level of economic activity. We shall consider in turn what policies are called for to use during periods of full employment when there is no inflation, during periods of recession and depression, and during periods of rapid inflation.

Full Employment with No Inflation: The Balanced Budget

What fiscal policy is appropriate when the economy's resources are near the full employment level and when, at the same time, no significant inflation is occurring? In terms of the equation of exchange, in a situation of this kind, total spending in the economy, both public and private, is changing in the same direction and at the same rate as the volume of trade. Both of these will be expanding even though there is full employment.[1]

If private spending alone is expanding enough to maintain full employment without inflation, it would appear that fiscal policy should be more or less neutral. This means that, as a first approximation, a balanced budget is in order. The government should add to the spending stream the same over-all amount that it removes from the spending stream through tax collections; that is, it should supplant the reduction in private spending with an equivalent amount of government spending.

There are qualifications to the supposed neutrality of the balanced budget. Things are not quite as simple as they seem. From whom were taxes collected? Were they collected from people who otherwise would have spent the money or from those who would have hoarded it? Further, what are the purposes of the expenditures? Will they generate new economic activity, for example, a road that opens up new trade possibilities, or are they made for services immediately consumed or for more or less nonproductive activities such as relief payment transfers? Generally speaking, the approximation of fiscal neutrality from a balanced budget is probably not too wide of the mark, but we should keep in mind that this policy is not always or necessarily neutral in its effects.

---

[1] Output would be expanding because the economy ordinarily is (1) adding to its stock of capital resources in terms of both quantity and quality, (2) improving its techniques of production, and (3) improving the quality and, perhaps, the quantity of its labor force during times of full employment.

Recessions and Depressions: The Budget Deficit

If a recession is underway or if unemployment seems to be at excessively high levels, what fiscal policy is recommended? Both total spending and output of the economy are too low, and thus an increase in total spending is in order. Such an increase will raise the price level, make business more profitable, and expand the volume of trade and employment. The appropriate fiscal policy, then, is a budget deficit—government expenditures should exceed tax revenues. A budget deficit increases total spending, since government spending in the deficit situation more than offsets the negative effects of tax collections on private spending.

The method of financing the deficit will determine how large the impact of a deficit will be on total spending. The government may finance its deficit by *creating new money,* either through borrowing from the Federal Reserve banks, through direct printing by the Treasury, or through borrowing from commercial banks when the latter have excess reserves. Or it may finance the deficit by *borrowing a part of the existing money supply;* that is, by borrowing from the general public.

Creation of New Money

The government may create new money to finance a deficit through the issuance and sale of new bonds and Treasury bills to the Federal Reserve banks in exchange for new Federal Reserve notes or for new deposits at the Federal Reserve banks.[2] The spending of these notes or deposits by the government creates new deposits in commercial banks in the names of those to whom the government makes payments. But even more important, the accompanying transfer of Federal Reserve notes or deposits from the government to the reserve accounts of member banks increases the excess reserves of the latter, making it possible for them to expand their loans and deposits by more than the amount borrowed and spent by the government. New money may also be created through direct printing by the Treasury, as was done in the case of U.S. notes issued during the Civil War. This money will also increase the deposits and the reserves of commercial banks when it is spent by the government and deposited by the recipients in commercial banks. The excess reserves that are generated set the stage for further increases in bank loans and demand deposits. The printing of paper money will be discussed in more detail later in the chapter.

Additionally, if the Treasury finances the deficit by selling new bonds to commercial banks, new money in the form of demand deposits may be created. If commercial banks have excess reserves—and this is the

---

[2] The government borrows by issuing and selling new government bonds and Treasury bills.

usual case during recession—they pay for the bonds by creating new deposits for the government. As the government spends them these deposits become deposits for the recipients of government payments, and a net increase in the money supply has occurred. Government expenditures so financed serve to increase total spending in the economy, since they are not offset by a decrease in private spending.

Financing a deficit by the creation of new money is a double-edged sword. Total spending is increased in the first instance by government spending that is not offset by tax collections from the general public. Second, the larger stock of money in the economy serves as a further stimulus to spending.

Borrowing from the Public

If the deficit is financed by the issuance and sale of new government bonds to people who would have spent the money for consumer goods and services or for capital goods, there will be no net effect on total spending. This method of financing government spending is similar to taxation, since just enough private spending is absorbed by the bond sales to offset the government spending. A deficit financed in this way serves only to increase the national debt and does not stimulate the economy.

If the borrowing is accomplished by the issue and sale of bonds to persons, businesses other than banks, and institutions (including government trust funds) that would otherwise have held idle money, total spending will be increased, although the money supply will not be. Idle money is drawn into the spending stream, increasing the velocity of circulation. Since private spending is not reduced, government spending in the amount of the deficit constitutes a net addition to total spending in the economy. The borrowing does add to the national debt, however.

Ordinarily, when the government engages in deficit spending and covers the deficit through borrowing, without creating new money in the process, a combination of the two foregoing possibilities occurs. Some bonds are purchased by the public with money that would otherwise have been spent in some other way. Some people, some businesses, and some institutions will purchase bonds with money that would otherwise have been hoarded or left idle. Total spending in the economy is increased, but not by as much as it would be if the deficit were financed by the creation of new money.

Inflation: The Budget Surplus

When resources are fully employed and the economy is plagued with inflation, the appropriate fiscal medicine is a budget surplus to reduce total spending. If tax collections exceed government expenditures, the reduction in private spending caused by tax collections is not fully offset by the government expenditures. Total spending will be less than it would be if the budget were balanced. This policy will attack directly the cause of the inflation, which is a rate of increase in total spending that exceeds the rate of increase in the volume of goods and services available to be purchased.

The Surplus Impounded

A budget surplus will have the greatest impact on total spending if the government simply impounds it. In the first place, the surplus in and of itself reduces total spending. But if the surplus is impounded, the quantity of money in circulation will be decreased, thus causing total spending to be reduced even further. Since the taxes giving rise to the surplus are paid with checks drawn by the public on commercial banks, the net effect is to reduce demand deposits in circulation by the amount of the surplus. Further, as the checks in the amount of the surplus are deposited by the government with the Federal Reserve banks and are impounded there, commercial bank deposits at Federal Reserve banks are transferred from commercial banks to the government's account. This reduces commercial bank reserves, and to the extent that it reduces them below required or desired levels, it induces banks to make further contractions in their deposits outstanding.

Retirement of Government Debt

Legislators and the public may want a surplus to be used to pay off government debt, that is, to purchase and retire outstanding government bonds. If the surplus is used in this manner, total spending may or may not be reduced, depending upon who owns the bonds that are retired. There are three possibilities: the bonds may be held by (1) Federal Reserve banks, (2) commercial banks, and (3) the nonbank public.

If a budget surplus is used to retire government bonds held by nonbank persons or business institutions who would then hold idle the money received for the bonds, the reduction in total spending occasioned by the surplus is the same as it would be if the surplus were impounded by the government. The stock of money in the economy is not changed by the surplus accrual and debt retirement;[3] however, the velocity of circulation

---

[3] Can you trace the changes in the balance sheets of the FRB and member banks to show that this is so? As a starting point, assume that a surplus of $5 billion is run by the government. How does this affect member-bank and FRB balance sheets? Now the government purchases government bonds from the nonbank public who maintain checking accounts or deposits in member banks. How does this affect member-bank and FRB balance sheets?

is decreased. Both the initial surplus and the reduction in the velocity of circulation operate to reduce total spending.

Suppose the budget surplus is used to retire government securities held by Federal Reserve banks. Government deposits at Federal Reserve banks are used to purchase the bonds from the latter and the FRB balance sheet shows equal reductions in its *government deposit* liability account and its *government securities* asset account. The total effect of the accumulation of a budget surplus and the use of the surplus to pay off government bonds held by Federal Reserve banks is precisely the same as it is when the government impounds the surplus.

Suppose now that the government uses the budget surplus to retire government bonds held by commercial banks that is, it uses its deposits at the Federal Reserve banks to buy bonds from commercial banks. On the Federal Reserve bank balance sheet government deposits decrease and member-bank deposits increase by the amount of the surplus so used. On member-bank balance sheets government securities accounts decrease and reserve accounts increase by the amount of the surplus so used. Thus member-bank reserves are raised to the level at which they stood *before* the budget surplus was accrued, permitting member-bank loans and demand deposits to expand to the level at which they stood before the budget surplus was built up. The primary reduction in total spending caused by the surplus is still effective, but since there is no net reduction in the money supply, secondary reductions in spending from this source are eliminated.

IMPLEMENTATION OF FISCAL POLICY

We consider now how fiscal policy should be put into effect. Should surpluses and deficits be effected by changes in government expenditures, in tax collections, or in both at the same time?

As a matter of fact, the structure of federal expenditures and of the tax system is such that expenditures and tax receipts change automatically in the right direction when economic fluctuations occur. The factors that cause these automatic changes to occur are referred to as *built-in*, or *automatic, stabilizers*. Over and above the automatic stabilizers, the government can take *discretionary action* to increase or decrease taxes and/or expenditures in the proper direction.

Built-In Stabilizers

Some of the expenditures of the federal government, and of state governments too, will tend to rise during periods of recession and depression and to fall during periods of high employment and inflation even though Congress and state legislatures take no action to increase or to decrease them. Social security and welfare expenditures make up the bulk of expenditures of this kind. Government payments of unemployment compensation and outright relief increase. Greater payments are made for farm price supports. Social security benefit payments increase as people, otherwise elgible but who had not been receiving them because their earnings in covered employments were too large, now are laid off and are placed on the full elgibility lists. All of these expenditures tend to decrease automatically during prosperous times.

Most of the built-in stabilizing effects of government budgets are on the tax side. Given an existing range of taxes and tax rates, depression and recession will reduce total tax receipts while high employment and inflation will increase them. Individual income taxes, corporation income taxes, excise taxes, and payroll taxes are the principal ones involved.

The individual income tax is the most important built-in stabilizer. As individual incomes increase during inflation the increase in the tax base itself increases the government's receipts from the tax. But an additional feature is operative—because the tax rate is progressive, more and more income is taxed at the progressively higher rates. The larger individual incomes grow, the greater becomes the proportion of total personal income that must be paid in taxes. These same forces work in reverse to decrease tax receipts in greater proportion than the decrease in income during recession and depression.

The corporation income tax, too, is highly sensitive to changes in the level of economic activity. During periods of recession and depression corporation incomes tend to fall more rapidly than does gross national product. The opposite tends to be the case during periods of expansion. The corporation income tax also has an element of progressivity in its rates. These two factors together tend to make corporation tax receipts respond to changes in economic activity in greater proportion than the changes that occur in gross national product.

Payroll taxes and excise taxes are not as sensitive as income taxes to changes in the level of economic activity. Nevertheless, they vary in the right directions for built-in stabilization. During periods of expansion payroll tax collections increase only to the extent that employment is increasing and that individual incomes are increasing up to the $7800 annual maximum on which the taxes are collected. As we have noted before, that part of an individual's income exceeding $7800 per year is not subject to the tax. Excise tax collections increase, of course, during periods of rising economic activity because the spending of the public on taxed items is increasing. The opposite occurs during recession and depression.

Discretionary Fiscal Policy

Built-in stabilizers alone ordinarily will not generate sufficiently large deficits or surpluses to prevent economic fluctuations from occurring. If economic stability at high levels of employment is to be attained, some additional *discretionary* changes in taxes and/or in expenditures usually are necessary.

Changes in Expenditures

Not all government expenditures can be manipulated in order to increase deficits or surpluses. Some functions of government are continuing ones requiring rather stable expenditures year in and year out. Among these are interest on the national debt, veterans' benefits and services, general government, and education. The magnitudes of some other functions, while not necessarily stable over time, are determined by forces other than whether or not the economy is undergoing economic fluctuations. Examples include national defense, space research and technology, and international affairs. But there is enough leeway in many government activities to permit some bunching of expenditures in periods of recession while reducing them to some minimum level in periods of high employment and inflation. The most important categories of expenditures of this type are (1) social security and welfare expenditures and (2) government investment in public works projects such as dams, highways, school buildings, government buildings, and the like.

Social security and welfare expenditures can be broadened in scope in periods of recession and high unemployment. Social security coverage can be expanded and payments increased. Direct welfare payments can be liberalized. And, as the Great Society program of the Johnson Administration well illustrates, a multitude of antipoverty programs can be initiated—area redevelopment programs, retraining programs, headstart programs for disadvantaged children, beautification programs, and others.

There are several things to be said for government investment in construction projects to create budget deficits during recession. First, it provides direct stimulation of capital goods industries, and it is these that exhibit the most marked contraction in recession. Second, an expansion of government projects will employ directly some of the unemployed. Third, the government goods can be obtained at lower cost during recession, since many of the resources used would otherwise remain unemployed. Fourth, from a psychological standpoint, employment and income earned from projects of this kind are preferable to direct welfare payments.

There are also some drawbacks to such discretionary expenditure changes for public works. One of the most serious is the problem of timing. For projects of any size, a lag of several months will generally elapse between approval of the project by the appropriate legislative body and the actual start of construction—and recessions are notoriously poor about holding still until action against them can be taken. Final plans must be drawn; bids must be obtained; and contracts must be let, assuming that expenditures have been authorized for the items to be constructed. Then, once a project is underway, expenditures cannot be turned off at precisely the right time. If a year or more is necessary to complete the project, the recession may have ended and the instability problem may have become one of inflation. If so, carrying the project through to completion may add fuel to the inflationary fires.

Another common argument against increases in government expenditures to incur deficits is that the practice tends to exhibit a ratchet effect. Once expenditures are increased, it is difficult to reduce them again. Social security coverage has been broadened and benefits have been increased, but no reductions have occurred. When any agency of the government has its scope of activities and its budget expanded, reductions at a future date become very difficult to accomplish. In any case, so the argument runs, the *level* of government expenditures should be based on whether or not the activities in which the government is engaging are desirable and economically sound in their own right rather than on whether or not a deficit or a surplus is needed for purposes of economic stabilization.

Changes in Taxes

Taxes seem to provide more promise for discretionary changes than do expenditures. If a deficit is desired to combat recession, both personal and corporation income tax rates can be lowered. Their exemptions and deduction features can be liberalized. Additionally, excise tax rates can easily be decreased or removed entirely. All of these can be changed in the opposite direction to eliminate a deficit or to run a surplus, although tax increases are harder to accomplish politically than are tax decreases. The massive tax cuts of 1964 and 1965 illustrate action aimed at reducing unemployment. Then, as inflationary pressure developed in 1966 and 1967, the political difficulties involved in increasing taxes became apparent. Not until mid-1968 could the Administration induce Congress to enact substantial tax increases to combat inflation.

Discretionary fiscal policy based on changes in taxes rather than in expenditures has the virtue of permitting government functions and government activities to be determined on their own merits apart from the pressures of recession or inflation. Highway construction or conservation projects, for example, can be considered on the basis of whether they represent the most productive uses of the resources that would be required to carry them out. Social security and welfare coverage and payments can be based on value judgments as to what is socially desirable rather than on the extent to which they make a direct contribution toward stemming recession.

The principal problems associated with tax variation are those of timing and the possible generation of uncertainty on the part of taxpayers. Tax changes of any considerable magnitude come about only after extensive hearings by Congressional committees and, ordinarily, lengthy debates in the House and the Senate.[4] Presidents have sought standby powers to change tax rates in order that the timing of changes might be improved, but so far Congress has not been willing to provide these. Not much need be said of uncertainty. It goes almost without saying that frequent changes in tax rates complicate tax planning both for individuals and for businesses.

Changes in Both Expenditures and Taxes

Changes in both expenditures and taxes each have their virtues and their flaws as means of implementing fiscal policy to combat economic fluctuations. If either practice is used alone, the magnitudes of the changes that must be brought about may from time to time be unduly large. Congress may balk at approving extraordinarily large changes in either expenditures or taxes. Private individuals or businesses may find that large tax changes generate enough uncertainty to interfere with sound economic decision-making. To mitigate the shortcomings of each when used alone, some combination of expenditure and tax changes of a discretionary nature may be in order to obtain deficits or surpluses large enough for fiscal policy to be effective. To enumerate the drawbacks of discretionary fiscal policy is not to discredit it. Rather, it serves the purpose of challenging us to devise ways to circumvent or eliminate the obstacles standing in the way of its use.

THE NATIONAL DEBT

Historically the federal government has generated larger and more frequent deficits than surpluses even though the deliberate use of discretionary fiscal policy has been very limited. This is evidenced by the growth of the national debt over time. There has been much public concern over

---

[4] Most economists were in agreement that further tax increases were in order in early 1967 to ease the inflationary pressures building up at that time. But there was much talk in Congress and no action during the year.

the size of the debt, with people commonly expressing two major fears. One is that the debt will become so large that the government will go "bankrupt." The other is that the present generation of taxpayers, by resorting to borrowing to finance government expenditures, is passing along the cost of those expenditures to future generations of taxpayers. Let us look first at the facts regarding the growth and size of the national debt. After examining these we shall consider the problem of transfers from taxpayers to bondholders within a given year and over a period of years. Finally, we shall consider the available alternatives to an increasing federal debt.

The Magnitude of the Debt

The total debt outstanding of the Federal government grew from $1.2 billion in 1915 to an estimated $351.6 billion in 1968. Table 26–1 shows the amounts for selected years to 1968. From 1850 through 1916 the total debt was relatively constant and was slightly above the $1 billion mark. Since 1915 there has been a 292 percent increase in its absolute size.

As we review the history of the 1915–1968 period we gain some insight into the causes of the changes in the debt. We can surmise that during World War I there was much deficit spending leading to the large debt increase from 1915 to 1920. Until the onset of the Great Depression the 1920s were generally prosperous, and budget surpluses permitted paying

TABLE 26–1
National Debt for Selected Years, 1915–1968

| YEAR | PUBLIC DEBT AT END OF YEAR | | YEAR | PUBLIC DEBT AT END OF YEAR | |
	AMOUNT (BILLIONS OF DOLLARS)	PERCENT OF GNP		AMOUNT (BILLIONS OF DOLLARS)	PERCENT OF GNP
1915	1.2	3.0	1950	257.4	97.7
1920	24.3	39.3	1955	274.4	72.5
1925	20.5	25.2	1960	286.5	57.8
1930	16.2	17.9	1965	317.8	48.8
1935	32.8	45.4	1966	320.4	45.0
1940	48.5	51.1	1967	326.7	42.8
1945	259.1	119.5	1968[1]	351.6	43.0

[1] Estimated.
SOURCE: *The Budget of the United States Government, 1969* (Washington, D.C., 1968), p. 544, and U.S. Department of Commerce, *Historical Statistics of the United States, 1789–1945.*

off some $8 billion of the debt. The depression years of the 1930s brought deficit spending to "prime the pump" of the economy—one of the first conscious uses of deficit spending to promote recovery from depression—and the debt increased correspondingly. The phenomenal debt increase from 1940 to 1945 is explained by World War II. Congress, the administration, and the general public were not willing to see tax levels raised sufficiently to cover the enormous (for that time) expenditures associated with the war.[5] Following World War II there was a sharp contraction of government spending and some reduction of the national debt. But since 1951 budgetary surpluses have occurred in only three years—1956, 1957, and 1960.

The "Bankruptcy" Fear

Dire predictions concerning the consequences of the increasing size of the national debt are not hard to find. Congress has expressed fears over the size of the debt by setting debt ceilings or limits beyond which the debt must not go; but whenever the debt presses against the limit, the ceiling is revised upward. The general public, businessmen and the financial community, in particular express fear that deficit spending and debt accumulation are leading the government down the road to "bankruptcy." Are these fears real or imaginary?

Government Debt versus Business Debt

We cannot progress toward answering the question just posed until we determine what people mean by bankruptcy. The meaning for a private business is clear enough: the business incurs losses to the extent that it cannot meet its creditors' demands, with the result that its assets are sold and the proceeds are distributed to these creditors. Can this happen to a government? Obviously it cannot. In the first place, a government is not a business enterprise operated for profits, or incurring losses, so bankruptcy is an inappropriate term to apply to it. Further, a national government can create the means of paying the interest and/or the principal on its debt. Private businesses cannot do this. What is it then that *really* concerns people who express fears of bankruptcy?

Excessive External Debt

We draw a distinction between the debt owed by a government to its own people and that owed by it to foreigners. The former is called the

[5] If the war had been financed largely by taxation, do you think the quantities of resources available to produce private goods and services would have been smaller than they were; that is, would the general public have been worse off than it actually was?

internal debt of the country while the latter is an *external debt*. Payments on the interest and the principal of a country's internal debt do not reduce the total amounts of resources available for the economy to use; that is, they do not cut down on the current size of the country's gross national product. Such payments transfer command over those resources from the rest of the economic units in the economy to those who receive the payments.

Payments on the interest and principal of externally held debt will reduce the amounts of resources that can be used currently to produce goods and services for domestic use. The payments enable foreigners to buy goods and services from the country; that is, to exercise command over some part of the economy's resources. Thus, from the point of view of the economy as a whole, the internal debt is not necessarily currently burdensome *per se*,[6] but the external debt is. Payments made on the latter reduce the current goods and services available for the country to use.

A country accumulating external debts may find that the servicing payments on the debt become more and more burdensome, although this is not necessarily the case and, presumably, never should be. If the money borrowed from foreigners is invested in an economically sound way, that is, so as to increase the country's productive power by more than enough to service the external debt, it is not really burdensome at all from a long-run point of view. If it is not used to increase the country's productive capacity, the servicing payments will reduce the country's living standards over the long run below what they would have been otherwise. The external debt of the United States is negligible, so any fears on this point by United States citizens are groundless. Such fears may be very real, however, for an underdeveloped country that has borrowed heavily from abroad and that has not used what it borrows to increase its capacity to produce.

Refusal To Pay Interest and Principal

Is there any likelihood that the national debt will reach such a magnitude that the government will default on its interest payments and on bond retirements? Table 26–1 provides data pertinent to this question. Although the debt has been increasing in absolute amounts, gross national product has been increasing at a faster rate. As a percentage of the value of the economy's annual total output, the debt decreased from 1945 to 1967. The larger the gross national product relative to the debt, the easier it becomes for the government to levy and collect the taxes necessary to service the debt. Thus, from this point of view, the

---

[6] Collection of taxes and payments of interest and principal may not transfer purchasing power in the most desirable directions, and they may lead to less efficient resource use in the economy, but these effects are not inevitable.

magnitude of the debt is of less consequence now than it was 25 years ago. Certainly there is no indication that the government has now or is likely to develop a financial position so shaky as to make defaulting on debt servicing a possibility.

As a matter of fact, as long as the government pays enough interest on government securities to make them attractive to investors, it will never need to pay off the principle unless it so desires. The debt can be carried at its present level or at higher or lower levels in perpetuity. As old bonds mature new ones can be issued and sold, and the proceeds of the new issue can be used to pay off the maturing issue. Paying off the debt does not really present a serious problem, since it need not be done.

Fear of Inflation

Will not the deficits that create the rising national debt cause inflation, reducing the value of the currency until the public loses confidence in it as a medium of exchange? As we have seen, the financing of a deficit through borrowing creates new money when commercial banks have excess reserves and when bonds are sold either to commercial banks or directly to the Federal Reserve banks by the Treasury. Whether or not inflation occurs depends upon the rate at which new money is created. With regard to the equation of exchange, if the increase in the money supply causes total spending to increase at the same rate over time as the volume of trade increases, no inflation is generated. If the creation of new money increases total spending faster than the volume of trade is increasing, inflation will indeed occur. But note that whether or not inflation occurs does not depend upon the *size of the debt;* rather, it depends upon *how rapidly the debt is increased.*

Fears that the national debt is approaching a level at which financial chaos will result thus appear to be unfounded. Inflation is probably the most serious financial consequence of debt accumulation, and even this need not occur. There may be problems associated with paying interest on the debt, but these are not problems of the ability or capacity of the government to pay; rather they are transfer problems and will be considered shortly.

The Transfer-of-Cost Fear

Many people believe that when the government finances some part of its expenditures by borrowing the present generation is obtaining those government services at no cost and that the burden will fall upon some future generation of taxpayers. An analogy usually is made with a private family. Suppose a man and his wife increase their current consumption by going in debt. Before the debt matures the couple die, leaving the debt to be paid by the estate—that is, by the couple's heirs, say their children. The couple lived beyond their means at the expense of the future generation.

Is this line of reasoning applicable to government borrowing? Suppose we consider the cost for the economy as a whole when the government resorts to borrowing to finance current expenditures. We shall look at three cases. In the first we shall suppose that there is full employment and that the government spends on a worthless project. In the second we shall assume that there is unemployment and that the government spends on a worthless project. In the third and fourth cases we shall assume that the government expenditure is a capital-creating one and that, alternately, there is unemployment and then full employment.

The Worthless-Project–Full-Employment Case

Suppose that certain government expenditures financed by borrowing are a total waste—for example, an irrigation system is built in a desert area where nothing will grow regardless of the amount of water used. Prior to the expenditures the resources of the economy were fully employed. What is the cost of the system and who pays for it? The cost of the project is clearly the value of alternative products that could have been produced with the resources used to build it. The primary economic cost is here and now, regardless of how the expenditures are financed. There will be secondary costs on future generations if the resources sucked into the building of the project could have been utilized to increase the economy's stock of capital had the project not been undertaken. Future stocks of capital will be smaller if the project is built than they would be if it is not. Thus the future output of the economy available to future generations would be smaller.

The Worthless-Project–Unemployment Case

Suppose that there are unemployed resources in the economy when the irrigation system is constructed and that the project draws only on these. In this case there is no primary economic cost, since no alternative products are forgone in order to build the system. There may even be secondary benefits or gains in the future from the activity. Incomes paid the owners of the resources used will be spent either in whole or in part, thus increasing demand for other products and drawing other unemployed resources into employment. The economy's output will be increased, thus permitting more capital accumulation than would occur otherwise. Future output will exceed what it would be in the absence of the project, and, rather than having a burden imposed on them, future generations benefit.

The Worthwhile-Project–Full-Employment Case

Suppose that the government activity financed by borrowing is one that creates capital—a hydroelectric project, for example—and it draws resources from the production of goods and services in the private sector of the economy. The current or primary economic cost is again the value of other products forgone by the diversion of resources into the construction of the project. The capital created by the government expenditure is expected to make positive contributions to future income flows generated by the economy. If the forgone private goods were consumer goods or less productive capital goods, future output would be increased by the project, making future generations better off.

The Worthwhile-Project–Unemployment Case

If the hydroelectric project financed by government borrowing is undertaken during a period when there is unemployment and if the resources that it employs are drawn from the ranks of the unemployed, the primary cost of the project is zero. No private goods need to be forgone in order for it to be constructed. Future generations will have the benefit of the project's output and thus, rather than having to bear the cost of an extravagance of the present generation, they stand to gain from an invesment made for them by the present generation.

Implications for the Transfer-of-Cost Fear

All four of the hypothetical cases point to a fundamental economic fact of life. The cost of producing anything today depends upon what must be forgone to produce it. If the government does the producing instead of private businesses, the principle is not altered. We are confronted here with a straightforward application of the alternative-cost doctrine. Whether the government project is financed by taxation, by borrowing, or by printing of new money is important only insofar as the method may determine from which private productive activity—if any—resources are to be drawn. Thus the fear of a transfer of cost from the present generation to future generations seems to be unfounded with respect to the internal debt of a country except for a situation in which the government uses resources less efficiently than they would have been used by the private sector of the economy.

Although a transfer of cost from present to future generations does not seem likely under most circumstances, there will be a transfer of *income* within a given future generation as the debt is serviced. Those who own the government securities will receive income from those who pay the taxes from which interest on the securities is paid. If bondholders are rich and taxpayers are poor on the average, this transfer may violate equity value judgments. If bondholders and taxpayers are by and large the same people, the only costs that are involved are those of collecting the taxes and of paying the interest.

Alternative to Increasing the National Debt

The increasing size of the national debt is mute testimony to the prevalence of budgetary deficits over the long run. To be sure, the largest deficits and the largest increases in the debt have occurred during war periods. Nevertheless, since 1945 the debt has increased by almost $100 billion. Why should deficits occur on the average during periods other than those of serious national emergencies?

Over the long run budgetary deficits may be expected to exceed surpluses because deficits provide a means of increasing the quantity of money in circulation. In a growing economy the volume of goods and services available to be purchased—the T in the equation of exchange—is increasing. In order to prevent the general price level, P, from falling, total spending, MV, must increase in approximate proportion to the increases in T. This means that the money supply must be expanded.

But is borrowing by the government the only way of increasing the money supply by the necessary amounts? We indicated earlier that an alternative is available. Instead of issuing interest-bearing bonds and increasing the quantity of money by selling those bonds to Federal Reserve banks and to commercial banks with excess reserves, the Treasury could (and has on occasion in the past) simply print and spend new paper money.

The printing of new paper money to finance a deficit has the virtue of not increasing the interest-bearing debt of the federal government. It achieves approximately the same results as does borrowing through the sale of government bonds to Federal Reserve banks; that is, it increases the money supply. Instead of moving toward this alternative, the federal government has taken positive steps in recent years to move away from it. Silver certificates and U.S. notes have been replaced in the currency supply by Federal Reserve notes. This means that the federal government is cutting itself off from the alternative to borrowing to finance deficits, or from the possibility of financing a deficit by means of the printing and issuing of new paper money by the Treasury.

By and large the idea of the Treasury printing new paper money to finance a deficit is appalling to most people—primarily because they do not understand that the value of money depends upon its scarcity or abundance—upon how much purchasing power is chasing the quantities of goods and services being made available for sale and not upon some kind of "backing" of the money by gold or silver. The public has seen countries misuse the printing press, flooding themselves with money and creating runaway inflation and financial chaos. The conclusion is that the printing press is at fault when the blame should be placed on those responsible for using it. Guns or automobiles are also dangerous in the hands of irresponsible people.

The practice of actually printing new money when an increase is needed in the money supply is as sound economically as the practice of creating new demand deposits through the sale of government bonds to the Federal Reserve banks and to commercial banks with excess reserves. The soundness (or unsoundness) of either method rests entirely with those responsible for using it—that is, with U.S. Treasury officials, Federal Reserve officials, and Congress. The direct printing of new money has the virtue of increasing neither the national debt nor the annual interest charges on that debt. Its use requires both responsible conduct and a great deal of knowledge on the part of the Treasury and Congress, but these requirements already rest on both.

There appear to be two reasons why many people prefer the debt-increasing method of financing deficits. First, it is not generally understood that the money supply is increased in the process. This reason obviously has no merit. Second, those who do understand the process of money creation hope that adverse reactions to the total size of the national debt will serve to control the extent to which new money is created. The debt itself is thought to force those responsible for increasing the money supply to act with restraint.

One final observation may be made here. Over time the national debt could be paid off rather easily if this were genuinely desired. All the elements of the process have been discussed above. Growth in the volume of goods and services being produced in the economy generates a need for a growing money supply. The additional money could be created by the Treasury via use of the printing press and injected into the economy through debt retirement, or the paying off of maturing government bonds, in whatever amounts are consistent with economic stability.

SUMMARY

Fiscal policy refers to the use by the federal government of tax and spending practices to influence economic activity. In general, a balanced budget tends to be neutral in its effects on total spending. Budgetary deficits tend to increase total spending in the economy and constitute the appropriate fiscal policy for combating recession and unemployment. Budgetary surpluses tend to reduce total spending and are therefore the recommended policy for halting inflation.

The inflationary or expansionary effects of budget deficits depend upon how they are financed. The primary methods of financing deficits are (1) through the issue and sale of government bonds and (2) through the printing of new paper money. The maximum effects will be obtained if the deficit is financed by the issue and sale of government bonds to Federal Reserve banks, or, alternatively, through the printing of new paper money. If the deficit is financed by borrowing, it is also possible that bonds may be issued and sold to commercial banks and/or to the general public. Some expansionary effects will occur if the banks that purchase the bonds have excess reserves and if the public buys bonds with money that would otherwise have been hoarded.

Surpluses exert their maximum effect in curbing inflation when the excess of tax collections over government expenditures is simply impounded by the government or is used to pay off bonds held by Federal Reserve banks. If the excess is used to pay off bonds held by commercial banks, the money supply will be decreased only if banks elect to hold the amounts so paid as excess reserves. If a surplus is used to pay off bonds held by the general public, total spending will be decreased only if the amounts so paid are hoarded.

Fiscal policy is implemented by the government either through built-in stabilizers or through discretionary changes in taxes and/or expenditures. Both the tax and the expenditure structure are such that total tax collections and government expenditures tend to vary automatically in the right direction for economic stability. But these built-in stabilizers can be supplemented with discretionary tax and expenditure changes by the government to bring about the desired results.

The national debt, represented by government bonds and Treasury bills outstanding, has been growing as the amounts of budget deficits have exceeded the amounts of budget surpluses. Much of this growth has resulted from such national emergencies as war, but some can be expected to result from growth in the output of the economy over time. The increasing size of the debt has caused many people to fear that the government will go "bankrupt." It has also induced a fear that the present generation is transferring the cost of present government services to future generations. Neither of these fears seems to be well grounded.

Continued growth of the national debt is not really necessary, since the alternative exists of printing new paper money to finance deficits of appropriate sizes for economic stability. This alternative is not held in high repute by a public that tends to confuse the means with the degree of responsibility to be exercised by those who use it. If responsibly used, the practice is in most respects equivalent to borrowing and has the further virtue of increasing neither the national debt nor its interest load. It could even be used as a means of reducing the size of the debt over time.

EXERCISES AND QUESTIONS FOR DISCUSSION

1. Is an increase in government expenditures always inflationary if full employment prevails in the economy? Explain in detail.
2. "The budget deficit of the United States has grown larger and larger. Interest payments are now in the billions of dollars. Our country is moving toward bankruptcy." Evaluate this statement.
3. What are the problems associated with the use of fiscal policy to control economic fluctuations? Should it be abandoned? What improvements can you think of in the means of implementing fiscal policy?
4. Suppose the economy is suffering from prolonged inflation (depression). What fiscal policy would you recommend to alleviate this situation? If a budget deficit is warranted, which method of financing would you employ?
5. In 1967 the United States was experiencing some inflation. At the same time, the government was running a budget deficit. Was this policy economically sound? What factors were responsible for this situation?

SELECTED READINGS

Buchanan, J. M., *The Public Finances*, rev. ed. Homewood, Ill.: Richard D. Irwin, Inc., 1965, Part VI.

Buchanan, J. M., and R. E. Wagner, *Public Debt in a Democratic Society*. Washington, D.C.: American Enterprise Institute for Public Policy Research, 1967.

Heilbroner, R. L., and P. L. Bernstein, *A Primer on Government Spending*. New York: Random House, Inc., Vintage Books, 1963.

Sharp, A. M., and B. F. Sliger, *Public Finance*. Homewood, Ill.: The Dorsey Press, 1964, Chap. 10–12.

National
Income
and Product
Concepts

CHAPTER 27

Whenever economists, journalists, government officials, and others attempt to evaluate the performance of the economy they ordinarily do so in terms of national income or national product concepts. National income and product data are used to determine whether economic growth is taking place and, if it is, the rate of growth. They also indicate the size and frequency of economic fluctuations. Additionally, on the basis of these concepts comparisons may be made between the actual and the potential performance of the economy.

Thus far in our discussions of economic fluctuations we have focused on the concept of gross national product. Actually, there is a group of related concepts, ranging from gross national product at one end to disposable income at the other, that is useful for analyzing economic performance as well as for collecting economic data.[1] This group of concepts provides the subject matter of the present chapter and lays the foundation for the more comprehensive analysis of national income in the chapters that follow. We shall consider three ways of viewing the value of the economy's output: (1) the value-of-product approach, (2) the income-received approach, and (3) the disposable-income approach.

VALUE-OF-PRODUCT APPROACH

The *value-of-product* approach to the national income and product concepts is the most common one and is the easiest to understand. This

[1] The Office of Business Economics of the U.S. Department of Commerce is the primary agency for collection of national income data. Some of the concepts defined in this chapter differ slightly from those of the Department of Commerce, but their magnitudes can be easily determined from the department's data.

is the one we have used implicitly wherever we have made use of the concept of gross national product. Basically it consists of valuing goods and services at their market prices, but as we shall see there are some things that cannot be valued in this way. In this section we shall refine the concept of gross national product, introduce and explain net national product, and examine the nature of intermediate goods along with problems of double counting.

Gross National Product

Gross national product, or GNP, is a convenient starting point for measuring the economy's output. It is defined as the total value of all goods and services produced in final form in the economy over a year's time. Units of each of the different goods and services comprising GNP are valued at their market prices, with the exception of some government goods and services, as noted later, and then are totaled to arrive at a figure for GNP. Expenditures made by the buyers of GNP ordinarily are classified into three major categories: (1) personal consumption expenditures, (2) gross private investment expenditures, and (3) expenditures for government goods and services. We can view these classifications, alternatively, as the values of (1) consumption goods and services, (2) gross private investment goods, and (3) government goods and services. As shown in Table 27–1, GNP for 1968 was approximately $852.9 billion.[2]

Consumption Goods and Services

Consumption goods and services are those placed in the hands of consumers during the year to be used directly in satisfying consumer wants. They are divided into three groups: (1) durable goods, (2) nondurable goods, and (3) services. *Durable goods* include such items as automobiles, furniture, and household equipment—products that are expected to last the consumer for several years. The *nondurable goods* group is composed of items used up more rapidly—clothing, food, gasoline, and the like. A wide variety of *services* can be listed. Some, such as barber and beauty services, are readily identified and their values easily determined. The quantities of others, such as household services, particularly those of housewives, are more difficult to estimate. All of these items are valued at their current market prices in estimating personal consumption, or C, for any given year. In 1968 C was approximately $527.9 billion, as indicated in Table 27–1.

[2] The latest estimate available at the time of writing was the rate for the second quarter of the year. If the second quarter is representative of the entire year, and it ordinarily is not far from this, GNP for the year will be $852.9 billion.

TABLE 27-1

National Income and Product Concepts, Second Quarter Rates, 1968 (billions of dollars)

VALUE OF PRODUCT		INCOME EARNED		DISPOSABLE INCOME	
CLASSIFICATION	AMOUNT	CLASSIFICATION	AMOUNT	CLASSIFICATION	AMOUNT
Consumption (C)	527.9	Indirect business taxes[2]	73.5	Household disposable income	586.3
Net investment[1] (I)	55.5	Corporate profits	89.2	Government disposable income	166.5
Government (G)	195.7	Proprietors' income	62.6	Corporate disposable income[3]	26.3
		Rental income	20.9		
		Net interest	25.8		
		Compensation of employees	507.1		
Net national product[1]	779.1	Net national income	779.1	Net disposable income	779.1
Depreciation[1]	73.8	Capital consumption allowances	73.8	Capital consumption allowances	73.8
Gross national product	852.9	Gross national income	852.9	Gross disposable income	852.9

[1] Gross investment (GI) is the sum of net investment and depreciation.
[2] Includes business transfers, subsidies less current surplus of government enterprises, and statistical discrepancy.
[3] Corporate disposable income only; that is, undistributed profits. All partnership and single proprietorship disposable income is included in household disposable income.
SOURCE: Computed from Survey of Current Business, September, 1968, Tables 1, 4, 6, and 10, pp. 7–9.

Gross Private Investment Goods

The *gross private investment* category is made up predominantly of capital goods purchased by business to be used in the further production of consumer goods. We frequently represent the entire group by the abbreviation *GI*. Capital goods are further subdivided into a *nonresidential group*, consisting of buildings and machinery, and a *residential group*, consisting of dwelling units. In addition, we shall include two other groups in the gross private investment category. One is the *net changes in business inventories* and the other is the *net foreign trade balance* of the country. Table 27–1 shows *GI* for 1968 at $129.3 billion.

Net additions to business inventories during the year are, of course, a part of the year's value of production. Reductions in business inventories during a given year represent goods sold that were produced in previous years and must therefore be deducted from the total value of goods sold in order to compute the value of the given year's output. Increases in business inventories during the year can be called investment goods legitimately because business firms must have committed funds to bring about the increases or must have invested in them just as they invested in plant and equipment. These inventories contribute to the consumption of goods and services in future years as surely as do plant and equipment. Decreases in business inventories during a given year are negative investments. Their sale releases the investable funds that were tied up in them.

The net foreign trade balance may be either positive or negative. It is found by subtracting the value of goods and services imported from the value of goods and services exported. If the net balance is positive, that is, if we have sold a greater value of goods and services abroad than we have bought, we have in effect some future goods and services coming to us from abroad or we have made an investment that will pay off in goods and services at some future date. If it is negative, that is, if the value of imports exceeds the value of exports, then we can think in terms of our owing some future goods and services to other countries.

Government Goods and Services

Goods and services produced by the government for the use of the general public have been discussed in detail previously. A large part of these are not sold in market places, that is, they are not directly priced; consequently, it is necessary to estimate their value. What, for example, is the yearly value of national defense services or of highway construction? The usual procedure is to value these at what it costs to provide them. The value of government goods and services, then, is taken to be total government expenditures—federal, state, and local—leaving out expenditures of a transfer nature that do not result in the creation of any new good or service. Government transfer expenditures represent a redistribution of purchasing power from taxpayers to those who receive the payments[3] rather than payments made for something produced during the year. We represent the value of government goods and services for the year with the letter G, and for 1968 it was estimated at $195.7 billion.[4]

The component parts of GNP can now be summed up conveniently in symbolic form. Let *GNP* represent the dollar value of *GNP* for the year, *C* the value of goods and services produced and sold for consumption, *GI* gross private investment goods produced, and *G* the value of government goods and services. Thus:

$$GNP = C + GI + G \qquad (27.1)$$

These components are shown graphically by the large rectangle on the left in Figure 27–1. The approximate magnitudes of each one, as well as for GNP for 1968, are listed in the value-of-product columns of Table 27–1.

Net National Product

GNP overstates the performance of the economy, for the entire amount of GNP is not available to use year after year unless productive capacity is not being maintained. Consider any given year. The total stock of capital on hand at the beginning of the year can be thought of as a gigantic machine, represented by the entire large rectangle on the left in Figure 27–2. In the process of producing GNP through the course of the year some of the economy's capital wears out, is used up, or becomes obsolete. We refer to all of this as *depreciation* of capital. If nothing were done about depreciation, the economy's stock of capital would be smaller at the end of the year than it was at the beginning by the amount of the depreciation. If this process were to continue over the years, eventually the stock of capital would disappear.

Now consider *GNP* for the year—the total value of the economy's output. Or is it? The component parts of *GNP* are C, G, and GI. Can we count all of this as the year's production? Some part of the *GI* component is required to take care of depreciation of capital, or to replace what wears out or becomes obsolete and to bring the stock of capital back to a condition equivalent to what it was at the beginning of the year. Thus the actual net usable production of the economy for the year is not *GNP*. It is

[3] Transfer expenditures are discussed later in the chapter.
[4] This figure is for all levels of government, federal, state, and local.

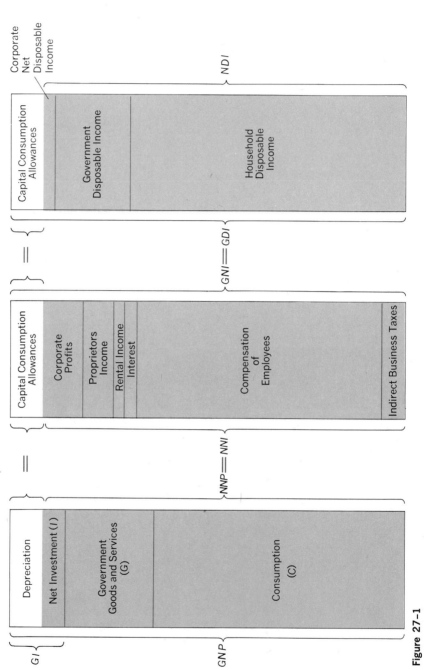

Figure 27-1

Gross national product, gross national income, and gross disposable income, their relations and component parts.

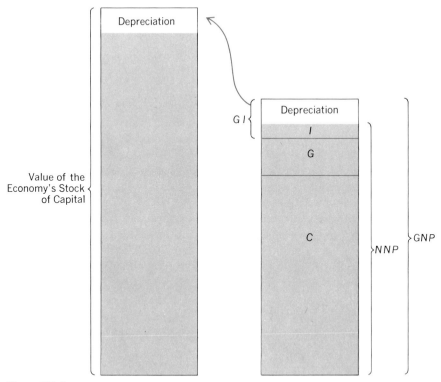

Figure 27–2
The relation between gross national product and net national product.

GNP minus that part of GI used to take care of depreciation. We call this remainder *net national product,* or *NNP.* In Figure 27–2, net national product for the year is the value of consumption goods and services produced, government goods and services, and *net investment* goods, the latter defined as gross investment goods minus the amount used to take care of depreciation. Algebraically,

$$NNP = C + I + G \qquad (27.2)$$

Suppose that during a given year the *GI* component of *GNP* is not sufficient to take care of depreciation of capital equipment. How do we compute *NNP,* or the net production of the economy? Nothing new or unusual is really involved; in equation 27.2, *I,* or net investment, is negative, thus *NNP* is less than the total of *C* and *G.* The economy is consuming private and government goods and services in excess of its production for the year. It is able to do this by converting some of its stock of capital —the depreciation not covered by *GI*—into goods and services. In essence, the general public "eats" a part of the economy's stock of capital, but the eaten part is not net production for the year.[5]

Double Counting

When *GNP* and *NNP* are computed by means of the value-of-product approach, double counting must be avoided. *Double counting* refers to counting at each stage the value of products used at several stages of a production process.[6] Goods that are likely to be double counted are *intermediate goods*, or goods produced to be used in the further production of higher-order goods. Suppose, for example, that the value of an automobile is counted as a part of *GNP* or *NNP*. Steel, glass, copper, rubber, paint, and other items were produced as intermediate goods during the year to be used in the manufacture of the automobile. The purchase price or value of the automobile includes the value of the intermediate materials used in its production. If the value of these materials were counted *in addition to* the value of the automobile, they would be double counted.

Frequently, to avoid double counting of items that go into the production of final goods, national income statisticians use a *value-added method* of computation. As we follow a basic product through its stages of production some value is added to it at each stage. The sum of the values added are the same as the value of the final product as it emerges in final form. Suppose, for example, that we follow a bushel of wheat through the stages of production transforming it into bread. In Table 27–2 a bushel of wheat is sold by a farmer to a miller for two dollars. The miller processes the wheat into flour and sells it to a baker for three dollars. The

TABLE 27–2
Use of Value-Added Computations to Avoid Double Counting

STAGE OF PRODUCTION	VALUE OF PRODUCT	VALUE ADDED
Wheat	$2.00	$2.00
Flour	3.00	1.00
Bread	4.00	1.00
	Sum of values added	$4.00

[5] This and the preceding paragraph hint at what is necessary for economic decline or for economic growth to take place. Since we are presently concerned only with the nature of the national income and product concepts, we shall not follow up on the hints at this point. They will be developed later in the analysis of national income determination.

[6] Strictly speaking, the problem is as much one of triple counting or quadruple counting, and so on, as it is of double counting. The term "double counting" is used as an umbrella to cover all of these.

baker makes the flour into bread and sells it for four dollars. The value of the product is shown at each stage of the production process in the center column of the table while the value added is recorded in the right-hand column. If the values of the wheat, the flour, and the bread were all counted, double counting would occur. If we total the value added at each stage of the production process however, we obtain a sum equal to the value of the final product.

THE INCOME-RECEIVED APPROACH

Every dollar's worth of goods and services produced during a year generates a dollar in income for those who furnish the resources required for its production. Suppose that a family spends $25,000 to have a new house built this year. Where does the $25,000 go? Part of it goes to carpenters, bricklayers, plumbers, and other workers in payment for labor services they have put into the house. Part of it goes to the suppliers of various kinds of materials. Part of it goes to the contractor who coordinated the use of resources and who may have used some of his own capital equipment on the project. The entire $25,000 paid for the house, the value of the product, becomes income received by those who contributed resources to its construction.

Gross National Income and Net National Income

If we extend the example of the new house to the entire range of goods and services comprising *GNP*, we arrive at a gross income figure for the entire economy. Suppose we call this *gross national income,* or *GNI.*[7] Gross national income is, of course, of the same magnitude as *GNP.* The production and sale of *GNP* generates an equivalent amount of income, *GNI,* for those who produce it.

Just as some capital equipment used up in the production of *GNP* is not a part of the year's net production, so some income used in the generation of *GNI* is not a part of the year's net income. The amount of income so used is that necessary to take care of depreciation, and we call it *capital consumption allowances.* It does not become net income for resource owners. Deducting the capital consumption allowances from *GNI,*

[7] The Department of Commerce does not define or use such a concept. However, it is easily determined from Department of Commerce data and is useful for completing the logical framework for national income and product accounting.

we arrive at a *net national income,* or *NNI,* magnitude that is identical to that of *NNP.*[8]

The Components of NNI

The net national income generated in the production of *NNP* is separated into six parts: (1) compensation of employees, (2) corporate profits, (3) indirect business taxes, (4) proprietors' income, (5) net interest, and (6) rental income. We met this classification earlier as the *functional distribution of income.* It represents a partial breakdown of income into categories according to the types of resources generating each category, but it does not go all the way in this respect. This will become evident as we discuss the list. The magnitudes of the parts are given in the center column of Table 27–1 and are represented pictorially in Figure 27–1.

Compensation of Employees

Included in *compensation of employees* is most but not all of the income earned by labor resources in the production of *NNP.* It includes the wages and salaries paid all employees of businesses as well as supplements to earnings such as employer contributions for Social Security, unemployment compensation, government retirement programs, and the like. It also includes employer payments on behalf of employees for private pension plans, medical and hospital insurance, and other similar programs. The earnings of labor resources *not covered* in this category are those of the self-employed. These are picked up in some of the categories listed below. From Table 27–1 we see that for 1967 compensation of employees was about $463.5 billion and was by far the largest of the six components of *NNI.*

Corporate Profits

Corporate profits as defined by the Department of Commerce form the next largest category of income earned by resource owners. The resource owners to whom they accrue are the owners of the assets of corporations—stockholders—and they are defined as the difference between corporate gross income from the sale of goods and services and the ex-

---

[8] Our definition of *NNI* is larger than the Department of Commerce definition of national income by an amount equal to *indirect business taxes.* In our judgment our definition is more consistent with and lends itself better to the analytical framework of national income analysis than that of the Department of Commerce. It is easily determined from Department of Commerce data.

penses of corporations as they are identified in current accounting practices. Corporate profits, defined in this way, are not the same thing as economic profits. In computing economic profits we treat average returns to stockholders on their investment as expenses, and *economic profits* is the amount left of the corporate profits after this is done. In accounting practice average returns to stockholders are not considered as a cost of engaging in business activity. Nevertheless, the entire amount of corporate profits can be thought of legitimately as being earned by the resources of corporation stockholders. Whatever is left of gross earnings after all accounting expenses are met is ultimately theirs.

Indirect Business Taxes

Indirect business taxes consist largely of sales and excise taxes collected by businesses from purchasers of goods and services and turned over directly to the government and of property taxes paid by businesses. They also include a number of miscellaneous fees and payments paid to the government by businesses, although the total amount of these is comparatively small. Additionally, when national income statisticians compute net national product using the value-of-products approach, and when they compute net national income using the income-earned approach, some items on one side or the other get lost in the shuffle, resulting in a small statistical discrepancy. For convenience we include that amount in the indirect business taxes category.

We do not treat indirect taxes in the same way as the Department of Commerce in setting up the various national income and product concepts. The Department of Commerce does not include this amount as a part of net national income. Rather, it deducts indirect business taxes from *NNP* to arrive at what it calls *national income.* We add the indirect business taxes to the Department of Commerce *national income* to arrive at what we call *net national income,* thus *our* net national income is equal in amount to *NNP*.

The justification for our treatment of indirect business taxes as a part of *NNI* is a simple and logical one. The *entire amounts* paid by buyers for *NNP* are earned by resource owners, regardless of whether the latter ever see the money. In this respect indirect business taxes are no different from the part of individual income taxes withheld by employers and paid directly to the government. The indirect business taxes paid by businesses to the government are partly the earnings of labor resources and partly those of capital resources, the amounts attributable to each depending upon the incidence of the taxes. Indirect taxes thus become disposable income for the government just as do any other tax receipts. They are in no way removed from the income flow of spending and are therefore identical to other kinds of government tax receipts.

Proprietors' Income

Consider now the total receipts of single proprietorships and partnerships. Although a large part of these are paid out to resource owners, becoming earnings in some other form, a small part, termed *proprietors' income,* remains. This is what the owners of the businesses have for themselves and is usually thought of as their "profit." The owners of single proprietorships and partnerships own capital resources used in the business and also furnish their own labor resources to the business during the year, so this net income or "profit" is really income earned by their labor and capital combined. A breakdown of this component into wage and salary, rent, interest, and return on investment entails such difficulties that the Department of Commerce does not attempt it and reports the entire amount as *proprietors' income.*

Net Interest Income and Rental Income

These last two classifications of income earned are almost self-explanatory. *Net interest income* is the net amount earned by those who have made loans to businesses and which the latter invest in plant, equipment, and inventories. *Rental income* is the amount earned by the owners of real property from renting the property out to others.

Transfer Payments

As we total up the amounts received during a year by businesses, private individuals, and the government in an attempt to arrive at *NNI* or *GNI* we must be careful to leave transfer payments to one side. *Transfer payments* are those made by one economic unit to another during the year *for which no services are performed by the ones receiving the payments* —that is, no contribution to the year's production is rendered for the payment. Such payments may be either (1) government transfer payments or (2) private transfer payments.

Government Transfer Payments

We met *government transfer payments* before. They are payments made by the government to individuals or businesses who make no contribution to the economy's output of goods and services. Welfare payments provide the clearest example. They represent purely and simply a transfer of purchasing power from the taxpayer to the welfare recipient. The payment is not made for work performed or for the placement of resources in the productive process.

Interest payments on government debt are classified by the Department of Commerce as transfer payments; however, there is some disagreement among economists concerning whether or not this is correct procedure. Some argue that such payments simply represent a transfer of purchasing power from taxpayers to bondholders. Others argue that bonds sold by government units provide funds that are invested in government capital—for example, the Tennessee Valley Authority—and that the investment yields returns to society at least sufficient to pay the interest. Both arguments have some merit. Some government borrowing is undoubtedly invested so that it yields a return. Just as surely some of it is not, and the interest paid on this part is of a transfer nature. We shall beg the question and follow the Department of Commerce procedure of treating interest on government debt as a transfer payment.

Private Transfer Payments

Private transfer payments are those made between private economic units for which nothing new is created. Suppose that Smith purchases a used car produced in some previous year from Jones. Nothing is added to *NNP* for the current year and consequently nothing is added to *NNI* by the transaction. The additions to *NNP* and to *NNI* occasioned by the production and sale of the automobile occurred in the year in which it was originally produced and sold, not this year. All that has happened this year is that an already existing piece of property has changed hands or has been transferred from one party to another. In addition to transactions in goods produced previous to the year in question, gifts from one person to another during the year are private transfer payments.

Product-Income Relation Restated

After the discussion on the component parts of *GNP* and *NNP* in the preceding section and of *GNI* and *NNI* in this one, a summary of the relations between the two sets of concepts is in order. Table 27–1 and Figure 27–2 are useful for this purpose. *GNP* is the total value of goods and services put in final form during a given year. Its production generates an equal amount of total income received, or *GNI*. Plant and equipment wear out or become obsolete in the process of producing *GNP*, so the net value of the economy's output, or *NNP*, is equal to *GNP* minus whatever value of goods and services is necessary to take care of such depreciation. On the income received side, businesses use a part of *GNI*, called capital consumption allowances, to take care of depreciation, so the net income earned by resource owners, or *NNI*, is equal to *GNI* minus capital consumption allowances. Net national income and *NNP* are equal, since depreciation and capital consumption allowances are equal.

Net national product, the net value of the economy's output for the year, is made up of three parts. These are the values of consumption goods, net investment goods, and government goods and services produced and they are summed up in the statement

$$NNP = C + I + G \qquad (27.2)$$

The production of *NNP* creates an equal amount of income, *NNI*, for resource owners. The component parts of *NNI* as they are computed by national income statisticians are compensation of employees, corporate profits, indirect business taxes, proprietors' income, net interest income, and rental income. This income received can be thought of as ending up in the hands of households, corporate business firms, and the government.

THE DISPOSABLE INCOME APPROACH

All of the income received during the year is available for spending and as such is called *disposable income.* The net amount of disposable income, or *NDI,* made available during the year is necessarily the same as *NNI,* but its distribution among economic units for spending purposes is not the same as the distribution of *NNI* as it is earned by resource owners. This is because some transfers of purchasing power occur between those who earn the income and those who have it available to spend. Households, corporate business firms,[9] and the government are the recipients of *NNI.* They are also the spenders of *NDI,* but the transfers take place between the time of earning and the time of spending.

Household Disposable Income

Before we can observe what constitutes household disposable income we must determine which parts of the components of *NNI* are received by households *before* any transfers take place. Obviously, all of the compensation of employees component is so received. A part of the corporate profits component is received by households in the form of dividends to

[9] Ideally, *all business firms* should be included here rather than just corporations. However, the Department of Commerce, in its national income and product classifications for data gathering and analysis, separates out corporations, placing proprietorship and partnership data with that of persons or households. To avoid confusion in the use of Department of Commerce data we shall follow the same practice.

stockholders. Proprietors' income is received by households, as is rental income and net interest income. Only the indirect business taxes component bypasses households completely.

What are the transfers that make household disposable income differ from the part of *NNI* that they receive as resource owners? Some part of household income is earned by labor resources working in employments covered by the Social Security Act. Social Security taxes must be paid, transferring purchasing power from households to the government. Households must also pay personal income taxes, personal property taxes, inheritance taxes, and such nontax payments as fees, fines, donations, and others to the government. But the transfers are not all in one direction. Some households, notably farmers, those who receive Social Security payments, welfare recipients, and government bondholders, receive transfers from the government. In the final analysis *household disposable income* consists of all income earned by households minus personal taxes and other payments made by them to the government, plus government transfer payments made to them. It is available to households to dispose of as they see fit—to spend or to save.

Business Disposable Income

Before transfers occur business firms are in possession of that part of the corporate profits component of *NNI* that is not paid to stockholders as dividends. The major transfers that occur from this amount are corporation income taxes and any other fees paid to the government by corporations. That part of profits remaining in the hands of the corporation after corporation income taxes have been paid and after dividends have been paid to stockholders is called *undistributed profits*. If we add to the undistributed profits any transfer payments to corporations from the government, say subsidies of one kind or another, we have *corporate disposable income*. This is income available to the corporation to spend as it desires.

Government Disposable Income

The government's direct receipts from the *NNI* pie consist of indirect business taxes. To this we add all tax receipts and other transfers from households and corporations to the government. Then we deduct all transfer payments from the government to households and corporations. The remainder is *government disposable income*, or the amount the government has available to provide the goods and services that it determines we should have.

Relation of NNP, NNI, and NDI Restated

The production of *NNP* generates an equal amount of *NNI* for the resource owners who furnish the resources to produce it. The income received by resource owners is subjected to transfers, and after these have been accomplished it becomes *NDI* in the hands of households, corporate businesses, and the government. The distribution of *NDI* will differ somewhat from the distribution of *NNI*, but no change in total income is brought about by the transfers. These relations are summed up in the statement

$$NNP = NNI = NDI \tag{27.3}$$

SUMMARY

This chapter lays the foundation for the analysis of national income developed in the ensuing chapters. Three sets of national income and product concepts are defined. Through the value-of-products approach we derive the concepts of gross national product and net national product. From the income-received approach we arrive at the concepts of gross national income and net national income, and from the latter concepts we move to those of gross disposable income and net disposable income.

From the value-of-products point of view *GNP* is the total value of all goods and services produced in final form in the economy per year. It is composed of three parts: (1) goods and services for personal consumption, or *C*, (2) government goods and services, or *G*, and (3) gross investment or capital goods, or *GI*. If we deduct from gross investment goods the capital goods needed to take care of the depreciation that occurs as *GNP* is produced, then (3) becomes net investment goods, or *I*, and the sum of the three makes up net national product, or *NNP*. In totaling the values of goods and services to find *GNP* or *NNP*, double counting of intermediate goods must be avoided. Intermediate goods are goods produced to further produce higher-order goods.

If we look at the income generated in the production of *NNP* and *GNP*, we have the concepts of net national income and gross national income, respectively, with *NNP = NNI* and *GNP = GNI*. The components of *NNI* are (1) compensation of employees, corporate profits, indirect business taxes, proprietors' income, net interest income, and rental income. If we add capital consumption allowances to these classifications, we arrive at *GNI*. Capital consumption allowances are the part of income received necessary to take care of depreciation and are equal to depreciation. The receipt of transfer payments must not be counted as a part of *NNI* or *GNI*.

The distribution of *NNI* as it is earned by resource owners is somewhat different from the distribution of *NDI* as it is available to be spent, although *NDI* is equal to *NNI*. Net disposable income consists of (1) household disposable income, (2) corporate disposable income, and (3) government disposable income. Household disposable income is what is left of household earnings after all tax and other payments to the government have been deducted and after transfer payments from the government have been added in. Corporate disposable income consists of undistributed profits plus government transfer payments to corporations. Government disposable income is composed of indirect business taxes plus all other tax revenues and government receipts minus government transfer payments.

EXERCISES AND QUESTIONS FOR DISCUSSION

1. Are the automobiles manufactured by General Motors final goods? Why are intermediate goods not included in *NNP* or *GNP?*
2. To compare *GNP* for two successive years we compare the market value of all final goods produced in the economy during those two years. Would a comparison of the physical outputs be a better measure of income growth? Why is this not done?
3. Can an economy's output and income earned be unequal in a given year? Explain.
4. In 1933 during the Great Depression net investment was negative. Does this mean that gross investment was negative also? Why or why not?
5. Which of the following goods or services would be included in *NNP* in 1968? In each case indicate why or why not.
   a. Flour.
   b. Sale of 1965 automobile.
   c. Sale of new wrist watch.
   d. Purchase of 100 shares of Texas Instruments stock.
   e. Services of housewives.
6. Which is the best measure of economic performance, *GNP, NNP,* or *NDI?* What reasons can you give for your answers?

SELECTED READINGS

Ackley, Gardner, *Macroeconomic Theory.* New York: Crowell-Collier and Macmillan, Inc., 1961, Chap. 3.

Chandler, Lester V., *The Economics of Money and Banking,* 4th ed. New York: Harper & Row Publishers, Inc., 1964, Chap. 13.

Ross, Myron H., *Income: Analysis and Policy.* New York: McGraw-Hill Book Company, Inc., 1964, Chap. 2.

The Level
of National
Income

CHAPTER 28

The step from the national income and product concepts of the last chapter to the forces that determine the level of economic performance is not a giant one. In fact, in developing the concepts and their relations to each other, the basic forces at work become almost self-evident. Though their broad outlines are simple, the details involved in their operation become rather complex. These details are introduced in this and the following chapter.

THE FRAMEWORK OF THE ANALYSIS

The foundations of national income analysis were laid by the noted British economist John Meynard Keynes in his celebrated *The General Theory of Employment, Interest and Money*.[1] An expert in the area of monetary theory, Keynes had long been troubled by the failure of the conventional economic theory of his day to come to grips with the causes of large-scale unemployment. His concern led to a whole new line of thinking with respect to the determinants of the level of economic activity, the causes of economic fluctuations and of unemployment, and policy prescriptions to correct some of the inherent defects of an economic system. Other economists have modified and developed Keynes's approach, adding an important dimension to economic analysis.

[1] John M. Keynes, *The General Theory of Employment, Interest and Money* (New York: Harcourt, Brace & World, Inc., 1936).

The Closed, Private Economy

In this chapter we limit our analysis to a closed, private economy. A *closed economy* is one that is self-contained; it carries on no transactions with other economies. By restricting the analysis to a closed economy we avoid the complications that international trade would introduce. A *private economy* is one in which there is no public or government sector. Such a situation is, of course, a figment of the imagination, but we must learn to crawl before we learn to walk. Once we understand the mechanics of national income analysis for the private economy, the extension to include the public sector is an easy one.

What are the implications of a closed, private economy for the national income and product concepts developed in the last chapter? Net national product consists of two parts instead of three. It is now the net value of goods and services produced for private consumption plus the value of net investment goods, or

$$NNP = C + I \qquad (28.1)$$

The only implication for net national income is that the indirect business taxes component drops out. Net disposable income is now concentrated in the hands of households and businesses. Government disposable income has disappeared. In the closed, private economy, then, net national product generates an equivalent amount of net national income, which, after certain private transfers are made, becomes net disposable income, or

$$NNP = NNI = NDI \qquad (28.2)$$

Spending, Saving, Investment, and Hoarding:[2] An Overview

What do the holders of the economy's net disposable income do with it? In the first instance they have a choice between spending for consumer goods and services or saving. Households will elect to spend some part of their disposable income on consumption and to save the rest. Businesses as such do not purchase consumer goods and services; therefore, we consider all of their disposable income as being saved. *Savings,* then, are that part of the economy's net disposable income that are not spent on consumption, or, letting S represent savings,

$$S = NDI - C \qquad (28.3)$$

---

[2] We shall defer discussion of the *determinants* of these to the latter part of the chapter. Here we are simply attempting to establish the mechanics of what makes income remain constant, rise, or fall over time.

Savings may be used to buy new capital goods or investment goods; that is, for the purchase of *net investment* goods. The actual channeling of savings into spending on new or net investment or capital goods is done in several different ways. Households may buy new issues of corporate stock with their savings, thus making available to corporations funds to invest in plant, equipment, and inventories. Sometimes they buy corporate bonds, the proceeds of which are invested in new capital by the corporation. Sometimes savings are deposited into accounts in commercial banks or savings and loan associations or are used to buy life insurance, whereupon these institutions make the funds available to businesses to invest in new capital goods. Additionally, there may be direct spending of business disposable income on investment or capital goods. This is usually characterized as "plowing earnings back into the business."

That part of *savings*—of both households and businesses—that is not spent on *investment goods* is *hoarded.* Care must be taken not to confuse hoarding with savings. They are not the same thing unless no spending for investment goods takes place. That part of *NDI not spent* on consumption is defined as savings. The savings are then available to be spent on investment goods or to be hoarded. That part of savings *not spent* on investment goods is defined as hoarding.

The disposition of net disposable income determines whether net national product will remain constant, rise, or decline over time. Although the production of net national product, the earning of net national income and net disposable income, and the spending of net disposable income are actually all occurring simultaneously, conceptually we can separate earning from spending. From the production of *NNP* an equivalent amount of *NDI* is generated.[3] This *NDI* now calls forth and is spent on the production of a new round of consumption goods and services as well as investment goods. The value of this new amount of consumption goods and services and investment goods—a new *NNP*—will be equal to the original one *if and only if* all current savings from the *NDI* are spent on investment goods and none are hoarded. If some of the savings are hoarded, or not spent for investment goods, then all of *NDI* is not spent and the value of consumption goods and services produced in response to spending will also be less than *NDI* and the original *NNP*. Under these circumstances *NNP* will decline over time. On the other hand, if households and businesses decide to spend *more* than the *NDI* currently earned—that is, if spending on investment goods exceeds the amount saved out of *NDI*, a new *NNP* greater than *NDI* and the original *NNP* will be forthcoming. This means that *NNP* will increase over time. We shall develop these processes in detail through the rest of the chapter.

[3] Since *NDI* is the same amount as *NNI*, we have left out the intermediate reference to *NNI.*

Period Analysis

An expository device called period analysis is useful in illustrating the forces that determine whether *NNP* remains constant, rises, or falls over time. We shall divide time into a succession of periods in order to separate analytically the earning from the spending of income.[4]

A Constant Level of NNP

The circumstances leading to a constant level of *NNP* over time are illustrated in Table 28-1. Suppose that in period (1) $700 billion worth of goods was produced. This amount is shown as *NNP* for period (1), and its production generates $700 billion in net disposable income (not listed separately in the table) available to be spent in period (2). We shall ignore the *NNP* figure for period (2) for the moment—we want to examine the process by which it is determined. Of the $700 billion available for spending in period (2) suppose that households elect to spend $600 billion for consumer goods and services. That part not spent on consumption is $100 billion and constitutes period (2) savings. The savings of period (2) can be spent in whole or in part for new or net investment or capital goods[5] and any remainder is defined as hoarding. Suppose, then, that the entire amount of savings is spent for $100 billion dollars worth of new investment goods.

TABLE 28-1
A Constant Level of *NNP* (billions of dollars)

	(1)	(2)	(3)
NNP	700	700	700
C		600	600
S		100	100
I		100	100

[4] The length of the period need not be specified, since it is an abstraction rather than a description of actual events. The values of *NNP, NDI*, and their components are assumed to represent annual rates—that is, to indicate what they would be for the entire year if they were to continue throughout the year at the same level shown in a given period. The essence of period analysis is that we assume income earned in any one period is disposed of (or partially hoarded) during the period immediately following.

[5] Why do we refer to *new* investment goods? Is it not possible that Mr. Throckmorton will use *his* savings to purchase stock in the Xerox Corporation from someone else rather than buying a newly issued share of Xerox? Of course, this is possible, but if Throckmorton so invests *his* savings the person from whom he is buying the stock is at the same time *disinvesting.* This transaction does not channel savings into investment for the economy as a whole. It simply transfers noninvested savings from Throckmorton to the party from whom he buys the stock. For the economy as a whole, savings can be invested *only* through the purchase of newly produced investment goods.

What is the total of *NNP* for period (2)? Consumer purchases of $600 billion worth of consumer goods means a $600 billion value for this component of *NNP*. Saver purchases of $100 billion worth of investment goods means a $100 billion value of the investment goods component. Net national product for period (2) must be $700 billion worth of product and is the same as it was for period (1). The $700 billion *NNP* for period (2) becomes *NDI* for period (3), and if all period (3) savings are invested —that is, if all of *NDI* for period (3) is spent—*NNP* for period (3) remains at the $700 billion level. The principle illustrated here is that *if current savings are all invested, total current earnings in the economy are all spent and NNP will remain constant over time.*

A Falling Level of NNP

The forces that lead to a decline in *NNP* are illustrated in Table 28–2. Again suppose that *NNP* produced in period (1) is $700 billion. This amount is *NDI* for period (2) and $600 billion of it is spent for consumer goods. Savings for period (2) are $100 billion. So far the example is identical to that for a constant level of *NNP*.

What happens to *NNP* if all savings of period (2) are not spent on investment goods? Suppose that only $50 billion of the savings is invested and that the other $50 billion is hoarded. Net national product for period (2) is $600 billion worth of consumer goods and services plus $50 billion worth of investment goods for a total of $650 billion—lower than it was in period (1) by the amount of the savings that is *hoarded* and *not invested.* The governing principle is that *if all current savings are not invested, total current earnings are not all spent and NNP will decline.*

What is likely to happen in period (3) and subsequent periods as a result of the decline in *NNP* from period (1) to period (2)? This question reaches ahead of what we are trying to establish at the moment. It will be handled in detail in the next chapter. However, we can take a brief look at its implications. Since *NNP* for period (2) has declined to $650 billion, *NDI* available to spend in period (3) has also declined to $650 billion as compared with the $700 billion available in period (2). House-

TABLE 28–2
A Declining Level of *NNP* (billions of dollars)

	(1)	*(2)*	*(3)*
NNP	700	650	610
C		600	560
S		100	90
I		50	50

holds, with less income to spend in period (3) than in period (2), are likely to reduce their over-all level of consumption. Suppose they reduce it by $40 billion to a level of $560 billion. Savings for period (3) are $90 billion. Now suppose that investment for period (3) is again $50 billion. Net national product for period (3) is $560 billion plus $50 billion, or $610. Net national product for period (3) is $610 billion, still lower than it was in period (2). (Compare the *cause* of the decline in *NNP* from period (1) to period (2) with the *cause* of the decline from period (2) to period (3). Are they the same?)

A Rising Level of NNP

The principles that govern the two preceding situations make the one associated with a rising level of *NNP* almost self-explanatory. *If businesses invest more than is being saved out of current income, more is being spent than is being earned in the economy and NNP will rise.*

Using the same starting point as before, we shall assume that investment in period (2) is $150 billion (see Table 28–3). Net disposable income available to be spent in period (2) is $700 billion, of which $600 billion is spent on consumption and $100 billion is saved. Investment for period (2) exceeds current savings by $50 billion. Since period (2) consumption is $600 billion and investment is $150 billion, *NNP* is $750 billion.

If investment in period (2) exceeds the savings of period (2), where do investors get the extra $50 billion to spend on investment goods? The answer is not hard to find. There are two sources of funds for investment readily available in addition to those provided by current savings. One such source is past accumulations of *hoarded savings.* Just as these were taken out of the spending stream in the past—as they were in the declinig *NNP* case—so can they be reinjected into the spending stream, augmenting current savings at any time the hoarders so desire. The second source is *newly created money,* ordinarily in the form of new demand deposits. If current savings are not sufficient to meet the demands of those wanting to invest in new capital goods, investors may go to the banks to borrow. If banks have excess reserves, new loans can be made and new deposits are

TABLE 28–3
A Rising Level of *NNP* (billions of dollars)

	(1)	*(2)*	*(3)*
NNP	700	750	790
C		600	640
S		100	110
I		150	150

created for the borrowers, thus increasing the funds available to investors over and above current savings.

Again, anticipating the analysis forthcoming in the next chapter, suppose we glance ahead at period (3). Net disposable income for period (3) is $750 billion, equal to the *NNP* of period (2). The rise in income available for spending in period (3) over that available in period (2) will surely stimulate additional spending on consumer goods and services. Suppose that the level rises to $640 billion for period (3). Savings in period (3) are $110 billion. If investment continues at the $150 billion level, *NNP* for period (3) is $790 billion.

DETERMINANTS OF NNP AND NDI

Although the general outlines of national income analysis are contained in the preceding section, a number of details must be filled in if we are to develop a useful theory that will round out our understanding of what determines the level of *NNP* or *NDI*, what causes them to fluctuate and to grow, and what government policies are likely to contribute to stability and growth. Much remains to be said about the nature of consumption, savings, and investment, as well as their interactions in the determination of net national product. We must begin to fill in the gaps.

Consumption

What are the main determinants of the annual spending of households on goods and services for personal consumption? Why, for example, as shown in Table 28–4, did expenditures of this type[6] fall from $79.1 billion in 1929 to a low of $46.5 billion in 1932 and then increase over the years to an estimated annual rate of $542.3 billion for the second quarter of 1968? Why do households consume a larger proportion of their disposable income in some years than they do in others; for example, compare 1949 with 1948. Again examine Table 28–4. There appear to be two primary determinants of the level of consumption. One is the level of disposable income available to households. The other is the psychological desire of consumers to spend on consumption as opposed to their desire to save some part of their disposable incomes. We shall refer to this desire as their *propensity to consume.*

---

[6] All *personal outlays,* defined by the Department of Commerce as *personal consumption expenditures* plus interest paid by consumers plus *personal transfer payments to foreigners,* are treated here as *spending for personal consumption.*

TABLE 28-4
Net National Product, Household Disposable Income, and Consumption,
Selected Years, 1929-1968

Year	Net National Product or Net Disposable Income	Household Disposable Income[1]	Consumption[2]
1929	95.2	83.3	79.1
1932	50.7	45.5	46.5
1935	65.4	58.5	56.4
1940	92.2	75.7	71.8
1945	200.7	150.2	120.7
1948	243.1	189.1	175.8
1949	239.9	188.6	179.2
1950	266.4	206.9	193.9
1955	366.5	275.3	259.5
1960	460.3	350.0	333.0
1965	624.0	402.2	433.1
1966	683.5	511.6	478.6
1967	720.5	546.3	506.2
1968[3]	779.1	586.3	542.3

[1] Equivalent to Department of Commerce "Disposable Personal Income."
[2] Equivalent to Department of Commerce "Personal Outlays."
[3] Second quarter estimates.
SOURCES: Department of Commerce, *The National Income and Product Accounts of the United States, 1929-1965* (Washington, D.C., 1966), pp. 12-13 and 32-33; and *Survey of Current Business* (September 1968), 8-9.

The Consumption Function

Ordinarily we expect the level of consumption to vary directly with the level of income available to households to spend—the higher the level of *household disposable income*, the higher the level of consumption. Table 28-4 confirms this expectation. The level of household disposable income in turn bears a direct relation to *net disposable income*, so we can say that consumption is a function of, or depends upon, net disposable income. Its dependence on *NDI* is not quite as strong as its dependence on household disposable income because of possible variations in the business disposable income component of *NDI*. However, in the analytical framework that we construct and use, we can avoid some complexities with little sacrifice of accuracy by relating consumption to *NDI*. This relation is called the *consumption function*, the term "function" being used in the mathematical sense to mean the *dependence* of consumption on *NDI*.

The nature of the consumption function for an economy is illustrated by Table 28-5 and Figure 28-1, but a little background work is in order before we look at the latter explicitly. In Figure 28-1, billions of dollars are measured along both the horizontal and the vertical axes. Now suppose that line *OE* is drawn upward and to the right from the origin in

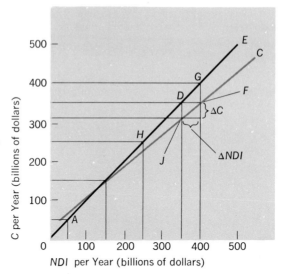

Figure 28–1
The consumption function.

such a way that each point on it represents the same amount measured along the vertical axis as it represents along the horizontal axis. Point A is $50 billion; point H is $250 billion; point D is $350 billion; and point G is $400 billion, in all cases both axes or either axis showing the correct measurements.[7] The OE line provides indispensable aid in the graphic representation of national income determination, its most valuable property being that for any given measurement along the horizontal axis it provides the same measurement vertically.

A typical consumption function, constructed from hypothetical data, is shown by columns (1) and (2) of Table 28–5 and is plotted as curve C in Figure 28–1. In Figure 28–1, net disposable income is measured along the horizontal axis, while expenditures on consumption goods and services are measured along the vertical axis. At an NDI level of $350 billion, households would want to spend $310 billion on consumption, and point J on the consumption curve is located. If NDI were $400 billion, C would be $350 billion, and point F is located on the consumption curve. Other points tracing out curve C are located in a similar manner.

Average Propensity to Consume

The consumption function in Figure 28–1 exhibits a characteristic that merits explanation. At relatively low income levels consumption exceeds

---

[7] If the scales of the two axes are the same, OE is a 45-degree line, or bisects the angle at the origin of the diagram.

NDI; at relatively high levels it is less than *NDI*; and the higher the income level, the smaller is the ratio or proportion of consumption to income. To say this another way, at relatively low levels of income the *average propensity to consume* is greater than 1; at relatively high levels of income it is less than 1; and as the income level increases, the average propensity to consume decreases. In this latter statement the *average propensity to consume* is defined as the proportion of the average dollar of disposable income used for consumption purposes. Mathematically it is expressed as

$$APC = \frac{C}{NDI} \qquad (28.4)$$

In Figure 28-1 we assume that at income levels below $150 billion the average propensity to consume is greater than 1—that the households of the economy consume a larger value of goods and services than they are currently producing. In order to do this the economy as a whole must transform some of its capital equipment into consumer goods and services or use up some of the inventories of goods and services carried over from previous years that comprise a part of the economy's total stock of capital. It fails to take care of all of the depreciation that occurs during the year. This almost happened in 1932.

At higher levels of income the pressure to consume is much less severe.

TABLE 28-5
A Hypothetical Consumption Function

(1) NET DISPOSABLE INCOME (*NDI*) (BILLIONS OF DOLLARS)	(2) CONSUMPTION (*C*) (BILLIONS OF DOLLARS)	(3) MARGINAL PROPENSITY TO CONSUME (*MPC*)
50	70	
100	110	0.8
150	150	0.8
200	190	0.8
250	230	0.8
300	270	0.8
350	310	0.8
400	350	0.8
450	390	0.8
500	430	0.8
550	470	0.8
600	510	0.8
650	550	0.8
700	590	0.8
750	630	0.8
800	670	0.8

People earn large enough incomes so that they need not consume on the average as much as they produce. Instead of spending the entire amount of the average dollar on consumption they can afford to save some part of it. And the higher the income level, the greater the proportion of the average dollar they can afford to save—or the smaller the proportion of the average dollar they feel compelled to spend for consumption. In any event, this is what the available data relating consumption to disposable income seem to indicate.

Marginal Propensity to Consume

The *marginal propensity to consume,* or *MPC,* plays an important role in the analysis of economic fluctuations and their control. Similar to the rest of the marginal concepts that we have used, it is defined as *the change in consumption per unit change in the level of income,* other things being equal. Mathematically it is expressed as

$$MPC = \frac{\Delta C}{\Delta NDI} \qquad (28.5)$$

In Table 28–5, in moving from one income level to the next, the marginal propensity to consume is 0.8, meaning that for each one dollar increase or decrease in *NDI* consumption will change by 80 cents. Consider, for example, an increase in *NDI* from \$350 to \$400 billion. The corresponding increase in consumption is \$40 billion worth of goods and services, the change from \$310 to \$350 billion. Thus

$$MPC = \frac{\$40 \text{ billion}}{\$50 \text{ billion}} = 0.8$$

The table has been constructed using the underlying assumption that the *MPC* is 0.8 throughout the range of possible income levels.

In Figure 28–1, the marginal propensity to consume for any small change in the level of income is measured by the slope of the consumption curve, *C,* for the change. Suppose again that the level of *NDI* is \$350 billion and that the level of consumption is \$310 billion initially, locating point *J* on the consumption curve. Now suppose *NDI* increases to \$400 billion and consumption increases to \$350 billion, moving up the consumption curve to point *F.* Again

$$MPC = \frac{\Delta C}{\Delta NDI} = \frac{\$40 \text{ billion}}{\$50 \text{ billion}} = 0.8$$

where $(\Delta C)/(\Delta NDI)$ is the slope of line segment *JF.*

Although we have shown the consumption function as a linear relationship, or as a straight-line consumption curve, many economists be-

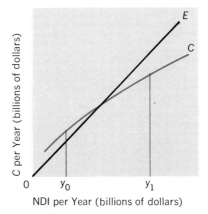

Figure 28-2
A nonlinear consumption function.

lieve that it is likely to be concave downward, as Figure 28–2 illustrates. In order for the consumption curve to be this shape, the marginal propensity to consume must be higher at low levels of disposable income than at higher levels—at Y_0 the slope of C must be greater than it is at Y_1. Is this plausible? If *NDI* is at depression levels, it seems reasonable to expect that households will spend a very large part of any increase in *NDI* on consumption, or that the *MPC* will be high. An affluent society with a relatively large *NDI* appears to be in a somewhat different position. An increase in *NDI* may not yield such a large increase in consumption because consumption is much less urgent than it is at lower income levels. Even if the consumption curve were concave downward, the theory of national income determination and change is essentially the same as it would be if the consumption curve were linear. Since linear curves are less complex to manipulate, we shall use the straight-line consumption function.

Changes in Propensity To Consume

We must distinguish between movements along a consumption function and shifts in the function itself. So far we have assumed that the over-all *propensity to consume* is fixed, thereby enabling us to identify a given consumption function. At different levels of *NDI* the average propensity to consume and the marginal propensity to consume may vary, but the over-all *propensity to consume* defines the range of consumption reactions of households to the whole range of possible alternative levels of *NDI*—it represents a given state of mind toward all possible alternative income levels.

The given state of mind, or the propensity to consume, may change.

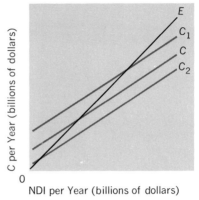

Figure 28–3
Shifts in the consumption function.

Households may be engulfed by a wave of optimism which induces them to consume more at each possible level of *NDI* than formerly and which shifts the entire consumption function upward from, say, *C* in Figure 28–3 to C_1. Or, on the other hand, pessimism—fear of a depression, for example—may shift it downward to a position like that of C_2. Another possibility is that income redistribution from the rich to the poor may occur in a society. Which group is likely to have the higher marginal propensity to consume? If *NDI* is transferred from those with lower *MPC*'s to those with higher *MPC*'s, at each of various levels of *NDI* the level of consumption will be higher than before—the consumption curve will be shifted upward.

Savings

Decisions to save are made by two groups of economic units, (1) households and (2) business enterprises. Household savings decisions must be made concurrently with decisions to consume. Business decisions to save, or to accumulate undistributed profits, are made concurrently with decisions concerning what part of corporate profits are to be paid out to stockholders as dividends. These decisions together define or locate the savings function for the economy.

The Determinants of Savings

When a household makes its consumption and savings decisions the desirability of saving must be weighed against the desirability of consuming, with the objective of reaching that distribution of disposable income between the two that will yield the highest level of satisfaction to the household. What are the factors that tend to make saving desirable? For one thing, an accumulation of savings can provide a degree of security against *unforeseen contingencies*—accidents, sickness, unemployment, death of the family breadwinner, or other adverse circumstances that can happen to anyone anytime. Second, members of households generally look toward *old age and retirement* and save to provide for themselves when they reach this period in their lives. Third, people may save for the explicit purpose of building a *source of additional income.* Toward this end they invest their savings in stocks, bonds, real property, businesses, and other income-yielding assets. Fourth, some people have read Benjamin Franklin's *Poor Richard's Almanac* or have come to value *thrift* as a virtue from other sources. Regardless of their income level they curtail their consumption and put some of their income into savings. Finally, some small part of household savings may be a *residual,* coming into existence simply because the households fail to spend their entire disposable income.

The volume of savings for households as a group will normally vary in the same direction as household disposable income. At relatively low income levels the need to consume is more pressing. But as disposable income increases, and as it becomes easier to fulfill some of the more important immediate wants, households can pay more heed to the various savings motives, holding more and more out of current consumption.

Business savings consist of corporate undistributed profits or of business disposable income. Since businesses do not consume goods and services, all of business disposable income is saved. Businesses save for two reasons. First, as in the case of households, it may be desirable to build some financial security against *unforeseen contingencies*—recessions, strikes, and so on. Second, businesses save in order to *invest in new plant and equipment.* Savings frequently provide a less expensive source of funds for expansion than the issuance of bonds or stocks. The total volume of business savings would be expected to vary directly with business disposable income, rising when income rises and falling when income falls.

Total savings, composed of both household and business savings, bears a direct relation to net disposable income of the economy. The whole is the sum of the parts in this case, since *NDI* consists of household and business disposable income combined. At depression levels of *NDI,* if household spending on consumption is greater than *NDI,* total savings of the economy must be negative.

The Savings Function

The *savings function,* or the relation between the level of savings and the level of *NDI,* is shown graphically in Figure 28–4(b). The position

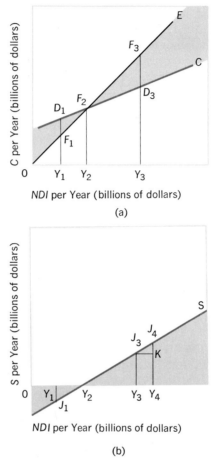

Figure 28-4
The relation between the consumption function and the saving function.

and shape of the savings curve, S, is interdependent with the shape and position of the consumption curve, C, of Figure 28–4(a). The NDI axes of the two diagrams are identical; however, in Figure 28–4(a) the annual rate of consumption is measured on the vertical axis while in Figure 28–4(b) the vertical axis represents the annual rate of savings.

Suppose that the consumption curve, C, is given and that we want to derive the savings curve from it. If the level of NDI is Y_3, what is the magnitude of savings? The OE line of Figure 28–4(a) enables us to answer the question easily and quickly. At income level Y_3, the level of consumption is Y_3D_3. The distance Y_3F_3 represents the same dollar amount as OY_3—the OE curve is constructed to make this so—and therefore is also a measure of NDI. Savings at income level Y_3, then, are represented by D_3F_3, the difference between NDI and consumption at that income level. In Figure 28–4(b), at income level Y_3, point J_3 is set so that Y_3J_3 is the same dollar amount as D_3F_3 in Figure 28–4(a) and it locates one point on the savings curve.

Suppose the process is repeated at income level Y_2. Total net disposable income is also measured by Y_2F_2. Spending on consumption, as indicated by the consumption curve, is Y_2F_2 at that income level, so savings are zero. In the lower diagram this is indicated by the point on the NDI axis at Y_2.

At income level Y_1, *dissaving* occurs; that is, savings are negative. Spending on consumption exceeds net disposable income. Consumers are either spending past accumulated stocks of household savings or businesses are drawing upon undistributed profits or savings of previous years to pay out more to their owners than their current corporate profits. In the diagram, net disposable income is measured by Y_1F_1 as well as by OY_1. Total spending on consumption is Y_1D_1. Total dissaving is F_1D_1. Point J_1 is located below the NDI axis in the lower diagram, so that J_1Y_1 is equal to F_1D_1.

Points such as J_1, Y_2, and J_3 trace out the savings function, SS, showing the relation of savings to net disposable income at various alternative income levels. In summary, the savings function is obtained by subtracting the consumption curve, C, vertically from the OE line. At any given level of NDI the level of savings is found by subtracting the level of consumption from that level of NDI.

Marginal Propensity to Save

The change in the level of savings in the economy per unit change in the level of NDI is called the *marginal propensity to save*. This is expressed as $\Delta S/\Delta NDI$ and is the same kind of concept as the marginal propensity to consume; in fact, the two are interdependent. Suppose, for example, that NDI increases by one dollar and that the MPC is 0.8. The level of consumption increases by 80 cents and the remaining 20 cents is added to savings. The marginal propensity to save, or MPS, is obviously 0.2. Mathematically,

$$MPC + MPS = 1 \qquad (28.6)$$

Since the $MPC = (\Delta C)/(\Delta NDI)$ and the $MPS = (\Delta S)/(\Delta NDI)$, then $MPC + MPS = 1$. That is, a one-unit change (or any other change) in NDI is necessarily divided between a change in consumption and a change in savings.[8]

[8] For any change in NDI,

$$\Delta NDI = \Delta C + \Delta S$$

or

$$1 = \frac{\Delta C}{\Delta NDI} + \frac{\Delta S}{\Delta NDI}$$

In Figure 28–4(b), for any given small change of *NDI* the slope of the savings curve shows the marginal propensity to save. If, for example, *NDI* rises from Y_3 to Y_4, savings increase by KJ_4. The change in savings per unit change in *NDI* is $(KJ_4)/(J_3K)$, or the slope of the line segment J_3J_4.

Investment

Who determines the annual rate of investment in new plant, equipment, inventories, and other capital goods? Most investment decisions are made by business firms, either those already in business or those in the process of entering. At any given time investment in some industries will be expanding while in others it will be contracting. Households are responsible for almost one third of net investment, mostly in the form of net additions to residential structures. The factors that seem to be most important in determining the magnitude of net investment are (1) the interest rate prevailing in the economy and (2) business expectations.

The Interest Rate

What is interest and the interest rate? We usually think of *interest* as the cost of borrowing money—what we must pay the bank or the mortgage company over time over and above the principal sum that we borrow. This is a correct definition but it does not go far enough. Business firms borrow to invest in inventories or in plant and equipment. They also raise funds in other ways, notably by selling stock or equities in the business. Dividend payouts, or the prospective earnings to stockholders in the form of appreciation in the value of their stocks, necessary to induce them to buy those stocks, are also *costs* of obtaining funds for investment. We shall refer to all such costs as *interest*. The *interest rate* is the percentage obtained by dividing the annual interest cost of a principal sum by the principal.

There is, of course, no such thing as "the" interest rate; there is a whole complex of interest rates. More risk is involved in providing investable funds to some businesses than to others, and the more risky business must offer a higher rate of return than others to compensate the supplier of funds for the possibility of not getting back either the full amount of the principal or the interest. Further, long-term use of investable funds usually implies a higher interest rate than short-term use. This is partly because of the greater risk associated with long-term commitments and partly because the supplier of funds loses control of them for a longer period of time. In any case, interest rates differ for different users of investable funds and for different time periods for which funds are committed. When we speak of "the" interest rate we refer to an index number of the complex.

How does the interest rate affect the amount of investment undertaken in the economy? If a business can invest $100 in plant and equipment and if that plant and equipment will yield a net income of $10 worth of goods and services per year—this amount over and above the amount necessary to take care of depreciation on the capital goods during the year—the *yield* on the investment is 10 percent per year. If the business can obtain investable funds from savers (or from itself as undistributed profits or business savings) for 8 percent per year, it is profitable to borrow or otherwise obtain the funds and to make the investment. However, if the cost of obtaining funds from savers is 12 percent per year, the investment will not be made, since it would result in a net loss.

The higher the interest rate, given business expectations, the less investors will be willing to invest. Suppose we know the positive net yield of all of the new investment projects that might be undertaken in the coming year and that we also know the costs of producing the investment goods to fulfill the projects. The total cost of such investment goods is measured in dollars along the horizontal axis in Figure 28–5. Now suppose that we arrange the projects along the horizontal axis so that those providing the highest yields are closer to the origin and those providing lower yields are farther from the origin. The line MEC is traced out by the yields as we accumulate the total costs of the projects, moving from the one with the highest yield to those with successively lower yields. A quantity of investment, I_1, will have a yield of r_1 percent or more; a quantity of I_2 will have a yield of r_2 percent or better; and so on, until we reach I, the total amount that will have a positive yield. This curve is called the *marginal efficiency of capital,* or the MEC curve.

Now suppose we look at r_1 and r_2 as alternative rates of interest or costs to investors of obtaining investable funds. If the interest rate were r_1, it would pay investors to undertake an amount of net investment of I_1. Investments up to this point would add more to investors' incomes than to their costs, since the yields would exceed the costs of obtaining the funds needed to effect the investments. Similarly, if the interest rate were r_2, investors would undertake investment in the amount of I_2. The amount of investment that would be undertaken, then, is inversely related to the interest rate.

Business Expectations

Business expectations is a blanket term covering everything that affects the general profit outlook of those who make business decisions. During periods of prosperity, such as 1963–1967, profit prospects are excellent and anticipated yields on new investments for the business community at large are relatively high. Exceptionally good expectations encourage larger amounts of investment at each possible level of the interest rate and thus shift the marginal efficiency of capital curve to the right, toward some position such as MEC_1. On the other hand, when profit prospects for business as a whole are adverse, as they were during the recession of 1960–1961, businesses are willing to invest less at each possible level of the interest rate because of smaller anticipated yields on new investment. The marginal efficiency of capital curve will lie farther to the left, toward some position such as MEC_0.

The Investment Curve

If the yearly rate of net investment depends on the interest rate and on business expectations rather than on the level of net disposable income, it is represented by a horizontal line when it is shown graphically on net disposable income diagrams such as those used to show the savings curve. Suppose that business expectations are such that MEC is the appropriate marginal efficiency of capital curve in Figure 28–5. Suppose also that the going interest rate in the economy is r_1. The level of investment is I_1. Figure 28–6 shows net disposable income on the horizontal axis, as did the savings diagram of Figure 28–4. The vertical axis measures investment. The investment curve is I_1, lying at I_1 dollars above the

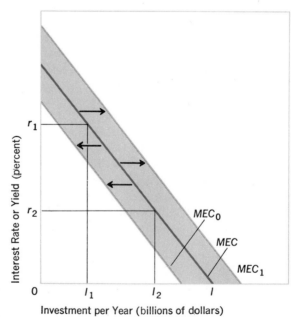

Figure 28–5
The marginal efficiency of capital curve.

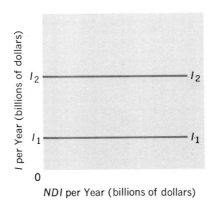

Figure 28-6
The investment curve.

horizontal axis for all levels of *NDI*. If the interest rate were to decrease to r_2 in Figure 28–5, investment per year increases to I_2, shifting the investment curve in Figure 28–6 upward to I_2.

The Equilibrium Level of NDI and NNP

A great part of savings decisions are largely accomplished by a different group of economic units than those who make investment decisions. Further, the factors underlying savings decisions are largely different from those underlying investment decisions. These observations lead to the conclusion that for any given level of *NDI* there is no compelling reason why investors would want to invest exactly the same amounts that savers want to save. If the amount of investment that investors desire to undertake differs from the amount of savings that savers desire to save, changes in *NNP* and *NDI* will be set in motion.

Suppose that the consumption function, the savings function, and the desired level of investment are those illustrated in Figure 28–7 by the *C*, the *S*, and the *I* curves, respectively. The *S* and the *I* curves are placed together in Figure 28–7(b). One new curve appears in Figure 28–7(a). This is the *C* + *I* curve, which shows the level of total spending on *both* consumption and investment for each possible level of *NDI*. It is located by adding the level of desired investment to the level of desired consumption for each possible level of *NDI*—that is, it is the vertical summation of the *C* and the *I* curves.

Rising NDI and NNP

If the level of *NDI* were Y_1, would *NNP* and *NDI* rise, fall, or remain constant? At that income level households want to spend Y_1C_1 dollars on

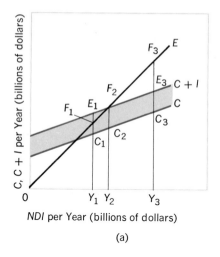

(a)

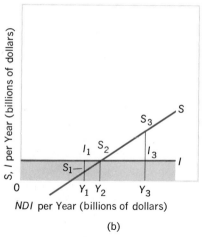

(b)

Figure 28–7
Determination of the level of net disposable income.

consumer goods and services, saving C_1F_1 dollars, as shown in Figure 28–7(a). Investors want to invest C_1F_1 dollars which is more than savers want to save. The consequences are that more will be spent than is being earned currently, inventories of goods and services will be depleted, and production will become more profitable because of rising demand. The economy's output of goods and services will rise in response to the more favorable profit opportunities, bringing inventories back to the desired levels. This, of course, means that NNP and NDI will rise.

The same situation is illustrated in Figure 28–7(b), since these two diagrams are completely interdependent. In Figure 28–7(b), the savings curve shows that at income level Y_1, the level of savings will be Y_1S_1. Investors desire to invest Y_1I_1 dollars which is more than is currently being saved. If desired investment exceeds savings, then more will be spent than is being earned currently and NNP and NDI will rise.

Falling NDI and NNP

What forces will be set in motion if the level of NDI is initially at Y_3? The level of consumption will be Y_3C_3, leaving savings of C_3F_3. Investment is only C_3E_3. Total spending is Y_3E_3 and E_3F_3 is hoarded. Total spending is less than the amount currently being earned. Falling demand for goods and services makes business less profitable and causes inventories to accumulate above desired levels. Production is curtailed, so NNP and NDI decline.

In Figure 28–7(b) at income level Y_3, savings are Y_3S_3 while investment is only Y_3I_3. Since savings are greater than investment, less is being spent than is being earned; I_3S_3 is hoarded; so NNP and NDI decline.

Equilibrium NNP and NDI

Net national product and net disposable income will be in *equilibrium* when there are no forces operating to make them rise or fall. In the rising income case, desired investment exceeded current savings, generating rising levels of NNP and NDI. But as NDI increases, savings increase also until at income level Y_2 they are equal, both being C_2F_2 in Figure 28–7(a) or Y_2S_2 in Figure 28–7(b). At this income level the forces generating the rise in income no longer exist and the increase will stop. In the opposite case, desired investment was less than current savings, causing NNP and NDI to fall. As NDI falls, savings decrease until at level Y_2 savings and investment are the same. The forces causing income to fall have faded away and the decrease in income stops. At income level I_2, at which savings and investment are equal, NNP and NDI are in equilibrium.

SECULAR EXPANSION OR CONTRACTION OF PRODUCTIVE CAPACITY

The principles of national income determination have been developed in this chapter as though the total quantity of resources available for use were fixed. This is a reasonable assumption to use for short periods of time, but secularly, or over a period of years, the total quantity of resources will surely change. These changes will usually increase, but on occasion they may decrease, the productive capacity of the economy.

Expansion of Productive Capacity

Throughout the analysis of income determination we have assumed that net investment is positive; that is, that net investment is occurring. What effects will positive net investment have on the economy's productive capacity? Consider Figure 28–8. Suppose we are observing the operation of the economy over a period of one year and that the economy's stock of capital at the beginning of the year is represented by the block labeled *initial stock of capital.* The production of *GNP* for the year, represented by the rectangle so indicated, would by itself reduce the stock of capital by the amount called *depreciation.* Of the *gross investment* component of *GNP,* some part is used to take care of depreciation, or to bring the stock of capital back to its initial amount. The rest of gross investment—*net investment*—represents *capital accumulation* for the year, and when added to the initial stock of capital brings the economy's stock of capital at the end of the year up to that shown as the *final stock of capital.*

Positive net investment then constitutes capital accumulation and a growing capacity of the economic system to produce. This is not inconsistent with the possibility that *NNP* and *NDI* may from time to time decrease. These may increase or decrease, even though the potential capacity of the economy to produce is increasing, as the actual levels of employment of resources of the economy are increased or decreased.

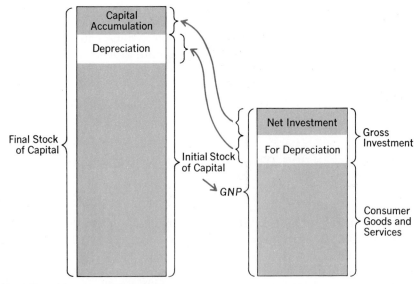

Figure 28–8
Positive net investment and capital accumulation.

Contraction of Productive Capacity

The possibility that net investment in an economy may be negative has been mentioned before. We would not expect long, sustained periods of negative net investment—an economic system where this occurs will not survive. Rather, we would expect short periods of negative net investment for economies undergoing some sort of crisis such as colossal mismanagement or a deep depression.

The circumstances of negative net investment and contraction of an economy's capacity to produce are illustrated in Figure 28–9. Again suppose that we observe the economy's operation for one year. The *initial stock of capital* is represented by the entire large rectangle on the left and is used to produce *GNP*. In the process the quantity of capital indicated as *depreciation* is used up. But this time the *gross investment* component of *GNP* is insufficient to cover all depreciation. That part of it not covered by gross investment is *net capital consumption* and can be thought of as being converted into consumer goods and services that are used up during the year. Thus the *final stock of capital* at the end of the year is less than the initial stock of capital by the amount of capital so consumed. This amount is the *negative net investment*. The shrinking stock of capital constitutes contraction of the economy's capacity to produce. (Can you illustrate and explain the circumstances under which the economy's stock of capital will remain constant over time?)

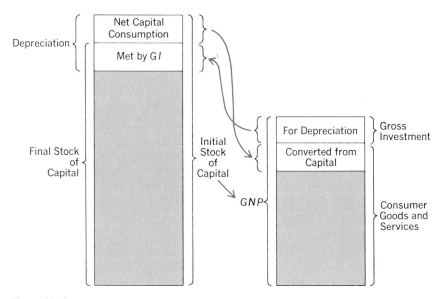

Figure 28–9
Negative net investment and net capital consumption.

SUMMARY

We study in this chapter the private economic forces that lead to a rising, a falling, or an equilibrium level of net national product and net disposable income. The relation of total spending to the amount of net disposable income currently being earned is the key element of the analysis and within this broad framework we examine the interplay among net disposable income, consumption, savings, investment, and net national product.

In the period analysis overview the spending process is separated conceptually from the earning process. That which is earned in one period is conceived of as being available for spending in the next. Of the net disposable income earned in any one period, households will elect to spend some part on goods and services for personal consumption. The remainder is household savings. Household savings together with business savings constitute total savings, the amount of net disposable income not spent on consumption during the second period. Spending for investment goods during the second period is done primarily by business firms, although household spending for new residential construction is considered a part of it. Net national product for the second period is the value of consumption plus the value of investment, and its production generates an equal amount of net disposable income that becomes available for spending in the third period. For net national product and net disposable incomes of the second period to be the same as net disposable income of the first period, investment in the second period must be the same as savings in the second period. If investment exceeds savings in the second period, *NNP* and *NDI* will rise. If investment is less than savings, *NNP* and *NDI* will fall.

The consumption function shows that the level of consumption in the economy depends on the level of *NDI* and the propensity to consume. The average propensity to consume is the change in consumption per unit change in the level of *NDI*.

The savings function indicates the level of savings at all possible levels of *NDI*. Savings decisions are made largely by households, along with their decisions to consume, but are also made by business firms. At any level of *NDI* savings are the difference between *NDI* and the level of consumption. The change in savings per unit change in *NDI* is called the marginal propensity to save.

The level of investment depends upon (1) the interest rate and (2) business expectations. The interest rate is the cost of obtaining investable funds to those who make investment decisions. It is the percentage of return that those who control the funds must have in order to be induced to make them available. Business expectations refer to the whole range of factors affecting the profit outlook for those who make business decisions.

Savings and investment decisions are made largely by different groups of economic units and for largely different reasons. At any given level of *NDI* the amount that investors want to invest is not necessarily the same as the amount that savers want to save. Any divergence between these amounts will cause the level of *NNP* and *NDI* to change until the amount that savers want to save is equal to the amount that investors want to invest. National income—*NNP* and *NDI*—is in equilibrium when this is the case.

Secular expansion or contraction of the economy's productive capacity is dependent on the level of net investment. If net investment is positive, the economy is accumulating capital or adding to its productive capacity. If net investment is negative, capital consumption is occurring and the productive capacity of the economy will be contracting.

EXERCISES AND QUESTIONS FOR DISCUSSION

1. If *I* is greater than *S*, the level of *NNP* and *NDI* will tend to rise until a full-employment equilibrium level of income is attained. Discuss.
2. "If the lower-income groups have a higher average propensity to consume than the higher-income groups and income is transferred from the higher groups to the lower groups, *NNP* will rise." Evaluate this statement.
3. Suppose all consumers decide to save more. What will be the effect on the equilibrium level of *NNP*? Beginning with the original equilibrium, discuss the causal process.
4. "If no hoarding takes place in the economy, investment will never exceed saving and the capacity of the economy will not grow." Discuss this statement critically.
5. Which of the following will affect the position of the consumption function? Why?
   a. An increase in the level of *NDI*.
   b. An increase in the *MPS*.
   c. A decrease in the *MPC*.
   d. A decrease in the *APS*.
6. "If net investment is positive, the equilibrium level of *NNP* will rise in the next period, since the productive capacity of the economy is increased." Evaluate this statement.

SELECTED READINGS

Chandler, Lester V., *The Economics of Money and Banking*, 4th ed. New York: Harper & Row, Publishers, Inc., 1964, Chap. 15.
Heilbroner, Robert L., *Understanding Macroeconomics*. Englewood Cliffs, N.J.: Prentice-Hall, Inc., 1965, Chaps. 4–7.
McKenna, Joseph P., *Aggregate Economic Analysis*, rev. ed. New York: Holt, Rinehart and Winston, Inc., 1965, Chaps. 6 and 8.

National
Income
and Public
Policy

CHAPTER 29

When net national product and net disposable income are in equilibrium, is the economic system behaving as we want it to behave? Are the problems of employment, instability, and growth that we have been attacking in the last eight chapters alleviated by the movement of national income to equilibrium levels? Not at all. There is nothing inherently desirable about an equilibrium level of *NNP* or *NDI*. As we shall see, the equilibrium level may be too low or too high. Further, it changes from time to time, leading to recession and depression on the one hand and to inflation on the other. In this chapter we relate national income analysis to the performance of the economy as a whole and we use it to round out our understanding of the causes of poor performance and of policy prescriptions intended to improve it.

NATIONAL INCOME AND ECONOMIC OBJECTIVES

As we have considered the performance of the economy as a whole thus far, three important objectives that we would like to see attained stand out. First, we would like to achieve full employment of the economy's resources. Second, we would like to have economic stability—freedom from recession and from inflation. Third, we want the productive capacity of the economy to grow. How does national income analysis relate to these objectives?

Full Employment and Stability

The objectives of full employment and stability overlap to such a degree that they can hardly be treated separately. The level of re-

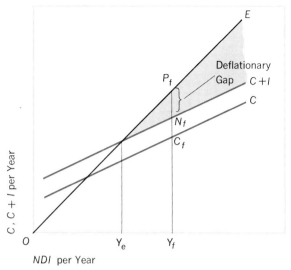

Figure 29-1
A deflationary gap.

source employment in the economy bears a direct relation to the level of national income up to the level at which full employment occurs. The higher the level of national income, the greater the level of employment up to that point.[1] If national income increases beyond that level, the increases are in money terms only, coming from price increases rather than from actual increases in the volume of goods and services comprising *NNP*.

The Deflationary Gap

Is it possible for national income to be in equilibrium at a less than full-employment level of resource use? It is not only possible, it happens. For *NNP* and *NDI* to be in equilibrium, it is necessary only that current savings be equal to intended investment—that all income currently being earned be spent. Savers decide what part of *NDI* they want to save for one set of reasons and investors decide how much they want to invest for another. If at a full-employment level of *NNP* savers want to save more than investors want to invest, the equilibrium level of *NNP* and *NDI* is necessarily below the full-employment level.

Such a situation is illustrated in Figure 29–1. Suppose that full employment would occur at income level Y_f. But at that level of income savers want to save $C_f P_f$ and investors are willing to invest only $C_f N_f$. Less will be spent than is being earned; *NNP* and *NDI* will fall to the

[1] See pages 377–385.

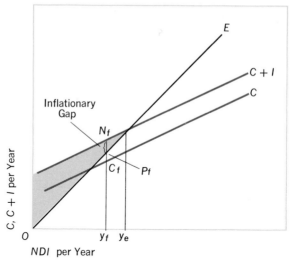

Figure 29–2
An inflationary gap.

equilibrium level Y_e; and at that level unemployment exists. The deficiency in total spending at Y_f, represented by $N_f P_f$, is referred to traditionally as the *deflationary gap*. Note that it is identical to the amount that would be hoarded at that level of income.

The Inflationary Gap

Can the equilibrium level of NNP and NDI be greater than the level at which full employment would occur? It most certainly can be and was during the immediate post-World War II years from 1946 to the middle of 1948. If at the full-employment level of NNP and NDI investors want to invest more than savers want to save, total spending will exceed total earning and, through inflation, the money level of NNP and NDI will rise. Real NNP cannot increase, however, if resources are fully employed.

The conditions giving rise to inflationary increases in NNP are illustrated in Figure 29–2. Suppose that Y_f is the full-employment level of NDI. Savers want to save only $C_f P_f$ at that level of income but investors want to invest $C_f N_f$. The excess of desired investment over current savings, $P_f N_f$, is called the *inflationary gap*.

Economic Growth

Economic growth, measured in terms of rising NNP—although more accurately in terms of rising real *per capita* NNP—is not assured by income levels that are merely in equilibrium. Although national income expands when given quantities of resources are used more efficiently, a primary source of growth lies in the accumulation of capital equipment over time—increases in the magnitude of the economy's productive capacity. As we noted at the end of the last chapter, capital accumulation occurs whenever net investment or I is greater than zero. If the general public spends all of its earnings on consumption, savings are zero. If at the same time there is no new investment in plant, equipment, and inventories, then savings and investment are equal at the zero level; national income will be in equilibrium; and no secular increase in NNP is possible. If savings and investment are equal at *negative levels*, secular contraction of productive capacity accompanied by falling NNP and NDI will occur.

Even when I is positive, some of the underdeveloped economies of the world find that per capita income increases very little, if at all, from year to year, and in some instances may even fall. India, for example, experienced virtually no increase in per capita income from 1900 to 1950, and since 1950 the increases have been small. In Chile between 1955 and 1963 there may have been a slight decrease in per capita income even though NNP was increasing somewhat. The problem in these and other countries is that population increases in almost the same proportion as NNP.

DESTABILIZING FORCES

Although deflationary and inflationary gaps lead to periods of recession and inflation, additional destabilizing forces are at work. Any given equilibrium level of NNP and NDI is determined by the existing level of the investment curve and the consumption or the savings function. Changes in one of these may occur, and when they do amplified changes in NNP and NDI are set in motion.

Changes in Investment

The amount of investment that business firms and households want to undertake is very volatile. Over short time periods business expectations can change rapidly for a variety of reasons. A major strike can bring on a wave of pessimism out of proportion to its real impact on the volume of business being done in the economy. So can an extensive government investigation like that of the American Telephone and Telegraph Company begun by the Federal Communications Commission in 1966. International events like the closing of the Suez Canal in 1967 in the Israeli-

Egyptian dispute or the Bay of Pigs disaster in 1961 may also have adverse effects. On the other hand, such things as a spectacular space exploit, the discovery of an extensive uranium deposit or an oil pool, or the signing of an international alliance or agreement may have favorable effects on business expectations. Over longer periods nothing buoys expectations like expansion and profits, and nothing is more devastating to them than economic loss and contraction. As expectations change, so does the level of investment.

Changes in the interest rate also affect the level of investment, although it is doubtful that these are as important as changes in expectations. An easy money policy on the part of the Federal Reserve System lowers interest rates and investment tends to increase. An easy money policy puts more money into the hands of the general public. It may permit more business borrowing by making excess reserves available to the banking system where none were available before. Both consumption spending and investment spending may increase simply because more money is available. In general, we would expect changes in the interest rate to reinforce changes in business expectations in bringing about changes in the level of investment.

The volatile nature of intended investment moves the latter now above and now below the level of savings. Both the savings and the consumption functions appear to be much more stable over time. As discrepancies between the level of desired investment and current savings occur, corresponding changes in the level of national income are set in motion.

The Multiplier

When changes in investment occur they bring about changes in the equilibrium level of *NNP* and *NDI* that exceed the magnitudes of the changes in investment; that is, they bring about amplified changes in national income, referred to as *multiplier effects*. To learn how they work we shall examine them first by means of period analysis and then by graphic methods.

Period Analysis

Let the equilibrium level of national income be $600 billion initially, as illustrated by periods (1) and (2) in Table 29–1. Suppose the level of consumption in period (2) is $500 billion, leaving $100 billion as savings. Let investment spending in that period also be $100 billion. Investment equals saving; all of the *NDI* earned in period (1) is spent in period (2); the *NNP* produced and the *NDI* earned in period (2) is $600 billion. Let the marginal propensity to consume be $\frac{4}{5}$; that is, a one dollar change in disposable income will bring about an 80 cent change in consumption.

Now suppose that a change in the interest rate or a change in business expectations or both causes investors to increase the amount they desire to invest in new capital goods by $10 billion per period, beginning in period (3). Of the $600 billion earned in period (2), $500 billion is spent on consumption in period (3), leaving savings of $100 billion. But $110 billion is invested, so income earned in period (3) rises to $610 billion. This rise in income in period (3) is equal to the *increase in investment.*

This is not the end of the matter if the level of net investment per period remains at $110 billion. The $610 billion earned in period (3) is the *NDI* available to be spent in period (4). This is $10 billion more than was available to be spent in period (3). Since the *MPC* of the consuming public is $\frac{4}{5}$, then $8 billion of the increase (10 billion times $\frac{4}{5}$) will be spent on consumption, raising the consumption level of period (4) to $508 billion. Savings of period (4) are $102 billion. With investment remaining at $110 billion, income earned in period (4) is $618 billion—up $8 billion, or by the *increase in consumption,* over the preceding period.

Another increase in *NNP* and *NDI* occurs in period (5). Of the extra $8 billion earned in period (4) and available for spending in period (5), $\frac{4}{5}$ of it, or $6.4 billion, will be spent on consumption, raising *C* to $514.4 billion. Savings are $103.6 billion and investment is assumed to remain at $110 billion. Thus *NNP* and income earned in period (5) is higher by $6.4 billion—the amount of the increase in *C*—than in the preceding period.

The increases in income will continue, becoming smaller and smaller in each successive period and eventually approaching zero. When they become small enough to be negligible, a new equilibrium level of *NNP* and *NDI* is for all practical purposes achieved, as shown for the periods marked (*N*) and (*N* + 1).

In summary, then, the initial increase in investment causes an increase

TABLE 29–1
Effects on National Income of a Change in Investment[a]
(billions of dollars)

	(1)	(2)	(3)	(4)	(5)	—	(N)	(N + 1)
NNP	600	600	610	618	624.4	—	650	650
C		500	500	508	514.4	—	—	540
S		100	100	102	103.6	—	—	110
I		100	110	110	110	—	—	110

[a]$MPC = \frac{4}{5}$.
$MPS = \frac{1}{5}$.

$$m = \frac{1}{1 - MPC} = \frac{1}{1 - \frac{4}{5}} = 5.$$

$$m = \frac{1}{MPS} = \frac{1}{\frac{1}{5}} = 5.$$

in *NNP* and *NDI* of an equal amount. The increase in income causes an increase in consumption, and the increase in consumption in turn causes a further increase in income that causes an increase in consumption that causes an increase in income, and so on. The new equilibrium level of *NNP* and *NDI* is $650 billion, with consumption at $540 billion, savings at $110 billion, and investment at $110 billion.

How do we determine the level at which national income will again be in equilibrium? As income and consumption increase, savings increase also. However, savings in periods (4), (5), and succeeding periods are less than investment. Not until income approaches $650 billion and the amount consumed approaches $540 billion will savings rise to the point at which they are as large as the amount that investors desire to invest. This can be verified by the laborious task of computing *C, S, I,* and *NNP* for a succession of periods following (5) in the same way that they were computed for (4) and (5).

There is, of course, an easier way to find the new equilibrium level of income. The change in *NNP* generated by the change in investment is a multiple of the change in investment, and the multiplying factor is called appropriately the *multiplier*. In the example the $10 billion change in investment generates a $50 billion change in *NNP*, so the multiplier is 5.

The size of the multiplier is determined by the marginal propensity to consume and it is found by summing a geometric progression. If the *MPC* is $\frac{4}{5}$, the effects of a one dollar increase in investment is found as follows[2]:

$$\Delta NNP = \$1 + \$\tfrac{4}{5} + (\$\tfrac{4}{5})^2 + (\$\tfrac{4}{5})^3 + \cdots + (\$\tfrac{4}{5})^n = \frac{\$1}{1 - 4/5} = \$5$$

The one dollar increase in investment increases *NNP* and *NDI* by one dollar, which, in turn, increases consumption by $\frac{4}{5}$ of a dollar, which increases *NNP* and *NDI* by the same amount, and so on. As the increases approach zero, the sum of the increases approaches $1/(1 - 4/5)$, or $5. Since a one dollar change in investment changes *NNP* by $5, the multiplier is 5. Whatever the *MPC*, the multiplier will be

$$m = \frac{1}{1 - MPC} \qquad (29.1)$$

or, since $MPS = 1 - MPC$,

$$m = \frac{1}{MPS} \qquad (29.1a)$$

and for any change in investment,

$$\Delta NNP = m \cdot \Delta I \qquad (29.2)$$

---

[2] This formula for finding the sum of a geometric progression can be found in any high school or college algebra textbook.

Applying this to the example of Table 29–1, we see that

$$\Delta NNP = 5 \times \$10 \text{ billion} = \$50 \text{ billion}^3$$

The multiplier works for decreases in investment as well as for increases. If the change in the level of investment had been a negative $10 billion, the new equilibrium level of income would have been $550 billion, a decrease of $50 billion. It will be instructive to work this out with period analysis similar to that of Table 29–1.

Graphic Analysis

The effects of a change in the level of investment on NNP and NDI are shown graphically in Figure 29–3. Although either (a) or (b) of the figure can be used alone to illustrate the analysis, in the interests of completeness and clarity we shall use both. For identification purposes we shall call diagrams such as Figure 29–3(a) *total spending diagrams* and those such as Figure 29–3(b) *savings and investment diagrams.* Suppose initially that the consumption function is represented by C; the corresponding savings function is S; the level of investment is I; and the consequent total spending curve is $C + I$. NNP and NDI are in equilibrium at level Y_e. All that is being earned is being spent.

What are the effects of an increase in investment amounting to ΔI? Both the investment curve of Figure 29–3(b) and the $C + I$ curve of Figure 29–3(a) are displaced upward by the amount ΔI to the new positions I_1 and $C + I_1$, respectively. At the original income level Y_e, desired investment exceeds current savings or, what amounts to the same thing, more is being spent than is being earned. This means that NDI rises, and as it rises consumption and savings rise too as we move along the C curve and the S curve to the right. When NDI has risen to level Y_1 savings are again equal to investment; earnings are again as great as total spending; and NNP and NDI are again in equilibrium.

Can the multiplier be illustrated graphically? Consider the savings and investment diagram. The slope of the savings curve or the MPS for the increase in NDI is measured by $(\Delta S)/(\Delta Y)$. Equation 29.1a defines the multiplier as the reciprocal of the MPS, or

$$m = \frac{\Delta Y}{\Delta S} \qquad (29.3)$$

From equation 29.2 we see that the change in NNP must be the change in investment multiplied by the multiplier, or

$$\Delta Y = m \cdot \Delta I \qquad (29.4)$$

---

[3] What would the multiplier be if the MPC were $\frac{2}{3}$? How would the $10 billion increase in investment affect NNP in the example of Table 29–1 if this were the MPC?

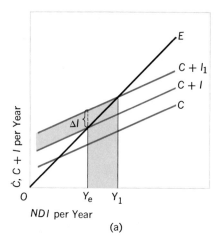

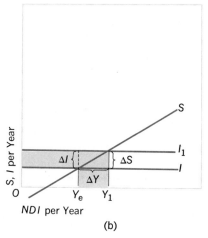

Figure 29-3
The effects of a change in investment.

Solving this equation for m, we find that

$$m = \frac{\Delta Y}{\Delta I} \qquad (29.5)$$

Since $\Delta I = \Delta S$ for the change in income, if we substitute ΔS for ΔI in equation 29.5 the equation becomes identical to 29.3; that is, the actual multiplier in this case—the reciprocal of the slope of the savings curve— conforms to the previously established definition of the multiplier.

A decline in the level of investment resulting from an increase in the interest rate or adverse business expectations or both should present no analytical difficulties. The I curve and the $C + I$ curve shift downward by the amount of the change. At income level Y_e savings exceed intended investment, and spending is less than current earnings. The level of national income falls until savings decrease to an amount equal to the new and lower level of investment. The new equilibrium level of NDI is lower than the original level by an amount equal to the change in investment multiplied by the multiplier.

Changes in Consumption

Changes in the equilibrium level of national income result from changes in the propensity to consume as well as from changes in the level of investment, although the consumption function tends to be much more stable than the level of investment. A change in the propensity to consume is reflected by a shift in the consumption function up or down. The consumption function shifts upward when there is a desire on the part of consumers to spend more on consumption at each possible level of NDI and it shifts downward with their desire to spend less. We must distinguish carefully between a movement *along* the consumption function and a *shift* in the function itself. A *shift* upward in the consumption function may be triggered by rising hopes and rising expectations on the part of consumers with respect to economic expansion. A movement from a lower to a higher point on a given consumption curve simply reflects a desire to consume more at higher levels than at lower levels of NDI, leaving out of account the kind of buoyancy in consumer hopes engendered by a period of rapid economic expansion. Changes or shifts in the consumption function will have multiplied effects on the level of NNP and NDI.

Period Analysis

Suppose that NNP is in equilibrium initially, as Table 29–2 shows from period (1) to period (2). In period (3) the expectations of consumers improve, shifting the consumption function upward and increasing the level of consumption by $10 billion at the $600 billion level of NNP and NDI. Savings of period (3)—found by subtracting consumption of period (3) from income earned in period (2)—decline by the same amount that consumption increases. The level of investment remains constant and the MPC is assumed to be $\frac{4}{5}$.

The increase in consumption causes NNP to expand. In period (3) the initial $10 billion increase in consumption increases NNP and therefore NDI by the same amount. Of the additional income earned in period (3) and available to be spent in period (4), $68 billion will be spent on consumption, since the marginal propensity to consume is $\frac{4}{5}$. The expansion sequence is identical to that occurring as the result of an increase in in-

TABLE 29–2
Effects on National Income of a Change in Consumption[a]
(billions of dollars)

	(1)	(2)	(3)	(4)	(5)	—	(N)	(N + 1)
NNP	600	600	610	618	624.4	—	650	650
C		500	510	518	524.4	—	—	550
S		100	90	92	93.6	—	—	100
I		100	100	100	100.0	—	—	100

[a]$MPC = \frac{4}{5}$.
$MPS = \frac{1}{5}$.

$$m = \frac{1}{1 - MPC} = \frac{1}{1 - \frac{4}{5}} = 5.$$

$$m = \frac{1}{MPS} = \frac{1}{\frac{1}{5}} = 5.$$

vestment. The increase in income of each period increases consumption of the next period by $\frac{4}{5}$ of that increase in income. Each increase in consumption increases NNP and income earned for the period in which it occurs by the amount of the increase in consumption. As the increases approach zero, NNP approaches the new equilibrium level shown by periods (N) and $(N + 1)$.

Again we find that a multiplier determined by $1/(1 - MPC)$ or $1/MPS$ is at work. With an MPC of $\frac{4}{5}$, the increase in NNP and NDI from the initial equilibrium level to the new equilibrium level is five times the consumption level increase that generated it. Thus the *consumption multiplier* and the *investment multiplier* are numerically the same.

Graphic Analysis

The graphic picture of a change in the propensity to consume is contained in Figure 29–4. The initial equilibrium level of NDI is Y_e. At this level of income in the total spending diagram the $C + I$ curve crosses the OE curve, showing that total spending, $Y_e B_e$, is the same as NDI. In the savings and investment diagram savings and investment are equal and are measured by $Y_e I_e$.

An increase in consumption, ΔC, shifts the C curve upward and the S curve downward by the amount ΔC. This also shifts the $C + I$ curve upward by ΔC. At income level Y_e, after the change in consumption, savings and investment are $A_e B_e$ and $A_e C_e$, respectively, in the total spending diagram, and they are $Y_e S_e$ and $Y_e I_e$, respectively, in the savings and investment diagram. Since desired investment is greater than current savings, total spending is greater than the current level of earnings, causing NNP and NDI to rise. As income rises savings rise also, until at

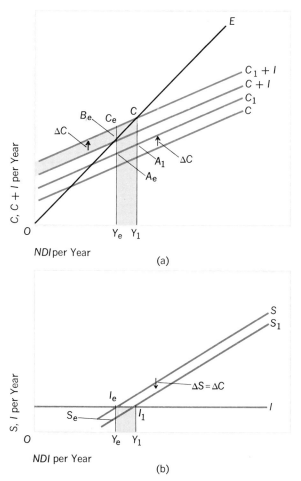

Figure 29-4
The effects of a change in consumption.

income level Y_1 savings and investment are equal at an amount Y_1I_1 in Figure 29–4(b) or A_1C_1 in Figure 29–4(a). Again all that is being currently earned is being spent, so Y_1 is the new equilibrium level of income.

Problems of the Private Sector

The analysis thus far serves to point up the economic problems of the private sector of the economy taken as a whole. A stable system, automatically generating full employment and economic growth, it is not. The system may be in equilibrium with a deflationary gap. In this case there will be unemployment and a subnormal growth rate. Or it may be in equilibrium with an inflationary gap, generating full employment but subjecting itself to the inequitable consequences and dangers of inflation. Or it may be unstable because of changes in the level of investment and changes in the propensity to consume, together with the multiplier effects of both.

In the discussion of changes in investment and in the propensity to consume we considered a single change in investment and the resultant multiplier effects and then we considered a single change in the consumption function with its resultant multiplier effects. Actually, during a period of economic expansion there may be a series of upward shifts in the level of investment, each one subject to multiplier effects and generating increases in income greater than the increases in investment. Less likely, but still possible, are upward movements of the consumption function, with multiplier effects that amplify the increases in national income over and above the increases in consumption. And all of these may work in reverse during a period of economic contraction. Small wonder that we worry continually about economic fluctuations or instability!

Having developed multiplier theory showing multiplier effects amounting to several times the initial changes in investment or consumption, depending upon the magnitude of the *MPC*, we must now back down to some extent. In developing the theory we assumed that a change in the level of investment or in the level of consumption set the process in motion. Then we assumed that no outside or additional disturbing forces were permitted to interfere with the process until it had completely run its course. The world does not run in this manner. As the multiplier effects of a change in investment or consumption are in process, other changes may occur that prevent them from exerting their full impact. Counteracting changes in investment or consumption may occur, or there may be changes in the *MPC* that change the magnitude of the multiplier. The multiplier is not a precise tool of analysis, at least not with the present state of economic knowledge. It should be thought of as a force tending to amplify the direct effects of changes in investment and consumption on national income.

MONETARY AND FISCAL POLICY

In isolating the forces leading to problems of unemployment, lagging growth rates, and instability in the private sector of the economy we have also isolated the points at which the problems can be attacked. The appropriate agency to attack them is, of course, the government, and the means of attack are monetary policy and fiscal policy. Both of these tools were examined earlier, and the task at hand is to fit them into the framework of national income analysis.

Monetary Policy

How does monetary policy operate within the framework of national income analysis? It would be expected to work by way of either the level of investment or the consumption function. It affects the level of investment through changes in the money supply and in the interest rate. It may have a direct impact on consumption spending.

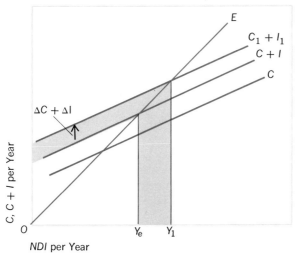

Figure 29–5
Monetary policy to combat unemployment.

Suppose that a deflationary gap exists, as Figure 29–5 illustrates, with the total spending curve initially at $C + I$, the equilibrium level of NDI at Y_e, and the full-employment level at Y_1. We learned previously that in circumstances of this kind an easy money policy is in order. Federal Reserve authorities engage in open-market purchases of government securities, lower the discount rate, and, if desirable, lower the required reserve ratio.

The major impact of an easy money policy tends to be on the level of intended investment, since most borrowing from banks is done by business firms. It may encourage business firms to modernize or expand plant and equipment by more than they would have in the absence of the easy money policy. It may also induce them to build larger inventories than they would have otherwise. This is because larger amounts of investable funds are made available to them at lower interest rates. Consumers may also be encouraged to borrow and spend more, particularly on consumer durable goods such as automobiles, household appliances, and the like, than they would have otherwise. To the extent that these results occur, the total spending curve shifts upward toward $C_1 + I_1$, reducing the deflationary gap and moving the equilibrium level of income toward the full-employment level.

Monetary policy can also be used to reduce the equilibrium level of income if an inflationary gap exists. A tight money policy on the part of Federal Reserve authorities is appropriate. To initiate it the Federal Reserve would engage in open-market sales of government securities, increases in the discount rate, and if desirable, increases in required reserve ratios. These measures decrease bank reserves and raise the interest rate, cutting down on the availability of investable funds. Consumption and investment are discouraged, both by the smaller quantity of money available to be spent and by the increase in the interest rate. The $C + I$ curve shifts downward, thus decreasing the equilibrium level of national income and reducing inflationary pressures.

Government Economic Activity

The introduction of fiscal policy into national income analysis becomes more complex, since the government produces directly a part of net national product and can coerce people into turning over a part of their incomes to the government in the form of taxes. The analytical model that we have been using must be expanded to include the government's economic activities. Net national product becomes the sum of the values of consumer goods and services, investment goods, and government goods and services; that is,

$$NNP = C + I + G$$

Correspondingly, the component parts of net disposable income now become household disposable income, business disposable income, and government disposable income, or

$$NDI = DI_h + DI_b + DI_g$$

The production of NNP generates, as before, an equivalent amount of NDI.

The expanded analytical model is illustrated in Table 29–3, in which national income is in equilibrium. Suppose that NNP in period (1) is $700 billion, generating $700 billion of NDI to be disposed of in period (2). With the government in the picture, not all of NDI is in the hands of households and business firms. Some of it—net tax collections or total

TABLE 29–3
National Income in Equilibrium
(billions of dollars)

	(1)	(2)	(3)
NNP	700	700	700
T		100	100
C		500	500
S		100	100
I		100	100
G		100	100

tax collections (and other receipts of the government) minus transfer payments to households and businesses—becomes *government disposable income*. We assume in Table 29–3 that this amount is $100 billion, as represented by *T* for period (2). Disposable income left in the hands of households and businesses in period (2) but not listed explicitly in the table will be $600 billion. Of this amount suppose consumers elect to spend $500 billion on consumption, leaving $100 billion saved. Suppose, further, that all savings are invested and that the government's disposable income or net tax collections is all spent, providing $100 billion in government goods and services to the public. The value of all goods produced in period (2) and the total income generated in its production is the sum of the values of consumption, investment, and government goods and services, or $700 billion. All that is being earned is being spent. A repetition of this pattern in period (3) and succeeding periods means that national income is in equilibrium.

It becomes immediately apparent in Table 29–3 that it is not strictly necessary that $I = S$ and $G = T$ in order for national income to be in equilibrium. Suppose, for example, that in period (2) we find $T = \$100$ billion and $S = \$100$ billion but that $I = \$90$ billion and $G = \$110$ billion. Substituting these values for those in the table, we see that *NNP* for period (2) is $700 billion, or the same as it was in period (1). Equilibrium exists, since *NNP* is neither growing nor contracting. Strictly speaking, then, national income is in equilibrium, or total spending is equal to the amount being earned, when *investment spending plus government goods and services provided* are equal to *savings plus taxes*.

Equilibrium in the expanded model is represented graphically in Figure 29–6. Looking first at the total spending diagram, we see that the vertical distance between the *OE* and the *C* curves at any given level of *NDI* must be *savings plus taxes* at that level of income. Consider an *NDI* level of Y_2, represented also by the distance Y_2F_2. Some of that amount of disposable income is paid to the government as taxes and is thus not available for households to consume. Of what is left after taxes are paid, some part is

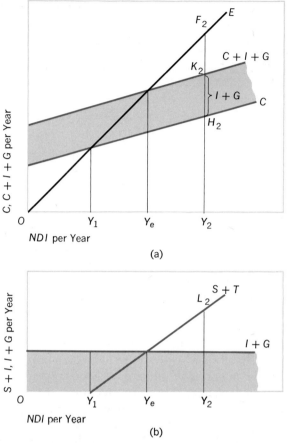

Figure 29-6
The national income model with the government sector included.

saved and the rest is consumed, thus the difference between *NDI* and consumption must be the combined amount of taxes and savings. Taxes plus savings are H_2F_2, plotted in the savings and investment diagram as Y_2L_2. The entire $S + T$ curve is obtained by subtracting the C curve vertically from the OE curve. The equilibrium level of national income is Y_e, the level at which total spending is the same as total earnings, or at which $I + G = S + T$.

Fiscal Policy to Control Recession

What fiscal policy measures are in order if actual national income is below its potential level—if the equilibrium level is below the full-employment level? From past discussion we know that a budgetary deficit is called for and that this can be achieved through (1) an increase in government expenditures with tax collections constant, (2) a decrease in tax collections with expenditures constant, (3) an increase in expenditures accompanied by a decrease in tax collections. Method (3) is simply a combination of (1) and (2) and does not require separate analysis. There is, however, another fiscal policy alternative that has not been considered previously. It consists of equal increases in tax collections and expenditures. We shall examine the effects of each of these. In each deficit case the government expenditure not covered by tax collections is assumed to provide government goods and services for the public and to be financed either from funds that would otherwise have been hoarded or from newly created money.

Expenditure Changes, Tax Collections Constant

In Table 29–4 we suppose that the initial $700 billion equilibrium level of income is a less than full-employment level and that in period (3) the government increases its expenditures in order to stimulate economic activity. Of the $700 billion earned in period (2), $100 billion is paid to the government in taxes and $500 billion is consumed in period (3). All of the $100 billion saved in period (3) is invested. The level of government expenditure rises by $10 billion, from $100 billion to $110 billion, thus increasing period (3) NNP by $10 billion over what it was in the preceding period.

The period (3) increase in NNP, and in the NDI available to be spent in period (4), sets in motion the familiar multiplier effect. Taxes in period (4) remain at $100 billion, but, assuming that the marginal propensity to consume is $\frac{4}{5}$, the extra $10 billion of NDI brings about an $8 billion increase in consumption. Savings increase to $102 billion. (Why?) Invest-

TABLE 29–4
Effects on National Income of an Expenditure Increase[a]
(billions of dollars)

	(1)	(2)	(3)	(4)	(5)	—	(N)	(N + 1)
Y	700	700	710	718	724.4	—	750	750
T		100	100	100	100	—	100	100
C		500	500	508	514.4	—	540	540
S		100	100	102	103.6	—	110	110
I		100	100	100	100	—	100	100
G		100	110	110	110	—	110	110

[a]$MPC = \frac{4}{5}$.
$MPS = \frac{1}{5}$.

$$m = \frac{1}{1 - MPC} = \frac{1}{1 - \frac{4}{5}} = 5.$$

$$m = \frac{1}{MPS} = \frac{1}{\frac{1}{5}} = 5.$$

ment remains at $100 billion and government expenditures continue at the $110 billion level. Period (4) *NNP* is higher than that of period (3) by $8 billion—the increase in consumption. In period (5) consumption, and consequently *NNP,* increase by $6.4 billion. In each succeeding period consumption and *NNP* increase by $\frac{4}{5}$ of the increase of the immediately preceding period. The increases eventually approach zero, and *NNP* approaches the new equilibrium level shown by periods (N) and ($N + 1$). in which taxes plus savings are equal to government expenditures plus investment.

The *government expenditures multiplier* is the sum of the increases in *NNP* resulting from a one dollar increase in government spending, this sum being the same kind of geometric progression as that of the multiplier derived from a change in investment or a change in consumption; that is,

$$m = \frac{1}{1 - MPC} = \frac{1}{MPS}$$

and, if the *MPC* is $\frac{4}{5}$, the multiplier is 5. The $10 billion increase in government expenditures would bring about a $50 billion rise in the level of *NNP* if the multiplier effects could work themselves out before other changes intervene. The increase in economic activity associated with the increase in *NNP* brings with it an increase in the employment level.

The effects of an increase in government expenditures are shown graphically in Figure 29–7. The equilibrium level of national income is initially Y_e, the income level at which the $C + I + G$ curve cuts the OE curve and at which $I + G = S + T$. All that is being earned is being spent, but the unemployment rate is assumed to be higher than that desired. The government now increases its spending on goods and services by ΔG in order to run a deficit. This shifts the $C + I + G$ curve upward by ΔG to $C + I + G_1$. The $I + G$ curve is shifted upward by the same amount to $I + G_1$. At the equilibrium level of income Y_e, investment spending plus government spending now exceeds savings plus investment. In the total spending diagram these are $A_e H_e$ and $A_e B_e$, respectively, while in the savings-investment diagram they are $Y_e K_e$ and $Y_e J_e$, respectively. Total spending exceeds the total amount being earned; national income expands; and savings increase until at income level Y_1 government spending plus investment is no greater than tax collections plus savings.

Changes in Tax Collections, Expenditures Constant

Suppose we look now at the effects on national income of a decrease in tax collections, assuming that government expenditures are held constant. As in the last subsection, we assume that any government deficit is

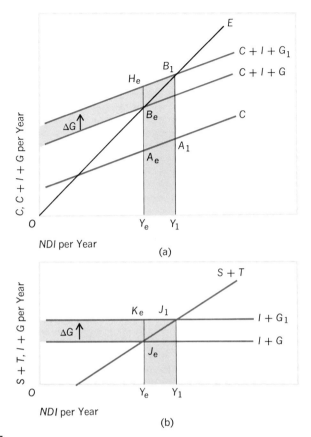

Figure 29–7
The effects of a change in G with T Constant.

financed with newly created money or with funds that would have been hoarded otherwise. We also assume that the entire amount of the tax decrease is left to consumers to spend; that is, it increases household disposable income by the amount of the decrease.[4] Again we suppose that national income is initially in equilibrium at a less than full-employment level; that initially $T = G$ and $S = I$, or $S + T = G + I$; and that the marginal propensity to consume is $\frac{4}{5}$.

In Table 29–5 the impact of a $10 billion decrease in tax collections is shown by means of period analysis. Income is in equilibrium at $700 billion from period (1) to period (2). In period (3) the tax decrease is

---

[4] This would tend to be the case if the tax cut were made in the personal income tax only. If corporation income taxes and excise taxes were decreased, business disposable income and household disposable income would both be increased and the analysis would be correspondingly more complex. We shall keep our case as straightforward as possible.

TABLE 29-5
Effects on National Income of a Tax Decrease[a]
(billions of dollars)

	(1)	(2)	(3)	(4)	—	(N)	(N + 1)
Y	700	700	708	714.6	—	740	740
T		100	90	90	—	90	90
C		500	508	514.4	—	540	540
S		100	102	103.6	—	110	110
I		100	100	100	—	100	100
G		100	100	100	—	100	100

[a]$MPC = \frac{4}{5}$.
$MPS = \frac{1}{5}$.

$$m_t = \frac{1}{1 - MPC} - 1 = \frac{1}{1 - \frac{4}{5}} - 1 = 4.$$

$$m_t = \frac{1}{MPS} - 1 = \frac{1}{\frac{1}{5}} - 1 = 4.$$

effected, leaving private disposable income for that period at $610 billion rather than at the $600 billion level of period (2). Of the extra $10 billion of private disposable income available in period (3), $8 billion will be spent on consumption, raising the level of period (3) consumption to $508 billion. Savings are $102 billion, investment remains at $100 billion, and government expenditures are constant at $100 billion. Net national product for period (3) will be $708 billion—greater than it was in the preceding period by the amount of the increase in consumption in period (3). The pattern of increases for succeeding periods is the familiar one. The new and higher equilibrium level of income is approached as $S + T$ approaches $I + G$ or as total spending is approached by total earnings of resource owners. The new equilibrium level of income is shown in the columns headed (N) and $(N + 1)$.

The multiplier for a tax change is smaller than that for a change in investment, in consumption, or in government expenditures. The reason for this is easily seen. A $10 billion increase in investment, in consumption, or in government expenditures in and of itself initially increases NNP by $10 billion, while a $10 billion decrease in taxes does not. The decrease in taxes increases private disposable income, which then increases consumption by an amount equal to the increase in private disposable income (or the decrease in taxes) multiplied by the marginal propensity to consume. Thus the initial effect of a $10 billion tax decrease on NNP when the MPC is $\frac{4}{5}$ will be only $8 billion, or $\frac{4}{5}$ of the tax decrease.

In effect, the geometric progression that we use to compute the tax-change multiplier is without the initial term in the series of numbers that we have been adding together. Whereas the sum of the geometric progression initiated by a government expenditure increase of one dollar when the MPC is $\frac{4}{5}$ is

$$1 + \tfrac{4}{5} + (\tfrac{4}{5})^2 + (\tfrac{4}{5})^3 + \cdots$$

that from a one dollar decrease in taxes is

$$\tfrac{4}{5} + (\tfrac{4}{5})^2 + (\tfrac{4}{5})^3 + \cdots$$

The initial one dollar increase at the beginning of the first summation is missing in the second, so that the total tax-change multiplier is 1 less than the investment, consumption, and government expenditure multiplier. Letting m represent the latter and m_t the tax-change multiplier, we can say while

$$m = \frac{1}{1 - MPC} = \frac{1}{MPS} \qquad (29.1)$$

that

$$m_t = \frac{1}{1 - MPC} - 1 = \frac{1}{MPS} - 1 \qquad (29.6)$$

If the MPC is $\frac{4}{5}$, then $m = 5$ and $m_t = 4$. So, for a tax decrease of \$10 billion, the increase in NNP will be \$40 billion if the tax-change multiplier can work itself out before other changes occur.

Figure 29–8 presents the graphic picture of the effects of a tax change. Suppose that Y_e is the equilibrium level of net disposable income, public and private. Total spending on consumption, investment, and government goods and services is $Y_e B_e$—indicated by the intersection of the $C + I + G$ curve and the OE curve—and is, of course, equal to NDI level Y_e. In the savings–investment diagram $S + T$ and $I + G$ are both at level $Y_e I_e$. We assume that at income level Y_e there is enough unemployment to cause concern.

What are the effects of a tax decrease of ΔT? First, it increases consumption by an amount equal to the extra income left in the hands of consumers multiplied by the marginal propensity to consume; that is, by $\Delta T \cdot MPC$. The consumption function is shifted upward by this amount from C to C_1, thereby moving the $C + I + G$ curve upward by the *same amount* to $C_1 + I + G$. Offhand it would appear that the $S + T$ curve would be shifted downward by the amount of the tax decrease, but this is not quite so. Of the ΔT dollars left in the hands of the public, a part, equal to $\Delta T \cdot MPS$, will be saved. Thus the $S + T$ curve can be thought of as shifting downward by ΔT then upward by $\Delta T \cdot MPS$. This is, of course, a net shift downward of $\Delta T \cdot MPC$ to position $S_1 + T_1$.

At income level Y_e more is now being spent than is being earned. The amount being earned is $Y_e B_e$ and the amount being spent is $Y_e H_e$. Or in

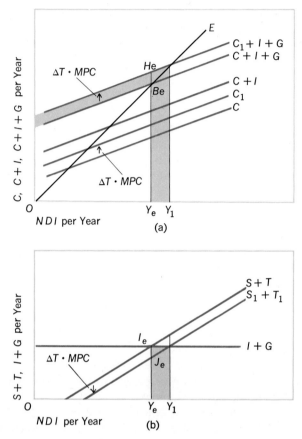

Figure 29-8
The effects of a change in T with G Constant.

terms of Figure 29–8(b), savings plus taxes are Y_eJ_e while investment plus government spending are Y_eI_e. Income increases until at level Y_1 savings have increased enough so that savings plus taxes are equal to investment plus government spending. All is being spent that is being earned and income is again in equilibrium at a level nearer to the full-employment level.

Equal Tax and Expenditure Changes

Thus far in analyzing the effects of government spending and taxation on the level of economic activity a balanced government budget with tax collections equal to expenditures has been treated as though it were neutral. This implies that, starting with a balanced budget, increases or

TABLE 29-6
Effects on National Income of an Equal Tax and Expenditure Increase[a]
(billions of dollars)

	(1)	(2)	(3)	(4)	—	(N)	(N + I)
NNP	700	700	702	703.6	—	710	710
T		100	110	110	—	110	110
C		500	492	493.6	—	500	500
S		100	98	98.4	—	100	100
I		100	100	100	—	100	100
G		100	110	110	—	110	110

[a]$MPC = \frac{4}{5}$.
$MPS = \frac{1}{5}$.
$m_b = m - m_t = 1$.

decreases in tax collections and expenditures by equal amounts would have no effect on the level of national income. With the tools of national income analysis we can demonstrate that this is not quite so. If tax collections and expenditures are increased by equal amounts, the level of national income will increase. If they are decreased by equal amounts, national income will decrease also.

The effects of equal increases in expeditures and tax collections are analyzed by means of period analysis in Table 29-6. The initial equilibrium $700 billion level of income is assumed to be a less than full-employment level. However, the government has a balanced budget with $G = T$, and at the same time $I = S$. The MPC is assumed to be $\frac{4}{5}$.

The increase in income is initiated in period (3). A $10 billion increase in taxes in that period leaves the private sector of the economy with $10 billion less in disposable income. If the MPC is $\frac{4}{5}$, consumption is reduced by $8 billion and savings are reduced by $2 billion. A corresponding increase in government expenditures of $10 billion raises G by that amount. Since investment spending has not been changed, the total value of goods produced in period (3) and the consequent income generated in that period is $C + I + G$, or $702 billion, an increase of $2 billion over that earned in the preceding period.

In subsequent periods the increases in income increase consumption, which increases income, and so on, with each increase in consumption and income in any given period equal to that of the preceding period multiplied by the MPC. In period (4), for example, the amount available for spending is $2 billion more than was available for period (3). Of this amount $1.6 billion will be spent on consumption, increasing consumption and income for period (4) by that amount. The sum of the increases in income in billions of dollars as the increases approach zero is

$$2 + 2(\tfrac{4}{5}) + 2(\tfrac{4}{5})^2 + 2(\tfrac{4}{5})^3 + \cdots = 2\left(\frac{1}{1 - \tfrac{4}{5}}\right) = 2 \cdot 5 = 10$$

The total increase in national income is just equal to the amount by which taxes and government expenditures are increased. The multiplier for this method of increasing the equilibrium level of national income is 1.[5]

Figure 29–9 presents the graphic analysis of the effects of equal tax and expenditure changes on the equilibrium level of income. Initial equilibrium is at level Y_e. With $S + T$ equal to $I + G$ and with $C + I + G$ crossing the OE line at that income level, total spending is just equal to total earnings per period.

How do we show the effects of an increase in tax collections of ΔT and of an increase in government expenditures of ΔG? The increase in tax collections alone would shift the $S + T$ curve upward by ΔT. However, since it also decreases private disposable income by ΔT, savings at all possible income levels are decreased by ΔT multiplied by the MPS. Consequently, the *net upward shift* of the $S + T$ curve will be $\Delta T - (\Delta T \cdot MPS)$, leaving the curve in the position $S_1 + T_1$. The increase in government expenditures amounting to $\Delta G \, (= \Delta T)$ shifts the $I + G$ curve of Figure 29–9(b) upward by that amount to $I + G_1$. Since the $I + G$ curve is shifted upward by a greater amount than is the $S + T$ curve (the extra amount being $\Delta T \cdot MPS$), more is being spent than is being earned at income level Y_e and income will rise to some amount Y_1. At Y_1, $S_1 + T_1$ is equal to $I + G_1$.

In terms of Figure 29–9(a) an increase in government expenditures of ΔG by itself would shift the $C + I + G$ curve upward by that amount. But the tax increase of $\Delta T \, (= \Delta G)$ would shift the C curve downward by $\Delta T \cdot MPC$. Consequently, the net upward shift of $C + I + G$ to $C_1 + I + G_1$ is equal to $\Delta G - \Delta T \cdot MPC$. At Y_e total spending exceeds total earning and Y will rise to the new equilibrium level Y_1.

A Comparison of the Fiscal Policy Alternatives

By way of a brief summary, any one of the three fiscal policy routes may be used to change the equilibrium level of national income. They are

[5] Another way to compute the multiplier is to add together the government expenditures multiplier for the expenditure increase and the tax-change multiplier for the tax increase. With an MPC of $\tfrac{4}{5}$, then

$$m = \frac{1}{1 - \tfrac{4}{5}} = 5 \qquad \text{and} \qquad m_t = \frac{1}{1 - \tfrac{4}{5}} - 1 = 4$$

so, letting m_b represent the balanced-budget multiplier

$$m_b = m - m_t = 5 - 4 = 1$$

The government expenditures multiplier will always be opposite in sign to the tax-change multiplier in computing the balanced-budget multiplier. (Why?)

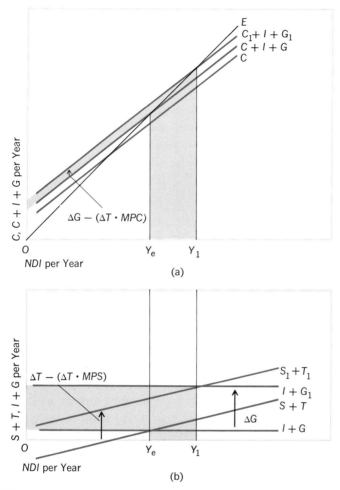

Figure 29-9
The effects of equal changes in G and T.

not all equally efficient, since the multiplier effects differ for each of the three. In the final analysis, value judgments are likely to determine which method or which combination of methods is to be used.

The multiplier effects are greatest for government expenditure changes used alone; they are less for tax changes used alone; and they are least for expenditure changes combined with equal changes in the same direction in tax collections. The multiplier for changes in government expenditures is the same as that for changes in investment and in consumption; that is, $1/(1 - MPC)$. The tax-change multiplier is 1 less than that; that is, $1/(1 - MPC) - 1$. When expenditure changes are accompanied by tax changes of the same magnitude and in the same direction, the multiplier is 1—the change in the equilibrium level of national income is equal to the tax expenditure change.

Value judgments regarding the desirable magnitude of government expenditures are important determinants of the fiscal policies to be employed. Should the government sector in relation to the private sector be larger, smaller, or is it about as it should be? The Kennedy and Johnson administrations, in order to stimulate economic expansion, in the first half of the 1960s placed much emphasis on the tax-decrease avenue. At the same time, expenditures were increasing as the pace of military activities in Vietnam were stepped up and as the War on Poverty was declared. During the 1966–1968 inflationary period the debate was over the use of a tax increase alone or whether a tax increase accompanied by an expenditure decrease was in order. The position of those advocating the latter course of action was based on the value judgment that the public sector of the economy was relatively too large.

SUMMARY

National income tends to move toward an equilibrium level, but there is nothing inherently "good" about equilibrium. An equilibrium level of income does not guarantee that there will be full employment, economic stability, and economic growth. Leaving government to one side, the savings function and the level of investment determine the equilibrium level of income. It may be an income level at which there is unemployment or it may be one that will generate inflation. If at the full-employment level of income more is saved than investors want to invest, there is a deflationary gap and national income will fall to a less than full-employment level. If at the full-employment level investors desire to invest more than is currently being saved, there is an inflationary gap and national income will rise in dollar terms but not in real terms. National income may also by chance be at a level at which there is full employment and price stability.

A change in the level of investment and/or a change in the position of the consumption function changes the equilibrium level of national income by more than the initial change in either the one or the other. Such changes are subject to multiplier effects. Instability of investment or of consumption over time leads to amplified changes in national income.

The multiplier, numerically equal to $1/(1 - MPC)$ or $1/MPS$, is a number that when multiplied by the initial change in the level of investment or consumption shows the change in NNP and NDI.

Monetary policy can be used to control fluctuations in national income or to move the equilibrium level up or down, depending upon the economic objectives sought. Monetary policy operates on the positions of the consumption function and the investment curve, an easy money policy tending to increase them while a tight money policy tending to make them contract. Any changes induced in either by monetary policy will produce amplified effects on national income by way of the multiplier.

Fiscal policy provides an additional means of governmental control over the level of national income. If expenditures are changed while tax collections are held constant, national income will tend to change in the same direction as the expenditures change, since G is a component of NNP. But the change in G will also generate the same kinds of *multiplier effects* on the equilibrium level of national income as do changes in the other two components of national income—consumption and investment.

Changes in tax collections with government expenditures constant bring about changes in private disposable income that in turn induce changes in the position of the consumption function. The shifts in consumption in turn exert multiplier effects on the equilibrium level of national income. However, the multiplier for tax changes is always 1 less than that for changes in investment, consumption, or government expenditures.

Changes in government expenditures accompanied by tax changes of the same magnitude and in the same direction have a multiplier effect of 1 on the level of national income. An expenditure increase by itself would have a positive multiplier effect. A tax increase of the same amount would have a negative multiplier effect that is 1 less than that for the tax increase. Subtracting the latter from the former leaves us with a magnitude of 1 for the equal tax-expenditure multiplier.

EXERCISES AND QUESTIONS FOR DISCUSSION

1. What is an inflationary gap? a deflationary gap? What fiscal and monetary policy measures could be used to eliminate each? Discuss the process by which a new equilibrium would be reached after the introduction of each type of policy measure.
2. Suppose the economy is suffering from inflation and yet its growth rate is less than satisfactory. Can the government do anything about these problems? Explain.
3. "If the economy is at full employment and the government needs to make more expenditures for, say, a war, the proper course to follow is to increase government expenditures with an equal increase in taxes." Evaluate this statement.
4. "During inflation most people's real incomes tend to fall. Therefore, the proper policy for the government to follow is one of decreasing taxes or increasing transfer payments to put more money in the hands of consumers." Comment critically.
5. Suppose the government has a balanced budget. If it now decides to increase

expenditures and decrease taxes, what will be the effect on *NNP* and *NDI*? Make the necessary assumptions and explain graphically and verbally.
6. An increase in investment will cause a multiple increase in *NNP*. Explain how this occurs. Will the final effect be larger or smaller than our theory would predict? Why?

SELECTED READINGS

Dernburg, T. F., and D. M. McDougall, *Macro-Economics.* New York: McGraw-Hill Book Company, Inc., 1968, Chaps. 5 and 6.

Heilbroner, Robert L., *Understanding Macroeconomics.* Englewood Cliffs, N.J.: Prentice-Hall, Inc., 1965, Chaps. 7, 8, and 10.

McKenna, J. P., *Aggregate Economic Analysis,* rev. ed. New York: Holt, Rinehart and Winston, Inc., 1965, Chaps. 5, 11, and 15.

Shapiro, Edward, *Macroeconomic Analysis.* New York: Harcourt, Brace & World, Inc., 1966, Chaps. 9 and 15.

PART 5 The World Economy

The economy of the United States, or of any other country, does not operate in isolation from the rest of the world. We carry on trade with other countries, opening up new opportunities for increasing the level of want satisfaction that all parties to trade can attain and, at the same time, creating some very serious problems. In Part 5 we examine both the opportunities and the problems.

The opportunities that are opened up by international trade are of the same basic nature as those arising from all voluntary exchanges. We read and hear so much about the problems arising from international trade and so little about the opportunities presented by it that many must wonder why we bother with it at all. Consequently, Chapter 30 is centered around the modification and application of principles already learned to the world economy so that we might see clearly at the outset why world trade is desirable.

The problems arise from the institutional arrangements that the countries of the world have devised for carrying on trade. In order to understand the problems we must understand the institutional arrangements. Thus, in Chapter 31 we examine the financing of international trade. Chapter 32 focuses on the factors that determine exchange rates and the causes of balance of payments surpluses and deficits. Tariff problems provide the subject matter of Chapter 33. Chapter 34 is concerned with one of the most challenging problems of our times—that of the economically underdeveloped countries.

The Basis
of International
Trade

CHAPTER 30

In this and the following chapters the economic horizons are expanded from those of a single economy to those of the world. Most of the principles developed thus far are as applicable to the world economy as they are to the more limited framework within which they were discussed. However, the world economy has certain unique characteristics that make it advisable to treat trade among its nations separately. Its special characteristics are nationalism, a sort of national consciousness or pride, and problems of exchange among different national currencies, both of which induce nations to restrict the free flow of people, capital resources, goods, and services across their borders. The gains possible from international trade are the same as those to be had from any voluntary exchange. But the principle that all parties gain from voluntary exchange is even less understood for the world economy than it is for national and local economies. Thus, some of the possibilities of gains from international trade are spelled out in this chapter in some detail.

PATTERNS OF TRADE

With whom does the United States trade and what are the principle items exchanged? Trade patterns are quite complex. We sell merchandise of many kinds to most countries of the world and we buy merchandise from them. In addition, we buy and sell such services as insurance and transportation for goods and services and for people. We invest in businesses in other countries and foreigners invest in U.S. enterprises. International borrowing and lending are commonplace. In this section we shall confine our attention to the more obvious merchandise trade which constitutes about three fourths of the total value of our foreign trade of all kinds.

Trade Patterns by Countries

The countries with whom the United States carries on a significant volume of trade are listed in Table 30–1 and are ranked by the value of U.S. merchandise exports to them. The value of our exports to Canada far exceeds that to any other single country. Exports to Japan are next in line, while those to the United Kingdom and West Germany follow. France and Mexico round out the six most important merchandise export markets.

On the import side Canada again heads the list. Japan is our second most important foreign supplier of goods, followed by West Germany and

TABLE 30–1

United States Trade in Merchandise[a] by Country, 1967
(millions of dollars)

COUNTRY	EXPORTS	IMPORTS
Canada	7,172.9	7,099.3
Japan	2,695.8	2,998.7
United Kingdom	1,960.3	1,709.8
West Germany	1,706.3	1,955.4
Mexico	1,223.3	748.9
France	1,025.1	689.8
Italy	972.9	855.6
India	955.4	297.6
Australia and New Guinea	894.1	411.5
Venezuela	587.5	981.6
Brazil	547.9	559.0
Philippines	428.2	380.5
Republic of South Africa	426.4	227.0
Pakistan	346.9	54.8
Chile	248.1	175.2
Argentina	230.3	140.3
Colombia	218.0	240.4
Indonesia	68.4	181.8
United Arab Republic	66.1	14.9
U.S.S.R.	60.2	41.0
Malaysia	49.2	195.6
East Germany	25.2	5.6
Total	30,934.4[b]	26,812.3[b]

[a] Excluding Department of Defense shipments.
[b] Columns will not total due to omissions of smaller trade figures.
SOURCE: *Survey of Current Business*, September 1968, s-21–22.

the United Kingdom. Imports from Venezuela are fifth, followed by Italy and Mexico.

There is little about these data that is surprising. For the most part our most important export markets and import suppliers are the economically advanced countries of the world—western European countries and Canada. Geographic proximity is important, too, as the comparatively large value of trade with Canada, Mexico, and Japan indicates.

In several instances there are rather large differences between the value of our exports to a country and that of our imports from it. Mexico, France, India, and Venezuela provide excellent examples. These differences may, among other things, reflect the *multilateral* character of much of our trade. We sell more to France than she buys from us. France may in turn sell more to the United Kingdom and other countries of western Europe than she buys from them. In turn, these other countries may sell more to us than they buy from us. Thus, although large differences may exist between the value of our exports to and that of our imports from a specific country, the difference between the value of our total exports to all countries and of our total imports from all countries will not be as great.[1]

Products Traded

The major groups of merchandise items, together with their values, that make up the trade of the United States with other countries are listed in Tables 30–2 and 30–3. Looking first at Table 30–2, we find that grain and cereal preparations head the list of our exports to other countries. When we consider the tremendous land resources available for agricultural purposes in the United States and the rapid development of agricultural technology referred to in Chapter 14, this is not surprising. Moving down the list we find that large amounts, measured in value terms, of automobiles, machinery, and manufactured goods are sold abroad. The relative abundance of our capital equipment makes us relatively efficient in the production of these items. Additionally, there is a very long list of other products that we export, lumped together in the "other" classification. No one of these is as important in value terms, however, as those listed, but in the aggregate they form the largest part of our exports.

On the import side the extensive overseas operations of U.S. oil companies, together with purchases of crude oil from foreign exploration and

---

[1] We obtain a better over-all look at what a nation earns abroad as compared with what it spends abroad in the next chapter. Table 30–1 is somewhat misleading in this respect, since it lists only the *merchandise items* that are traded.

TABLE 30-2
United States Merchandise Exports, 1967

Commodity Group	Millions of Dollars
Chemicals	2,801.6
Motor vehicles and parts	2,733.9
Grain and cereal preparations	2,681.4
Electrical machinery	2,098.2
Construction machinery	1,038.0
Soybeans	771.6
Beverages and tobacco	648.7
Agricultural machinery	614.7
Iron and steel manufactured goods	561.2
Petroleum and products	538.9
Textile manufactured goods	530.9
Other	16,123.0
Total	31,142.1[a]

[a] Department of Defense shipments are not separated out in this classification, hence the total is larger than that of Table 30–1.
Source: *Survey of Current Business,* September 1968, s-22.

TABLE 30-3
United States Merchandise Imports, 1967

Commodity Group	Millions of Dollars
Automobiles and parts	2,259.4
Petroleum and products	2,088.1
Nonferrous metals	1,562.3
Iron and steel manufactured goods	1,372.8
Electrical machinery	1,139.8
Metal ores	973.9
Coffee	962.7
Chemicals	957.9
Newsprint	863.7
Textile manufactured goods	811.9
Beverages and tobacco	698.1
Meats and preparations	645.0
Sugar	588.4
Other	11,888.3
Total	26,812.3

Source: *Survey of Current Business,* September 1968, s-22–23.

drilling companies, are responsible for the largest value-of-import group. Next we see the results of our tastes for foreign automobiles. We import large amounts of nonferrous metals to be used in manufacturing a number of end products. We also import directly large amounts of iron and steel manufactured goods. The electrical machinery group rounds out the classifications of imports that were valued at over $1 billion dollars each for 1967.

We seem to be both important exporters of and importers of some specific products—iron and steel manufactured goods, electrical machinery, automobiles and parts, and chemicals are cases in point. Actually, most exchanges of this sort arise from specialization of different countries on specific kinds of goods within each of the categories. General classifications are likely to hide or mask such internal differences.

THE GAINS FROM TRADE

Why do countries carry on trade with one another? Why does the United States import crude oil, steel, cameras, watch movements, and a host of other items? Why do we sell automobiles, wheat, and electrical machinery abroad? Surely our production possibilities are diverse enough so that we could produce as many of these things as we really need to live in reasonable comfort. In this section we consider the bases of trade among countries, with the primary objective being to show why trade is advantageous to all the parties that engage in it voluntarily. We are not at this point interested in determining the exact terms at which trade will take place.

Specialization and Exchange

Specialization and exchange are characteristic of the modern economic world. We do not expect any one family to produce all that it consumes. Aside from the personal services that its members render for one another, one family may produce nothing of what it consumes. Its resources usually do not produce a complete product of any kind but contribute to the making of parts of products only. Each family's resources are specialized to these parts of productive processes and the incomes that they earn from placing those resources in employment are used to buy the complete products and services that the family consumes. The resources of many families contribute to the production of the goods and services so purchased.

Similarly, communities and regions of any one country trade with one another, each specializing in the production of certain products or parts of products. One community produces crude oil but another may refine it. One region produces iron ore but another may smelt it. Still another community builds automobiles. All carry on exchange with one another and all the finished products.

Nations trade with one another in essentially the same way. We purchase rubber from Malaya, watch movements from Switzerland, and bananas from Central America. We sell textiles, automobiles, and many kinds of manufactured goods to the countries from which we buy. But why do nations (or regions or individuals) find such specialization and exchange advantageous?

Principle of Comparative Advantage

Specialization of countries in the production of certain goods and services and the resulting exchange among them makes larger supplies available to each country than would be possible otherwise. Thus consumers in each of the countries are able to obtain larger quantities of the goods and services they want than they could in the absence of trade. Voluntary trade raises the standards of living of each participating country.[2] The underlying principle involved is called the *principle of comparative advantage.* Essentially it states that if countries (or regions or individuals) specialize in producing the things that they can produce with *relatively* greater efficiency than other countries, trading some of these for other goods and services, all parties to the exchanges can gain. The remainder of this subsection explains and elaborates on this common sense principle.

Alternative Costs Revisited

The principle of comparative advantage depends so heavily on a thorough understanding of the *alternative cost doctrine,* or the *principle of opportunity costs,* that a restatement of that concept is in order.[3] Suppose that a country's resources can be used to produce either alarm clocks or eggbeaters and that its resources are fully employed, producing some combination of the two. What is the real cost of an alarm clock? For the consuming public as a whole the cost of an alarm clock can only be the amount of eggbeaters that must be forgone to produce it. A one-unit in-

---

[2] The actions that different countries take to *restrict* their trade with other countries would appear to refute these statements. Surely the governments of *all* countries want the highest possible standards of living for their citizens! Unfortunately, the best interests of the general public within a country do not always coincide with the best interests of particular producing groups that want to suppress competition from abroad and who have the ears of lawmakers. Unfortunately, too, we do not seem to be able to devise a system of international payments that will permit a free flow of goods and services among the countries of the world.

[3] See page 123.

crease in the production of alarm clocks draws resources away from the production of eggbeaters, reducing the eggbeater output. If a one-unit increase in the output of alarm clocks reduces the output of eggbeaters by three units, then the cost of an alarm clock is three eggbeaters. Similarly, the cost of an eggbeater is one third of an alarm clock. The real cost of a unit of any good or service, therefore, is the quantities of alternative goods and services that must be forgone in order for that unit to be produced.

Production Possibilites without Trade

Now let there be two countries, *A* and *B*, with resources suitable for producing both alarm clocks and eggbeaters. Suppose that resource prices in each country are given and fixed. If they remain constant throughout the analysis, we can measure the total resource supplies in each country in terms of their total value in whatever monetary units are used. To avoid exchange rate problems—to be discussed in Chapter 32—suppose that both countries use dollars. Suppose, also, that in each country the average and marginal costs of producing both alarm clocks and eggbeaters are constant, that is, they do not vary as outputs per unit of time are changed.[4]

If the total resource supplies available per unit of time in country *A* are worth $400; if the money cost of producing an eggbeater is $4; and if the money cost of producing an alarm clock is also $4, the production possibilities of the country are easily determined. If no alarm clocks are produced, the economy can turn out 100 eggbeaters. Or, if no eggbeaters are produced, 100 alarm clocks are possible. If the economy is currently producing 100 alarm clocks and wants 10 eggbeaters, the latter can be obtained by giving up 10 alarm clocks, using the released resources to produce the eggbeaters. The real cost of an eggbeater in country *A* is thus one alarm clock, and the real cost of an alarm clock is one eggbeater. Country *A*'s production possibilities are listed in the "without trade" columns of Table 30–4 for 10-unit changes in the level of production of both alarm clocks and eggbeaters, but if we so desire we can interpolate the additional production possibilities lying between any two of those listed. In Figure 30–1 the production possibility curve of country *A* is the line *KL*.

Turning to country *B*'s production possibilities, let us suppose that $1500 worth of resources are available, that it takes $15 worth of resources to produce an alarm clock, and that $5 worth of resources are required to produce an eggbeater. If no alarm clocks are produced the

---

[4] None of these assumptions is critical to the results that we shall develop. They do reduce greatly the complexity of the analysis.

TABLE 30–4

Production Possibilities of Country A

WITHOUT TRADE[a]		WITH TRADE[b]	
ALARM CLOCKS	EGGBEATERS	ALARM CLOCKS	EGGBEATERS
100	0	100	0
90	10	90	20
80	20	80	40
70	30	(1) 70	60
60	40	60	80
50	50	50	100
40	60	(2) 40	120
30	70	30	140
20	80	20	160
10	90	(3) 10	180
0	100	0	200

[a] Assume that resource prices are given and fixed; that $400 worth of resources are available; that $4 worth of resources are necessary to produce one alarm clock; and that $4 worth of resources are necessary to produce one eggbeater.

[b] The terms of trade are one alarm clock for two eggbeaters.

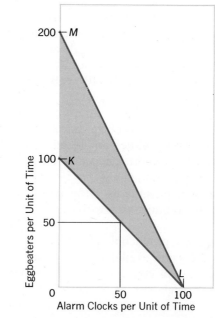

Figure 30–1

Production possibilities of country A before and after trade.

output of eggbeaters could be 300. If no eggbeaters are produced the resources of the country would permit the production of 100 alarm clocks. In order to increase the rate of alarm clock output by one unit, three eggbeaters per unit of time must be given up. Conversely, a one-unit increase in the rate of eggbeater output requires the sacrifice of one third of an alarm clock per unit of time. Some of the alternative combinations that could be produced are listed in the "without trade" columns of Table 30–5. All possible combinations are shows by *RS* in Figure 30–2.

Comparative Costs of Production

How does the cost of producing an eggbeater in country *A* compare with that in country *B*? We have assumed that only $4 worth of resources are required to produce one unit in country *A* while $5 worth are necessary in country *B*, so it appears that country *A* can produce them at lower cost. *But the comparative money costs are misleading*—the alternative cost doctrine comes forth to save us from making this common mistake! In country *A* one alarm clock must be given up to obtain an eggbeater, so this is the *real cost* of producing an eggbeater in that country. In country *B only one third of an alarm clock* must be given up to obtain an eggbeater, so the *real cost* of producing an eggbeater is lower in country *B* than it is in country *A*. Country *B* has a comparative advantage in the production of eggbeaters.

The real cost of producing alarm clocks is lower in country *A*. In country *A* an alarm clock requires the sacrifice of one eggbeater. To produce an alarm clock in country *B*, three eggbeaters must be given up. Country *A* has a comparative advantage in the production of alarm clocks.

Production Possibilities with Trade

Suppose that each country specializes in the production of the product for which it has a comparative advantage—country *A* in alarm clocks and country *B* in eggbeaters. Country *A* has a real cost advantage in producing alarm clocks—the cost is only one eggbeater as compared with three eggbeaters for country *B*. Country *B* has a real cost advantage in producing eggbeaters—the cost is only one third of an alarm clock as compared with a whole alarm clock for country *A*.

Limits within which *terms of trade* must fall are determined by the comparative real costs of production in the two countries. Country *A* will not be willing to accept *less* than one eggbeater for each alarm clock given up, since it can itself produce an eggbeater by giving up an alarm clock. Country *B* will not give up *more* than three eggbeaters for an alarm clock because it can itself produce an alarm clock by giving up three egg-

TABLE 30–5

Production Possibilities of Country B

WITHOUT TRADE[a]		WITH TRADE[b]	
ALARM CLOCKS	EGGBEATERS	ALARM CLOCKS	EGGBEATERS
100	0	150	0
90	30	135	30
80	60	120	60
70	90	105	90
60	120	(3) 90	120
50	150	75	150
40	180	(2) 60	180
30	210	45	210
20	240	(1) 30	240
10	270	15	270
0	300	0	300

[a] Assume that resource prices are given and fixed; that $1500 worth of resources are available; that $15 worth of resources are necessary to produce an alarm clock; and that $5 worth of resources are necessary to produce an eggbeater.
[b] The terms of trade are one alarm clock for two eggbeaters.

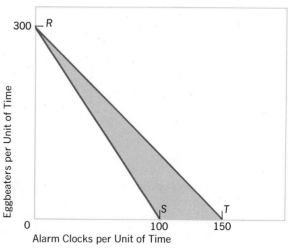

Figure 30–2
Production possibilities of country B before and after trade.

beaters. The terms of trade must fall between one alarm clock for one eggbeater and one alarm clock for three eggbeaters. Suppose they come to rest at one alarm clock for two eggbeaters.

Through specialization on alarm clocks country *A*'s production possibilities are improved by these terms of trade. Before trade country *A* could obtain only one eggbeater for each forgone alarm clock. Now, by giving up an alarm clock, two eggbeaters can be obtained. Formerly by giving up 10 alarm clocks only 10 eggbeaters could be produced. Now 10 alarm clocks can be traded for 20 eggbeaters. The "with trade" columns of Table 30–4 and the line ML in Figure 30–1 show the new production possibilities.

We refer to the combinations of goods available to country A through trade with country B as "production" possibilities, although strictly speaking eggbeaters are not produced directly by country A—they are traded for. Yet, it is exactly as though country A had discovered some new technique for producing eggbeaters that enabled her resources to turn out a 100 percent larger volume of eggbeaters at a given cost than before. This is precisely what international trade does for a country. Whenever goods can be imported at a cost lower than would be required to produce them at home their importation at the lower cost is analytically identical to the discovery and use of lower-cost technology in producing them at home.

The "with trade" columns of Table 30–5 and the line RT in Figure 30–2 show the production possibilities to country B available from specialization in the production of eggbeaters and from trading for alarm clocks. Whereas before trade country B found it necessary to give up three eggbeaters to obtain an alarm clock, with trade only two eggbeaters need be sacrificed. If all of country B's resources are used in eggbeater production, a total of 300 per unit of time can be produced. By giving up 30 of these 15 alarm clocks can be obtained. Still another 30 eggbeaters can be traded for an additional 15 alarm clocks, making a combination of 30 alarm clocks and 240 eggbeaters available to consumers of the country. Other possible combinations are listed in the table and are plotted in Figure 30–2. Through specialization and trade the efficiency with which alarm clocks can be obtained is increased by 50 percent.

Note that the gains from trade do not in any way depend upon money costs of production being lower in a country than in those with which it trades. Resources in country A may be cheap relative to resources in country B. Country A may be able to produce both alarm clocks *and* eggbeaters at lower *money costs* than country B—in fact, in the illustration this is assumed to be the case. Still, both countries can be better off with trade. All that is necessary in order for both parties to gain is that the *eggbeater cost* or *real cost* of producing alarm clocks be different in country A than in Country B and that, correspondingly, *alarm clock costs* or *real costs* of producing eggbeaters be different in the two countries. (In order to grasp this point firmly, rework the entire set of illustrations, assuming that in Country A the *money costs* of producing alarm clocks and eggbeaters are each two dollars instead of four dollars each. What do you think, now, about the commonly expressed idea that as a nation it is to our disadvantage to import goods made with "cheap foreign labor?"

THE BASES OF TRADE

Hopefully, the gains from trade available to countries as a result of specialization in the production of goods and services in which they have a comparative advantage and trade for those in which they have a comparative disadvantage are clearly understood. In this section we probe beneath the surface to determine why it is that comparative advantages crop up for some products while comparative disadvantages appear for others. The reasons are not tremendously profound or complex—indeed, they are rather ordinary—but they need to be catalogued.

Differences in Resource Endowments

Comparative advantages or disadvantages in the production of specific goods and services arise among countries partly because of differences in resource endowments. Countries differ in their holdings of both capital resources and labor resources. We shall consider each in turn.

Capital Resources

The so-called natural resources comprise one general class of capital resources that are very unequally distributed among nations. Some countries have an abundance of rich agricultural land while others have arid desert areas and wastelands. There are a limited number of areas especially suited for growing coffee beans; grapes cannot be cultivated in all areas with equal efficiency; some regions favor the growth of forests. Most of us find that the land we own does not contain substantial deposits of gold, oil, diamonds, or uranium—each of these seem to be clustered in relatively small parts of the world. Diversity among countries in available natural resources is characteristic of the world economy.

Countries also differ widely in the quantities and kinds of capital equipment that they have accumulated over time. The Scandinavian countries have accumulated large quantities of ocean-going vessels. The United States has accumulated much equipment for producing heavy machinery, automobiles, and even agricultural products. Some of our less fortunate world neighbors have accumulated relatively small amounts of capital and thus have comparative disadvantages in producing products requiring large ratios of capital equipment to labor.

Labor Resources

Large qualitative differences exist among the labor resources of different countries. General skill levels tend to vary directly with the amount of education available to the labor force, so that countries with better educational facilities for the whole population tend to have relatively more highly skilled workers. Within specific skill levels the types of skills are likely to be very different among different countries. German and Japanese laborers are noted for their skill in producing optical equipment. Labor in the United States is particularly adept at tasks requiring mechanical aptitude. India and Mexico have some of the world's best bronze and silver craftsmen.

In terms of quantities, some economies are comparatively long on labor resources and short on capital resources while others have smaller ratios of labor to capital. In the Far East birth rates are high, per capita incomes are low, and capital accumulation is slow, so that labor is comparatively abundant and inexpensive. Countries in such areas tend to have a comparative advantage in producing products requiring high ratios of labor to capital. In other economies the ratio of labor to capital is much smaller, permitting labor to be more productive and consequently much more expensive relative to capital. Countries like these tend to enjoy a comparative advantage in the production of goods for which low ratios of labor to capital are needed.

Differences in the Resource Mix

The diversity among countries with respect to resource endowments makes it inevitable that there are areas of comparative advantage for some products and of comparative disadvantage for others for any given country *vis-à-vis* the world economy. Certainly we would not expect any two countries to have the identical mix of resources, and therefore it would indeed be surprising to find that the real costs of production of *all* products in one country are the same as they are in another.

Among most countries differences in the proportions in which resources are available are abundantly evident. With respect to the United States, Brazil clearly has a comparative advantage in the production of coffee and a comparative disadvantage in the production of machine tools. Although the United States could in some areas grow coffee of a sort, the terrain and climatic conditions of Brazil are much better suited for this type of endeavor. On the other hand, the capital equipment available and the special skills for machine-tool making that have been developed over time in the United States make it evident that the latter has a comparative advantage in this line of production.

Particularly glaring are the differences that exist in the capital to labor ratios of different countries. By and large the highly developed countries of western Europe, Great Britain, the United States, and Canada have relatively large proportions of capital to labor, while the underdeveloped areas of South America, Africa, and Asia have much lower capital to labor ratios. This means that the highly developed countries tend to have comparative advantages in *capital-intensive* kinds of production, or lines of production requiring high capital to labor ratios. The comparative advantages of the underdeveloped areas tend to lie in more *labor-intensive* lines of endeavor. This state of affairs is not at all to the liking of many underdeveloped countries and, rather than pursuing the gains available from their comparative advantage, they often attempt to develop relatively high-cost lines of industrial production by shutting out competitive industrial imports, a practice that makes industrial goods more costly to them than they would be otherwise.

Differences in Technology

Specific lines of comparative advantage and disadvantage also arise partly because of differences in the technology used in different countries. Among different countries we can identify (1) different general levels of technology and (2) different types of technology. Both are, of course, closely related to the differences in the resources available to the countries.

Different Levels of Technology

We find wide variations in the general levels of technology used as we look at the underdeveloped countries of the world on the one hand and at the advanced countries on the other. In India, for example, agricultural methods are primitive compared with those used in the western world, with water buffalos still widely used for pulling walking plows. In South American wheat production grain separators that have not been seen in the United States for 20 years provide a common method of threshing wheat. In most African countries neither the know-how for producing electrical appliances nor the electricity required for operating them is generally available.

Simply to list such examples is to point to why differences in technology come into being. Advanced levels of technology stem from two primary sources: (1) comparatively high levels of educational attainment and (2) adequate stocks of capital equipment on which technical know-how can be put to work. The extent to which these are available differs greatly among countries.

Different Types of Technology

Different countries of the world tend to develop their own special kinds of technological proficiencies, heavily influenced by the kinds of resources available in each. Countries with abundant coal and iron ore deposits are likely to develop an efficient steel-making technology. Maritime economies may develop more sophisticated fishing or ship-building techniques. In view of the vast land areas of the United States, is it any wonder that this country is relatively strong in the production of various kinds of transportation equipment?

Economies of Scale

It is often advantageous to countries, particularly small countries, to specialize in a particular type of production and to trade even if they have almost identical resources and production techniques. This is so because of economies of scale.

Suppose that two countries both produce automobiles and refrigerators before trade. Let country A's resources be such that she can produce and consume 500,000 automobiles and 500,000 refrigerators annually. Country B is in the same position. Suppose that in each country both the output of automobiles and of refrigerators is too small for the firms producing them to utilize optimum scales of plant.

If country A's resources were *all* devoted to automobile production, suppose that the economies of scale realized would permit production of 1,200,000 automobiles. If country B's resources were *all* devoted to refrigerator production, suppose that economies of scale could be realized to the extent that 1,200,000 refrigerators could be produced. Under these circumstances it would be to each country's advantage to specialize and trade. Together they could produce 1,200,000 automobiles and 1,200,000 refrigerators. By trading 600,000 automobiles for 600,000 refrigerators they could each have 600,000 automobiles and 600,000 refrigerators—a net gain of 100,000 of each product for each country over what it could have without trade. Other combinations yielding advantages to both countries are, of course, possible.

A real-life counterpart of this example exists in western Europe. Between World War I and World War II tariff barriers erected by the various small countries of western Europe limited the market in many industries of each country to the country itself. The European Economic Community, usually called the Common Market, established in 1957, is directed toward the elimination of such trade barriers among member countries. It appears that, among other factors, the broadening of the markets available to specific industries in each has contributed to improvements in productive efficiency in the member countries.

SUMMARY

International trade is carried on for the same reasons as trade among individuals and among communities and regions within a country; all parties to voluntary exchange expect to gain from it. But because of such factors as nationalism and currency differences, special problems are associated with trade among nations. This chapter examines how and why trade is mutually advantageous to the parties engaging in it.

Patterns of trade for the United States are examined first. Canada, Japan, the United Kingdom, West Germany, France, and Mexico were our largest export markets in 1966. For the same year our most important suppliers of imports in terms of value of goods imported were Canada, Japan, West Germany, the United Kingdom, Venezuela, Mexico, and Italy. Trade is not necessarily a two-way exchange between two countries but is typically multilateral in character, involving several countries in complex trading patterns. The United States exports a multitude of products, the three most important in 1966 being grain and cereal preparations, chemicals, and motor vehicles and parts. We also import a great many products, with petroleum and its products, automobiles and parts, and nonferrous metals heading the list.

The mutual benefits possible from international trade are rooted in the principle of comparative advantage. According to this principle, if a country specializes in producing goods and services in which its productive efficiency is greater relative to other goods and services and trades for goods and services in which its productive efficiency is relatively less, its "production possibilities," or the total of all goods and services available to the trading parties, will be greater than they would be in the absence of trade. The alternative costs of trading for goods in which a country has a comparative disadvantage are less to the country than the alternative costs involved in producing such goods itself. Specializing in the production of goods and services in which the country has a comparative advantage and trading for those in which it has a comparative disadvantage yields the same benefits to the country as would the discovery of some cost-reducing technique for producing the latter group.

Every country of the world has a comparative advantage in the production of some goods and a comparative disadvantage in the production of others. This is so because of differences in resource endowments and in levels and kinds of technology among countries. Small countries, whose internal markets for some goods are not large enough to permit taking advantage of possible economies of scale, may find that specialization in some products and trade for others will permit the trading parties to expand outputs of those goods sufficiently to reduce average costs of production. Where this is possible, the trading parties benefit from the higher productive efficiency in each country.

This chapter demonstrates the potential of trade. In the next three chapters we discover the complications that arise in the course of trade and the almost inevitable attempts on the part of some people to restrict its volume.

EXERCISES AND QUESTIONS FOR DISCUSSION

1. Compare the exchange of goods among countries and among individuals. Must one party lose whenever the other party gains? Explain.
2. "If Japan can make transistor radios cheaper than we can make them, we should import radios from Japan." Evaluate this statement.
3. Is the principle of comparative advantage applicable only on an international plane? If not, explain where else it might apply.
4. "The United States as compared with Nigeria has as absolute advantage in all manufacturing lines. It would not, therefore, be mutually advantageous for trade to occur between these countries." Evaluate this statement.
5. Discuss the difference between the real cost of producing a good and the money cost of producing it. Which is relevant for international trade? Elaborate.
6. Is multilateral trade more advantageous economically to the countries involved than is bilateral trade? Explain.

SELECTED READINGS

Ellsworth, P. T., *The International Economy*. New York: Crowell-Collier, Macmillan, Inc., 1964, Chaps. 4–5.

Kenen, P. B., *International Economics*. Englewood Cliffs, N.J.: Prentice-Hall, Inc., 1964, pp. 7–17.

Kindleberger, C. P., *International Economics*, 3d ed. Homewood, Ill.: Richard D. Irwin, Inc., 1963, Chap. 5.

Snider, D. A., *Introduction to International Economics*, 3d ed. Homewood, Ill.: Richard D. Irwin, Inc., 1963, Chap. 3.

The Financing
of International
Trade

CHAPTER 31

Differences in the currencies or monetary units used by countries engaging in international trade lead, unfortunately, to some highly vexing problems. The framework within which international trade is carried on should be such that all mutually beneficial trade can occur with a minimum of effort. Instead, we permit financial arrangements to become so tangled that some trade that would have benefited trading parties is not carried on at all. A major challenge, clearly, is to find and to institute a set of arrangements that will promote a free flow of trade. This chapter sets the stage for understanding the financing of international trade. First, we shall consider the simple mechanics of an international transaction; second, we shall discuss a country's balance of payments, with particular reference to the situation of the United States; third, we shall examine the nature of deficits and surpluses in the balance of payments; and fourth, we shall briefly survey the recent history of the U.S. balance of payments.

INTERNATIONAL TRANSACTIONS

In this section we reduce a set of international transactions to its simplest terms. Then, in the remainder of this chapter and in the next we move into the more complex aspects of the financing of international trade.

Suppose that a U.S. oil company wants to import crude petroleum into the United States from Mexico. Suppose also that an enterprise in Mexico wants to import automobiles from the United States. We will first consider each transaction in isolation from the other and then we will view them as a part of regular, continuing trade between the two countries.

Isolated Transactions

If the only transaction possible between a business in Mexico and one in the United States is the export of an automobile from the latter to the former, in all probability no transaction at all will take place. If no other transactions of any kind have occurred and if none is contemplated between Mexico and the United States, the Mexican business firm will have no dollars and will be able to make payments in pesos only. But the potential seller of the automobile wants dollars, since this is the medium of exchange in which he makes his sales, meets his costs, and computes his profits. He will not want pesos if no other trade with Mexico is to occur, since he would be unable to use them.

The same stalemate will exist if the only possible transaction is the export of crude petroleum from Mexico to the United States. The seller of petroleum operates his business in terms of pesos. He has no use for dollars if no other transactions are or will be possible.

Continuing Trade

The situation is quite different if the prospective parties to an international sale or purchase of a good or service are confident that the contemplated exchange is only one of many that will occur over time. A U.S. seller of automobiles will gladly accept 62,500 pesos for an automobile if he knows that there are parties in the United States who import goods from Mexico. He can sell the pesos to the oil company, say, for $5000,[1] thus obtaining the kind of money that he wants and needs to carry on his business. With the 62,500 pesos the oil company can buy crude oil from a Mexican producer. Both transactions are complete and both sellers are paid in the monetary units that they desire.

The transactions could have been accomplished the other way around. The U.S. oil company could buy $5000 worth of crude oil from a Mexican producer, paying the producer in dollars. The Mexican automobile importer could then buy with pesos the $5000 from the crude oil producer and use the dollars to import an automobile from the United States.

[1] A United States dollar does, in fact, currently exchange for 12.5 pesos. We shall see in the next chapter how exchange rates are determined.

Again both sellers would have what they desire, payment in their own money for the goods that they have sold.

Foreign Exchange Markets

The financial aspects of international trade can be readily generalized. Transactions need not be paired. Import and export activities carried on over time by a great many different businesses and persons have caused markets to be established for foreign currencies. These are called *foreign exchange markets,* with the term "exchange" meaning "money," and they are usually operated by banks as a part of their regular business. Anyone in the United States desiring to import from another country can buy with dollars the appropriate foreign money in the foreign exchange market; that is, at his bank. Anyone in the United States who sells abroad can sell for the money of the country to which he exports, and the foreign money or foreign exchange can then be sold for dollars in the foreign exchange market.

With organized foreign exchange markets in operation it is not even necessary that the exporters and importers of a country trade with the same foreign country. Payments on a *multilateral* basis are possible. Suppose, for example, that the United States exports automobiles to Mexico and imports wine from France. Suppose, further, that France imports silver from Mexico. The pesos earned from the sale of automobiles to Mexico may be used to buy French wine and, in turn, used by French importers to buy Mexican silver.

THE BALANCE OF PAYMENTS

Most countries keep records of those international economic activities that give rise to what they owe, or to their demands for foreign exchange, and to what is owed them, or to the supplies of foreign exchange that are placed on the market; or in the absence of complete records they attempt to estimate the demand and supply magnitudes involved. A statement of its international accounts is called a country's *balance of payments.* That for the United States for 1967 is given in Table 31-1. For analytical convenience we classify balance of payments items into five categories: (1) goods and services, (2) unilateral transfers, (3) capital movements, (4) unrecorded transactions, and (5) the balance on liquidity basis. The first four can be thought of as the *basic classifications* determining how much is owed a country and how much the country owes others. The fifth is a *balancing classification* showing how the net amounts that a country owes,

TABLE 31-1

Balance of Payments of the United States, 1967
(millions of dollars)

	WE OWE (DEBITS)	OWED US (CREDITS)
I. Goods and Services		
Exports		
Merchandise, adjusted[a]		30,468
Military sales		1,240
Services		7,190
Income on U.S. investments abroad		6,858
Total value of exports		45,756
Imports		
Merchandise, adjusted	26,991	
Military purchases	4,340	
Services	7,366	
Payments on foreign investments in the U.S.	2,293	
Total value of imports	40,990	
(Section I balance)		(4,766)
II. Unilateral transfers		
Private (net)	835	
Government[b] (net)	2,241	
Total unilateral transfers	3,076	
(Sections I and II balance)		(1,690)
III. Capital movements		
Transactions in U.S. private assets (net)	5,504	
Transactions in U.S. Government assets[c] (net)	2,411	
Total transactions in U.S. Assets (net)	7,915	
Transactions in foreign assets in the U.S.[d]		3,185
(Sections I, II, and III balance)	(3,040)	
IV. Unrecorded Transactions	531	
(Sections I, II, III, and IV balance)	(3,571)	
V. Balance on liquidity basis		
Transactions in U.S. official reserve assets[e] (net)		52
Transactions in foreign liquid assets (net)		3,519
		3,571
Total balance on liquidity basis	52,512	52,512

[a] Excluding transfers under military grants.
[b] Excluding military grants.
[c] Excluding official reserve assets.
[d] Excluding liquid assets.
[e] Transactions in official U.S. reserve assets (millions of dollars):

Gold	1170
Convertible currencies	−1024
Payments into IMF in gold	− 94
Total	52

SOURCE: Survey of Current Business, September 1968, p. 3.

or that is owed it, are settled. The first four or basic classifications are discussed in this section, leaving the balancing classification for the next section.

Goods and Services

The goods and services accounts make up the largest part of the balance of payments. In fact, when most people think of international trade these are the items that they have in mind. However, as we shall see, other international transactions are important too. The sales of goods and services, or exports, to other countries generate amounts owed us, and as these amounts are paid *supplies* of foreign exchange are placed in the foreign exchange markets from the viewpoint of the selling country or "our" country. These are referred to as *foreign exchange credits* for the selling country. On the other side of the fence we owe for purchases of goods and services or imports from other countries. What we owe creates *demands* for foreign exchange, or foreign exchange *debits,* on our international accounts.

Credits or Receipts

Four kinds of transactions are usually included in a country's sales of goods and services abroad. One is the very large *merchandise* account made up of the goods listed in Table 30–2—agricultural products, automobiles, machinery, and a large number of other goods. The second kind of transaction, *military sales,* consists of sales of military equipment to foreign governments, mostly for the use of military personnel that they have stationed in the United States. But note that other countries want to pay what they owe in their own money, and thus supplies of foreign exchange are generated just as though the goods were actually shipped to those countries.

Sales of *services,* the third category, is made up of transportation, travel, and miscellaneous services. We sell transportation services to other countries. We carry their freight and passengers and they pay for these in their own currencies, creating supplies of their currencies in foreign exchange markets. When foreigners travel in the United States foreign exchange supplies are also generated. They must give up their money for dollars to pay for their travel in their own money. In a very real sense we are "exporting" vacations or travel services to them. Miscellaneous services, the "catch-all," consists of insurance that we sell to foreigners together with a host of other small items.

Income on investments abroad refers to interest and dividends or other forms of returns on investments that we have made abroad in the past. In essence, we are selling foreigners the continuing services of our investments in their plant and equipment. When we are paid what they owe us for these, the payments—in foreign currencies—generate foreign exchange supplies.

Debits or Payments

Our purchases abroad are direct counterparts of our sales to foreigners, and these transactions create demands for foreign exchange. We purchase *merchandise* items of the kinds listed in Table 30–3. For our military personnel stationed abroad we buy certain supplies from the countries in which they are deployed, giving rise to *military expenditures*. In the *services* classification we purchase transportation, insurance, and other services from foreign firms. We also demand foreign currencies in exchange markets to pay interest and dividends on investments that foreigners have made at past dates in U.S. businesses. They desire these payments in their own monetary units.

Unilateral Transfers

Unilateral transfers refer to gifts and grants that the government and private parties in the United States make to governments and private parties elsewhere in the world. They also refer to gifts and grants that come from foreign countries to the United States. *Net* unilateral transfers represent the difference between payments of this kind that are made to us from abroad and those that we make. They can result either in net demands for foreign exchange or net supplies of foreign exchange, depending upon which set of payments is greater. In 1967, net demands of $3.1 million were generated, that being the net amount that was paid abroad by private parties in the United States and by the federal government.

An example of private remittances is money sent by persons in this country to relatives or friends living in another country. Another consists of contributions made for any kind of project being undertaken or for any sort of "cause" being carried out in another country. The recipients want their own money, so transfers of this kind generate demand for foreign currencies.

Government unilateral transfers work the same way. Government grants and gifts abroad for foreign aid form the bulk of the $2.2 million shown in Table 31–1. We can think of the U.S. government as buying the necessary foreign exchange and giving it to foreign governments or to private organizations. If the foreigners use it directly to import U.S. goods, no actual foreign exchange transactions are really necessary. The amount of a grant showing up in this section of the balance of payments may be matched by a like value of goods and services exports. However, the grant may be used for other purposes.

Capital Movements

Balance of payments capital account items consist of changes in long-term U.S.-owned assets in other countries and in long-term foreign-owned assets in the United States. "Long term" is taken arbitrarily to mean a period exceeding one year. When U.S.-owned assets in other countries are increasing or when foreign-owned assets in the United States are decreasing, a *movement of capital out* of the United States is said to be occurring. The opposite of this, a decrease in U.S.-owned assets in other countries or an increase in foreign-owned assets in the United States, is called a *movement of capital into* the United States from abroad. We divide capital account transactions into three groups: (1) transactions in U.S. privately owned assets in other countries, (2) transactions in U.S. government-owned assets in other countries, and (3) transactions in foreign-owned assets in the United States.

Transactions in U.S. Privately Owned Assets

Private parties, individuals, and businesses invest rather large amounts abroad. The Cessna Aircraft Company purchases a French aircraft manufacturing concern. The Ford Motor Company opens up a manufacturing branch in Great Britain. Drug companies establish branches in Latin American countries. Stocks or bonds of foreign companies are purchased by U.S. investors. U.S. residents open bank accounts in francs in Switzerland. All of these create demands for foreign exchange, or represent *capital movements out* of the United States. Any of these working in reverse—liquidation of U.S. investments abroad—creates supplies of foreign exchange; that is, they are *capital movements into* the United States.

Transactions in Government-Owned Assets

Transactions in U.S. government-owned assets abroad are predominantly in the form of extending loans and credits to other countries and in the repayment of these loans and credits. When these are extended, they create demands for the currency of the country to which they are made.[2] When they are repaid, the repayments generate supplies of the currencies of the repaying countries on the foreign exchange market as it looks to those in the United States.

Transactions in Foreign-Owned Assets

When foreigners increase the quantities of assets that they own in the United States, or are investing in the United States, supplies of foreign exchange are placed on the market. Their investments in the United States are the counterpart of U.S. investments abroad; however, the composition of their investments is different. Most of their investments in U.S. assets are in private stocks and bonds and in savings accounts, while most U.S. investment abroad is direct investment in plant and equipment for U.S. businesses operated in other countries.

Unrecorded Transactions

Not much can be said about this part of the classification system. Some international transactions of parties in the United States go unreported. Perhaps a few articles on which high duties are levied are smuggled in. Or people on vacations abroad engage in exchange transactions that are never reported to data-gathering agencies. Statistical discrepancies from other parts of the balance of payments are entered here also.

INTERNATIONAL RESERVES, DEFICITS, AND SURPLUSES

It is possible, but not likely, that for a given year a country's basic international transactions—goods and services, unilateral transfers, capital movements, and unrecorded transactions—are such that it owes other countries exactly the amounts that they owe it, or that its sales to and gifts from other countries generate exactly the amounts of foreign exchange needed to pay for its purchases from and gifts to other countries. It is more likely that on balance either more or less foreign exchange is earned than is owed and that, correspondingly, a country has either a

---

[2] Suppose that the receiving country is free to use the loan obtained as it desires; it would want the loan in terms of its own monetary units. Even if a loan were made conditional on its being spent in the United States, the actual loan can be thought of as being made to the borrowing country in units of its own currency—that is, as giving rise to demand for foreign exchange. When it is spent, and the spending should be thought of as a separate transaction, the spending would then place supplies of the foreign exchange on the market from the point of view of the United States.

balance of payments *surplus* or a balance of payments *deficit* for any given year's international transactions. We shall look first at what constitutes a country's *international monetary reserves* and then at deficits and surpluses in the balance of payments.

International Reserves

Broadly speaking, a country's *international reserves* consist of whatever it has available to settle its international transactions; that is, they are made up of the things that represent purchasing power in international markets. What items can a country use for these purposes? One of the most obvious media for making international payments is gold. It has long been so used and, in fact, has little other monetary use in modern economic transactions. Another is the country's holdings of foreign money or foreign exchange. Foreign exchange can be held by both the government and private persons or institutions. It consists mostly of bank accounts owned in other countries, but it also includes any direct holdings of foreign currencies.

Other kinds of liquid assets are also included as parts of a country's international reserves. If the people and the government of the country own liquid assets of other countries—that is, short-term debt is owed them by parties in other countries—these can be used as a means of paying for foreign goods and services. Not quite so obvious, but certainly as important, is the amount of debt that the country in question is willing to build up or owe to other countries and that the other countries are willing to accept. For example, a business in the United States may sell $5000 worth of goods to a party in Italy. If the Italian party is willing to accept a U.S. bank account, a check in dollars may be written for the goods. The Italian party simply deposits the check in a U.S. bank, opening up a checking account in its name. This, in effect, is an increase in the amounts owed by people in the United States to people in Italy. Alternatively, the U.S. buyer might simply give the Italian seller a promissory note or, perhaps, even U.S. government securities such as Treasury bills. Thus the amount that a country is willing to go into debt to foreigners and that the latter are in turn willing to permit can be used by the country as international purchasing power and may be said to constitute international reserves.

The last statement should be qualified. Only the potential accrual of *liquid* liabilities to foreigners is generally considered to be a part of a country's international reserves. Long-term debt, as it is accrued to foreigners, ordinarily represents a desire on the part of foreigners to make investments in the country for the purpose of earning a return rather than a means by which foreigners are paid for things purchased from them.

As such, its accrual represents a capital movement into the country. Liquid liabilities are ordinarily taken to be those maturing or payable within one year. But the line between that which is a capital movement into a country and that which represents a decrease in the country's international reserves via an increase in what it owes foreigners is hard to draw with accuracy.

Deficits and Surpluses

Deficits

We have been hearing for several years about the U.S. balance of payments deficit. What is it? Essentially, a balance of payments *deficit* is said to occur when a country is drawing down or using up its international reserves. If during a given year what a country owes others for the basic first four sections of the balance of payments as illustrated by Table 31–1 shows a *net* excess over what others owe it, a balance of payments deficit exists. Some of the country's international reserves are used to finance the net amount due others.

Let us review Table 31–1 part by part, paying close attention to who owes how much to whom at each step of the way. The figures in parentheses show cumulative net balances. First, in part I, we note that U.S. goods and services exports generated some $45.8 billion in foreign exchange due it. But goods and services imports used up $41.0 billion of that amount, leaving $4.8 billion owed the United States as a result of the complete set of transactions. Moving into part II, we find that on balance unilateral transfers abroad exceeded unilateral transfers in by $3.1 billion, thus using up that amount of foreign exchange due us and leaving a balance of only $1.7 billion owed us. Capital movements out of the United States—increases in United States-owned foreign assets or foreign investment—exceeded capital movements in, not only using up all of the $1.7 billion owed us but creating a balance *owed abroad* of $3.1 billion. Add to that the $0.5 billion that we owed on unrecorded transactions and we find that for the first four basic classifications of the balance of payments for 1967 we ended up owing a total of $3.571 billion to other countries. This figure represents the U.S. balance of payments deficit, or the amount by which our international reserves, both official and private, were depleted for the year.

How were the different components of U.S. international reserves affected by the deficit; that is, how did we finance the deficit? The balance on liquidity basis, part V of Table 31–1, provides the pertinent information. Almost $0.052 billion came from U.S. official reserves. The other

$3.519 was made up of increases in U.S. assets owned by foreigners, or in U.S. indebtedness to them.

U.S. *official reserve assets* are defined by the Department of Commerce as the government's (and its agencies') holdings of gold, convertible currencies, and its reserve position in the International Monetary Fund. The gold holdings are self-explanatory. Convertible currencies are those that can be converted into dollars or other currencies in foreign exchange markets without restrictions of any kind. The reserve position of the United States in the International Monetary Fund represents rights of the United States to draw foreign currencies from that agency almost automatically up to its full amount. Its amount is determined by U.S. gold subscriptions to the International Monetary Fund.[3] All of these official reserve assets are readily available for settling U.S. international accounts.

The details of the 1967 decrease in U.S. official reserves are shown in footnote *e* to Table 31-1. The United States made payments in gold to other countries amounting to $1,170 million and it decreased its gold subscription to the International Monetary Fund by $94 million. The total amount of gold given up by the United States for the year was thus slightly over $1 billion. However, at the same time, the U.S. government acquired $1,024 million in access to foreign currencies, in the form of drawing rights on the International Monetary Fund, so the net decrease in U.S. official reserves was $52 million.

The decrease in international reserves other than official reserves, or the increase in U.S. indebtedness to foreigners, took several forms. Private persons and businesses in the United States gave foreigners short-term (less than one year) promissory notes for some of what was owed them. Foreigners were also paid by checks drawn in dollars on U.S. banks, which they then deposited in accounts of their own in U.S. banks. Foreigners also accepted payment in the form of U.S. government securities with maturity dates of less than one year.[4] Almost all of the net balance owed other countries was financed in these ways.

Surpluses

Once balance of payments deficits are understood, not much need be said about surpluses. A surplus arises for a country when the basic classifications show that for a given year it is owed more than it owes. Its basic international transactions generate more foreign exchange than they require the country to pay out during the year.

The balancing transactions for the country with a surplus will

---

[3] See pages 636–638 for a discussion of the International Monetary Fund. See also *Federal Reserve Bulletin,* November 1967, pp. 1992–1993.

[4] Purchases of U.S. government securities with longer maturities were accounted for as capital movements *into* the United States in section III of the balance of payments.

strengthen its international reserve position. The amounts due the country may be paid partly in gold. Additionally, the debtor countries will use some of their foreign exchange reserves, held in the form of the given country's monetary units (or other convertible currencies), to pay some part of it. These may well be bank balances of the debtor countries that they own in the given country. Other short-term debt obligations of the surplus country to the debtor countries that were built up in the past may be used. And, finally, the surplus country may accept short-term debt obligations of the debtor countries. It may accept their promises to pay in the form of promissory notes from the debtors and in the form of bank balances in the banks of the debtor countries. All of these increase the international reserves of the country with the surplus.

Historical Record of the United States

With the exception of the 1942–1945 war years, the United States experienced balance of payments surpluses in the period from 1933 to 1950. From 1933, when the U.S. government fixed the price of gold at $35 an ounce,[5] through 1941 the surpluses brought to the U.S. Treasury large amounts of gold and international reserves in other forms. Vast U.S. expenditures overseas during World War II brought on deficits for 1942 through 1945, but from 1946 through 1949 large surpluses were again the order of the day. By the end of 1949 the United States held some two-thirds of the world's stock of gold used for monetary purposes.

The surpluses and the consequent accumulation of gold and other international reserves by the United States meant, of course, deficits and the loss of gold and other international reserves by other countries. These losses pressed on the allied countries of western Europe with especial severity as they imported heavily from the United States in the late 1930s after war had broken out on the Continent. They experienced "dollar shortages," or shortages of the foreign exchange that they needed most, and to meet as large a part of them as possible they shipped gold to the U.S. government and incurred indebtedness to both the U.S. government and private sellers of goods and services. Again, after the cessation of hostilities in 1946, the countries that had been devastated by the war turned to the United States for goods and services that they wanted but were not able to produce. The dollar shortage appeared to be chronic.

From 1946 through 1950 forces were being set in motion that would reverse the long-standing surplus position of the United States with respect to the countries of western Europe and Japan, the countries with whom the United States carried on most of its international trade. The

---

[5] Purchases were made from anyone wishing to sell gold, but sales were made primarily to foreign central banks and central government treasuries. U.S. citizens could purchase or hold gold for commercial uses only.

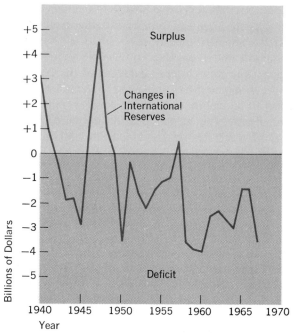

Figure 31-1
Changes in U.S. international reserves, 1940-1966.

TABLE 31-2
Changes in International Reserves of the United States

YEAR	MILLIONS OF DOLLARS	YEAR	MILLIONS OF DOLLARS
1940	2,890	1955	−1,145
1941	1,119	1956	− 935
1942	− 205	1957	520
1943	−1,979	1958	−3,529
1944	−1,859	1959	−3,743
1945	−2,737	1960	−3,881
1946	1,261	1961	−2,370
1947	4,567	1962	−2,203
1948	1,005	1963	−2,670
1949	175	1964	−2,798
1950	−3,580	1965	−1,335
1951	− 305	1966	−1,357
1952	−1,406	1967	−3,571
1953	−2,152		
1954	−1,550		

SOURCES: U.S. Department of Commerce, *Business Statistics, 1965,* pp. 12–13; and *Survey of Current Business,* September 1968, p. S–3.

Marshall Plan and other foreign assistance programs elevated U.S. uni-lateral transfers to these countries. As they rebuilt and improved their capacities to produce, they were able to increase their exports to the United States. Expanding foreign economies became attractive outlets for investment by U.S. businesses and individuals. By 1950 U.S. balance of payments surpluses had turned to deficits. The changes are recorded in Table 31–2 and in Figure 31–1.

Not until the late 1950s did the continuing deficits arouse alarm in the United States. The accumulation of international reserves, including most of the world's monetary gold, that had occurred prior to 1950 gave the impression that the United States had almost unlimited international purchasing power. But the continuing drain through the 1950s served to shake world confidence in the capacities of the United States to meet an unlimited series of deficits. The world's dollar shortage of the pre-1950 era turned to a surfeit of dollars in foreign exchange markets following that date. And the solution to the problem is not yet in sight.

SUMMARY

This chapter introduces the financing of international transactions. Different countries use different currency systems and, since sellers of goods ordinarily desire payment in their own currency, some system for making international payments must be arranged if trade is to be car-ried on. The present system consists of foreign exchange markets in which those who receive payments from other countries may sell any foreign currencies that they obtain and in which those who make payments to other countries may purchase the necessary forcign currencies with their own currency.

The international economic transactions of a country that create either supplies of or demands for foreign exchange are summed up in its balance of payments. Items making up the balance of payments can be classified into two major groups: (1) the basic group, which includes all of the transactions occurring autonomously and which give rise to amounts owed by any one country to others and the amounts owed it by others. and (2) the compensating, or balancing group, which shows how net amounts owed are paid or financed.

Within the basic group items are classified as (1) goods and services, (2) unilateral transfers, (3) capital movements, and (4) unrecorded trans-actions. Exports of goods and services by a country increase the supplies of foreign currencies available to the country while imports of goods and services draw them down. Unilateral transfers—gifts or grants—to other countries draw down a country's foreign exchange holdings while unilateral transfers from other countries increase them. Capital movements out of a country, or investments in foreign assets, decrease a country's stock of foreign exchange. Capital movements in, or foreign investments in the country, generate increases in foreign exchange holdings of the country. Unrecorded transactions is a catch-all classification for transactions that escape official records and takes into account errors and omissions in other classifications.

The balancing group of items records changes in the international reserves or international purchasing power of the country. A country's international reserves consist of its official reserves, that is, government-held international purchasing power, plus whatever private and government debt to foreigners it is willing to build up and which foreigners are willing to permit. The exact composition of the country's international reserves is difficult to determine, because the line between what constitutes a capital movement and what constitutes a balancing transaction is blurred. In the United States official reserves are taken to mean gold plus foreign currencies owned by or available to the government, including drawing rights on the International Monetary Fund. To official reserves we add the potential amount of debt that we are willing to incur to foreigners and that they are willing to accept.

Balance of payments deficits or surpluses may arise depending upon who owes whom as a result of the basic transactions. A deficit occurs for the country that on balance owes other countries and must therefore decrease its international reserves. A surplus occurs for the country that on balance is owed amounts by other countries. Surpluses increase the country's international reserves.

The U.S. balance of payments position has shifted from one extreme to the other in the years since the Great Depression. Surpluses and the acquisition of gold and other international reserves were accumulated, except for the World War II years, from 1933 through 1949, and the rest of the world was said to be experiencing a dollar shortage. Since 1949, balance of payments deficits have existed, except for a small surplus in 1957. The dollar shortage of the rest of the world has turned to a dollar glut. Many of these surplus dollars owned by foreigners have been used to purchase gold from the United States, hence the gold outflow that is causing so much concern.

EXERCISES AND QUESTIONS FOR DISCUSSION

1. "A country can import more goods than it exports and still have balance of payments equilibrium." Evaluate this statement.
2. What, if any, are the limits to the size of the deficit a country can run in its balance of payments? Explain.

3. If gold were not used as a means of making international payments, could world trade continue? If so, how?
4. "The U.S. balance of payments deficits of the past few years have resulted from American fiscal and monetary irresponsibility." Discuss this statement.
5. President Johnson in early 1968 requested restrictions on foreign travel by U.S. citizens and a cutback on foreign investment by U.S. firms. How would these proposals affect the balance of payments? What alternatives are available to alleviate the balance of payments deficit?
6. If the U.S. budget deficit were funded by the selling of long-term government bonds to foreigners, how would this affect the U.S. statement of international accounts?

SELECTED READINGS

Balassa, Bela, ed., *Changing Patterns in Foreign Trade and Payments.* New York: W. W. Norton and Company, Inc., 1964, pp. 8–25.

Ingram, James C., *International Economic Problems.* New York: John Wiley and Sons, Inc., 1966, Chaps. 2 and 5.

Kenen, Peter B., *International Economics.* Englewood Cliffs, N.J.: Prentice-Hall, Inc., 1964, pp. 51–58.

Exchange Rates and International Payments

CHAPTER 32

If you take a trip to Europe this summer, one of the first facts of life that will confront you is that you must have the currency of the country you are visiting in order to pay the porter at the airport, the taxi driver who takes you to your hotel, and for any other goods or services that you may require while abroad. You could have used dollars to purchase the needed foreign currencies before leaving the United States, but more likely you will exchange dollars for the appropriate currency in each country that you visit. In Great Britain you will pay about $2.40 for each pound sterling that you buy; in France a franc will cost you approximately 20 cents; and a West German mark will cost about 25 cents.

What determines the rate at which the money of one country can be converted into that of another? In this chapter we shall examine the mechanism by which *exchange rates* are determined in uncontrolled or free markets and the means by which the rates may be "pegged" or fixed artificially in controlled markets. We shall consider the relations between exchange rates and balance of payments disequilibria, how countries seek to control their balance of payments deficits, and the issue of flexible versus controlled exchange rates. Finally, we shall summarize international financial developments of the present century.

FREE MARKET EXCHANGE RATES

How would the exchange rate between the currencies of two countries be established in an ordinary competitive market situation? Several hints were advanced in the preceding chapter. The fact that the people who receive payments from abroad like to be paid ultimately in the currency of their own country leads to the establishment of foreign exchange markets. The operation of foreign exchange markets is ordinarily but not necessarily conducted by banks. In any given country supplies of foreign currencies come into such a market from the export of goods and services, from unilateral transfers into the country, and from capital movements into the country. Demands for foreign currencies arise from import activities, from unilateral transfers out of the country, and from capital movements out of the country. These provide the basis for the determination of exchange rates, or for the establishment of the prices of the various foreign currencies in terms of the monetary units of the home country.

Demand for a Foreign Currency

To establish the home country demand schedule or demand curve for a foreign currency, we should think of the currency as though it were a commodity. The demanders are those who want to make payments to parties in the other country. Suppose, for example, that the United States is the home country and Great Britain the foreign country. The demand schedule or demand curve would show the quantities of pounds sterling per unit of time that people in the United States would be willing to buy at alternative dollar prices of the pound, other things being equal.

The demand curve for pounds sterling would be expected to slope downward to the right, as does *DD* in Figure 32–1; that is, the lower the dollar price, the greater the quantity of pounds per year (or whatever the appropriate time unit is) that people in the United States would be ex-

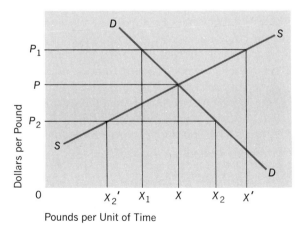

Figure 32–1
Exchange-rate determination.

pected to want. Why is this so? The lower the dollar exchange rate on the pound, the less expensive are British goods in terms of dollar prices. Consider, for example, a British product priced at one pound sterling per unit. If the exchange rate were three dollars to one pound, the price to the U.S. buyer would be three dollars (ignoring transportation costs). But, if the exchange rate decreases to two dollars per pound sterling, each unit of the product will cost two dollars instead of three. This means that British goods and services become cheaper relative to goods and services produced in the United States, and residents of the United States are induced to substitute some of the British goods for some of those produced at home. Of course, the larger the quantities of British goods that are purchased, given their prices in pounds sterling, the larger the quantities of pounds sterling demanded.

Supply of a Foreign Currency

The supply schedule or supply curve of a foreign currency, say British pounds sterling to the United States, can be established in a similar way. Suppliers of pounds are the British who purchase goods and services from the United States. The supply curve can be defined as showing the quantities of pounds that would be placed on the market at alternative dollar prices of the pound, other things being equal.

The supply curve of pounds is illustrated by SS in Figure 32–1, and usually it will slope upward to the right, as do most supply curves. The determining factor in whether it does or does not slope upward to the right is the elasticity of British demand for U.S. goods when the demand curves are expressed in terms of pound sterling prices. Consider Figure 32–2(a), in which some sort of composite units—basketfuls—of U.S. goods and services imported by the British are measured along the horizontal axis and the price per basket in pounds sterling along the vertical axis. Suppose that initially a pound sterling exchanges for two dollars and that U.S. sellers sell baskets of goods for two dollars each. Thus the pound sterling price of a basket will be one pound and, according to our demand curve, the British will purchase 1000 baskets of goods, providing a supply of £1000 on the foreign exchange market.

The resulting point on the supply curve of pounds sterling to the United States is shown as point A in Figure 32–2(b). In this diagram we measure the exchange rate in dollars per pound on the vertical axis and the quantity of pounds made available per unit of time on the horizontal axis, just as in Figure 32–1. Point A shows that at an exchange rate of $2 = £1$, a quantity of £1000 will be forthcoming.

Now suppose that the dollar price of the pound, or the dollar exchange rate on the pound, rises to $3 = £1$. With reference to Figure 32–2(a), a

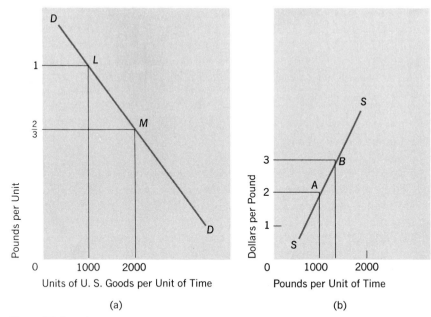

Figure 32–2
Supply of a foreign currency.

basketful of U.S. goods, imported by the British and still priced in the United States at $2 per basket, now costs only two thirds of a pound per basket. At this lower pound sterling price the demand curve *DD* shows that the British are willing to purchase 2000 baskets per time period. The total expenditures of the British on the imports are £1333⅓. Transferring this data to Figure 32–2(b), we plot point *B*, showing that at $3 = £1, the quantity supplied will be £1333⅓. Points *A* and *B*, along with other points similarly determined, trace out the pound sterling supply curve *SS*.

A brief review of the basic relations between the elasticity of demand and the total expenditures made on a product, together with another look at the *DD* curve in Figure 32–2(a), should suffice to complete the supply picture. If the British demand curve for imports from the United States is *elastic* for pound sterling price decreases,[1] as we have assumed it is for the movement from *L* to *M*, the British pound sterling expenditure for U.S. goods and therefore the quantity supplied of pounds sterling in the foreign exchange market will increase. This will make the supply curve of pounds sterling of Figures 32–1 and 32–2(b) slope upward to the right. We would expect that by and large this would be the usual case—the British demand for U.S. goods would tend to be elastic, since

[1] Keep in mind that we assume these are brought about by *increases* in the dollar price of the pound.

U.S. sellers must compete with sellers from other countries for British markets. However, if the British demand curve for U.S. goods is of unitary elasticity, the supply curve of pounds sterling will be vertical. If it is inelastic, the supply curve of pounds will be backward sloping for higher dollar prices of the pound. (Can you explain why these two statements are so?)

The Equilibrium Exchange Rate

The determination of the *equilibrium exchange rate* in a free market is a pricing problem similar in nature to other pricing problems. At relatively higher dollar prices of the pound the British are encouraged to import more from the United States, giving rise to relatively larger quantities supplied of pounds sterling. Imports to the United States from Great Britain are discouraged, curtailing relatively the quantities demanded of pounds sterling. At relatively lower dollar prices of the pound the opposite occurs. Quantities demanded of pounds sterling will be relatively larger and quantities supplied will be relatively smaller.

Equilibrium exchange rate determination is illustrated in Figure 32–1. At an exchange rate of P_1 dollars per pound sterling, quantity X_1 will be demanded and quantity X_1' will be supplied. Surpluses of pounds sterling are accumulating in the foreign exchange market. This induces sellers of foreign exchange to undercut each other, thus lowering the dollar exchange rate on the pound. When the exchange rate has been reduced from P_1 dollars to P dollars, the quantity demanded and the quantity supplied of pounds sterling will be the same and equilibrium will exist.

At an exchange rate of P_2 dollars per pound, those wishing to make payments to Great Britain will want X_2 pounds per unit of time. But transactions giving rise to supplies of pounds are discouraged by the low exchange rate and only X_2' pounds are made available. The shortage induces demanders to bid the price up to the equilibrium level P.

PEGGED EXCHANGE RATES

The major trading countries of the world have not been willing to let free market exchange rates among their currencies prevail throughout most of the present century. Rather, they have preferred to fix, or *peg*, their exchange rates at specific levels. Historically, two methods of pegging have been used. Prior to the 1920s an *international gold standard* was widely used. In more recent years countries have moved to what might be called a *major currency exchange standard*. We shall examine the main characteristics of each.

The International Gold Standard

Countries participating in an *international gold standard* system each define their monetary units in terms of gold content, or what amounts to the same thing, they each set a fixed price in terms of their own currency on an ounce of gold. Suppose the United States has fixed the price of gold at $35 per ounce and that Great Britain has established a fixed price at £14.6 per ounce. If one ounce of gold is worth $35 in the United States or £14.6 in Great Britain, and if both countries stand ready either to buy or sell gold at these prices, the exchange rate between the two currencies cannot fluctuate far from $2.40 = £1.[2]

If the demand for and the supply of pounds sterling from the point of view of the United States were DD and SS, respectively, in Figure 32–3(a),

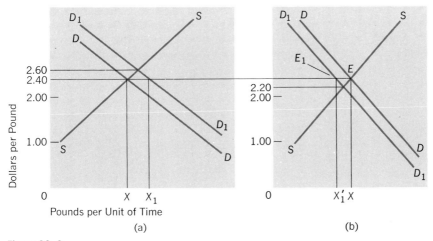

Figure 32–3
Exchange rates under an international gold standard.

then $2.40 = £1 would be an equilibrium exchange rate. At that exchange rate the total payments that the British want to make to the United States are X pounds sterling. This is exactly the quantity of pounds sterling needed by people in the United States to make all the payments to the British that they want to make at that exchange rate.

What would be the effects of an increase in U.S. demand for British goods? First, the demand for pounds sterling would increase, shifting the demand curve to the right to some such position as D_1D_1. The shortage of pounds at the original equilibrium price would be XX_1 and would cause the price of the pound to rise. If it were to rise to $2.60 = £1—that

---

[2] Since $35 = 1 ounce of gold and £14.6 = 1 ounce of gold, then £14.6 = $35 and £1 = $2.40.

is, to the new equilibrium level—forces would be set in motion to return it to the $2.40 level. Anyone with a pound sterling to invest can go into the foreign exchange market and buy dollars—$2.60 with each such pound. He can put 20 cents in his pocket, use the remaining $2.40 to buy a chunk of gold from the U.S. Treasury, and sell the gold to the British Treasury for one pound sterling. He can then repeat the process again and again. But note what is happening. *Additional* pounds sterling are coming into the foreign exchange market and an equivalent pound sterling value of gold is flowing from the U.S. Treasury into the British Treasury. As long as the dollar price of pounds sterling is above the $2.40 level, it pays those with pounds to buy dollars, purchase gold, and sell the gold to the British Treasury. This in turn places enough extra pounds sterling on the market to bring the dollar price of the pound back to the $2.40 level. In Figure 32–3(a) XX_1 pounds sterling worth of gold will be shipped to Great Britain per unit of time, generating an equivalent amount of pounds sterling—enough to fill the shortage at the $2.40 price—for the foreign exchange market.

The process can work the other way around as well. Suppose that U.S. demand for British goods decreases, shifting the demand curve for pounds sterling to the left in Figure 32–3(b) to D_1D_1 and decreasing the equilibrium dollar price of the pound to $2.20. People with dollars can now take $2.20 into the foreign exchange market and buy £1. The pound sterling can be taken to the British Treasury and sold for a chunk of gold. The gold can in turn be taken to the U.S. Treasury and sold for $2.40—its fixed price—and 20 cents has been made on the deal. Transactions of this kind bring about a flow of gold from Great Britain to the United States. The increased dollar demand for pounds sterling to buy gold raises the exchange rate back to its original level of $2.40. In effect, the British Treasury by selling gold at £14.6 per ounce generates a dollar demand for pounds sufficient to support the price of the pound at $2.40. For the decrease in the market demand for pounds to D_1D_1 an amount of gold valued at $X_1'X$ pounds must be shipped, creating an equivalent extra demand for pounds.

Actually, because of shipping and insurance charges for gold movements, the exchange rate could fluctuate slightly above or slightly below $2.40 = £1$. Suppose that on a $2.40 chunk of gold these costs are one cent. The exchange rate must go above $2.41 = £1$ to set in motion a gold movement out of the United States. It must fall below $2.39 = £1$ in order to cause a gold movement in.

A Major-Currency Standard

An alternative method has been used by some countries to peg their exchange rates. Instead of defining their respective monetary units in terms of gold, they define them in terms of the currency of one of the major trading countries of the world—say the pound sterling of Great Britain or the dollar of the United States. If the major currency so selected by a country is in turn defined in terms of gold, the country is said to be on a *gold-exchange* standard. To keep the price of the major currency constant in units of the home currency, the home country must stand ready to buy or sell the (foreign) major currency at the established pegged price.[3]

Suppose, for example, that West Germany defines the mark as one fourth of a dollar; that is, it sets the price of the dollar at four marks. Suppose in Figure 32–4(a) that price P, the equilibrium price, is at this level. There is neither a shortage nor a surplus of dollars. Suppose now that U.S. demand for West German goods increases, moving the supply curve of dollars to West Germany to the right to S_1S_1. A surplus of dollars comes on the market and tends to drive the mark price of the dollar down. The West German government in this case engages in price-support operations by going into the market and buying the excess of XX_1 dollars per unit of time. The West German government will be accumulating foreign exchange.

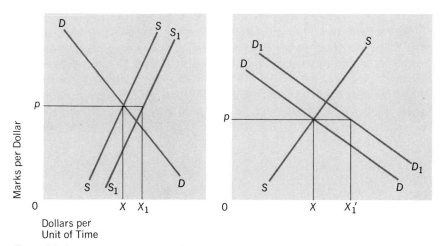

Figure 32–4
Exchange rates under a major-currency standard.

Suppose now that in Figure 32–4(b) the initial equilibrium price of the dollar is again P marks but that an increase in West German demand for U.S. goods occurs. The demand curve for dollars will shift to the right to D_1D_1 and a shortage of dollars occurs at the designated exchange rate. Now, in order to prevent the exchange rate on the dollar from rising, the

---

[3] Alternatively, it may put exchange controls into effect or take other actions to control directly its foreign trade. These alternatives will be considered later.

West German government must supply dollars in the amount of XX_1' per unit of time.

Countries on major-currency exchange standards historically have established *exchange stabilization funds* to engage in the buying and selling operations just described. Since 1945 the operations of their exchange stabilization funds have been supplemented by, and in some cases supplanted by, foreign exchange drawing rights on the International Monetary Fund.[4]

Depreciation and Devaluation

Whenever the price of a foreign currency in terms of a given country's monetary units goes up, the currency of the given country is said to have *depreciated* with respect to that of the foreign country. Or, to put it directly in terms of exchange rates, a country's currency is said to have depreciated with respect to a foreign currency whenever its exchange rate on the foreign currency rises. Thus, if in Chile the escudo price of the dollar rises from three escudos equals one dollar to four escudos equals one dollar, the escudo has been depreciated relative to the dollar. Its purchasing power in the United States has been decreased.[5]

We hear the term "devaluation" used much more frequently than the term "depreciation." In the strictest sense, *devaluation* of a country's currency means that the country has decreased the gold content of its monetary unit, or what amounts to the same thing, has increased the price at which it stands ready to buy or sell gold. When the United States in 1933 raised the price at which it would buy or sell gold from $21 to $35 per ounce, this was a devaluation of the dollar. When one country devalues its currency and others do not the effect is to raise the exchange rate of the country's currency on that of the others. In addition, the country's currency has *depreciated* in terms of the others. However, if one country devalues its currency and its trading partners devalue theirs by proportionate amounts, there will be no changes in exchange rates and, hence, no depreciation of the currency.

Devaluation has come to be used in a broader sense to mean any increase in the pegged exchange rate of one country's currency for others. Thus the 1967 increase in the British pound sterling exchange rate for other currencies was termed a devaluation of the pound. From the point of view of the United States, the dollar price of the pound was decreased from $2.80 to $2.40. From the British point of view, the pound price of the dollar was increased from £0.35 to £0.42 per dollar.

---

[4] See pp. 636–638.

[5] If the exchange rates between the dollar and other countries with which Chile trades do not change, the escudo will also have depreciated with respect to the other countries' currencies. The international purchasing power of the escudo will be less.

BALANCE OF PAYMENTS DISEQUILIBRIA

The situations of the preceding section in which the United States experiences either a gold outflow or a gold inflow, or in which West Germany either accumulates or uses up dollars are obviously examples of balance of payments disequilibria. A country accumulates gold and foreign exchange when it has a balance of payments surplus and it loses gold and foreign exchange when it has a balance of payments deficit. Surpluses cause countries little concern—their international purchasing power is increasing. But deficits are a different story. A country facing a shortage of the means of making international payments will exhibit great concern —witness that of the United States through the decade of the 1960s. It is with deficits that we shall be concerned here.

Most countries cannot meet a prolonged balance of payments deficit without imposing controls or restrictions of some kind on the availability of foreign exchange, on imports, and on other payments abroad or without taking some kind of corrective action to eliminate the causes of the deficit. An outflow of gold or the using up of its stocks of foreign exchange to keep the home-country price of foreign exchange from rising must be short-run expedients for a country. The long-run solutions lie elsewhere.

Causes of Deficits and Surpluses

Balance of payments deficits and surpluses arise as a result of changes in a country's conditions of supply of or demand for foreign exchange when its exchange rate is pegged at a level that is initially in equilibrium. Another way of looking at the same thing is to view exchange rates as being pegged above or below the equilibrium levels that would prevail under differing sets of demand and supply conditions. To get at the fundamental causes of deficits and surpluses, then, we must look to the causes of the demand and supply changes.

Components of Demand and Supply

The major components of the demand for foreign exchange are readily apparent from the balance of payments classification of the items entering into international transactions. For the United States the major part of demand is for the import of goods and services items, including the "importation" of trips abroad. Unilateral transfers to other countries—especially U.S. foreign aid grants—constitute a much smaller, but a significant, source of demand. More important than unilateral transfers to other countries, but less important than goods and services imports, are capital movements out—new loans and investments made abroad by both the government and private businesses.

The sources of supply of foreign exchange are the same set of items moving in the opposite direction. For the United States the major source consists of exports of goods and services. Capital movements in—investments and loans made in the United States by other countries—are usually second in importance. Unilateral transfers from other countries to the United States tend to be of least significance; however, for some countries that receive massive aid from others, this may be a sizable source of foreign exchange.

Monetary and Income Causes

One set of causes of changes in a country's demand for and supply of foreign exchange has *monetary and income* origins. A country may find itself in a situation in which its price level is rising relatively faster than the price levels in the countries with which it trades. Or it may find that its national income level is rising relatively faster than those of the countries with which it trades, even though no relative price-level changes are evident. These two forces frequently work in the same direction; however, one may be operative without the other, and in some instances they may work in opposite directions.

To illustrate the effects of relative price changes, suppose in Figure 32–5 that U.S. demand curve for and the supply curve of pounds sterling

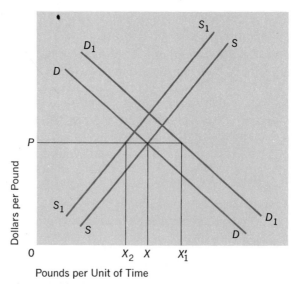

Figure 32–5
Balance of payments disequilibrium from relative price-level changes.

are DD and SS, respectively. The equilibrium exchange rate is P dollars per pound. Suppose that the exchange rate is pegged at this level.

What would be the effects of rising prices in the United States relative to those in Great Britain? As British prices decrease relative to U.S. prices, U.S. buyers shift their purchases toward British goods and import activity is increased, causing an increase in demand for pounds sterling from DD in Figure 32–5 to D_1D_1. At the same time U.S. exporters find that the rising price level in the United States increases their costs of production, shifting their product supply curves to the left and increasing the prices that the British must pay for those products. U.S. exports and British imports decrease, shifting the supply curve of pounds sterling to the left to S_1S_1. At the pegged exchange rate P there will be a shortage of foreign exchange or a balance of payments deficit of X_2X_1'.

The effects of an income increase in the United States relative to that in Great Britain is illustrated in Figure 32–6. Again we suppose that P is initially the equilibrium exchange rate and that it is then pegged at that level. As income in the United States increases, that is, as U.S. purchasing power grows, the demand for import goods and services from Great Britain also increases. Rising affluence in the United States may also increase unilateral transfers, or gifts and grants, abroad. It will most certainly increase the desire to lend and to invest abroad. All of these factors serve to shift the demand curve for pounds to the right, toward some position such as D_1D_1. But in this case, since no change is assumed in U.S. costs of production or in British purchasing power, there will be no change

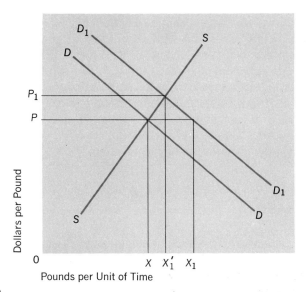

Figure 32–6
Balance of payments disequilibrium from relative income-level changes.

in the British desire to import from the United States or in the supply curve of pounds. The U.S. balance of payments deficit will be XX_1 in terms of pounds sterling.

Structural Causes

The other principal causes of changes in the demand for and supply of foreign exchange are *structural* in nature. They result from changes in the structure of demands for goods and services or from changes in the desire to give gifts abroad or to lend and invest abroad when these changes are not induced by relative price-level and/or income-level changes. In addition, they may result from changes in the supply curves of goods and services—from changes in the quantities and qualities of resources available or from changes in technology in different countries.

For purposes of illustration, suppose that technology in British industries, including export industries, advances rapidly, substantially lowering production costs and shifting British product supply curves to the right. The resulting lower prices of British goods to the United States will induce people in the United States to make larger expenditures for imports from Great Britain, provided the United States demand for those goods is elastic, as it is very likely to be. Consequently, U.S. demand for pounds sterling will shift to the right, as illustrated again by the movement from DD to D_1D_1 in Figure 32–6, creating a balance of payments deficit of XX_1 pounds at an exchange of P dollars per pound.

The effects of other structural changes in trade patterns and trade relationships can be handled in a similar fashion. Changes in U.S. demand patterns for foreign goods and services relative to domestic goods and services—or in their demand patterns for U.S. goods and services relative to their own—bring about changes in the U.S. demand for and supply of foreign exchange. An increase or decrease in unilateral transfers abroad will increase or decrease demand, as will capital movements out or capital movements in. In a changing world the trade patterns change and, with fixed exchange rates among the currencies of the world, balance of payments deficits and surpluses are bound to occur.

Control of Deficits

Short-run balance of payments deficits may be met in most cases through the depletion of the deficit country's stock of gold and/or its other international reserves. But what can a country do to correct a chronic or long-term balance of payments deficit? The major possibilities are (1) to bring about a relative contraction of national income and/or a relative decrease in the price level, (2) government control or rationing of foreign exchange, (3) other measures to restrict imports and payments abroad, and (4) depreciation of the currency.

Income and Price-Level Adjustments

In the nineteenth century the classic method of adjustment to a balance of payments deficit was a relative contraction in the deficit country's national income. The major trading countries were on gold standards and the adjustment mechanism worked automatically. A country developing a deficit lost gold to the country (or countries) with a surplus. Since the money supply of each country was tied to the quantity of gold that it had, the money supply of the deficit country contracted while that of the surplus country increased.[6] The decrease in the money supply of the deficit country reduced aggregate demand or total spending, including demand for imports. The expansion of the money supply increased aggregate demand, including the demand for imports, in the surplus countries. Thus the demand for foreign exchange was decreased and the supply of foreign exchange was increased for the deficit country, thereby reducing and eventually eliminating the deficit. If the income contraction in the deficit country was accompanied by falling prices and if the income expansion in the surplus countries was accompanied by rising prices, so much the better. Foreign goods became more expensive to the deficit country, encouraging still less importation from abroad. Deficit country products became less expensive to the surplus countries, encouraging them to purchase more from the deficit countries.

In terms of national income analysis a balance of payments surplus has the same effect on national income as net investment—in fact, it means net investment in the deficit countries by the surplus countries. So the development of a surplus leads to an expansion of national income and an increase in the country's imports. The development of a deficit for the deficit country amounts to a decrease in net investment; in and of itself the deficit represents negative net investment. This leads to income contraction in the deficit country and a consequent reduction in its demand for imports.

In the twentieth century, as countries have gone off the gold standard and have learned more and more about using monetary and fiscal techniques to stabilize and stimulate their own economies, income adjustments are no longer permitted to exercise their corrective influences. What country would be willing to deliberately undergo recession and court de-

---

[6] Think of gold as constituting the currency and the reserves of a country's banking system. A loss in gold thus decreases both the currency component and the demand deposit component of the country's money supply. An increase in gold has the opposite effect.

pression in order to correct a balance of payments deficit? Certainly not the United States in the 1960s! Still, some lip service is paid to the income method of adjustment. Countries with deficits are encouraged to subject themselves to "balance of payments discipline," but this is usually intended to mean that they should control any inflationary tendencies that they might have rather than that they should actually contract income and the employment level.

Exchange Controls

Exchange controls provide an alternative means of controlling a chronic balance of payments deficit. They require government operation of the deficit country's foreign exchange market. In the typical situation all receivers of foreign exchange must sell what they receive to the government at the official or pegged rate. Then any party desiring to import, invest abroad, or otherwise make payments abroad must go to the government to obtain the necessary foreign exchange.

The economics of exchange control are not new to us. The problem is essentially one of rationing. The balance of payments deficit, or the shortage of foreign exchange, indicates that its price is fixed below the equilibrium level. If price or the exchange rate is not used to ration available supplies of foreign exchange, then some other rationing mechanism must be employed. An exchange control system provides such a mechanism.

Black markets in foreign exchange frequently arise where exchange controls are in effect. Those who want foreign exchange are willing to pay a price higher than that fixed by the government for the quantity that is available, and there are usually persons around who are willing and able to accommodate them—illegally, of course. If the black market were permitted to develop, no transactions would occur at the official exchange rate. Those with foreign exchange to sell would sell it in the black market rather than to the government. The black market rate, which would be the equilibrium rate in such a case, would prevail and the exchange rate at which transactions occur would no longer be pegged.

To prevent black markets from developing, countries resorting to exchange controls use various methods to insure that all foreign exchange supplies will be turned over to the government. *Export licensing* is one such device. This means that a permit must be obtained from the government before exports can be shipped out, thus a record of the transaction and the foreign exchange to received are in the government's possession from the outset. Additionally, laws or decrees are put into effect, making it illegal for anyone to dispose of any foreign exchange except to the appropriate government agency.

The government of a country employing exchange controls is put in the position of determining what kinds of payments to other countries are to be permitted and the quantities in which those payments can be made. Those desiring to make payments abroad are required to make applications for the necessary foreign exchange and ordinarily must specify the purposes of the payments. The pattern of imports can be determined by the government through the control of the allocations of foreign exchange. Frequently, imports that compete with home-produced goods are restricted. Capital movements out are generally curtailed.

Other Control Measures

A deficit country may resort to still other means of restricting the amounts that can be spent abroad. One of the most venerable methods is the tariff, and its use raises such important issues that most of the next chapter will be devoted to it. Another effective method of limiting the importation of goods is through the use of import quotas. Still others are direct limitations on amounts that can be invested abroad, curtailment of dividend and interest payments abroad, and taxes or direct limitations on foreign travel. Most of us, as we read about and listen to the debate over the U.S. balance of payments deficit in the 1960s, can readily extend the list.

Depreciation of the Currency

A country with a prolonged balance of payments deficit may find it necessary to raise the exchange rate of its currency on other currencies or to depreciate its currency. Great Britain took this step in 1949 and again in 1967. Deficits occur when a country's exchange rate is pegged below the equilibrium level. We would expect, then, that an increase in the price of foreign currencies could eliminate the deficit.

The basic mechanism can be demonstrated with the aid of Figure 32–6. Suppose there is an increase in the demand for pounds from DD to D_1D_1. At the pegged exchange rate P a deficit of XX_1 per time period comes into existence for the United States. Suppose now that the currency of the United States is depreciated by an increase in the pegged exchange rate level P to P_1. At the higher dollar price of the pound, it becomes more expensive to the United States to make payments abroad for whatever reason, cutting down on the quantity of pounds demanded. At the same time, it becomes less expensive to the British to make payments to the United States for imports, for investment purposes, and for any other reason. The higher price of the pound brings forth a larger quantity supplied and induces demanders to ration themselves to that which is made available. Both quantity demanded and quantity supplied will be X_1' at the new exchange rate P_1.

The next corrective step beyond adjustments in the pegged level of exchange rates is simply not to have them pegged at all. Rates that are free to move in response to changes in supply and demand, both monetary and structural, are generally referred to as *flexible exchange rates*. A growing group of economists has been advocating a system of flexible exchange rates instead of the currently used system of pegged exchange rates in order to eliminate both balance of payments problems and problems of shortages (of deficit countries) of international reserves.

Pegged versus Flexible Exchange Rates

Most countries of the world today adhere to pegged exchange rates, and those experiencing balance of payments deficits exercise restrictions over payments abroad rather than permitting exchange rates to rise to equilibrium levels. Why is this so? The answers are not clear-cut. Economists are not agreed on whether pegged exchange rates with restrictions on payments abroad are best for deficit countries or whether it would be best to avoid deficits altogether by means of flexible exchange rates.

Arguments for Pegged Exchange Rates

A principal argument made in favor of pegged exchange rates is that major currency countries such as the United States have an obligation to protect the many holders of their currencies from fluctuations in their international values. Many countries, for example, hold U.S. dollars in their central banks as central bank reserves. It is considered "unfair" to let the dollar depreciate, since this would reduce the international purchasing power of the dollars they hold. It is also thought by many to be unfair to such countries for the United States to let the value of the dollar rise—that is, to let the dollar prices of the currencies of such countries fall—when the United States has a balance of payments surplus and the latter countries have deficits. Appreciation of the dollar means depreciation of the international purchasing powers of their currencies.[7]

Another major argument in favor of pegged exchange rates is that speculation of a destabilizing nature would occur if exchange rates were free to fluctuate. There is a large amount of money in currencies of different countries, so the argument runs, in the hands of persons who would rush this money from country to country in the pursuit of differences in short-term earnings opportunities on it. Suppose, for example, that short-

---

[7] The important question that arises here is that of what constitutes a "fair" exchange rate. What makes the current pegged exchange rates the "fair" or "correct" ones?

term speculators believe that the dollar price of the pound sterling is going to rise above its present level. They will sell their dollars on foreign exchange markets and demand pounds sterling. The effect, of course, will be to drive up the dollar price of pounds sterling. In a very short time the entire movement could be reversed, driving the dollar price of the pound down again (or, what amounts to the same thing, driving up the pound price of the dollar). This *hot money* may rush from country to country, causing rapid and extensive changes in exchange rates. These, in turn, would have adverse effects on international trade because of the uncertainties they may generate regarding their course over time.

A third reason why deficit countries often prefer pegged exchange rates is that the pegged rate permits them to import at lower prices in terms of their own currencies than would be the case if the price of foreign currencies were permitted to rise. The deficit country's currency is *overvalued* in terms of foreign currencies, and this means better *terms of trade* for the deficit country. Suppose that Chile has a deficit with respect to its trade with the United States and that the exchange rate is pegged at five escudos to one dollar. Ignoring transportation costs, an import from the United States priced at five dollars will cost Chileans 25 escudos at the pegged rate. Now, if the market price of the dollar were permitted to rise to 7 escudos, the same item would cost Chileans 35 escudos. Thus an overvalued escudo permits importation of U.S. goods on more favorable terms.[8]

Still other arguments are brought to bear by those who favor fixed exchange rates. An important factor in the maintenance of pegs, although not an argument usually brought forward by proponents, is that a decrease in the value of a country's currency in terms of that of other countries has come to be regarded as an international loss of face. Such a decrease in the value of the currency is considered an admission of financial irresponsibility on the part of the country concerned. Witness the dialogue over the 1967 British devaluation of the pound and the expressed determination of U.S. authorities to "protect" the dollar.

Arguments for Flexible Exchange Rates

A principal argument for flexible exchange rates has been advanced already. A system of flexible exchange rates would avoid balance of payments disequilibria and consequent problems of international reserve shortages. Restrictions on payments abroad would be unnecessary. There would be no need for exchange controls, import restrictions, controls on

---

[8] Export industries of the deficit country are subjected to adverse discrimination. The artificially low escudo price of the dollar means lower escudo receipts for exporters than they would receive if the escudo price of the dollar were permitted to rise. The country's supply of dollars will be smaller because of the lower volume of exports.

foreign investment, or travel abroad to alleviate balance of payments problems.

Another point often made is that flexible exchange rates would place the values of foreign goods in proper relation to those of domestic goods. If U.S. demand for French goods and services expands relative to that for domestic goods, it should be expected that the dollar price of the franc will rise to reflect the relatively higher value placed by U.S. residents on those goods and services. Exchange rate changes would thus properly reflect the structural changes occurring among the trading countries of the world.

A third argument in favor of flexible exchange rates is that they permit individual countries to pursue independent monetary and fiscal policies with minimum effects on the economies of other countries. Suppose, for example, that the United States experiences rapid inflation while France does not. With fixed exchange rates, U.S. goods become more expensive to Frenchmen, thus cutting down on the amounts that France can import. At the same time, the export industries of France are stimulated by rising U.S. demand for the now relatively cheaper French goods. The combination of these two effects means that in real terms the French have smaller amounts of goods and services to consume. The U.S. inflation is thus harmful to the French.

Suppose now that in the face of relatively more inflation in the United States than in France exchange rates are flexible. Rising U.S. prices cut down on the quantities demanded of U.S. goods by the French, thus decreasing the supply of francs made available to the United States. Rising U.S. demand for French goods increases the demand for francs in the United States. As francs become short in the United States, the dollar price of the franc rises until the shortage is alleviated. The rising dollar price of the franc, or the falling franc price of the dollar, thus again makes French importation from the United States attractive, tending to offset the adverse effects of the U.S. inflation. Similarly, the rising dollar price of the franc makes French goods look less attractive to U.S. buyers, thus tending to offset the stimulating effects of the U.S. inflation on French export industries. In summary, the disrupting effects of inflation in one country on its trade with other countries tends to be offset by exchange rate adjustments under a system of flexible exchange rates. This counter-mechanism is missing where exchange rates are pegged.

Proponents of free market exchange rates question whether hot money movements would lead to highly unstable exchange rates. They argue that speculation and forward markets may well serve to stabilize exchange rates in the same way that they stabilize commodity markets in the very short run. They expect speculators to be trying consistently to purchase relatively cheap currencies, thus driving their prices up at times when their values tend to be low. They expect that when currencies become relatively expensive they will be sold, thus driving their prices below what they would be otherwise. These activities are expected to prevent extreme fluctuations from occurring.

Twentieth-Century World Financial Developments

Pre-World War I

International trade in the nineteenth century became rather highly developed, with most countries of the world pursuing production and trade largely along comparative-advantage lines. Restrictions to multilateral trade were minimal. Differences in the rate of technological development among countries and the discovery of new resource supplies in some but not in others brought about changing production patterns among different countries. Although rather severe adjustments were necessary at times, these were made without prolonged balance of payments difficulties.

Many economists attribute the successful adjustments of the period to the gold standards that formed the basis of the monetary systems of most countries. Countries that developed excesses of imports over exports, or rather whose payments exceeded their foreign exchange receipts, lost gold. The effect was a contraction of their money supply and a relative deflation. Deflation curtailed their payments abroad and augmented their receipts from abroad, thereby tending to correct the difficulty. The correction was furthered, too, by some degree of inflation in the gold-receiving countries, since their exports were discouraged and their imports were stimulated.

World War I through World War II

During World War I the "old" international payments system experienced severe dislocations. The Great Depression of the 1930s, followed by World War II, administered the *coup de grace*. Disruptions in trade patterns and gold losses by some countries induced them to abandon gold standards. Pegged exchange rates, balance of payments problems, and trade restrictions became the order of the day. The gold standards of the interwar years of countries professing to be on gold standards were different creatures from those of the old days. Governments were beginning to assume the responsibility for the control of their own money supplies. They were beginning to use monetary and fiscal policies both to offset the deflationary forces of gold drains and the inflationary forces of gold receipts that had characterized the "old" gold standards. With individual nations pursuing independent national monetary and fiscal objectives, relative changes in price levels and national incomes could no longer perform balance of payments equilibrating functions as they had under the "old" gold standards with pegged exchange rates. Under the "new" gold standards, gold was used only to define the monetary unit and to make international payments. It no longer served as an effective control agent over national money supplies.[9]

By defining their monetary units in terms of given amounts of gold, the "new" gold standard countries automatically established pegged exchange rates among their currencies. In this respect the "new" gold standards were no different from the "old." But the pursuit of independent monetary and fiscal policies by the different countries made it impossible for some of them to maintain gold reserves at the fixed exchange rates. Great Britain went off the gold standard in 1931 and several other countries followed suit. By the late 1930s only five countries—the United States, France, Belgium, the Netherlands, and Switzerland—still claimed to maintain gold standards.

Post-World War II

The chaotic state of international trade and exchange rates—partly controlled and partly uncontrolled—in the 1930s and through World War II brought home the idea that international understanding and cooperation would be desirable. The United States invited 50 nations to participate in an international financial conference at Bretton Woods, New Hampshire, in 1944. Out of this conference came the International Monetary Fund (IMF) and the International Bank for Reconstruction and Development (the World Bank). Only the former will occupy our attention at this juncture; we will consider the World Bank in Chapter 34.

The IMF commenced operations in 1947 with four major objectives. One was to provide a forum for consultation on problems of international payments among nations of the world. A second was to promote stability of exchange rates and a means of making orderly adjustments when these seemed to be in order. A third was to assist particular countries in the removal of direct controls over foreign exchange. A fourth purpose was to provide financial aid to countries experiencing *temporary* shortages of foreign exchange.

Toward these ends each member nation, as a condition of membership, must fulfill a quota subscription to the IMF of either gold or dollars and of its own currency, with the size of the quota depending upon the coun-

---

[9] This discussion is not intended to imply that the old gold standard was superior to present-day independent monetary standards. Most economists, including myself, argue that the classic gold standard is inferior—that changes in national income in gold-losing and gold-receiving countries represent a hard and inefficient way of adjusting to balance of payments disequilibria.

try's size and economic strength. Of its total quota, 25 percent must be paid in gold or dollars and the remainder may be paid in the country's own currency.

Member countries define their currencies in terms of either gold or dollars and these are submitted to IMF officials for approval. Once they are approved, exchange rates are, of course, determined. Member nations experiencing fundamental balance of payments deficits may devalue or depreciate their currencies by as much as 10 percent, but a greater devaluation or depreciation may be allowed to correct persistent deficits. This was the case in the British devaluation of 1967. However, it is expected—but not always accomplished in fact—that international consultation through the medium of the IMF will precede devaluation or depreciation.

From quota subscriptions the IMF has at its disposal a large assortment of foreign exchange which member nations may borrow to meet temporary balance of payments deficits. In any one year a member may borrow—that is, purchase with its own currency—foreign currencies amounting to 25 percent of the value of its own quota. When the total amount of foreign currencies purchased reaches a point such that the IMF holds 200 percent of the particular country's quota in the currency of the country, its purshasing rights are used up and the IMF will assist the country in correcting what has developed into a fundamental disequilibrium.

The extent of IMF success in smoothing out international monetary arrangements is difficult to measure. Certainly it has provided an important forum for discussion of international financial problems. Although intended by its founders to provide short-run stability to exchange rates while permitting long-run flexibility (through devaluation of deficit country currencies), it has in fact brought about a large measure of inflexibility in exchange rates, a situation that has created serious problems for some countries which have not been satisfactorily resolved.

In its early years the IMF was confronted by serious balance of payments deficits in Great Britain and western Europe. World War II had played havoc with the domestic productive capacities of these countries, restricting the production of goods and services for export as well as for domestic consumption. The United States, on the other hand, emerged from the war with greater productive capacity than before. Sales of these countries to the United States were small and their purchases from the United States were large. Additionally, their overseas investments, together with their merchant marines, were reduced materially during the war, curtailing foreign exchange earnings from these sources. The deficit countries were not willing to let exchange rates of their currencies on U.S. dollars rise to what would have appeared at the time to be fantastic levels in order to achieve balance of payments equilibrium. Great Britain at last depreciated the pound by some 30 percent in 1949, and France depreci-ated the franc in both 1957 and 1958.

Since 1950 the shoe has been on the other foot. The United States has been running persistent balance of payments deficits since that time, with the exception of 1957, and has given up large quantities of gold to Euro-pean countries as a result. By early 1968 the dwindling gold stock of the United States had created concern both in the United States and in the major countries of Western Europe to induce them to agree to restrict their gold purchases and sales to official transactions among themselves. Greater restrictions on payments abroad have been put into effect and more severe measures are being considered. The official U.S. position is that devaluation and depreciation of the dollar are out of the question. But intensive study of the alternatives facing the country is in order. Which would be the least costly to us and to the world in the long run: (1) restrictive monetary and fiscal policies leading to relative income- and price-level adjustments; (2) exchange controls and restrictions on other transactions, leading to payments abroad, or (3) depreciation of the dollar?

SUMMARY

The exchange rate between any two currencies is simply the price of one in terms of the other. In a competitive market the equilibrium ex-change rate would be determined by the forces of demand and supply in the same way that any competitive price is determined. Alternatively, exchange rates may be pegged or fixed at given levels. Countries may peg their exchange rates by defining their monetary units in terms of gold. The resulting system is called an international gold standard. Pegging can also be accomplished among different countries by means of their defining par values for their currencies in terms of the currency of some major trading country such as the United States or Great Britain. This system is referred to as a major currency standard.

When countries peg their exchange rates, balance of payments prob-lems may be created by monetary and income factors and by structural factors. These bring about long-run changes in demand for and supply of foreign exchange for any given country. Balance of payments deficits (surpluses) arise when the pegged exchange rate is below (above) an equilibrium level.

Countries employ a number of measures to control long-run deficits. Under the old gold standards of the nineteenth century national income and price changes occasioned by gold flows from country to country provided the equilibrating machinery. In the world today countries are not willing to let their national incomes or their prices rise or fall in accordance with balance of payments needs. Rather, they attempt to pursue monetary and fiscal policies geared to full employment, stability, and economic growth. Exchange controls and other restrictions on payments abroad, designed to conserve the limited supplies of foreign exchange available, are used instead. Countries sometimes depreciate their currency to eliminate the cause of the deficit.

Although it is widely agreed that flexible exchange rates would avoid balance of payments disequilibrium, countries—and many economists— prefer pegged exchange rates. They argue that stability and fairness in the international monetary system depend upon exchange-rate stability. They maintain, further, that speculation in exchange markets would render free market exchange rates highly unstable. In addition, deficit countries like the terms of trade provided them by exchange rates that overvalue their currencies. In general, countries believe that any deterioration in the exchange rate of their currencies for others would mean an international loss of face.

Proponents of free market exchange rates argue that such a system would eliminate balance of payments problems and would place the import prices of foreign goods in proper relation to prices of domestic goods. They would insulate countries from the effects of irresponsible monetary and fiscal policies used by others. They argue that speculation in exchange markets would more likely be stabilizing than destabilizing.

In 1944 the major trading countries of the world agreed to establish a mechanism to assist in international payments problems. Subsequently the International Monetary Fund commenced operation in 1947. It promotes stability in exchange rates by making foreign exchange available on a loan basis to countries experiencing temporary balance of payments deficits. On a long-run basis it is supposed to provide the mechanism for alleviating deficits through adjustments in exchange rates. However, it appears in practice to have made exchange-rate adjustments by deficit countries more difficult than they were prior to its existence.

EXERCISES AND QUESTIONS FOR DISCUSSION

1. A recent article stated, "The international gold standard is like the Bible. It is the best kind of guide available, but we do not have to use it." Comment on this statement.
2. If exchange rates were allowed to move freely in response to foreign exchange demand and supply conditions, would the U.S. balance of payments predicament worsen or improve? Explain.
3. If, by allowing its currency to depreciate, a country can improve its balance of

payments position, why are most countries hesitant to permit depreciation of their currencies? Explain in detail.

4. Suppose that you as an importer increase your purchases of French bicycles by $10,000 worth per month. Explain the impact of your purchases on gold flows and exchange rates between the United States and France under (a) the international gold standard, (b) a major currency standard, and (c) flexible exchange rates.

5. Distinguish between devaluation and depreciation. Can a country's currency be devalued and yet not depreciated? If so, how? What domestic or international factors might dictate the devaluation of a country's currency?

6. In order to release gold stocks Congress removed the 25 percent "backing" required for U.S. Federal Reserve notes. Is this action sound with respect to our current balance of payments deficit? Discuss.

SELECTED READINGS

Balassa, Bela, ed., *Changing Patterns in Foreign Trade and Payments.* New York: W. W. Norton and Company, Inc., 1964, Part III.

Ingram, James C., *International Economic Problems.* New York: John Wiley & Sons, Inc., 1966, Chaps. 4 and 7.

Kenen, Peter B., *International Economics.* Englewood Cliffs, N.J.: Prentice-Hall, Inc., 1964, Chap. 5.

Tariffs
and Trade
Organizations   CHAPTER 33

Why does Wedgwood pottery cost less in the Bahamas than in U.S. shops, or why is an Irish linen tablecloth less expensive in Panama City than in the United States? A practical answer, of course, is that the United States places a special tax called a *tariff* on pottery and on Irish linen imported into the United States. These are examples of a long list of items on which the United States levies import duties—and U.S. tariffs are not as extensive as those of most countries. The Bahamas and Panama at the other extreme provide well-known examples of free trade areas.

In this chapter we shall examine the reasons why tariffs are levied and what implications they have for economic efficiency. The tariff issue has served so well as a focal point for political campaigns that it has become difficult for people to separate fact from fiction and logic from emotion. We shall attempt to pull these apart. In the latter part of the chapter recent international efforts to reduce tariffs are summarized.

THE RATIONALE OF TARIFFS

"The free traders win the arguments but the protectionists win the votes," so the saying goes. In Chapter 30 the principle of comparative advantage that underlies all voluntary trading relations was examined in detail. We learned there that trade along comparative-advantage lines can operate for a country in exactly the same way as any technological development that increases the outputs attainable from given quantities of resources. Yet for centuries governments have persisted in throwing obstacles into the way of international trade. Among the restrictive devices used, tariffs—duties or taxes on imports—loom large. Why have governments insisted on placing tariff barriers in the way of importation of goods and services? Some of the reasons have been discussed already and will be treated in a summary fashion. Others will require more elaboration.

For Revenue Purposes

Tariffs have been used for several centuries to provide revenue to governments. The greater part of U.S. government budgetary receipts came from this source in the late 1700s and early 1800s. Among the large, economically advanced countries, other revenue sources have been developed, and the contributions of tariffs to total government receipts are relatively small today. But among many of the less economically advanced nations tariff collections still constitute a significant part of government revenue.

Tariffs or import duties, like the sales taxes that they are, may be levied either as specific or as *ad valorem* duties. Specific duties are based on such physical measures of product quantity as volume or weight, while *ad valorem* duties are levied as a percentage of a product's price.

A tariff levied for revenue purposes should never be high enough to shut off the importation of the product to which it is applied. Elasticity principles determine the tariff level at which revenue from the tariff will be maximized. Given the demand for importation of the product, the quantity imported will vary inversely with the level of the tariff. If the elasticity of the quantity imported with respect to the level of the tariff is greater than 1, total tariff collections can be increased by lowering the tariff. If the elasticity is less than 1, an increase in the tariff will increase revenue collections from it. Tariff collections are maximum at the tariff level at which the elasticity of the quantity imported with respect to the tariff is 1.

The tariff for revenue cannot be faulted completely—no more so than can a sales tax. But one can ask whether there are alternative ways of raising revenue that may be superior. Tariffs for revenue share the faults —and virtues—of sales and excise taxes, for the latter are essentially what they are. They make the goods on which they are levied more costly relative to goods that escape them, thus inducing buyers to discriminate against the covered goods in favor of those that are not covered. It is frequently argued that the burden of the tariff is on the foreign seller, but its incidence, like that of any excise tax, is usually split in some way between the seller and the buyer, the split depending upon the elasticities of demand and of supply.

For Balance of Payments Purposes

Balance of payments deficits have provided an important stimulus to countries to increase their tariffs. Underdeveloped countries experiencing rapid inflation have used them extensively for this purpose. But major countries, too, when confronted by shortages of foreign currencies have resorted to import duties in an attempt to reduce the size of the deficit.

The anticipated effects of the tariff for this purpose are simple enough. The tariff is expected to increase the prices that importers must pay for their imports, thereby reducing the quantities demanded. Since the duties themselves are paid in the currency of the country that imposes them, the smaller volume of imports requires smaller quantities of foreign exchange to pay to foreigners. The reduction in the demand for foreign exchange is expected to reduce the shortage.

Unfortunately for the deficit country, other countries do not always sit still when it enacts tariffs on the goods that it imports from them. Suppose, for example, that in Figure 33–1 the demand for and the supply of French francs are DD and SS, while the dollar price of francs is P_1. At that price the United States has a franc deficit of $F_1'F_1''$. Now suppose that the United States raises tariffs on imports from France, cutting back demand for francs to D_1D_1 in order to eliminate the franc deficit. France

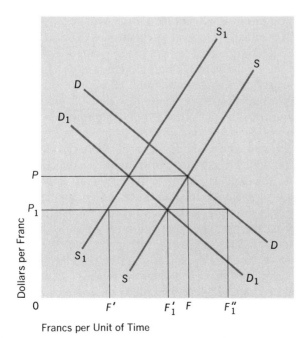

Figure 33–1
The effects of retaliatory tariffs.

is quite likely to retaliate, raising its tariffs on goods imported from the United States. This countermove on the part of France cuts down on the goods purchased from the United States and moves the supply curve of francs to the left. If France succeeds in cutting its value of imports from the United States by as much as U.S. imports from France were cut, the new supply curve for francs will be S_1S_1. The deficit $F'F_1'$ will be as large as it was before and both countries will be denying themselves the advantages of international specialization and exchange.

For Promotion of Economic Development

Tariffs have been widely used by underdeveloped countries in an attempt to promote economic development. At least two overlapping subcategories of tariff objectives within the general category can be distinguished: (1) the protection of infant industries and (2) the promotion of industralization.

Infant Industries

The *infant-industry* argument for a tariff relies for its support on the principle of comparative advantage along with the possibility that the expansion of an industry can lead to economies of scale and long-run decreasing costs. The argument is that a new and/or small industry of a country may be a relatively high-cost operation as compared with the country's other productive activities and, consequently, the country may have a comparative disadvantage in this line of production. Another country (or countries) would thus have a comparative advantage and the given industry, subjected to competition from abroad, would never have a chance to expand and become more efficient. Protection from competitive imports that are less costly is thought to be necessary in order for the industry to develop its potential. It is thought that if a tariff is imposed with rates sufficiently high to make the competitive imports more expensive to users than the domestic product, the desired results can be obtained. During the period of protection the infant industry is expected to prosper and grow, and as growth takes place average production costs are expected to decline relative to those of the country's other productive activities. It is expected that eventually the relative decline in the costs of producing the product will give the country a comparative advantage in its production. If so desired, the tariff can then be eliminated.

On the face of it the argument appears to be logical enough. One possible trouble spot is that when a country has a comparative advantage in the production of some items it must necessarily have a comparative disadvantage in the production of others. As the infant industry grows and, as we assume it does, develops a position of comparative advantage, the country must at the same time be developing a comparative disadvantage in some product or products in which it previously had a comparative advantage. A position of comparative advantage in all products is not possible. The switch in the products in which a comparative advantage is held is not necessarily adverse, although under some circumstances it may be. Once the new industry is in a comparative-advantage position it may contribute more to the country's economic growth than the ones it displaces. Then, again, it may not.

The infant industry argument is usually challenged on grounds of practice and experience with tariffs levied to protect the infants. First, many question whether government officials or legislators—or economists for that matter—have the information and the analytical tools necessary to determine what infant industries of a country show the greatest promise of developing a comparative advantage at some future date. Second, they argue that infant industries that are really promising will not need protection to grow up but will develop on their own. Third, they point out that high-cost infant industries usually become high-cost adult industries and continue to require tariff protection for their existence. The babies never really grow up. Textile production and pottery production in the United States are often cited as examples.

Industrialization

Some countries, especially the less developed ones of Asia, Africa, and South America, use tariffs partly in the hope of spurring their economic development by so doing. They hope and expect that the tariffs will help them *industrialize,* or develop manufacturing industries, and industrialization is thought to be an essential ingredient in economic development. Through the selective use of tariffs it is thought that the composition of the country's imports can be controlled in such a way that growth in the industrial sector will be accelerated.

The typical tariff pattern of a country following this course of action favors the importation of industrial raw and semifinished materials while it discriminates against any manufactured products that are likely in any way to compete with home products. High tariffs are placed on the importation of expensive goods deemed to be luxury goods. Automobiles, for example, are frequently subjected to extremely high tariffs, if their importation is permitted at all. On the other hand, capital goods such as industrial machinery will carry low tariff rates or be admitted duty free. So, too, will industrial chemicals and fuels not produced domestically. Sometimes the country chooses specific industries to be promoted—for example, the steel industry or the fish-meal industry—and provides favorable treatment for imports that are needed for the industry's operation while imposing tariffs on imports of a competitive nature.

The shadowy point in this line of reasoning is whether industrialization is really a prime mover of economic development. Many people believe that it is, but there are some cogent economic arguments that will deny it. Economic development depends upon improvements in techniques of production and accumulation of *capital in general*—in agriculture, mining, services, and *all* lines of endeavor—not just in the area of manufacturing. Capital accumulation within a country requires that some part of *NNP* be saved to add to the country's stock of capital. The higher the country's *NNP,* the greater the possibilities for saving and for capital accumulation.

Tariffs used for any purpose, including the promotion of manufacturing or industrialization, limit the size of the country's *NNP* by denying the country the additional product that it can obtain through specialization and exchange along the lines of its comparative advantage. When they are used to favor manufacturing industries, these industries are promoted at the expense of the other sectors of the economy, including the export sectors. It is precisely the development of products for export that will make it possible for a country with small internal markets to grow and develop. Although there may be some correlation between economic development and industrialization, it is possible that industrialization follows or results from rather than precedes and causes economic development.

For Purposes of Protection

Another reason for the existence of tariffs is simply that of protecting certain domestic producers from foreign competition. This is the international trade manifestation of the almost universal desire to monopolize, to exclude as much competition as possible from the markets in which domestic producers sell.

Particular Interests versus the General Interest

Although we have demonstrated that countries can gain through international trade based on comparative advantages, not everyone within a specific country loses when trade is inhibited by the imposition of tariffs on the import of particular products. Producers of products sheltered from foreign competition and those who furnish resources to those producers ordinarily gain. The imposition of the import duties makes it relatively more expensive to purchase those products from abroad. Consumers shift away from consumption of the imported items toward consumption of the domestic substitutes. The increase in demand for the domestically produced products generates the same sort of gains for those furnishing resources to the industry as does an increase in demand from any other source.

The advancement in the economic well-being of those associated with the protected industry cannot be generalized to the entire economy. In fact, the principle of comparative advantage leads us to the conclusion that the opposite occurs. The tariff simply increases the cost of importing goods in which the country has a comparative disadvantage, thus reducing the total amount of product available to the country through trade below what it could be in the absence of the tariff. From a slightly different point of view, the tariff that increased demand for the protected products makes the latter more costly to consumers. The general price level is raised somewhat and the real income of consumers in general declines correspondingly. The direct economic effects of the tariff are, then, that it serves the particular interests of those engaged in producing the protected item, but it is contrary to the interests of consumers in general.

Cheap Foreign Labor

One common argument made for protective tariffs in the United States is that they protect us from the competition of products made by "cheap foreign labor." Thus Congress is urged to enact tariffs on the importation of Japanese toys, transistor radios, and other products. The fear seems to be that U.S. producers will be undersold across the board by the cheaper foreign-made goods and that unemployment of U.S. labor along with lower living standards will be the end result.

At the outset it may be noted that cheap labor does not always enable foreign firms to produce at a lower money cost than U.S. firms that use more expensive labor. At existing exchange rates between the rupee and the dollar, can India, for example, using large amounts of inexpensive labor, build an automobile comparable to a Mustang at as low a dollar cost as the Ford Motor Company? Probably not. The point is that comparative dollar costs per unit of producing a given kind of product do not necessarily depend upon comparative hourly costs of the labor used in producing the product. Comparative costs of *all* resources used, together with comparative technologies, determine comparative dollar costs of production.

More important, differences in the absolute money-cost levels of producing given products among countries are not the determinants of the gains to be obtained from engaging in trade. If the United States and Canada consume products *A* and *B*, with the United States holding a comparative advantage in the production of *A* while Canada does likewise with *B,* trade will permit gains for both countries even if costs of producing both products are higher in the United States. If the United States by giving up production of a unit of *B* can increase production of a unit of *A* by more than can Canada, and if Canada by giving up production of a unit of *A* can increase production of *B* by more than can the United States, then if the United States concentrates on the production of *A,* trading for *B,* while Canada concentrates on the production of *B,* trading for *A,* both countries can obtain larger amounts of *A* and *B* regardless of the money cost of labor or other resources in one country or the other.[1]

It should be reiterated that even though the interests of the consumers of a country are best served by the absence of a tariff seeking to exclude products made with cheaper foreign resources, some particular producing groups in the country will be better off with such a tariff. These are the groups who would produce domestically the products that the tariff would exclude. If they were engaged in producing the product prior to the time the threat of competition from abroad became a reality, the foreign competition would indeed hurt them. But the case does not differ in principle from any other dislocation of resource owners coming from dynamic changes in the economy. Temporary dislocations of certain groups of resource owners are the price we pay for economic progress and a growing national income.

For National Self-Sufficiency

Sometimes tariffs are levied in an effort to make a country less dependent on other countries for certain goods and services. Reasons for self-sufficiency policies vary. Nationalistic zeal coupled with a "we don't need anyone else" attitude may provide the motivating force. Another may be that a country is desirous of strengthening certain industries that it believes to be vital to its national security. These include the merchant marine, aircraft manufacturing, steel, oil, rubber, and others providing products and services that if not available in time of war would lead to disaster. In both cases the country is willing to sacrifice immediate economic well-being for the attainment of other goals.

Some countries may pursue self-sufficiency policies because they fear having their own economic destiny tied to that of countries with which they trade. Prior to the Great Depression of the 1930s Chile depended heavily on foreign trade. Its chief exports were nitrate up to 1920 and copper through the decade of the 1920s. Import restrictions were relatively mild and a wide range of goods were imported. Between 1929 and 1933 the world market for copper collapsed, severely curtailing the quan-

[1] See pp. 587–594.

tities of foreign exchange that the country could earn and its ability to import goods and services. There was a precipitous drop in living standards. Experiences of this kind are not easily forgotten and lead to import duties in order that "import-substitute" industries may be developed at home—albeit at production costs above the costs of importing the goods during more stable times.

TOWARD TARIFF REDUCTIONS

Not quite all the votes are won by the pro-tariff interests. Countries have been somewhat ambivalent in their expressed attitudes toward trade. At times they have pressed toward formidable restrictions and at other times they have sought to reduce them. Sometimes, in the 1960s, for example, they have tried to work both sides of the street at the same time. Over the last 100 years we find an ebb and flow of trade restrictions by the United States and the other trading countries of the world. At the time of writing, uncertainty over trade policies exists. While lip service is paid to further reductions in trade barriers among nations, balance of payments disequilibria seem to be forcing deficit countries toward greater trade restrictions.

U.S. Tariff Policies

From the time it was established as an independent nation until 1934 the United States pursued policies of generally increasing tariffs, which were the major sources of government revenue until the end of the nineteenth century. Since then their percentage contribution to federal government receipts has dwindled to the point at which they are negligible. Throughout most of this period those supporting high tariffs were well aware of their protectionist elements as well as of their revenue-raising capabilities. The infamous Hawley-Smoot Tariff of 1930 raised U.S. tariffs to their historicaly all-time high level and, together with retaliatory tariffs levied by other countries, undoubtedly contributed toward the breakdown of world trade during the Great Depression of the 1930s.

In 1934 the United States began a long, slow process of liberalizing its import restrictions. The Reciprocal Trade Agreements Act passed in that year empowered the President to negotiate reciprocal tariff reductions with the governments of other countries. The act included a policy that the United States had followed even before the act was passed. This was the *most-favored-nation* policy—any tariff concessions or benefits granted to a given country would be extended to all other countries without the necessity of concessions in return. Further, any concession granted a third party by the given country with which the United States was negotiating must also be extended to the United States. The Reciprocal Trade Agreements Act was to be effective for three years. At the end of the three-year period it was extended, as it was at each subsequent expiration date until 1962. Under the act and its extensions tariffs were reduced to somewhere in the neighborhood of one fourth of their 1930 levels.

The Trade Expansion Act of 1962 replaced the Reciprocal Trade Agreements Act expiring in that year. It renewed and expanded the authority of the President to negotiate tariff reductions with these countries. Notably it permitted him to negotiate the elimination of tariffs on items for which the United States and the European Economic Community countries together account for 80 percent or more of world exports. In this respect the act was intended to discourage the countries of such an organization from becoming regional trading blocs, trading freely within their own memberships and discriminating heavily against imports from countries outside the group.

Gatt, 1947

Following World War II representatives from the major trading countries of the world drew up a charter for a proposed International Trade Organization (ITO). The ITO was intended (1) to promote the reduction of tariffs, of other barriers to trade, and of discriminating trade treatment of some countries by others; (2) to promote the economic development of underdeveloped areas; and (3) to provide a forum for the discussion and solution of problems relating to international trade. Congress refused to ratify the charter and thus effectively scuttled the ITO. In its place, a much weaker General Agreement on Tariffs and Trade, generally referred to as GATT, was set up in 1947.

The main purpose of GATT is to encourage the negotiation of tariff reductions among signatory countries. Its effects are made multilateral through the inclusion of a *most-favored-nations clause* like that of the United States Reciprocal Trade Agreements Act. Though by no means a powerful organization for sweeping away tariff restrictions, GATT has provided a medium through which discussions of trade problems among countries can be conducted.

Regional Economic Integration

The reduction of tariff barriers and other restrictions to international trade tends to be more easily accomplished with one's neighbors than with countries that are geographically and ideologically more remote. Thus in recent years there have been several moves among the countries of specific regions of the world to band together in groups for purposes of freeing themselves from at least some of the restraints on the trade among them. These groups are said to be seeking *regional economic integration,* that is, to move toward integration of their productive capacities along comparative-advantage lines.

Regional organizations of countries for trade purposes are frequently classified as common markets, customs unions, or free trade associations. A *common market* in its pure form is an association in which no restrictions are placed on sales of goods and services or movements of resources among the participating countries. The economies of the countries are truly integrated. The closest approximation to a pure common market occurs among the states of the United States. A *customs union* imposes much less interdependence on the participating countries. The usual objective of a customs union is to eliminate the tariff barriers against goods moving among the countries that comprise it, but for the group as a whole to confront outside countries with a common set of tariffs. The *free trade association* is even less demanding on its members. The ultimate objective is free trade among member countries, but each one is left to make whatever trade arrangements it desires with outside countries. Suppose we look at the major examples of organizations of these types.

The European Economic Community, 1957

The European Economic Community, or EEC, created by the Treaty of Rome in 1957, has common market characteristics. It evolved from the Organization for European Economic Cooperation that was established by the United States and the western European countries following World War II for the allocation of funds sent to that area under the Marshall Plan to aid in the reconstruction of war-torn Europe. Originally it was hoped in official circles in the United States that all of the countries of western Europe would join in setting up the European Economic Community. But several countries, Great Britain in particular, were fearful of tying their economies as closely to those of other countries as the objectives of the common market would require. Consequently the EEC included only France, Germany, Italy, Belgium, Luxembourg, and the Netherlands. Since 1961 Great Britain has made belated attempts to join the group; however, every attempt thus far has been vetoed by France. Had Great Britain been admitted, it is likely that the northern European countries would have followed suit and the EEC would have embraced almost the whole of western Europe.

The avowed purpose of EEC is to remove restrictions on economic transactions among member countries. Toward this end the Treaty of Rome calls for (1) the gradual removal of tariffs, import quotas, and other kinds of trade restrictions among the member countries; (2) a uniform tariff among the member countries on goods imported from outside the group to any one of them; (3) the free movement of both labor and capital resources among member countries; (4) the coordination of monetary and fiscal policies of the members; and (5) the establishment of common policies with respect to agriculture, business, labor, and social security. These objectives are to be accomplished over a 12–15 year period.

What economic benefits may be expected to be derived from an arrangement of this kind? A first and most obvious set includes those that arise from specialization and exchange in accordance with the principle of comparative advantage—the ordinary gains that always arise from voluntary exchange. Second, it can expand the markets available to specific industries of given countries. Third, it may increase the amount of competition that exists among the sellers of products in the member countries. The first point has been discussed in detail previously. Some elaboration of the second and third points is in order.

With respect to the benefits to be derived from market expansion, we should keep in mind that a great many countries of the world are small and that the internal markets available to the industries of such countries are limited in size. Consequently, it may not be possible for a firm selling only to the internal market to produce a large enough volume of a product to take advantage of economies of scale. Suppose that such a country has only 300,000 automobiles operating within its borders. How large a market will exist for automobile jacks? A free trade arrangement with other countries may expand the markets available to such a firm, permitting larger output rates, economies of scale, and lower costs of production.

Increasing competition among sellers of products in a region where trade barriers are reduced will ordinarily be expected to benefit consumers of the region. Domestic sellers in a small country may well be monopolists in the sale of their products. The small size of the internal market, together with tariffs against competing imports, may make it so. If tariffs among countries of the region are reduced, the producers in the country may not only find their markets larger but may at the same time find themselves subjected to competition from abroad. This erosion of their monopoly positions tends to bring about improvements in the quality of the products, larger quantities of the products, and lower prices for consumers.

The precise impact of the EEC on the member countries is hard to measure, but it appears that it has been positive. There have been large increases in GNP, employment, and productivity in the region since its inception. Large increases in trade among the member countries and in the trade of the group with the rest of the world have occurred. But it is difficult to say how much of this would have taken place if the EEC had not existed.

European Free Trade Association, 1960

In 1960 Great Britain, Norway, Sweden, Denmark, Austria, Switzerland, and Portugal signed a treaty creating the European Free Trade Association, or EFTA. The Association was formed as a countergroup to the EEC. Great Britain had not been willing to go all the way with the common market characteristics of the EEC, and when it became apparent that the EEC would be formed anyway, the British countered with a proposal for a free trade area including all of the countries now members of the two groups. The Treaty of Rome, giving birth to the EEC, was signed while the British proposal was under discussion, eliminating the six EEC countries from possible membership and leaving the others to establish the Association.

Some measure of success has been achieved by EFTA in reducing tariffs among the member countries. In fact, reductions have been similar to those accomplished by EEC. However, there has been no intent on the part of the group to establish a customs union or a common market. The tariff policy of each member country toward countries outside the group is considered to be its own affair. Comparison between the economic performance of EFTA countries and the EEC countries may or may not be meaningful because of differences in the economic circumstances in which member countries of the two organizations find themselves. However, for whatever it is worth, trade among EFTA countries and between EFTA countries and outsiders appears to have increased about on a par with that of EEC countries.

The Central American Common Market, 1958

In 1958 the countries of Costa Rica, El Salvador, Guatemala, Honduras, and Nicaragua set up the Central American Common Market. According to the generally accepted definition of a common market, this is somewhat of a misnomer. The first objective of the organization is to establish a free trade association, lowering trade restrictions among the member countries so that after 10 years trade would be free. The free trade association is then expected to evolve into a customs union, with common tariffs on imports into member countries.

Again, measurement of the degree of success is not an easy task. Tariffs have been reduced and many goods now flow across the borders of member countries duty free. Trade has increased greatly both internally and externally over the last few years, but the extent to which the organization has made this so has not yet been determined. In any case it has introduced the idea that reductions in trade barriers are beneficial where not so long ago the pressures were exerted in the other direction.

The Latin American Free Trade Association, 1960

The major countries of South America, plus Mexico and with the exception of Venezuela, formed the Latin American Free Trade Association (LAFTA) with the signing of the Treaty of Montevideo in 1960. The objectives, according to the framers of the treaty are: (1) to expand the South American markets of member countries, (2) to expand the trade among member countries relative to that with the rest of the world, and (3) to achieve greater economic integration and complementarity among the industries of the participating countries. These statements recognize the importance of increasing the size of the market for the industries of a member country beyond the country itself. However, they avoid giving the impression that competition among the industries of the participating countries will be permitted to increase. Many Latin Americans are distrustful of competition. The treaty leaves the impression that planned *industrial complementarity* will be sought among the countries of the association—that is, that specific major industries will be assigned to certain countries and will not be permitted to develop in others.

The treaty provides for a 12-year program of tariff reductions. Annual negotiations are to reduce average tariff barriers against each country's imports from the others by 8 percent per year. By the end of 12 years trade among the countries is supposed to be free. The first year's round of negiotiated reductions came off well, with most of the reductions being made where special interest groups were hurt least. But in succeeding rounds, seeking to remove the protection afforded larger important industries, negotiations became progressively more difficult. Free trade appears to be a remote goal. Again it is difficult to draw any conclusions as to the impact of the association on trade among the countries. However, the member countries at least have the reduction of tariff barriers under discussion.

SUMMARY

The economic impact of tariffs has been a subject of debate since the birth of economics as an area of systematic study. Although it can be demonstrated by means of the principle of comparative advantage that in most cases the national income of trading countries will be greater without tariffs than with them, countries have persisted in building up tariff walls against imports. One reason is that tariffs can provide revenue for the central government. Another, and a more important one today, is that they can be used to restrict imports into countries with balance of payments deficits. A third reason is the belief that tariffs can hasten industrialization and thus the economic development of underdeveloped countries. A fourth is to provide protection of home producers from competition from abroad, a simple monopolization motive in which the protected producing interests gain at the expense of the rest of the economy. A fifth reason for tariffs is to promote self-sufficiency on the part of individual countries.

Historically tariff policies of the world's trading countries have evidenced periods of increasing tariffs and periods of decreasing tariffs. U.S. tariffs moved generally upward from 1850 to 1934. Since 1934, under the Reciprocal Trade Agreements Act and the Trade Expansion Act of 1962, they have moved downward. At the present time what appears to be a chronic balance of payments deficit seems to be forcing the United States toward increasing trade restrictions.

A number of agreements have been signed and organizations have been formed among the countries of the world to reduce trade barriers. On a multicountry basis, the General Agreement on Trade and Tariffs established in 1947 has provided a forum within which negotiations can be conducted for tariff reductions. Additionally several organizations to promote liberalization of trade barriers among member countries are in operation. These include the European Economic Community, the European Free Trade Association, the Central American Common Market, and the Latin American Free Trade Association. The economic success of these organizations is difficult to assess, but they represent substantial steps in the direction of unrestricted trade.

EXERCISES AND QUESTIONS FOR DISCUSSION

1. "The U.S. must sooner or later form or join a common market or free trade association. Otherwise its position in international trade will be weakened." Discuss.
2. Can the infant-industry argument be justified with respect to the principle of comparative advantage? Explain.
3. American beef producers argue that the elimination of tariffs on Argentine beef would drive down the price of beef in the United States to a level at which small producers could not continue in business. Is this sufficient reason to warrant the continuance of a protective tariff? Elaborate.
4. "German labor works for much less money than American labor. This is why Volkswagens are less expensive than American cars. If tariffs were removed from

these automobiles thousands of U.S. workers and their families would be affected." Are these statements valid? Expand.

5. Make a list of several goods that now carry import tariffs. What would be the
likely effect on the U.S. industries involved if these tariffs were lifted? on the U.S.
economy? on the world?

6. Can you think of any industries today that clearly should have protective tariffs?
If so, why should they be allowed such protection?

SELECTED READINGS

Balassa, Bela, ed., *Changing Patterns in Foreign Trade and Payments.* New York:
W. W. Norton and Company, Inc., 1964, Part Two.
———, *Trade Liberalization among Industrial Countries: Objectives and Alternatives.*
New York: McGraw-Hill Book Company, Inc., 1967.
Ingram, James C., *International Economic Problems.* New York: John Wiley & Sons,
Inc., 1966, Chaps. 3 and 6.
Kenen, Peter B., *International Economics.* Englewood Cliffs, N.J.: Prentice-Hall, Inc.,
1964, Chap. 3.

Underdeveloped Economies

CHAPTER 34

A large part of the world's population lives under adverse economic circumstances. Some two thirds of all mankind live in countries producing not more than one third of the world's income. The large concentrations of poverty-ridden people are in Asia, Africa, and Latin America. Most of those that we call poor in Australia, New Zealand, Europe, and North America are relatively much better off. No analysis of the world economy would be complete without a discussion of the economically underdeveloped countries and their problems, nor can we find a better capstone for an introduction to economic theory. The underdeveloped economies present one of the major challenges facing the world today.

MEANING AND MEASUREMENT OF UNDERDEVELOPMENT

Underdeveloped countries are those in which a large proportion of the population is very poor. A number of means have been used to measure the level of well-being of different countries—daily per capita calorie intakes, infant mortality rates, life expectancies, literacy rates, and others—but all of these add up to low income levels. The almost universally used measures of comparative levels of development are per capita income figures.

Although per capita income data have certain shortcomings for purposes of comparing countries on the basis of level of development, they provide one of the best measures available. One shortcoming is that income distribution is left out of account. The poor of a country can be very poor indeed, yet there may be enough extremely wealthy people in the economy to pull per capital income figures up to a level tending to mask the poverty that exists. We should also keep in mind that such data do not provide a fine measure of the comparative economic well-being of persons in different countries. The typical bundle of consumer goods in one country is not the same as in another. Further, if one country's currency is pegged in foreign exchange markets so that it is substantially overvalued, its per capita income will appear unduly high relative to that of a country whose currency is undervalued. But despite factors such as these that reduce the accuracy of per capital income comparisons, the differences among countries are so large that the general validity of the comparisons is not seriously affected.

Table 34–1 gives some idea of the relative levels of development of a representative group of countries. It is apparent that a vast difference exists between the highest and the lowest countries, the former being almost 62 times the latter. The countries usually considered to be relatively advanced economically are clustered in the $1000 and above range. Where income levels are below $1000 we can guess that a rather large proportion of the population lives in acute poverty. Casual observation tends to confirm that in many of the countries in the $400–$1000 range there are substantial disparities in income distribution. In Venezuela, for example, the lower classes are as poor as in most other Latin American countries, but

TABLE 34–1
Per Capita Gross National Product
Estimates for Selected Countries, 1966
(1965 Prices)

COUNTRY	EXCHANGE RATE PER DOLLAR		U.S. DOLLARS	COUNTRY	EXCHANGE RATE PER DOLLAR		U.S. DOLLARS
United States			3,648	Greece	30	drachmas	708
Sweden	5.17	kronor	2,584	Argentina	202	pesos	700
Canada	1.981	C $	2,553	South Africa	0.714	rands	545
Switzerland	4.3	S francs	2,384	Chile	4.8	escudos	501
New Zealand	0.36	NZ $	2,055	Mexico	12.5	pesos	470
France	4.937	F francs	1,984	Peru	26.8	soles	378
Germany	4.0	D. M	1,945	Guatemala	1	quetzal	314
Australia	0.893	A $	1,911	Brazil	1,400	cruzieros	271
United Kingdom	0.357	pounds	1,817	Ghana	0.857	cedis	269
Netherlands	3.62	guilders	1,584	Taiwan	40	NT $	231
Austria	26	shillings	1,317	Bolivia	12	pesos	149
Israel	3	I pounds	1,308	Thailand	20.8	baht	128
Italy	625	lire	1,150	Nigeria	0.357	pounds	117
Japan	360	yen	922	India	4.76	rupees	104
Venezuela	4.5	bolivares	895	Pakistan	4.76	rupees	99
Spain	60	pesetas	747	Ethiopia	2.5	E $	59

SOURCE: Agency for International Development, *Gross National Product, Growth Rates and Trend Data*, March 31, 1967.

per capita income is higher because there is a proportionally larger number of wealthy people. The economic circumstances of the large majority of the population in countries with per capita incomes under $400 per year are self-evident.

RECENT CONCERN WITH AN OLD PROBLEM

Although poverty is as old as mankind itself, the urgency for economic development that is making itself felt throughout the world today is of comparatively recent origin. World War II and the ensuing Cold War seem to have been the catalytic agents. Prominent among the factors contributing to such world-wide concern have been: (1) the travel and social interchange that took place during and following World War II, (2) the Cold War struggle for power between the Communist countries and those of the Western world, (3) expansion in the distribution and use of mass communications media, and (4) the decline in colonialism and the emergence of nationalism in the underdeveloped areas of the world.

Travel and Social Interchange

Never in the history of the world were so many people transported to so many different countries and exposed to so many different cultures as was the case during World War II. Military personnel from the advanced countries stationed in the Pacific islands, Asia, and Africa saw firsthand and for the first time the grinding poverty in which the majority of the world's population lives. At the same time, soldiers from the underdeveloped areas found themselves in countries where living standards were almost beyond their wildest dreams. Too, the civilian populations in the underdeveloped areas became acquainted with what to them appeared to be high income levels and lavish spending habits of North American, Australian, and European troops. Out of the exchange came an awareness on both sides of what economic conditions in the rest of the world are like.

Travel abroad has become commonplace, albeit on a smaller scale than during World War II; growing investments abroad by Western firms have induced a flow of technical personnel and their families to the countries where the investments are made; international loans and aid to underdeveloped countries by the governments of advanced countries have done the same thing; student and teacher exchanges are on the increase; tourism has flourished. All of these exchanges have been beneficiaries of the transportation revolution brought about by the advent of jet aircraft.

The Cold War

The ideological competition between the Communist world and the West for the allegiance and support of the smaller, and in many cases underdeveloped, countries has undoubtedly contributed to a greater awareness of and concern for the underdeveloped countries. The Marshall Plan, to provide aid in the reconstruction of war-torn Europe, demonstrated the possibilities arising from massive loans and grants to other countries to help them build up their productive capacities. This program was followed by U.S. aid to underdeveloped countries, first through the Point Four program and later through the Agency for International Development (AID). The Soviet Union entered the field of aid to underdeveloped countries in the mid 1950s.

The fear on the part of the United States and western European nations that the less advanced countries would turn to communism as a route to development has played an important role in recent concern for the underdeveloped areas of the world. By the same token, the Soviet Union and Communist China have worked the other side of the street. Rivalry between the two blocs has been strong in Africa, Asia, and in Latin America.

Mass Communications Media

Technological developments in communications media since World War II have brought people in all parts of the world in closer touch. Developments in radio—particularly the transistor—enable people to hear, even if they cannot read, of events and conditions outside their own areas. In most underdeveloped areas a transistor radio is a much sought after and highly prized possession. Widespread distribution of motion pictures has had an impact, and some countries that were formerly rather isolated now have limited access to television.

Nationalism

The growth of nationalism and the dismantling of colonial empires have played important roles in the recent interest in economic development. Newly independent nations have sought to establish the superiority of home rule over rule by an outside power in the development of their economies. Pakistan and India provide major examples. Over 30 small independent nations have come into being in Africa. World-wide interest has been generated in the successes and failures that these countries have experienced as they attempt, among other things, to improve their economic performance.

REQUISITES OF ECONOMIC DEVELOPMENT

How does economic development of a country come about? The economic requisites for growth in per capita income are easily stated, but the cultural, social, psychological, and political underpinnings necessary to bring them about pose formidable problems. Growth in national income results from the accumulation of more and better resources and from increases in the efficiency with which they are used. But population growth also means more mouths to feed. Per capita income can grow only if national income is increasing at a greater rate than is population. Suppose we examine the forces at work.

Capital Accumulation

Capital accumulation is, of course, a basic ingredient in economic development. If national income is to grow, the economy must accumulate capital, and if per capita income is to grow, capital per worker must be increasing, assuming that the labor force increases at least as fast as does the population. We should keep in mind that an economy's capital is made up of all of its nonhuman resources—communications and transportation facilities; educational facilities; tools, machines, and factories for producing industrial goods; mining equipment; agricultural land and tools; ore deposits and other "natural" resources; and so on. All of these contribute to the total output of the economy.

If an economy is to accumulate capital without outside help, it must refrain from consuming its entire net output. Some part of its output must be in the form of new capital goods, over and above the amounts used to keep the economy's capital resources intact or to take care of depreciation. Thus the size of the economic machine and its capacity to produce will grow over time. The rate of growth in the productive capacity of its capital resources depends upon the willingness of the populace to forgo consumption in order that resources that would otherwise be employed to produce consumer goods can be used to produce capital goods.

Capital accumulation is not confined to increases in the quantities of the capital resources available; it can also take the form of improvements in the qualities of resources. Soil fertility can be increased; through careful selection of seed stocks crop yields can be expanded; river channels can be widened and deepened; better educational facilities can be made available; dams built to control erosion and to store up water supplies for irrigation can also frequently be made to yield electrical energy.

Technological Development

Through technological development not only can the quality of resources be improved but better and more efficient ways of using resources of given qualities are devised. Technological advancements go hand in hand with capital accumulation and with advancing educational levels. Education provides the foundations underlying technological development. But in order for ideas to bear fruit—or even to survive—the means of testing them and putting them into practice must be available. Capital resources provide the laboratory for this purpose. High levels of technology are rarely developed in capital-poor countries.

In the world today underdeveloped economies seldom find it necessary to come up with entirely new technological developments on their own. They can borrow from the more advanced countries. They can send students abroad to be trained as engineers and as scientists and to bring home technical knowledge in a wide range of fields. They can also import complete sets of techniques, as the Japanese have done with great success since World War II. They can bring in from the advanced countries the ways and means of producing electrical and other kinds of energy. They can copy—and perhaps improve upon—manufacturing techniques of many kinds. And, as in the case of Japan, these can give them a strong boost along the way to higher per capita incomes without subtracting from the incomes of those from whom the techniques are borrowed.

Qualitative Improvements in Human Resources

Higher literacy rates, higher average levels of educational attainment, and training and development in specific skills constitute essential ingredients in the economic growth of any economy. As Galbraith has aptly put it, "Literate people will see the need for getting machines. It is not so clear that machines will see the need for getting literate people."[1]

In order to increase its per capita income a poor economy must educate its population so that a climate is provided in which capital accumulation and technological development can thrive. Through primary and

[1] John K. Galbraith, *Economic Development* (Cambridge, Mass.: Harvard University Press, 1964), p. 42.

secondary education of a general nature, as well as through higher education in the liberal arts, a spirit of inquiry can be encouraged and initiative
for the improvement of one's lot can be instilled. The correlation between
average levels of general education and per capita incomes is high and
positive within the United States. From the data available, it appears to
be equally strong throughout the world.

In addition to raising its literacy rate and advancing its general level
of education, a developing country must increase the technical competence and skill levels of its work force. We expect technical training to increase the capacities of workers to contribute directly to the economy's
output of goods and services. We also know that without it technological
advancements are not likely to occur. The accumulation of capital by a
developing economy must necessarily be accompanied by the acquisition
of skills on the part of a larger and larger proportion of its labor force.
Trade schools, technical schools, adult education classes, and on-the-job
training all contribute toward this end.

Improved Employment and Allocation of Resources

National income and per capita income of an economy can be increased through improvements in the employment and allocation of whatever resources it has. Underdeveloped economies typically have rather
high unemployment rates; or, in the event that obvious unemployment
does not occur, labor may be *underemployed,* that is, more man hours
are used to perform specific tasks than are really necessary.

Capital too can be underemployed. For example, land tenure systems
may be such that most of the agricultural land is held in very large farms
owned by the aristocratic wealthy class of the society. The owners may
take little interest in the actual operation of the farms. Traditional
methods rather than the best ones available, used by peasants who have
little interest in efficiency, may hold productivity far below what it could
be. Mineral deposits and forest areas may not be contributing as much as
they are capable of contributing to national income.

In underdeveloped economies there is usually a large possibility of
increasing national income through a more efficient allocation of resources among alternative employment opportunities. Whenever resources are pulled out of less productive uses and placed in more
productive ones, the gains more than offset the losses and national income rises.[2] Suppose, for example, that land is being utilized to grow
lentils but that most people do not think much of lentils as a form of
nourishment. They value the yearly product of an acre of land used in

---

[2] See pp. 304–305.

producing lentils at $100. Suppose that the public values the amount of beans that the same acre could grow each year at $150. Clearly, national income would rise if land were reallocated from the production of lentils to the production of beans. Similarly, reallocation of labor from less productive to more productive employments will cause national income to rise.

INTERNAL OBSTACLES TO ECONOMIC DEVELOPMENT

The economic forces that contribute to growth in national income are easy to list, yet it is difficult for underdeveloped countries to bring them into being under their own steam. Many obstacles stand in the way of capital accumulation, technological advancement, improvements in labor force quality, and more efficient use and allocation of resources. Among these are the country's initial state of poverty, its social structure, inflation, political instability, and population growth. Others could be listed but these seem to be among the most important.

Initial State of Poverty

In countries with low per capita incomes the forces leading to growth are extremely difficult to set in motion. How can a country that produces barely enough food to keep its population alive divert resources from the production of consumer goods to the production of capital goods in large enough quantities for significant capital accumulation to take place? How can it shift resources away from production of the bare essentials of living toward provision of the education necessary for technological advancement and for upgrading the quality of the labor force? Those countries most in need of rapid economic development are precisely the ones that find it most difficult to generate development. The relatively rich countries find it much easier to forgo a large measure of current consumption and to use the resources thus released to expand the productive capacity of the economy.[3]

The internal means of generating growth for many underdeveloped countries may be limited to the new capital they can produce or the additional education they can achieve through increasing the efficiency with which existing resources are used. If unemployment and underemployment can be reduced, gains in national income are possible. Some

---

[3] See pages 547–549.

further gains may be obtainable through reallocation of resources from less to more productive uses. Any additions to net national product thus obtained conceivably can be used for capital accumulation and education purposes. However, if living standards are initially at very low levels, there is no certainty that gains of this sort will not be consumed. As a matter of fact, not much optimism is warranted for the possibilities of increasing the efficiency of resource use. Apathy on the part of the general public and gross administrative ineptness on the part of governments are the rule rather than the exception in low-income countries.

Social Structure

In many underdeveloped countries social and economic class lines are rather strongly drawn and the resulting class structure is not conducive to economic growth. In India, for example, the caste system, even though abolished by law, still exists in fact and tends to prevent workers from moving out of hereditary caste employments such as sweeping, personal service, cooking, laundering, and so on, into occupations that may be more productive and more remunerative. In Latin America the aristocracy tends to be an aloof, exclusive group that the present working classes can never hope to join. The aristocrats are wealthy; the working classes are poor. The latter work for the former in their family businesses and on their farms, and there is no burning desire on the part of the aristocracy to see the economic and social order change—it serves their ends well.

There is some evidence that class structures are cracking. In many low-income countries the poorer classes are obtaining representation in government and are pressing for measures that will change the status quo. In many such countries there is a growing middle class of businessmen, entrepreneurs, and professionals. The step from the working class to the middle class is much smaller than that to the aristocracy and as time passes it can be taken by working-class people. As the middle class grows it accumulates capital and generates employment opportunities. Too, the aims of the poor and the middle class may be furthered by their growing political strength.

Inflation

Many underdeveloped countries have experienced rates of inflation high enough to be detrimental to economic development. Inflation in most underdeveloped countries is generated by large-scale deficit financing of government expenditures. Goverments are reluctant to collect sufficient taxes to cover their expenditures for fear that they will be replaced if taxes appear onerous. Welfare-minded governments establish expenditure levels too high for the tax-collecting mechanism to support. Special interest groups generate fiscal policies with inflationary biases by pressing for public expenditures to further their particular ends. There is pressure at the same time from such groups to obtain relief from tax loads. In almost all underdeveloped countries these forces create large government deficits and large increases in the money supply. Increases in total spending outstrip increases in output and price levels rise.

The argument is frequently made that inflation is conducive to economic development. It is said that a constantly expanding monetary demand for goods and services will provide profit incentives to use production facilities at capacity. Also, through deficit spending, it is said that the government can bid resources away from the production of consumer goods and services and use them to produce capital goods.

To be sure, an excess of expenditures over tax collections can be used by a government to accumulate capital. Government demand for goods and services, effected through increases in government expenditures, increases relative to private demand. The government then *can* bid resources away from the private production of consumer goods and *can* put them to work building dams, roads, schools, steel mills, and so on. The decrease in consumer goods available for the general public to buy, coupled with constant consumer purchasing power, causes prices to rise and the real income of the general public to fall, Inflation of this sort has the same general effect as a tax—real purchasing power is transferred from the public to the government.

There is, however, little evidence to support the theory that inflation has in fact stimulated the real growth of underdeveloped economies. More often it seems to have repressed growth, both by discouraging direct investment in new plant and equipment and by inducing government units to enact control measures that inhibit growth.

On the first point, the inflation of most underdeveloped countries is highly erratic. It is not deliberately planned to stimulate the economy. Rather, it occurs because the governments concerned are unable or unwilling to take the necessary steps to prevent it. In one year price levels may rise by 20 percent. The next year the increase may be 80 percent. The following year it may be 30 percent. The effect is to create a high degree of uncertainty on the part of would-be investors concerning the real rate of return on investment. Consequently, only those investments offering an extraordinarily high rate of return are likely to be undertaken.

In addition, inflation tends to cause investment to be channeled into already existing items that are known to increase in price at a rate at least as high as that of the general price level. Real estate and objects of art are outstanding examples. But investment in these creates no additional jobs and no increases in productive capacity; it simply causes their prices to rise to higher levels.

On the second point, the government is likely to take steps to suppress inflation. Price ceilings are often set on a select list of the most important consumer goods. Suppose, for example, that a ceiling price is put on fluid milk but not on manufactured dairy products such as butter and cheese. The latter become relatively more profitable to produce and dairying resources are shifted from the production of milk to the production of butter and cheese. This situation, however, represents a worse rather than a better allocation of resources, since resources move from uses where they are valued more highly (but where the price ceiling prevents that value from being expressed in the market place) to uses in which they are not so highly valued. The principle can be generalized. A system of partial price controls will cause resources to be shifted out of the production of the products where controlled prices are effective and into the production of those where prices are free to move. The former are the goods most valuable to consumers as a whole while the latter are the ones least valuable.

Price controls may also be established on certain resources deemed to be important, strategic, or critical to the economy. If the controls are effective, shortages will occur and government agencies will be assigned the task of allocating these materials or resources to the producing units or business firms that use them. Under the best of circumstances the administrative machinery is cumbersome. Delays in allocations occur; manpower and machines lie idle while firms wait. Further, administrative techniques in underdeveloped countries are usually far from perfect and their shortcomings add to the built-in problems of allowing scarce resources to be allocated by government agencies rather than by prices.

Underdeveloped economies generally develop balance of payments problems as a result of inflation and thus they are prevented from obtaining full measure from international trade based on comparative-advantage principles. Underdeveloped countries typically have a rate of inflation higher than that of the advanced countries with which they trade. Their desire to import is stimulated and the incentives for export are dampened, creating either foreign exchange shortages or rising prices of foreign currencies. Like most of the rest of the world, these countries attempt to peg their exchange rates, but the pegged rate tends to be below equilibrium levels because of inflation and foreign exchange shortages result. In order to live with this situation a variety of trade restrictions are put into effect. These include exchange controls, import quotas, tariffs, restrictions on investment abroad, and others. The countries are placed in a situation in which they are unable to import what they desire of the capital goods they so urgently need from the advanced countries. At the same time, they penalize through overvaluation of their currencies the export of primary goods in which they have a comparative advantage and which provide their sources of foreign exchange.

Political Instability

Political instability exercises a significant retarding influence on economic growth in underdeveloped countries. The mortality rates of governments in Latin America and in the new countries of Africa have been high. Even in countries such as India, where political processes have been more orderly than in most, the number of different political groups and the diversity among them have made the promulgation of policies conducive to growth difficult. Economic development is not likely to occur in the absence of political stability. At the same time, political stability in and of itself will not assure growth.

The causes of government instability and inefficiency in underdeveloped countries are not hard to find. They are rooted in poverty. In countries where most of the population lives in poverty and is largely uneducated there is a dearth of qualified persons to serve in government positions. Many of those selected, whether by democratic processes or otherwise, are inept under the best of circumstances and corrupt under the worst. Even governments that are doing their best to establish and administer policies to promote growth will find themselves severely criticized. Growth may not come fast enough or be tangible enough to convince the public that the government is doing all it can, with the result that pressure mounts to have the group in power replaced.

Political instability has several adverse effects on economic growth. Capital accumulation may be handicapped if there is uncertainty concerning the attitude of the government toward private property, since there is little incentive to accumulate when the possibility of confiscation is present. Another deterrent is the inflation that almost inevitably accompanies political instability. Additionally, inconsistent policies and rapid changes in policies over time may place restraints on already meager productive efforts.

Population Growth

In some underdeveloped countries population growth seems to be an important obstacle to economic growth or to rising per capita income. Table 34–2 indicates that Ghana, India, Brazil, and Venezuela all have relatively high rates of population growth and relatively low rates of increase in per capita income. Other countries, such as Taiwan and Thailand, have high rates of population growth *and* high rates of growth in per capita income. But from Table 34–1 we see that the per capita incomes of all of these countries are still very low. A large proportion of the underdeveloped countries have high rates of population growth, and even those with high rates of increase in per capita income could undoubtedly do better if their populations were inceasing more slowly.

In the latter part of the eighteenth century a Scotsman by the name of Thomas R. Malthus handed down what has become known as the Malthusian principle. Wages, said Malthus, can never be much above the subsistence level because the world's food supply tends to increase in

TABLE 34–2
Gross National Product Per Capita and Population, Average Annual Growth Rates (percent)

| COUNTRY | GNP PER CAPITA | | POPULATION |
	1960–1966	1966[a]	1966[a]
Greece	8.3	8.9	0.5
Japan	8.3	6.8	2.8
Spain	7.7	8.6	0.8
Taiwan	6.8	4.5	2.8
Israel	4.5	− 1.3	2.6
Italy	4.3	4.5	0.7
Thailand	4.1	4.8	3.1
Sweden	4.1	3.4	0.6
Canada	3.8	4.2	1.9
France	3.8	3.9	1.0
Austria	3.5	3.9	0.5
Netherlands	3.5	2.7	1.3
Peru	3.4	3.0	3.1
South Africa	3.4	2.4	2.3
United States	3.4	4.2	1.2
West Germany	3.3	2.3	1.2
Guatemala	3.2	3.0	3.3
Switzerland	3.0	1.7	1.2
Nigeria	2.9	3.2	2.1
Pakistan	2.9	2.0	2.6
Mexico	2.7	3.3	3.5
Bolivia	2.7	3.0	2.4
New Zealand	2.7	3.5	1.4
Australia	2.2	− 0.9	1.8
United Kingdom	2.2	0.0	0.8
Chile	2.1	3.3	2.4
Ethiopia	2.1	2.1	1.4
Venezuela	1.6	1.5	3.4
Brazil	1.2	0.4	3.0
India	1.1	3.3	2.4
Argentina	1.0	− 2.5	1.6
Ghana	− 0.9	− 5.9	2.7

[a] 1966 average over 1965 average.
SOURCE: Agency for International Development, *Gross National Product, Growth Rates and Trend Data*, March 31, 1967.

arithmetic proportion while the population tends to increase in geometric proportion. Therefore, the population will always be pressing on the food supply, with famine, pestilence, and war wiping out the surplus people. Although the Malthusian principle appears to have little or no relevance in the advanced economies, it may have a glimmer of truth with respect to the underdeveloped ones.

Economic growth of underdeveloped areas brings with it forces tending to reduce the death rate, which is initially high in most of them. With economic growth come improvements in nutrition and better systems of sanitation. Health measures are effected that combat communicable diseases, decrease deaths from infection, reduce infant mortality, and increase longevity.

The birth rate, which is also typically high, does not respond correspondingly to economic growth. Folkways and mores concerning reproduction and birth are not as amenable to change as are the forces governing the death rate. As a consequence, even if a country can bring about a respectable rate of growth in GNP—say 4 or 5 percent per year—it may find that the gain is wiped out, wholly or in part, by population increases.

The population problem has, of course, been widely recognized and in some countries positive steps are being taken to bring it under control. The Indian government, for example, has adopted family limitation as a matter of national policy and actively engages in the dissemination of knowledge concerning methods of birth control. Further, it has established a system of small payments to those who undergo sterilization operations. But population control measures are touchy subjects, particularly where religious beliefs oppose them. The discipline of economics has little to say on this matter—it can only point out the consequences of population growth for economic development.

EXTERNAL AIDS TO ECONOMIC DEVELOPMENT

Since World War II the economically advanced countries have provided economic assistance to most of the underdeveloped countries. One reason for aid of this type is undoubtedly a humanitarian one, with those in more fortunate circumstances helping those in less fortunate circumstances. But this is not the only reason. Rivalry in giving aid has developed between the Communist countries and those of the Western world. Each bloc uses its assistance program for ideological purposes—but not always with overpowering success.

Aid is supplied jointly and individually by the advanced countries. An important part of the joint effort on an international level is made through the International Bank for Reconstruction and Development (the World

Bank), together with its affiliate organizations, the International Development Association and the International Finance Corporation. Its activities are discussed in the next section. Other international organizations operating in this area include the Organization for Economic Cooperation and Development, the United Nations Development Program, the Inter-American Development Bank, the European Development Fund and the European Development Bank, the African and Asian development banks, and others. In addition, individual countries have their own aid programs, the United States Agency for International Development (AID) being a good example. In 1965 total Free World governmental aid to underdeveloped countries through joint and individual country sources amounted to some $6.3 billion, of which $3.7 billion was contributed by the United States.[4] Aid from private institutions and individuals amounted to roughly another $3 billion.[5]

United States Assistance

Government Aid

Approximately half of the assistance provided underdeveloped countries by the U.S. government is channeled through AID. All but a small fraction of this, as Table 34–3 indicates, consists of (1) developmental loans, (2) technical assistance grants, and (3) supporting assistance grants.

TABLE 34–3

United States Agency for International Development, Estimated Funds Available, Fiscal Years 1967 and 1968 (thousands of dollars)

	1967	1968
Developmental loans	1,088,992	1,440,375
Technical assistance	320,272	378,815
Supporting assistance	718,754	745,350
Contingency fund, general	51,020	60,000
International organizations and programs	147,720	140,985
U.S.-sponsored schools and hospitals abroad	11,000	14,029
Preinvestment assistance	1,664	2,200
Administrative expenses	63,163	65,151
	2,402,585	2,846,905

SOURCE: Agency for International Development, *Proposed Foreign Aid Program, FY 1968* (Washington, D.C.: U.S. Government Printing Office, 1967), pp. 296–297.

[4] See Agency for International Development, *Proposed Foreign Aid Program, FY 1968* (Washington, D.C.: U.S. Government Printing Office, 1967), pp. 53–62.
[5] Estimates for 1964 were about $2.7 billion. See Wolfgang G. Friedmann, George Kalmanoff, and Robert F. Meagher, *International Financial Aid* (New York: Columbia University Press, 1966), p. 16.

Development loans at low interest rates, repayable in dollars, are made for a host of purposes. They are used to help underdeveloped countries accumulate capital—to build industrial facilities such as power plants, steel mills, and cement plants; to build communications and transportation facilities; and to develop agricultural facilities. They are also used to enable recipients to import U.S. goods and services, presumably essential to development, which they cannot afford from their own supplies of foreign exchange or cannot finance from regular commercial sources. (Why do you suppose foreign exchange for these purposes is not available?) Among such items are fertilizers, raw and semifinished materials, industrial equipment, and spare parts.

Technical assistance is intended to accomplish two objectives: (1) to help develop special skills and technical competence where there seem to be critical man-power needs and (2) to help provide the framework and the facilities within which such trained personnel can function effectively. AID turns much of its technical assistance effort toward increasing agricultural productivity, improving educational levels, and raising public health standards. Grants are made to build educational and health facilities. Technical personnel from the United States are sent to develop demonstration farms, to assist and advise in plant and animal genetics, and to provide instruction in how to increase agricultural productivity. Education specialists consult and advise on matters of educational curricula and teacher training. Tax experts help devise more effective tax laws and more efficient collection procedures. Additionally, persons from underdeveloped countries are sent to the United States to acquire new areas of competence or to improve on what they have. Universities in the United States have been heavily involved in the technical assistance programs, both in supplying specialists to underdeveloped countries and in training persons sent to the United States from those countries.

Supporting assistance grants differ from technical assistance grants in that their primary purpose is to advance U.S. foreign policy. Presumably, wherever possible, they are used for developmental purposes also, but these are incidental to their use to avert political instability and to deter communism in underdeveloped areas. The greater part of supporting assistance grants go to Vietnam and other Southeast Asian countries.

In addition to the AID programs, the United States provides aid to underdeveloped countries through the Food for Peace program (Public Law 480) and through other agencies. The Food for Peace program made available some $1.7 billion worth of surplus agricultural products in 1966 to countries of Asia, Africa, and Latin America. Through other agencies— the Export-Import Bank, the Peace Corps, the Inter-American Development Bank, the International Development Association, and others—some $1.3 billion more was made available.[6]

Military assistance is still another avenue of aid to underdeveloped countries. Like supporting assistance grants of AID, it is geared more to the security requirements of the United States than to the economic development of poverty-stricken countries. Military assistance provides grants and loans to countries for the procurement of military hardware from the United States; to train foreign military personnel in the United States; and to place specialists in the recipient countries to serve as advisers and consultants to their military establishments.

It is difficult to differentiate clearly between nonmilitary and military aid. For example, nonmilitary aid provided a country may be used to release resources in the recipient country from production of civilian goods and services for the production of military goods and services, with the net effect being the same as if military aid had been extended. Or, in the reverse case, military aid may be used to release resources in the recipient country from the production of military goods and services for the production of civilian goods and services.

Private Aid

As indicated earlier, a sizable portion of the aid provided underdeveloped countries by the United States comes from private sources. The Ford Foundation and the Rockefeller Foundation have done much in this respect, especially in the provision of technical assistance to both the government and the private sectors of recipient countries. These foundations have also provided fellowships and research grants for U.S. personnel to work and study in other countries and to make it possible for promising scholars from underdeveloped countries to study in the United States.

Business firms as well as individuals make private investments in underdeveloped countries where the prospective rates of return are attractive, or higher than they are at home. These investments, of course, contribute to capital formation or capital accumulation in the recipient countries. Much of the investment from these sources is direct, involving the setting up of branch plants or new firms. Standard Oil of New Jersey sets up a foreign subsidiary in Venezuela. Sears, Roebuck opens a retail store in Lima, Peru. Another avenue of private investment in underdeveloped countries is the purchase by private parties in the United States of securities of firms established and operated by the nationals of those countries.

Private investment in such countries by U.S. businesses or individuals

---

[6] Agency for International Development, *op. cit.,* pp. 287–290.

tends to be looked upon with a jaundiced eye by the recipient countries. Nationalism rears its head in such cases, with the United States or other foreign companies being looked upon as exploiters of the local economy.[7] An economy should be run by its own citizens, the argument runs.

A small and underrated source of private aid to underdeveloped countries is that of eleemosynary institutions such as church mission groups and the Salvation Army. The work of these organizations has seldom been of a spectacular nature, since they do not build dams or steel mills. But they have done much in the way of providing educational and medical facilities. They have provided orphanages and foster-home care for homeless children. They have often been able to develop a sense of community pride and community responsibility where none existed before. These efforts are, of course, supported by private contributions.

The World Bank

The International Bank for Reconstruction and Development, commonly called the World Bank, along with the International Monetary Fund, grew out of the Bretton Woods Conference of 1944. It was established originally to make long-term loans for reconstruction following World War II and for economic development purposes. Today, with its affiliate organizations, the International Development Association and the International Finance Corporation, most of its activities are in the latter area.

The Bank makes loans for developmental projects to any one of the over 100 countries that comprise its membership. Loans are made to private enterprises as well as to governments. Loan applications are carefully screened by the Bank's management and loans are made only for projects that appear to be financially sound and that show every promise of paying off both interest and principle. The Bank has been extremely successful in this respect and has been subjected to much criticism as a result. It is often argued that if the Bank's loan standards were lowered, loan activities and aid could be expanded far beyond that which has actually been accomplished.

Funds for loans come from two major sources. Member countries each fulfill a basic capital subscription to the Bank. Additionally, the Bank can sell its own bonds and notes in member countries to obtain appropriate foreign exchange for loans. Its hard-nosed reputation has made it possible

---

[7] Does the principle of mutual gain from voluntary exchanges provide any enlightenment on this issue?

for the Bank to resell the financial paper representing loans or parts of loans that it has made to private financial institutions such as banks, insurance companies, and the like in member countries.

SUMMARY

Underdeveloped economies are those with relatively low per capita incomes. Although not a perfect measure of a country's state of development relative to other countries, per capita income provides the best that is currently available. A large part of the world's population lives in countries in which per capita income amounts to less than $500 per year.

The present world-wide concern with economic development dates largely from World War II and was brought about by several factors. First, during and since the war there has been an increasing amount of travel and social interchange between the citizens of the advanced and the underdeveloped countries. Another contributing factor has been the ideological struggle between the Communist countries and the West. A further factor has been the advances made in communications media and the distribution of the latter throughout the world. The rise of nationalism and the decline of colonialism that has been occurring in recent years has also helped focus attention on the underdeveloped countries.

The factors necessary to bring about economic growth are easily identified from the nature of economic activity. Economic growth, or rising per capita income, comes partly from the accumulation of capital resources by an economy. Capital accumulation is aided and abetted by technological advancement. Qualitative improvements in the labor force constitute another essential ingredient. Growth can be further enhanced by putting unemployed resources to work and by reallocating employed resources from less to more productive employments.

A number of obstacles stand in the way of self-development of underdeveloped countries. Among the most important is the initial state of poverty of a country, a situation that almost precludes capital accumulation. Social and economic class lines make it difficult for an economy to use its resources in a more efficient way. Among other things, they tend to stifle entrepreneurship. Inflation is another deterrent to economic development, and so too is political instability. Additionally, population growth may be spurred by increases in GNP to the detriment of increases in per capita incomes.

External aid is provided to most underdeveloped areas by the advanced countries. The U.S. government through the Agency for International

Development makes loans and grants to underdeveloped countries for a wide range of projects. Private foundations have also made substantial contributions, mostly in the form of technical assistance and fellowship programs. Eleemosynary institutions have provided a considerable amount of unheralded aid. On an international basis the International Bank for Reconstruction and Development through long-term loans has provided the major avenue for joint or international efforts to help underdeveloped countries.

EXERCISES AND QUESTIONS FOR DISCUSSION

1. In 1966 annual per capita GNP (in 1965 prices) in Sweden was $2584 while in Pakistan it was $99. How do you account for this difference?
2. Per capita GNP in Sweden increased at a rate of 4.1 percent per year from 1960 to 1966. In the same period the rate of increase in Thailand was also 4.1 percent. What conclusions can you draw from this comparison?
3. From 1960 to 1966 the growth rate of per capita income in India was 1.1 percent. What forces seem to have been responsible for a rate as low as this?
4. Do you think that loans and grants made by the Agency for International Development should be made with no strings attached or that they should be made for specific, approved projects, with their expenditure by the recipient government or private institution carefully supervised by U.S. experts? Explain your answer carefully.

SELECTED READINGS

Agency for International Development, *Proposed Foreign Aid Program, FY 1968.* Washington, D.C.: U.S. Government Printing Office, May 1967.

Baldwin, R. E., *Economic Growth and Development.* New York: John Wiley & Sons, Inc., 1966.

Galbraith, J. K., *Economic Development.* Cambridge, Mass.: Harvard University Press, 1964.

Johnson, H. G., *Economic Policies toward Less Developed Countries.* New York: Fredrick A. Praeger, 1967, Chaps. I and II.

Kindleberger, C. P., *Economic Development,* rev. ed. New York: McGraw-Hill Book Company, Inc., 1965, Chaps. 1, 15, and 20.

Index

DATE DUE